WELFARE STATE FUTURES

Edited by

STEPHAN LEIBFRIED

Centre for Social Policy Research, University of Bremen

Contributors

Giuliano Bonoli, Francis G. Castles,
Maurizio Ferrera, Anton Hemerijck,
Karl Hinrichs, Franz-Xaver Kaufmann, Stein Kuhnle,
Herbert Obinger, Bruno Palier, Martin Rhodes
and Fritz W. Scharpf

CAMBRIDGE
UNIVERSITY PRESS

PUBLISHED BY THE PRESS SYNDICATE OF THE UNIVERSITY OF CAMBRIDGE
The Pitt Building, Trumpington Street, Cambridge, United Kingdom

CAMBRIDGE UNIVERSITY PRESS
The Edinburgh Building, Cambridge CB2 2RU, UK
40 West 20th Street, New York, NY 100011-4211, USA
10 Stamford Road, Oakleigh, Melbourne 3166, Australia
Ruiz de Alarcón 13, 28014 Madrid, Spain
www.cambridge.org

©Academia Europaea 2001

This book is in copyright. Subject to statutory exception
and to the provisions of relevant collective licensing agreements,
no reproduction of any part may take place without
the written permission of Cambridge University Press.

First published 2001

Printed in the United Kingdom at the University Press, Cambridge

Typeset in Times

A catalogue record for this book is available from the British Library

Library of Congress cataloguing in publication data

ISBN 0 521 00512 4 paperback

Contents

And I saw people coming through the round valley,
They were silent and weeping, advancing at the pace
Penitential processions use in the world.

As my gaze sank more deeply into them,
Each one of them seemed to be twisted round
Between the chin and the point where the thorax begins;

So that the head was turned, back to front,
And they were therefore obliged to walk backwards,
No longer being able to look the other way.

(A classic punishment addressed to "future seekers" –
fortune tellers, prophets, wizards of all trades. Extract
from *The Divine Comedy* by Dante Alighieri – Inferno,
Canto XX –, translated by Charles H. Sisson, Oxford
1998, pp. 127–131, here p. 127. Used by permission
of Oxford University Press.)

European Review, Vol. 8, No. 3, 277–289 (2000) © Academia Europaea, Printed in the United Kingdom

1 Welfare state futures. An introduction

STEPHAN LEIBFRIED* and HERBERT OBINGER*

The Five Beveridge Giants (negatives!): Want, Disease, Ignorance, Squalor and Idleness (Beveridge Report 1942).

The Five Giddens Giants (positives!): Autonomy, Active Health, Education, Well-being and Initiative (Giddens 1998).

What the British, since the 1960s, have come to call the 'welfare state', is labelled by the Germans *Sozialstaat*, the French *l'état providence*, the Dutch *Verzorgingsstaat* and Swedes the Folkhemmet. In the US there is no such catch-all term: 'welfare' is closely associated with poor relief only, and 'Social Security' is typically understood as pension insurance. In the social sciences, however, the term 'welfare state' has now been commonly used for some time to connotate that *higher degree of legitimate state intervention* aimed at increasing public welfare – with the US liberal type of society as the implicit contrast, and the UK somewhere in-between.

From the moment of its inception in Germany in the 1880s, what was later (in the 1930s) to be called the *welf*are state – in contrast to the *war*fare state – was said to have no future: the welfare state was alleged to be ill-conceived, to be conducive to dependency – then called 'pension hysteria' – and to lead straight into a permanent state of receivership. But 'crisis', as Kaufmann's contribution suggests, may be just a misnomer for a constitutive feature of the welfare state itself, the permanent challenge for politics to achieve new synergies, again and again, in the conflict between the dynamics of the economic system and the demands of the social welfare system.[1] No self-fuelling process of a welfare state race to the bottom is in sight – institutional integrity is not (as yet) threatened, although 'globalisation' is seen as a major challenge by Kaufmann, Scharpf, Ferrera *et al.* in their contributions in this volume. What is often labelled a crisis of the welfare state may simply be a crisis of a blocked and veto-ridden political system (Zacher 2000; Schmidt 2000: table 7). The challenge would then be one to the democratic mechanisms that are to achieve such synergies. The problem here is, of course, that the same political rules which produced the status quo are supposed to facilitate a way out.

Welfare states are always, in Esping-Andersen's (1985) words, 'politics against markets', are always about a needs-driven expansion of social regulation in which affordability, or budgetary soundness, takes a back seat. Most of the major welfare state reforms, e.g. in the 1880s, 1930s or 1950s, would never have taken place if the only means at disposal for redistribution had been the growth dividends at hand. Even in the 'Golden Age' – the immediate

* Centre for Social Policy Research, University of Bremen, Parkallee 39, 28209 Bremen, Germany. E-mail: stlf@zes.uni-bremen.de; hobinger@zes.uni-bremen.de.

post-World War II period – the welfare state appears only in retrospect as a growing piece of an expanding pie, an outcome of increased distributive potentials. At the time these reforms were fought through, they were cheques drawn on empty accounts – to be filled later, somehow.[2]

In recent years, many social policy scholars often with a 'generalist' disciplinary background – in economics, political science and sociology – have become pessimistic about the future of the welfare state. This contrasts regularly with the stance of social policy and social administration specialists, who have weathered more than one storm and are, in their empirical tradition, alleged simply to 'count lampposts' (Mann 1998). The pan-disciplinary consensus seems to be: *the welfare state is having hard times*. Since the mid-1970s, most OECD countries have experienced declining economic growth and rising unemployment, accompanied by high inflation and increasing public debt. Today some of these problems are well under control, but the deterioration of the exceptional economic performance – the basis for 'Golden Age' welfare capitalism – is irreversible: this has slowed down welfare state expansion, provoked debates on 'European welfare futures' (Bonoli *et al.* 2000), and radically shifted the ground for discussion.

The welfare state, until then anchored deeply and unquestioned in most Western democracies' postwar consensus, has increasingly been challenged by a new market-liberal world view. The welfare state is now seen as part of the problem, not as part of the solution, as it was in the earlier Keynesian view. In the economic crises from the early 1970s onwards, the Keynesian postwar consensus was overpowered, and replaced more and more by a set of market-liberal ideas (Rieger 1999). More specifically, the welfare state was alleged to hamper economic growth, to encourage unemployment by undermining work incentives, to set poverty traps, to be unaffordable and a burden on the economy, to diminish international competitiveness,[3] etc. Conservative governments deeply beholden to such ideas took power in the United Kingdom in the late 1970s and in the US in the early 1980s. They entered office with a strong commitment to roll back the welfare state and to unleash market-driven economic dynamics.[4] As this market-revolution unfolded, conservative ideology featured prominently among both academics and then governments of other OECD countries, including those of social-democratic persuasion, and spilled over to the European Community level.

So what happened? How did OECD countries respond to these welfare challenges? At the start of the 21st century, in the wake of the 'conservative revolution' of the *fin de siècle*, where do we find ourselves? In this volume we take stock of 'the state of the welfare state'[5] from several angles, profiting from one academic growth industry of the 1990s, i.e. comparative welfare state studies:

- Franz-Xaver Kaufmann assists us 'Towards a theory of the welfare state' and focuses on the connection between welfare issues and the theory of the state, of economic order etc. His reflections span much of the historical welfare state trajectory and all of the primary welfare state dimensions: personal services, income redistribution and labour protection. He shows how facile contrasts between 'faith in the market' and 'belief in the state' fail to do justice to the complex reality of the 'social welfare sector', its 'intermediary realms' as well as its social services and family dimensions. As a new theoretical point of reference, he proposes 'welfare production', which includes the household perspective. His sober across-the-board assessment of the present condition of the welfare state also provides a look behind the veil of crisis rhetoric, which feeds on the contrast with a 'Golden Age' and on mistaking the real world for the 'land of milk and honey'. He also looks at the consequences of 'globalisation' (cf. Rieger and Leibfried 2001), which are discussed in more detail by Scharpf and Ferrera *et al.* in this volume. We get a broad continental perspective on 'welfare' and its state – contrasted with the liberal US trajectory.

- Francis Castles points us to 'The dog that didn't bark: economic development and the postwar welfare state'. Why is it that most comparative studies have failed to establish linkages between postwar economic and social policy development? More specifically, why has research on advanced capitalist nations failed to uncover a link between economic affluence and levels of social spending? Why has it proven so difficult to establish a connection between economic growth and post-war expansion of the welfare state? Why is it that economic slowdown has not been more directly adduced as a factor accounting for the changed trajectory of welfare state development in recent years? This dog didn't bark, but it did bite – albeit differently in rich Protestant nations than in poor Catholic ones. The story is of a canny canine, whose overall impact can be discerned only by taking a non-linear approach to the post-war development of the welfare state.

- Giuliano Bonoli and Bruno Palier ask 'How do welfare states change?' and look at 'Institutions and their impact on the politics of welfare state reform'. They focus our attention on 'path dependency' as the basic pattern of resistance to institutional change. They look at reforms of unemployment insurance, old-age pensions and health care systems in two prominent and starkly contrasting welfare states: the United Kingdom and France. How differently did these contrasting institutional settings frame the politics of social reform in the last two decades? In France, a middle class bias automatically protected against cuts while Britain's targeted 'welfare' state was prone to a downward slide. In addition, the presence or absence of corporatism shaped the nature and scope of the 'trimming' – the politics of cost-saving – of these welfare states.

- Then Karl Hinrichs takes a closer look at the one welfare state sector central for most welfare states' profile: old-age pensions. He follows 'Elephants on the move' and observes 'Patterns of public pension reform in OECD countries', focusing on the 'social insurance' species. On this elephant march, policy changes have not led to clear convergence among countries. Although the herd is not as scattered as it once was, its points of divergence have, for the most part, merely taken a different form. Moreover, in pensions, political elites are nervously geared to instinctive continuity, a 'steady hand' and calming exercises according to the maxim: 'Don't irritate the elephants. Beware, stampede!' Political rule may be directly destabilised. Nevertheless, the postwar period's quasi-natural 'politically stable equilibrium' (Heclo 1998: 72) surrounding 'social insurance' has vanished, as has the ideological hegemony of once-closed expert policy communities. This has been due to counter-mobilisation in mass media, research institutes, financial services industries etc, and, at least in Europe, has been accompanied by a growing counter-chorus of Basic Income advocacy (cf. Parijs 1995, 2000).

- Stein Kuhnle now puts 'The Nordic welfare state in a European context: dealing with new economic and ideological changes in the 1990s' (see also Kautto *et al.* 1999). He does so to the tune of 'The welfare state is here to stay' – even in 'Scandinavia', where its withering away, or meltdown, has been sighted on numerous occasions in recent years.[6] Its role may change as societal wealth and incomes increase. Perhaps most striking is the Finnish experience of the 1990s. Its advanced, universalistic welfare state actually helped the country cope with the unexpected economic crisis, and extreme external shocks, more rapidly and steadfastly than a less comprehensive welfare state would have, and with less social damage inflicted. Could 'Look to Finland' become a new directive by the World Bank or a new model propagated by the OECD?

- Fritz Scharpf steps back from the welfare state and the institutional approach. From the perspective of political economy he takes a broad comparative look at 'The viability of advanced welfare states in the international economy: vulnerabilities and options', based on the extensive comparative study in Scharpf and Schmidt (2000). His is probably the most sceptical appraisal of 'the state of the welfare state' in this volume. However, he also draws our attention to the strategic dimension that (and how) all of these national welfare states differ greatly in their vulnerability to international economic pressures, in the specific problems they thus most urgently need to address, and in the policy options available to them. There is no 'One best way' for the advanced welfare state to maintain its viability.

- In conclusion Maurizio Ferrera, Anton Hemerijck and Martin Rhodes, squarely confront the future and report from the summit on 'Recasting European welfare states for the 21st century'. They recapitulate the European Community's present social agenda, where the search for 'new value combinations' is seen to be most actively undertaken. They then discuss the nature of the adjustment challenges faced by the presently 15 European welfare states, address their different needs for re-calibration – a new word for reform – and present core components of an optimal adjustment strategy that could reconcile growth with solidarity. Finally, they return to the European Community and its future role in preserving and developing the 'European social model' (Jacques Delors).

So, where are we now?[7]

Most of these accounts strike us as a more or less soft version of 'new institutionalism'. Past commitments, the political weight of welfare constituencies and the inertia of institutional arrangements go a long way in political circumstances in which the median voter has a substantial stake in the welfare state, as is now the case in most OECD countries. This situation might be characterised as the *developed* welfare state. It dates to the late 1960s and 1970s rather than to the 1950s and early 1960s, which was the 'take-off' phase. An examination of Goodin *et al.* (1999) reveals that almost every voter in the Netherlands has a substantial interest in welfare state outcomes, a clear majority has one in Germany (Manow 2001), while in the US only a substantial *minority* is similarly affected. The developed welfare state marks the watershed in welfare state development, and only then did the welfare state come into its own, becoming an independent, politically broadly supported system which was solidly anchored in electoral majorities. The welfare state had now gained parity with market forces. This produced a permanent instability of a higher order, which Janowitz (1976) had already noted, now with two classes of possessive individuals counter-balancing each other, the old and new propertied. Perhaps here continental European welfare states, from Finland to Germany, stand out most, as Bonoli and Palier reveal in their sample of the UK and France. Schemes that mainly redistribute horizontally and protect the middle classes well are more likely to be resistant against cuts. Their support base is larger and more influential compared with schemes targeted at the poor. The contrast between the overall resistance of the French social insurance system to cuts and the withering away of its British counterpart is telling, and also speaks for (at least) two worlds of welfare state reform. But also, as Kuhnle reveals, the Scandinavian welfare states have proved to be quite resistant to a fundamental rollback. Here also, middle-class inclusion in the arrangements of social security has helped avert major benefit cuts and a *Gestalt-switch*.

A core message of all the contributions is: *The race to the bottom has not taken place.* On the contrary, a glance at the latest social spending data provided by the OECD[8] reveals that in the last two decades, with the exception of the Netherlands, all nations continued to expand their welfare state. However, this picture looks less bright if one allows for cross-national variation in the factors pushing social spending, such as the level of unemployment or the age profile. Nevertheless, if convergence took place at all it was 'divergent convergence', as Hinrichs here and Scclcib-Kaiser elsewhere (1999, 2000) have pointed out. Consequently, we find different national trajectories of welfare state adjustment in response to broadly similar challenges. The welfare state does not follow a unified logic, nor do its reforms.[9] The different reform paths pursued are, in turn, influenced and shaped by a series of factors: the partisan complexion of government, the power resources and aggregation capacity of trade unions and employers, the system of interest mediation, the room for manoeuvre granted by a nation's polity and, last but not least, the institutional legacy of the welfare state regime – including the different sets of problems associated with each regime.

However, no contribution sounds an *all clear* sign for the huge welfare state steamer. Kuhnle's happy postwar affair between welfare state and the nation state in the golden economic age of full employment ended in the 1970s and is now history. All welfare states on the ground are exposed to a variety of challenges touched upon in these essays, and these challenges look somewhat different in each national case. This is a story about reconfiguring the welfare state, about it being 'locked in' by past needs and deeds, not about its crisis and demise. Kaufmann summarises the changing times in an interesting metaphor: 'Politics of the future will resemble more the attempt to steer a sailing-ship dependent on fair winds than the task of commanding a steamer dependent on the power of its own engine.' But, sailing boats may sail against the wind (doing even better than steamers), and in their modern, developed versions also have strong engines. In Europe, the major challenge of the 21st century may turn out to be the broken link between the nation – the national communality and community of fate – and the welfare state, a link that may not be completely re-forged via European integration. In addition, the reform trajectory will unfold differently in countries that never fully crossed the welfare state threshold, such as the United States (Katznelson 1986, 1988;

Heclo 1995; Glazer 1988; Amenta and Skocpol 1989). The future will look quite different as well in the countries of 'East Asia'; South Korea (Kwon 1998) and Taiwan are examples where the institutions we have come to label 'welfare state' may mask a radically different historical-political and socio-cultural reality (Rieger and Leibfried 1999). Essentially, then, we are facing the future of the *European* welfare state.

Within the European perspective as well, the challenges confronting welfare states vary considerably across national boundaries. Restructuring the welfare state and adjusting it to a new environment is a multi-dimensional undertaking. Several problems emerged or were not adequately addressed in the past, problems that vary again with the institutional arrangements chosen in each country. To begin with, the social foundations that originally provided the firm ground for consolidating and expanding the European welfare state have been weakened or eroded altogether (see Esping-Andersen 1999). These developments are well known: they are the transformation of the traditional family structure and the male bread-winner model. The diminishing role of continuous and 'life-long' full-time employ-ment and the increasing diversity of careers are only some of the phrases which attempt to capture this most recent 'great transformation'. Welfare states, like all institutions, lag behind such developments since they are mostly tailored to fixed assumptions about social structure in times long past. In a certain sense, welfare states freeze social structure and much depends on their capacity for self-guidance, self-steering, and their different institutional potentials for endogenous self-limitation (see Rieger and Leibfried 1998: 282). New social risks have emerged which do not fit the old assumptions. The high incidence of poverty among single-parent families may serve as an example, or the distinct dynamics of today's Continental poverty, which calls for an *activating* welfare state rather than a passive transfer or support state (Leisering and Leibfried 1999). Most welfare states still maintain their well-developed safety nets for those who fit the 'Golden Age' criteria on which the national models of social security were built. So welfare states tend to overreach by looking back, and are inclined to underreach in looking at the present or the future.

A similar selectivity takes place in the interaction of the welfare state with the labour market – a field that is under-researched compared with work on the institutions of the welfare state itself.[10] Rapid technological change has widened the gap between low and high skilled workers (Nickell 1998). Regulations designed to protect insiders in the labour market, when low-skilled labour had a prominent place in the market, now function as major obstacles for low-skilled outsiders to find a job. Here the welfare state produces 'closure'. In particular, Continental welfare states, still inclined to the family wage and thus to high contribution rates, do not provide much of an incentive to employers to hire low-skilled and not-so-productive workers. In addition, the employment potential of the 'service society' and the attendant expansion of the tertiary sector may not be exhausted. Moreover, policies and strategies pursued by trade unions contribute little to covering this Achilles heel of 'conservative' welfare regimes. The structure of funding and benefits can thus also be seen as a source of unemployment. This does not necessarily lead down a market-liberal path of reform. Scaling down social benefits will not solve the problem. But intelligent reforms can shape incentives in the direction of an 'activating welfare state'. The unemployed or the recipients of Social Assistance often face marginal tax rates of close to 100% if they take up a job, although they keep health insurance benefits, which their counterparts in the US lose after one year. The latter do not regain health benefits in much of the low end of the labour market, since health insurance reform failed in the US and thus never closed the gap (Stone 1993; Hacker 1997; Skocpol 1997). Redesigning incentive structures combined with social investments aimed at human capital formation could be steps towards enhancing employment, as Scharpf has argued repeatedly.

Systematically speaking, the issue here is that we know from T. H. Marshall's 1949 lecture (1964) that welfare states are systems that produce their own social inequality independent of the market system. The welfare state may reinforce primary inequality by positively privileging winners, and thus create double losers, or it may compensate for primary inequality, and thus protect losers, or it may mix both approaches. We need to understand better the combination of these two selective systems. When we look at the tax–benefit balance sheet over recent years it may already seem that, in quite a few places, market losers are already negatively privileged by the welfare state (Goodin *et al.* 1999), which radically diminishes the welfare state's potential for social integration and for buffering social change.

There is also some evidence that the welfare state has contributed to speeding up demographic changes common to OECD countries. Again the Continental regime stands out. Continental countries have low fertility rates since there is a trade-off between career and family formation (Esping-Andersen 1996), which is neither mitigated by social services or flexible and temporary opting-out opportunities as in the Nordic countries, nor by the broader US private labour market option. Consequently, Continental welfare states also need to forge a new 'gender contract'.[11] As European as well as third-country immigration into most European nations continues to fill some of the fertility gap, this will necessitate a new 'ethnic contract' as well, as the homogeneity of most European societies that made for closely related 'social citizens' – all more or less pre-integrated into one self-perceived communality and community of fate – disappears. In addition, a top-heavy demography, combined with a different labour market fate of the younger cohort, will require a new 'generational contract'. Consequently, a new (at least) triple 'social contract' will be required to reshape the new 'communities of fate' in the making and to underpin the reformation of the welfare state.

In light of such challenges, it becomes clear that the welfare state definitely has a future. New social problems have emerged while others have been solved, or have even disappeared. Also, as the welfare state was built and a richer society evolved, 'problems' have transformed. The original five negatives attacked by the Beveridge Report in 1942 may now largely be reformulated as five positives to be pursued (Giddens 1998/2000). Indeed, some are already highly institutionalized, like the shifts from 'disease' to 'health' and from 'ignorance' to 'education'. But does the welfare state provide the right tools to pursue these goals or do market-based instruments look more promising? Is it still true that the highly developed 'new' economies need to maintain social cohesion and political stability through some automatic stabiliser in the form of welfare state institutions? The lumbering old welfare state steamer is unlikely to be able to cope with this heavy sea of new challenges. Kaufmann's flexible sailing ships may be needed, especially if they have some motors of their own. Redesigning the welfare state is the critical analytical and political issue, not retrenchment.[12] But even sailing ships are not 'nano-machines' – they have (leaner) bureaucracies, are still bound by entitlements (the rule of law) and are regularly entrusted to professionals, to experienced sailors. 'Activating' welfare states, therefore, may not fully facilitate the leap from 'want' to 'autonomy' or from 'idleness' to 'initiative', as Giddens would wish.

In several respects, issues of the 'hidden welfare state' will come to the fore in the future. This will go beyond 'occupational welfare' (Titmuss 1958) as we knew it. It will involve the linkage between the tax system and the welfare state, which pertains to much more than just the *Earned Income Tax Credit* (*EITC*) in the USA (Howard 1999; Myles/Pierson 1997), but also to the status of the family in the tax system (see Kaufmann in this volume), and also includes the relationship between public and private pensions (Shalev 1996). This will relate as well to the level of equality or inequality of primary income distribution, which interacts with the scope and depth of secondary redistribution, i.e. the welfare state monetary transfers – touched upon by Kaufmann and others; and to the interaction between the 'private insurance' industry in general and the public welfare state, a relationship that has become increasingly unstable in the European Community (Leibfried/Pierson 2000: 285f.). In a sense, what is usually called the 'welfare state' is just the public tip of the iceberg. Much of its future will depend on those other 'institutions' hidden under water, not just on raw social issues and their political processing. To switch the metaphor, we are dealing with a system of interconnected pressure valves of which the welfare state is only one and the complex dynamics of these various interacting pressures has become a force for social reform in several countries.

Specifically on the Continent, a major important 'hidden issue' is the formation of 'social capital.' In Anglo-American social science and administrative thinking, 'education' always figured as an important part of social policy, so much so that the growth of higher education in 19th century America was seen as functionally equivalent to the development of social insurance in Germany (Heidenheimer 1981).[14] So, one of Beveridge's five giants was naturally 'ignorance', and one of Giddens' five positives is naturally 'education'. In Germany and France, and probably in many other Continental countries, 'education' is not a sub-sector of social policy but a distinct field of its own, tied to institutionalised notions of cultivating status and maintaining culture, also dating from the 19th century. Consequently, welfare state reform is seen as not related to education and vice versa.[15] Only against resistance and in the negative – a synthetic look at 'poverty' and education[16]– may these two fields be brought together (Allmendinger 1999). To move from a 'welfare state' to a 'social investment state,'[17] as Giddens (1998) advises, would seem a particular challenge here, as the walls between 'social' and 'education' policy would need to be broken down – walls often cemented additionally by federal structures.

In sum, welfare states have a future, but ones which may turn out to be quite different from their Golden Age past. This is not hard to see once we lift the veil of crisis rhetoric. The time to come may also hold some surprises: the welfare state's future may not so much be challenged by 'globalisation' as that the welfare state itself might develop into a major institution, destined to sustain the new era of international interdependence. After all, the welfare state has grown into a central buffer institution protecting the interlinked economic order of most of the OECD world. As Dani Rodrik remarked:

In essence governments have used their fiscal powers to insulate domestic groups from excessive market risks ... At the present however, international economic integration is taking place against the background of receding governments and diminished social obligations. ... Yet the need for social insurance for the vast majority of the population that remains internationally immobile has not diminished. If anything, this need has become greater as a consequence of greater integration. The question therefore is how the tension between globalisation and the pressures for socialisation of risk can be eased. If the tension is not managed intelligently and creatively, the danger is that domestic consensus in favour of open markets will ultimately erode to the point where a generalised resurgence of protectionism becomes a serious possibility. (Rodrik 1997: 6; see also Rieger and Leibfried 1998, 2001)

A major problem will be whether this buffering 'hidden hand' of a modern welfare state can also be made to work visibly. The early postwar growth of the welfare state provided a broad window of opportunity for a new era of free trade, globally and via European integration. But this was an unintended consequence of institutionalising welfare states, which were built for purely domestic purposes. While there are now majorities for such welfare states, there may be no stable majorities for such re-calibrated welfare states aimed directly at fulfilling the buffer function in a more adequate way. Electoral support gaps of this kind may turn out to be the decisive Achilles heel of welfare state reform in the 21st century.

Notes

1. Ira Katznelson calls this the 'welfare state as a permanently contested institutional idea' (Katznelson 1988, see also 1986).
2. With the coming of the developed welfare state after the 1970s, i.e. with the median voter being solidly anchored in the welfare state, occasionally, in good times, the availability of 'pie' would drive the expansion of the welfare slice. However, since the 1980s we have returned to the normalcy of 'politics against markets' in most OECD nations.
3. A leading European student of this issue in economics remains agnostic: 'The studies of the aggregate relationship between economic performance and the size of the welfare state ... do not yield conclusive evidence. The results of econometric studies of the relationship between social transfer spending and growth rates are mixed: some find that high spending on social transfers leads to lower growth, others find the reverse. The largest of the estimated effects – in either direction – do not, however, seem believable' (Atkinson 1999: 184).
4. For a comparison of the – *comparatively* modest – results see Pierson (1994, 1996) and Atkinson (1999), and on the US future see Weir (1997).
5. For other stock-taking exercises see lately Atkinson (1999), Bonoli *et al.* (2000), Clayton and Pontusson (1998), Ebbinghaus and Manow (2000), Ferrera, Hemerijck and Rhodes (2000), Ferrera and Rhodes (2000), Huber and Stephens (2001), Iversen (2000), Kuhnle (2000), Leibfried and Wagschal (2000), Pierson (2001), Stephens, Huber and Ray (1999), and Sykes *et al.* (2000).
6. That the Swedish welfare state remained intact is not for want of extremely critical neoliberal arguments (see Lindbeck 1997).
7. For a recent overview see Leibfried (2000).
8. OECD, Social Expenditure Data Base, CD-Rom, Paris: OECD. For the OECD view on welfare state futures see also OECD (1997, 1999).
9. See the pioneering study of Visser and Hemerijck (1997; and now 2000) on the Netherlands and its reform trajectory, and now especially Scharpf and Schmidt (2000) for an evaluation of such reforms in 12 countries across the OECD.
10. For a good first overview see Jochem and Siegel (2000).
11. On gender and the welfare state see O'Connor *et al.* (1999) and Lewis (1993).
12. The focus on redesign will then lead to distinguishing the different kinds of policy changes involved (see Bonoli and Palier (1998).

9

13. These stark differences in primary distribution point to different welfare *capitalisms* already at 'the point of production'. Here the debate over 'varieties of capitalism' (Hall and Soskice 2000; Soskice 1999) has one crucial interface with welfare state analysis (Ebbinghaus and Manow 2000).
14. When education is seen as part of social policy, the trade-offs between the different paradigms of securing equality – equality of opportunities versus equality of results – may be studied more easily within one nation, and not just cross-nationally, as Heidenheimer (1981) did.
15. Illustrations for this abound in Germany. The regular federal 'Social Report' (*Sozialbericht/Sozialbudget*) addresses social transfers and social services (but not education services, excepting those that are directly part of active labour market policy) – thus 'welfare state cuts' can never be conceived as potential 'education state' gains; the recognition of years of education in the pension formula has been slowly marginalised – the years recognised fell to three from thirteen in several steps – without any consideration of the 'social capital' effects and the necessary reshaping of the linkage between 'time for qualification' and the shape of the 'social wage' (especially for women for whom extended recognition contributed strongly to lifting them out of poverty).
16. About 10% of each age cohort do not pass the A-levels (*Hauptschulabschluß*) in Germany each year, a 'must' to enter the German labour market at any level. Ethnic minorities are strongly over-represented in this 10%, which could result in long-term, cumulative social exclusion.
17. The move towards a 'welfare society' would seem less of a problem (see Leisering and Leibfried 1999: 294, 308–312).

References

Allmendinger, J. (1999) Bildungsarmut. Zur Verschränkung von Bildungs- und Sozialpolitik (Educational Poverty – On Interrelating Education and Social Policy), *Soziale Welt*, **50**(1), 35–50.
Amenta, E. and Skocpol, T. (1989) Taking exception: explaining the distinctiveness of American public policies in the last century. In: F. C. Castles (ed), *The Comparative History of Public Policy*, Cambridge: Polity Press, pp. 292–333.
Atkinson, A. B. (1999) *The Economic Consequences of Rolling Back the Welfare State*, Cambridge MA: MIT Press.
Beveridge, W. H. (1942) *Report on Social Insurance and Allied Services* (Beveridge Report), London: HMSO (Cmd 6404).
Bonoli, G. and Palier, B. (1998) Changing the politics of social programmes. Innovative change in British and French welfare reforms, *Journal of European Social Policy*, **8**(4), 317–330.
Bonoli, G., George, V. and Taylor-Gooby, P. (2000) *European Welfare Futures: Towards a Theory of Rentrenchment*, Cambridge: Polity Press.
Clayton, R. and Pontusson, J. (1998) Welfare-state retrenchment revisited: entitlement cuts, public sector restructuring, and inegalitarian trends in advanced capitalist societies, *World Politics*, **51**(1), 67–98.
Ebbinghaus, B. and Manow, P. (eds) (2000) *Varieties of Welfare Capitalism. Social Policy and Political Economy in Europe, Japan and the USA*, Routledge: London (in preparation).
Esping-Andersen, G. (1985) *Politics against Markets. The Social Democratic Road to Power*, Princeton NJ: Princeton University Press.
Esping-Andersen, G. (1996) Welfare states without work: the impasse of labour shedding and familialism in continental European social policy. In: Gösta Esping-Andersen (ed), *Welfare States in Transition. National Adaptations in Global Economies*, London: Sage, pp. 66–87.
Esping-Andersen, G. (1999) *Social Foundations of Postindustrial Economies*, Oxford: Oxford University Press.

Ferrera, M., Hemerijck, A., and Rhodes, M. (2000) *The Future of Social Europe. Recasting Work and Welfare in the New Economy*, CELTA: Oeiras, Portugal.

Ferrera, M. and Rhodes, M. (eds) (2000) Recasting European welfare states, *West European Politics* (special issue), **23**(2).

Giddens, A. (1998) *The Third Way*, Cambridge: Polity Press (extracted as 'Positive welfare' in C. Pierson and Castles 2000: pp. 369–379).

Glazer, N. (1988) The American welfare state: incomplete or different? In: N. Glazer, *The Limits of Social Policy*, Cambridge MA and London: Harvard University Press, 168–192, 204–205.

Goodin, R. E., Headey, B., Muffels, R. and Dirven, H.-J. (1999) *The Real Worlds of Welfare Capitalism*, Cambridge: Cambridge University Press.

Hacker, J. (1997) *The Road to Nowhere: The Genesis of President Clinton's Plan for Health Security*, Princeton NJ: Princeton University Press.

Hall, P. and Soskice, D. (eds) (2000) *Varieties of Capitalism: The Institutional Foundations of Comparative Advantage*. Cambridge University Press (in preparation).

Heclo, H. (1995) The social question. In: K. McFate, R. Lawson and W. Julius Wilson, (eds), *Poverty, Inequality, and the Future of Social Policy*, New York: Russell Sage Foundation, pp. 665–691.

Heclo, H. (1998) A political science perspective on social security reform. In: R. D. Arnold, M. Graetz and A. H. Munnell (eds), *Framing the Social Security Debate. Values, Politics and Economics*, Washington DC: The Brookings Institution Press, pp. 65–89.

Heidenheimer, A. J. (1981) Education and social security entitlements in Europe and America. In: P. Flora and A. J. Heidenheimer (eds), *The Development of Welfare States in Europe and America*, New Brunswick NJ: Transaction Books, pp. 269–306.

Howard, C. (1999) *The Hidden Welfare State: Tax Expenditures and Social Policy in the United States*, Princeton NJ: Princeton University Press.

Huber, E. and Stephens, J. D. (2001) *Political Choice in Global Markets: Development and Crisis of Advanced Welfare States*, Chicago, IL: University of Chicago Press.

Iversen, T. (2000) The dynamics of welfare state expansion: trade openness, de-industrialization and partisan politics. In: Pierson 2001: pp. 45–79.

Janowitz, M. (1976) *Social Control of the Welfare State*, Chicago and London: University of Chicago Press.

Jochem, S. and Siegel, N. (2000) Wohlfahrtskapitalismus und Beschäftigungsperformanz – Das 'Modell Deutschland' im Vergleich (Welfare Capitalism and Employment Performance – The 'German Model' Compared), *Zeitschrift für Sozialreform* **46**(1), 38–64.

Katznelson, I. (1986) The welfare state as a contested institutional idea, *Politics & Society* **16,** 517–531.

Katznelson, I. (1988) Rethinking the silences of social and economic policies, *Political Science Quarterly* **101,** 307–325.

Kautto, M., Heikkilä, M., Hvinden, B., Marklund, S. and Ploug, N. (1999) *Nordic Social Policy. Changing Welfare States*, London: Routledge.

Kitschelt, H., Lange, P., Marks, G. and Stephens, J.D. (eds) (1998) *Continuity and Change in Contemporary Capitalism*, Cambridge: Cambridge University Press.

Kuhnle, S. (ed) (2000) *Survival of the European Welfare State*, London: Routledge.

Kwon, H.-J. (1998) *The Welfare State in Korea: The Politics of Legitimation*, Basingstoke: Macmillan.

Leibfried, S. (2000) National welfare states, European integration and globalization: a perspective for the next century, *Social Policy & Administration* **34**(1), 44–63.

Leibfried, S. and Pierson, P. (2000) Social policy. Left to courts and markets? In: H. Wallace and W. Wallace (eds), *Policy-Making in the European Union*, 4th edn, Oxford: Oxford University Press, pp. 267–292.

Leibfried, S. and Wagschal, U. (eds) (2000) *Der Deutsche Sozialstaat: Bilanzen, Reformen,*

Perspektiven (The German Welfare State – Status, Reforms, Perspectives), Frankfurt a.M.: Campus.

Leisering, L. and Leibfried, S. (1999) *Time and Poverty in Western Welfare States. United Germany in Perspective*, Cambridge: Cambridge University Press.

Lewis, J. (ed). (1993) *Women and Social Policy in Europe: Work, Family and the State*, Aldershot Hants.: Edward Elgar.

Lindbeck, A. (1997) *The Swedish Experiment*, Stockholm: SNS Förlag.

Mann, K. (1998) The welfare state and postmodernity, *Critical Social Policy* **18**(1), 85–93 (reprinted in Pierson and Castles 2000: pp. 360–368).

Manow, P. (2001) Social protection, capitalist production. Explorations into the political economy of the German welfare state (in preparation).

Marshall, T. H. (1964) Citizenship and social class. In: T.H. Marshall, *Class, Citizenship and Social Development*, Garden City NJ: Doubleday, pp. 65–122 (first published 1950, first held 1949 as Marshall Lecture at Cambridge University).

Myles, J. and Pierson, P. (1997) Friedman's revenge: the reform of 'liberal' welfare states in Canada and the United States, *Politics & Society* **25**(4), 443–472.

Nickell, S. (1998) The collapse in demand for the unskilled: what can be done? In: R. B. Freeman and P. Gottschalk (eds), *Generating Jobs. How to Increase Demand for Less-Skilled Workers*, New York: Russell Sage Foundation, pp. 297–319.

O'Connor, J., Orloff, A. S. and Shaver, S. (1999) *States, Markets, Families. Gender, Liberalism and Social Policy in Australia, Canada, Great Britain and the United States*, Cambridge: Cambridge University Press.

OECD (1997) *Societal Cohesion and the Globalising Economy. What Does the Future Hold?* Paris: OECD.

OECD (1999) *A Caring World*, Paris: OECD.

Parijs, P. van (1995) *Real Freedom for All*, Oxford: Oxford University Press.

Parijs, P. van (2000) Basic income and the two dilemmas of the welfare state. In: Pierson and Castles 2000: pp. 355–359.

Pierson, P. (1994) *Dismantling the Welfare State? Reagan, Thatcher, and the Politics of Retrenchment*, Cambridge: Cambridge University Press.

Pierson, P. (1996) The new politics of the welfare state, *World Politics* **48**(2), 143–179.

Pierson, P. (ed) (2001) *The New Politics of the Welfare State*, Oxford: Oxford University Press (in preparation).

Pierson, C. and Castles, F. G. (2000) *The Welfare State Reader*, Cambridge: Polity Press.

Rieger, E. (1999) Global capitalism and the politics of social policy reform in Germany and the United States. In: C. Lankowski (ed), *Responses to Globalization in Germany and the United States. Seven Sectors Compared*, Washington DC: American Institute for Contemporary German Studies, The Johns Hopkins University, pp. 101–129 (AICGS Research Report no. 10).

Rieger, E. and Leibfried, S. (1998) Welfare state limits to globalization, *Politics & Society* **26**(4), 363–390.

Rieger, E., and Leibfried, S. (1999) Wohlfahrtsstaat und Sozialpolitik in Ostasien. Der Einfluß von Religion im Kulturvergleich (Welfare state and social policy in East Asia. The comparative influence of religion). In: G. Schmidt and R. Trinczek (eds), *Globalisierung. Ökonomische und soziale Herausforderungen am Ende des zwanzigsten Jahrhunderts*, Baden-Baden: Nomos, pp. 413–499.

Rieger, E. and Leibfried, S. (2001) *Grundlagen der Globalisierung. Perspektiven des Wohlfahrtsstaats* (Foundations of Globalization – Perspectives for Welfare States), Frankfurt am Main: Suhrkamp (in preparation).

Rodrik, D. (1997) *Has Globalization Gone too Far?* Washington DC: Institute for International Economics.

Scharpf, F. W. and Schmidt, V. A. (eds) (2000) *From Vulnerability to Competitiveness: Welfare and Work in the Open Economy*, Oxford: Oxford University Press, 2 vols.

Schmidt, M.G. (2000) *Demokratietheorien* (Theories of Democracy), 3rd edn, Opladen: Westdeutscher Verlag.

Seeleib-Kaiser, M. (1999): Wohlfahrtssysteme und Bedingungen der Globalisierung: Divergenz, Konvergenz oder divergente Konvergenz? (Welfare Systems and the Conditions of Globalization: Divergence, Convergence and Divergent Convergence), *Zeitschrift für Sozialreform* **45**(1), 3–23.

Seeleib-Kaiser, M. (2000) *Globalisierung, Politische Diskurse und Wohlfahrtssysteme* (Globalization, Political Discourse and Welfare Systems) [book draft]

Shalev, M. (ed) (1996) *The Privatization of Social Policy? Occupational Welfare and the Welfare State in America, Scandinavia and Japan*, London: Macmillan.

Skocpol, T. (1997) *Boomerang: Health Care Reform and the Turn against Government*, New York: W.W. Norton.

Soskice, D. (1999) Divergent production regimes: coordinated and uncoordinated market economies in the 1980s and 1990s. In: Kitschelt *et al.* 1999: pp. 101–134.

Stephens, J. D., Huber, E. and Ray, L. (1999) The welfare state in hard times. In: Kitschelt *et al.* 1999: pp. 164–193.

Stone, D. A. (1993) The struggle for the soul of health insurance, *Journal of Health Politics, Policy and Law*, **18**(2), 287–317.

Sykes, R., Palier, B. and Prior, P. (eds) (2000) *Globalization and European Welfare States: Challenges and Changes*, London: Macmillan.

Titmuss, R. M. (1958) The social division of welfare. In: R. M. Titmuss, *Essays on the Welfare State*, London: George Allen and Unwin, pp. 34–55.

Visser, J. and Hemerijck, A. (1997) *A Dutch Miracle. Job Growth, Welfare Reform and Corporatism in the Netherlands*, Amsterdam: Amsterdam University Press.

Visser, J. and Hemerijck, A. (2000) Die pragmatische Anpassung des niederländischen Sozialstaates. Ein Lehrstück? (Pragmatically Adjusting the Dutch Welfare State. A Lesson for Others?). In: Leibfried and Wagschal 2000: pp. 452–473.

Weir, M. (1997) *The Social Divide. Political Parties and the Future of Activist Government*, Washington DC and New York: Brookings Institution/Russell Sage Foundation.

Zacher, H. F. (2000) Der deutsche Sozialstaat am Ende des Jahrhunderts (The German Welfare State at the End of the Century). In: Leibfried and Wagschal 2000: pp. 53–90.

About the Authors

Stephan Leibfried is Professor of Social Policy and Social Administration at the University of Bremen. He is Director of the Centre for Social Policy Research and the Research Centre on Life Courses Studies. He has written extensively on welfare state development, especially on poverty in the US, UK and Germany and the effects of European integration on national welfare states.

Herbert Obinger is Research Assistant at the Center for Social Policy Research. His research interests are in social policy and comparative political economy. A recent publication is *Politische Institutionen und Sozialpolitik in der Schweiz* (Political institutions and social policy in Switzerland).

European Review, Vol. 8, No. 3, 291–312 (2000) © Academia Europaea, Printed in the United Kingdom

2 Towards a theory of the welfare state

FRANZ-XAVER KAUFMANN*

The understanding of welfare states hitherto suffers from characteristic biases – national, political and disciplinary. This paper proposes a generalized framework for international comparative research designed to be as immune as possible to such biases. The guarantee of social rights for all and the issue of societal reproduction are taken as reference points to define the political criteria for social welfare. However, politics and social policies remain a partial aspect of the production of welfare in a given society. A theory of the welfare state has to take into account the interactions among household production, market production and associative forms of welfare production, on the one hand, and political interventions on the other.

The lack of theory of and for the welfare state

What is usually termed the 'welfare state' ekes out an existence without theory in the space between jurisprudence, economics, and relevant analyses in sociology and political science. In the German-speaking world, the activity of the 'Verein für Socialpolitik' provided, from 1873, an early academic foundation for applied social policy, and in Britain such questions have been treated in the framework of an independent discipline, 'Social Administration'. Essentially, however, the discussion focuses on history, institutions, individual measures and their reform. Historical and international comparisons of the developments in social and economic policies, which the British call 'the welfare state', the Germans 'der Sozialstaat', the French 'l'état providence', the Dutch 'Verzorgingsstat' and the Swedish 'Folkhemmet' have been undertaken only recently. In the USA, on the other hand, 'welfare' is understood solely as poor-relief and a 'welfare state' is distrusted for creating 'dependency'. To be sure, other terms such as 'social protection', 'social security' or 'social services' are also used, but no term mobilises political passions and academic scrutiny like 'the welfare state' and its equivalents in other languages.

Since social policies evolved independently in different nations, they differed in their legitimisation, in the political issues that came into focus and in the shape of the institutions which emerged from the political controversies. The same may be said about democracy and even about market capitalism, which exhibit national, or at least cultural, characteristics. Although there is an extensive international debate about the conception of democracy or a

* Graf-von-Galen Strasse 5, D-33619 Bielefeld, Germany. E-mail: f.x.kaufmann@uni-bielefeld.de.

market economy, there is no comparable discussion about the concept of the welfare state. Comparative inquiries are dominated by the inductive method, and comparisons focus almost entirely on easily comparable issues such as social budgets or legal norms. Social services as such are rarely compared (see Alber 1995).

To this day, there have been few attempts to connect systematically social welfare issues with questions of theories concerning the state, the economic order, political guidance, social structure or ethics, and to the extent that such an attempt is made, it has usually been done with a characteristic disciplinary one-sidedness. Moreover, the scientific treatment of issues often suffers from political and ideological biases. Liberal authors mistrust state intervention *a priori*, while Social-Democratic and Christian-Democratic authors all too easily take social problems as evidence of the state's responsibility to solve problems, without considering the restrictions on administrative policy suggested by the structure of the problems or by the requirements of the economic system.

Various reasons can be adduced for this situation. The most important – in the political and economic sciences alike – is itself of a theoretical nature and stems from an inadequate conceptualization of the societal context. Legal and political science distinguish between the 'state' and 'society', and economics distinguishes between the 'market economy' and the 'state', thus these two fields do not share the same concept of the state. Hegel, to whom we owe the theoretical distinction between the 'state' and 'civil society', already knew a third principle of association, namely the 'family'. Yet, the welfare-creating services of private households are conceptually ignored by both points of view. The manifold services of private associations, as well as corporatism, fit equally poorly into this scheme. The dominance of legal and economic thought has led to the development of an abstract antithesis between the 'market' and the 'state' that serves as the starting point for all considerations about systematic economic policy today. However, modern societies command a greater arsenal of principles of control and administration, and, as will be shown, such societies depend on the complementarity of these principles.

A less visible reason for the dominance of the sterile opposition between market and state stems from differences between US and continental European conceptions of the state and society. The Americans' individualistic idea of society is based on the experience of the 'frontier' ('Go west, young man') and the repeated necessity of forming a community 'from the bottom up'. In Europe, by contrast, the state, including an efficient state administration, preceded the liberalisation of markets and also democratisation. Britain is an exception, where the 'civil service' was not built up until almost two centuries after the 'Glorious Revolution'. As is well known, the state administration in the United States is very unevenly professionalised, even to this day. Another cultural difference is the absence of Roman law in the English-speaking countries. The 'state' as a *unified order* of government, administration and jurisprudence, created by positive constitutional and statutory law is, strictly speaking, unknown. The term 'government' used in the Anglo-Saxon world covers a substantially narrower area (see Dyson 1980).

Thus, the continental European and Anglo-Saxon political cultures display characteristic differences, precisely in terms of the conception of the state, and this manifests itself in a different degree of trust in the state's ability to solve problems. However, in continental Europe there is a greater acceptance of arguments based on public interest and, consequently, of the legitimacy of state intervention. This essay focuses on a more general conception of the welfare state, which transcends the idiosyncrasies of national or ideological perspectives, although it cannot systematically discuss all the pertinent questions.

Starting points for a general idea of the welfare state

What we generally term the welfare state refers not only to the state, but also, as German social scientists precisely formulated in the mid-19th century, to civil society. The 'mediation' between the private sphere of the market economy and the public sphere of government under law was referred to around 1850 as 'Sozialpolitik' (Pankoke 1970; Kaufmann 2000). 'Sozialpolitik' may be translated into English as 'social policy' or 'social politics'. In the German context the main concern addressed by social politics was the political and social integration of the emerging working classes into the newly constituted German Reich. In the British and Scandinavian tradition there was, for a long time, no comprehensive concept for the emerging policies of labour protection, social security and social services. The term 'welfare state' was accepted in Scandinavia in the 1930s, but was only widely used in Great Britain after World War II.[1] 'Welfare state' here is less concerned with social politics than with social policies. It covers 'the institutional outcome of a society's assumption of legal and therefore formal and explicit responsibility for the basic well-being of all of its members' (Girvetz 1968: 512).

Political theories start with the state, and economic theories start with the (market) economy; thus, each approach has a one-sided view of the specific characteristics of social welfare. However, even the social scientists' metaphors of 'mediation' or 'mixture' cannot serve as keys to solving the problem, for they do not acknowledge, and reveal the reasons for, the inadequacy of the mere separation of the spheres of the rule of law – enforced by compulsion – and the free market economy. As is well known, these reasons, thematised under the term *social question*, originally referred to the pauperism of the transitional period and, later, to the problematical situation of the workers in general. Legally (for example, in terms of the right to vote and the right of free association), as well as economically (in poverty and precarious employment), workers were excluded from the status of both citizen and bourgeois. The abolition of feudal ties had given them legal and contractual rights, but not the right to own the means of production, which was considered a prerequisite of bourgeois society. From the outset of industrialisation, it was not implausible that, with the necessary diligence, someone could save enough money to go into business for himself. Even economic liberalism recognised a 'right to work' for independent workers; no one was to be excluded from a trade by guild or state restrictions. However, Karl Marx showed in his analysis of capitalism that the competitive mechanism had an intrinsic tendency toward the 'centralisation of capital' and thus that the dependent employment of unpropertied workers was not only a biographical phase of youth, but a lasting condition of an economic class. In parallel, Lorenz von Stein (1850) developed the idea of state mediation in the conflict between the classes of proprietors and workers. This involved protection of private property, but also the conferral of rights on workers and their education and protection.

Not only the situation of the individual worker was at stake, but also that of his family. This aspect was neglected in the German discussion, but became the centre of the discussion in

France where, influenced by Frédéric Le Play, Christian entrepreneurs very early on experimented with family wages. As long as child labour was not forbidden, family income at least tended to increase with family size. However, the ban on child labour and the introduction of universal compulsory education deprived parents of their children's working capacity, putting children exclusively on the debit side of the family budget.

English liberals had reason to oppose the ban on child labour on the basis of the systematic economic policy principle 'government shall not interfere', for every state intervention results in new problems and political demands. However, the moral objections to child labour practices uncovered by commissions of inquiry proved more compelling than such liberal ideological convictions, even in England (see Frazer 1984: 11ff.). In France and Prussia, these arguments were supplemented early by national political justifications, such as the weakening of military power, which also came to bear in Great Britain during the Boer War. Today, demographic arguments and arguments based on the theory of human capital, in particular, point out the family's indispensable reproductive services to society (Myrdal 1934; O'Neill 1994).

We have, thus, identified two starting points for the development of a general conception of social welfare – the first concerns social rights and the second, societal reproduction.

(1) As early as 1949, T. H. Marshall designated social rights, as anchored in the United Nations General Declaration of Human and Civil Rights, to be a systematic supplement to the civil and political rights accompanying citizenship (Marshall 1964). Like political rights, these are not defensive rights against state intervention, but participatory rights; they refer to participation in social life. That makes these rights ambivalent for systematic economic policy since they can be guaranteed only by state intervention in economic and social relationships, which the liberal credo would exclude. Expanding on T. H. Marshall, Talcott Parsons and Niklas Luhmann have coined the term *inclusion* to underscore this characteristic of welfare-state responsibility. For Parsons, inclusion means the recognition of a person as a member of a social community, i.e. primarily a moral state of affairs with legal consequences. In contrast, Luhmann defines the term functionally: 'Each person must be able to gain access to all functional realms. Everyone must have legal status permitting him to start a family, take part in exercising or at least in supervising political power; everyone must be educated in schools, be able to obtain medical care if necessary, and to take part in economic activity. The principle of inclusion replaces that of solidarity based on belonging to one and only one group'[2] (Luhmann 1980: 30). The requirement of inclusion is here clearly applied to societal modernisation, i.e. the abolition of feudal bonds. This made possible personal freedom on the one hand, but at the same time abolished the previously existing rights to protection and participation. At the same time, modernisation means that social functions performed by the system's differentiated parts become routine, and their services indispensable, as a rule, for the lives of individuals. Political and social rights are supposed to ensure that individuals get the opportunity to participate in the different realms of life. Here, social rights refer first to the protection of wages and working conditions; then to financial transfers to secure existence where other income is insufficient; and, finally, to personal health, education and social services.

(2) The second starting point is the problem of societal reproduction. To the extent that human life proceeds in the form of a delimitable, imagined collective whose participants recognize each other as members, a basic solidarity can be assumed. The recognition of *people*

18

like myself is the foundation of all social life which, of course, does not rule out systems of social ranking or multiple memberships. The normative implications of such basic solidarity are culture-bound and also depend on existing network structures. For the idea of the social welfare state, the politically constituted society of the nation state appears to be the relevant reference point for now. In Europe, the recognition of the right to life for every human being can be assumed to be culturally normative;[3] but the recognition of full membership rights in the sense of the quality of citizenship always remains tied to specific preconditions, which also mark the boundary of the collective. Each collective needs to gain new members; in the case of states, this can proceed only through biological reproduction and education or through the assimilation of immigrants. Since there are limits to the latter, not only the state but also all societal system parts depend quantitatively and qualitatively on the services of families to guarantee their recruiting potential. These services must be systematically included in any theory of the welfare state.

Finally, a theory of the welfare state must assume political power and legislation as a systematic reference point in the construction and maintenance of social solidarity. This assumption has lost some of its self-evidence under the influence of so-called globalisation. We will address the problems which this raises later. Here, we will start by clarifying the necessity and the limits of state responsibility for social welfare.

The production of welfare as a general reference point

Family services are mobilised by neither the mechanism of trade nor that of coercion, but instead are motivated by a mixture of emotional bonds and considerations of expediency, as well as by moral and (in the case of conflict) legal obligations. As a rule, family services are carried out within a common household, but can also go beyond a single household, for example in assisting relatives. Political and economic theories presuppose these generally unpaid family services as given, but the more affluent a society becomes, and hence the higher the opportunity costs of family services, the more difficult it is to take them for granted. In reaction to egalitarian Napoleonic inheritance law, the French started having fewer children in the 19th century, and in the 20th century birth control became widespread. Within the three years after 1989, the birth rate in the territory of the former East Germany fell by half, showing that, today, the population of a country is able to adjust its reproductive behaviour rapidly and significantly to changes in its living conditions. The introduction of nursing care insurance in the Federal Republic of Germany in 1994 is another indication that family services may no longer be taken for granted.

Despite the displacement of self-sufficiency by market-mediated production and consumption, the private household has not become a mere unit of consumption, as posited by economic theory (Teichert 1993). Here, economic theory goes astray because it regards 'one who raises pigs… as a productive member, and one who raises people as an unproductive member of society' (List 1922: 231). The services characteristic of the modern family household no longer have to do with the production of goods, but with personal services, in particular with education, care, counsel and assistance, as well as with emotional support. Additionally, monetary and commodity transfers still take place within households and within kinship relations which go beyond individual households.

19

Social services have developed essentially as a supplement to and partial substitute for these family services. The development of systems of social security and of service organisations in the educational, health and social spheres has supplanted very few market-mediated services; rather, these organisations provide, in an organised and professional form, services previously performed in rudimentary or undifferentiated form in the framework of private households. As international comparison shows, these transfer and service systems often arose as collective self-help organisations (e.g. friendly societies) on the one hand or, on the other hand, in the context of private and church charity (schools for the poor, hospitals) or service institutions (private schools, private practices and clinics). State interventions then extended them universally, whereby different countries exhibit substantial differences in the degree of state control of these institutions.

What is today generally termed the 'welfare state', i.e. all institutions of social security together with publicly financed social services, appears to be not necessarily a state institution like the police and courts; their degree of state control is historically contingent. One should, therefore, employ a more neutral term such as the 'social welfare sector', since the kind and extent of these services is, for the most part, independent of the degree of their control by the state. This change of name allows for a more precise terminology in several ways.

First, we need a term allowing us to think of all social welfare services – market-mediated, non-profit, state, as well as unpaid services performed within kinship or other social networks. This enables us to conceive of them all from a common perspective. To this end, we follow Zapf (1984) in suggesting the term *welfare production*. This encompasses all individual services that arise through transferable sources, regardless of who performs them.

The sum of these welfare-producing services is substantially greater than the gross national product, since it includes more than paid services. A representative time-budget survey by the German Federal Statistical Office found the annual volume of paid and unpaid work in Germany in 1992 to consist of 60 billion hours of paid work (36%), 10 billion hours of transportation (6%), and 95.5 billion hours of unpaid work (58%); unpaid work included the time for household production, network assistance and volunteer activities. 'In a macro-economically reasonable estimation, unpaid work in what was already the Federal Republic of Germany before unification had a value of 1,125 billion DM in 1992. This is only 9% less than the total of all the gross wages and salaries in the West German economy, the entire (i.e. paid and unpaid) economic production is thus 42% higher than the gross domestic product.' If other methods of evaluation were used, 'the value of unpaid work could be even twice as high' (Blanke *et al.* 1996).

This view of welfare production is heuristically fertile in two ways. First, it allows the thematisation of sectoral shifts in welfare production, whether in regard to the relationship between paid and unpaid work or in regard to the relationship between market-controlled, associative and state-controlled forms of service production. If, as can be assumed, the market and state sectors have expanded at the expense of household and network production, the consequence is that the actual gain in welfare due to economic expansion is much lower than the official economic growth rates. As in the case of environmental consumption, here, too, we have to consider social costs when household services are commodified, e.g. losses of transaction utilities from emotional relationships. If the services of households and networks are taken into account, the welfare balance sheet for overall economic development is substantially less favourable than the official economic figures show.

Second, the perspective of welfare production allows us to incorporate the highly diverse forms of industrial relations into the framework of a theory of the welfare state. The influence of law and government ranges from nearly full abstention (as in Great Britain until Margaret Thatcher) to the regulation of bargaining systems (e.g. in the Federal Republic of Germany) to tripartite corporatistic wage policy arrangements (e.g. in the Netherlands and Sweden), to minimum wage legislation (e.g. in France). The determination of wages is, of course, a central element in the distribution of productivity gains and, thus, of shares in the national product and the distribution of welfare. The fact that state intervention here assumes manifold forms and degrees within the political arrangements of welfare states renders industrial relations hard to localise from a state-centred perspective. However, they fit easily into a more comprehensive framework of welfare production.

The social welfare sector

In the relationship between market-controlled and non-market-controlled production, only the services of the social welfare sector are of interest here. In an initial approach we note that, for historical and systematic reasons, it is a part of neither the genuine state nor the genuine market sector. It contains two functional segments – fiscal redistribution and public or non-profit services – that aim directly at the improvement of living conditions. Income redistribution as such is only indirectly related to the idea of welfare production, since it does not actually produce anything. Public and non-profit services may be differentiated in the provision of infrastructure and of personal social services. We focus our attention on personal services as they represent by far the most expensive services in the social sector and partially substitute for unpaid forms of welfare production.

Personal services

Personal services lack the specific qualities typical of commodities as emphasised by economic theory: they are mobile only to a limited degree, they cannot be stored, and they generally depend on the active co-operation of their 'consumers', which is why in everyday language instead they are called clients, students, or patients (Gartner and Riessman 1974). The limits to the rationalisation of personal services are thus very narrow; and the scope for increases in profits due to growth in the size of operations (economies of scale) remains modest as well. The distinction between production costs and transaction costs becomes irrelevant, at least at the level of interactive services. Product quality cannot be standardised, but remains dependent on the interaction of the persons involved in the individual case. All this is true, not only for paid services, but also for unpaid services. The transition is typically fluid, as shown, for example, by reimbursements to volunteer workers or by social insurance payments to family members providing care.

Thus, there is much evidence that conventional economic distinctions in this area do not apply. This area is characterized by the proximity between the formal and the informal economy. Whether the formal or informal economy is more advantageous is a matter of

21

perspective: should we rely on differentiated professional services or on 'lay' or, perhaps more precisely, 'amateurish' provision of these services (parents and caring spouses or husbands being amateurs in the original sense of the word)? In self-help groups and many associations, the aims officially pursued are embedded in broader social relationships, so that the participants often receive not only instrumental assistance, but also emotional support and, under some circumstances, they can even unite to pursue common interests *vis-à-vis* third parties. In the 1980s in Germany, the number of psycho-social and health self-help groups alone was estimated at 45,000 (Hondrich and Koch-Arzberger 1992).

Seen from an economic perspective, it seems helpful to distinguish between the utility of transactions themselves and the utility of results. Market theory knows only of the utility of results: all that is traded on markets are results of production processes, which are turned into consumer or investment goods through third-party use.[4] In personal services, however, production and consumption become inseparable; the utility evolves in the interactive process between the professional and the client, and it cannot be distinguished from the interaction between the participants. This becomes especially clear in consulting processes, but is also true for pedagogical and most therapeutic processes; it is only to the degree that the process itself is experienced as useful (i.e. that transaction use arises) that utilities can be expected which go beyond the interactive process. Interest in the utility of results generally dominates in paid service production, but in unpaid services, interest in the necessary interaction, i.e. the utility of the transaction itself, is often paramount (for example, in families or self-help groups).

Paid personal services thus stand in a close complementary or substitutive relationship to informal forms of welfare production (Evers and Olk 1996). Here, we must especially consider differences in quality and unquantifiable positive and negative side effects, which can be adequately controlled neither with the help of legal norms nor with the aid of economic incentives. The participants' personal motives and competencies play a central role here. From the perspective of institutional theory, we can expect that the formation of a common ethos, whether professional, company, group or family, is of central importance.

To summarise, the area of personal services is substantially larger and more influential for lasting welfare production than is generally assumed (Anheier and Seibel 1990). Welfare state debates typically address only a particular segment of the overall field. And this segment cannot be adequately investigated within the conceptual framework *market versus state*, whether in regard to efficiency or ethics. In such debates, qualitative aspects related to the mutual responsibility of the participants play a central role. Thus, quite distinct from state or market co-ordination, we can speak here of *co-ordination by solidarity* (cf. Hegner 1991).

The special character of social services has also been recognised in the theory of public goods. Here, we examine justifications for state interventions, although the services in question do not match the defining characteristics of 'pure' public goods; the problem is treated under the term *merit good*. In principle, the supply of these services could be controlled by the market. However, it can be expected that, under the sole influence of market prices, demand would be much lower, especially from the lower-income segments of the population. This expectation becomes all the more plausible the more the relative price of personal services rises in relation to the price of goods; and this is the trend, due to services' lower potential for rationalisation while the productivity of goods-manufacturing increases.

From the perspective of liberal economic theory, this problem of inadequate demand should not be solved by subsidising providers, nor through the public provision of services. If a solution is considered necessary at all, it is seen in income transfers to those with lower incomes, or in credits in kind. The leading argument relies on 'distorted preferences', i.e. the idea that state interventions are necessary because the recipients underestimate the long-term utility of such services and give priority to short-term over long-term needs. However, the argument of distorted preferences cannot explain by itself why there should be any intervention in consumer sovereignty. Additional valuations of the side effects of the neglected use of these services are required, valuations that transcend the typified actor's horizon of experience. Here, reference is often made to a public interest, for example in regard to the education of future generations (the formation of human capital) or to the avoidance of severe disease and early invalidity, i.e. to the expectation of higher costs otherwise to be borne by the general public or by an insurance community. Whether and how such a public interest can be justified is one of the most controversial issues between the proponents and critics of the welfare state. Market control can solve only the problem of the allocation of resources, not that of an appropriate distribution of goods. Pareto optimality is compatible with extremely different patterns of distribution of income and goods.

Income redistribution

Political debate as well as comparative scientific inquiry about the welfare state focuses not on non-cash benefits and services, but on income subsidies. However, there are substantial differences among welfare states as to the priority given to services in kind versus cash transfers. The Scandinavian states are strong in investing in social services, whereas Germany is strong in income redistribution.

The so-called secondary income distribution is carried out by siphoning off income-dependent levies from primary income; in addition to direct and indirect taxes, this also includes social insurance contributions. Again, there are substantial international differences in how the social welfare sector is financed. In Sweden, for example, the social budget was, until very recently, financed almost exclusively by general taxes and, to some extent, by employer's contributions. On the continent, the social insurance principle prevails, in which the burden is normally shared among the insured and their employers. The redistributive effect from the rich to the poor is normally stronger when financing is done by taxes rather than by contributions. However, the effect also depends upon the nature of the taxes and the way in which tax laws are implemented.

Let us take Germany as an example. In German social insurance, the amount paid to the insured individual is based on the amount of contributions previously paid (equivalency principle) and there is no guarantee of a minimum benefit. International comparison clearly reveals the low weight assigned to need in the assigning of income transfers in the German social insurance system, for example, payments are not connected to family status. Accordingly, contribution-financed payments are essentially limited to redistribution between various phases of life or between generations ('horizontal' redistribution); redistribution between varying abilities to pay or varying degrees of need ('vertical' redistribution) takes place exclusively through tax-financed payments (for example: child benefits, housing subsidies, social assistance). One would expect that such a system would produce rather high levels of income inequality, but this seems not to be the case, which points to higher pre-welfare state income equality. Calculations of the Gini-Index for standardised household incomes show that, among EU members in 1993, Germany exhibited the second lowest value. Only Denmark had a more egalitarian income structure (Alber 1998). This counter-intuitive effect may be explained by the interaction of corporate wage policies, tax policy and social redistribution. Due to the power of trade unions, but also to cultural factors fostering equality, the wage differentials in Germany are rather restricted and the income-tax rather progressive.

Functionally, social insurance essentially replaces feudal, guild and kinship obligations of solidarity. In pre-industrial times, the essential economic rights of disposal were based on land; accordingly, risk communities were oriented primarily toward the ground rules of the local agrarian system and toward land ownership. The disappearance of the feudal system and the privatisation of land destroyed this basis of social security; and, with the spread of dependent wage labour, the 'free' labour contract prevailed over the patriarchal operating principle. 'Free' contracts expressed not only the freedom of the parties to contract, but also the separation of the work relationship from all other considerations. The principle 'wage for labour' considers neither the worker's state of health nor his family obligations.

The wide variety of organised aid funds which were founded in the second half of the 19th century constituted early attempts, on a money-economy basis, to protect against the risks of life now separated from working life and to form new communities of solidarity. In some countries the state stepped in to protect and subsidise these funds. The contribution-financed social insurance schemes – which, with the exception of Bismarck's earlier 'worker insurance', were established in the 20th century – followed a distinct but similar principle. An alternative can be seen in the tax-financed, exclusively needs-oriented 'people's pension' which was first introduced in Sweden in 1913 to replace the earlier poor relief and which has moulded basic old-age security in the Scandinavian states to this day. In 1948, Switzerland introduced an interesting mixed model of needs-oriented, but contribution-financed basic security with substantial vertical redistribution; in the broad segment of medium incomes, the principle of equivalency of contributions and benefits is preserved, while the higher contributions of the wealthy compensate for the otherwise inadequate coverage among those with low incomes.

Along with insuring against income losses due to invalidity and old age, the second problem not considered by labour contracts is how to finance the raising of the next generation. This problem was first recognised in France, where experiments with family wages had failed. Then regional trans-company family equalisation funds were established and today, in generalised form, they provide the organisational core structure of the French system of social security. In Germany, the problem of equalising family burdens as a task for the 'social state' remained a neglected aspect of social policy until the late 1980s; since then, the Supreme Court has ruled repeatedly in favour of family needs. In many European countries there is still little concern about family policy, but the needs-oriented systems of protection against poverty (e.g. in Great Britain) or the concern for gender equality (e.g. in Sweden) may provide equivalents.

A third complex of problems in income security lies in the temporary loss of income among adults due to sickness or unemployment. The situations in question here are less clearly defined than age, invalidity and parenthood, and they are more dependent on the behaviour of the risk-bearer, i.e. more exposed to 'moral hazard'. At the same time, they are more closely related to the employment relationship and the labour market; indeed, they are greatly influenced by general economic development and by the economic health of companies. Here, we find a multi-layered area of overlap between economic and social policy; but its organisation is particularly controversial and thus attracts the most attention in political and economic debates. Most of the economists' objections to social policy's productivity-inhibiting incentive structures refer to this area alone, although it is small in relation to the entirety of social welfare measures.

Worker protection and industrial relations

Mostly excluded from the international debate is a third aspect of the development of welfare states, namely the regulation of industrial work, i.e. occupational health and safety, the labour contract and the occupational rights of workers. Together with poverty, this was the first field of state intervention for the sake of social welfare, but it developed quite unevenly among nations.

The forerunner in industrialisation was Great Britain. Laws forbidding trade union organisation were abolished there as early as 1824, and by 1875 the right to strike was attained. Male workers were conferred the franchise between 1867 and 1884. Thus, the workers' movement developed gradually and experienced the strength of self-help by creating trade unions, friendly societies, co-operatives for different purposes, and eventually their own Labour Party. In the industries employing mainly male workers, labour conditions became regulated through bargaining within local trade boards consisting of representatives of employers and of workers of a defined trade. Labour legislation remained restricted to child and female labour, and wages were considered to be exclusively a matter of private bargaining. Until the 1980s, the prevailing employment pattern remained clearly outside of state regulation. Even judicial control remained weak. The same pattern of non-intervention developed in the United States, although the labour movement succeeded only temporarily and in certain domains in combating the much more ruthless behaviour of American employers. In both countries, problems of unemployment were not defined as a collective issue of public concern but remained a problem to be solved solely at the individual level.

In Scandinavia, likewise, industrial relations developed without strong state support. National associations of trade unions and employers were formed as early as 1900 and their bargaining patterns set the example for the evolving regulation of labour and wages. Problems of unemployment became defined primarily as a structural problem necessitating public intervention. Labour market policies were considered to be an integral part of welfare policies.

By contrast, labour legislation was a dominant issue of social politics in Germany from the start. Bismarck was opposed to the imposition of labour regulation on industry, and this became a lasting political conflict until World War I, and again in the Weimar Republic. Under the pressures of industrial conflicts, the determination of wages also came under public influence. The 'Workers' Question' (Arbeiterfrage) remained the focus of social policy until legislation in the 1950s eliminated the remaining differences between industrial workers and employees and secured rights to co-determination in industry. The emergence of state regulation of labour and, occasionally, of wages, became central to the development of the German welfare state, as it did in most other continental nations. Labour market policies are less developed than in Scandinavia although some public responsibility for full employment is acknowledged.

So we begin to understand why the international concept of the welfare state does not necessarily include the regulation of labour, even though from a continental European perspective this is seen as indispensable. Labour regulation also needed to be included from the theoretical perspective of welfare production presented above. If one sees state intervention as only one route among many in the development of welfare production, than nothing stands in the way of including the Anglo-Saxon and Scandinavian models of regulating labour through industrial relations in our analytical framework. Labour-market and full-employment policies affect both the working and living spheres of welfare, so it seems reasonable to include them, even though they belong more to the realm of economic than social policy.

Political arrangements of social welfare

It should be clear by now that a theory of the welfare state needs to be more complex than allowed by the debate between liberal 'faith in the market' and the 'believers in the state', who consider themselves socially responsible. Also, the question of income redistribution, at the centre of current disputes, is only one part of the complex issues related to the welfare state. The welfare state must now be defined more precisely in terms of the role of the state as well as in terms of criteria for judging redistributive processes. At the same time, we have to make clear in what respects welfare states differ from other political arrangements of social welfare, such as liberal welfare capitalism or socialist modes of welfare production.

In German constitutional law, Article 20 (I) of the 'Grundgesetz' defines the German republic as a 'sozialer Rechtsstaat', a social state under the rule of law. This formula is anything but clear, but what has prevailed is the interpretation that the state has a responsibility toward the weak and to 'effect their sharing in the economic goods in accordance with the principles of justice and with the goal of ensuring a life with human dignity for everyone' (Zacher 1993). This formula accords with the social-ethical postulate of a common responsibility for the guarantee of equal rights for all, as well as with the sociological derivation of the inclusion principle sketched above. According to another classic formulation, the goal of the 'social state' is to guarantee the 'social preconditions for the realisation of constitutional freedom' (Böckenförde 1976) – this version is more closely related to a liberal understanding of the constitution. In the English-speaking world, Girvetz (1968) declares similarly: 'The welfare state is the institutional outcome of a society's assumption of legal and therefore formal and explicit responsibility for the basic well-being of all of its members. Such a state emerges when a society or its decision-making groups become convinced that the welfare of the individual … is too important to be left to custom or to informal arrangements and private understandings and is therefore a concern of government.' On the level of international developments, the Social Charter of the European Council (1961), the UN Covenant on Economic, Social and Cultural Rights (1976) and similar standards of the European Union define the goals of public welfare development.

The formulation of this political, or even constitutional, commitment to individual welfare still says nothing about the methods to be used in its pursuit, or about the extent of direct state intervention, and this is where disagreement often occurs. In the following, I suggest an interpretation of the welfare state that remains as open as possible to different solutions.

Despite differences in detail, certain features are shared by all welfare states and distinguish them as an independent, modern form of society, from the liberal type of society approached in the United States of America and from the socialist type of society in the former Eastern European bloc. The defining properties are (cf. Kaufmann 1997):

(a) In the sphere of production, private property and entrepreneurial freedom of disposition are preserved. However, these freedoms are limited by recognised rights of employees and their public protection. National welfare states differ in the type of limitations that prevail: state bans, tort law, procedural rules, or systems of supervision and negotiation. They differ, further, in the extent to which they regulate labour market issues and promote full employment.

(b) In the sphere of distribution, primary income distribution – in accordance with the principles of a market economy – is exclusively oriented toward payment for production. The price of labour is determined not only by individual, but also by collective bargaining. There is no 'social wage' as in the socialist system. Instead, the primary distribution of incomes is corrected with secondary income distribution based on legislation. This secondary income distribution directly or indirectly ensures a minimum subsistence to those who have no income from capital or labour. National social welfare states differ in the method of financing these income transfers through taxes or contributions, as well as in the system of entitlements and in the organisation of the system of social security.

(c) In the sphere of reproduction, the services of private households are supplemented and supported by publicly regulated and subsidised or entirely publicly financed services of education, health and social aid. National welfare states differ in the proportions of state, local, non-profit and business responsibility for the service-providing institutions, as well as in the nature and extent of their state financing and legal control.

To be sure, there are strong links between these three dimensions at the level of individual welfare and some effects are, in part, mutually substitutive. Others impinge on the welfare production of households/families/networks which, as we have seen, remain a major form of welfare production.

Seen historically, welfare state development hinges on a compromise between employer and union interests, which in many countries has found expression in explicit agreements between employers' associations and unions, often the product of vehement labour disputes.[5] Seen functionally, welfare states try to combine the advantages of the liberal entrepreneurial economic system with those of more egalitarian access to economic, social and cultural resources.

The political arrangement of social welfare which we call the welfare state differs markedly from the liberal type of welfare capitalism the latter is characterized by a fundamental separation between the state and the market economy, whereas the former foresees a higher degree of legitimate state intervention: the state is recognised, and so in principle is its ability to increase welfare by public intervention. In the paramount 'liberal' case of the United States, differences relative to the Western European pattern can be attributed to the weaker idea of the state and the more radical individualism of American culture, which is less influenced by ideas of Roman law and Western metaphysical thought. Moreover, it is mostly race, and not class, that matters in the politics of social inequality in the US.[6] To be sure, there exist substantial differences in social protection between regions and states. Some states, like Wisconsin, pioneered social policies under European influence. However, the decisions of the Supreme Court worked against most federal interventions. Up until now, the United States is, together with South Africa, the only developed country not to have signed the UN International Covenant on Economic, Social and Cultural Rights.[7]

The welfare state differs from the socialist type of society in its guarantee of the independence of the entrepreneurial function and in the separation of primary and secondary income distribution. Principles of need affect only secondary income distribution, whereas the primary distribution of incomes is determined by the price of the utility. This is linked to the more basic difference between these two economic systems. The socialist economy is considered to be dominated by a politically controlled planning system in which decisions about the distribution of incomes go hand in hand with decisions about the allocation of resources.[8] In welfare states, on the contrary, allocative decisions are free, whereas the distribution of the resulting incomes is influenced by collective bargaining, taxation and social policies.

Compared to the imagined pure liberal and socialist forms, the social welfare state form is less elegant, more tension-laden, and also more complex. It proceeds from the idea that it is possible simultaneously to increase individual freedom and collective provisions, i.e. that state intervention and spontaneous self-direction can co-exist. Here, the market and the state are not seen as opposites, but as complementary principles of control based on different 'logics'. Freedom is not regarded as a pre-constitutional condition (John Locke), but as the result of political processes forming a constitution and thus institutional givens, which also influence the distribution of opportunities to act.

Sociologically, the hypothesis that political intervention and social self-direction can be increased simultaneously is specified best by relying on a theory of social differentiation of functions. In the course of modernisation, societal contexts became differentiated into functionally oriented sub-systems which complement one another in their efficient one-sidedness and which also provide checks for one another.[9] The development of the market economy and the rise of the modern state are understood as processes of functional differentiation and growing institutional autonomy, whereby these two partial systems of society specialise in different problem areas and develop their own institutional fits and, with the help of their respective sciences, their own distinct 'logics'. The tension between the economic sciences on the one hand and the legal and social sciences on the other underscores precisely this real tension in modern societies, a tension that became constitutive with functional differentiation. This tension manifests itself in the rise of 'social problems' and cannot be fundamentally resolved. The tension between the dynamics of the economic system and the demands of the social welfare system is thus a constitutive feature of welfare states. It is a permanent challenge for politics to achieve synergies, again and again, among economic and social policies.

The need to mobilise the state to address problems stemming from the independence of the economic system, problems which resulted from the spread of private property and the institutionalisation of economic freedoms, seemed manifest in Europe. Here, in contrast to the United States, the development of the state historically preceded liberalisation, and the problems of intensified competition could not be meliorated through territorial expansion. This mobilisation occurred in paternalistic as well as in democratic states in reaction to similar socio-economic challenges. The development of the welfare state is an essential outcome of the processing of problems that derive from the mutual structural independence of the market economy and the state. The welfare state, thus, does not follow a unified logic; rather it strives toward a synthesis of differing political, economic, and ethical-social 'logics'. This is why it typically needs to be studied in an interdisciplinary way and cannot be adequately grasped from the viewpoint of a single discipline.

Therefore, we should speak of a political arrangement of social welfare in the form of a welfare state wherever an independent political system is legitimised to react with continuing legal and organisational interventions to the undesired consequences of unfettered competition within an independent economic system. Problematical effects emerge mainly in the working and living conditions of individuals and their families. As a result of these interventions, a social welfare sector arises, controlled by state regulation. In this context, the central political task consists in guiding and moulding the interaction of the four realms – state, economy, social welfare sector and households/families – toward as synergetic, i.e. mutually fostering, relationship as possible (Kaufmann 1994).

Is there a crisis of the welfare state?

Immediately after the 1973 oil crisis, which ended the 'short dream of everlasting prosperity', a discussion began in the social sciences about the 'crisis of the welfare state'. This discussion has lasted for a quarter of a century and continues today. The most important diagnoses of the crisis can be typified as follows.

(a) Fiscal crisis: The expansion of social expenditures after the Second World War was furthered by a historically unique phase of economic growth. Once growth petered out, the scope for distribution was massively reduced. Postponing outstanding distributive conflicts by increasing government debt leads to inflationary pressures; and since the liberalisation of financial markets and the intensification of international site competition, national freedom of action in labour and social policy has been limited. The financial constraints now faced by welfare states assume various forms, depending on the institutional structure of the country's social sectors, but all welfare states face the task of restoring the lost synergy between economic and social policy. To this end, limitations on social services and wage restraint have been recommended.

(b) Demographically induced crisis: Throughout Europe, the decline in the birth rate, which has continued throughout the 20th century with only temporary reversals, is leading to a long-term shift in the population's age distribution. As a result of welfare state interventions and of retirements, occupational activity is increasingly concentrated in the age group of the 20 to 60-year-olds. This makes social policy dependent on demographic development, which has become one of the most important determinants of the extent of income redistribution. As a result of the long-term decline in the mortality rate and the attendant increase in life expectancy, in the coming decades the share of the retired generations will increase disproportionately at the expense of the occupationally active generations. Most welfare states leave the support of the succeeding generation to families, but have widely collectivised the support of the older generation. This not only provides a continued incentive to limit births, but also increasingly burdens the systems of social security for old age and disease, thus further intensifying the problems of distribution.

(c) Crisis of control: Various arguments support the suspicion that the state is no longer able to make efficient social policy decisions to maintain the prerequisites for a successful arrangement of welfare production. Thus, the 'entitlement society' thesis proposes that democratic systems have a tendency to overextend social expenditures because all parties believe they can gain votes through 'social good deeds'. Marxist theoreticians see in the intensification of distribution conflicts a re-eruption of the basic antagonism between capital and labour. Liberal critics point to undesirable side effects of social welfare state development, effects the social welfare state cannot master, namely a weakening of the work ethic and of competitiveness as well as an erosion of the family's potential for self-help. They also lament the expenses and the inefficiency of administratively controlled services. Critics from the field of political science fear that democratic institutions will be overburdened with demands for decisions ('crisis of governability'), or overruled by corporatistic bargaining. In addition, critics from sociology point to the lack of quality and effectiveness in legally and bureaucratically controlled service production.

(d) Crisis of trust: Along with the utility of social services for individual recipients, their public or collective merits have always been underscored by proponents of social welfare state activities. Thus, social policy itself has macro-economic value, e.g. in increasing labour productivity or in stabilising macroeconomic demand. Above all, its pacifying and socially integrating value is emphasized; social policy meliorates class conflicts and contributes to a just social order, thus increasing the legitimacy of the connection between the state and the market economy. The social welfare state has released 'utopian energies' of hope for a just social order, but these are becoming exhausted under the impression of intensifying distributional conflicts (Habermas 1985). The worsened perspectives for the future, especially in regard to security in old age, have led to a loss of trust in the state security systems and, thus, to a loss of solidarity on the part of the younger generations. These negative expectations feed mistrust in the problem-solving capacities of politics and, thereby, contribute to social disintegration.

Especially taken together, the arguments sketched here suggest a scenario of the collapse of the welfare state – a collapse, however, that has not yet actually occured anywhere. Financial difficulties and distributional conflicts have increased everywhere, but in most welfare states there have been no substantial signs of political disintegration; and even political movements (for example, tax protests) have remained too marginal even to cast doubt on existing constellations of parties. All empirical studies show that the population has a high regard for the central institutions of the social welfare sector as well as a willingness to accept restrictions in their services or increases in contributions in order to ensure these institutions' ability to function. Apparently, the institutional integrity of the institutions of the social welfare sector is not yet threatened by financial difficulties and cuts in services alone. No self-accelerating process of mutually exacerbating crisis scenarios has begun.

In strongly developed welfare states like Denmark, Sweden and the Netherlands, reforms aimed at reducing services show that the 'welfare state compromise' between employers and unions can also prove effective politically. In Germany, the 'posturing' of representatives of employers' associations and trade unions should not be taken at face value. Nevertheless, before the 1998 parliamentary elections, there was a backlog of overdue reforms, not only in the realm of social services legislation, but also in the financing framework and in the federal structure. Overall, there are substantial conflicts of interest, but there is no sign that we will not be able to solve them within the framework of the constitutionally provided political processes.

Despite a wide variety of crisis rhetoric, we cannot seriously speak of any lasting economic threat to the welfare state arrangement.[10] So far, the conflict between optimal allocation and equalising distribution, as formulated in economic theory, has not been evident over a long period. Societies organised along democratic and market-economy lines are highly flexible, allowing them to adjust to various institutional solutions to the distribution problem (cf. Scharpf and Schmidt 2000). Structurally, the distribution conflict is characteristic of all political arrangements of social welfare; the welfare state should not be confused with a 'land of milk and honey'. Between the end of World War II and the 1980s, the development of the welfare state led primarily to an equalisation of income and supply conditions, but more recent developments have tended to restore greater socio-economic inequality.

Globalisation

Recently, the diagnoses of the crisis of the social welfare state have received new nourishment from the debate on globalisation. In this connection, three different but mutually reinforcing developments have to be distinguished.

(a) Internationalisation: This has to do with the increasing importance of border-crossing transactions. Thus, the economy is internationalised with the rising proportion of imports and exports; the population is internationalised with the increasing proportion of cross-national migration; public opinion is internationalised under the influence of international mass media, etc.

(b) Globalisation: In the narrower sense this can be understood as the world moving closer together, operationally and cognitively. Thanks to technological progress, international agreements and political liberalisation, the worldwide networking of information and transportation has decreased transmission times and reduced the importance of spatial distance, so that local events are perceived and become effective worldwide with less and less delay. For the first time in history, routine intercontinental co-operation is emerging – along with conflict with regard to environmental problems, human-rights abuses and the international confrontation between wealth and poverty.

(c) Transnationalisation: Increasingly, institutional structures and collective actors are emerging that transcend national legal systems and thus can no longer be controlled by nation states. This development is especially marked in the area of large firms that merge into multi-national corporations and seek an optimal business site. The emergence of transnational economic relations, especially in the currency and financial markets, clearly reduces the scope for autonomous policy in the respective nation states. This must be distinguished from explicit renunciations of sovereign rights in the context of multilateral agreements in international law, such as the creation and intensification of the European Union or the GATT, and now WTO, agreements. In the latter, transnational regimes are created that typically remain limited to specific functional areas; unlike nation states, these regimes cannot claim any fundamental universal responsibility.

These developments, which have accelerated in recent decades, become problematic against the backdrop of the still prevailing consciousness of sovereign nation-statehood. Under the influences sketched above, the idea of the nation state as a self-governing (democratic) community of shared fate and responsibility, solidified through the combination of common socio-cultural (national) and political (state) characteristics, is becoming less and less realistic. More and more clearly, the various sectors of human existence are gaining different spatial and social ranges; in reality, and increasingly in consciousness, they are less and less exclusively bound to the boundaries of the nation state.

Consequences for the welfare state

In several ways, these developments provoke far-reaching challenges for the nation state's responsibility for social welfare.

(a) Since the mobility of capital is much greater than that of labour, the liberalisation of the commodity and financial markets entails a shift in power relations in favour of capital. This development was further supported by the collapse of socialism. The tension between the dynamics of the rapidly expanding international financial markets and the attempts of individual states to conduct economic and monetary policy in their own interests have also increased the capital owners' preference for liquidity; falling interest rates have further intensified this. Capital has become more site-sensitive and responds more rapidly than before to fiscal burdens, be they taxes or social contributions. This has often thrown existing modes of financing the social sector into question.

(b) Public debt is less and less able to ease the financial pressure in the social sector, because the inflationary tendencies that public debt unleashes induce the international financial and currency markets to lower the external value of a currency. It is hard to avoid an intensification of internal distributional conflicts as a consequence. Conflicts arise, first, over the relationship between the employed and those dependent on transfer income, and second, over the relationship between various groups of transfer recipients, for example pensioners, families, the unemployed and the handicapped. Public arguments capable of generating consensus are especially lacking in the second type of conflict, because there are various forms of social need that must be weighed against one another.

(c) As the degree to which individual groups (e.g. the self-employed, civil servants) have the ability to escape from redistributive pressure grows, an increasing diminution of solidarity can be expected. This is also expressed in the deteriorating power of employers' associations and unions to keep, and to discipline, their members and, thus, in the loss of the binding power of collective bargaining agreements for complete sectors or the economy as a whole. The decreasing power of the nation state favours the revival of regional interests. All these developments are not simply about an individualisation of interests, but rather about a pluralisation of horizons of solidarity. It is becoming clear that the concentration of all collective interests in the solidarity horizon of the nation state is an historical exception of the last one-and-a-half centuries. However, the ideas of the welfare state that have prevailed until now presume precisely this unified national horizon of solidarity. To the degree that the latter dwindles, cognitive and normative re-orientations become necessary; and these have already begun here and there, but have not yet led to clearly recognisable new structures. In the context of these processes of reorientation, the importance of the nation state is not simply eroded; rather, it becomes focused on a few fundamental decisions.

There is no visible legitimate alternative to the democratic formation of will in the form of state legislation, by means of which rights and duties are defined and the community of solidarity is constituted. However, these relatively unwieldy procedures are no longer well suited to address the growing complexity of social reality and its dynamics. The processes of European unification, in particular, will probably involve extremely far-reaching political re-structuring that, to increase problem-solving capacity, will end in a separation of the responsibilities and powers of various levels of political decision-making. Seen from the perspective of functional efficiency, one could argue that regulations in the realm of market-oriented production should operate on the European level, income re-distribution on the national level, and regulation of personal services on a regional or local level. Accordingly, it appears quite conceivable that the facilities of the social sector, too, will fall more clearly under the jurisdiction of various political decision-making levels and that the extent of the state's central regulating activity will be reduced. Thus, the nation state's freedom to structure will be limited, but it will not be lost completely, as is often claimed.

A predictable consequence of European unification is the increasing business-site competition among regions and communities. However, we need not expect that these processes of competition will be decided by price alone, and thus be explicable through conventional economic analysis. On the contrary, immaterial site factors will gain in importance, and these include not only such aspects of the quality of life as culture and natural surroundings, but also social peace, infrastructure, the quality of human capital, and security obtained through a well-functioning legal system. Welfare production remains a multidimensional process that will still be controlled by policy, economic decisions, solidarity and associations. There will be political communities that fare better or worse than others in finding synergetic solutions for economic attractiveness and generalised qualities of life.

For this reason, the components of the existing arrangements of social welfare will not evaporate under the pressure of transnationalisation, but merely re-order themselves (Leibfried and Pierson 1995). Growth in fiscal and social welfare is contained by the processes of globalisation, at least in states with an especially high level of welfare and security. Increasing international competition will probably lead to more equalisation of the average level of welfare in expanded contexts – for example, continental or intercontinental contexts – while the level of security of the presently leading social welfare states will suffer at least relative losses (Pierson 1998). From the perspective of universal ethics, however, these developments must be welcome, even if they are painful for the populations or population segments affected. In this context, we have to expect an intensification of distributional conflicts and an increase in social inequality, both on the level of interpersonal patterns of distribution and on the regional level. These two dimensions of inequality remain contingent, however. The degree of interpersonal redistribution is more dependent on cultural and political factors than on economic ones.

It would be short-sighted to turn the growing opportunities for reduced solidarity into an argument for the legitimacy of greater inequalities, for legitimacy cannot be merely a question of power relations. Rather, one could even argue that liberal fears that welfare politics lead to institutional sclerosis are losing importance as the balance of power tips from politics to markets. The danger of the foreseeable future no longer appears to be political, but economic overconfidence. Politics still faces great disappointments. It will have to learn to make decisions under conditions more difficult than any since World War II. In the future, politics will resemble more the attempt to steer a sailing-ship dependent on fair winds than the task of commanding a steamer dependent on the power of its own engine. It is the task of social science to redefine and to explore empirically the boundaries between the dynamics of markets and their social consequences in a multi-tiered political system.

Acknowledgements

Most sections of this chapter have been published in German as parts of: Sozialstaaatlichkeit unter den Bedingungen moderner Wirtschaft. In: *Handbuch der Wirtschaftsethik*, edited by Wilhelm Korff, ibid., Gütersloher Verlagshaus Gütersloh 1999, Vol. 1, 803–833. Thanks to Mitch Cohen (Wissenschaftskolleg Berlin) for the translation of this text which has, however, been substantially shortened and revised for the present international audience, and also to Benjamin Veghte for his intensive revisions. Thanks also to Stephan Leibfried whose comments have been eye-opening.

Notes

1. In Germany, the now generally accepted term 'Sozialstaat' was coined by Lorenz von Stein, the main founder of a theory of the welfare state (cf. Stein 1850/1964; Roth 1968). The term 'Wohlfahrtsstaat' was occasionally used in 1876 by the eminent member of the 'Verein für Sozialpolitik', Adolph Wagner; its current use is, however, more in a pejorative sense, i.e. insinuating exaggerated state intervention.
2. German quotations generally have been translated into English.
3. The development of the doctrine of Human Rights has evident sources in the teachings of the Christian gospel and its impact on European history, cf. Kaufmann (1988, 1997a: 93f.); for the different development of social policies in the Confucian context see Rieger and Leibfried (1999).
4. Consequently, Adam Smith considered most services, including government, as non-productive, cf. *The Wealth of Nations*, II, 3.
5. The earliest of these agreements was the 'September-Agreement' in Denmark (1900); other important agreements were the 'Stinnes-Legien-Abkommen' (1918) at the start of the Weimar Republic, the Agreement in the Swiss Metal industry (1937), and the Swedish 'Agreement of Saltsjöbaden' (1938). The French 'accord de Matignon' (1936) failed, whereas the 'accords de Grenelle' (1968) still contribute to the pacification of the class conflict which nowhere in the West was as bitter as in French History. In recent times the 'Akkoord van Wassenaar' (1982) has laid the foundations for quite successful revisions of welfare politics in the Netherlands.
6. Substantial overviews pertaining to the American politics of welfare can be found in Weir *et al.* (1988) and in Noble (1997).
7. For the history of this covenant and the withdrawal of the United States, see Köhler (1987: 924ff).
8. For descriptions of the economic and the social welfare system of the USSR, see Madison (1968); Osborn (1970) and Lane (1985).

9. Drawing on Max Weber, Emil Durkheim, Georg Simmel and Talcott Parsons, this theory has been developed mainly by Niklas Luhmann (1977).
10. This is also the result of most serious inquiries into the question, cf. e.g. Pfaller *et al.* (1991); Esping-Andersen (1996); Pierson (1996); Alber (1998).

References

Alber, J. (1995) A framework for the comparative study of social services, *Journal of European Social Policy*, **5**, pp. 131–149.

Alber, J. (1998) Der deutsche Sozialstaat im Licht international vergleichender Daten, *Leviathan*, **26**(2), pp. 199–227.

Anheier, H. K. and Seibel, W. (eds) (1990) *The Third Sector. Comparative Studies of Non-profit Organizations*, Berlin – New York: De Gruyter.

Blanke, K., Ehling, M. and Schwarz, N. (1996) *Zeit im Blickfeld. Ergebnisse einer repräsentativen Zeitbudgeterhebung*. Schriftenreihe des Bundesministeriums für Familie, Senioren, Frauen und Jugend, Bd. 121. Stuttgart: Kohlhammer.

Böckenförde, E.-W. (1976) *Staat, Gesellschaft, Freiheit. Studien zur Staatstheorie und zum Verfassungsrecht*. Frankfurt/Main: Suhrkamp.

Dyson, K. (1980) *The State Tradition in Western Europe*, Oxford: Robertson.

Esping-Andersen, G. (ed.) (1996) *Welfare States in Transition. National Adaptations in Global Economies*, London: Sage.

Evers, A. and Olk, T. (eds.) (1996) *Wohlfahrtspluralismus. Vom Wohlfahrtsstaat zur Wohlfahrtsgesellschaft*, Opladen: Westdeutscher Verlag.

Frazer, D. (1984) *The Evolution of the British Welfare State*. 2nd edn, London: Macmillan.

Gartner, A. and Riessman, F. (1974) *The Service Society and the Consumer Vanguard*, New York: Harper & Row.

Habermas, J. (1985) Die Krise des Wohlfahrtsstaats und die Erschöpfung utopischer Energien. In: J. Habermas, *Die neue Unübersichtlichkeit*, Frankfurt a. M.: Suhrkamp, pp. 141–163.

Hegner, F. (1991) Comparing solidarity, hierarchy, and markets: institutional arrangements for the coordination of actions. In: Kaufmann (ed.) (1991) *The Public Sector — Challenge for Coordination and Learning*, Berlin — New York: De Gruyter, pp. 417–439.

Hondrich, K. O. and Koch-Arzberger, C. (1992) *Solidarität in der modernen Gesellschaft*, Frankfurt/Main: Fischer.

Kaufmann, F.-X. (1988) Christentum und Wohlfahrtsstaat, *Zeitschrift für Sozialreform*, **34**(2), pp. 65–89.

Kaufmann, F.-X. (1994) Staat und Wohlfahrtsproduktion. In: *Systemrationalität und Partialinteresse*. Festschrift Renate Mayntz. ed. by Hans Ulrich Derlien *et al.*, Baden-Baden: Nomos, pp. 357–380.

Kaufmann, F.-X. (1997) *Herausforderungen des Sozialstaates*. Frankfurt a. M.: Suhrkamp.

Kaufmann, F.-X. (1997a) Religion and modernization in Europe, *Journal of Institutional and Theoretical Economics (JITE)*, **153,** pp. 80–96.

Kaufmann, F.-X. (2000) Der Begriff Sozialpolitik und seine wissenschaftliche Deutung. To be published in: *Geschichte der Sozialpolitik in Deutschland seit 1945*, Baden-Baden: Nomos, Vol 1.

Köhler, P. A.(1987) *Sozialpolitische und sozialrechtliche Aktivitäten der Vereinten Nationen*, Baden-Baden: Nomos.

Lane, D. (1985) *Soviet Economy and Society*, Oxford: Blackwell.

Leibfried, S. and Pierson, P. (eds) (1995) *European Social Policy: Between Fragmentation and Integration*, Washington D.C: Brookings.

List, F. (1922) *Das nationale System der politischen Ökonomie* (1841). Repr. 4th edn 1922, Jena: Fischer. (Engl. London 1928).

Luhmann, N. (1977) The differentiation of society, *Canadian Journal of Sociology*, **2**(1), 29–53.

Luhmann, N. (1980) *Gesellschaftsstruktur und Semantik*, Frankfurt a.M.: Suhrkamp.

Madison, B. Q. (1968) *Social Welfare in the Soviet Union*, Stanford: Stanford University Press.

Marshall, T. H. (1964) *Class. Citizenship and Social Development*, Garden City and New York: Doubleday.

Myrdal, A. and G. (1934) *Kris I Befolkningsfragan*, Stockholm.

Noble, C. (1997) *Welfare As We Knew It. A Political History of the American Welfare State*, New York: Oxford University Press.

O'Neill, J. (1994) *The Missing Child in Liberal Theory. Towards a Covenant Theory of Family, Community, Welfare, and the Civic State*, Toronto: University of Toronto Press.

Osborn, Robert J. (1970) *Soviet Social Policies: Welfare, Equality, and Community*, Homewood Ill: Dorsey.

Pankoke, E. (1970) *Sociale Bewegung — Sociale Frage — Sociale Politik. Grundfragen der deutschen 'Socialwissenschaft' im 19. Jahrhundert*, Stuttgart: Klett.

Pfaller, A., Gough, I. and Therborn, G. (1991) *Can the Welfare State Compete?* London: Macmillan.

Pierson, P. (1996) The new politics of the welfare state, *World Politics*, **48**(2), pp. 142–179.

Pierson, P. (1998) Irresistible forces, immovable object. Post-industrial welfare states confront permanent austerity, *Journal of European Public Policy*, **5**(4), pp. 539–560.

Rieger, E. and Leibfried, S. (1999) Wohlfahrtsstaat und Sozialpolitik in Ostasien. Der Einfluß von Religion im Kulturvergleich, in: Gert Schmidt/Rainer Trinczek (eds), *Globalisierung. Ökonomische und soziale Herausforderungen am Ende des zwanzigsten Jahrhunderts*, Baden-Baden: Nomos, pp. 413–499.

Roth, G. (1968) Stein, Lorenz von. In: *International Encyclopedia of the Social Sciences*, **15**, pp. 257–259.

Scharpf, F.W. and Schmidt, V. A. (eds) (2000) *From Vulnerability to Competitiveness: Welfare and Work in the Open Economy.* 2 vols., Oxford: Oxford University Press.

Stein, L. von (1964) *The History of the Social Movement in France 1789–1850.* Introduced, edited and translated by Kaethe Mengelberg, Totowa, NJ: Bedminster Press. (In German: 1850)

Teichert, V. (1993) *Das informelle Wirtschaftssystem. Analyse und Perspektiven von Erwerbs- und Eigenarbeit*, Opladen: Westdeutscher Verlag.

Weir, M., Orloff, A. S., Skocpol, T. (1988) *The Politics of Social Policy in the United States*, Princeton N.J.: Princeton University Press.

Zacher, H. F. (1993) Das soziale Staatsziel. In: H. F. Zacher *Abhandlungen zum Sozialrecht*, Heidelberg: C.F. Müller, pp. 3–72.

Zapf, W. (1984) Welfare production: public versus private, *Social Indicators Research*, 14, pp. 263–274.

About the Author

Franz-Xaver Kaufmann is Professor Emeritus of Sociology and Social Policy at the University of Bielefeld. His special interest has been in issues of welfare states developments, family policy, and sociology of religion. He most recently co-edited in English *Family Life and Family Policies in Europe*; earlier books were *The Public Sector: Challenge for Coordination and Learning, Social Intervention: Chances and Constraints,* and *Guidance, Control and Evaluation in the Public Sector.*

European Review, Vol. 8, No. 3, 313–332 (2000) © Academia Europaea, Printed in the United Kingdom

3 The dog that didn't bark: economic development and the postwar welfare state

FRANCIS G. CASTLES*

This paper focuses on the linkages between postwar economic and social policy development. Examining the relationship between affluence and levels of welfare over the period as a whole reveals a tendency for social expenditure effort to be higher in moderately affluent then in extremely affluent nations. Turning to the question of how economic growth impacted on welfare expansion in the early postwar decades, the paper argues that growth was a necessary, rather than a sufficient, condition of welfare development. Finally, analysis of the era of welfare containment suggests that domestic economic performance has been the main factor conditioning expenditure change

Introduction

Two decades of extensive comparative research on the determinants of social spending have had little to say concerning the relationship between economic development and the size and growth of the postwar welfare state. This silence is curious for at least three reasons. First, there is the fact that much of the early theorising in the field posited a direct developmental connection between economic growth and the expansion of the state (for a review of the literature, see Ref. 21). Second, the modernisation paradigm, from which this notion derived, made it wholly natural to interpret postwar welfare state expansion as the immediate consequence of the unparalleled extent of postwar economic growth in the decades following 1945.[7, 40, 42] Finally, the coincidence of the end of the 'Golden Age' of capitalism and the 'Golden Age' of welfare expansion has been repeatedly noted in the scholarly literature, with the 1970s oil shocks widely regarded as harbingers of reduced economic growth, increased unemployment and emergent welfare state crisis.[11, 20]

Yet, although linkages of these kinds are amongst the standard assumptions informing our understanding of the dynamics of the postwar political economy, they have not featured prominently in recent comparative research on the development of the postwar welfare state. This discrepancy stems from a difference in analytical focus. The broader currents of analysis

* Political Science Programme, Research School of Social Sciences, Australian National University, Canberra, ACT 0200, Australia. E-mail: francis.castles@anu.edu.au.

noting the connections between economic and social policy development have based their conclusions on changes occurring as countries became more economically developed or on differences between countries at widely different economic levels. In contrast, analyses of the determinants of welfare expenditure levels and change have tended to focus on comparisons of advanced, democratic states at roughly comparable levels of economic and political modernisation. From the late 1970s onwards, these analyses began to suggest that politics – and, in particular, national differences in the partisan composition of government – provided a more persuasive account of the diversity of welfare spending than did differences in levels of economic development.[5, 15, 32]

In subsequent decades, the comparative literature has grown in scope and sophistication, but economic development has never been a major focus of attention. On occasions, the complex statistical modelling exercises, which are a feature of much of this work, do contain terms for level of per capita GDP and/or for the rate of economic growth. Almost invariably, though, this is as a backdrop to the analysis of factors considered as being of greater theoretical interest. In this literature, politics remains a central focus, but is now conceived more broadly. Many scholars now see the structure of governmental institutions as having just as great an impact on outcomes as does the partisan composition of government.[12, 17, 37] Cultural factors are also regarded as important. In particular, the impact of religious doctrine on social policy ideas has been singled out as a formative influence on welfare policy choices.[3, 36, 41] Although contemporary researchers are far more willing than were their predecessors to concede the multiplicity of causal factors associated with social policy development, levels of economic development and trajectories of economic growth are rarely seen as being of sufficient significance to merit extended analysis.

The primary goal of the comparative literature has always been to account for cross-national differences in the development of the welfare state. Recently, however, attention has shifted from the factors accounting for social policy expansion to those responsible for the tendencies to contraction of recent years. Again, despite the universal recognition that such tendencies stem from fundamental changes in the functioning of the capitalist economy, there has been surprisingly little research on how deteriorating economic performance impacts on trajectories of social expenditure development. Instead, scholars have been preoccupied by two controversies. One concerns the role of politics in the new environment of welfare containment. The issue here is whether a 'new politics' of the welfare state has emerged, cutting across traditional lines of support for social pro-grammes,[27, 33] or whether more traditional class- and partisanship-based accounts retain their explanatory relevance.[6, 30] The other controversy concerns the impact of economic globalisation, which some commentators see as hugely restricting the autonomy of national governments to pursue welfare state strategies[29] and which others see as being much exaggerated.[14, 35]

In one Sherlock Holmes story, the key to unravelling the mystery is the fact that a guard dog failed to give a warning, suggesting to the great detective that the criminal he sought was the dog's master (*The Memoirs of Sherlock Holmes*, 1893). In this paper, I examine a no lesser mystery of the absence of expected effects by inquiring why it is that most comparative studies have failed to establish linkages between postwar economic and social policy development. My inquiry concentrates on three key questions, highlighting areas in

38

which the failure to uncover such impacts is most puzzling. The first is why research on the advanced nations of Western capitalism has failed to uncover a link between economic affluence and levels of social spending. The second is why it has proved so difficult to establish a connection between economic growth and postwar expansion of the welfare state. The final question is why it is that economic slowdown has not featured more directly as a factor accounting for the changed trajectory of welfare state development in recent years.

My discussion of these questions draws on evidence from some 21 advanced, democratic, OECD nations (for a listing of countries, see Table 1) over the period 1950–1995. Some of this evidence is necessarily of a quantitative kind, and the paper contains a number of tables reporting social expenditure levels and growth rates. However, in order to make the argument as widely accessible as possible, I have avoided all statistical analysis in the text and have relegated supporting evidence of this nature to a few statistical appendices. Otherwise, the presentation here is wholly non-technical in character. Its aims are to provide a broad overview of the changing character of the linkages between economic development and the welfare state during the postwar years and simultaneously to locate what it is about those linkages which has made them so relatively impenetrable to comparative research.

Economic affluence and welfare provision

Early work on the sources of welfare state development was strongly predisposed to see a link between economic and social policy development. The basic framework of discourse was a structural-functional analysis focusing on industrial modernisation as the key to economic, demographic, social and political change. Industrialisation created wealth, reduced mortality and extended life expectation, undermined traditional family ties and community structures and produced pressures for democratic participation. Most of all, modernisation made for a whole range of profound new social problems. Rapid urbanisation produced slums, epidemic diseases and popular disorder. Industrial development created not only wealth, but also substantial groups superfluous to the requirements of the new economic order and outside its rewards structure (most conspicuously, the aged infirm and those surplus to the employment needs of industry). A modernisation perspective makes it natural to interpret the enhanced role of the state as a provider of urban services and social benefits as a response to changing patterns of social needs and citizen demands.

In broad terms, such an account makes sense of gross disparities between levels of state intervention in rich and poor nations and in countries prior to and after economic modernisation. What it does not seem to make sense of is the historical sequence of welfare state development in the more advanced Western nations or the present-day variation in levels of welfare expenditure amongst these nations. Flora and Alber[13] have demonstrated that the sequence through which European nations adopted social insurance programmes from the late 19th century onwards cannot be understood in terms of socio-economic development alone. Rather, patterns of early and late policy adoption only become comprehensible when we take into account both the extent of working class mobilisation and the character of constitutional development. Despite lower socio-economic levels than in liberal democracies such as Britain, it was the authoritarian regimes of Germany and Austria that were the 19th century's social insurance pioneers, utilising such concessions to retard the growth of working class politics.

Table 3.1 Postwar expenditure on the welfare state

	1950 ILO	1960 OECD	1974 OECD	1983 OECD	1995 OECD
Poor Nations	POR **4.9**	POR **(4.7)**	POR **(7.8)**	POR 11.6	GR 16.8
	GR •	GR **7.1**	GR **8.4**	GR 14.7	POR 18.3
	JAP 4.0	JAP 4.1	IRE **15.2**	IRE **18.5**	SP 21.5
	SP •	SP **(4.0)**	SP **(11.7)**	SP **18.1**	IRE **19.4**
	IRE **7.2**	IRE **8.7**	JAP 8.1	IT **21.4**	NZ 18.8
	IT **8.4**	IT **13.1**	IT **19.3**	UK 20.9	FIN 32.0
	AU **12.4**	AU **15.9**	AU **19.2**	AU 23.3	IT **23.7**
	Mean 7.4	Mean 8.2	Mean 11.6	Mean 18.4	Mean 21.5
Middling Nations	GER **14.8**	FIN 8.8	UK 14.9	JAP 11.0	AU 26.2
	FIN 7.4	BEL **(15.3)**	NOR 18.6	BEL **27.3**	BEL **27.1**
	FR **11.5**	NOR 7.8	FIN 15.1	NL **31.1**	UK 22.5
	NOR 6.2	FR **13.4**	BEL **22.1**	NZ 18.0	NL **27.8**
	BEL **11.6**	UK 10.2	GER **23.5**	FIN 21.4	FR **30.1**
	NL **8.0**	NL 11.7	NL **26.7**	DK 28.5	SWE 33.0
	DK 7.9	GER **18.1**	DK 22.7	FR **26.5**	GER **28.0**
	Mean 9.6	Mean 12.2	Mean 20.5	Mean 23.4	Mean 27.8
Rich Nations	UK 9.6	DK **(11.7)**	FR **17.7**	GER **24.4**	JAP 13.8
	SWE 9.7	CAN 9.1	NZ 11.1	SWE 31.3	DK 32.0
	CAN 6.2	SWE 10.8	AUS 10.5	NOR 19.0	SWI 21.0
	NZ 9.7	AUS 7.4	SWE 21.0	AUS 13.5	AUS 15.7
	SWI 5.9	SWI 4.9	USA 12.8	SWI 15.0	CAN 18.2
	USA 4.0	USA 7.3	SWI 11.5	USA 14.2	USA 15.8
	Mean 7.1	Mean 8.8	Mean 14.1	Mean 19.1	Mean 20.6

Sources and notes: The first column reports total social security expenditure as a percentage of GDP from the International Labour Organization, *The Cost of Social Security*, Geneva, 7th International Inquiry, 1973. Columns 2 and 3 report total social expenditure as a percentage of GDP from OECD, *New Orientations for Social Policy*, Social Policy Studies, no. 12, Paris, 1994. Where there are missing data for these columns, International Labour Organization data for the nearest corresponding time-points are reported in parenthesis. Columns 4 and 5 report total social expenditure as a percentage of GDP from the *Social Expenditure Data Base (SOCX)*, Paris, 1998. Countries are ordered from the least to the most affluent in terms of real GDP per capita measured in 1985 US $ (data from Summers and Heston, 1991 – for 1995, brought up to date using data from Ref. 23). Means are for thirds of each distribution — poor, middling and rich nations. Countries in bold are those classified as having strong Catholic cultures; others are non-Catholic. This classification is to be found in Ref. 4.

Turning to the data in Table 3.1 on postwar welfare state expenditure levels in 21 OECD nations underlines the same point. For each time-point – from 1950 through to 1995 – these countries are ordered from the least to the most affluent. Yet there is no obvious correspondence between level of GDP per capita and welfare spending as a percentage of GDP of the kind implied by the modernisation thesis. In particular, the division into three groups of poor, middling and rich nations demonstrates that, at every time-point, average levels of spending in the middling nations markedly exceeded those in the rich nations. Nor does Table 1 provide any systematic evidence that the countries we classify as rich spent significantly more than those we classify as poor. Given these findings, it is hardly surprising that the bulk of comparative research in recent times has tended to focus on the factors that differentiate nations with advanced welfare states from both the very poor and the very rich nations with much lower levels of welfare state expenditure. The factors most prominently identified in this literature have been population ageing[26, 40], partisanship[1, 10, 16] political institutions[17] and the social policy impact of religion.[36]

The correspondence between expenditure and income implied by the modernisation thesis is both linear and positive. The argument is that the more wealthy a nation is, the greater will be its social expenditure level. However, while the scholars who have shown the absence of such a correspondence between expenditure and income in the advanced nations of Western capitalism have simply assumed that this must mean that the variables are unrelated, this is not necessarily the case. Variables can be systematically linked in ways other than through a linear correspondence. The division of the advanced nations into poor, middling and rich groups demonstrates an alternative form of correspondence, which statisticians describe as curvilinear. What this means is that a positive relationship between the variables over one part of the distribution is replaced at some point by a negative one. At all five time-points in the postwar period, middling nations have significantly higher levels of welfare expenditure than poor nations, but at every time-point rich nations are significantly lower spenders than are middling ones. The degree of curvilinearity of the relationship appears to have been getting stronger with the passing of time.

As already noted, the standard focus of attention in the literature has been on what makes the middling nations differ from both the poor and the rich nations. The question to be addressed here is why a group of very rich countries – countries I describe as *rich welfare state laggards* – behave in a manner systematically different from that of other Western nations. Conspicuous amongst these nations are four that have featured in the rich group throughout the postwar period. They are Australia, Canada, Switzerland and the USA. Excluding these nations from the analysis always produces a significantly linear picture. With them, all signs of linearity disappear.

In order to account for such a phenomenon, it is necessary to locate a parameter, which might make income a positive source of expenditure in some countries and a negative source of expenditure in others. A possible clue to such a parameter is the difference that appears to exist between social policy beliefs and welfare state forms in countries in which prevailing religious doctrines are different. Catholic social policy is built around the twin notions of the 'just wage' and 'subsidiarity'.[36] The 'just wage' concept implies that all members of a society – wage-earners and welfare beneficiaries alike – are deserving of an income adequate to maintain a civilised standard of existence. Subsidiarity implies a preference for avoiding direct state intervention and for utilising contributory social insurance as the means of financing income transfers. The adequacy of standards and contributory financing forge links between income levels and social spending. A civilised standard implies that benefit levels will increase with increasing affluence. Basic insurance principles guarantee that contribution levels will keep pace with wages. At a minimum, this means that social spending will remain proportional to per capita national income. Moreover, with greater affluence, the notion of a civilised standard is likely to be continuously redefined and upgraded to include an ever-wider range of programme commitments and an ever-greater degree of benefit generosity. These consider-ations suggest that the relationship between economic development and social spending levels in Catholic nations will be both linear and positive.

The way in which the data in Table 1 are presented allows us to see whether this is, in fact, the case. Countries marked in bold are those designated as characterised by a Catholic culture. Three points should be noticed. First, looking down each column, and examining only those entries in bold, it is clear that Catholic countries are arrayed more or less as one would expect on the basis of the linear hypothesis. Second, it is apparent that this linear pattern becomes markedly stronger over time. Indeed, by 1995, there is only one exception, and that a minor one, to the rule that, amongst Catholic countries, the higher the income level the higher the expenditure. For these countries, modernisation theory seems to provide a progressively more satisfactory account of cross-national differences in the size of the welfare state. Finally, we may note that, with only two exceptions – France in 1974 and Germany in 1983 – Catholic countries fall in the poor or middling income ranges. What that means, of course, is that rich welfare state laggards are almost exclusively non-Catholic in cultural orientation.

Given that the overall distribution is best described in terms of a curvilinear correspondence between expenditure and income and that the relationship in Catholic countries is both linear and positive, the relationship in the non-Catholic nations must take a different form. In fact, the relationship changes over time. In 1950 and in 1960, it mirrors the curvilinear distribution of the entire sample and is statistically significant. In 1973 and 1983, no association of any kind is observable. However, by 1995, the relationship has become linear and negative (i.e. higher income leads to lower expenditure), although, in this very small sample of countries, the finding is not statistically significant. In all instances, the fact that the group of consistent and conspicuous rich welfare state laggards have welfare spending values often as much as a third lower than the mean for the middling countries is what leads to the significant curvilinearity of the sample as a whole.

There are two standard explanations in the literature for these nations' laggard status: demography and politics. The non-Catholic grouping consists of two quite distinct families of nations. [2] On the one hand, there are the Scandinavian social democracies and, on the other, the English-speaking nations plus two countries fitting into no clearly defined geographical grouping, Japan and Switzerland. This latter grouping closely resembles that which has been identified as the 'liberal' world of welfare capitalism.[10] Most accounts suggest that the combination of an ageing population and a high level of Left (or non-Right) partisan mobilisation characterising the Scandinavian countries for much of the postwar era is sufficient to account for welfare expenditure levels which by the 1990s were consistently higher than in other Western nations.

However, the identification of the rich welfare state laggards as being almost exclusively non-Catholic suggests the possibility that cultural preferences and institutional arrangements may also be relevant. In much the same way that Catholic doctrines of the 'just wage' and of subsidiarity create a dynamic of welfare state expansion, Protestant doctrines of individual self-reliance and of giving succour only to the needy make for inherently self-limiting systems of welfare provision. In countries imbued with such values, programmes have often been introduced relatively late by international standards and have frequently been selective in character, with tests of means used to restrict eligibility to the very poor. Most important of all, the notion of need, and hence of poverty, has tended to be defined in absolute rather than in relative terms. This has had two consequences. On the one hand, it has made for a focus on minimum rather than on adequate levels of benefit. On the other, given that, all other things being equal, absolute need is likely to decline with increasing affluence, it has also provided the dynamic for a negative linkage between the level of economic development and the extent of social spending in those countries where Protestant social policy doctrines are prevalent.

All the non-Catholic (and, with the exception of Japan, essentially, Protestant) nations started out with means-tested welfare programmes (see Ref. 25). However, in the early postwar years, left mobilisation won out over Protestant virtue when both Britain and Scandinavia abandoned selectivity for universal citizen benefits. In social democratic Scandinavia, the Protestant social policy heritage was jettisoned with the introduction of a wide range of universal services and earnings-related income transfers designed to win the hearts and minds of middle class voters.[9] That left the rich welfare state laggards of the liberal world of welfare as the only ones in which a culturally shaped logic of the proper functioning of social policy institutions served to make affluence a reason for welfare restraint rather than for welfare generosity. Under Margaret Thatcher, Britain sought to return to a liberal mainstream, only hesitatingly and incompletely rejected by Beveridge and the postwar Labour government.

Because there are a variety of possible explanations for the observed behaviour of non-Catholic nations, further analysis requires the elaboration of more complex, statistical models. In this paper, the findings of that analysis can only be noted and summarised (see the Appendix). For the latest time-point for which we have data (1995), much of the account presented here is broadly confirmed. For the sample as a whole, we locate a significant curvilinear term for GDP per capita, a negative term for Right partisanship and a positive one for population ageing. Decomposing the sample into Catholic and non-Catholic nations, we find that all that matters for Catholic countries is the positive effect of affluence, while, for non-Catholic ones, partisanship, population ageing and the *negative impact* of affluence are all highly significant predictors of total social expenditure level. These findings suggest that those who have discounted the influence of economic development on postwar social expenditure have missed an important dimension of the story.

Comparative research on levels of welfare spending has neglected the role of economic development for two reasons. One was the insistence of the prevailing modernisation thesis that the only relationship likely to exist between expenditure and income levels was linear and positive. This made it extremely difficult to identify the dog that did not bark, i.e. the consistently anomalous behaviour of the nations described here as rich welfare state laggards. The other was the fact that it was only possible to locate the vital parameter of the curvilinear correspondence between affluence and expenditure once it was established that social policy could be shaped by cultural and institutional factors. Thus, in an odd way, we come full circle. Comparative research is only able to identify the role of economic development in shaping welfare performance, once the notion is abandoned that economic modernisation is the be-all and end-all of social progress.

Economic growth and welfare expansion

Our understanding of the relationship between economic growth and the expansion of the

43

welfare state is made more complex by the way in which comparative research conceptualises welfare effort. In order to compare nations at quite markedly different levels of affluence, it is normal to standardise by expressing expenditure as a percentage of Gross Domestic Product. However, that procedure necessarily obscures an obvious sense in which social spending is linked to economic growth: that, all other things being equal, greater income permits greater expenditure. This relationship is frequently stressed by national governments in the hope of demonstrating that policies designed to improve economic performance, simultaneously have welfare payoffs.

A simple way of measuring expenditure change without standardising for GDP is to examine real expenditure growth rates. For the group of OECD nations with which we are here concerned, the relationship between economic growth and the rate of growth of real social expenditure is consistently positive and strongly statistically significant. This is true for the postwar period as a whole and for all possible sub-periods that can be derived from the data in Table 1. Looking at expenditure growth rates also provides perspectives quite different from those deriving from Table 1. Growth rate measures favour nations starting from lower levels of expenditure and experiencing substantial economic growth. Compared in this way, 1950–1995 expenditure growth was faster in countries like Japan and Portugal than in social democratic Scandinavia. This measure also produces some unfamiliar country pairings. For the period as a whole, Australia and Germany both had expenditure growth rates of 4.7% per annum and Sweden and the US both had rates of 4.8%. All four nations were at and around the OECD median for welfare expansion measured in this way.

Such comparisons are not trivial. Growth rates of spending may be as relevant to attitudes to the welfare state as are levels or changes in expenditure expressed in GDP terms. Table 1 shows Japan to be consistently the smallest welfare state in the OECD throughout the postwar period. However, the fact that it was also the OECD country with the fastest rate of social expenditure growth may help to explain why Japanese governments were not under greater pressure to do more. Other bases of comparison produce other perspectives. Measuring change in absolute dollar terms favours countries that start out affluent, since a given percentage increase in spending translates into more dollars and cents spent on welfare than in countries which start out poorer. Again, these differences may be relevant to attitudes. The United States may be a consistent, rich welfare state laggard in terms of Table 1, but its absolute increase in postwar welfare spending was only marginally less than that of Austria, a country commonly seen as in the European welfare state vanguard. Almost two decades of welfare backlash in the United States may seem anomalous when we consider that country's low spending as a percentage of GDP. It is less so when we consider change in absolute terms.

The reason that comparativists have avoided using measures of expenditure growth and of absolute change is not that they misrepresent the trajectory of expenditure development, but rather that what they capture is as much a function of a country's economic performance as of its commitment to welfare. Standardisation of expenditure by measuring it as a percentage of GDP is designed to get around this difficulty. The procedure removes automatic effects of economic growth on measured welfare effort and leaves open the question of whether economic growth enhances or impedes expenditure development.

Once automatic effects are out of the equation, the likely impact of economic growth is less certain. Adolf Wagner, writing in the latter part of the 19th century, enunciated a 'law of increasing state activity', which postulated that, as a nation's real per capita income increased, so too would the proportion of national income it devoted to public purposes (for discussion, see Refs. 21 and 39). This hypothesis was premised on the notion that, as countries industrialised, there would be ever increasing demands for state action to address the collective action problems created through the modernisation process. However, whilst Wagner's law broadly fits with most national profiles of public expenditure development this century, it may well be less pertinent in an era and for a group of nations in which the industrialisation process is more or less completed.

In any case, it is by no means clear that Wagner's law, however applicable to national expenditure trajectories over time, will always show up in cross-national comparison. His argument was that public spending increased faster than income, or, as modern economists would put it, that such expenditure was income-elastic. He did not argue that the degree of income-elasticity would be roughly the same in all countries, which is what would be required in order to produce a positive relationship on a cross-national basis. Moreover, public expenditure meets needs other than those arising from industrialisation. In particular, when economic circumstances are adverse, the state is often called in to compensate or alleviate the condition of the losers, which suggests the possibility of a negative relationship between growth and spending. That fast-growing economies, like Japan, were able to combine substantial expenditure growth with only a modest increase in spending as a percentage of GDP, points in the same direction.[38] Despite arguments in the comparative literature for both positive and negative relationships, the standard finding of most cross-sectional studies of welfare state development in the postwar era has been that economic growth and expenditure change are unconnected. As in the case of the similar finding for the link between affluence and welfare provision, this has led to a tendency to downplay the direct role of the economy in shaping welfare policy outcomes and to see ideology, institutions and demography as the main forces driving postwar welfare state development.

Once again, however, we may be missing the dog that does not bark. There are good reasons for thinking that the relationship between economic growth and spending may itself be contingent on the extent of growth. This possibility rests on the notion that there must be some threshold level, below which attempts to promote welfare reform run up against limits imposed by the availability of economic resources. Beneath the threshold, welfare expansion is severely constrained, but, above it, the prospect of continuing high levels of economic growth transforms the context of expenditure choice, leaving nations free to expand the reach of the state largely on the basis of their ideological or cultural preferences. Seen in this light, a moderately high level of economic growth becomes a necessary, but not a sufficient, condition for welfare state expansion (for further discussion, see Ref. 4). Above the threshold, the relationship between growth and expenditure is likely to be subject to contradictory forces. On the one hand, the fact that countries with identical growth rates but different welfare preferences will have quite different trajectories of expenditure suggests an indeterminate pattern of outcomes. On the other hand, the fact that, in countries with similar welfare preferences but different rates of economic growth, the countries with the fastest growth will experience the least change measured in GDP terms implies that the relationship will be negative.

Overall, the nature of the link between growth and expenditure is likely to depend on the distribution of growth rates in the countries being compared. Where most countries experience low to moderate growth rates, resource constraints on those below the growth threshold suggest the probability of at least a modest positive relationship between growth and spending. Where most countries experience moderate to high growth rates, the tendency for higher growth to go along with lower measured expenditure change implies the likelihood of some sort of a negative relationship. Where countries are evenly distributed across the growth spectrum, linear tendencies of either kind seem most improbable.

It is a distribution of this latter type that has characterised the OECD nations for much of the postwar period. Table 2 provides data on economic growth and expenditure for the years 1950 to 1983. The 1950 beginning point is the first year for which we have data. The early 1980s end point is chosen because it marks the first time that the onward march of the postwar welfare state was halted, or even, in some countries, reversed.

There are at least three reasons why such changes had not occurred earlier with the onset of the first oil shock recession in the early 1970s. First, there was the power of inertia. Major social spending programmes initiated in the years of plenty could not readily be reversed. Second, the recessions of both the early 1970s and early 1980s led to higher unemployment and, hence, to increased expenditure. Third, in the aftermath of the early 1970s oil shock, some governments deliberately expanded public social expenditure as a device of Keynesian demand management. In 1983, with the end of the second oil shock recession almost in sight, these factors were largely played out. The majority of programmes had reached maturity, unemployment was (temporarily) on the decline and prolonged demand management had come up against the roadblock of increasing deficit levels. Over the entire period 1950–1983, average OECD welfare expenditure increased by 0.41 percentage points of GDP per annum. Between 1974–1983, the rate of increase was no less than 0.49 percentage points per annum. However, between 1983 and 1989, the year preceding the next recession, the average rate was actually marginally negative at -0.06 percentage points per annum. This makes it reasonable to see the early 1980s as a decisive turning point in the postwar history of the welfare state.

Table 2 clearly shows the very considerable range of economic growth during this period, with New Zealand at one end of the distribution with a rate 1.5% per annum and with Japan at the other with 6.1% per annum. The table shows no less clearly the absence of any linear relationship between economic growth and expenditure change during these three decades of uninterrupted welfare state expansion. Dividing the OECD nations into low, medium and high growth groupings does, however, reveal a quite distinct pattern, at least in respect of the first two groupings. Low growth countries, with the single, but important, exception of Sweden, were also countries of weak welfare state development, with annual rates of change within the narrow range of 0.24 to 0.33 percentage points. In contrast, all the medium growth countries were countries of strong expenditure growth, with a much wider range of rates of change from 0.72 to 0.40 percentage points per annum. Finally, the high growth nations lack any distinct profile. Change rates within this grouping vary from very low to moderately high, but with an overall average markedly lower than that of the medium growth grouping.

There are at least two ways in which we might interpret the data in Table 3.2. One is in terms of what has now become the standard account in the literature: that partisan ideology is the primary factor influencing the growth of the postwar welfare state. As a simple means of gauging how well this account fits the data, we identify in bold those countries that

Table 3.2 Economic growth, rightist incumbency and expenditure development, 1950–1983

		Percentage points growth in welfare state spending			
		LOW	<0.35%>	HIGH	
Economic growth rate	LOW <2.50>	**NZ**	**0.24**		
		USA	**0.30**		
		AUS	**0.23**		
		UK	**0.33**		
		SWI	0.26		
				SWE	0.72
		CAN	0.31		
	MEDIUM			DK	0.61
				NL	0.72
				BEL	0.50
				IRE	0.49
				NOR	0.48
				FR	0.54
				FIN	0.40
	HIGH <3.70>	**GER**	**0.29**		
				AU	0.36
				IT	**0.52**
				(SP)	
		POR	**0.16**		
		(GR)			
		JAP	**0.24**		

Sources and Notes: The figures in the table are the annual average percentage point change in social security spending for the period 1950–1983 from ILO, *The Cost of Social Security*, Geneva, various editions. Countries are ranked according to their growth rates, with 1950–1983 average annual rates of economic growth calculated from Ref. 34. Countries in bold are those in which the major party of the Right held more than the median percentage of cabinet seats over the period as a whole. The major party of the Right is defined as in Ref. 1 and the data comes from Ref. 30. The expenditure development profiles for Greece and Spain are based on an extrapolation of the data in Table 1.

experienced more than a median degree of government by a unified party of the Right in the period 1950 to 1983. Of the countries which experienced low rates of expenditure change, only two – Switzerland and Canada – were not ruled primarily by unified parties of the Right and, in the Swiss case, some commentators would suggest that a long-term governing coalition including three right-of-centre parties amounted to much the same thing. Of the countries that experienced high rates of expenditure change, only two – Italy and Spain – had right-wing governments for much of the period, with much of the Spanish expansion post-dating the fall of the Franco government in 1975. There is, then, a very strong *a priori* case for arguing that partisan control of government does make a major difference.

An alternative interpretation rests on the fact that both the low and the high growth nations manifest lower rates of change than the medium growth nations. This suggests the possibility of a relationship taking the same curvilinear form as that identified earlier between levels of economic development and levels of welfare spending. However, although the countries showing up as having the lowest rates of economic growth in the period 1950–1983 are precisely those that were earlier identified as being the most affluent in 1950, statistical tests do not confirm a curvilinear relationship in respect of growth. Instead, Table 2 reveals a radical discontinuity within the OECD grouping during this period. All but one of the countries in the low growth category also manifest low rates of expenditure change. However, as growth rates increase to around 2.5% per annum, there is a step up to much higher rates of expenditure change, with a tendency for subsequent decline as growth rates increase further. This is, of course, precisely the kind of threshold effect that would be expected if the unusually high economic growth rates experienced in this period were a necessary condition for the expansion of the postwar welfare state. The negative relationship above the threshold is also as predicted, given the way in which high rates of economic growth reduce expenditure change measured in GDP terms.

So which of these accounts provides the most convincing story: the impact of parties or the removal of economic constraints? Almost certainly, the sensible answer is that, for many countries, these factors were complementary. Countries like New Zealand, the US, Australia and Britain missed out on the postwar welfare revolution – growing slowly in real as well as in GDP terms – partly because of an absence of political will and partly because of the lack of the necessary economic means. Prevailingly rightist governments undertook few welfare state initiatives, while interludes of more progressive government were generally frustrated by economic crisis. In contrast, in countries like Sweden, Denmark, the Netherlands and Belgium, rightist governments were few and far between and economic growth was sufficient to allow progressive forces to contemplate welfare reform on a major scale. However, moderate growth plus big ambitions added up to expenditure change on a massive scale. By contrast, faster rates of growth in other non-rightist countries, like Norway, Finland and Austria, allowed high growth rates of real expenditure and a more modest increase in the size of the welfare state measured as a percentage of GDP. Finally, in countries like Portugal, Greece and Japan, the combination of high growth and a strong right-wing presence in government produced results similar to those of the English-speaking nations in expenditure change terms, but radically different in terms of the growth of real spending.

The linkages between economic growth and expenditure change discussed here also provide a reinforcing mechanism for the religious dynamic underlying the curvilinear relationship between economic development and welfare spending identified in the previous section. The social policy heritage of Protestantism was not the only factor militating against expenditure growth in the countries that started out the postwar period as rich welfare state laggards. They were also, without exception, countries whose postwar economic growth performance fell below the 2.5% threshold. The coincidence between affluence and low economic growth was not accidental, but an aspect of the strong convergence tendency of economic growth during the postwar period (see Ref. 8). It meant that countries with already low levels of welfare expenditure experienced lesser expenditure growth in the years that followed. Within the Catholic grouping, economic growth also amplified the thrust of the welfare dynamic imparted by religious doctrine. The Catholic countries are all to be found in the medium to high economic growth categories, making for a negative (and statistically significant) relationship between growth and welfare expansion during the period. Amongst these countries, welfare spending as a percentage of GDP grew most rapidly in the middling rich nations of moderate economic growth, which were already welfare state leaders, and grew least strongly in the poorer nations of rapid economic growth, which started out in the welfare state rearguard.

In this section I have pointed to evidence that the unusually high economic growth rates of the early postwar decades were a precondition for the large-scale, welfare state expansion experienced by many countries during that period. However, this discussion of the expenditure trajectories of countries experiencing higher and lower degrees of economic growth during the heyday of the postwar welfare state provides only a part of the relevant evidence. What is also required is a comparison of welfare expenditure trajectories in periods of greater and lesser economic growth. In the next section of this paper, I examine data for the years 1983 to 1995 with a view to understanding the role of economic factors in an era widely regarded as one of welfare state crisis and containment. Since this was also a period of much weaker economic growth than that examined here, comparison of findings for the two periods will enable us to take the analysis further.

Economic slowdown and the welfare state

The two major controversies concerning the contemporary development of the welfare state in the advanced countries of Western capitalism both concern the continued salience of partisanship in an era of welfare constraint. One argument is that partisanship has been rendered irrelevant by the emergence of a 'new politics' of the welfare state. According to this view, the postwar expansion of the welfare state has itself reshaped the institutional parameters of modern public policy.[27] Whereas the initial adoption of welfare programmes was shaped by ideological agendas, their maintenance is now a function of the coalitions of interest they serve. Welfare claimants and welfare employees seek to defend the programmes which benefit them and governments wishing to be re-elected seek to avoid the blame for welfare cuts. This helps to explain why, despite economic slowdown and ideologically motivated attacks on the public sector, so few countries have manifested major cuts in the size of the welfare state in recent years. The other argument is that partisanship has been rendered irrelevant by the globalisation of the international economy. According to this view, the welfare state expansion of the early postwar decades rested on the economic policy autonomy of the nation-state.[19, 28] However, greater exposure to international trade and greater international capital mobility has left governments with less and less room for manoeuvre in economic policy. This makes partisan differences on the scope of the welfare state more a matter of rhetoric than of reality and creates pressures for a downward convergence in cross-national social expenditure levels.

The evidence in support of the proposition on which these arguments agree – the irrelevance of partisanship to the present trajectory of welfare state development – seems quite incontrovertible. Research by Stephens *et al.*[33] has demonstrated that, for the period 1979–1986, neither Social Democratic nor Christian Democratic incumbency made any difference to a wide range of welfare-related policy outcomes. Similarly, a statistical analysis of the data presented in Table 3 on change in aggregate social spending for the period 1983–1995 provides no evidence of a relationship between expenditure change and Right partisan incumbency of the kind that was identified in the previous section (see Ref. 2). This evidence is in no way at odds with our earlier findings that, as recently as the mid-1990s, cross-national variation in the level of social expenditure reflected partisan differences and that partisanship was the strongest single influence on expenditure change in the period 1950–1983. Any apparent contradictions are easily resolved if one contrasts the extent of change manifested in Tables 3.2 and 3.3. Between 1950–1983, when partisanship had a major impact, welfare spending as a percentage of GDP in the average OECD nation grew by 13.4 percentage points; between 1983–1995, it grew by 3 percentage points. The story, then, is that the extent of change in the recent period, when partisanship has been irrelevant, has been of insufficient dimensions to affect either the overall trajectory of postwar change or the cross-national expenditure relativities established in the heyday of welfare expansion.

Although the arguments we are discussing here agree on the irrelevance of partisanship, they differ on the reasons for that irrelevance and on the probable trajectory of social expenditure change. The obvious implication of the 'new politics' thesis is that countries with extensive social programmes are likely to be better protected from retrenchment initiatives than countries with weaker welfare state development. In contrast, the globalisation thesis seems to suggest that the countries likely to be under the greatest pressure to make cuts will be those with the highest initial expenditure levels. The evidence provided by Table 3.3 is mixed. The fact that three of the four Scandinavian nations – Denmark, Finland and Norway – experienced substantial welfare expansion in this period fits with the 'new politics' interpretation. On the other hand, the fact that the Netherlands and Belgium, both in the welfare state vanguard in 1983, were the only countries to experience a decline in spending in the ensuing period fits with the globalisation hypothesis. Although expenditure as a percentage of GDP did not actually fall, the Swedish experience was quite similar. The evidence is no less mixed at the other end of the distribution. Some welfare state laggards (Australia, Greece and the USA) grew slowly after 1983; others (Portugal and Switzerland) grew much faster than the OECD average.

Apart from their rejection of the relevance of partisanship, the 'new politics' thesis and the globalisation hypothesis have one other thing in common: both downplay the potential impact of the domestic economy on the trajectory of expenditure development. Again, this must be attributed to the comparative literature's fixation with the politics of the welfare state. It is, however, quite extraordinary in an era widely characterised in terms of problematic domestic economic performance and where linkages between economic performance and expenditure change are often quite transparent. Some propositions follow from the analysis of economic growth rate distributions in the previous section. If, as argued there, a moderate to high rate of economic growth is a precondition for welfare state expansion on any scale, we would expect the slow growth era of the early 1980s to the mid-1990s to be one of only modest social expenditure change. Moreover, if the majority of countries fall below the threshold level for major welfare state expansion identified in the previous section, we would expect to locate at least a modestly positive relationship between economic growth and expenditure change during this period.

Apart from direct effects of economic development, other aspects of domestic economic

Table 3.3 Economic growth, unemployment change, public indebtedness and expenditure development, 1983–1995

		Percentage points growth in welfare state spending		
		LOW	<0.20%>	HIGH
				(SWI) 0.50
				FIN 0.88
		SWE 0.14		
	LOW	GR 0.17		
		(NZ) 0.07		
				FR 0.30
		CAN 0.17		
	<1.94>			GER 0.30
		USA 0.13		
Economic		BEL −0.02		
growth	MEDIUM			AU 0.24
rate		**IT** 0.19		
		AUS 0.19		
		NL −0.28		
	<2.20>			DK 0.29
		UK 0.13		
				NOR 0.72
	HIGH			SP 0.28
				JAP 0.23
				POR 0.56
		IRE 0.07		

Sources and Notes: The figures in the table are the annual average percentage point change in social security spending for the period 1983–1995 from Ref. 24. Countries are ranked according to their growth rates, with 1983–1995 average annual rates of economic growth calculated from Ref. 34 (updated from Ref. 23). Countries in bold are those in which the increase in unemployment in the period 1983–1995 was above the median for these nations. Unemployment change calculated from Ref. 23. Countries which are underlined are those in which the 1983 level of gross financial liabilities of general government as a percentage of GDP (i.e. public indebtedness) was above the OECD median for these nations. Countries in parentheses have missing data for this variable. Gross financial liabilities from Ref. 23.

performance are also likely to be relevant to outcomes. Cross-national differences in unemployment rates and the successes or failures of governments in bringing unemployment under control have direct implications for the welfare budget. The existence of unemployment benefit schemes throughout the OECD means that increasing unemployment will necessarily have a positive impact on spending levels in the short- to medium-term, although, in the longer term, greater obligations to the unemployed may induce governments to seek cuts in other social programmes.[33] In contrast to the positive effects of unemployment, high levels of public indebtedness are likely to put a brake on further welfare expansion. Arguably, those nations, which used deficit financing to fund welfare expansion in the 1970s, had a price to pay in enhanced retrenchment pressures in the 1980s and 1990s. Arguably, too, this is a factor, where the border between the domestic and international economy is extremely fuzzy. Governments are likely to be more vulnerable to international market pressures when they run large deficits or have high aggregate debt levels. The Maastricht Treaty obligation to bring deficit levels down to an acceptable level was an institutional recognition of this reality and a potent force for social expenditure containment in many European countries in the early to mid-1990s.

A simple way to assess the overall impact of economic slowdown on the trajectory of social expenditure change is to superimpose the cut-off points of Table 3.2 on the data contained in Table 3.3. Of the 21 countries in Table 3.3 only five – Ireland, Japan, Norway, Portugal and Spain – experienced economic growth rates above the 2.5% growth threshold identified in Table 3.2. In the earlier decades of welfare expansion, two thirds of the OECD nations exceeded this average growth rate. According to the reasoning of the previous section, we would expect the 16 countries falling beneath the growth threshold in the period from 1983 to 1995 to manifest expenditure change below the Table 3.2 cut-off point of 0.35 percentage points per annum. The fact that only two of these countries – Switzerland and Finland – exceeded this level of expenditure change strongly supports the conclusion that large-scale welfare expansion generally occurs only when economic growth is unusually high.

The Swiss and Finnish exceptions do, however, require some explanation, since it was these countries that had the lowest levels of growth in the OECD between 1983 and 1995, a finding difficult to square with both the threshold notion and the hypothesised positive link between growth and spending under circumstances of economic constraint. For a positive relationship to exist despite these countries' aberrant performance, both would have to manifest extreme values on a range of other variables strongly related to welfare expansion. Table 3.3 identifies two variables, which might account for these countries' exceptional welfare expansion. Countries marked in bold are those with above median increases in levels of unemployment and countries underlined are those with higher than median levels of public indebtedness. Even casual inspection shows that, in this period, greater increases in unemployment were positively associated with greater increases in welfare spending and that higher levels of initial indebtedness were associated with weaker subsequent expenditure development.

Finland's extraordinary rate of welfare expansion becomes far more explicable when we recognise that it began the period with the lowest level of indebtedness in the OECD and experienced much the OECD's greatest increase in unemployment in the years thereafter. Low debt levels allowed Finland to embark on an ambitious programme of welfare catch-up in the 1980s, and a massive increase in unemployment in the early 1990s made it impossible to scale back social expenditure growth, despite several years of negative GDP growth. While data on Swiss levels of public indebtedness are unavailable, that country's reputation for budgetary prudence suggests that it, too, is likely to have been near the bottom of the OECD league table in this respect. Switzerland started the period with the lowest joblessness rate in the Western world, but was one of a number of low unemployment countries in which the dam finally burst in the early 1990s, recording the OECD's fourth largest increase in unemployment over the years 1983–1995. Thus, although the Swiss trajectory of change was not as dramatic as that of Finland, it appears to have been driven by quite similar forces.

The data in Table 3.3 suggest a moderately strong correspondence between various aspects of domestic economic performance and the trajectory of welfare expenditure change in the period 1983–1995. As previously, in discussing the factors associated with cross-national differences in welfare spending as a percentage of GDP, further analysis requires statistical modelling, the results of which can only be noted here (see Appendix B). This modelling confirms the main lines of the analysis above. All three aspects of domestic economic performance are significantly associated with expenditure change – economic growth and unemployment change positively and indebtedness negatively. On the other hand, Rightist incumbency, which proved so significant an influence on 1995 expenditure levels and on change during the 1950–1983 period, had absolutely no impact on change in the later period. Finally, although not shown below, the inclusion of initial spending levels in the 1983–1995 change model has a wholly negligible effect. This means that predictions as to the trajectory of expenditure change deriving from both the 'new politics' thesis and the globalisation hypothesis are invalidated. Neither add anything to an account based on domestic economic performance alone.

Conclusions

The main conclusion that follows from this study is that comparative research on the welfare state has been mistaken in neglecting the role of economic development in influencing postwar social expenditure outcomes. Throughout, it has been a case of the dog that did not bark. From 1950 right up until the present, the relationship between affluence and welfare provision in the countries of the OECD has been curvilinear, with rich Protestant nations marching to the step of a quite different drummer to that of their Catholic cousins. In the early postwar decades, when the welfare state was expanding rapidly, moderate to high rates of economic growth served as a vital background condition of large-scale expenditure change. In the most recent period of economic slowdown, aspects of domestic economic performance appear to have been the main forces shaping the growth path of social spending, with higher rates of economic growth amongst the factors permitting some continuing modest expansion of social spending. In every period, then, the wealth of nations has had a significant role in shaping the trajectory of welfare state development.

Acknowledging the importance of such economic factors does not, however, mean that they should now become the exclusive or even the main focus for comparative research in this area. Rather, the proper lesson of our story is that affluence, economic growth and the role of the domestic economy, more generally are often likely to be key elements in what will invariably be a multi-causal account of welfare state development. At various points in this analysis, we have shown that demography, culture, partisanship and institutional choice, as well as a variety of aspects of economic performance, have variously influenced the size and growth trajectory of postwar welfare state development. We have also shown that different influences were more or less salient at different times. In 1950, social spending levels in the majority of OECD countries were below 10% of GDP. Five decades later, the average is more than 20%. Indeed, the extent of change is still greater, since, over these same years, OECD per capita GDP levels have themselves increased threefold in real terms. Those who examine changes of this magnitude should almost certainly assume that what they study will variously reflect the impact of all those economic, social and political forces which have so hugely transformed modern societies in the second half of the twentieth century.

Appendix A

Robust models with curvilinear terms for the relationships between GDP per capita and various components of public expenditure for the years 1960 and 1973 are to be found in Ref. 4 and between GDP per capita and total social expenditure for the years 1960, 1973 and 1993 in F. G. Castles, 'Social protection in the postwar era: the OECD experience', *Social Security* (1999) **56**, 138–60 [in Hebrew]. The 1995 data for total social expenditure in column S of Table 3.1 can be modelled as follows: 1995 EXPENDITURE $= -17.482 + 0.004$ (2.90) 1995 GDP PER CAPITA — 1.48 SE. -7 (2.91) 1995 GDP PER CAPITA SQUARED $+1.512$ (406) 1995 AGED POPULATION — 0.131 (5.56) 1950–95 RIGHT CABINET SEATS. Adj. $R^2 = 0.803$. 21 cases in regression. For the Catholic nations, the result is 1995 EXPENDITURE $-5.285 + 0.001$ (4.66) 1995 GDP PER CAPITA $+1.022$ (1.97) 1995 AGED POPULATION -0.041 (1.07) 1950–95 RIGHT CABINET SEATS. Adj. $R^2 = .867$. 10 cases in regression. For the non-Catholic nations, it is 1995 EXPENDITURE 33.997 -0.001 (3.15) 1995 GDP PER CAPITA $+1.018$ (2.29) 1995 AGED POPULATION $-.164$ (6.25) 1950–95 RIGHT CABINET SEATS. Adj.$R^2 = 0.90$. 11 cases in regression. Figures in parentheses are t-statistics. Data on the age structure of the population from Ref. 23; data on Right cabinet seats calculated from Ref. 31. All other sources are as in Table 3.1. It should be noted that the location of a curvilinear relationship in the full model for 1995 is dependent on the inclusion of the Greek case. Given the small number of cases in the smaller samples, it is hardly surprising that the model for the non-Catholic countries is not robust. However, in the Catholic model, the inclusion or exclusion of individual cases makes no difference to the significance of the income term.

Appendix B

The data for expenditure change in Table 3.3 can be modelled as follows: 1983–1995 EXPENDITURE CHANGE $= 0.108 + 0.124$ (2.41) 1983–1995 PER CAPITA GDP GROWTH $+0.052$ (3.88) 1983–1995 UNEMPLOYMENT CHANGE — 0.005 (2.65) 1983 GROSS FINANCIAL LIABILITIES OF GENERAL GOVERNMENT $+0.002$ (1.29) RIGHT CABINET SEATS. Adj. $R^2 = 0.609$. 19 cases in regression. Figures in parentheses are t-statistics. All sources as in Table 3.3. It should be noted that the findings in respect of both unemployment and initial levels of indebtedness remain significant irrespective of the exclusion of individual cases. The finding for economic growth is, however, dependent on the inclusion of the Portuguese case.

References

1. Castles, F. G. (1982) The impact of parties on public expenditure. In: Castles, F. G. (ed), *The Impact of Parties*, London: Sage Publications, pp. 21–96.

2. Castles, F. G. (ed), (1993) *Families of Nations: Patterns of Public Policy in Western Democracies*, Aldershot: Dartmouth.

3. Castles, F. G. (1994) On religion and public policy: does Catholicism make a difference?, *European Journal of Political Research*, **25**, 19–40.

4. Castles, F. G. (1998) *Comparative Public Policy: Patterns of Postwar Transformation*, Cheltenham: Edward Elgar.

5. Castles, F. G. and McKinlay, R. (1979) Does politics matter?: an analysis of the public welfare commitment in advanced democratic states, *European Journal of Political Research*, **7**, 169–86.

6. Clayton, R and Pontusson, J. (1998) Welfare-state retrenchment revisited: entitlement cuts, public sector restructuring, and inegalitarian trends in advanced capitalist societies, *World Politics*, **51**(1), 67–98.

7. Cutright, P (1965) Political structure, economic development and national social security programmes, *American Journal of Sociology*, **70**, 537–50.

8. Dowrick, S. and Nguyen, D. T. (1989) OECD comparative economic growth in the postwar period: evidence from a model of convergence, *American Economic Review*, **7**(5), 1010–1030.

9. Esping-Andersen, G. (1985) *Politics Against Markets. The Social Democratic Road to Power*. Princeton, NJ: Princeton University Press.

10. Esping-Andersen, G. (1990) *The Three Worlds of Welfare Capitalism*. Cambridge: Polity Press.

11. Esping-Andersen, G. (1996) After the golden age? Welfare state dilemmas in a global economy. In: G. Esping-Andersen, (ed), *Welfare States in Transition*, London: Sage.

12. Evans, P. B., Rueschemeyer, D and Skocpol, T, (eds) (1985) *Bringing the State Back In*, Cambridge: Cambridge University Press.

13. Flora, P. and Alber, J. (1981) Modernization, democratization, and the development of welfare states in Western Europe. In: Flora, P and Heidenheimer, A. J. (eds.) *The Development of Welfare States in Europe and America*, New Brunswick: Transaction Books, pp. 37–80.

14. Garrett, G. and Lange, P. (1991) Political responses to interdependence: what's left for the Left?, *International Organization*, **45**(4), 539–564.

15. Gough, I. (1979) *The Political Economy of the Welfare State*. London: Macmillan.

16. Hicks, A. and Swank, D. (1984) On the political economy of welfare expansion, *Comparative Political Studies*, **17**(1), 81–119.

17. Huber, E. Ragin, C. and Stephens, J. D. (1993) Social Democracy, Christian Democracy, constitutional structure and the welfare state, *American Journal of Sociology*, **99**(3), 711–49.

18. International Labour Organization (1973 and other numbers) *The Cost of Social Security*, Geneva.

19. Jessop, B. (1996) Post-Fordism and the state. In: Greve, B. (ed) *Comparative Welfare Systems: The Scandinavian Model in a Period of Change*, New York: St Martin's Press.

20. Kitschelt, H., Lange, P. Marks, G. and Stephens, J. D. (eds) (1998) *Continuity and Change in Contemporary Capitalism*, Cambridge: Cambridge University Press.

21. Larkey, P. D., Stolp, C. and Winer, M. (1981) Theorizing about the growth of government: a research assessment, *Journal of Public Policy*, **1**(2), 157–220.

22. OECD (1997) *Economic Outlook*, Paris.

23. OECD (1997) *Historical Statistics 1960–1995*, Paris.

24. OECD (1998) *Social Expenditure Data Base (SOCX)*, CD Rom, Paris.

25. Overbye, E. (1994) Convergence in policy outcomes: social security systems in perspective, *Journal of Public Policy*, **14**(2), 147–74.

26. Pampel, F. C. and Williamson, J. B. (1989) *Age, Class, Politics, and the Welfare State*. Cambridge: Cambridge University Press.

27. Pierson, P. (1996), The new politics of the welfare state, *World Politics*, **48**, 143–179.

28. Rhodes, M. (1997) The welfare state: internal challenges, external constraints. In: Rhodes, M., Heywood, P. and Wright, V. (eds), *Developments in West European Politics*, London: Macmillan.

29. Scharpf, F. W. (1987) *Crisis and Choice in European Social Democracy*. Ithaca: Cornell University Press.

30. Schmidt, M. G. (1996) When parties matter: a review of the possibilities and limits of partisan influence on public policy, *European Journal of Political Research*, **30**, 155–83.

31. Schmidt, M. G. (1996) *Die parteipolitische Zusammensetzung von Regierungen in demokratischen Staaten (1945–1996)*. Heidelberg: Institut für Politische Wissenschaft.

32. Stephens, J. D. (1979) *The Transition from Capitalism to Socialism*. London: Macmillan.

33. Stephens, J. D. Huber, E. and Ray, L. (1998) The welfare state in hard times. In Kitschelt, H., Lange, P. Marks, G. and Stephens, J. D. (eds), *Continuity and Change in Contemporary Capitalism*, Cambridge: Cambridge University Press.

34. Summers, R. and Heston, A. (1991) The Penn World Table (Mark 5), *Quarterly Journal of Economics*, **106**(2), 327–68.

35. Swank, D. (1992) Politics and the structural dependence of the state in democratic capitalism nations, *American Political Science Review*, **86**, 38–54.

36. Van Kersbergen, K. (1995) *Social Capitalism: A study of Christian Democracy and the Welfare State*. London: Routledge.

37. Weaver, R. K. and Rockman, B. A. (eds) (1993) *Do Institutions Matter? Government Capabilities in the United States and Abroad*. Washington, D.C.: The Brookings Institution.

38. Wildavsky, A. (1975) *Budgeting. A Comparative Theory of Budgetary Processes*. Boston: Little Brown.

39. Wildavsky, A. (1985) The logic of public sector growth. In: Lane, J-E. (ed) *State and Market: The Politics of the Public and the Private*, London: Sage Publications, pp. 231–70.

40. Wilensky, H. L. (1975) *The Welfare State and Equality*. Berkeley, CA: University of California Press.

41. Wilensky, H. L. (1981) Leftism, Catholicism, and Democratic Corporatism: the role of political parties in recent welfare state development. In: Flora, P and Heidenheimer, A. J. (eds) *The Development of Welfare States in Europe and America*, New Brunswick: Transaction Books, pp. 345–82.

42. Wilensky, H. L. and Lebeaux, C. N. (1957) *Industrial Society and Social Welfare*. New York: Russell Sage Foundation.

About the Author

Francis Geoffrey Castles is Professor of Political Science in the Research School of Social Sciences, Australian National University. His interest is in the area of comparative politics. His most recent books are *Families of Nations* (1993), *The Great Experiment* (1995) and *Comparative Public Policy* (1998).

European Review, Vol. 8, No. 3, 333–352 (2000) © Academia Europaea, Printed in the United Kingdom

4 How do welfare states change? Institutions and their impact on the politics of welfare state reform in Western Europe

GIULIANO BONOLI* and BRUNO PALIER**

In the 1980s and 1990s West European welfare states were exposed to strong pressures to 'renovate', to retrench. However, the European social policy landscape today looks as varied as it did at any time during the 20th century. 'New institutionalism' seems particularly helpful to account for the divergent outcomes observed, and it explains the resistance of different structures to change through past commitments, the political weight of welfare constituencies and the inertia of institutional arrangements – in short, through 'path dependency'. Welfare state institutions play a special role in framing the politics of social reform and can explain trajectories and forms of policy change. The institutional shape of the existing social policy landscape poses a significant constraint on the degree and the direction of change. This approach is applied to welfare state developments in the UK and France, comparing reforms of unemployment compensation, old-age pensions and health care. Both countries have developed welfare states, although with extremely different institutional features. Two institutional effects in particular emerge: schemes that mainly redistribute horizontally and protect the middle classes well are likely to be more resistant against cuts. Their support base is larger and more influential compared with schemes that are targeted on the poor or are so parsimonious as to be insignificant for most of the electorate. The contrast between the overall resistance of French social insurance against cuts and the withering away of its British counterpart is telling. In addition, the involvement of the social partners, and particularly of the labour movement in managing the schemes, seems to provide an obstacle for government sponsored retrenchment exercises.

What distinguishes Western Europe from the rest of the world, it is often remarked, is its

* Department of Social Work and Social Policy, University of Fribourg, 11 rte des Bonnesfontaines, 1700 Fribourg, Switzerland. E-mail: giuliano.bonoli@unifr.ch
** CEVIPOF — MSH 54 Bd Raspail, 75006 Paris, France. E-mail: palier@msh-paris.fr

welfare state. Unlike other world regions with similar levels of economic development, such as North America and East-Asia, all western European countries have developed comprehensive social protection systems that take care of citizens who are exposed to a range of risks, such as old age, unemployment, sickness, and parenthood. These comprehensive social protection systems are common to all European countries and may provide a nucleus for a developing European identity around a distinctive 'European Social Model'. However, if one takes a closer look, particularly at the national level, one finds an impressive degree of variation in how individual nation-states have gone about developing their own systems of social protection. Different histories, political economies, and political struggles have given rise to systems of social protection that fulfil a similar social function, but they do so with distinctly different instruments (Ebbinghaus 1999).

Since the mid-1970s these social protection systems have been exposed to new, but similar socio-economic challenges to which governments have been forced to respond, be it reluctantly or with enthusiasm. In this process, however, welfare states have proved rather resistant to change. Most commentators would now agree that the gloomy predictions made in the 1970s and early 1980s about the bleak future of the welfare state were simply wrong. However, the resilience of welfare state arrangements did not mean the absence of change. On the contrary, the 1980s and, even more so, the 1990s were decades of intense 'renovation' for most systems. These systems were subjected to strong pressures, but so far they have generally adapted and remained viable.

These processes of change have not all been of the same cut. Different countries responded in different ways and at different times to similar and simultaneously occurring problems. In spite of economic and political trends towards more integration, and even though these welfare states are to a large extent facing common challenges, the European social policy landscape today probably looks as varied as it did at any time during the 20th century.

Our strategy to explaining the persistence of diversity focuses on institutions. The 'new institutionalism' approach[1] seems particularly helpful to account for the outcomes observed, and explains the resistance of different structures to change through past commitments, the political weight of welfare constituencies and the inertia of institutional arrangements. These different factors lead to institutional continuity or 'path dependency'. Within this strand of argument, our contribution focuses on the special role of welfare state institutions in framing the politics of reform, such that we can explain trajectories and forms of policy change. The institutional structure of existing social policies poses, in our view, a significant constraint on the degree and direction of change. In other words, the choice of a given policy path in any country can only be understood against the backdrop of the institutional set-up prevailing at the time reform began.

Identifying, first, the key institutional variables determining the nature of a social programme, and particularly its distributional and political dimensions, we will see how these affect the patterns of support and opposition in which the programme is embedded. Specifying how these variables crucially determine the kind of problems a welfare state confronts and the kind of reform that is politically feasible in a given system. Our model is applied to observed policy developments in two European countries, the UK and France, which both have developed welfare states although with very different institutional features. This illustrates the influence of the institutional variables identified and shows their likely impact on policy developments.

Welfare state variations in Western Europe

Comparative sociology has been interested for some time in the institutional variation of welfare states, which has been mapped out according to different criteria in several studies. Among the most influential attempts to categorise welfare states is Gøsta Esping-Andersen's (1990) work on the *Three Worlds of Welfare Capitalism*, where he develops a trinity of *welfare regimes*, of social protection systems embedded in a given structure of political economy and labour market. However, here we prefer to capture welfare state diversity by focusing on key *institutional variables* that define welfare state schemes rather than on welfare regimes.

Previously we found (following Ferrera 1996a: 59) four institutional variables to be helpful in describing social protection systems (Bonoli and Palier 1998). These four variables tend to vary together across countries and to cluster in a way not very different from Esping-Andersen's typology. However, because these variables impact individually on the overall character of a welfare scheme, they are better looked at separately. In addition, these institutional variables are important because they influence the kind of politics that a scheme allows for, in other words, these variables determine who gains and who loses in a given scheme, and, as a result, who is likely to support and to oppose it.

In general, a welfare state scheme may be characterised by four institutional variables:

- *Mode of access*, for example citizenship, need, work, the payment of contributions, or a private contract.
- *Benefit structure*, where a structure may be means-tested, flat-rate, earnings-related, or contribution-related.
- *Financing mechanisms*, which can range from general taxation, employment-related contributions to premiums.
- *Actors who manage the system*; those who take part in the management of the system can include: the state administration, the social partners (representatives of employers and employees) and the private sector.

International comparisons show that each social protection system combines these four variables in its own special and principled, although not exclusive, way. This combination allows us to distinguish and compare national systems. These four variables combine in most cases in a rather similar way throughout the programmes in a given country. Thus, we can identify *four families of welfare states* in Europe (European Commission 1995; Ferrera 1996a). (1) In the *Nordic countries* (Denmark, Finland, Iceland, Norway and Sweden) the logic of universality has been developed furthest even before Beveridge. Social protection is a right for all citizens who can enjoy substantial access to free services. Most benefits are flat-rate, generous and paid automatically when a contingency arises. However, employees also receive supplementary benefits through compulsory occupational protection schemes. These systems are financed principally through taxes (particularly in Denmark). These schemes are totally public and placed under the direct responsibility of central and local public authorities. Only unemployment insurance is not integrated into the public social protection system of these countries.

(2) The *English-speaking countries* (the UK and Ireland) have not entirely followed Beveridge's ideal of universality. Although in these countries access to social protection is not significantly related to being employed, only the National Health Service is truly universal and provides the same access for everyone free-of-charge. With cash benefits (sickness benefit, unemployment benefit and retirement benefit provided through the national insurance system), those who do not work or earn enough are not entitled to national insurance benefits. These flat-rate benefits are distinctly less generous than in Scandinavian countries; private insurance schemes and company social protection programmes, therefore, play an important role in these countries. For the poorest there is a well-developed extensive safety net of means-tested benefits. The social protection system is also financed through taxes (about 50 %), whereas Beveridge had advocated social contributions. Some of the flat-rate benefits of the national insurance system are financed through contributions. The public system, which is highly integrated, is wholly managed by the state. The social partners play a peripheral role in these systems.

(3) In the *core of the European continent* (Germany, France, the Benelux countries and Austria), the Bismarckian social insurance tradition is strongest. Entitlement to benefits is linked to payment of contributions and social benefits directly depend on employment status (with the exception of the Netherlands, where some programmes are universal). Social insurance schemes are compulsory, except health insurance for those with the highest incomes in Germany and the Netherlands. Cash benefits are contributory and earnings-related. The level of both benefits and contributions may vary with the occupational group covered. The contributions paid by employers and employees provide the lion's share in financing these systems (France beats all others, with almost 80% of the system being financed by social contributions). These schemes are devolved to institutions, which are relatively independent from the state level and are managed by representatives of the social partners. Individuals who are not or no longer covered by social insurance can fall back on a last safety net of means-tested minimum benefits financed through taxes. These benefits have become more important in recent years, although they have not developed into a coherent and harmonised system as they did in the English-speaking countries. In these continental countries, the social partners play an important role in the decision-making and management of social protection.

(4) The *countries of Southern Europe* (Italy, Greece, Portugal and Spain) are sometimes described as a distinct group of European welfare states. In their principal characteristics they are close to the continental or Bismarckian model, featuring social insurance schemes providing benefits to protect labour income. Nevertheless these countries display some special characteristics which justify a fourth family. There is a high level of occupational segregation of social insurance schemes, often particularly generous to public sector employees; universal national health services, which emerged in all of these countries between 1975 and 1985 and the gradual and rather recent establishment of a last safety net guaranteeing a minimum income; and, especially in Italy, the weakness of the state accompanied by inefficiencies and irregularities in public administration, such as clientelism and fraud (Ferrera 1996b).

Institutions and the problems welfare states confront

This institutional variation across the European continent contrasts with the common challenges European welfare states face. Population ageing and high levels of unemployment affect the whole continent in a similar way. Where more people are in work, as in the UK, many face problems of low pay and insecure employment. Moreover, virtually all governments have budgetary problems, due in part to the growing financial requirements of their comprehensive social protection systems.

These socio-economic challenges translate into somewhat different day-to-day problems in the various national institutional contexts, and they subsequently generate different policy responses. Although European countries are faced with broadly similar difficulties, international comparisons of social policy-making confirm that the problems that emerge, and how these problems are construed, vary from country to country, as do the policy responses.

In the UK, the conservative governments headed by Margaret Thatcher and John Major defined three key issues: to reduce the costs of the welfare state and, as a result, to lower public deficits; to increase the efficiency of the delivery systems, particularly to reduce the number of patients on the waiting lists in the National Health Service; and to decrease the work disincentives allegedly generated by some cash benefits. All of these problems clearly relate to the institutional set-up of the British welfare state. The fact that social expenditures are predominantly financed by the government – and not by social insurance funds – means that increased spending will immediately put pressure on the government budget. Similarly, the extent of the incentive problem directly derives from the strong reliance on means-tested provision, which inevitably creates the 'Why work?' or 'Why save?' dilemmas. The new policies adopted in the UK, as will be seen below, responded to these problems generally by increasing the role of the market in social protection systems and, also, by modifying the incentive structure of targeted benefits. Overall, these reforms have reinforced the liberal and residual dimension of the British social protection system, but also the repressive and social control aspects of providing for the poor (Castles and Pierson 1996).

In the 1980s and 1990s, the Nordic countries whose small and open economies were particularly affected by changes in the international economy have seen the emergence of high unemployment and a sharp increase in interest rates. The problems that emerged from these developments were how to maintain full employment and, then, how to reduce public deficits. Since the Nordic countries relied strongly on the state as an employer of first resort, increasing structural unemployment generated higher public expenditure and, given the already high levels of taxation, it increased public deficits as well. At the same time, the inclusive character of the Nordic model preserved strong levels of public support, making the liberal route chosen by Britain impractical (MIRE 1999).

Looking at policy responses, Nordic countries, particularly Sweden, started by reinforcing their active labour market policies, and by expanding the state's role as employer of first resort. As it became more difficult to maintain a costly welfare state in the face of economic internationalisation in the 1990s, the overall direction of social policy making shifted somewhat. Sweden, for instance, started to privatise public enterprises, to decentralise decision-making, and to introduce private sector management techniques in the state sector. Sweden was also forced to retrench some of its welfare state programmes by restricting eligibility and lowering benefit levels. Overall, however, most commentators agree that the Nordic regime has remained relatively stable. Its main strength is the high level of public support it enjoys with the electorate (Stephens 1996; Benner and Vad 2000).

In continental and Southern Europe, debates on social protection have focused on two key issues. First, there is concern about the present and future costs of the welfare state – which are expected to increase as a result of demographic ageing – and about the fact that these costs are mostly born by labour through employment-related contributions. This results in high and increasing non-wage labour costs, generally held to be responsible for the high unemployment rates in these countries. Second, the welfare states of continental and southern Europe, which are mostly contribution-based, do not deal very effectively with social problems such as long-term unemployment and social exclusion. Those most in need of protection are generally those who never were involved in paid work, and are therefore not covered by standard social insurance programmes. The emergence of these two particular problems clearly relates to the institutional structure of these welfare states, as do the reform solutions put forward.

Again, the main changes adopted remain within the logic of these systems. Pension reforms in France and Germany have modified pension formulas restrictively, but did not challenge the logic of the insurance systems (Bonoli 2000). Similarly, cost containment in health care has not affected the insurance character of the French and German systems. Germany has demonstrated how attached it remains to the social insurance model of social protection when it set up a new Long Term Care Insurance scheme in the early 1990s. It is structured just like the main German welfare state programmes: by contributions equally split between employers and employees and by contributory benefits.

Institutions and the politics of social programmes

Institutions determine the shape socio-economic problems take. However, they also impact on future policy developments by limiting the realm of the technically and politically feasible. The four institutional variables already identified – mode of access, benefit structure, financing mechanisms, and actors who manage the system – are useful for detecting such institutional effects, as they shape the kind of politics generated by a given programme. Depending on how these different variables are set we encounter different patterns of support and opposition. This is how we expect these variables to influence the politics of social programmes:

(1) *Mode of access*. This factor is crucial for shaping the politics around a given social programme, as it delimits the beneficiaries and thus the likely supporters of a scheme.[2] The mode of access also relates to the objectives of a programme: income maintenance, poverty alleviation or equality. As a result, support for a scheme might come from groups with an ideological orientation congenial to one of these objectives. Generally, Left-wing parties have tended towards equality, Christian-Democrats have supported income maintenance and Liberal parties have been keener to alleviate poverty (Esping-Andersen 1990: 53ff.)

(2) *Benefit structure*. To some extent this variable is related to the previous one, as typically earnings-related benefits are granted on a contributory basis while universal ones are flat-rate. There are some exceptions though, which are politically significant. For instance, the UK's basic pension builds on a contributory basis but grants flat-rate benefits. Flat-rate benefits are

less likely to be supported by the middle classes than are earnings-related ones. With flat-rate benefits, the higher someone's income, the less the benefit contributes to his or her living-standard. Politically, a low level, flat-rate benefit structure might be related to lack of programme support from the middle and upper classes. As earnings inequality increases in many industrial countries, it will become ever more difficult to set a flat-rate benefit which is at the same time affordable and significant for a majority of the population.

(3) *Financing mechanisms*. While related to the two previous factors, this variable has some significance in its own right. If the mode of access determines the beneficiaries of a programme, the financing mechanisms reveal who is paying for it. Generally these two groups overlap although, in fact, most contributory schemes are also subsidised by general taxes. The political support for a financing mechanism is likely to be stronger if those who pay for a programme are identical with those who receive the benefits. The looser the link between benefit and payment, the less likely the financing mechanism is seen to be legitimate. As a result, there is a crucial difference between tax- and contribution-financed schemes in their ability to attract public support. In a contributory system, the amounts paid in are seen as 'deferred wage'. From a political point of view, contributions are raised much more easily than taxes, especially income taxes.

(4) *Actors who manage the system*. This dimension determines the accountability and legitimacy of different actors. The more the state controls a system and its generosity, the more political class is likely to be held responsible for any changes. When benefits are increased, the government is credited, when benefits are reduced it gets blamed (Pierson 1996). When management is shared with trade unions and employers, responsibility tends to be diluted. This variable also determines the range of actors seen as legitimately participating in welfare reform debates. In a state controlled system the debate is confined to political parties. When the management is handed to the social partners, their participation in the debate is legitimised, and then trade unions are also seen as important actors in social policy-making. They are widely regarded as defending the current system against retrenching governments. This institutional setting gives rise to tensions between governments (often regardless of political persuasion) and the trade unions on the control over social security. Union involvement in the management of social security grants unions a *de facto* veto power against welfare state reforms.

Institutional effects on social policy developments in the UK and France

We will now analyse recent social policy developments in the UK and France in view of such institutional effects. Comparing these two countries is particularly instructive, since our four institutional variables vary considerably across the programmes of these two countries. Generally speaking, France tends to rely on contributory schemes that deliver earnings-related benefits, financed almost exclusively through employment-based contributions and which are jointly managed by the social partners. In contrast, in the UK, besides some minor contributory schemes, mainly means-tested programmes obtain. Benefits are generally flat-rate, including most of the contributory ones, and are financed through a mix of contributions and general taxes. Control rests exclusively with the state. France and the UK, thus, are two cases at extreme opposites as regards most of our four variables. This promises to be fertile empirical ground to gauge the impact of these variables on current social policy change.

Our account of welfare reforms in the UK and France covers three key areas of social protection: unemployment compensation, pensions and health care. These areas were selected because, in both countries, they account for the bulk of social expenditures, they have become prime targets for cuts in this respect, and also because they mix means-tested, contributory and universal provision. For each sector we briefly describe the institutional structure of the schemes and key developments of the 1980s and 1990s.

Unemployment compensation

Both the UK and France have a two-track system of unemployment compensation that distinguishes between contributory and means-tested benefits. The relationship between the two benefit tracks, however, differs substantially between the two countries. In the UK, both benefit tracks are flat-rate and set at virtually the same level. In practice, the only relevant difference between the insurance (Unemployment Benefit) and assistance (Income Support) benefits is that the former is not means-tested while the latter is. In contrast, in France, the Insurance Benefit may provide replacement rates of up to 75% of the salary insured, while the main non-contributory means-tested benefit (*Revenu Minimum d'Insertion* – RMI) is set at less than half of the minimum wage. The lack of a clear distinction between Unemployment Benefit and Income Support in the UK means that both tracks are often lumped together insofar as they provide for the unemployed. In contrast, in France, the Insurance Benefit and RMI are seen as two distinct tracks of intervention. The former is managed and controlled jointly by the social partners, who are responsible for setting contribution rates and benefits, whereas the latter is a government-run and tax-financed scheme, even though it is delivered by the Family Benefits Funds. The two countries also rely on the first track to a different degree: in the UK only 18% of the unemployed are covered by the Unemployment Benefits, while the same figure for the Insurance Benefits in France is 70% (Evans 1996: 11).

In the UK, unemployment compensation policy has been characterised by three trends in the last 15 years: downward pressure on the level of benefits, increased targeting, and the removal of work disincentives. Levels of benefits have been modified on numerous occasions. Atkinson and Micklewright (1989) provide a list of the main changes in benefits for the unemployed adopted between 1979 and 1988. Altogether they identify some 32 individual regulations in the decade they cover: they see 23 of these measures as disadvantageous to the unemployed, seven as being of undetermined effect and four as favourable (Atkinson and Micklewright 1989: 21). It is widely accepted among experts that the unemployed were the main losers of the social policy changes introduced by the Thatcher governments (Barr and Coulter 1990: 333; Pierson 1994: 102).

As a result, over the last decade, the benefit value for the unemployed has remained more or less constant in real terms, but did decline relative to average earnings from 16 to 13.5%. This is a trend also found in other cash benefits and is generally referred to as 'erosion'. This results from a decision taken in the 1980s to index benefits to consumer prices only – rather than to prices or wages, whichever is higher. This slow piecemeal process generates substantial savings for the government budget in the long run and also reduces the generosity of benefits radically.

The 1980s and 1990s are also marked by a shift away from insurance-based provision for the unemployed to means-tested assistance. First, an earnings-related supplement to the insurance benefit was abolished in 1980, making the Unemployment and the Assistance Benefit virtually identical. Secondly, in 1996, the maximum duration of the Unemployment Insurance Benefit was reduced from one year to six months. These changes dramatically increased the role of means-tested benefits for the support of the unemployed. Currently only about 5% of benefit expenditures for the unemployed are insurance benefits (Erskine 1997: 138). In the area of unemployment, the reforms of the 1980s and 1990s reinforced some of the key liberal and residual features of the British system, and abandoned the few social insurance elements that existed until then.

Finally, the incentive problem was also addressed in the 1990s, a compulsory workfare scheme was introduced for the able bodied unemployed, as was a negative income tax programme for low-wage workers plus a minimum wage. Given these measures and the ungenerous level of means-tested benefits in the UK, workers are less likely to be exposed to a 'Why work?' dilemma, since they are regularly much better off in work than 'on the dole'.

In France, the policies towards the unemployed were quite different. In the 1980s, early-retirement and job-creation in the non-market sector were the typical instruments that dealt with unemployment, accompanied by the simplification of a complex, although generous Unemployment Insurance. Also important was the introduction in 1988 of a brand new non-contributory scheme, aimed mainly at the long-term unemployed. Known as RMI, the new programme combines a guarantee of minimum monetary support with re-insertion measures. Some retrenchment measures were adopted in the early 1990s, disbanding the early retirement instruments and adopting the Unemployment Insurance Reform of 1992.

Early retirement as an employment policy instrument was used most prominently in the early 1980s. The government policy aimed at controlling labour supply by removing older workers form the labour market. This was achieved by lowering the official retirement age from 65 to 60 in 1981, and by encouraging early retirement. The early 1980s brought a rapid increase in the numbers of early retirees, from 84 000 in 1975 to 159 000 in 1979, 317 000 in 1981 and 705 000 in 1983 (cf. Bichot 1997: 132). Government policy at the time also included 'protected jobs' (*emplois aidés*) for the young and the long-term unemployed. This role of the state as employer of last resort can be illustrated by the numerous contracts proposed to the unemployed in different 'insertion policies'.[3] The 're-insertion' dimension of the RMI may be seen as a major policy innovation in this perspective. Towards the end of the 1980s, however, these 'human' policies for the unemployed were viewed as too costly, and scaled down, especially as regards early retirement. By 1988, the number of workers taking early retirement had fallen to 433 000 (Bichot 1997: 132).

Unemployment Insurance was created in 1958 – outside the state – through an agreement between the social partners. From 1982 to 1992, several attempts ware made to rationalise the system and to stabilise the benefit level, which remained generous compared with the UK. In 1982, the replacement rate was 80% in the first year.[4] The benefit level then fell to 75% for the next 9 months (Join-Lambert 1997: 575). The main problem during the 1980s may have been different 'group' schemes of unemployment insurance benefits, at least five programmes existed and it was difficult to control and rationalise the development of the system. Unemployment Insurance appeared to be out of state control and difficult to manage by agreements between the social partners. A further, now major, reform was adopted in 1992. The different unemployment insurance programmes were now replaced by a single benefit known as *Allocation Unique Dégressive* (AUD).

This new unemployment insurance benefit is paid for a limited time only and according to the contribution record. The amount of benefits paid decreases over time. For instance, a person who worked for at least 14 months during the two-year period prior to his or her claim will receive the full benefit for the first 9 months and then lose 17% of the benefit in six-month intervals. Claimants with a shorter contribution record would be awarded benefits for a shorter period. While entitlement to the main unemployment insurance benefit ends after a maximum of 30 months, a variety of measures extend the coverage of the scheme. The most important of these is *Allocation de Solidarité Spécifique* (ASS), a means-tested programme, but still with a contributory spin (Join-Lambert 1997).

Due to the 1992 unemployment insurance reform, and the stricter time limits and contributory requirements it imposed on benefits, the unemployed are increasingly turning to RMI as their last safety net. In December 1998 there were over 1.1 million recipients of RMI; if spouses and children are included, the grand total reached 2.1 million, or 3.5% of the French population (CNAF 1999). More than half the recipients are single persons and 20% are single parents. The average age of the recipient population is falling; since 1996 more than 50% are younger than 35.

Comparative summary

In unemployment compensation, insurance benefits seem to have suffered more in the UK than in France. This supports the hypotheses discussed above. The more generous French benefits, with wage replacement rates between 75 and 57.4%, have proved less vulnerable than their much cheaper UK counterpart, with a replacement rate of only 23% of average net earnings. This distinct difference in the resistance of unemployment benefits to cuts can be explained by the stronger degree of middle class integration of the French programme, which is due to the benefit structure and the benefit levels. French benefits have also been cut, but the cuts are effective only after 6 months of unemployment and thus do not affect recipients who re-enter the labour market after short spells of unemployment, which is more regularly the case for skilled middle-class workers.

The involvement of trade unions in the management of the French scheme might also account for its stronger resistance to change, as the reform impasse in the 1980s shows, and also for the fact that the 1992 reform resulted from an agreement between the social partners. If we compare the evolution of insurance and means-tested benefits in France, we find that insurance benefits (run by employers and trade unions) were even moderately increased in recent years, while means-tested benefits (ASS and RMI, financed and controlled by the state) remained frozen since the late 1980s. When the state has direct and exclusive control over the benefit level (as is the case for all benefits in the UK, and for ASS and RMI in France), retrenchment is likely to be politically easier than in systems that involve the social partners in their administration.

Old age pensions

Both the UK and France have two-tiered pension systems, which combine a basic pension with compulsory supplementary pensions. In the UK, the basic pension is flat-rate and contributory while, for supplementary provision, employees can choose between a state earnings-related supplement (SERPS), an occupational pension (if provided by the employer) or an individual pension in the private market place. In France, both first and second tier pensions are earnings-related and jointly managed by employers and trade unions. The French pension system is very fragmented, as different occupational groups are covered by quite different pension schemes. The British and French systems differ markedly in the generosity of pension provision. In the UK, the combined replacement rate (of the basic and the supplementary pension) for an employee with a complete contribution record and lifetime average earnings amounts to 33% of final gross earnings, assuming the choice of SERPS (Atkinson 1991: 12). In France, anyone earning less than the ceiling on social security contributions can expect a pension of about 75% of final gross earnings. Both countries also provide a means-tested benefit for pensioners whose income is below a certain threshold: Pensioners' Income Support in the UK, which is higher than income support for working age people, and the *Minimum vieillesse* in France.

In the UK, pension policy over the last two decades has been characterised by two trends: an eroding value of state benefits and a shift of providing for retirement from the state to the private sector. The erosion of state benefits mainly results from a change of the indexing mechanism for the basic pension pushed through by the Thatcher government in the early 1980s. Until then, the benefit was indexed to prices or wages, whichever was higher. Since 1982, the basic pension was indexed to prices only. The value of the basic pension relative to average earnings has constantly diminished (see Table 4.1). If this trend is not stopped the value of the basic pension relative to earnings will continue to decline, and the basic pension will eventually become irrelevant. The government of the day may then easily get rid of the basic pension altogether (Glennerster 1995: 182).

A second series of changes was adopted in 1986 following a comprehensive review of the social security system (Bonoli 2000: 52–85; Nesbitt 1995). The formula of SERPS was changed from 25% of earnings during the best 20 years to 20% of average career earnings. In addition, the 1986 reform allowed employees to opt out of SERPS and to buy an individual pension in the private insurance market. This reform was a revised version of a more radical proposal put forward in an earlier Green Paper (DHSS 1985), which had argued for totally abolishing SERPS. First, the government had to withdraw its radical plan as it had generated widespread opposition, also from within the government – as the Treasury opposed the measure

Table 4.1 The UK – basic pension in percent of average gross earnings of a single person (1986–1995)

1986	1987	1988	1989	1990	1991	1992	1993	1994	1995
21.0	19.8	18.8	18.2	17.8	18.2	18.0	17.7	17.7	17.3

Source: Recalculation of data from DSS (1997, Table 3.13, p. 56 and Table 6.14, p. 143).

because of its fiscal implications. The 1986 reform resulted in a massive outflow of some 5 million employees from SERPS into private pensions. The lowering of SERPS benefits, the general lack of support for state provided pensions, and aggressive marketing by private insurance carriers persuaded many to turn to the private sector for their pensions.

These trends had a significant impact on British pension policy. First, the UK is one of the few industrial countries that seems to have no financing problem of public pensions due to population ageing (OECD 1995). Second, the erosion of state benefits has resulted in a move of a large number of employees to the private sector. However, private provision is not necessarily adequate for all of them. As Waine (1995) has noted, a private pension is a viable option for people with relatively high earnings, otherwise the charges paid to service providers consume too high a proportion of the contributions. As a result, people on low income, whether they opted out of SERPS and bought a private pension, or whether they stayed in the scheme, face the prospect of inadequate income in retirement.

The Labour government picked up this issue in a Green Paper (DSS 1998). Plans under review include a quality label for private pensions that meet certain standards; the introduction of a means-tested pension replacing income support for older people, and the abolition of SERPS, which will be replaced by a State Second Pension providing flat-rate benefits for low wage workers who are ill-served by the private sector. As with unemployment compensation, British pension policy in the 1980s and 1990s has seen the reinforcement of liberal principles of private sector involvement and means-testing. Things have not changed much after the election of a Labour government aiming to improve social policy effectiveness of the current private/public pension mix, but not to alter its overall balance.

In France, concern over the issue of financing pensions grew in the 1980s. Between 1985 and 1993 a series of government mandated reports was published that took a rather pessimistic view of the future of pension policy. Pension reform, however, was widely perceived as a politically sensitive issue so, throughout the 1980s, governments of the left and the right were inclined to procrastinate. In 1993, a newly elected right-wing government adopted a reform of the main basic pension scheme covering private sector employees. This became possible because the reform package was carefully designed: it included both cuts and concessions to the trade unions as regards their role in managing and controlling pensions. Thanks to such logics of political exchange, the government was able to reform pensions (Bonoli 2000: 118–149). Due to the institutional design of both basic and supplementary pension schemes, the French government had to negotiate reforms with the trade unions and always faced strong and well-entrenched popular opposition to its initiatives.

The 1993 changes were threefold: first a '*Fonds de solidarité vieillesse*' was created, which funds non-contributory benefits. Secondly, the qualifying period for a full pension was extended from 37.5 to 40 years; the period over which the reference salary is calculated was extended from the best 10 to the best 25 years. The changes are being introduced gradually in a ten-year transition period. Finally, the indexation of benefits is based on prices – as opposed to earnings – for a five-year period[5] (Ruellan 1993: 919).

In the long run, the impact of these reforms on pension expenditures could be quite substantial. Without the 1993 reforms, contribution rates in 2010 were projected to increase by about 10 percentage points. With the reform, especially if price-based benefit indexation is maintained, this figure could fall to between 2.73 and 7.26 percentage points. The 1993 reforms will have an impact on the pension levels and on the actual age of retirement. Since the qualifying period has been extended to 40 years, some employees are expected to delay their retirement to obtain their full pension, in spite of the reform. The extension of the reference period will also impact on pension levels by reducing benefits by 7 to 8% for high salaries, but this will not affect minimum wage earners, as they will receive a minimum pension (*minimum vieillesse*), which remains untouched by the reforms (Ruellan 1993: 922).

In 1995, the Juppé government attempted to extend these measures to the pension schemes of public sector employees. This measure was prepared secretly, and there were no negotiations with the trade unions. The result was a massive protest movement, led by a rail workers strike, which forced the government to abandon its plans (Bonoli and Palier 1997; Bonoli 1997). Finally, in 1997, a new law was passed, encouraging the introduction of pension funds. However, it is not yet in force, as the subsequent Socialist government has refused to adopt the necessary implementing regulations.

Comparative summary

In pensions, the UK shows a militant tendency towards more market plus more means-testing, while France displays a strong resistance to change of the contributory pension schemes jointly run by the social partners. Similarly to unemployment benefits, these divergent outcomes can be explained by the high level of public support for the relatively generous French social insurance system and by the strong involvement of the social partners in managing and controlling and defending the French pension system.

Health care

Health care may be the sector where institutional differences explain most of the divergent developments in these two countries. The health care systems of France and the UK have been challenged by distinct, if not opposite, problems in recent years. In the UK, health care is altogether a state service, thus it was relatively easy for the government to control the development of expenditure for health, basically by freezing the budget of the National Health Service. The main problem is: how do you achieve an efficient and adequate health care system with the limited resources the government makes available? In contrast, in France, the government does not directly control health care expenditures. There are no budgetary limits or freezes, but there is a system of reimbursing health care expenditures first incurred by the insured person. The problem here is an uncontrolled upward trend in health expenditures. The problems confronted by the health care system of each country are at polar opposites; while in the UK waiting lists are the key issue, in France cost containment is on the top of the agenda.

In the UK, tight control over the budget of the National Health Service during the 1980s checked the pressures for increasing health spending relatively successfully. However, this resulted in 'underfunding'. Towards the end of the 1980s, a Parliamentary Select Committee estimated a gap of £2 billion to exist between spending on health and the amount required to satisfy the health care needs of the nation (Holliday 1992: 25). As a result, increasing numbers of patients were being forced onto waiting lists. The number of individuals waiting for hospital treatment increased from 622 000 in 1982 to 915 000 in 1992 (Holliday 1992: 31).

Towards the end of the 1980s, the pressure on the Thatcher government to 'Save the NHS' increased, which led to a major review of the system. One of the reform options considered, was to shift financing towards a social insurance model as it exists in France. The Treasury, however, opposed such plans as it would make cost containment more difficult, since direct control over the health care budget would be reduced (Glennerster 1995: 203). The response of the government to the funding crisis of the NHS was eventually to increase the funds available, and to introduce an internal market in the system, designed to improve the efficiency of the NHS (Klein 1995).

The French development confirms that a social insurance system in health care does make expenditure more difficult to control. Since the beginning of the 1970s health care expenditures increased much faster than the economy grew. Health expenditure measured as a proportion of GDP increased from 7.6% in 1980 to 9.7% in 1994 – compared with 5.8% in 1980 and 6.9% in 1994 in the UK (Join-Lambert 1997: 510). Since the mid-1970s, successive governments have relied on two kinds of instruments for coping with this problem: in the 1970s and 1980s, a series of rescue plans (*plans de sauvetage de la Sécurité sociale*) aimed simultaneously at increasing resources available and cutting expenditures. Since the early 1990s, a new tool was employed: agreements were struck with the medical professions in order to contain health care expenditures. Moreover, since 1995, a structural reform was implemented in the French health care system.

Over the years, numerous measures were taken to deal with the financial difficulties of the health insurance funds. On average, every 18 months since 1975, a new rescue plan[6] was adopted. Typically these plans combine increases in the contributions paid by employees with cuts. Measures adopted have included retrenchment clauses, such as increasing user charges in health care and reducing the level of reimbursement of medical expenses. Governments have also adopted measures to raise additional revenues, such as increasing health insurance contributions and improving the yield of different taxes[7] (Bonoli and Palier 1997). In 1997, the government decided to replace the health insurance contributions paid by employees with the CSG.[8]

These plans did not contain the growth in demand for health care, which turned out to be unstoppable. As a result, policy shifted towards greater state control over the health care system. This was the case with the *plan Juppé* of November 1995, which brought about a higher degree of statism and state leverage in the whole social protection system, but mainly in the area of health care (Hassenteufel 1997). Even though the social partners are still in charge of managing the system, several measures are likely to weaken their position and to further reduce their influence. In France, trade unions are the main defenders of the Bismarckian components of the system. To weaken them will make room for additional shifts in the direction of the institutional logic: the shift in health insurance financing towards taxation increases the government's influence over the system. Tax-raised funds, paid by the whole of society, are controlled by the government, while only employment-related contributions (paid by employers and employees) can justify joint management by the social partners.

Comparative summary

Both the French and the British health care systems have undergone a series of structural reforms in the last two decades. These programmes may contribute to the convergence of both systems, since more market was introduced into the state-controlled system (UK), and more state control into the system where medical professionals are self-employed and where patients are clients (France). To understand these changes we have to consider the financial pressures affecting health care systems throughout the industrial world. How such pressures are translated into actual policy problems, however, largely depends on the institutional structures typical for each country. The solutions therefore fit the different national institutional environments.

Institutions and the different national trajectories

This account of policy developments in three core areas of the British and French welfare states suggests that major policy trends are a mix of convergence and divergence. The four institutional variables identified are useful again to make sense of the variation observed in policy outcomes.

The two countries are, as already mentioned, at two polar opposites in respect to most of the variables. As concerns the politics of embedding social programmes, France scored high on all variables that relate to stronger middle-class support. Overall, the French welfare state provides a good bargain to the middle classes: thanks to the contributory and earnings-related nature of most benefits these classes are not forced into large scale redistributive processes but, nevertheless, receive good quality protection against major social risks. In contrast, in the UK, the near irrelevance of contributory and earnings-related benefits leads the middle classes to see themselves as the net contributors to the system. If they are to support social programmes, a stronger moral effort is necessary for them than for their French counterparts. This observation applies more neatly to cash benefits than to health care, since most middle class voters in the UK believe, rightly or wrongly, that they benefit from the NHS. Conversely, the French health insurance scheme effects more vertical redistribution than does any other social insurance programme.

The two countries are also at polar opposites in how they manage their welfare state systems. In the UK, the central government controls its welfare state with little interference by external actors. In contrast, the French system, with its high degree of devolution to the social partners, has proved much less controllable. The UK, thus, has a welfare state that combines poor middle class integration with strong central government control over the administrative machinery. France is exactly the UK's mirror-image: a system with strong middle-class integration is governed by the social partners and by the state, with the division of responsibilities between the two remaining uncertain and forever disputed.

The policy developments observed are much better understood in the light of this distinction. The UK, in fact, has seen, above all, a kind of purification of its model. The earnings-related elements, that were alien to it, were removed or are in the process of being purged. Similarly, the contributory principle has not been abolished, but certainly lost much of its significance. Contributory benefits did not guarantee an income higher than means-tested programmes, and their overall significance is likely to decline even further in the future. Together with the removal of what may be seen as alien elements in the British system, a policy change has also reduced the generosity and diminished the significance of social programmes. The British welfare state has not proved particularly resistant to economic crises and political attacks.

In France, reflecting its different starting point, the opposite developments have taken place. First, retrenchment was limited and came about only after several years of major budget deficits. At the same time, however, more profound changes took place, which contributed to change the original Bismarckian cut of the French social security system, and moved it towards a state-run, tax-financed system, at least in health care, family benefits and anti-poverty policy, a direction quite alien to the French postwar tradition of welfare. French reforms impacted less on beneficiaries than did British reforms, but they led to more profound changes in the governance of the system, and, particularly, modified the institutional variables that affect the politics of its social programmes. The result might facilitate further reforms, including more radical retrenchment policies, which so far has proved unfeasible (Bonoli and Palier 1998; Palier 2000).

Conclusions

Policy developments in France and the UK have revealed the link between the institutional set-up of social protection systems and the direction of policy change. Two institutional effects in particular emerged. First, schemes that mainly redistribute horizontally and protect the middle classes well are likely to be more resistant against cuts. Their support base is larger and more influential compared with schemes that are targeted on the poor or are so parsimonious as to become insignificant for the majority of the electorate. The contrast between the overall resistance of French social insurance against cuts and the withering away of its British counterpart illustrates this point. Secondly, the involvement of the social partners, and particularly of the labour movement in managing the schemes, seems to provide an obstacle for government-sponsored retrenchment exercises. What often matters more than the legal position of the trade unions as 'co-managers' is the perception the general public has of the unions' role. In France, for instance, the labour movement, as it is involved in the management of social security, can legitimately claim a right to be consulted and listened to on social security reform.

These institutional effects may be generalised, with due caution, to other systems that share the essential features of the French and British welfare state. If the starting point is similar, than the institutional effect is likely to be present. However, this effect might occur together with other ones, which possibly override it completely and lead to a completely different outcome. In general, institutional explanations are better for understanding developments *ex post* than for predicting them *ex ante*. As Ellen Immergut argued: 'Political institutions do not predetermine policies. Instead, they are an integral part of the strategic context in which political conflicts take place. Political institutions set boundaries within which strategic actors make their choices' (Immergut 1992: 242).

When assessing the usefulness of institutional explanations, we must always remember that they make sense only together with socio-economic and political explanations. The institutional explanations advanced here can help account for the persistence of diversity in public policies in general. Obviously, institutional variables are intermediary in nature: They mediate the impact of socio-economic and political developments on policy-making. A focus on institutions should never go hand in hand with the neglect of other factors. If welfare states are being changed in the first place, it is because they are having financial problems or they are unable to deal with new social problems or, perhaps, they are losing their political support bases. Given these developments, however, the institutional structure of a welfare state can still impact substantially on what will eventually surface as policy reform.

Notes

1. Currently there is a large body of literature on 'New Institutionalism'. On the general approach see: March and Olsen (1989); Steinmo *et al.* (1992); North (1990); Weaver and Rockman (1993); Hall and Taylor (1996); and Kato (1996). In relation to social policies consult above all Pierson (1993, 1994); and Immergut (1992).
2. As Ferrera (1993) noted, we should look at who benefits from welfare state programmes – as opposed to 'how much' they get – because this is likely to generate insights into the political interactions that produce certain policy outcomes.
3. See for instance the *Stages de réinsertion en alternance, Action de réinsertion et de formation, contrats de retour à l'emploi* (Outin 1997).
4. This rate is relevant for about 50% of the unemployed.
5. The measure expired in 1998 but price-based indexation has been prolonged on a yearly basis.
6. *Plan Durafour* (December 1975), *plan Barre* (plan B September 1976), *plan Veil* (April 1977 and December 1978), *plan Barrot* (July 1979), plan Questiaux (November 1981), *plan Bérégovoy* (November 1982 and March 1983), *plan Dufoix* (June 1985), *plan Séguin* (July 1986, December 1986 and May 1987), *plan Evin* (September 1988 and December 1990), *plan Bianco* (June 1991), *plan Veil* (August 1993) and *plan Juppé* (November 1995).
7. Taxes on alcohol and tobacco, or creating new taxes like the *Contribution sociale généralisée*, CSG in 1991.
8. The *CSG* (*Contribution Sociale Généralisée*) is a new tax introduced by the Socialist government in 1990. Unlike social insurance contributions, it is levied on all sorts of incomes (not only on wages), including capital incomes and welfare benefits. Unlike income tax it is a proportional tax. It also applies to low incomes. The proceeds are ear-marked for non-contributory welfare programmes. Despite the use of the term 'contribution', the *CSG* is best understood as a tax (the French equivalent for contribution is *cotisation*).

References

Atkinson, T. (1991) *The Development of State Pensions in the United Kingdom*, London: London School of Economics (Welfare State Programme Discussion Paper No. 58).

Atkinson, T. and Micklewright, J. (1989) Turning the screw: benefits for the unemployed 1979–1988. In: A. Dilnot and I. Walker (eds), *The Economics of Social Security*, Oxford: Oxford University Press, pp. 17–51.

Barr, N. and Coulter, F. (1990) Social security: solution or problem? In: J. Hills (ed), *The State of Welfare. The Welfare State in Britain since 1974*, Oxford: Clarendon Press, pp. 274–337.

Benner, M. and Vad, T. (2000) Sweden and Denmark: hanging places in defence of welfare. In: F. Scharpf and V. Schmidt (eds), *From Vulnerability to Competitiveness: Welfare and Work in the Global Economy*, Oxford University Press.

Bichot, J. (1997) *Les politiques sociales en France au 20ème siècle*, Paris: Armand Colin.

Bonoli, G. (1997) Pension politics in France: patterns of co-operation and conflict in two recent reforms, *West European Politics*, **20**(4), 160–181.

Bonoli, G. (2000) *The Politics of Pensions Reform. Institutions and Policy Change in Western Europe*, Cambridge: Cambridge University Press.

Bonoli, G. and Palier, B. (1997) Reclaiming welfare. The politics of social protection reform in France. In: M. Rhodes (ed), *Southern European Welfare States. Between Crisis and Reform*, London: Francis Cass, pp. 240–259.

Bonoli, G. and Palier, B. (1998) Changing the politics of social programmes: innovative change in British and French welfare reforms, *Journal of European Social Policy*, **8**(4), 317–330.

Castles, F. and Pierson, C.(1996) A new convergence? Recent policy developments in the United Kingdom, Australia and New Zealand, *Policy and Politics*, **4**, 233–245.

CNAF (1999) Revenu Minimum d'Insertion au 31 décembre 1998, *Recherche, prévisions et statistiques*, May.

DHSS (1985) *Reform of Social Security, Green Paper* (3 vol.), London: HMSO (Cmnd. 9517–9).

DSS (1997) *Social Security Statistics*, London: HMSO.

DSS (1998) *A New Contract for Welfare. Green Paper*, London: HMSO (Cmnd. 3805).

Ebbinghaus, B. (1999) Does a European social model exist? Can it survive? In: G. Huemer, M. Mesch and F. Traxler (eds), *The Role of Employer Associations and Labour Unions in the EMU. Institutional Requirements for European Economic Policies*, Aldershot: Ashgate.

Erskine, A. (1997) The withering of social insurance in Britain. In: J. Clasen (ed), *Social Insurance in Europe*, Bristol: Policy Press, pp. 130–150.

Esping-Andersen, G. (1990) *The Three Worlds of Welfare Capitalism*, Cambridge: Polity Press.

European Commission (1995) *Social Protection in Europe*, Brussels: European Commission, DGV.

Evans, M. (1996) *Means-testing the Unemployed in Britain, France and Germany*, London: London School of Economics (Welfare State Paper No. 117).

Ferrera, M. (1993) *Modelli di solidarietà*, Bologna: Il Mulino.

Ferrera, M. (1996a) Modèles de solidarité, divergences, convergences: perspectives pour l'Europe, *Swiss Political Science Review*, **2**(1), 55–72.

Ferrera, M. (1996b) The southern model of welfare in social Europe, *Journal of European Social Policy*, **6**(1), 17–37.

Glennerster, H. (1995) *British Social Policy since 1945*, Oxford: Blackwell.

Hall, P. A. (1986) *Governing the Economy: The Politics of State Intervention in Britain and France*, New York: Oxford University Press.

Hall, P. A. and Taylor, R.C.R. (1996) Political science and the three new institutionalisms, *Political Studies*, **XLIV**, 936–957.

Hassenteufel, P. (1997) Le 'plan Juppé': fin ou renouveau d'une régulation paritaire de l'assurance maladie?, *Revue de l'IRES*, spring-summer (special issue on 'Le paritarisme, institutions et acteurs'), 175–189.

Holliday, I. (1992) *The NHS Transformed*, Manchester: Baseline Books.

Immergut, E. (1992) *Health Politics. Interests and Institutions in Western Europe*, Cambridge: Cambridge University Press.

Join-Lambert, M.-T. (1997) *Politiques Sociales*, Paris: Dalloz.

Kato, J. (1996) Review article: institutions and rationality in politics — three varieties of neo-institutionalism, *British Journal of Political Science*, **26**(4), 553–582.

Klein, R. (1995) *The Politics of the NHS*, 3rd edn, London: Longman.

March, J. and Olsen, J. (1989) *Rediscovering Institutions: The Organisational Basis of Politics*, New York/London: Free Press/Collier Macmillan.

MIRE (1999) *Comparing Social Welfare Systems in France and Northern Europe*, Paris: Rencontres et Recherches de la MIRE (vol. IV, Copenhagen Conference).

Nesbitt, S. (1995) *British Pension Policy Making in the 1980s. The Rise and Fall of A Policy Community*, Aldershot: Avebury.

North, D. C. (1990) *Institutions, Institutional Change and Economic Performance*, Cambridge: Cambridge University Press.

OECD (1995) Effect of ageing populations on government budgets, *Economic Outlook*, **57**, 33–42.

Outin, J. L. (1997) Les politiques d'insertion. In: M. Vernières (ed), *L'insertion professionnelle, analyses et débats*, Paris: Economica.

Palier, B. (2000) Defrosting the French welfare state, *West European Politics* (special issue, M. Ferrera and M. Rhodes, eds) **23**(2), 114–137.

Pierson, P. (1993) When effects become cause. Policy feedback and political change, *World Politics,* 45(4), 595–628.

Pierson, P. (1994) *Dismantling the Welfare State? Reagan, Thatcher and The Politics of Retrenchment*, Cambridge: Cambridge University Press.

Pierson, P. (1996) The new politics of the welfare state, *World Politics*, **48**(1), 143–179.

Ruellan, R. (1993) Retraites: l'impossible réforme est-elle achevée?, *Droit social*, **12**, 911–929.

Steinmo, S., Thelen, K. and Longstreth, F. (eds) (1992) *Structuring Politics: Historical Institutionalism in Comparative Analysis*, Cambridge: Cambridge University Press.

Stephens, J. (1996) The Scandinavian welfare states achievements, Crisi, and prospects. In: G Esping-Andersen (ed) *Welfare States in Transition*, London, Sage, pp. 32–65.

Waine, B. (1995) A disaster foretold? The case of personal pension, *Social Policy & Administration* **29**(4), 317–334.

Weaver, K.R. and Rockman, B.A. (eds) (1993) *Do Institutions Matter? Government Capabilities in the United States and Abroad*, Washington DC: The Brookings Institution Press.

About the Authors

Giuliano Bonoli is a Lecturer in the Department of Social Work and Social Policy, University of Fribourg, Switzerland. He has been involved in comparative public policy research with a focus on the political dynamics of welfare state adaptation. Among his recent publications are (with Vic George and Peter Taylor-Gooby) *European Welfare Futures. Towards a Theory of Retrenchment* (Polity Press 2000); *The Politics of Pension Reform. Institutions and Policy Change in Western Europe* (Cambridge University Press 2000).

Bruno Palier is a researcher at the (CNRS) Institut d'Etudes Politiques de Paris, and works on the transformation of the French social protection system. From 1994 to 1999 he organised the comparative programme on social welfare systems in Europe for MIRE in the French Ministry of Social Affairs, which resulted in the publication of four books. He chairs the working group on 'Globalisation, European Integration and Welfare State Changes' of the EC-level COST programme 'Reforming social protection systems in Europe' (COST A15) and is French correspondent for the European bi-annual report *Social Protection in Europe* ('DG V'). He is author of several recent essays on welfare state reform written from an institutionalist perspective, such as: Defrosting the French welfare state, *West European Politics*, **23**(2), 114–137 (2000); (with G. Bonoli) Changing the politics of social programmes: innovative change in British and French welfare reforms, *Journal of European Social Policy*, **8**(4), 317–330 (1998).

European Review, Vol. 8, No. 3, 353–378 (2000) © Academia Europaea, Printed in the United Kingdom

5 Elephants on the move. Patterns of public pension reform in OECD countries

KARL HINRICHS*

Among OECD countries there are two clusters of old-age security systems: (1) 'Social insurance' countries had, by the end of the 1960s, fashioned the core of old-age security as public, contributory, earnings-related and unfunded insurance schemes; (2) a diverse collection of countries that, after 1970, topped up their basic pension arrangements with funded occupational pension schemes with (almost) universal coverage. 'Social insurance' countries, on which this essay focuses, reveal at least six common trends in pension reform, all about improving the financial sustainability of public schemes. Although the repertoire of incremental adjustment strategies is quite limited, policy changes since the early 1980s have not led to a clear convergence among 'social insurance' countries (or across the two clusters). Their original diversity has been somewhat diminished, but it has for the most part merely taken a different form. Public pension reforms regularly harmed (future) beneficiaries. Nevertheless, most reforms were actually based on broad political consensus. The success of attempts to introduce retrenchment policies depends on prior negotiation with – and support obtained from – collective actors above and beyond a simple parliamentary majority. This peculiar prerequisite ensures success in the sense of a sustained implementation of the measures taken and of actual improvement in public trust in 'reliable' pension schemes.

Welfare state regimes and public pension policy

Since the early 1980s, public pension reform has (repeatedly) been on the political agenda of most OECD countries. The foreseeable accelerating rise in the ratio of the elderly population to that of working age during the decades to come, a common trend in all industrialised nations, sparked efforts to keep government-provided support systems for the elderly financially viable and to check sharpening intergenerational inequities – or, at least, those concerns played a major role in legislation. In the wake of these debates and policy changes, interest grew almost

* Zentrum für Sozialpolitik, Universität Bremen, Parkallee 39, D 28209 Bremen, Germany. E-mail: hinrichs@zes.uni-bremen.de. Karl Hinrichs acknowledges gratefully linguistic assistance from Ben Veghte.

77

everywhere in learning about the arrangement of old-age security systems in other countries and their respective reform strategies. To this end, international organisations (e.g. the ILO, OECD and World Bank) provided additional comparative information and evaluations. A main motivation of policymakers, administrators, media commentators, academics and others for looking beyond their national borders are 'lessons' that can be drawn for a rational reorganisation of old-age security systems in their own country. The search for concrete reform elements worth adopting (so-called 'best practices') is, however, not the focus of this article. Rather, the aim is to contextualise pension policy developments during the last two decades in a number of OECD countries. This effort is delimited to a selection of countries with a similar structure of public pension schemes. Therefore, it is necessary first to identify countries with a comparable institutional starting point, then to show common developmental trends and, finally, to look into the similar versus differing backgrounds of reforms as well as patterns of decision-making in public pension policy. 'Lessons' thus mainly relate to the consequences of differing institutional starting points and the modes of compromise-building in the political process of pension reform.

In conceptual perspective, this article critically departs from Gøsta Esping-Andersen's (1990) 'regime approach', which has substantially influenced comparative welfare state research in the 1990s. Relevant to this article however is a central argument of Esping-Andersen, which suggests that a country's affiliation to one of the three ideal-typical 'worlds of welfare capitalism' is permanently fixed, and that the welfare state landscape is thus 'frozen'. The path once entered upon as a result of specific power constellations and political coalitions cannot be deserted – welfare states do not (or very rarely) *mutate*, and they reproduce their character constantly anew (Esping-Andersen 1999: 86–7, 165). Path deviation (or non-deviation), however, is an empirical-historical question, and on this account the static regime approach – more capable of explaining stable conditions (policy outputs and structures of interest) than of coming to grips with change – has been repeatedly criticised (Borchert 1998; Cox 1998). If dynamics affecting welfare states in their totality can be ascertained then this should be even more true for their parts, which thus deserve special attention. Conversely, if path dependencies (or 'policy legacies') exist these can be identified only at the level of individual social policy programmes. Indeed, it is only at the programme level that 'history matters', for political decisions only rarely affect the welfare state as a whole.

A further objection to Esping-Andersen's analysis stems from the institutional complexity and high degree of internal heterogeneity of welfare states which, in only a few cases, allow for an unconditional assignment to one regime cluster. Esping-Andersen (1990: 28–29, 49) admits that, as *real* types, they are impure, but for the sake of the elegance of an *ideal*-type construction – to capture the 'distinct overall logic' – he suppresses this insight: '*One programme does not define a regime*' (Esping-Andersen 1999: 92, 88). Given that comparable programmatic arrangements can be found in more than one regime cluster, if one is seeking to compare reform policies it seems appropriate not to be guided by regime affiliations but rather to emphasize that every social policy programme has its specific conditions of development, functioning and perpetuation. Old age security, health care, family welfare policy, unemployment protection – every component of the welfare state is distinguished by peculiar institutional arrangements (e.g. modes of redistribution reflecting policy-specific intuitions of fairness), different interest formations, degrees of popular support, and enabling conditions or constraints of policy development.

Finally, employing a *programme approach* and putting regime affiliation last against similar institutional arrangements when comparing reform policies is justified due to another argument from Esping-Andersen. Evaluating the adjustment strategies and opportunities by regime type, he identifies the conservative welfare states of the European continent (namely the 'pensioner states', Germany, Italy and France) as particularly unable to modernise as their demographics carry them passively into increasingly aged-biased distributions of transfers. The objectives of justice and efficiency fall by the wayside because 'the evermore aged median voter' and status quo-oriented interest groups prevent a redirection (Esping-Andersen 1999: 167, 165; 1996). Population ageing, however, is not confined to this group of welfare states and, likewise, pronounced resistance against reform is a general feature of public pension schemes. These schemes are *distinct*, for public pension expenditure regularly represents the largest single item of their nations' total social spending. They are the 'grey giants' of the welfare state and, like fully grown elephants, difficult to move. The most important cause of this immobility is that public pension schemes particularly enjoy high esteem and support among citizens of all ages. Living up to current and future beneficiaries' expectations of reliable income security nonetheless poses a difficult challenge for public policy. Reform considerations of policymakers in this area of social policy are typically shaped by a very long time frame, stretching well beyond one parliamentary period.

One question I will turn to in the following is whether, as a result of comparable changes in their environment, old-age security systems are converging. Now that the elephants have been set in motion, are they moving in the same direction? A change affecting all industrialised countries to roughly the same extent, and particularly concerning old-age security systems, is the ageing of the population, due both to the decline in fertility and to the fact that ever more people actually enter retirement (regularly at an earlier age) and remain pensioners for longer than before. Beside demographic trends, concerns about a nation's competitiveness in the face of globalisation are an additional factor putting pressure on (not only) public pension schemes, especially if going along with a general advancement of liberal market ideology. The question of convergence directly challenges the regime approach because it explicitly opposes the assumption of linearity, i.e. the impossibility of convergence (Esping-Andersen 1990: 3, 18). This leads to a second question. If a universal direction of development can be ascertained, are there nevertheless peculiarities in pension reform politics reflecting certain institutional characteristics of distinct welfare states? I will address this question as well.

At first glance, old age security policy seems to be an area in which it is quite easy to carry out international comparisons. In contrast to health care or education policy, there are few (collective) actors involved. Benefit providers with corresponding income and professional interests are not present. It is predominantly money that is (re-)distributed, and even in countries with a federalist state structure, public pension policy is always under the jurisdiction of the central government.

However, differently or to a much larger extent than other arrangements of protection (income replacement in the case of unemployment or sickness, the provision of health care), income security during retirement is regularly marked by components of *private* welfare. Everywhere we find a differently composed mix of minimum pensions, public and/or occupational earnings-related pensions and supplementary private pensions, which together constitute total retirement income. Typically, the *non*-public components are not completely private, but are shaped by public regulation and fiscal welfare, such that tax advantages for individuals and firms can be secured only under the condition of adherence to regulatory standards. The resulting 'income package' may differ from the distributional and security objectives of the state's schemes for providing social welfare in old age because, empirically, everywhere there is considerable variation in the composition and level of total retirement income. Usually, in elderly households at the lower end of the income distribution, public transfers predominate, whereas at the upper end, occupational pensions and elements of private provision play a much larger role. Thus, the degree of income inequality (and poverty) among retirees is largely influenced by the share of public transfers (Kangas and Palme 1991; Korpi and Palme 1998). The presence of different components of retirement income and their interrelationship complicates a comparative analysis.

It, therefore, does not suffice to focus exclusively on public pension scheme expenditures – and not merely because monetary figures do not provide an optimal yardstick for international comparisons. More important is that present changes in expenditure are, to a large extent, the result of political decisions reached (very) long ago, and recent reforms sometimes change the expenditure and revenue situation with an extended time-lag.[1] Moreover, changes in expenditure levels reflect the balance of programme expansions and restrictions in the past as well as demographic changes. A comparison of old-age security policies, which takes into account these peculiarities, must engage national policies in considerable detail. It has to analyse in depth the institutional set-up, decision-making processes and the policy changes.[2] Such a qualitative approach precludes consideration of a large number of countries in the analysis. Hence, in the following section, a number of OECD countries are singled out and, subsequently, they will be given special attention.

From Bismarck and Beveridge to new models of old-age security policy[3]

In order to cut a path through the variety of national old-age security systems, I will fall back upon a formerly quite common classification which takes the historical origin of public pension schemes as the starting point of differentiation, namely Bismarck versus Beveridge countries. It is known that Bismarck countries are considered those in which, right from the start (or after a short 'detour'), the development of modern social policy was founded on the social insurance principle. The 'employment centredness' of social security results in status maintenance having priority over poverty prevention. The latter objective usually prevailed in Beveridge countries. Coming from the 'poor law' tradition, in these countries a universal, tax or contribution-financed basic ('people's') pension system was established. Initially, the flat-rate benefits paid when reaching a certain age or, in case of disability, were means-tested. In some countries a 'needs test' still holds (or, at least, for certain components over and above a uniform basic grant) and, as a rule, the benefit level is tied to the length of residence and differentiated by marital status. The basic pension is not actually poverty preventing in every Beveridge country: in Switzerland and the United Kingdom, for example, elderly people without further retirement income are dependent on supplemental, means-tested benefits.

Most OECD countries can be assigned unambiguously to one or the other type. It is unproblematic here that, for a few countries, this classification only partially applies because, for our purposes, it is the trajectories, goal shifts and goal enhancements of old-age security systems in Beveridge countries that are at the centre of interest.

Countries belonging to the Bismarck tradition are, in addition to Germany – Austria, Italy, France and Belgium (see Figure 5.1). By legislative decisions of 1935 and 1939, comprising the organisation of the core of retirement provision as social insurance, the United States joined this group. Shortly after, so did Japan, as it gradually enacted a contributory two-tier system consisting of an earnings-related employees' pension insurance and a basic ('national') pension scheme. In the course of their development, those social insurance schemes expanded in three dimensions: in terms of benefit levels, the range of entitlements, and coverage of the compulsorily insured. Moreover, it was important that in all these countries (with the exception of Germany[4]) a 'basement' of minimum protection was established for those elderly whose contribution record led to insufficient benefit entitlements. Either a (tax-financed) minimum pension was separated from the general system of social assistance (like the *Ausgleichszulage* in Austria or *minimum vieillesse* in France), or was institutionalised at the same time as the inception of the social insurance scheme (like *Supplementary Security Income* in the USA).

More interesting for the purpose of this article are changes that occurred within the Beveridge countries, which can now be divided into two or three groups (see Figure 5.1). First, there is a large group of countries in which the basic pension scheme was *topped up* with a second pillar aiming at income continuity during the life course. These countries can be further divided into two groups: the *early birds* and the *latecomers*. The early birds were Sweden (1959) and Finland (1961) and, somewhat later, Canada (1965) and Norway (1966). In view of favourable economic and demographic conditions at that time, these countries established a second *public* pillar, which was contribution-based, unfunded (at least in principle), yielded an earnings-related supplementary pension and included redistributive provisions in varying degrees. As these complementary pension insurance schemes matured, the relevance of the 'basic pension' pillar declined in relative or even absolute terms. In effect, these four countries thus metamorphosed into Bismarck countries.[5]

The latecomers, i.e. Beveridge countries which had *not* established a mandatory public complementary pension scheme until the early 1970s, combined the traditional solidarity principle (minimum pensions, financed out of general tax revenues or tax-like contributions) with the equivalence principle (aimed at status maintenance) by different means: an earnings-related topping-up was attained via *occupational* pension schemes that were either mandated by law (Switzerland, Australia[6]) or arose through collective agreements (Netherlands, Denmark). In the latter case, coverage of nearly all employees was achieved by legal provisions of extension. In these four countries the second pillar is funded and private, but – in order to protect the employees who orient their strategies of retirement provision toward those benefits – publicly regulated and controlled. In the Netherlands, Denmark and Australia, the inception *viz.* generalisation of the second pillar was predominantly the result of union pressure.[7]

A further latecomer, constituting a special case, is the United Kingdom. The introduction of SERPS (State Earnings-Related Pension Scheme) in 1978 brought the UK into the group of social insurance countries. However, the reforms carried out by the Thatcher and Major governments in 1986 and 1995 reversed this course. The public supplementary scheme's

81

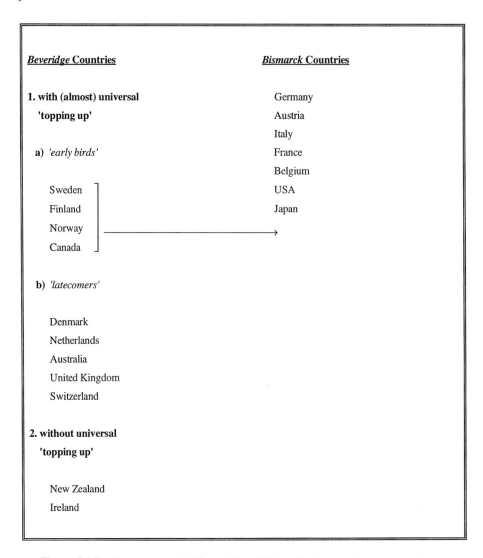

Figure 5.1 Pension systems in 'Bismarck' and 'Beveridge' countries – changes in 'Beveridge' countries

benefits were substantially reduced, rendering SERPS unattractive for younger cohorts of employees and increasingly marginal. Presently, it covers no more than about a quarter of all employees. The permitted alternatives to SERPS (contracting out) – occupational pension schemes and the heavily tax-subsidised private pension plans (APPs) – clearly predominate (Davis 1995: 63–64; Liu 1999). The New Labour government's 'stakeholder pension' proposal will bring no substantial changes for the majority of employees (Department of Social Security 1998).

In both groups of countries where topping up took place, personal responsibility for retirement income was increased relative to the citizenship component. In those latecomer countries where complementary occupational pension schemes attained broader coverage only in the last two decades, individual strategies of providing for old age (still) play a greater role (notably in Australia, where the acquisition of owner-occupied housing is very important). *Per se*, the occupational or personal pension schemes in the latecomer countries (as everywhere) do not contain elements of systematic redistribution. However, clearly regressive redistributive effects result from tax advantages once pension capital is built up. Tax expenditures are considerable (Davis 1995: 77–90).

From the originally numerous Beveridge countries there are only two countries left, namely Ireland and New Zealand, where no comparable topping up occurred. In New Zealand, the basic pension (which is now called *New Zealand Superannuation* and has not been explicitly means-tested since 1938) is supplemented by voluntary private provision and scattered occupational pension schemes (both variants contain no tax advantages). In Ireland, complementary occupational pension schemes have spread, but are not (yet) obligatory and thus the coverage rate is substantially lower than in the latecomer countries. If one leaves aside these two countries, then the structures of old age security in the OECD countries examined is still bifurcated: on the one hand, there are the latecomer countries, and on the other hand, there is the enlarged group of social insurance countries. In the discussion of the patterns of public pension reform below, it is appropriate to restrict the comparison to the latter group of countries (albeit some of the ascertained trends also apply to the latecomer countries; see the following section). Methodologically, they represent 'most similar cases'. Before embarking on this task, a few explanatory remarks are necessary to explain the selection of countries.

Whereas the latecomer countries either belong to Esping-Andersen's 'liberal' or 'social democratic' regime type, social insurance countries can be found in all three regime clusters. It will become clear that regime clusters are rather meaningless *here*, because – and this is important to note – the latecomers (the Netherlands, Australia, Denmark, Switzerland, and the UK) have, compared with the social insurance countries, established a different welfare state for the elderly by adopting a *private* and *funded* supplementary pillar. Thus, demographic ageing presents itself as a *political* problem in a different manner as well. Despite the macroeconomic consequences of the ageing of the population, these countries will not have to extract taxes and/or contributions to the same extent as social insurance countries in order to fund pensions. On the contrary, the more those not yet matured private pension systems expand, the more spending on public minimum pensions declines in a natural way (this is expected to happen in Australia when *Superannuation* matures). Likewise, those schemes' benefits can be scaled back more easily – for example by stricter targeting,[8] cutting supplementary benefits, or modifying indexing procedures (so that there is no real growth of minimum pension levels). Moreover, increasing the standard retirement age is already underway in several of these latecomer countries.[9]

With regard to the funded supplementary pension schemes, the risks of increasing longevity, of an unexpected poor performance of the pension funds, or of declining asset values (when, due to the demographic shifts, more retirement savings are dissolved than added) rest either with the sponsors of those schemes (i.e. the employers if they run a *defined benefit* scheme, as in the Netherlands and in the UK) or with the (future) beneficiaries if included in *defined contribution* arrangements (prevailing in Australia, Denmark and Switzerland). As long as indexation rules are not prescribed or agreed upon, the retirees additionally bear the inflation risk during the whole period of annuity receipt. Moreover, employees approaching the end of their working careers have to face the insecurity of not knowing the status of financial markets (interest rates, equity prices) when retirement assets are required (or intended) to be converted into an annuity.

While in the 'old' (Germany, Austria, etc) and 'new' (Sweden, Finland, etc) social insurance countries, due to the susceptibility of those predominantly unfunded pension schemes to demographic shifts, retrenchments have been undertaken or are in part already effective, in the latecomer countries, a further expansion of old age security is thoroughly conceivable. A convergence of the retirement income schemes of these two groups, however, appears most unlikely. This will be shown in the next section.

Public pension reforms in social insurance countries

The central difference between the *latecomer* and the *social insurance* countries is that, in the former, earnings-related retirement income is (overwhelmingly) *non*-publicly provided, whereas in the latter it is effected through public schemes. This does not necessarily imply a marginal or stagnating role of 'private' complementary provision in *social insurance* countries. Dependent on the standard benefit level and to what extent the replacement ratio drops for employees with above-average wages, additional components of retirement provision have developed, resulting in varying 'public-private mixes' of retirement income in this group of countries. For example, in the USA the non-public sources of retirement income, especially in the case of formerly high-wage earners, play a much larger role than in Austria, Italy or Finland, where the replacement ratio of public pensions (and, thus, payments as a percentage of GDP) is considerably higher. Obviously, a given institutional design of public pensions gives rise to distinct collective bargaining and individual strategies for supplementing pensions or for compensating missing income replacement through (firm-specific or industry-wide) occupational and private provision. The design and extent of non-public provision itself is also influenced by public policy (regulation and tax subsidies). Nevertheless, *none* of the 'old' and 'new' social insurance countries have a layer of *funded* occupational pensions, covering almost *all* employees, over and above the earnings-related public pension scheme. In the USA, for example, coverage is below 50%; in Sweden, due to collective bargaining, occupational pensions are nearly universal but not fully funded in an actuarial sense. Those differences, developments and feedback mechanisms are not at the centre of this section, but rather the reforms of the public pension schemes are considered.

All countries where a contributory, unfunded pension scheme plays the dominant role in retirement income allocation have legislated reforms of varying scope. These schemes' financial stability is threatened from two sides: first, from the *revenue* side, when economic and/or structural developments on the labour market lead to a decrease of covered earnings or this contribution base does not keep pace with predetermined expenditure. Problems from the *expenditure* side arise if, due to demographic change, there is an increase in the number of beneficiaries or the average period of benefit receipt and, thus, the dependency ratio rises. Thus, a doubly destabilising effect follows from growing numbers of early retirees: higher benefit outlays have to be met out of a reduced contributory base. If scheme provisions are not adjusted and if no accumulated reserve funds are available, those changes result immediately in deficits or in the necessity to raise the contribution rate. Presently, the effects of contributory financing on (non-wage) labour costs give rise to demands for retrenchment. In the long term, imminent demographic change puts pressure on the schemes' generosity because, if benefit levels were to remain at their present real levels, the unavoidably rising contribution rate would not only endanger the employment rate and international competitiveness, but would also violate notions of intergenerational fairness, undermining the schemes' legitimacy.

In the case of a current or future 'crisis', there is only a limited repertoire of policies that can stabilise the expenditure or revenue side of a public pension scheme (OECD 1996: 17–22, 44–46; Weaver 1998). These policy changes can affect either the insured (contributors), the pensioners, or the state's engagement in terms of co-financing or improving the framework conditions (see Figure 5.2; Hinrichs 1998: 16–18). The scope and the mix of adjustment strategies, and thus eventually the allocative and distributional outcome, is determined by the respective institutional design as well as by the interests of the political actors involved, i.e. *pension politics*. If one studies the reforms of public pension schemes that have been initiated since the mid-1980s in view of acute imbalances or long-term threats to the systems' stability, then six broad trends can be identified that are valid for all, or at least several, of the *social insurance* countries.

(1) Almost everywhere, the reforms have strengthened the *equivalence principle* and thus reduced elements of interpersonal redistribution.[10] The requirements for receiving a full pension, i.e. the target benefit level, were tightened by modifying the respective *benefit formula* in various ways. For example, the reference periods were lengthened, giving individual equity more weight or, when computing the individual benefit, earnings of more or all contribution years were taken into account instead of, hitherto, those of a few 'best years' or of the 'last years' prior to retirement. Alternatively, non-contributory periods, which hitherto had increased one's entitlement, were eliminated or reduced and, at the same time, in a number of places deductions from the benefit level for early retirement were introduced or increased to (almost) actuarial amounts. All these measures imply lower pension benefits for those with a less than full employment record and/or whose earnings rise with age, or a lower benefit level for all if accrual rates were reduced.

In this respect, the most far-reaching changes in benefit calculation will become effective in Sweden and Italy after the transition to a defined contribution system has been completed. Without factually giving up the pay-as-you-go mode of financing, a funded scheme is mimicked when contributions paid according to a defined rate earn an interest rate corresponding to the growth of wages or of the gross domestic product. At retirement – the age of entry is optional within a certain range – the benefit is computed as the annuity equivalent to the accumulated 'capital', actuarially adjusted for the age at first pension receipt. A post-retirement adjustment of benefits is effected through a combined index of wage and consumer price inflation (Sweden) or according to price inflation alone (Italy).[11] In both of these countries, but even more so in Italy, these rule changes imply a departure from the principle of income maintenance through *public* pension benefits.

Implicit demographic parameters to stabilise the schemes were introduced in Germany

I.	*Measures concerning current/future contributors*	

1. increasing the contribution rate
2. utilising parts of an increased contribution rate to build up a fund reserve
3. broadening the contribution base
   - a) making hitherto non-covered employed liable for mandatory insurance
   - b) increasing the ceiling of earnings subject to contributions
4. calculating employers' contribution share on value adding items (profits, interest revenue, depreciation)
5. differentiating the employees' individual contribution rate according to the number of children

II.   Measures concerning current/future beneficiaries

1. changing the benefit formula
2. suspending automatic benefit indexation and/or changing the indexing formula
3. raising the standard retirement age
4. increasing benefit reductions for early retirees up to actuarial level
5. tightening the eligibility rules for disability pensions
6. reducing/eliminating derivative/auxiliary benefits

III.   Measures concerning the state's engagement

Directly:
1. increasing/introducing subsidies out of general taxation to public pension schemes
Indirectly:
2. intensifying population policy (fertility, migration)
3. increasing the employment ratio (reducing the unemployment level, facilitating higher female labour force participation)
4. promoting investments in physical and human capital to facilitate higher productivity growth rates

Figure 5.2 Measures to cope with the effects of population ageing on the financing of public pension schemes

(1992), Austria (1993) and Japan (1994): the adjustment of pensions is calculated on the basis of preceding *net* (instead of gross) wage growth, so that higher contribution rates (predominantly stemming from the ageing process) slow down pension spending. The new benefit computation procedure in Sweden is explicitly targeted at compensating for the 'longevity-conditioned transfer gains' of pensioners which occur at the immediate expense of covered employees. The (increasing) life expectancy of every birth cohort is taken into account when the notional pension capital is converted into a monthly pension payment. In Germany, a 'demographic factor' to be applied when computing new and annually adjusting current pensions was meant to achieve the same end. However, the implementation of this central part of the *Pension Reform 1999* was suspended and, as of early 2000, it remains undecided whether it (or a modified version) will take effect at all. Post-retirement indexation of public pensions has been changed to the disadvantage of beneficiaries in other countries as well – mostly tying it to consumer prices, cutting off the retired from participation in the real wage growth of the working-age generations. Furthermore, indexation as such has been temporarily suspended or discretionarily changed in the USA, Belgium, Sweden, Finland, Italy, Germany and Austria.

(2)   In nearly all the countries, the reforms are aimed at increasing the *age of entry into retirement*, be it by gradually raising the standard retirement age or by blocking pathways into early retirement. The latter included measures of tightening access to disability pensions (e.g. by restricting eligibility to exclusively medical grounds) and attempts to remove distorting incentives for early retirement. The hitherto prevailing consensus that the labour market chances of younger workers ought to be improved by providing older employees attractive opportunities to exit working life prematurely has, almost everywhere, been superseded by attempts to reverse the trend of ever lower employment rates in the upper age brackets.[12] To this end, sometimes, workers were given the opportunity to combine part-time work with the receipt of a partial pension. Moreover, incentives were established even to stay in the labour force beyond standard retirement age. Countries with comparatively high employment rates of older workers were no less eager in their attempts to raise the actual age of entry into retirement than others. At the same time, in those countries where standard retirement ages hitherto differed by gender, reforms have aimed at equalisation, i.e. the lower retirement age for women was raised.

(3)   In almost all countries under consideration, *unpaid family work* was incorporated into benefit calculation. Raising children and/or taking care of frail relatives now results in (higher) benefit claims in Canada, France, Norway, Austria, Italy, Belgium, Germany and Sweden (since 1997, also in the Swiss basic pension scheme). The applied procedures and the produced benefit increases differ considerably and cannot be described in detail here. To the extent that these 'family credits' not only compensate for other benefit cuts (e.g. as a result of changed benefit formulas particularly affecting women, or the setbacks of survivors' pensions) they represent the sole expansionary element among the recent reforms. Although the reduction of horizontal disadvantages when performing 'family duties' was the proclaimed objective, at least implicitly pronatalist considerations played as much a role as the gender equity issue.

(4)   *Increased tax financing* of the hitherto exclusively or predominantly contribution-financed public pension schemes can be identified as a further trend. Independent of the various justifications given, the intention combined with these (additional) subsidies out of general revenues to the (fiscally separated) public pension schemes was to contain, or even reverse, increases in the contribution rate – in particular, to relieve employers of non-wage labour costs. Those refinancing strategies were applied in Belgium, Italy, the USA (in an indirect way), France, Germany, Sweden and Japan. In the three countries mentioned last, the relationship between strengthened individual equity on the one hand, (newly added) redistributional elements aiming at social adequacy on the other, and increased tax financing is obvious: non-contributory components of the benefit package are financed out of taxes, and hence, technically, the demarcation relative to entitlements earned through contribution payments becomes more visible, rendering the schemes more transparent and acceptable (see also OECD 1988: 93–94).[13]

(5)   In so far as special pension schemes existed for public employees (and workers in publicly owned enterprises), it was attempted to *harmonise* them with the schemes for employees in the business sector. One strategy pursued was gradually to reduce privileges of public employees, e.g. with regard to retirement age or replacement level, which formerly had been targets of workers in the private sector. This happened in Austria, Finland and Italy. Another strategy, applied in the USA, made public sector employees increasingly compulsory members of the core scheme. In Germany and France, however, where different rules for public and private employees are strongly pronounced, no such reforms were (successfully) launched. While the first strategy aims at lowering the total wage costs of the state as employer in the long run, the second strategy shovels (but only temporarily) additional contribution revenues into the funds of the social insurance scheme(s). This purpose is also served when certain groups of employees hitherto exempted from insurance become mandatory members (like marginal part-time workers in Austria and, most recently, in Germany).

(6)   More and more countries which have paid a *basic pension* regardless of individual need are now fully or partially taking into account other retirement income. While in Canada only the very well-off pensioners have been affected (after plans for elaborate income testing were withdrawn in 1998; see McCarthy 1998), in Sweden and Finland the universal, flat-rate 'people's pension' has been abolished and replaced by an income-tested 'guarantee pension'. Only Norway and Japan have stuck with a non-targeted basic pension.

Finally, two further changes are worth mentioning: the USA (in 1983) and Canada (in 1997) have modified the pay-as-you-go mode of financing such that the contribution rate is set higher than currently necessary to cover annual pension spending, causing trust fund reserves to grow considerably. One goal is to increase the national savings rate so that the economic growth base is enlarged, particularly if the surpluses are not invested (only) in government bonds but, as in Canada, in a more diversified portfolio of securities. Irrespective of whether this strategy succeeds, the second objective is to 'tunnel through' the ageing process, accumulating capital reserves which will then melt away as the population ages during the coming decades, allowing a lower contribution rate to be asked from the then employed than otherwise would be necessary.

A second change leads to a comparable, but with regard to distributional consequences, not equivalent, result. It is the expansion of individual and occupational pension schemes, either by mandating participation (Sweden) or by improving incentives, mainly through augmented tax advantages as in Italy and – not yet finally legislated – France and Germany. The amount of tax expenditures grows inasmuch as enterprises and individuals actually deduct eligible savings from taxable incomes (or make use of corresponding tax credits) and as pension fund income is exempted from taxation. Those foregone taxes will be recovered much later and only partly because of the generally lower marginal tax rate on retirement income. At the same time, those persons partaking in non-public retirement saving schemes will have the opportunity to compensate for more modest public pension benefits resulting from reforms mentioned above, whereas in the first case (USA and Canada), future pensioners 'prepay' (largely) maintained public benefits when presently made subject to higher contribution rates.

Both strategies can attain their respective ends only if the *political* and *economic* context provides the chance to translate them into action well before the massive demographic shifts develop. That is, the public scheme's contribution rate has not yet reached a prohibitively high level, a large majority of wage earners can afford additional savings for retirement, or public budgets can currently cope with corresponding tax expenditures.

These two strategies also exemplify that social insurance countries with large, matured, unfunded public pension schemes can hardly emulate the latecomer countries and create an old age security system with a predominantly funded component and an absolutely or relatively shrinking public component providing basic security as it is emphatically demanded by the World Bank (1994) and now also by the OECD (1998). The present generation of pensioners and those of working age who have paid contributions have earned entitlements which they legitimately expect to be honoured by succeeding generations.[14] In view of the virtual impossibility of dismissing these earned and property-like claims, which represent the implicit debt of a public insurance scheme, it is fiercely contested among economists whether a 'pareto-efficient' transition of the mode of financing is viable without impairing any generation's welfare. The assumption prevails that members of a number of birth cohorts would have to carry a 'double burden' if they had to save for their own funded retirement income and at the same time redeem claims earned in the unfunded scheme with contributions, now bearing an explicit tax character. At best, only the very young cohorts of employees (and those not yet of working age) may expect a more efficient (cheaper) provision for retirement income if payments into funded pension schemes actually yield a higher rate of return than those into a public pay-as-you-go scheme.

Such a constellation makes the transition to a fully funded old age security system politically almost impossible. It cannot be ruled out, however, that in social insurance countries the non-public, funded components of retirement income will gain ground. This is safe to say because the process of reforming old age security systems has not come to a halt in the 1990s. Proposals to change further the parameters of public pension schemes, largely proceeding along the patterns mentioned above and, increasingly, those concerning the regulation of the non-public components of retirement income, are at different stages of the policy-making process in France, Germany, the USA, Italy, Japan and Austria. Whatever these proposals aim to change in detail, in social insurance countries the general direction is to reduce entitlements further by various means and to relieve the contribution rate so as to obtain more leeway for prefunding future retirement income, preferably from non-public sources.

Shifting the relative share of pension components is, however, a very slow process, as can be shown from projections made by the Advisory Council to the German public pension scheme (Sozialbeirat 1999: 133–8). They are based on the assumption that the reform proposals of the Red–Green government of June 1999 regarding the public pension scheme will be actually implemented, including the obligation to save an additional 2.5% of gross earnings (starting with a rate of 0.5% in 2003, gradually increasing to the final level in 2007) for a personal pension. If these compulsory savings were to yield a constant interest rate of 5.5%, the personal pension accrual would amount to no more than 11% of the standard pension (after 45 years of covered employment) for a worker retiring in 2030. Since the portion of retirement income presently stemming from funded sources amounts to less than 20%, it is thus unlikely that Germany (or most other social insurance countries) will attain the unfunded/funded income mix of latecomer countries like the Netherlands or the United Kingdom in the foreseeable future. This assertion is further supported by the fact that reforms of the pension schemes along the lines mentioned above will not prevent a further rise in public pension spending (as a portion of GDP). Such a development defines limits on what can reasonably be expected from working-age generations to reinforce their *private* efforts to provide for old-age pensions.

Lessons from the public pension reform process

Based on the findings in the preceding section, I will now turn to some conclusions. First, the question of (reduced/revised) diversity will be addressed. The circumstances of reform initiatives and the politics of pension reform policy will then be discussed. Finally, I will look into the implications of recent reforms, particularly, the preconditions of quite substantial retrenchments.

Convergence

Have the reforms initiated since about the mid 1980s in social insurance countries reduced the diversity of public pension schemes? No definite answer can be given because it is dependent on the criteria defined for convergence, which can either be the structural design, the outcome, the instruments, or the goals. If one focuses, like Overbye (1994), on the question of whether a *dual structure* of old age security – a poverty alleviating basic pension supplemented by an earnings replacing component (or vice versa) – has developed as a combined result of risk exposition, political institutions and actor strategies, then convergence is most obvious and also includes the latecomer countries. However, this perspective blurs precisely those differences that are crucial for present (and future) problem constellations and political adjustment strategies.

Johnson (1999) looks for evidence of a convergence in the outcomes of public pension schemes. Instead of using (inadequate) expenditure data or indirect outcome measures (like income inequality or poverty rates), he concentrates on the 'pure' impact of the pension scheme's (changed) rules on 'hypothetical individuals'. Apart from the fact that this approach is too 'stylised' (or synthetic) because standard cases are becoming ever less representative and rule changes affect insured persons selectively,[15] it cannot adequately grasp the 'final state' when rule changes are fully implemented after (extensive) phasing in/-out periods. People live through, as Johnson (1999: 604) points out correctly, 'both their personal career history and the institutional history of their national pension system'. While he summarises the findings of his simulations on the long-term trends as inconclusive, Johnson (1999: 615) states that 'since the mid 1980s ... retrenchment has reversed a trend towards harmonisation and has increased the variance across countries in the level of income provided for similar individuals through the public pension system'.

If one borrows from Hall's (1993: 278) distinction of the kinds of policy change (goals, techniques and levels) and reviews the trends ascertained earlier, conspicuously more uniformity of the applied techniques and levels of these instruments can be observed These regard standard retirement ages, pension credits for unpaid family work, or benefit formulas geared to a tighter relationship between contributions (or, lifetime earnings) and benefits. This evolution is less a result of 'emulation' (Bennett 1991) which presumes a transnational diffusion of information on problems and solutions as well as lessons drawn, but stems rather from a limited set of incremental (or parametric) adjustment options (see Figure 5.2 above), furthering parallel development: 'There is always a finite repertoire of possible responses to emerging policy problems' (Bennett 1991: 220). Undoubtedly, a convergence of the profile of the reformed Swedish public pension system with the German approach is discernible if one considers the introduction of (tax financed) contribution payments covering non-employment periods (child care, unemployment, sickness, military service), the contributions becoming evenly split between employers and employees (not fully realised yet), benefit calculation on the basis of all years of insurance, or the reduction of intragenerational redistribution. The 'Germanisation' is also true for the Austrian, Finnish and, to some extent, the Italian pension scheme after the latest revisions, which in their central respects again resemble the Swedish reforms. Policy changes may indeed occasionally be borrowed from the toolboxes of others. The deliberate sounding out of exemplary policy solutions ('best practices'), eventually leading to a transfer presumes, however, a high degree of rationality in the policymaking process. The feasibility of such tool transfers also depends on the phase of the policy cycle at which foreign reform elements are fed in.[16]

Taking the concept of 'path dependency' seriously, one can thus expect that similar challenges, dealt with in different institutional contexts with a correspondingly different course of issue processing and dissimilar actor coalitions, result in policy changes which, above all, *revise* the original diversity. Only a very detailed comparison of chosen or accessible reform strategies can inform about changed goals of public pension systems or altered conceptions regarding the future mix of retirement income and its social distribution and, hence, settle the question of whether diversity was actually *reduced*. Obviously, in this respect, again, the reconstruction of the Swedish old age security system implies the most far-reaching *goal shift* (or 'third order change'; Hall 1993) towards re-commodification. The 'citizenship' principle has been replaced with an income test for the new guaranteed pension (also true for Finland).[17] Furthermore, instead of adhering to distinct features of the Social Democratic welfare regime, e.g. to 'maximise equality' or to 'minimise … market dependency' (Esping-Andersen 1999: 78–9), the new *inkomstpension* scheme is far less redistributive and will provide benefits that are more differentiated due to its strictly contribution-based formula. Finally, the paramount role of the state in providing retirement income will be reduced when about 14% of the total contribution amount goes into the premium reserve scheme, thus enlarging the weight of private welfare. These shifts away from traditional policy objectives raise serious doubts about the *immutability* of regimes and whether at all the regime approach, as such, is relevant if one focuses on particular policy areas, since traits assumed to be central to the Social Democratic regime vanished under Social Democratic rule and without social upheaval.

Timing and consensus politics

When examining which governments have initiated the predominantly retrenching reforms, it is striking to note that they were led by Christian Democratic or Conservative parties (mostly in coalition with Liberal parties), 'Grand Coalitions' including Social Democrats, as well as (coalition) governments led by Social Democrats. If the 'colour' of the governments is obviously less relevant for the choice of roughly similar adjustment strategies, it is more

91

interesting to ask *when* the reform projects were started and *which* alliances over and above the government parties supported the reform.

Weaver's (1998) observation on the circumstances of reform initiatives holds true for most countries. Either looming deficits of pension schemes, their impending 'insolvency' (1983 in the USA), growing deficits of the public budget, an unrestrained increase in pension spending, or the contribution rate rising due to massive labour market induced early retirement represent immediate policy challenges. Additionally, and further explaining why reforms occurred increasingly in the 1990s (and another wave is in the making), pressure stemmed from imminent EU membership (Austria, Finland) or the advancing process of European integration (in Italy and France, the problem to meet the EMU convergence criteria). The perception of a need for reform was intensified by generally advancing market liberal positions asserting consequences detrimental to economic development such as financial unsustainability, loss of international competitiveness and distorting tax wedges if public pension schemes were not substantially reformed. Of at least equal importance was increased attention towards pessimistic scenarios of ageing, mainly preoccupied with rising old age dependency ratios. However, the extent of the predicted demographic shift and its consequences hardly made a difference in making it a political issue or in the intensity of the reform debate. A largely accepted crisis definition provided for the necessary thrust to get the reform process going and, in the course of the respective process, not only acute problems, but also long-term challenges, were tackled. *A priori*, taking a time horizon well beyond urgent repairs cannot be expected from politicians striving for success in the next election. The peculiarities of the *politics* of public pension policy offer an explanation of why politicians dare to burden themselves with even more unpopular decisions whose consequences go beyond the current parliamentary period.

Almost always and everywhere pension policy has differed from legislative changes in other areas of the welfare state in that decisions largely came about in a consensual manner. For one thing, this is due to pension law being a rather complicated and technical matter, and thus experts, representatives of the programme administration and special commissions play a decisive role in preparing reforms. Within those policy communities issues are de-politicised and long-term 'technical' solutions are favoured. On the other hand, taking a long planning horizon is demanded because present decisions extend far into the future, and bringing the planning period in line with the even longer time horizon of the insured (covering about 60 years – from entering employment for the first time until termination of benefit payments) is all the more important. This is needed in order to convey to the scheme's participants of all ages the guarantee of institutional stability so that their institutional trust is sustained. Reliable rules, if supported by a broad majority in parliament and thus not endangered in case of a change in government, are decisive for the participants in an unfunded pension scheme to experience 'security' regarding their life planning and also for maintaining the institution's legitimacy. The pension consensus in Germany, established in 1957 (and lasting until the mid 1990s) and constantly referred to by political parties and the social partners, was not untypical but probably more well-developed than elsewhere.

If these conditions were valid (and quite easy to fulfil) during the expansionary phase, a consensus appears to be all the more necessary if retrenchments are considered. Governments regularly attempt to win over others for supporting a compromise because its interest is to spread responsibility for concrete impairments affecting large parts of the electorate, or for having caused general insecurity (Pierson 1996), so that 'the ability to avoid blame is a key component of loss imposition' (Ross 1997: 190). Obviously, far-reaching retrenchments in public pensions, even if they only take effect gradually, become fully implemented and gain acceptance among policy-*takers* if (a) their necessity is uncontested; (b) they are perceived as a coherent redesign of the scheme in response to a problem, but not a systemic rupture; (c) they are negotiated and (broadly) consented to, (d) and therefore ensure a socially balanced (fair) distribution of burdens, (e) accrue in small doses when being phased in over a long period.

In almost all social insurance countries, where in order to stabilise the public pension scheme, attempts to contain the increase in pension spending were undertaken, these considerations were politically relevant. The making of the *Pension Reform Act of 1992* in Germany was guided by the eventually successful endeavour to reach a consensus among political parties and social partners. In the USA, the 1983 reform of *Social Security* was based on a compromise reached by a 'bipartisan commission', which included trade unions and employers (Hinrichs 1993). The principles of the Swedish public pension reform, decided upon in 1994, followed the recommendations of a committee composed of members of the four bourgeois parties and the Social Democrats (but not the social partners) that strove for consensual responses to problems ascertained in a broad political investigation (1984 to 1990). Likewise, these five parties supported the subsequent legislation on the details of reform and thus provided for a 90% majority vote in parliament. In Canada, only after an agreement on the reform had been reached with (most of) the provincial governments (of different party compositions) did the federal government start the legislation process in 1997. The 'Great Coalition' in Austria (Social Democrats and the Christian-Conservative party) was successful in integrating both social partners in the multi-stage reform process (in 1997, however, only after intense conflicts with the trade unions) and, hence, was able to broaden the legitimatory basis for the resulting sacrifices (Tálos and Kittel 1999: 155–160).

Italy, France and Germany provide an interesting contrast: although it began already in the 1980s, the permanent project of reforming the excessive Italian public pension system did not make substantial progress until 1992 ('Amato reform') and 1995 ('Dini reform'), under the auspices of a (revived) concertation with the social partners. The changes originally proposed by the Dini government of 'technocrats' were moderated upon consultation with the trade unions before they could pass parliament with the support of the Left parties. Again, the 'refinements' of 1997 (which mainly meant an acceleration of the harmonisation of different schemes and of phasing out provisions) were preceded by agreements with the unions. In contrast, the Berlusconi government was incapable of attaining such an understanding. The trade unions' fierce struggle against the proposals for an overhaul of the pension system contributed to the eventual fall of the Berlusconi government at the turn of 1994/95 (Klammer and Rolf 1998; Levy 1999; Mairhuber 1998: 127–149). The decisive role of trade unions' consent to pension reforms can also be seen in France: whereas the Balladur government pursued a consensus strategy – and after making concessions to the trade unions they refrained from protests against the reform –, the confrontational approach of the Juppé government two years later failed when it attempted to extend to public-sector employees the measures adopted in 1993 for the private sector and to change the trade unions' role in the management of social insurance schemes (Bonoli 1997). The succeeding government has abstained from putting into practice all legislative changes that remained from the Juppé plan.

In Germany, traditional consensus politics, which still governed the reform act of 1989 (which went into effect in 1992), came to a (temporary) halt when the Christian Democratic–Liberal government enacted substantial retrenchments in 1996 and 1997 on their own. Although not all reform elements were controversial, the trade unions opposed further impairments affecting the pensioners and disabled workers, and the Social Democrats announced they would undo these parts after winning the election in autumn 1998. The new Red–Green government indeed suspended parts of the not yet effective reform of its predecessor, legislated changes to keep in check the contribution rate (against the opposition of the former government parties), and proposed elements for another 'structural reform' in June 1999. Very reluctantly, the parties agreed to strive for an inter-party consensus, which, however, has not yet been achieved as of spring 2000 (Hinrichs 1998, 2000a).

If there is any *lesson* to be learned from an international comparison, it is not that some highly innovative policy changes can be detected by scanning pension reforms in other countries. The feasible set of incremental changes, as well as the restrictions of non-parametric reforms within a country's given institutional framework, are known and, at least partly, tested. Rather, the first lesson relates to the success of retrenchments in that they trigger no popular discontent and, ultimately, become (fully) implemented. Successful reforms are contingent upon support reaching well beyond the necessary majority in parliament, i.e. that either the main opposition party backs the government proposal or from the social partners at least the trade unions agree (if they hold a vested power position). The second lesson concerns the pre-conditions for broad support. Establishing a special pension reform commission is a promising political strategy to attain a consensus, as can be learned from the reforms in the USA (1983), Japan (1985; see Kato 1991), Germany (1992 reform act), and Sweden (1990s). If furnished with a clear mandate and authority, because social and political interests as well as programme administrators and other experts are included, such committees provide an opportunity (but no guarantee) to remove conflicts from the parliamentary arena, to internally settle issues, and to evolve a compromise *package* of items on which, otherwise, achieving unanimity would prove more difficult. A commission's compromise package that somehow balances desired and disapproved elements for all actors involved and committed to reform policy, limits the possibilities for concerted action by opponents. In contrast, a government which comes forward with a reform proposal that has not been negotiated in advance is more likely to fail to achieve broad support.

Implications

Elephants can be moved! The German public pension reforms of the last decade may serve as an example: before enacting the reform of 1992, the equally unacceptable alternatives were either to exempt retirees from any benefit cuts, and then gradually have to increase the contribution rate from about 18 to 36% in 2030, or to cut benefits by half while maintaining a stable contribution rate. Estimates calculated by the Sozialbeirat (1998: 242) show that the cumulative reform effects would reduce the expected contribution increase by 13 percentage points (36.4% before the 1992 reform; 23.5% if the 1999 reform was fully implemented). Although one may doubt the accuracy of the projected figures, the *difference* is astonishing and provides at least two lessons.

First, reforms legislated within eight years and producing such a large financial impact contradict assertions that pension insurance schemes are highly resistant to change ('Contributory 'rights' and privileges, spanning perhaps fifty years, become sacrosanct' – Titmuss 1976: 60). Rather, it is proof of considerable institutional elasticity because, due to the schemes' evolved complexity, a multitude of 'adjusting screws' can be moved without transgressing the boundaries of incremental (or 'system-immanent') reform.[18] Second, in Germany (and elsewhere), in one way or another the present and, still more, the future cohorts of pensioners will have to carry the main part of the adjustment burden, while the contributors and the general taxpayer will shoulder the smaller (and now reduced) part of the consequences of demographic ageing. Apparently, that one third of the 1998 electorate in Germany is 55 years or older, turns out disproportionally highly at elections and has an immediate interest in pension benefits, represents no insurmountable hindrance to the democratic process being able to carry out substantial retrenchments – despite the fact that public pension benefits constitute the predominant or even sole source of income for the large majority of retirees.

It is easily conceivable that political parties initiating such retrenchments are not punished by voters if their identity is based on a *reputation* for pursuing foresighted, purposeful policies, which they try to utilise for increasing their appeal to the electorate. The risk of losing voters in subsequent elections is small and, hence, increases the willingness to engage in, ultimately, substantial retrenchment efforts, provided that generous phasing in/out provisions can be established. It requires operating with a long planning horizon (see above) and shows that procrastination does not pay off. Government parties and opposition parties alike might be motivated not to postpone 'hardships' since they reappear as more intensive reform urgency, but then with less leeway to spread the burden over a longer period. While phasing in/out stipulations reduce the number of immediate 'losers' and thus the possibility of protest, automatisms and (changed) formulas—thresholds triggering certain responses or the predetermination of which birth cohorts will be affected by a higher retirement age or by a new mode of benefit calculation—help to depoliticise the actual implementation of reforms. They relieve policymakers from being held responsible for the retrenchment effects. The inclination to engage in a timely and large-scale pension reform should be increased if one can benefit from the 'blessing of a lack of transparency' (Zacher 1987: 594–595) which impedes an exact calculation of the individual outcome of rule changes and thus provides another 'blame avoidance' option (Weaver 1986).[19] Taken together, the strategies of gaining reputation (turning 'vice into virtue' – Levy 1999), distributing burdens over time, extending 'automatic government' and lowering the visibility of reform outcomes have been used to enlarge the scope for public pension reforms and to minimise their impact on subsequent elections.

Conclusions

It has been shown that, in OECD countries, old-age security systems have developed along two different lines. Among the traditional and new social insurance countries, as well as among the latecomer countries, one finds welfare states that are assumed to belong to different *regimes*. Substantial path changes were thus indeed possible and have occurred. Due to the central significance of old age security systems for the profile of welfare states, these long-term developments must not be underestimated because they have, in varying degrees, remodelled the structural interplay of (labour) market, state and private households in producing welfare, as well as modified the landscape of political interests.

In the course of recurrent attempts of social insurance countries to stabilise their old-age security systems, the design has been reshaped too, although political elites have been anxious to convey to the public an image of institutional continuity. Despite sometimes producing quite substantial cumulative effects, the retrenchments enacted during the last two decades corresponded to the traditional pattern of incremental changes (OECD 1988: 11, 65–6). Radical reform proposals, which might possibly be adequate for an economic and demographic constellation 20 or more years from now, are hardly capable of gaining a majority in parliament, to say nothing of a consensus among the relevant political actors, because they involve considerable insecurity regarding goal attainment and currently imply political rule instability (Lindbeck 1994) to such an extent that the system's legitimacy could become endangered.[20]

The intensified dispute on 'privatising' US *Social Security* which, according to the latest projections, will not be confronted with contribution rate increases or solvency problems during the next three decades, may serve as an example: the report of the Advisory Council on Social Security (1997) came forward with three proposals, each supported by a group of economists, of which the least radical one opts for marginal changes of the programme in order to make it financially sound for the next 75 (!) years. The most extreme one would imply a shift away from the social insurance approach and move the USA to the group of latecomer countries. Arnold (1998) is probably right when he expects that none of the three proposals (or one of their numerous variants) will ultimately have a chance to become enacted but, rather like the 1983 reform, only a bipartisan commission (including non-parliamentary actors) might be able to resolve the present conflict.

A negotiated compromise package that takes into account the expectations of the young and the old generation alike would presumably not amount to the retirement-income model of the latecomer countries. The current debate in the USA also shows that the window of opportunity for substantial changes in social insurance countries has become larger since the once 'coherent policy paradigm' (Hall 1993: 210) has been shaken. In view of (overdramatised) doubts about sustainability, transnational diffusion of experience with reform policies and advancing reform proposals of market-liberal provenance, the model of a contributory, pay-as-you-go public pension scheme, committed to a balanced blend of individual equity and income adequacy (solidarity), is no longer situated in a 'politically stable equilibrium' (Heclo 1998: 72). It no longer functions as an uncontested point of reference of actors rallying in this policy area. In the USA and Germany (Hinrichs 2000a) at least the once closed policy communities have lost their interpretative hegemony, mainly due to the counter mobilisation of external actors (coming from mass media, research institutes, the financial services industry etc), who have become more capable of re-framing pension policy issues (Quadagno 1999). Concomitantly, the focus of public pension reforms has changed: starting as attempts to save the present scheme, increasingly the *leitmotiv* is to design a sustainable system of different components of retirement income. It implies that public policy has become engaged more frequently in shaping the non-public components.

Notes

1. This is also true for the income situation of today's retirees, being the result of institutional arrangements and individual behaviour oriented to those rules, incentives, or obligations when they were at working age.
2. Huber and Stephens (1993: 323), for example, are well aware of the limits of their *quantitative* analysis and demand: '(R)esearchers will have to examine individual pension systems in greater detail … (and) devote more attention to qualitative aspects of pension systems.'
3. This section is very much inspired by the work of, and discussions with, John Myles (see Myles 1998; Myles and Quadagno 1997; Myles and Pierson 2001; see also various chapters in Overbye 1998). For references to background material not explicitly mentioned in this and the subsequent section see Hinrichs 2000b.
4. It is interesting to note that, in Germany (and most recently in Italy too), an opposite route was taken: existing (albeit insufficient from the outset) elements of minimum protection were eventually removed in 1957 from the public pension scheme. As of early 2000, the fate of the Red–Green government's proposal to introduce a special needs-tested minimum benefit for retirees that would be tax-financed, but administered by the public pension scheme, remains to be seen.
5. These (second pillar) statutory pension *insurance* schemes of comparatively recent vintage (to which, in this case, one might add the USA) are marked by some peculiarities relative to the schemes of the original *Bismarck* countries: from the outset (nearly) the *total* workforce was included in *one* scheme (exception: Finland where a more 'semi-public' system of six decentralised funds, controlled by the social partners, was established). There were no, or very high, contribution ceilings (exception: Canada), and in Sweden, Finland, and Canada reserve funds play(ed) a larger role. However, the schemes in these three countries are far from being fully funded and do not aspire this.
6. On developments in Australia since the mid 1980s and the 1991 legislation, see Edey and Simon 1998; Pierson 1998 – The basic pension in Switzerland (*AHV*), concluded in 1948, has never been a universal, flat-rate pension. It is financed through 'contributions' levied on almost all income categories without an upper ceiling (factually, it is a proportional income tax), while benefits are capped and show a small spread (the maximum pension amounts to double the minimum benefit). Starting in 1985, this scheme was supplemented by a second, occupational 'pillar', which is mandatory for all employees with annual earnings above a certain threshold.
7. In 1964, Denmark introduced a *public* (and funded) supplementary pension scheme. Unlike Sweden or Norway, benefits are not earnings-related (rather, they are differentiated by the insurance period and contributions paid according to weekly working hours) and comparatively *modest* even after a full working career (Kangas and Palme 1991).
8. In Denmark the income-tested elements as a relative share of the maximally attainable 'people's pension' were already increased to almost 50% (for single pensioners).
9. The argument of this paragraph does not imply that population ageing will cause no problems for the financing of *latecomer* countries' basic pension schemes. These challenges will vary according to the relative benefit level. Having the most generous basic pension, the Netherlands already established a reserve fund which is expected to

melt away after 2020 in order to keep the contribution rate to the *AOW* scheme continuously at its present level. Remaining deficits will be covered by subsidies out of general taxation (Oorschot and Boos 1999).

10. It is only in Norway where a *weakening* of the contribution-benefit link has occurred and which is expected to bring considerable expenditure savings in the future: in 1992, the progressiveness of the benefit formula was increased, such that even fewer credits are granted out of covered earnings above a certain multiple of the 'base amount', and the income threshold above which benefit claims are earned underproportionally has been lowered to almost the average earnings of industrial workers. Moreover, the (gross) replacement rate, attained after 40 years of employment, is to decrease from 45 to 42%. Taken together, these measures will result in a lower benefit level with a compressed spread at the upper end.

11. For details on the reforms in Italy and Sweden see Artoni and Zanardi (1997); Klammer and Rolf (1998); Mairhuber (1998); Ministry of Health and Social Affairs (1998); Palmer (1998); Scherman (1999); Sundén (2000). It has been contested whether it is justified to actually consider this so called 'Notional Defined Contribution' approach (NDC) as a new paradigm. Cichon (1999) argues that largely the same results can be a attained by a linear accrual rate (as in Germany where all years of covered employment are in like manner included in the benefit formula). Moreover, the reformed public pension schemes in Italy and Sweden do not rule out financial instabilities and the need for political modifications in future.

12. Governments' attempts to close pathways into the early labour market exit is offset by collective agreements when both enterprises and unions have an interest in substitutive provisions or, in contradiction to their policy of increasing the retirement age, governments themselves are tempted somehow to support alternatives as long as unemployment stagnates at high levels (like in Germany).

13. Since 1993, in Belgium, the revenues of a new energy tax are utilised to reduce employers' social insurance charges by 1.5 percentage points (largely limited to industrial enterprises in the exposed sector). It preceded a similar approach in Germany where, beginning in 1998, a gradually increasing 'ecology tax' serves to lower the contribution rate to the public pension scheme for both employers and employees.

14. It was precisely due to the fact that the public earnings-related scheme in the United Kingdom (SERPS) had collected contributions for less than ten years and thus was 'unmatured' that the Conservative government had the opportunity to undertake substantial retrenchments and to embark on a different path of old-age security policy (Pierson 1996).

15. For example, women in Germany benefit from certain of the recent rule changes and lose from others, but not in a uniform way across and between birth cohorts.

16. An example is the proposal of the German Minister of Labour and Social Affairs to *mandate* savings of 2.5% of annual earnings for a personal pension (exactly matching the Swedish pattern). It leaked to the public in June 1999 and immediately stirred vehement protests from all directions (trade unions, opposition parties, the media etc) and was dropped after one week. Being 'burned' at a very early stage, it is somewhat unlikely that this proposal will be part of a reform package coming out of inter-party negotiations aiming at a renewed 'pension consensus'.

17. Esping-Andersen admits that 'this implies a qualitative retreat from the principle of universalism: the notion of solidarity of risks is being rewritten' (1999: 80, see also 88, n. 16)

18. It might still be true that tax-financed basic pension schemes in the *latecomer* countries (or those components in *social insurance* countries) can be cut much faster and more discretionary because the benefits do not represent *earned entitlements* (Myles and Quadagno 1997).

19. Sweden entered a politically risky strategy when increasing the system's transparency: Annual statements explicitly show the (notional) 'return' of contributions to the individual accounts of the *public* scheme provides and the (real) return obtained from paying into the mandatory and likewise non-redistributive *private* pension funds. If the 2.5 percentage points of the total contribution rate of 18.5% diverted to the latter yield a (much) higher rate of return, people might ask why they should contribute to the less profitable public scheme at all.

20. This points to a pension *political* dilemma: far-reaching reforms which create long-term stabilisation in one go, are difficult to put through and therefore rarely occur (possible exception: Sweden; Scherman 1999: 44–47). In contrast, incremental changes are more likely to gain a (broad) majority, but when recurrently put on the political agenda and rule changes happen frequently (as in Italy, Austria or Germany during the 1990s), 'security expectations' on the part of the public might get lost. Confidence in the system's reliability should dwindle even more if reform necessity is a permanent issue in the political debate but no decisions are taken (as in the USA).

References

Advisory Council on Social Security (1997) *Report of the 1994–1996 Advisory Council on Social Security, Vol. I: Findings and Recommendations*, Washington, DC: Government Printing Office.

Arnold, R.D. (1998) The Politics of Reforming Social Security, *Political Science Quarterly*, **113**, 213–240.

Artoni, R. and Zanardi, A. (1997) The Evolution of the Italian Pension System, in: Ministère de L'Emploi et de la Solidarité, Mission Recherche et Expérimentation (MIRE), *Comparing Social Welfare Systems in Southern Europe*, Vol. 3, Florence Conference, Paris, pp. 243–266.

Bennett, C.J. (1991) Review article: what is policy convergence and what causes it?, *British Journal of Political Science*, **21**, 215–233.

Bonoli, G. (1997) Pension politics in France: patterns of co-operation and conflict in two recent reforms, *West European Politics*, **20**(4), 111–124.

Borchert, J. (1998) Ausgetretene Pfade? Zur Statik und Dynamik wohlfahrtsstaatlicher Regime, in: S. Lessenich and I. Ostner (eds), *Welten des Wohlfahrtskapitalismus. Der Sozialstaat in vergleichender Perspektive*, Frankfurt/New York: Campus, pp. 137–176.

Cichon, M. (1999) Nominelle beitragsbestimmte Systeme: Alter Wein in neuen Flaschen?, *Internationale Revue für Soziale Sicherheit*, **52**(4), 105–126.

Cox, R.H. (1998) The consequences of welfare reform: how conceptions of social rights are changing, *Journal of Social Policy*, **27**, 1–16.

Davis, E.P. (1995) *Pension Funds: Retirement-Income Security and Capital Markets. An International Perspective*, Oxford: Clarendon Press.

Department of Social Security (1998) *A New Contract for Welfare: Partnership in Pensions*, Cm. 4179, London: The Stationery Office.

Edey, M. and Simon, J. (1998) Australia's retirement income system, in: M. Feldstein (ed), *Privatizing Social Security*, Chicago/London: The University of Chicago Press, pp. 63–89.

Esping-Andersen, G. (1990) *The Three Worlds of Welfare Capitalism*, Princeton, NJ: Princeton University Press.

Esping-Andersen, G. (1996) Welfare states without work: the impasse of labor shedding and familialism in continental European social policy, in: G. Esping-Andersen (ed), *Welfare States in Transition*, London: Sage, pp. 66–87.

Esping-Andersen, G. (1999) *Social Foundations of Postindustrial Economies*, Oxford/New York: Oxford University Press.

Hall, P.A. (1993) Policy paradigms, social learning, and the state: the case of economic policymaking in Britain, *Comparative Politics*, **25**, 275–296.

Heclo, H. (1998) A political science perspective on social security reform, in: R.D. Arnold *et al.* (eds), *Framing the Social Security Debate*, Washington, DC: Brookings Institution Press, pp. 65–89.

Hinrichs, K. (1993) Public pensions and demographic change: generational equity in the United States and Germany, Universität Bremen, Zentrum für Sozialpolitik, ZeS-Arbeitspapier Nr. 16/93, Bremen.

Hinrichs, K. (1998) Reforming the public pension scheme in Germany: the end of the traditional consensus?, Universität Bremen, Zentrum für Sozialpolitik, ZeS-Arbeitspapier Nr. 11/98, Bremen.

Hinrichs, K. (2000a) Von der Rentenversicherungs- und Alterssicherungspolitik. Reformen und Reformprobleme. in: K. Hinrichs *et al.* (eds), *Kontingenz und Krise. Institutionenpolitik in kapitalistischen und postsozialistischen Gesellschaften*, Frankfurt/New York: Campus, pp. 291–317.

Hinrichs, K. (2000b) Rentenreformpolitiken in OECD-Ländern. Die Bundesrepublik Deutschland im internationalen Vergleich, *Deutsche Rentenversicherung* No. 3–4, 188–209.

Huber, E. and Stephens, J.D. (1993) Political parties and public pensions: a quantitative analysis, *Acta Sociologica*, **36**, 309–325.

Johnson, P. (1999) The measurement of social security convergence: the case of European public pension systems since 1950, *Journal of Social Policy*, **28**, 595–618.

Kangas, O. and Palme, J. (1991) The public–private mix in pension policy, *International Journal of Sociology*, **20**(4), 78–116.

Kato, J. (1991) Public pension reforms in the United States and Japan: a study of comparative public policy, *Comparative Political Studies*, **24**, 100–126.

Klammer, U. and Rolf, G. (1998) Auf dem Weg zu einer gerechteren Alterssicherung? Rentenreformpolitik in Deutschland und Italien im Vergleich, *Zeitschrift für Sozialreform*, **44**, 793–817.

Korpi, W. and Palme, J. (1998) The paradox of redistribution and strategies of equality, *American Sociological Review*, **63**, 661–687.

Levy, J.D. (1999) Vice into virtue? Progressive politics and welfare reform in continental Europe, *Politics and Society*, **27**, 239–273.

Lindbeck, A. (1994) Uncertainty under the welfare state – policy-induced risk, *The Geneva Papers on Risk and Insurance*, **19**, 379–393.

Liu, L. (1999) Retirement income security in the United Kingdom, *Social Security Bulletin* **62**(1), 23–46.

Mairhuber, I. (1998) Soziale Sicherung in Italien, in: E. Tálos (ed), *Soziale Sicherung im Wandel: Österreich und seine Nachbarstaaten*, Wien/Köln/Weimar: Böhlau, pp. 103–170.

McCarthy, S. (1998) Martin backs off seniors plan, *The Globe and Mail*, July 29, A1 and A4.

Ministry of Health and Social Affairs (1998) *The Pension Reform. Final Report*, June 1998, Stockholm.

Myles, J. (1998) Discussion: insights from social security reform abroad, in: R.D. Arnold *et al.* (eds), *Framing the Social Security Debate*, Washington, DC: Brookings Institution Press, pp. 237–248.

Myles, J. and Pierson, P. (2001) The comparative political economy of pension reform, in: P. Pierson (ed), *The New Politics of the Welfare State*, Oxford: OUP, pp. 305–333.

Myles, J. and Quadagno, J. (1997) Recent trends in public pension reform: a comparative view, in: K.G. Banting and R. Boadway (eds), *Reform of Retirement Income Policy: International and Canadian Perspectives*, Kingston, Ontario: School of Policy Studies, Queen's University, pp. 247–271.

OECD (1988) *Reforming Public Pensions*, OECD Social Policy Studies, No. 5, Paris: OECD.

OECD (1996) *Ageing in OECD Countries: A Critical Policy Challenge*, OECD Social Policy Studies, No. 20, Paris: OECD.

OECD (1998) *Maintaining Prosperity in an Ageing Society*, Paris: OECD.

Oorschot, W. van and Boos, C. (1999) Dutch pension policy and the ageing of the population, *European Journal of Social Security*, **1**, 295–311.

Overbye, E. (1994) Convergence in policy outcomes: social security systems in perspective, *Journal of Public Policy*, **14**, 147–174.

Overbye, E. (1998) *Risk and Welfare: Examining Stability and Change in 'Welfare' Policies*, Norsk institutt for forskning om oppvekst, velferd og aldring, NOVA Rapport 5/98, Oslo: NOVA.

Palmer, E. (1998) The Swedish pension reform model – framework and issues, Stockholm (mimeo.).

Pierson, C. (1998) Globalisation and the changing governance of welfare states: superannuation reform in Australia, *Global Society*, **12**, 31–47.

Pierson, P. (1996) The new politics of the welfare state, *World Politics*, **48**, 143–179.

Quadagno, J. (1999) Creating a capital investment welfare state: the new American exceptionalism, *American Sociological Review*, **64**, 1–11.

Ross, F. (1997) Cutting public expenditures in advanced industrial democracies: the importance of avoiding blame, *Governance*, **10**, 175–200.

Scherman, K.G. (1999) The Swedish pension reform, International Labour Office, Social Security Department, Issues in Social Protection, Discussion Paper No. 7, Geneva: ILO.

Sozialbeirat (1998) Gutachten des Sozialbeirats zum Rentenversicherungsbericht 1998 und Stellungnahme zu einigen weiteren Berichten zur Alterssicherung, in: Bundesregierung, *Rentenversicherungsbericht 1998*, Deutscher Bundestag, Drucksache 13/11290 (v. 17.07.98), Bonn, pp. 239–251.

Sozialbeirat (1999) Gutachten des Sozialbeirats zum Rentenversicherungsbericht 1999, in: Bundesregierung, *Rentenversicherungsbericht 1999*, Deutscher Bundestag, Drucksache 14/2116 (v. 02.12.99), Berlin, pp. 131–147.

Sundén, A. (2000) How will Sweden's new pension system work?, Center for Retirement Research at Boston College, Issue Brief, No. 3/2000, Chestnut Hill, MA.

Tálos, E. and Kittel, B. (1999) Sozialpartnerschaft und Sozialpolitik, in: F. Karlhofer and E. Tálos (eds), *Zukunft der Sozialpartnerschaft. Veränderungsdynamik und Reformbedarf*, Wien: Signum, pp. 137–164.

Titmuss, R.M. (1976) Pension systems and population change, in: *Essays on 'The Welfare State'*, 3rd edn, London: George Allen & Unwin Ltd., pp. 56–74 (first: 1958).

Weaver, R.K. (1986) The politics of blame avoidance, *Journal of Public Policy*, **6**, 371–398.

Weaver, R.K. (1998) The politics of pensions: lessons from abroad, in: R.D. Arnold *et al.* (eds), *Framing the Social Security Debate*, Washington, DC: Brookings Institution Press, pp. 183–229.

World Bank (1994) *Averting the Old Age Crisis: Policies to Protect the Old and Promote Growth*, New York: Oxford University Press.

Zacher, H.F. (1987) Grundtypen des Sozialrechts, in: W. Fürst *et al.* (eds), *Festschrift für Wolfgang Zeidler*, Bd. 1, Berlin: Walter de Gruyter, pp. 571–595.

About the Author

Karl Hinrichs is a Research Associate at the Centre for Social Policy Research at the University of Bremen and teaches political science at Humboldt University in Berlin. In 1989/90 he was a John F. Kennedy Fellow at the Center for European Studies, Harvard University, and in 1999 Visiting Professor at Berlin's Humboldt University. His main area of research is the German welfare state in comparative perspective. His English language publications include: 'Health care policy in the German social insurance state: from solidarity to privatization?', *Policy Studies Review* 2000, **17** (forthcoming); (with William K. Roche and Carmen Sirianni, eds.) *Working Time in Transition: The Political Economy of Working Hours in Industrial Nations* (Temple University Press, Philadelphia, 1991).

European Review, Vol. 8, No. 3, 379–398 (2000) © Academia Europaea, Printed in the United Kingdom

6 The Nordic welfare state in a European context: dealing with new economic and ideological challenges in the 1990s

STEIN KUHNLE*

Within the framework of a general discussion of 'the state of the welfare state' in economically advanced West European democracies, this paper offers an account and interpretation of how the Nordic welfare states, often perceived as the most comprehensive and 'generous' welfare states, met a number of challenges in the 1990s. Economic problems were most critical in Finland and Sweden in the early 1990s, and social policy reform activities with the aim of modifications of programmes and cutbacks in expenditure have been most pronounced in these countries. A single common denominator for Nordic welfare state development in the 1990s is a somewhat less generous welfare state, but Norway is generally an exception. The basic structure of the welfare systems has been preserved, and social, health and welfare issues are consistently of high priority for governments and voters. The welfare state is highly valued in Scandinavia, but more space for market and other non-governmental welfare solutions is likely to grow in the future.

Introduction: persistence of national welfare states

Most European welfare states experienced some serious challenges of one kind or another in the 1980s or 1990s. It has not gone unnoticed in the academic and media world that the Nordic welfare states were among these. Sweden, in particular, has come under closer international scrutiny, with observations of problems often mixed with a dose of *schadenfreude*, perhaps to compensate for previous envy at, or disbelief of, the social and economic success of her 'welfare model'. Finland was the other Nordic welfare state to face severe problems, even more so than Sweden, but attracting less international attention thanks to her existence in the shadow of her bigger Scandinavian sister.[1] Denmark, and especially Norway, were economically less challenged, but in these countries also, the 1990s were marked by social reform activity, although not always for the purpose of welfare retrenchment.

I prefer the concepts of 'problems' or 'challenges' rather than the dramatic concept of 'crisis' which has been with us in various disguises for some time. From the 1970s, various theorists

* Department of Comparative Politics, University of Bergen, Christiesgate 15, N-5007, Bergen, Norway. E-mail: stein.kuhnle@isp.uib.no.

have claimed a fiscal crisis (O'Connor 1973); a crisis of government overload (e.g. Rose and Peters 1978); a crisis of legitimacy (e.g. Habermas 1976); a crisis of liberal democracy (e.g. Crozier *et al*. 1975). If by crisis is meant breakdown or radical institutional change, none of the theories can be said to have 'succeeded' empirically, so far.[2] Challenges to welfare state institutions and principles of state welfare are nothing new. According to Alber (1988), the financial implications of the emerging social insurance policies in Germany in the early 1900s were considered a huge problem by many politicians, i.e. at a time when social expenditure in Germany made up only 1.4% of gross domestic product. In the most recent decade, abundant theorising on the crisis has focused on the increased internationalisation or globalisation of the economy, aptly epitomised in the question: 'Has the happy, post war marriage between the nation state and the welfare state come to an end?' (Hagen 1998). Given the persistence of the best-selling crisis perspectives, one may wonder if, and to what extent, the alternative conception of a 'happy marriage' was ever true.

In my view, crisis perspectives have tended to be overblown, but may have served the purpose of political warnings to forestall systemic breakdowns. A more fitting interpretation, though, is that the possibility of processes of piecemeal, democratic adaptation to changing social, economic and political circumstances and challenges appears to have been underestimated. One might even argue that the marriage between nation state and welfare state has never been stronger than today. Divorce is hardly in question, but perhaps a reasonable long-term perspective might be that the relationship between nation state and welfare state has moved from loose, scattered co-habitation (limited coverage, weak rights, means-testing) through stable, 'eternal' marriage (universal coverage, strong entitlements, generous benefits) towards a future of legally regulated, binding co-habitation (universal coverage, basic rights, adequate benefits)? The nation state is – not least because of the welfare state – a different state than it was 40, 80 or 100 years ago, but any state of today is also part of an entirely different international environment. For reasons of endogenous, as well as exogenous, factors, the Nordic and other European welfare states are likely to change. However, we do not necessarily have to exclaim 'crisis!' every time social or welfare reforms are made: it would indeed be a strange capitalist conservative-liberal-social democratic society that did not experience continuous social reform activity.

Contrary to anticipations promulgated by crisis theories, the welfare states of Western Europe continued to grow during the 1980s and 1990s in terms of expenditures and beneficiaries, and in many instances also in terms of employees. The overall scope of the welfare state is probably nowhere in Western Europe much less in 1999 than it was in the early 1980s. Why is that? A number of reasons can be listed: established social rights and entitlements have automatically led to an increase in expenditure as the composition of the population changed, first and foremost an increase in the number of old age pensioners, but also a significant increase in numbers of disability pensioners, unemployment income compensation beneficiaries and social assistance recipients; the effect of conscious political decisions to improve social security or welfare schemes or to establish new programmes; the ability of the welfare state – and especially the health system – to meet more needs than earlier, which again has led to increased demand; the growing saliency of some known problems, such as unemployment; and of some relatively new 'problems' or needs, resulting from an increase in divorces and single-parent households.

No doubt, the welfare state has met, and will in the future face, great challenges. Empirical research on changes in European welfare states during the last two decades has shown that, almost everywhere, successful attempts to reduce benefit levels in selected social security or welfare programmes have taken place, but that there appears to be no uniform pattern of cutbacks, and are few signs of radical or fundamental change. Welfare cutbacks and reforms have been strictly limited in scope (Pierson 1994, 1996). Popular electoral support for the welfare state has remained strong all over Europe, but whether this is a good or bad indicator for the future viability of the welfare state can be questioned. High expectations of more state welfare may have to be adjusted downwards in light of public budgets, public debts and unemployment levels and expenditure. West European welfare states face some similar challenges, and assumed unifying forces generated by accelerated European economic integration may give further impetus to this perspective. However, great institutional variations between European welfare states persist – variations as to coverage or access to social programmes; to benefit structures; to financing regulations; and to organisational arrangements. At the macro-institutional level, it is still meaningful to talk about (at least) 'four social Europes' (Ferrera 1997) in Western Europe.[3] Different types of welfare states may also face different kinds of challenges, and be equipped with different political and institutional capabilities to cope with specified challenges.

Against the background of a general reflection on 'the state of the welfare state' in developed, West European welfare states, I shall give an account of recent social reform activity in the Nordic welfare states, which are sometimes perceived as the 'most advanced', 'most developed' or at least – in more neutral terms – as the most expensive and comprehensive welfare states in terms of governmental effort put into welfare provision. In the final section I shall round off with a reasoned perspective on the sustainability of European and Nordic types of welfare states.

Although the European Union and processes of European economic integration do, and will, play a role – directly or indirectly – in the future configuration of welfare states and societies in Europe (e.g. Leibfried and Pierson 1995; Scharpf 1997; Teague 1998), I shall focus almost exclusively on within-nation developments affecting welfare state trajectories. This limitation of the discussion below does not mean that I do not consider within-nation contexts to be (increasingly) influenced by international social, economic and political development, but I subscribe to the view that fundamentally 'welfare states are [still] national states' (Swaan 1990).

Limits to state welfare

In all societies, welfare is provided by a mixture of providers: the state (central and/or local government); firms (based on market demand or welfare for own employees); households/families; and voluntary organisations. These providers – and interrelationships between them – have varying importance over time and across the 'four social Europes': e.g. the state and public sector have overall importance in Scandinavia; families and voluntary organisations relatively more importance in Southern Europe. Much research has gone into why different types or 'models' of welfare states have developed in Europe: different pre-industrial social structures, historically different state–society relations, different political institutions and timing of democratisation, degree of homogeneity of population and cultural characteristics, state capacity and characteristics of the state of 'social knowledge', all of which frame different debates, problem perceptions and induce different preferences for institutional solutions to social problems, needs or demands. New ideas and solutions to (old and new) problems hit or fall upon political systems and societies at different points in 'developmental time'.

Currently, with much economic determinism dominating political debate and public policy studies in general and welfare state studies in particular (e.g. the claim that 'globalisation of capital mobility leads to less state welfare' – without taking political agency into consideration) we do well to remind ourselves that social insurance was a political invention, a politically motivated invention leading to the establishment and cross-national spread of institutions which in the beginning were weakly correlated with scope of industrialisation, level of economic development, 'social problem pressure', degree of democracy and visions of a socially just society. Thus, social insurance – and a variety of different principles of coverage, financing and organisation – was instituted in different economic, social and political institutional settings, and different relationships between different welfare providers, and different weight to different providers, were established. 'Heavy' pre-social insurance structures and institutions (e.g. the supra-national Catholic Church, the family in Southern Europe; a merged state and church bureaucracy, local government in Scandinavia) undoubtedly have a long-lasting impact, as do the early institutions of social insurance that were established. Everything else being equal (which everything else tends not to be), institutional inertia is one factor why *different* welfare models persist in Europe, and one factor why *welfare states* persist and are likely to do so: politics and institutions matter.

Since the early 1980s there has been growing attention to the welfare role played by the market, family and voluntary organisations among political and bureaucratic elites, mass media, social science researchers and, to some extent, voters. Paradoxically, this new attention based on sharp criticism of the welfare state emanated from political leaders of the 'less advanced' of Western welfare states: Thatcher in Britain and Reagan in the USA, but this paradox serves to emphasise the importance of political rather than economic factors for policy change. Likewise, welfare cutbacks have subsequently not been shown to be more pronounced in the expensive and comprehensive Scandinavian countries than in leaner welfare states.

A more general indicator of an increased attention devoted to non-state welfare providers came in an OECD-publication some 20 years ago: 'New relationships between action by the state and private action must be thought; new agents for welfare and well-being developed; the responsibilities of individuals for themselves and others reinforced. It is in this sense that the emergence of the Welfare Society is both inevitable and desirable' (OECD 1981: 12). This political statement, usually more directly wrapped in terms of economic rationalism, was based upon perceptions of demographic and economic challenges and implied a clear ambition to shift the burden of welfare responsibilities among the various possible welfare providers. Modifications of welfare programmes have occurred all over Europe since then, but without much affecting the overall cost of the welfare state (given demographic composition, entitlements, increasing welfare needs). The new awareness of other possible welfare providers than the state may have been induced by perceived economic or financial imperatives and constraints, and thus modifications of schemes could be looked upon as simply pragmatic adjustments to 'economic realities' as defined by those in a position to define. The new awareness can also be interpreted as an indicator of a major ideological shift: that state 'monopoly' of welfare provision is not a good thing, that maximum state organised welfare is not necessarily an expression of the most progressive welfare policy, that voluntary organisations offer other qualities in welfare provision, that market competition can stimulate both better and more efficient health and other welfare service delivery. On the rhetorical-ideological level, the welfare state has also been claimed to undermine individual initiative, threaten economic prosperity, and create a 'dependency culture' (as if markets, organisations and families do not create dependencies).

These arguments and beliefs to justify less state welfare may be fictional or 'real' according to some inter-subjective standard. We still lack a model that explains how and why the boundaries between market, state, voluntary agencies and the family in the provision of social welfare change over time and across countries (Paci 1987). It is also an empirical, under-researched question to what extent boundaries, in fact, have changed. One hypothesis could be that, controlled for demographic composition, as people and countries become richer, more resources will be spent on welfare because meeting welfare needs has high priority for individuals as well as for governments in democratic societies. Thus, although there have been cuts and adjustments of benefits in many social security schemes in European countries, the overall governmental expenditure effort has increased in absolute terms. What may have happened since the 1980s at a general level is that welfare provided by other 'agents', other resource allocation mechanisms, has increased at the same time. Thus, we may observe not so much a shift in the welfare mix formula as a simultaneous growth of all kinds of welfare provision. Statistics on welfare provision offered by non-governmental agencies, institutions and companies are not systematically collected or readily available, so this must remain a hypothesis as this stage. However, the logic of the argument is valid: welfare provision is not a zero-sum game between providers.

Ideology and rhetoric aside, why is it likely that the relative role (if not necessarily the absolute role, at least not in the first place) of the state will decline in the decades ahead? My argument would go like this: more wealth in society and higher incomes for a large part, for a large majority, of the population in a country give greater meaning to the concept 'freedom of choice', or to use the concepts and theory developed by Hirschman (1971): greater individual economic resources make 'exit' from an organisation possible, and greater individual resources make it more likely that possible alternative providers will arise as a reaction to subjectively felt poor quality, or declining quality of services, or unmet demand, in – in this case – the public state welfare system (e.g. waiting lists for health operation; infrequent home help services; low income replacement in public pension scheme). As long as the state provides a near monopoly of social insurance, health and welfare services, the use of a political voice to demand better or more services is realistically the only option open for dissatisfied voters. When the majority of the population was relatively less well off, one would expect – at least, for historical reasons, in a Scandinavian context – that demands for equal or universal access to welfare resulted in a political pressure for more state welfare.

Income and wealth means freedom of choice, and one hypothesis could be that people are rather pragmatic as to choosing between public and private providers of welfare, as long as services are considered good, satisfactory and efficient. If one values equality of quality of services, or equal access to the best possible services, the problem is of course that a dual public-private welfare system most likely will become differentiated in the way that the private providers pay better wages for professional employees as well as provide better services catering to the economically well-off in society, and that the economically well off will gradually lose interest in paying taxes for a public system they do not need for their own welfare demands, thus causing further differentiation of private and public service provision and deterioration of the public system. Still, the possibility of 'exit' does not necessarily lead to massive exit. The threat of exit can be efficient, and the use of 'voice' can be more productive once the threat of exit is real. There is also the possibility that public versus private welfare provision are not substitutes: people can have both, or even more, kinds of welfare provision at the same time.

There is also a third possibility (and fourth, if we consider the family) beyond the dichotomy public versus private or market welfare provision: namely, provision by voluntary organisations and institutions, which have been, and can be, more or less dependent upon, or integrated with, either the market or government. Weisbrod (1977) argues that changes over time and across countries in the substitution ratios among the three sectors can be explained in terms of political demand and changes in per capita income levels: until a political majority is able to demand public provision of a collective good, the minority will have to remain satisfied with voluntary organisations. As sufficiently coherent political demand emerges and as society generates sufficient national income, it moves to supplant traditional family or charitable provisions with public welfare. Once per capita income reaches a relatively high level, however, consumers develop diversified needs and seek market substitutes for the public provision of goods.[4]

This perspective may supplement the exit–voice perspective. A graphic illustration of one element of this hypothesis applied to the size of the welfare state would be an inverted U-curve for the relationship between the size of the welfare state and income levels in society. As income increases, market and other substitutes or supplements to public welfare are likely to develop because consumers (in the roles of voters, parents, children, in-laws, patients, clients, gainfully employed, etc) develop, and can act upon their, more or less diversified needs (determined by a number of factors), thus causing market and 'third sector' welfare provision to develop as complements or supplements to public welfare. An overall increase in the demand for welfare may thus subsequently lead to a greater supply of welfare provision. Paci (1987) claims that there is a revival of the voluntary sector that seems to confirm a long-waved cyclical development of the complex system of social protection. I am not so sure it is revived as much as it is rediscovered. Whether the voluntary sector in relative terms plays a more important role today than 30–40 years ago is questionable, but it may play a different role because it relates differently to both market and the state, and voluntary organisations themselves may be of a different character and function differently (Selle and Øymyr 1995).

My expectation would be, though, that in Nordic and European societies with high levels of income, a large middle class, a large and growing class of well-off, highly educated pensioners, and in a situation where welfare needs enjoy high priority and increasing welfare needs are not easily met by the welfare state, more space for market and 'third sector' solutions will be opened. Once this space is being filled, the relative importance of the state will decline, and the longer term scenario will be that more mixed welfare provision will give new generations a different experience from older generations, thus, perhaps, slowly reducing expectations towards the welfare state and the high demands for state welfare that have been evident during most of the post World War II period. Younger generations will grow accustomed to finding non-public solutions, and most likely, more frequently, also solutions outside the nation state. With the EU and the European Economic Area (EEA), the market for welfare, health and social insurance services is no longer limited to the territory of the nation state: supply and demand will grow across national boundaries, something that will also in itself reduce the near public monopoly (in Scandinavia) of welfare provision today. The likely development of a greater proportion of trans-national households may also undermine the 'monopoly' position of national welfare states, and a likely more heterogeneous (ethnic, cultural) composition of 'national' populations may also make it more difficult to preserve or create the political consensus for unified state welfare solutions (Barry 1983; Baldwin 1997; Østerud 1999).

In all likelihood, welfare policies and institutions will be, and must remain, largely national, but a possible weakening national integration, due both to European and global integration (leading to individualisation?) on the one hand and the resurgence of regional identities at the sub-national level on the other, may reduce the possibilities of nationwide solidarity and redistribution. Both changes in social structure and the demographic transition will most likely affect institutional adjustments and changes of welfare states. Developments towards more segmented welfare states, 'dual welfare states', are likely, although national governments may still maintain regulatory and taxation tools to control the growth of market-based and other non-governmental welfare provision in such a way that universal access to quality welfare provision and relatively equal distributions of income and welfare are politically possible. These will remain domestic issues and choices for which national governments can, to a large extent, be held politically accountable. However, the social and political bases for state-organised solidarity are changing and, perhaps, so is the possibility of certain forms of organised solidarity.

On the other hand, new forms of solidarity may develop on a trans-national or trans-regional basis – state boundaries, will to a lesser extent than before, constrain such solidarity from developing. Tendencies towards more space for the market, through fiscal and occupational welfare, and greater emphasis on voluntary welfare, and the tendency towards more European, cross-national private 'social' insurance and welfare provision, can result in organisational fragmentation, social segmentation and complexity of the welfare system, which is not easily 'corrected' at the national level, even if a political majority within a nation should wish to change its course. This kind of Europeanisation is brought about not by 'positive' political decisions at the European level, but indirectly by the opportunities for organisations, business and individuals created by the common market and the four freedoms, or by what is called 'negative integration' (Leibfried and Pierson 1995), or what I would prefer to label 'passive integration'.

The trajectory of Nordic welfare states into the 1990s[5]

The idea of national social insurance dawned on European countries at different stages of social and economic development and political institution-building at the end of the nineteenth century. In the relatively poor Norway, with industrialisation in its infancy, the concept of a

109

'people's insurance' was coined in political debates earlier than elsewhere and already at the time of entry into the twentieth century. Soon afterwards, Swedish social democrats adopted the term 'people's home' to market the vision of the welfare society to be developed. The term embodies an all-inclusiveness that, even now, characterises the Scandinavian welfare states. More than elsewhere in Europe 'peasants were carriers of freedom and equality' (Sørensen and Stråth 1997: 8) in Scandinavia. The combination of relatively egalitarian pre-industrial social structures and homogenous (and small) populations in terms of language, religion and culture, was very likely conducive to the gradual development of comprehensive, principally tax-financed, redistributive and universal social and welfare policies.

That the state (and local government as the more or less autonomous arm of the state) came to be the prime welfare provider can probably be attributed to the observation that no major competing welfare provider existed. The secular state did not have to relate to a supra-national church with its separate institutions for education and health services. Thanks to the Lutheran Reformation during the first half of the 1500s, the Church and State bureaucracies were fused under the mantel of the State. 'The market' was not much of an alternative for social insurance in Scandinavia when conservative Bismarck's radical idea for social insurance quickly spread northwards in the 1880s (Kuhnle 1981), and the 'civil society' of voluntary non-governmental organisations was of limited scope. For historical-institutional reasons, the role of the state is, even at the end of the twentieth century, seen as legitimate, perhaps more so than elsewhere in Europe. Scandinavian societies are more 'state-friendly', indeed, 'state' and 'society' are sometimes used to mean the same thing (Allardt 1986).

The Scandinavian (or more precisely the 'Nordic'[6]) welfare states share a number of common characteristics, such that researchers tend to group them into one specific category of 'welfare regime' (Esping-Andersen 1990), 'model' (Leibfried 1993), 'family of nations' (Castles 1993), or 'type of welfare state' (Ferrera 1997; Kuhnle and Alestalo 2000). Concepts and classifications of various 'social Europes' are based on different sets of more or less precise indicators of institutional characteristics and/or institutional and public policy outcomes. The unpretentious concept of 'type of welfare state' suggests that countries and welfare states can be classified by characteristics of the 'welfare mix' of the four major providers of welfare in society: the state, the market, the civil society and the family. Thus, although all four possible providers have been, and still are, active (and interactive) in Scandinavian countries as elsewhere in Europe, the dominant role of the state is paramount in the Scandinavian setting.

International winds of welfare state criticism and warnings quickly reached the Scandinavian shores during the 1980s, but have hardly seemed to rock the solid historical position of the state (meaning both central and local government; the public sector) in the welfare state. Despite some significant economic problems, especially at the beginning of the 1990s in Sweden and Finland, Scandinavian countries have fundamentally maintained and, to some extent, also strengthened, their welfare states during the last decade. In the Scandinavian case(s) of the 1990s, economic rather than ideological factors must, however, be said to have catalysed reforms. The 'stateness' of the welfare state has been fundamentally preserved. Political solutions have been tempered by institutions and normative legacies.

Among the Nordic countries, Sweden and Finland experienced the most critical economic problems in the early 1990s, Finland the most severe backlash. The Finnish case was a result of the combined effect of international recession, effect on trade of the fall of the Soviet Union, and of the decision to link the Finnish Markka to the Deutschmark at a time when the latter was extremely solid (Heikkilä and Uusitalo 1997). Gross domestic product declined in each of the three years 1991–93, in 1991 by almost 8%. From an average unemployment rate of 4.8% during the 1980s, the figure during 1991–97 averaged 15% (OECD 1997a), with a peak figure of 17.7% as an average in 1993 (Ploug 1999: 82). This is a Nordic post World War II record: Denmark reached 12.4% in 1993 (Nososco 1997: 8), the rate in Sweden jumped from 1.3% in 1989 to a postwar peak of 8.2% in 1993 (not counting those on labour market programmes), while the rate in oil-rich Norway peaked at about 6% in 1993 (Marklund and Nordlund 1999; Ploug 1999). The unemployment rates have been steadily falling across the Nordic countries since the mid-1990s. The Finnish budget deficit peaked at 70% of GDP in 1995 (OECD 1996). A declining GDP combined with high unemployment pushed social expenditure as a proportion of GDP up to the level of 37.8% in 1993. The struggle to regain control of public finances led to more radical policy changes in Finland than in the other Nordic country in some serious trouble, Sweden.

Sweden lived through its worst economic recession since the 1930s in the early 1990s. Besides the soaring unemployment figures, GDP declined during each of the three years 1991–93. Central government budget deficits increased substantially, and government debt as a percentage of GDP reached the level of 83–85% during the period 1993–96 (OECD 1997d). Primarily because of unemployment and a declining GDP, social expenditure as a proportion of GDP peaked at 40.3% in 1993. The Swedish economy started to grow again in 1994, resulting in increased exports, large and growing surplus on foreign trade and on the balance of payments (Nososco 1997: 17).

Denmark has had quite high unemployment figures since the 'first oil-crisis' in the 1970s, and started restructuring the public finances and the welfare state in the 1980s. Denmark achieved solid economic growth during the mid-1980s, and again from 1992–93 (OECD 1997b). During Europe's 'annum horribilis' in 1993, the Danish economy showed a solid balance of payments, foreign trade surpluses, and ultralow inflation. Since 1993, unemployment has fallen consistently to about 7% in 1999. For the first time in ten years, the state budget showed a surplus in 1997.

Although Norway was affected by the international recession and experienced an economic setback around 1990, the economy has grown persistently every year since 1989. Large revenues from the oil and gas sector makes Norway a unique case. The average annual GDP growth rate was 3.5% during 1990–96, compared to an OECD average of 2.5%, and the EU average of 1.7% (OECD 1997a). Unemployment has fallen to a level below 3% as of September 1999. For the first and only time since 1950, the general government financial balance was in the negative in 1992–93, but is now well back on the plus side – with the biggest surplus (estimated at 6.8% of GDP) in Europe in 1997 (OECD 1997c).

All four nations were affected by the international recession around 1990, but to a greatly varying degree. Judging from indicators of economic development, one should expect Sweden and Finland to be much more active in welfare reform activities than Denmark and Norway, including efforts to cut back on welfare spending. This has also been the case. All have striven to reduce spending by the public sector at large, but governmental final consumption per capita has increased rapidly since the early 1980s through the mid-1990s in Norway, while the trend in Sweden has been the opposite. Denmark was, by 1995, the most costly Nordic country, and has also overtaken Sweden in terms of public spending (Marklund and Nordlund 1999: 24–25), although public expenditure as a percentage of GDP declined in Denmark during the latter half of the 1990s (Goul Andersen 2000). In all four countries, trade surpluses have been growing in the 1990s, thus indicating that the economies have recuperated and are strong at the end of the 1990s.

All four Nordic countries under review had universal coverage of old age pension systems, sickness insurance, occupational injury insurance, child allowance and parental leave schemes at the time of the international recession around 1990. The unemployment insurance was in principle compulsory only in Norway, while only union members were covered in the other three countries, although unemployment cash assistance would normally be available for the non-insured. The same overall institutional pattern existed at the end of the 1990s, although the introduction of a partial income-test of the 'pension-supplement'-part of the basic old-age pension in Denmark in 1994 can be seen as a potentially significant change towards some element of means-testing of the amount of pension benefits. In a similar vein, the pension reform passed in Sweden in 1998, to be implemented in 2001, which restricts the payment of the previously universal basic amount to people with no, or low, employment-derived pension, can be seen as important. The Finnish pension reform of 1996–97, similarly, limits the hitherto universal minimum national pension to pensioners with employment-derived pensions below a certain limit. In all countries, however, all citizens/residents will still automatically be entitled to an old-age pension. With the exception of Denmark, all countries had an earnings-related supplementary pension scheme for all employees and self-employed both at the start and end of the 1990s. In Denmark, with the most generous basic pension of the Nordic countries (Nososco 1997: 103), all employees (only) have been entitled to a modest non-earnings-related supplement, but a labour market pension scheme agreed between the labour market partners in 1989 has given Denmark a *de facto* earnings-related pension system.

In all four countries, some reduction of pension benefit levels or income replacement rates has been decided in the 1990s, most markedly in Finland and Sweden. In Norway, the earnings-related part was modified in 1992, while the basic minimum pension was substantially increased in 1998. In Finland, the old-age pension system has seen several changes in the 1990s: index-linking and cuts in the employment-derived part; lowering of age limit for part-time pensions; and the increase of retirement age for some groups in the public sector. The pension reform of 1996–97 implies a stronger link between contributions and pensions, and a greater importance of work history. The Swedish parliament initiated a reform process in 1994 through a solid and broad cross-party effort, and passed a law in 1998 which implies a move from a 'defined benefit' to a 'defined contribution' system, thus also creating a closer link between contributions and payments.

There has been no change in the principle of universal coverage of sickness insurance in any of the countries during the 1990s, but a tightening of the qualifying conditions has been made in Finland and Sweden, but not in Denmark and Norway. Only in Norway has the wage replacement rate remained stable (100% up to a maximum of six times the so-called 'basic amount' in the insurance scheme), while it has been significantly reduced in the three other Nordic countries. Only Denmark and Norway have maintained a system free of waiting days.

The sickness cash benefit scheme is the most frequently and extensively reformed area of the Swedish social security system in the 1990s.

All four countries have introduced stricter qualifying conditions for unemployment insurance during the 1990s. The income replacement rate has been significantly reduced in Sweden, which has also introduced waiting days. Denmark has now the only scheme without waiting days, on the other hand the maximum period for which benefits could be paid has been reduced from a very generous nine to a still (comparatively speaking) generous five years. All countries offer support for the education of unemployed, and active labour market programmes have been improved in the 1990s. In Finland, a partially means-tested benefit known as 'labour market support' was introduced in 1994 to secure the basic livelihood of long term unemployed and young people with no job experience.

All countries have held on to their universal child allowance schemes and had, in a European comparison, generous schemes for maternity benefits and maternity/parental leave. The parental leave period has been significantly extended in Norway, from 28/35 weeks to 42/52 weeks leave at 100/80% wage compensation, from the beginning to the end of the decade, but Sweden has kept its 'leading' position with 64 weeks of parental leave, although the wage compensation level has, as in Finland, been reduced markedly (as for sickness insurance). In all four countries the schemes allow for a father's period of leave, and this period has been increased in Denmark and Norway during the 1990s. Kindergarten coverage was relatively high in 1990, especially in Denmark and Sweden (64 and 48% coverage for children 0–6 years, but in Norway only 33%). By 1995, the coverage had increased in all four countries, in Norway and Sweden in particular, indicating a real and important welfare priority during a period of economic downturn (in Sweden).

Almost all health and social care services are funded from tax revenues and provided by public authorities in Scandinavia. The principle of universalism covers not only social security schemes, but also access to health and social care services, with the partial, but important, exception of dental treatment for adults. In the health sector, user charges for services have gradually been introduced in Finland, Norway and Sweden, but with rules which set a defined maximum payment of user charges. Medical treatment is still free of charge in Denmark, and to be expected, there are more medical consultations per capita in Denmark than in the other countries (in 1994 there were 4.8 consultations per capita, in Sweden 3.0; Nososco 1997: 88). Hospital service is still mainly a public issue as there are few private hospitals in Scandinavia but, partly as a response to the problem of 'health queues', there has been a trend of develop-ment of private health centres with out-patient clinics/'policlinics' which charge market prices for treatments. The organisation of the health sector is otherwise primarily the responsibility of the municipal and/or county authorities. In all countries, dental treatment for children and young people has remained completely or partly free of charge, while the rest of the population generally pays all costs for treatment themselves, or is reimbursed a small part of the costs.

Public expenditure on health per capita was significantly higher in Sweden than in the other Nordic countries in the early 1980s, but by 1994 Norway was on top (Lehto *et al.* 1999: 106–107). Expenditure per capita increased during the first half of the 1990s in Denmark, and especially Norway, but declined in Finland and Sweden. Expenditure on services for the elderly and handicapped has increased enormously in Norway since the early 1980s and in the 1990s, and also markedly in the temporarily 'crisis-ridden' Finland and Sweden during the first half

Table 6.1 The Nordic countries: Social expenditures as a percentage of GDP; social expenditure per inhabitant, 1995-prices, in national currencies (Kr/Fm); relative share of expenditures on services and cash benefits/transfers, 1990 and 1995.

	Social expenditure		Share of expenditure (%)	
	As % of GDP	Per inhabitant	Services	Cash transfers
Denmark				
1990	29.7	51104	34	66
1995	33.7	62288	35	65
Finland				
1990	25.7	28988	37	63
1995	32.8	35322	30	70
Norway				
1990	26.4	50503	35	65
1995	27.4	58181	42	58
Sweden				
1990	34.8	67481	41	59
1995	35.8	66692	39	61

Sources: Nososco 1992, 1997

of the 1990s. Denmark has had only a small increase, but had the most expensive system of social care services in place by the early 1980s.

A major comparative study of health and social care services in the Nordic countries concludes that 'the Nordic model of social and health services has not significantly weakened in the 1990s. As a matter of fact, the model is providing even better childcare. The differences between the Nordic countries decreased in the 1980s. There are some areas where the economic hardships of Sweden and Finland in the 1990s seem to have led to an increase in differences between them and the better off Norway and Denmark' (Lehto *et al.* 1999: 130). All countries, except Sweden, spent substantially more public resources per capita in real terms on social purposes in 1995 than in 1990 (see Table 6.1). The increase in absolute terms was about 22% in Denmark and Finland, 15% in Norway, and the slight decline in Sweden was about 1%. In both years, Sweden spent the highest share of GDP on social purposes. Despite substantial cuts in cash benefit levels, a declining share of social expenditures was spent on services in Finland and Sweden. In Denmark and Norway, with little or no cuts in cash transfer benefits, the share of expenditure for services went up, and this was particularly marked in Norway. The reasons for these patterns are that increasing unemployment levels resulted in a sharp increase in cash transfer benefits in the two 'eastern' Nordic states, while the two 'western' Nordic states expanded services as responses to persistent or increasing needs and demand. The limit to welfare state growth in absolute terms seems not yet to have been reached in the Nordic area.

Let me put Scandinavia in some European perspective. A comparison with the other group of most expensive European welfare states shows that, in 1990, social expenditure as a proportion of GDP was on average slightly lower in the Nordic countries compared with the average for Continental European countries:[7] 28.1% versus 29.6%; however, by 1995 the Nordic average had reached 32.1%, while Continental Europe stood at 30.1% (Kuhnle and Alestalo 2000). However, Scandinavian 'exceptionalism' really stands out in terms of one indicator of the 'stateness' of the welfare states: in 1990, government employment as a percentage of total employment was, on average, 26.9% while, on average, 18.7% in Continental Europe, while in 1995, after the phase of the severe economic downturn in Finland and Sweden, the average Nordic figure had, perhaps surprisingly, increased to 29.4%, while it was still only 18.8% in Continental Europe[8] (Kuhnle and Alestalo, 2000). Not only government employment, but employment levels as a whole are generally higher in Scandinavia (and the United Kingdom), with the highest levels of female employment (mostly for welfare state provision of services) in the OECD area (OECD 1997: 41).

Contrary to the general recipe proposed by the OECD crisis report from 1981, i.e. stimulate non-state welfare provision, Scandinavian countries have consolidated state welfare solutions and employment. This has happened whether countries have been through periods of serious economic turmoil or not in the 1990s, and the four countries have all entered a new period of steady economic growth in the latter half of the 1990s. Perhaps one may be justified in declaring that history has proven the OECD 1981 diagnosis to have been ideologically motivated, or alternatively, to have been wanting in imagination as to how welfare states can adjust to changing economic, demographic and other circumstances, and how welfare state growth and economic growth can still go hand in hand in 'advanced' welfare states. A possible lesson can be drawn or reiterated: it is not so much a question of *how much* public money is spent on welfare, but *how* money is spent, which seems important.

Public support for the welfare state in Scandinavia has traditionally been high. New studies show no declining long-term trend in support for the welfare state (Goul Andersen *et al.* 1999: 255–256). Universal welfare schemes are, in all countries, more popular than selective ones, in accordance with findings beyond the Nordic area. Universal health care and old-age pension programmes are the most popular. Programmes for social assistance, housing benefits and unemployment benefits are less popular. Among voters, the division between the political left and right is very small in Norway, more marked in Sweden. Such contrasts reflect historical differences between the more polarised 'class politics' in Sweden and the more 'consensual' politics in Norway during the post World War II period.

The politics of Scandinavian welfare reform in the 1990s, mostly reducing the generosity of schemes, is characterised by efforts to create compromises across competing parties and across the government–opposition division. This may be seen as joint efforts of 'blame avoidance'. Politics in general has been pushed towards more compromises simply because majority coalition governments or minority governments have become the order of the day. The era of one-party (social democratic) majority government (in Norway and Sweden only) seems to be gone for ever: not since 1961 in Norway and 1970 in Sweden have one party majority governments existed in Scandinavia (Petersson 1998). More governmental 'instability' has given parliaments and opposition parties more power. Thus, changes in the way the main political institutions work against any government proposals for radical changes in policies, unless support from at least part of the parliamentary opposition is secured.

The situation invites compromises over welfare policies, and trade-offs between various policy areas. No major political party or political actor in any of the Nordic countries has called for state withdrawal from central spheres of health and social security, although parties on the right are favourable to more private alternatives and supplements. Both at mass and elite levels widespread support for public responsibility for welfare provision persists. Signs that, in the 1990s, welfare reforms are, to a greater extent, achieved through compromises across traditional (left-right) political cleavages are most evident in Finland, with its 'Rainbow-co-alition' government of 1995, made up of representatives from the Conservatives, Greens, Left-wing Alliance, Swedish People's and Social Democrats Party.

Nordic and European welfare states likely to stay

Despite the assessment that 'the Nordic welfare states had truly "grown to limits", be it in terms of comprehensiveness, universalism, or benefit generosity' (Stephens 1996), it has been shown above that Nordic welfare states, with the slight exception of Sweden, continued to grow significantly in terms of real social expenditure per capita in the 1990s. The Norwegian welfare state definitely grew both in comprehensiveness (parental leave scheme) and benefit generosity (minimum pensions, child allowances), while expenditure growth in Finland typically, even with substantial cuts in benefit levels, reflected an increase in the number of beneficiaries with entitlements. If one should extract a single common denominator for the welfare state development in the Nordic countries in the 1990s, it would be a *less generous welfare state*, but Norway – 'the Kuwait of Scandinavia' – does not fit into the picture. The basic structure of the welfare systems has been preserved, with the partial exception of the pension reforms in Denmark (1994), Finland (1996) and Sweden (1998). Although all of the Nordic countries are now more open for private initiatives in the fields of health services, social care services and social insurance than before, a trend which not only reflects strained public budgets but also large, well-to-do middle classes preferring diversified responses to welfare needs of various kinds, no political party – and very few voters – favour a deconstructed welfare state.

The observation that the Nordic countries seem to have overcome the 'crisis' or dramatic economic challenges of the early 1990s with reasonable economic success towards the end of the decade, and with welfare state institutions and programmes largely intact, makes it less likely that the Nordic type of welfare state can be judged fit for the dustbin of history. The Nordic welfare states stood the test, and the Finnish case is particularly illustrative. The Finnish experience may teach other governments a lesson: an advanced, universalistic, welfare state is not a handicap when a sudden, unexpected economic crisis occurs. On the contrary, the type and format of the welfare state may have helped the Nordic countries, and Finland especially, more rapidly through the 'crisis' than a welfare state of another, less comprehensive, type might have done, and with less social damage[9]. 'Advanced' welfare states may be better prepared for crisis management and economic recovery. The Nordic experience in the 1990s shows that the universal and comprehensive welfare state can be a vital shock absorber that stabilises the economy and social conditions in such a way that the economy can recuperate fast and well.

Cutbacks in social security and welfare programmes in Western Europe have, on average, been modest during the 1980s and 90s, and real social expenditure has – for various reasons – continuously, in some places, substantially increased, during the last 15 years in most countries, i.e. after the period of 'Growth to Limits' (Flora 1986, 1987). The sustainability of the welfare state is given a high priority among voters (Ferrera 1993), a fact that sets European voters in general apart from voters in other parts of the world, the USA in particular: less than one third of the Americans were, in 1986, in favour of government responsibility for basic income for all, and for reducing income differences, and less than half of the US population were in favour of the government being responsible for creating jobs for all, whereas more than two thirds of the Europeans (from UK, Germany, Netherlands, Italy, Hungary) supported all these forms of state intervention (Flora 1993). In spite of a number of similar financial, employment and demographic problems and challenges, and common external challenges associated with European and global economic integration, European welfare states remain institutionally strong with solid support from voters and major political parties. Citizen welfare will continue to be a prime responsibility of the nation states.

The importance of the European Union is still very limited. In fact, the strength of national welfare states appears to make the need for the European level to be engaged less imminent. It is too early (if ever possible!) to say what kind of political entity the EU will become, but a stronger 'Political Europe' to match the 'Economic Europe' is likely to prove conducive for relatively advanced or comprehensive national welfare states – a 'Social Europe' – to survive.

The state is, however, likely to play a relatively less dominant role in the future social Europe given large, economically well-off middle classes that may demand exit options, choice and differentiated services. More space for market and other non-governmental welfare solutions has been opened within and across European nation states, and although more dual public–private welfare states are likely to appear, national governments enjoy a number of policy instruments to regulate and control developments in order to affect access to quality welfare services for all and relatively egalitarian income distributions. Whether to maintain and develop welfare states, and what kind of welfare states to develop, are questions of institutional persistence or 'conservatism', of 'strong' rights and entitlements, of vested interests, but also of political preferences and choices by governments, organisations, firms and individuals – choices that are influenced by institutions, experience, values, socio-structural change and economic opportunity.

We should make note of the apparent paradox that, at the same time as markets (of all kinds) are globalised, national state barriers lowered, many more nation states have been created during the last 15 years. This combined process of global economic integration and politicisation of territorial organisation has also meant that social security and other principles of original European welfare state policies, seem to undergo a process of globalisation. The world has more sovereign nation states than 10 years ago, and the number may still be increasing, even in Western Europe (e.g. Flanders, Scotland, Catalonia). More nation states than ever have now introduced at least one kind of social insurance scheme: 165 countries have introduced social insurance of one kind or another, most frequently an occupational injury insurance or pension scheme (Social Security Programmes Throughout the World 1995). The more nation states, the more public social security institutions in the world.

A number of major 'welfare state reforms' were made in East and Southeast Asia during the most recent 'economic miracle' period (1985–95), particularly in Korea, Taiwan, China and Thailand and there are, in spite of more poverty and social misery, few signs of 'welfare state dumping' after the 'crash of Summer of 1997' (Hort and Kuhnle, 2000). In fact, the lag between industrialisation and major state intervention for social protection was greater in Europe than it has been in industrialising Asia, in spite of the assumed or contended (continued) importance of Confucian values and traditions of family welfare provision. If America is not the leader here, a number of Asian countries are looking to Europe – and, more particularly, to the Nordic countries – for solutions for state welfare policies. These trends of Asian welfare development, which may embody somewhat different principles of organisation and financing than in European countries, are no guarantee for the survival of European welfare states, but the observation that state welfare schemes are spreading in the globalised world may indicate that some of the external pressure for retrenchment and down-scaling of European welfare states may be alleviated. In fact, because of fairly well-developed welfare states, Europe and Scandinavia may – if not in the immediate short-term – be better prepared to meet the challenges of demographic and socio-structural change in the modern world than other regions of the globe.

Scandinavian countries in particular, in which, for example, comprehensive social policies to support families (kindergartens, parental leave schemes, cash transfers, home help for the elderly, public support for institutional care) exist, may be better prepared for global competition than countries in which welfare provision is solely or primarily a family responsibility. It seems evident that family- and children-friendly policies have been more protected against cuts and retrenchment than other social policies in recent periods of economic and public budget strain. It would not be unreasonable to make the interpretation that strength of family and children oriented policies in Scandinavia correlates with strength of the incorporation of women in politics – in political parties, parliaments and governments – and in the government and 'welfare state' bureaucracy.

Thus, ultimately thanks to women's political mobilisation and integration into decision-making bodies, expensive Nordic countries may have developed a 'comparative advantage' if it can subsequently be shown that it is the type and scope of 'family-friendly' welfare state policies that secure relatively high fertility rates and (almost) population reproduction. The Nordic countries have, at the end of this century, Europe's highest proportions of female employment, the most comprehensive welfare states, and (with Ireland) the highest fertility rates. These characteristics seem interconnected.

Many factors influence decisions about investments, production and location of production facilities – not only low wages and maximisation of profit. Skilled labour, efficient public bureaucracy, little corruption, little poverty, limited social inequalities, public safety, safe environment, social and political stability, democracy and political accountability, are all factors that have a bearing upon decisions about where, how and at what cost to produce goods and services. An economically integrated Europe, with or without further political integration, may in this context also be a 'comparative advantage'.

European welfare states may, with a number of continuous adjustments and a different welfare mix, fare well. In my view, Nordic and European welfare states are likely to maintain, or advance, universal coverage of major welfare rights, but may in the longer run attend more to basic rights than to rights which today are earned through gainful employment: income and welfare security beyond basic levels may be left to individual and voluntary decisions and the market and other non-governmental welfare providers. The format of the welfare state may in the coming decades become different from that in the period of the most intense 'happy marriage between the nation state and the welfare state': less generous state welfare, and a slightly different mix of welfare provision.

Interpretations of history and anticipations of future development differ. It does not appear immediately likely that one of the major international actors in the globalised world, the World Bank, will announce to the world: 'Look to Europe!' It is even less likely to exclaim: 'Look to Scandinavia!' This might, nevertheless, be a good idea, and perhaps a look at Finland, which has experienced the most severe challenges of the Nordic welfare states in the 1990s, would be the most interesting and instructive start.

Acknowledgement

I thank participants at 'The Welfare State' seminar at the Research School of Social Sciences, Political Science Programme, Australian National University, 13 October 1999, for critical comments to a draft version.

Notes

1. For reasons I do not know, a 'nation' is normally referred to in the feminine, as is a 'ship' – and sometimes nations are also referred to as ships!
2. See van Kersbergen (2000) for a *tour de* crisis literature.
3. The conception of 'four social Europes', or similar conceptions of various types of West European welfare states, implies a distinction between a liberal, 'residual' or Anglo-Saxon type, a Continental, Bismarckian or 'corporatist' type, a Southern European, Catholic or 'rudimentary' type, and a Scandinavian, 'institutional' or 'social democratic' type.
4. One would imagine that not only income per capita is important, but also the distribution of income. A relatively equal income distribution in a rich country would imply a large, well-to-do middle class that it is assumed will form a stable basis for substantial non-governmental or private welfare provision.
5. More comprehensive analyses of social policy developments and the politics of welfare reform can be found in Eitrheim and Kuhnle (2000), and Kuhnle (2000).
6. 'Scandinavia' most correctly denotes Denmark, Norway and Sweden, while 'the Nordic countries' include also Finland and Iceland, and the semi-independent Greenland and Faroe Islands (under Denmark) and the Aland Islands (under Finland). Since the concept of 'Norden' has not yet entered the English language, it is seen as permitted to use 'Scandinavia' to encompass Finland and Iceland. Iceland is not included in the present analysis.
7. As Continental European countries, here are included: Austria, Belgium, France, Germany, the Netherlands.
8. Note that the figures indicate unweighted averages of proportions. The OECD definition of government employment is used and stems from the System of National Accounts. The definition covers 'producers of government services', those who are employed by central or local bodies in administration, defence, health, education and social services. The definition excludes most public enterprises.
9. According to Heikkilä and Uusitalo (1997), restructuring and benefit adjustments in the Finnish welfare state have been achieved without creating greater inequality in distribution of disposable income. Incomes are distributed roughly in the same way in 1997 as in the mid-1970s.

References

Alber, J. (1988) Is there a crisis of the welfare state?, *European Sociological Review*, **4**(3), 181–207.

Allardt, E. (1986) The civic conception of the welfare state in Scandinavia. In: R. Rose and R.Shiratori (eds) *The Welfare State. East and West*. New York: Oxford University Press, pp. 107–125.

Baldwin, P. (1997) State and citizenship in the age of globalization. In: P. Koslowski and A. Follesdal (eds) *Restructuring the Welfare State: Theory and Reform of Social Policy*. Berlin: Springer-Verlag, pp. 95–118.

Barry, B. (1983) Self–government revisited. In: Miller, D. and Siedentop, L. (eds), *The Nature of Political Theory*. Oxford: Clarendon Press.

Castles, F. G. (ed.) (1993) *Families of Nations: Patterns of Public Policy in Western Democracies*. Aldershot: Dartmouth.

Crozier, M., Huntington, S. P., and Watanuki, J. (eds) (1975) *The Crisis of Democracy*. New York: New York University Press.

Esping-Andersen, G. (1990) *The Three Worlds of Welfare Capitalism*. Cambridge: Polity Press.

Eitrheim, P. and Kuhnle, S. (2000) Nordic welfare states in the 1990s: Institutional stability, signs of divergence. In S. Kuhnle (ed) *Survival of the European Welfare State*. London: Routledge, pp. 39–58.

Ferrera, M. (1993) *EC Citizens and Social Protection. Main Results from a Eurobarometer Study*. Brussels: EC Commission, Div. V/E/2.

Ferrera, M. (1997) Four social Europes between universalism and selectivity. In: Y. Meny and M. Rhodes (eds) *A New Social Contract*. London: Macmillan, pp. 81–96.

Flora, P. (ed) (1986, 1987) *Growth to Limits. The Western European Welfare States Since World War II*, Vols. 1 and 2 (1986), Vol. 4 (1987). Berlin: Walter de Gruyter.

Flora, P. (1993) The national welfare states and European integration. In: Moreno, L. (ed) *Social Exchange and Welfare Development*. Madrid: Consejo Superior de Investigaciones Cientificas, pp. 11–22.

Goul Andersen, J. (2000) Welfare crisis and beyond: Danish welfare policies in the 1980s and 1990s. In: S. Kuhnle (ed.) *Survival of the European Welfare State*. London: Routledge, pp. 235–261.

Goul Andersen, J., Pettersen, P. A., Svallfors, S., and Unsitalō, H. (1999) The legitimacy of the Nordic welfare states: trends, variations and causes. In: M. Kautto, M. Heikkila, B. Hvinden, S. Marklund and N. Ploug (eds) *Nordic Social Policy. Changing Welfare States*. London: Routledge.

Habermas, J. (1976) *Legitimation Crisis*. London: Heinemann.

Hagen, K. (1998) Towards a Europeanization of social policies? A Scandinavian perspective. Paper presented at MIRE Conference (Comparing Social Welfare Systems in Nordic Countries and France), Gilleleje, Denmark 4–6 September (*mimeo.*).

Heikkilä, M. and Uusitalo, H. (eds) (1997) *The Cost of the Cuts*. Helsinki, STAKES.

Hirschman, A. O. (1971) *Exit, Voice, and Loyalty*. Cambridge: Harvard University Press.

Hort, S. and Kuhnle, S. (2000) The coming of east and southeast Asian welfare states?, 2000 in *Journal of European Social Policy*, **10**(2), 162–184.

Kuhnle, S. (1981) The growth of social insurance programmes in Scandinavia: outside influences and internal forces. In: P. Flora and A.J. Heidenheimer (eds) *The Development of Welfare States in Europe and America*. New Brunswick: Transaction Books, pp. 125–150.

Kuhnle, S. (2000) The Scandinavian type of welfare state in the 1990s: challenged, but viable. In: M. Ferrera and M. Rhodes (eds) *Recasting European Welfare States*. London: Frank Cass, and in *West European Politics*, **23**(2), 209–228.

Kuhnle, S. and Alestalo, M. (2000) Introduction: growth, adjustments and survival of European welfare states. In: S. Kuhnle (ed) *Survival of the European Welfare State*. London: Routledge, pp. 3–18.

Lehto, J. Moss, N. and Rostgaard, T. (1999) Universal public social care and health services?, M. Kautto *et al.* (eds) *Nordic Social Policy*. London: Routledge, pp. 104–132.

Leibfried, S. (1993) Towards a European welfare state? On integrating poverty regimes in the European Community. In: C. Jones (ed) *New Perspectives on the Welfare State*. Oxford: Blackwell, pp. 133–156

Leibfried, S. and Pierson, P. (1995) Semisovereign welfare states: social policy in a multitiered Europe. In: Leibfried and Pierson (eds) *European Social Policy: Between Fragmentation and Integration*. Washington DC: Brookings, 43–77.

Marklund, S. and Nordlund, A. (1999) Economic problems, welfare convergence and political instability. In: M. Kautto *et al* (eds) *Nordic Social Policy*. London: Routledge, pp. 19–53.

Nososco (1992) Social trygghet i de nordiske land: omfang, utgifter og finansiering 1990, Statistical Reports of the Nordic Countries no 58. Copenhagen: Nordic Social–Statistical Committee.

Nososco (1997) Social protection in the Nordic countries: scope, expenditure and financing 1995, Nordic Social–Statistical Committee no 7:97. Copenhagen.

O'Connor, J. (1973) *The Fiscal Crisis of the State*. NY: St. Martins Press.

OECD (1981) *The Welfare State in Crisis*. Paris: OECD.

OECD (1996) *Economic Surveys: Finland*. Paris: OECD.

OECD (1997) *Economic Outlook*, no.59. Paris: OECD.

OECD (1997a) *Economic Outlook*, no. 61 Paris: OECD.

OECD (1997b) *Economic Surveys: Denmark*. Paris: OECD.

OECD (1997c) *Economic Surveys: Norway*. Paris: OECD.

OECD (1997d) *Economic Surveys: Sweden*. Paris: OECD.

Østerud, Ø. (1999) *Globaliseringen og nasjonalstaten*. Oslo: AdNotam Gyldendal.

Paci, M. (1987) Long waves in the development of welfare systems. In Maier, C. (ed) *Changing Boundaries of the Political*. Cambridge: Cambridge University Press, pp. 179–200.

Petersson, O. (1998) *Nordisk politik*. Stockholm: Norstedts Juridik.

Pierson, P. (1994) *Dismantling the Welfare State? Reagan, Thatcher, and the Politics of Retrenchment*. Cambridge: Cambridge University Press.

Pierson, P. (1996) The new politics of the welfare state, *World Politics*, **48**(2): 143–79.

Ploug, N. (1999) Cuts in and reform of the Nordic cash benefit systems. In: M. Kautto *et al.* (eds) *Nordic Social Policy*. London: Routledge, pp. 79–103.

Rose, R. and Peters, G. (1978) *Can Government Go Bankrupt?*.

Scharpf, F. (1997) European integration, democracy, and welfare states, *Journal of European Public Policy*, **4**(1), 18–36

Selle, P. and Øymyr, B. (1995) *Frivillig organisering og demokrati* (Oslo: Samlaget).

Social Security Programmes Throughout the World 1995. Washington DC: Social Security Administration.

Sørensen, O. and Stråth, B. (1997) Introduction: the cultural construction of Norden in O. Sørensen and B. Stråth (eds) *The Cultural Construction of Norden*. Oslo: Scandinavian University Press, 1–24.

Stephens, J. (1996) The Scandinavian welfare states: achievements, crisis, and prospects. In: G. Esping–Andersen (ed) *Welfare States in Transition*. London: Sage, pp. 32–65.

Swaan, A. de (1990) Perspectives for transnational social policy. Paper, World Congress of Sociology, 9–13 July, Madrid (mimeo).

Teague, P. (1998) Monetary Union and social Europe, *Journal of European Social Policy*, **8**(2), 117–38.

Van Kersbergen, K. (2000) The declining resistance of welfare states to change? In S. Kuhnle (ed) *Survival of the European Welfare State*. London: Routledge, pp. 19–36.

Weisbrod, B.A. (1977) *The Voluntary Non–Profit Sector: An Economic Analysis*. Lexington, MA: Heath.

About the Author

Stein Kuhnle is Professor of Comparative Politics in the Department of Comparative Politics, University of Bergen, Norway. He has written extensively on the history and development of Scandinavian and European welfare states. His most recent book is *Survival of the European Welfare State* (London: Routledge, 2000).

European Review, Vol. 8, No. 3, 399–425 (2000) © Academia Europaea, Printed in the United Kingdom

7 The viability of advanced welfare states in the international economy Vulnerabilities and options[1]

FRITZ W. SCHARPF*

The paper presents a preliminary and partial analysis of the information collected in a comparative 12-country study of the adjustment of national employment and social-welfare policies to the increasing internationalisation of product and capital markets. After the postwar decades, when national governments were still able to control their economic boundaries, the first international challenge came in the form of the oil-price crisis of 1973/74, which confronted industrial economies with the double threat of cost-push inflation and demand-gap unemployment. It could be met if countries were able to achieve a form of 'Keynesian agreement' in which expansionary monetary and fiscal policies would defend employment while union wage restraint could be relied on to fight inflation. For this solution, 'corporatist' industrial-relations institutions were a necessary, but not a sufficient, condition. Since the second oil-price crisis of 1979–80 was met by restrictive monetary and expansionary fiscal policies in the United States, the steep increase of real interest rates in the international capital markets forced other central banks to raise interest rates accordingly. As a consequence, employment-creating investments could only be maintained if the share of profits in the national product was significantly increased. Under the pressure of rapidly rising unemployment, unions in most countries were forced to accept this massive redistribution from labour to capital. In the 1990s, finally, the international integration of product and capital markets has been constraining private sector employment as well as the financial viability of the welfare state. Now, however, institutional differences among different types of revenue systems, welfare states and employment systems – Scandinavian, Anglo-Saxon and Continental – are creating important differences in vulnerability that can no longer be met by standardised responses. This paper concludes with an examination of the specific

* Max Planck Institut für Gesellschaftsforschung, Paulstr. 3, 50676, Köln, Germany. E-mail: scharpf@mpi.fg.
koeln.mpg.de.
This article appears at full length under the same title with some revisions in the *Journal of European Public Policy* 2000, **7**(2)(June), 190–228. For the current article some of the detailed documentation (9 figures and 6 tables) have been omitted, but the argument is presented in full. For the full documentation the article in the *JEPP* should be consulted.

problems faced by, and the solutions available to, the different countries included in the study.

Introduction

Since the second oil-price crisis of 1979–80 was met by restrictive monetary and expansionary fiscal policies in the United States, the steep increase of real interest rates in the international capital markets forced other central banks to raise interest rates accordingly. As a consequence, employment-creating investments could only be maintained if the share of profits in the national product was significantly increased. Under the pressure of rapidly rising unemployment, unions in most countries were forced to accept this massive redistribution from labour to capital.

In the 1990s, finally, the international integration of product and capital markets has been constraining private sector employment as well as the financial viability of the welfare state. Now, however, institutional differences among different types of revenue systems, welfare states and employment systems – Scandinavian, Anglo-Saxon, and Continental – are creating important differences in vulnerability that can no longer be met by standardised responses. This paper concludes with an examination of the specific problems faced by, and the solutions available to, the different countries included in the study.

The rise of the capitalist welfare state

Modern welfare states have their roots in the last decades of the19th century and the first decade of the 20th century, when the international integration of capitalist economies had reached a high plateau. However, they only achieved their full development in the 'golden age' of the early postwar decades, under conditions of nearly closed national economies. After the rampant protectionism that followed the Great Depression and the complete breakdown of world markets in World War II, most currencies were not freely convertible, capital transfers were tightly controlled and internal financial markets were strictly regulated in most countries. The restoration of international trade in product markets was a slow process. Export dependence and import penetration were still limited, and the range of economic activities that were sheltered against international competition was quite large. Services were protected almost everywhere, as was agriculture in most countries, while manufacturing was generally more export oriented, except for Australia and New Zealand, which relied on agriculture and raw materials exports to sustain highly protected manufacturing industries. If the competitiveness of internationally exposed sectors became insufficient, the Bretton Woods system of fixed exchange rates allowed negotiated adjustments to restore the balance of payments.

Thus, while it would be wrong to speak of totally closed national economies in the early postwar decades, nation states were able to control both their own economic boundaries and the conditions under which trans-national economic transactions took place. Behind these protective barriers, national governments and unions could more or less ignore the exit options of capital owners, taxpayers and consumers. Government interest rate policy was able to determine, and vary, the minimal rate of return that captive capital owners could expect in the market for longer-term investment opportunities. By the same token, the level and the type of taxes that governments could impose on captive taxpayers were primarily limited by political, rather than economic, constraints. If governments and unions were able to impose uniform regulations, taxes and wage increases on all competing firms, the higher production costs could generally be passed on to captive consumers without endangering the profitability of capitalist production.

Under these conditions, advanced industrial democracies were able to achieve the 'Great Transformation' (Polanyi 1957) that allowed them to exploit the economic efficiency of dynamic capitalism without having to accept its recurrent crises and highly unequal distributional consequences. Since they were able to control trans-national capital movements, most governments learned to dampen macro-economic fluctuations through Keynesian demand management, and to achieve and maintain relatively high rates of economic growth and full employment. At the same time, national control over external trade gave governments and unions great freedom to shape the conditions of production. Moreover, boundary control combined with the power to impose nationwide rules allowed redistribution of primary incomes through cross-subsidisation in the private sector, as well as secondary redistribution through public services and transfers financed through progressive taxation. Hence, a suitable wage policy could compress wage differentials between low-skill and high-skill groups with little regard for actual differences in labour productivity. Energy policy could require the use of domestic coal in electricity generation; agricultural policy could keep inefficient farms in business; national health systems could offer medical care free of charge to everybody; and national systems of social assistance, unemployment and disability benefits and pensions could provide generous levels of non-wage incomes.

However, even though all capitalist democracies used their new-found freedom of market-correcting political action to pursue full-employment, social security and egalitarian goals, the employment and welfare-state structures through which these common goals were realised differed greatly with regard to:

- the division of labour between formal employment and household production – in particular of services for the young, the sick and the aged;
- the importance of formal employment in the public or private sectors;
- the importance of the state, 'corporatist' bargaining, and the market in regulating wages and the conditions of formal employment;
- the relative importance of the formal welfare state or of the employment system in achieving aspirations of social security and social equality;
- the relative importance of social transfers or of social services in the formal welfare state;
- the relative importance of income maintenance or of basic security in social transfers;
- the relative importance of general tax revenue or of insurance contributions in financing the formal welfare state;
- the relative importance of opportunity oriented or outcome oriented egalitarian policies; and
- the relative importance attached to primary incomes or secondary redistribution in outcome oriented equalisation policies.

125

This list of institutional and structural differences (which could easily be extended) is sufficient to show that, of the 12 advanced welfare states that we have studied in detail, no two are truly alike. Nevertheless, there are greater or lesser differences among countries along each of the dimensions mentioned, and a cluster analysis of these differences seems to agree with the distinction between 'Scandinavian', 'Continental' and 'Anglo-Saxon' welfare states proposed by Esping-Andersen (1990).[2] I will return to the characteristic differences between these three clusters of welfare states in the concluding section of this paper.

What matters here is the fact that, during the postwar decades, all advanced industrial democracies were able to achieve their respective welfare-state goals without endangering the viability of their capitalist national economies. However, institutional differences began to matter from the early 1970s onward, when major changes in the international environment did increase the economic vulnerability of advanced welfare states. This is not meant to deny the importance of endogenous challenges, among which were the ageing of the population and the erosion of traditional family structures that also differed in their impact on different types of postwar welfare states. We will focus, however, on the impact of external economic challenges. In the period from the early 1970s to the mid-1980s, these were in the nature of macro-economic shocks; whereas, in the later period, and at present, they are characterised by intensified competition in international capital and product markets.

Challenges and responses of the 1970s and early 1980s

For most industrialised countries, the end of the postwar 'golden age' coincided with the breakdown of the Bretton Woods system of fixed but adjustable exchange rates and with the OPEC oil-price crisis in the early 1970s. The first of these created an environment of floating exchange rates and accelerated the growth of 'offshore' capital markets that were not under the control of any of the major central banks. The second confronted oil-dependent industrial economies with the double challenges of 'stagflation', i.e. the simultaneous impact of cost-push inflation, caused by the fourfold increase within a few months of the price of crude oil, and of demand-gap unemployment, caused by the diversion of purchasing power to OPEC countries that could not immediately 'recycle' their new wealth into additional demand for industrial products. Under these conditions, governments committed to Keynesian demand management were confronted with a dilemma. If they chose to fight unemployment with monetary and fiscal demand reflation, they would generate escalating rates of inflation. If, instead, they fought inflation with restrictive fiscal and monetary policies, the result would be mass unemployment.

In the 1970s, as I have shown elsewhere, this dilemma could only be avoided if, in addition to fiscal and monetary policy, wages could also be employed as a tool of macro-economic policy. What was needed was a form of 'Keynesian concertation' where the government would prevent job losses through demand reflation while the unions would reduce inflationary cost pressures through wage restraint (Scharpf 1991). On the government side, the success of that strategy depended on a close coordination between fiscal and monetary policy. In the face of strong inflationary pressures, however, that coordination did require either convergent (Keynesian) beliefs of policy makers in both areas, or a clear dominance of the government over the central bank. On the union side, a necessary (but by no means sufficient) precondition was a degree of organisational concentration and centralisation that allowed the adoption of strategies that accepted the short-term sacrifice of real-wage losses in the interest of longer-term employment benefits.

The closest approximation to Keynesian concertation was achieved in Austria. In Germany and Switzerland, by contrast, governments were unable to reflate the economy because monetary policy was determined by an independent central bank that was unconditionally committed to the defence of price stability, which meant that the bank's tight-money policy would neutralise expansionary fiscal impulses. The same was true in Denmark, the Netherlands or Belgium, where the government tried to stabilise the exchange rate with the Deutschmark which, regardless of the institutional independence of the central bank, implied a restrictive monetary regime. Under these conditions, major job losses were unavoidable. They could only be ameliorated if real wages were quickly adjusted downwards. This was the case in Germany and Switzerland, but not in the other hard-currency countries that practised an imported (and perhaps less clearly understood) version of the Bundesbank's monetarism.

In countries where the central bank was willing to accommodate the rise of oil prices, government deficit spending was generally able to avoid major job losses in the 1970s. Inflation would then, however, escalate unless it was counteracted by effective wage restraint. In the absence of unemployment, and at a time when their real-wage position was eroding, this was more than most unions could have delivered even under favourable institutional conditions. Instead, they generally tried to defend the real wages of their members by pushing for settlements that anticipated (and thus generated) further price increases. This was particularly damaging in countries where public sector salaries, pensions and welfare benefits were automatically adjusted to the rise of private sector wages. As a result, the rate of inflation rose to very high, often two-digit levels. Moreover, the attempt to stabilise employment through demand reflation left most governments with very high budget deficits at the end of the 1970s.

By the end of the decade, therefore, governments and central banks in most countries had come to define loose money policies and fiscal irresponsibility as the critical policy failures of the 1970s. This greatly increased their willingness to switch to monetarist and hard-currency policy responses when the second oil crisis seemed to replay the challenges of the 1970s. The result was that unemployment rates now also rose steeply in most of the former soft-money countries that had been able to avoid major job losses in the 1970s.[3] Most important, however, was the fact that the monetary policy of the United States was no longer ready to accommodate oil-price inflation. As a consequence, real dollar interest rates, which had been close to zero or negative through most of the 1970s, rose steeply to very high positive levels of 3.1% in 1981, 5.4% in 1982, 7.2% in 1983 and 8.1% in 1984. Since the internationalisation of capital markets had progressed rapidly during the 1970s, most countries had become heavily indebted to them. National central banks, regardless of their institutional independence and theoretical orientations, were forced to raise interest rates accordingly, in order to avoid massive capital outflows (as had happened in France before the monetarist turnaround in 1983). This had major distributional consequences. Since minimal profits expected from real investments have to be significantly above the interest income from risk-free government bonds, the dramatic rise of real interest rates meant that the share of capital incomes in the national product had to rise at the expense of government and labour shares if investment and business employment were to be maintained. The only question was whether the change in distribution was realised through reduced wage claims and tax 'reforms' favouring capital incomes, or whether it was realised through dis-investment and job losses in the private sector.

On the whole, therefore, the success or failure of countries during the crises of the 1970s depended primarily on their capabilities for macro-economic management, that is on the coordination between the fiscal and monetary policy choices of the state, and on the capacity and willingness of unions to practise effective wage restraint in the face of oil-induced inflation. In the early 1980s, however, avoiding inflationary wage increases was no longer enough. Now, private sector employment could only be stabilised if the share of labour in the social product was being reduced. Organisationally strong unions in countries with centralised or coordinated wage-setting systems were generally able to implement the shift from wages to profits through voluntary wage restraint which, in the Netherlands, Denmark, and Australia, was facilitated by the sense of a deep crisis at the beginning of the 1980s. In Belgium, the government was able to impose effective wage restraint in the face of continuing ideological divisions among unions. In countries with highly decentralised wage-setting systems (as they existed in the United Kingdom and, after the early 1980s, in France), market pressures alone were eventually sufficient to achieve this effect.[4] Thus, in the second half of the 1980s, private sector employment was again increasing in countries with either weak unions and decentralised wage setting (Britain, France and, to a lesser extent, Switzerland), with 'statist' wage determination (Belgium), or with 'corporatist' industrial relations systems (Sweden, Denmark, Austria, Germany, Australia). Business employment continued to decline only in New Zealand, with strong unions and highly decentralised wage bargaining, and in Italy, with centralised but competing unions in a confrontational industrial relations system.

After the mid-1980s, international macro-economic shocks had spent their force. Oil prices declined and, while real interest rates remained high, they had come down from the extreme levels reached in 1984. In most countries, employment was increasing again, and budget deficits could be reduced. At the same time, however, the internationalisation of markets for goods, services and capital was now reaching levels that equalled, and then exceeded, the degree of international economic integration that had existed in the decades before World War I.

Capital exchange controls, which had still protected the domestic financial markets of most countries in the early 1970s, had practically disappeared by the early 1990s.[5] Moreover, the European Community had decided to liberalise financial services, and most countries had deregulated their domestic financial markets as well. As a consequence, financial capital was again internationally mobile, and the minimal rate of return that investors can expect is no longer defined by reference to interest rates set by the national bank, but by the attractiveness of competing worldwide opportunities for speculative, portfolio, or real investments.

At the same time, successive rounds of GATT and WTO negotiations had progressively lowered the tariffs and quantitative restrictions protecting national markets for goods, services and investments. In Europe, the Single-Market programme had also eliminated the non-tariff barriers that still impeded the full integration of product markets. It had introduced international competition in a wide range of services and utilities, including telecommunications, postal services, rail, air and road transport, or electricity supply, which, previously, had been provided either by the state itself or by state-controlled monopolies and cartels. Moreover, the completion of the internal market was followed by the commitment to create a Monetary Union.

This would not only remove monetary and exchange rate policy from the control of national governments, and impose severe constraints on the conduct of national fiscal policy, but it would also remove the last important barrier to real-capital mobility: firms would now be able to choose the lowest-cost location of production within the territory of the Monetary Union without having to consider either non-tariff barriers or exchange-rate fluctuations that might affect their access to the home market. By the same token, it has become much easier to move mobile tax bases, in particular business profits and other forms of capital incomes, to locations offering the least burdensome tax regimes.

As a consequence of these cumulative changes in the international economic and legal environment, national governments and national labour unions are no longer able to rely on the protective barriers that facilitated the achievement of their policy goals in the postwar decades. The internationalisation of capital markets has reduced the effectiveness, and increased the budgetary costs, of Keynesian full employment policies in the 1980s, and the exit options of investors, tax payers and consumers are constraining the capacity to regulate processes of production and to tax the profits from production. In that sense, it is indeed plausible to conclude that 'Polanyi's Great Transformation is over' (Cerny 1994: 339).

This is not meant to say that countries have lost all capacity to pursue the welfare goals they had chosen in the postwar decades, but it does imply that these goals must again be pursued within the constraints of international capitalism. It suggests that the vulnerability of national solutions will be the greater the more these had in the past relied on direct interventions into the operation of capital, product and labour markets. However, before it is possible to discuss the greater or lesser vulnerability of different countries, it seems necessary to specify more precisely the mechanisms through which the pursuit of employment, social security and social equality goals is constrained by economic internationalisation. In the following sections, I will focus on the two areas that are most directly affected – private sector employment and the financial viability of the welfare state.

Private sector employment

In the course of the last two decades, the international product markets served by advanced industrial economies have changed in two respects. On the one hand, lower-cost competition from newly-industrialising and Central and Eastern European countries is forcing producers in high-cost countries to automate production, or to specialise in 'up-market' industrial products of high technical or aesthetic quality, or in highly productive services. Assuming that wages and non-wage labour costs are downward inflexible, skill requirements will rise, and demand for unskilled workers will shrink as a consequence.[6] On the other hand, competition among advanced industrial countries has also become more intense, contributing to the greater volatility of increasingly specialised markets for 'diversified quality production' (Streeck 1997). Hence employment in internationally exposed sectors of the economy can only be maintained through continuous product and process innovations that reduce the costs of production and allow flexible adaptation to the volatile demand in specialised market niches (Streeck 1999). In other words, international competition will

129

necessarily drive up productivity in those firms that are able to survive. In the aggregate, this will limit employment opportunities even in those countries that are doing well in the international markets. In fact, employment ratios in the exposed sectors of the economy[7] have declined practically everywhere in the advanced industrial countries since the early 1970s. Employment gains were achieved only in the sheltered branches of ISIC 6 and 9, i.e. in 'wholesale and retail trade, restaurants and hotels' and in 'community, social and personal services'.

From a social policy point of view, it is even more important that, in internationalised and liberalised markets for goods and services, firms have become price takers, and that among the member states of the European Monetary Union, governments have also lost the option of correcting a loss of international competitiveness through adjustments of the exchange rate. As a consequence, above-average cost increases can no longer be passed on to captive consumers. At the same time, firms are now facing investors who are no longer limited to national investment opportunities but will compare (post tax!) rates of return achieved by real or portfolio investments to benchmarks defined by the most profitable investment opportunities available internationally.[8] Moreover, the resulting pressures are felt not only in the exposed sectors of the economy, but also in sheltered branches supplying local goods and services to internationally exposed firms, as well as in capital-intensive branches providing services that are locally produced and consumed. This is comparable to the situation in the media, in wholesale and retail trade or in hotels.

As a consequence, private sector firms are now much less able to cross-subsidise between highly profitable and less profitable lines of production, or between highly productive and less productive jobs. Instead, and most obviously within the European Monetary Union, each product and, in the extreme, each job, must now earn its full costs of production plus an adequate rate of return on capital at internationally uniform prices.[9] For governments and unions this implies that the employment risks associated with strategies aiming at the 'de-commodification of labour' (Esping-Andersen 1990) have greatly increased. Solidaristic union wages, government minimum-wage legislation, social policies raising the reservation wage of unemployed job seekers, and taxes and regulations imposing non-wage labour costs are all now more likely than before to entail job losses if they raise production costs above the level that is compatible with expected earnings. Obviously, these risks will most directly affect service jobs whose productivity cannot easily be increased, and hence will reduce the employment opportunities of less skilled workers.

In summary, then, more intense international competition in product markets is driving up productivity and skill requirements, and it tends to limit or reduce employment opportunities in the exposed sectors of the economy in particular, for less skilled workers. The effect is reinforced by the higher rates of return demanded by internationalised capital markets, and this also affects employment in capital-intensive branches of the sheltered sector. As a consequence, it is now generally more difficult than before to instrumentalise private sector employment relations for the achievement of egalitarian welfare goals. If such purposes were, in the past, pursued through collective bargaining and government regulations of employment conditions, their continuing realisation will now depend to a larger degree on the formal welfare state and the tax system. These options, however, are also constrained by the impact of economic internationalisation on welfare state revenue.

Welfare state revenue

In the average OECD country, the proportion of taxes and social security contributions in GDP rose until the mid-1980s, but tended to stagnate thereafter. In Sweden, it is true, taxes have come down from a temporary peak of 55.6% of GDP in 1990 to 52% in 1996, and Italy has greatly increased its tax revenue from 34.2% in 1985 to 43.2% in 1996. However, annual figures otherwise seem to fluctuate cyclically at about the level reached in the mid-1980s. Remarkably, however, differences between countries have remained about as high as before. Australia and Switzerland have tax shares a little above 30% of GDP, the United Kingdom and New Zealand around or above 35%, Germany somewhat below, and Austria, Belgium, France and the Netherlands significantly above 40%, and Denmark and Sweden above 50%. In other words, there seems to be no convergence over time. Instead, the stagnation of tax revenues seems to have had, more or less, the same constraining effect on Scandinavian high-tax countries, Anglo-Saxon low-tax countries, and the Continental welfare states with their intermediate levels of taxation.

In order to understand this pattern, we must consider the upward as well as the downward pressures on public sector revenue. The upward pressures that had increased tax burdens everywhere in the 1970s and early 1980s have, of course, not abated. Unemployment, poverty, pensions and health care for an ageing population, rising demands on education and business-oriented infrastructure, all would, under earlier circumstances, have required – and justified – further increases of taxation. As for the downward pressures, the usual suspects are governments competing for revenue from internationally mobile tax bases (in particular, from corporate profits and capital interest) and for internationally mobile investments and production.[10] As a result, most countries have significantly cut the nominal rates of taxes on capital incomes since the mid-1980s. However, as is frequently pointed out in the literature, one nevertheless cannot observe a general 'race to the bottom' of *effective* rates of capital taxation (Garrett 1998a, 1998b; Quinn 1997; Swank 1998).[11] Instead, countries that cut their top rates have generally tried to defend their revenue position by simultaneously broadening the tax base. Even though the economic logic of that solution seems somewhat doubtful,[12] countries seem to have been pushed toward it by the disadvantages associated with the alternative courses of action, which they would have had to choose among if revenues from mobile sources were significantly reduced.

These alternatives include a sustained increase in public sector deficits, significant reduction of public expenditure, and a shift from mobile to less mobile bases of taxation. Closer inspection reveals, however, that each of these options is confronted with obstacles or associated with negative side effects that reduce their feasibility or attractiveness (Genschel 1999).

Deficit spending had increased in most countries during the 1970s and, even though it was continued in the 1980s, its budgetary costs increased dramatically with the rise of real interest rates. In the 1990s, the Maastricht criteria for membership in the European Monetary Union had the effect of foreclosing the deficit option for most European welfare states. Under conditions of high capital mobility, all other countries were also constrained to demonstrate their fiscal conservatism in order to avoid paying high risk premiums on their public debt. In short, deficit spending had ceased to be a sustainable national strategy in the 1990s. At the same time, however, significant cuts in public expenditures were difficult to adopt in multi-party and corporatist political systems where hard choices depend on broad agreement among multiple actors. They were also difficult in Westminster-type two-party systems, where the governing party must fear political opposition and negative electoral reactions to significant and visible cuts in welfare benefits (Pierson 1994, 1996). In most cases, therefore, expenditure cuts were not, and are not, a solution that governments could pursue without incurring heavy political costs.[13] This shifts the emphasis to burden-shifting strategies. Among the less mobile tax bases, the ones with the largest revenue potential are taxes on consumption, social security contributions, and taxes on income from labour, all relatively immune to international tax competition.[14] In taking that course, however, governments need to consider the potential impact of tax increases on the costs of labour and, hence, on employment.

Contrary to widespread expectations, the statistical association between the *total* burden of taxes and social security contributions (measured as a share of GDP) and *total* employment (measured as a share of the working-age population) appears to be very weak. In fact, Denmark, the country with the highest tax burden, does as well or better in employment terms than the lowest-tax economies of the United States and Japan. Among the 12 countries covered by our project, the highest employment ratios are achieved by low-tax Switzerland together with high-tax Denmark and Sweden, while the low-tax Anglo-Saxon countries have intermediate and the remaining moderate-tax Continental countries have the lowest employment scores (Table 7.1).

If we look at the distribution between public and private sector employment, more systematic differences emerge. As is to be expected, high-tax Scandinavian welfare states are characterised by extremely high levels of public sector employment and relatively low private sector employment, whereas low-tax Switzerland and the Anglo-Saxon countries have very high employment in the private sector and low scores for government employment. More surprising is the employment performance of Continental welfare states with intermediate tax burdens: on average, they have as little private sector employment as the Scandinavian countries, and as few public sector jobs as the Anglo-Saxon countries.[15] Looking even more closely, it appears that the Continental deficit in private sector employment cannot be located in the manufacturing sector (where Germany actually has the highest employment ratio) but seems to be due to a lack of private service jobs. For these, employment in the branches included in ISIC 6 (wholesale and retail trade, restaurants and hotels) seems to be a good proxy.

While *total* taxation does not seem to have an influence on *total* employment, it seems plausible to search for causal effects by examining differences in the structure of employment as well as differences in the structure of taxation.

On the employment side, the first distinction is between public and private sector employment. As is to be expected, there is a positive association between the total tax burden and government employment ratios. The relationship is not very strong, however, and if Sweden, Denmark and Norway[16] were left out of the picture, it would disappear. Apparently, it is only these highly developed Scandinavian welfare states that have systematically translated high tax revenues into high levels of publicly financed social services, whereas Continental countries tend to cluster below the regression line.[17] The expected negative association between total taxation and business employment appears to be stronger, with

Table 7.1 Total and sectoral employment as % of the population 15–64, 1996

	Total Employment as % of Pop. 15–64	Government Employment as % of Pop. 15–64	Business Employment as % of Pop. 15–64	Industrial Employment as % of Pop. 15–64	Employment in ISIC 6 as % of Pop. 15–64
Australia	68.7	10.3	58.1	9.8	17.2
New Zealand	61.8	8.8	53.0	12.0	14.7
United Kingdom	69.3	9.6	59.1	13.2	13.7
Switzerland	79.1	11.0	68.3	15.7	15.2
Austria	62.6	14.2	49.5	14.5	14.4
Belgium	55.3	10.3	44.7	10.4	10.1
Germany	61.7	9.5	52.3	16.4	11.0
France	58.8	14.5	44.3	11.3	9.9[a]
Italy[b]	56.0	8.9	47.1	12.1	10.9
Netherlands[c]	51.4	6.8	44.8	10.2	13.4
Denmark	73.4	22.2	51.1	14.4	12.1
Sweden	72.2	22.4	49.6	13.5	10.6
OECD 18	66.5	12.6	52.7	13.0	13.0

a Data for 1989.
b Data for Italy in Columns 1–3 include estimates for jobs in the 'unofficial economy'.
c Data for the Netherlands in Columns 1–3 are full-time equivalents.

Sources: Columns 1–3: OECD Economic Outlook 1998;
Columns 4–5: OECD Labour Force Statistics 1998

Denmark and Sweden doing better, and Continental countries generally doing less well than would be expected on the basis of relative tax burdens.

Continuing on private sector employment, it is clear that diverse branches are included whose sensitivity to tax burdens may differ considerably. One theoretically meaningful distinction is between employment in those branches that are or are not exposed to international competition. According to the definition proposed above, the exposed branches include primary and secondary production and production-related services (ISIC 1–5 and 7 + 8). Contrary to the usual assumptions in political and economic debates, there is practically no statistical association between the overall tax burden and employment in the exposed sectors. It is also remarkable that both high-tax countries like Denmark and Sweden and medium-tax countries like Austria and Germany have more jobs in the exposed sectors of the private economy than is true of the United States, one of the two countries with the lowest tax burden. The conclusion seems to be that employment in those branches that are facing international competition is relatively insensitive to the overall tax burden. By implication, this suggests that the strongly negative impact of tax burdens on business employment must primarily affect private services that are domestically produced and consumed. In OECD statistics, these services are included in ISIC 6 (wholesale and retail trade, restaurants, and hotels) and ISIC 9 (community, social and personal services), but, since the latter category includes both public

133

and private sector jobs, employment in ISIC 6 should provide a clearer test for the causal effect of taxation on domestic service employment. In fact, it is strongly negative.

The next question is whether differences in tax structures may explain some of the observed variance in negative employment effects. Distinguishing between three major blocks of revenue (personal and corporate income taxes, consumption taxes and social security contributions), it appears that the high-tax Scandinavian welfare states as well as the low-tax Anglo-Saxon countries rely primarily on personal and corporate income taxes for their revenue, whereas, in most of the Continental welfare states, social security contributions provide the lion's share of revenue. There is less of a clear pattern with regard to consumption taxes (Table 7.2).

Considering private sector employment as a whole, one might conclude from current policy debates that taxes on corporate and personal incomes, which are thought to depress demand and discourage business investments should have the strongest negative effect. Remarkably, this expectation is again not supported by the data.[18] There is no statistical association between business employment and the GDP share of personal and corporate income taxes. That leaves social security contributions and consumption taxes, which are generally considered the most promising targets of burden-shifting policies, because they are relatively immune to international tax competition. Taken separately, each of these has a clear negative effect on overall business employment as well as on employment in ISIC 6. In combination, their joint effect on ISIC-6 jobs is very strong, accounting for just about all of the negative impact of the total tax burden.

We can, thus, conclude that the tax system does indeed affect private sector employment, but that these effects vary greatly on both the employment and the tax-side of the relationship.

Table 7.2 Taxes and social security contributions as % of GDP, 1996

	Total Taxation as % of GDP	Social Security Contributions as % of GDP	Taxes on Goods and Services as % of GDP	Personal & Corporate Income Tax as % of GDP
Australia	30.5	2.1	8.9	16.8
New Zealand	36.5	0.4	12.6	19.1
United Kingdom	35.5	6.2	12.7	13.1
Switzerland	33.7	12.4	6.2	12.5
Austria	41.5	18.1	11.7	10.4
Belgium	46.3	15.2	12.0	17.5
Germany	39.2	15.5	10.9	10.8
France	44.5	20.4	12.2	7.8
Italy	41.2	13.2	11.3	14.8
Netherlands	44.0	18.3	12.0	11.6
Denmark	50.2	1.8	16.7	29.7
Sweden	49.7	15.5	12.0	20.5
OECD 18	39.8	10.9	11.2	15.7

Source: OECD Revenue Statistics

Employment in internationally exposed industrial and service branches seems hardly affected at all by the size of the overall tax burden. Instead, negative effects seem to be concentrated in branches in which services are produced and consumed locally. On the tax-side, in turn, it seems that private sector employment is not affected by differences in the levels of personal and corporate income taxes, whereas social security contributions and consumption taxes have strongly negative employment effects.[19]

The interpretation of these patterns is straightforward. Employment in manufacturing, but also in transport, communication or financial services is little affected by the overall tax load, since high productivity allows the burden to be shifted either to consumers or (more likely in competitive markets) to workers whose relatively high take-home pay is reduced accordingly. In contrast, the market-clearing wages of less productive services might be at or near the level of social assistance benefits that define the lowest net reservation wage in advanced welfare states. Hence, the cost of taxes and social security contributions levied on such jobs cannot be shifted to employees but must be borne entirely by the employer, with the consequence that such services may be priced out of the market.

The same argument explains the variation in the impact of different types of taxation. Consumption taxes reduce demand for all products, but they fall most heavily on services whose low productivity makes them vulnerable to automation, to self-service (Gershuny 1978) or to tax evasion. Similarly, social security contributions are usually (except in the Netherlands[20] and in Britain[21]) raised as a proportional tax on total wages, with a cap at medium wage levels. Hence, they fall heavily on low-wage jobs, while the burden on highly productive and highly paid jobs is relatively smaller. In contrast, personal income taxes are not collected on wages below a basic-income exemption and, since their rates are generally progressive, taxes on the income elements that exceed the exemption begin at lower rates. Thus, the burden of income taxes on the cost of low-wage jobs tends to be minimal and, while they may have some effect on investments and on the ability of firms to attract high-wage professionals from low-tax countries, their negative impact on business employment is much weaker than is true of consumption taxes and social contributions.

If these effects are well understood, governments should seek to resist the temptation of shifting the tax burden from mobile capital to the less mobile bases of consumption taxes and social security contributions. Negative effects on employment would be smaller, it is true, if reduced rates on capital incomes were compensated by further increases in the taxation of high incomes from work. Here, however, political opposition is likely to be very strong in a period in which the real-income position of skilled workers has been declining while the tax resistance of high-income professionals has been reinforced by the dominant neo-liberal ideology.

Thus, under the pressure of international tax and investment competition, countries ought to cut taxes on capital and, under the pressure of high unemployment, they ought to cut taxes on labour inputs and on the consumption of services. Moreover, under the constraint of international financial markets, they ought to reduce public sector deficits. They could comply with these economic imperatives by raising personal income taxes or by cutting public expenditures. However, while these options might be economically innocuous, they have proven to be politically unpalatable in most cases. In other words, fiscal constraints have generally become tighter after the mid 1980s, and there is no obvious way in which they could be relaxed through strategies that are feasible at the national level.[22] Moreover, these constraints seem to operate at all levels of taxation, and there is no reason to think that low-tax countries should be under less pressure than high-tax countries. In fact, even countries like the United Kingdom and New Zealand, which have converted to radical versions of the neo-liberal creed, have not been very successful in reducing the total tax burden.

Characteristic challenges and options

Overall, then, the constraints imposed by international product and capital markets on employment and the welfare state may be summarised in the following conclusions.

- employment in the exposed sectors is generally shrinking and can be maintained only under conditions of high and rising productivity;
- employment losses in the exposed sectors can be compensated for by employment gains in the sheltered service sectors;
- the level of public-sector service employment is only weakly determined by the level of public sector revenue;
- opportunities for increasing public sector revenue have become severely constrained;
- employment in the sheltered private sector services is particularly vulnerable to the negative impact of social security contributions and consumption taxes;
- opportunities for egalitarian cross-subsidisation in private sector employment relationships, through solidaristic wage policy and social policies raising reservation wages, are generally being reduced.

From the perspective of welfare state goals, however, it matters more that these constraints are confronted by very different types of welfare states, with different employment structures, different revenue structures and different policy legacies. These all affect their greater or lesser vulnerability to competitive pressures, the major problems that they presently have to face, and the policy options that might be effective in coping with these problems.

In spite of the fact that no two countries in our project are alike with regard to all of the dimensions discussed above, it seems useful to discuss their differences by reference to distinctions between the Scandinavian, Anglo-Saxon and Continental regimes presented in Esping-Andersen's *The Three Worlds of Welfare Capitalism* (1990).

Scandinavian welfare states

In our project, the Scandinavian, or 'social democratic', regime is represented by Sweden and Denmark. Both of these countries are characterised by:

- very high levels of total employment;
- very high levels of female participation in the labour market;
- very high levels of taxation;
- very generous social policy, providing high levels of income replacement in cases of involuntary inactivity and in old age as well as comprehensive social services for the young, for the sick and handicapped, and for the aged;
- very low levels of wage differentiation and income inequality.

Both countries have succeeded in creating a virtuous cycle, in which the expansion of publicly provided child care, pre-school education, health care, and home care for the aged has freed married women to seek employment in the formal labour market, while providing both the jobs they could fill and the political support to sustain higher levels of taxation. As a consequence, public sector employment in the Scandinavian countries is almost twice the OECD-18 average.

Business employment, by contrast, is slightly below average. However, industrial employment as well as overall employment in the exposed sectors are above the average in both countries. Sweden, it is true, suffered a dramatic decline in the 1990s – which was, however, caused by a combination of unfortunate domestic policy choices and international conditions that do not seem related to specific vulnerabilities of the Swedish welfare state to international competition. Thus, the relative weakness in business employment must be located in the sheltered sector. In some fields (ISIC 9), private services are crowded out by the large public sector, but the weakness is also visible in ISIC 6 where public services play no role.

The explanation for the relative weakness of private service employment seems straightforward. Both Denmark and Sweden have strong unions committed to solidaristic wage policies which, together with reservation wages pushed up by generous income replacement ratios, have reduced wage differentials to the lowest level among OECD countries. In other words, unskilled worker receive relatively high wages in Sweden and Denmark. As a consequence, one should expect that the less productive consumer and household services would be squeezed out of the market (Iversen and Wren 1998), presumably by self-service and do-it-yourself activities and by the 'unofficial economy'.

In fact, given the extremely low wage dispersion and the very high tax burden, it seems more surprising that employment in ISIC6 services should not be even further below the OECD average. For the reasons discussed above, that should be due, at least in part, to a relatively employment friendly tax structure (Table 2). Denmark, in particular, benefits from the fact that it primarily relies on income taxes, rather than on social security contributions for financing its generous welfare state. While the revenue from consumption taxes is also very high, much of it is due to high rates on (imported) 'luxury' goods that have little effect on domestic employment.

At the same time, however, private sector employment in Denmark benefits from two other deviations from the Swedish model. First, there is very little job security. Employment can be terminated at low cost and with short notice. This is considered socially acceptable since workers with average wages are assured of exceptionally generous unemployment benefits, replacing up to 90% of their income from work for a maximum of five years. In recent years, however, these benefits have been coupled with an obligation of recipients to participate in retraining and other 'activation' measures, and to accept suitable job offers. As a consequence, unions and workers will not resist layoffs when demand falls, and firms are willing to hire even if a perceived increase in demand seems insecure. Sweden, by contrast, has maintained the rules regarding employment protection that are generally characteristic of countries with highly developed welfare states and powerful unions. The Danish system of collective bargaining has never attempted to achieve the degree of centralisation that was the pride of the Swedish model and, after the dramatic failure of the 1970s, it has moved to a two-tier system, which leaves considerable space for differentiated settlements at the level of individual branches and regions.

If Scandinavian welfare states are vulnerable, it is on the revenue side. Until the mid-1980s, the expansion of welfare transfers and services had depended on rising tax revenues and, in certain periods, heavy public sector borrowing. By the second half of the 1980s, however, the rise of tax revenues as a share of GDP had come to an end, partly as a result of the internationalisation of capital markets and the pressures of tax competition, and partly as a result of political tax resistance. At the same time, Denmark kept public deficits well below the 3% line defined by the Maastricht criteria, whereas Sweden was forced into excessive borrowing by the economic crisis of the early 1990s which, after the mid-1990s, was brought under control by drastic measures of fiscal consolidation.

In response to fiscal constraints, both countries have reduced the share of social expenditures in GDP after a peak in the early 1990s, but Sweden has done so to a greater extent – going from 37.4% of GDP in 1993 to 33.4% in 1995. Denmark reduced total social expenditures only from 33% in 1994 to 31.9% in 1996. This difference seems to explain the fact that the public sector employment ratio in Denmark remained stable at about 22% throughout the decade, whereas in Sweden it fell from 26.1% in 1989 to 21.9% in 1997. Since both countries have about maintained their levels of total taxation during the same period, the difference may be explained in part by the fact that Denmark has come to finance an increasing share of social services for families and for the elderly through means-tested co-payments.[23] Sweden, so far, has maintained its near-exclusive reliance on tax revenues for financing universal social services without regard to income differences.

In international comparison, however, both countries are still doing well on overall employment, and they are also doing very well on social security and social equality. The main problems that they confront are: first, difficulties in financing very expensive welfare states under conditions of high capital mobility and rising political tax resistance; and, second, a need to expand private sector employment to compensate for the stagnation or decline of employment opportunities in the public sector. It seems that Denmark is presently better placed than Sweden for coping with both problems because of its more employment-friendly tax system, its greater use of co-payments in the financing of public services, and because of its more decentralised wage-setting institutions, and more flexible regulations of conditions of employment. Nevertheless, even Sweden – which fell into a deep crisis in the early 1990s – seems capable of achieving economic and fiscal recovery without sacrificing the basic structures of its social-democratic welfare state.

Anglo-Saxon welfare states

In our project, the Anglo-Saxon or 'liberal' welfare states are represented by Australia, New Zealand and the United Kingdom. In some respects, Switzerland is also sufficiently similar to these to be discussed in the same context. All four countries are characterised by:

- high (in the case of Switzerland, very high) levels of total employment;
- relatively high levels of female participation in the labour force;

- low to moderately low levels of taxation;
- low to moderate levels of social expenditure, providing low to moderate (except in Switzerland) levels of income replacement in cases of involuntary inactivity and in old age, and low (except in the United Kingdom) levels of social services for the young, for the sick and handicapped, and for the aged;
- moderate to high levels of wage differentiation and income inequality.

Given their low levels of taxation, all four countries have low (but not exceptionally low) levels of public sector employment, whereas business employment is generally, and in Switzerland significantly, above the OECD average. Only in Switzerland, however, is this associated with exceptionally high employment ratios in the exposed sectors. Instead, the relative success of liberal welfare states is mainly due to jobs in the sheltered-sector services. Some of the explanations for this pattern are a mirror image of the ones discussed above with regard to the Scandinavian model.

In Australia and New Zealand, average replacement rates of unemployment insurance are quite low, whereas social assistance has been reformed in the 1980s according to principles of a 'negative income tax'. In the United Kingdom, similarly, unemployment benefits are flat-rate, rather than income related, and relatively generous levels of social assistance have been reformed to place greater emphasis on in-work benefits. As a consequence, there are fewer incentives to remain in socially supported inactivity, while seeking low-paid or part-time work is being financially rewarded. In New Zealand and the United Kingdom, moreover, labour markets have been deregulated while unions have recently lost their former power to determine wage rates and employment conditions through collective-bargaining agreements. In Australia and Switzerland, by contrast, collective bargaining has remained effective, but is practised in highly decentralised forms that allow for considerable differentiation and flexibility (which is reinforced in Switzerland by the continuing role of seasonally employed foreign workers in the service branches). In short, wage differentiation and flexible employment conditions have greatly facilitated the expansion of private services.

At the same time, the liberal welfare states also benefit from relatively employment friendly tax structures. Switzerland and Australia are significantly below average on consumption taxes, whereas the reliance on social security contributions is relatively low in New Zealand, Australia and the United Kingdom. As a consequence, overall labour costs are not greatly pushed up by either the industrial relations systems or the social benefits or the taxation systems of liberal welfare states. Hence, they all have relatively high employment ratios in the less productive service branches of the private sector.

Beyond that, patterns diverge. Switzerland has high shares of industrial employment based on a well-trained labour force, cooperative industrial relations and a specialisation on export-oriented high-quality production in the chemical and engineering industries. At the same time, the country has maintained its traditional strengths in financial and business services and in high-class tourism. Moreover, the Swiss welfare state, which has traditionally relied heavily on (publicly subsidised) private insurance, has in recent decades expanded the coverage of collectively financed unemployment and pension insurance. In combination with very high

139

levels of employment, therefore, Switzerland has not been affected by the inequality and poverty problems that otherwise are characteristic of the liberal welfare state.

Australia and New Zealand had traditionally relied on highly competitive agricultural and raw materials exports to cross-subsidise incomes in highly protected industrial and service sectors. Social security and a relatively high degree of social equality had been achieved by the unique combination of a very lean welfare state, providing mainly low, flat-rate benefits, with a highly regulated employment system in which import protection ensured full employment while state arbitration courts ensured an adequate 'family wage' for full-time workers in all sectors. When the deterioration of export markets undermined the economic viability of these arrangements, so that both countries were forced to liberalise their manufacturing and service sectors, their paths diverged.

In New Zealand, the post-1984 Labour government imposed radical liberalisation on product and capital markets, while strong but decentralised unions continued to strike for highly inflationary wage increases. The result was massive job losses, which were only reversed in the 1990s after a Conservative government had scrapped the arbitration system and substituted individualised for collective wage bargaining in the Employment Contracts Act of 1991. In Australia, in contrast, post-1983 Labour governments managed to negotiate a series of corporatist 'Accords', in which unions were willing and able to trade wage restraint for more gradual liberalisation and an increase of social assistance benefits. Employment increased rapidly after the mid-1980s, and fluctuated thereafter at high levels while wage inequality remained moderate.

In the United Kingdom, industrial employment fell precipitously in consequence of Margaret Thatcher's switch to monetarism and a hard-currency policy after 1979. In addition, the power of the labour unions was severely weakened by the elimination of earnings-related unemployment benefits and by industrial relations legislation outlawing secondary strikes. Employment conditions were deregulated and collective bargaining, to the extent that it still takes place in the private sector, became even more decentralised than before. In the exposed sectors, the continuing loss of manufacturing jobs (in spite of the rise of foreign direct investment) was not fully compensated by the steep increase of employment in the financial and business services. Thus, the relatively positive overall trend is, again, owed to the expansion of services in the sheltered sector.

In effect, New Zealand and Britain have moved to extremely deregulated labour markets and highly decentralised, or even individualised, wage setting. They have, thus, no problem with wage differentiation and employment flexibility. There is also no more organised resistance to the rapid introduction of process and product innovations. Neither, however, is there much investment in skills and in the practices of trustful cooperation between management and labour that are important for highly productive and high-quality industrial production. It is perhaps indicative that, after investing years of managerial effort and hundreds of millions of pounds, BMW never achieved German levels of quality, productivity and profitability in its British Rover plant. In contrast, Britain seems to be doing very well in some high-tech industrial branches and in financial services, where success depends on the creativity and motivation of highly skilled professionals, on the availability of venture capital, and on the freedom to capture the profits from rapid innovation in deregulated markets.

On the whole, therefore, the liberal welfare states have been able to achieve high rates of private-sector service employment, at both high and low skill levels. At the same time, their overall tax burdens are relatively low, and their welfare states are relatively lean. In comparison, therefore, neither employment nor the financing of the welfare state appears to be an acute problem. What is a problem in Britain and New Zealand, however, is increasing social inequality and the poverty of workers in low wage service jobs and their families. A partial solution is provided by forms of social assistance and of in-work benefits that are modelled on the Earned Income Tax Credit in the United States. By combining earned incomes with social incomes according to the logic of the negative income tax, these programmes allow low-skilled workers to accept low-wage service jobs without becoming victims of extreme poverty. In order to reduce the increasing inequality of life chances, however, they would still need to be complemented by measures that provide opportunities for training and upward mobility for those who enter the labour market by accepting low-skilled and low-wage jobs (Esping-Andersen 1999).

It needs to be noted, however, that among the liberal welfare states, Australia and Switzerland have achieved similar or superior levels of business employment without accepting nearly the same degree of insecurity and inequality as has been the case in Britain and New Zealand. There is reason to think, therefore, that the socially disintegrative consequences of 'classical' Anglo-Saxon liberalism can be greatly mitigated without endangering its superior economic efficiency.

Continental welfare states

The last group of countries is more heterogeneous. Nevertheless, it is possible to say that, in general, Continental or 'Christian-Democratic' welfare states are characterised by:

- low or very low rates of total employment;
- low or very low rates of female participation in the labour market;
- moderate levels of taxation;
- moderate levels of social expenditure, providing relatively high levels of income replacement in cases of involuntary inactivity (except for Italy) and in old age, but only limited social services for the young, the sick and handicapped, and the old;
- low or moderate levels of wage differentiation and income inequality.

With the exception of Austria and France, Continental welfare states have not converted their intermediate levels of taxation and social spending into correspon – ding levels of public sector employment. In the tradition of the 'Bismarck model', they are transfer intensive, but not service intensive, providing income-maintaining insurance for the (male) breadwinner and his family, but relying mainly on the unpaid services of mothers, wives, and daughters to provide care for the young, the sick and the aged (Esping-Andersen 1990). Remarkably, however, Continental welfare states also have lower rates of business employment than their intermediate tax levels would lead one to expect.

In those sectors of business employment that are exposed to international competition, however, Austria and Germany are above the OECD average, and while the Netherlands are still below the average, it is the only country in which exposed-sector employment has increased significantly since the mid 1980s. By contrast, employment ratios in Belgium, Italy, and France are considerably below the OECD average. On the assumption that exposed-sector employment and, in particular, manufacturing employment in high-cost countries has become increasingly vulnerable to above-average wage increases and increasingly dependent on productivity-increasing forms of work organisation and industrial relations (Streeck 1999), it seems plausible to think that differences in the structures of industrial relations systems would make a difference here.

Austria, Germany, and the Netherlands have relatively strong industrial unions and patterns of 'coordinated' sectoral wage bargaining that normally permit the effective adjustment of *average* wage increases to given macro-economic conditions and to the pressures of international competition. In the Netherlands, the traditional patterns of corporatist bargaining were disrupted by political conflicts in the 1970s, but were re-established in the early 1980s. Since then, a strategy of sustained, competitiveness-oriented wage restraint has contributed to the dramatic turnaround of Dutch employment (Visser and Hemerijck 1997). At the same time, there are strongly institutionalised forms of vocational training and of worker participation at the firm level, which facilitate high-quality production and cooperative adjustment and innovation. The downside, under present conditions, seems to be a tendency to over-regulate employment relationships, to over-protect existing jobs, and to over-standard-ise wages and working conditions. These dangers are most manifest in Germany, where wage compression has actually increased in the last decades, while Dutch and Austrian industrial relations have allowed more differentiation and flexibility.

In Belgium, France and Italy, in contrast, unions are politically divided and industrial relations were traditionally highly conflictual, with a correspondingly large role for state intervention in the wage setting process. In the 1970s, however, intervention had failed to control wage-push inflation an all three countries. From the early 1980s onward, Belgian governments were finally able to impose effective wage restraint but only at the price of an increasing compression of wage scales. In France, in contrast, private sector unions were nearly destroyed by legislation that was intended to facilitate plant-level worker participation. Since the state also ceased to intervene in collective bargaining, private-sector wage negotiations have become extremely decentralised and settlements highly differentiated. Nevertheless, the state still legislates on working conditions and working hours, and it also continues to define statutory minimum wages. However, in both countries, government intervention cannot substitute for a lack of organised cooperation that would facilitate 'productivity coalitions' between management and organised labour at the level of industries and individual firms. In Italy, finally, the state was never strong enough to exercise control over the wage-setting process but, in contrast to France, unions remained strong, and in the 1990s they were finally willing and able to coordinate their bargaining strategies with a view to the macro-economic requirements of European monetary integration. In the process, Italian industrial relations have also become transformed in ways that approximate to the 'corporatist' model.

With regard to sheltered sector employment (ISIC 6 + 9), all Continental countries are below the OECD average[24] which in part reflects the generally low levels of public sector employment. Focusing more narrowly on private services in ISIC 6, it appears that Austria and the Netherlands are somewhat above, and France, Belgium, Italy, and Germany, significantly below the OECD average. As was pointed out above, an explanation for this generally poor performance is provided by the fact that Continental welfare states have traditionally relied not on general taxation but on social insurance contributions from workers and employers to pay for social expenditures. These are particularly damaging in their effect on the less productive private services. The position of Austria as an extreme positive outlier remains a puzzle that is probably not completely explained by above average employment in tourism. The Netherlands, by contrast, seem to have benefited from the fact that social security contributions were integrated into the income-tax schedule in 1990.[25]

In addition, several of the factors that constrain private service employment in the Scandinavian countries are also present in Continental welfare states. In most countries (except for Italy), relatively generous social assistance and income maintaining benefits for the unemployed have the effect of raising the reservation wages of job seekers in the private sector. At the same time, employment is highly regulated, dismissals are expensive, and firms hesitate to start hiring in the face of uncertain demand in their product markets. In Belgium, Germany, and the Netherlands, wage scales are also compressed by minimum wage legislation or by the solidaristic wage policies pursued by strong unions. In Austria, in contrast, very high wage differentials seem to favour private service employment.[26]

With regard to the fiscal constraints, the comparatively high dependence of Continental welfare states on social insurance contributions also creates specific vulnerabilities. On the one hand, job losses will, at the same time, reduce the revenue of insurance funds and increase the expenditures for unemployment and other forms of subsidised inactivity. On the other hand, the fact that social security is institutionalised in the form of compulsory insurance programmes tends to create entitlements (or even legally protected property rights) in expected benefits that are more resistant against cutbacks or against means testing than is generally true in the case of tax-financed benefits. As a consequence, job losses will typically create a need to raise the rates of social security contributions. In other words, Continental welfare states are vulnerable to a vicious cycle in which rising unemployment will lead to increases in non-wage labour costs that will further reduce employment opportunities in private sector services.

Given these conditions, all Continental welfare states are presently confronted with two major problems, insufficient employment and an over-committed transfer system. These problems are closely connected. On the one hand, the financial viability of a generous transfer system is undermined if the size of the inactive population that depends on welfare transfers increases relative to the size of the active population. On the other hand, cost-sensitive private sector employment will shrink if the increasing burdens of the welfare state are primarily financed as a surcharge on wages. At the same time, the political cleavage between those who are asked to pay for, and those who depend on, the welfare state is likely to become sharper. The consequence is that the political viability of governments is undermined by massive political opposition, regardless of whether they try to respond to the dilemma by increasing tax burdens or by cutting welfare-state benefits. In other words, there is a huge financial and political premium on solutions that will increase overall employment levels.

Fiscal problems are most acute in Continental countries where, with partial exceptions for the Netherlands and Italy, public transfers are expected to provide status-maintaining unemployment, disability, sickness, and retirement incomes through pay-as-you-go insurance systems that are financed through surcharges on labour. These are most obvious in the field of old-age pensions. While they are similarly generous, the Scandinavian, Dutch and Swiss pension systems are typically three- or four-tiered, combining (1) a universal and tax-financed[27] basic pension at or near the social-assistance level with (2) a compulsory but limited supplemental-pension insurance, (3) a funded and income-related labour-market pension financed through (compulsory or collectively negotiated) wage-based contributions, and (4) voluntary but tax-subsidised private insurance or pension funds. Whereas the first and second tiers are strongly redistributive, the third and fourth tiers presuppose strict equivalence between contributions and benefits. In a financial squeeze, therefore, it is possible for governments to increase the redistributive effect of first- and second-tier pensions by introducing means testing, whereas entitlements in the third and fourth pillars must be treated as sacrosanct property rights.

The typical continental pension system (except for the Netherlands, whose three-tiered pension system resembles Scandinavian models) combines redistribution and equivalence in a single scheme which, because it is redistributive, is resented as a (highly regressive!) form of taxation. Because it is organised as a contribution based insurance system it does not allow means-testing and other forms of discretionary retrenchment. From a social security point of view, the lack of a basic pension means that persons with incomplete work biographies that include longer stretches of inactivity or part-time work will not be able to have retirement incomes above the social-assistance level. From an employment point of view, this form of pension insurance reinforces the male-breadwinner pattern and discourages part-time work, which is even more true if the income-tax system also privileges non-working wives.

To the extent that the need to increase employment (as distinguished from efforts to reduce open unemployment) has been accepted as a policy priority, Continental welfare states seem to concentrate efforts on improving the international competitiveness of exposed-sector industries. Since significant increases of industrial employment are not to be expected, the emphasis should be on the highly productive information, communication, financial and business services. However, even if growth is facilitated by the deregulation of product markets, these branches will provide jobs only for highly qualified workers. Thus, if the employment deficit of Continental welfare states is to be overcome, major gains will also have to occur in the less productive consumer-oriented, household-oriented and personal services.

In order to realise such gains, however, several preconditions must be met. On the demand side, Continental countries need to reduce the excessive burden of non-wage labour costs that so far prevent the development of a low-wage market for private services. Important steps in that direction were taken by the integration of social security contributions into the income-tax schedule in the Netherlands in 1990, and by the French decision to relieve employers from social-insurance contributions for low-wage workers in 1999. On the supply side, it would be useful for Continental countries to follow the Anglo-Saxon tendency to shift from social assistance to in-work benefits that eliminate the prohibitive taxation of the earned incomes of welfare clients. Moreover, some deregulation of product markets and of employment relations may be necessary if private services are to expand in areas that are presently not included in the formal economy.

With regard to fiscal constraints, the main challenge confronting Continental welfare states seems to be the difficult transition from all-inclusive pay-as-you-go insurance systems to solutions that separate interpersonal redistribution and basic-income support from arrangements insuring individual risks or providing for status-maintaining retirement incomes. While the former should be compulsory or tax-financed, and pay-as-you-go, the latter could be based on income-related contributions, funded, and in part voluntary. However, while the desirability of such changes is widely accepted, the main obstacle is the design of transition strategies that avoid the double burden on the presently active generation, who would have to finance both the benefits to pensioners entitled under the present regime and the contributions necessary to build up their own retirement funds (Miegel and Wahl 1999).

Conclusions

Compared with the decades after World War II, economic internationalisation has confronted all advanced welfare states with new challenges. In the 1970s, these could have been met by more effective macro-economic coordination but, in the 1980s and 1990s, internationalisation came to have a more direct effect on the structures of national employment and social-policy systems. In product markets, international competition intensified and spread to sectors of national economies that had previously been sheltered. At the same time, mobile firms were enabled to choose among national production locations, and mobile capital is now able to seek the most attractive investment opportunities worldwide. As a consequence, the terms of trade between capital, labour, and the state have shifted in favour of capital interests, and national powers to tax and to regulate have become constrained. Governments and unions wishing to maintain employment in the exposed sectors of the economy must seek ways to increase productivity, rather than redistribution. At the same time, welfare state revenue is constrained by international tax competition, by the need to reduce non-wage labour costs, and by the need to avoid public sector deficits, while welfare state retrenchment is encountering massive political opposition.

Under these conditions, all countries are under pressure to increase private sector employment, to increase the efficiency of welfare state spending and, in particular, to reduce the employment-impeding effects of welfare state financing and welfare state benefits. But these pressures are affecting countries that differ greatly with regard to levels and structures of employment, with regard to levels and structures of welfare state spending, and with regard to levels and structures of public sector revenue. As a consequence, national welfare states differ greatly in their vulnerability to international economic pressures, and in the specific problems that they need most urgently to address. They differ also in the policy options that they could reach under the path-dependent constraints of existing policy legacies, and under the institutional constraints of existing veto positions. There is, in other words, not one best way through which advanced welfare states could maintain their economic viability in an environment of internationalised capitalism without abandoning their employment, social security and egalitarian aspirations. However, as countries such as Denmark, Switzerland, Australia, or the Netherlands demonstrate, there is also no reason to think that economic viability should be incompatible with the successful pursuit of these aspirations.

Notes

1. This paper draws on the preliminary results of a conference project, directed jointly by Vivien A. Schmidt (Boston University) and myself, that compares the adjustment of employment and social policy to economic internationalization after the 1970s in 12 advanced welfare states (Austria, Australia, Belgium, Denmark, France, Germany,

Italy, the Netherlands, New Zealand, Sweden, Switzerland and the United Kingdom). The country reports, special studies and comparative analyses produced by the project are published this year, co-edited by Vivien A. Schmidt, in two volumes as *Welfare and Work in the Open Economy: From Vulnerability to Competitiveness* by Oxford University Press.

2. Based on indicators for household production (participation of women in the labour force), public sector employment, total employment, social security contributions, and D5/D1 wage differentials, a Cluster analysis produced the following three groups of countries: Sweden/Denmark; Australia/New Zealand, United Kingdom and Switzerland; Austria/France, Germany/Belgium, the Netherlands, and Italy.

3. One exception was Sweden, where the incoming Social Democratic government chose to stimulate export demand through a massive devaluation in 1982 (while embarking on a policy of fiscal consolidation), and where the export-sector unions were finally willing and able to practise wage restraint that did maintain the competitive advantage through most of the decade. By contrast, France, which had tried Keynesian reflation when the Socialists came to power in 1981, failed to contain inflationary pressures and escalating deficits, and was forced into a late and painful monetarist turnaround in 1983.

4. It should be noted, however, that even with significantly higher unemployment, real-wage increases in the mid 1980s were higher in Thatcherite Britain than in Germany – mainly because decentralised wage setting did allow bargainers to exploit the above-average ability to pay off profitable firms, while workers in less successful firms were still able to fight for adherence to 'comparability' norms.

5. According to an indicator of capital-exchange liberalisation constructed by Dennis Quinn on the basis of IMF data (where a score of 14 marks total liberalisation), in 1970 11 of 20 OECD countries had scores below 10, and only one country (Germany) had a score of 14. By 1993, only one country (Greece) still scored below 10, and nine countries now had a score of 14.

6. Given these conditions, the dispute about the major cause of the deteriorating position of low-skilled workers (technical change or competition from low-wage countries) seems quite pointless: If low-wage competition does not displace production in high-wage countries, it will speed up productivity-increasing technical change.

7. Since competition works at the margin, we are not relying on indicators measuring differences in the 'openness' of economies (which in any case are highly correlated with the size of countries), but have chosen to define all industries as being 'exposed' in which imports and exports play any role at all. Hence, our definition includes employment not only in manufacturing industries but also in primary production and in a wide range of production-related services, such as transport, communications, financial and business services (i.e. ISIC 1–5 and 7 + 8, according to the International Standard Industrial Classification of all Economic Activities).

8. In effect, target rates of return for business investments continue to rise even though real interest rates for long-term government bonds have long come down from the peak reached in the mid-1980s. It is unclear to what extent this divergence reflects higher risk premia associated with increasingly speculative markets for equity investments or the self-reinforcing effects of shareholder-value oriented management techniques (Vitols 1997).

9. In other words, competitiveness is no longer defined by national *averages* of cost and productivity increases. That is why the disappearance of the 'special relationship' between the German Bundesbank and the German metal workers' union under the EMU regime will not have the destabilizing effects feared by Soskice and Iverson (1997). Within the Monetary Union, each national branch union is in direct competition for jobs against unions organising the same branch in other member

countries. Thus, above-average wage increases will be punished by job losses regardless of whether the European Central Bank will target its Europe-wide monetary policy toward the German or the European economy.

10. Competition for revenue and competition for investments will often, but not invariably, imply similar tax-cutting strategies. The differences are explicated by Ganghof (1999).

11. On the difficulties of empirical confirmation or falsification, see Ganghof (1999).

12. Presumably, rational investors would consider effective, rather than nominal, tax rates. Moreover, the elimination of exemptions could reduce the relative attractiveness of real as compared to portfolio investments (Sinn 1990; Ganghof 1999).

13. Obviously, however, party-political constellations do matter: Margaret Thatcher faced a divided opposition, in New Zealand the neo-liberal policies introduced by a Labour government were not challenged by the conservative opposition, and in the Netherlands, welfare cuts were adopted by inclusive coalition governments (Green-Pedersen 1999).

14. For consumption taxes in the form of the value-added tax, that is true as long as they are raised according to the 'country-of-destination' principle, by which exports are exempted and imports taxed at the domestic rate. Even though that does constitute a (bureaucratic) burden on international trade, the European Commission seems to have abandoned its former efforts to switch to the country-of-origin principle for VAT.

15. For the Netherlands, OECD figures for government and business employment represent full-time equivalents, while all other data include full-time and part-time jobs.

16. The Norwegian position is, of course, influenced by the availability of oil revenues, which do not count as taxes.

17. The Dutch position as an extreme low outlier is in part explained by the statistical anomaly mentioned in note 15, and in part by the fact that some social services are subsidised by the state but provided by charities (as is also true in Germany).

18. Here Dutch figures are comparable with those of all other countries.

19. I have presented only bivariate relationships. But the patterns reported here have survived first attempts at multivariate analysis.

20. In the Netherlands, social security contributions were integrated into the income-tax schedule after 1990. Thus, they are only collected on incomes above the basic exemption of Dfl 8500 per year, and they are also progressive.

21. In the United Kingdom, social security contributions are progressive.

22. I leave out a discussion of the obstacles to international or European tax harmonization, and of the chances that they might be overcome.

23. Denmark is also the only OECD country where, between 1960 and 1990, private expenditures for health care have increased more rapidly (from 0.4 to 2.7% of GDP) than did public expenditures (from 3.2 to 5.0 percent of GDP) (Schmidt 1999, Table 1).

24. The relatively high scores for the Netherlands are affected by a change in the statistical series, which is reflected in an increase of 3.1 percentage points from 1986 to 1987. The largest annual increase in other years between 1974 and 1996 was 1.1 percentage points.

25. Thus, contributions are only collected on incomes above the basic exemption of about Dfl 8500 per year – which in comparison with most other countries constitutes a considerable subsidy to low-wage and part-time employment.

26. Even though Austrian unions are highly centralised, wage equalisation between skill groups, sectors and regions was never a salient union goal, whereas in Germany sectoral unions have traditionally tried to achieve disproportionate gains for low-wage groups, and to match the percentage increases achieved by the 'wage-leader' union

(usually the metal workers). In Belgium, increasing wage equalisation was the price governments had to pay for imposing wage restraint on non-cooperative unions during the 1980s and 1990s.

27. The Swiss pension system is structurally similar, with a first pillar that relies on income-based 'social security contributions' to pay for what is, in effect, a tax-financed and highly redistributive basic pension system.

References

Cerny, P. G. (1994) The dynamics of financial globalization: technology, market structure, and policy response, *Policy Sciences* **27**, 319–342.

Esping-Andersen, G. (1990) *The Three Worlds of Welfare Capitalism*. Princeton: Princeton University Press.

Esping-Andersen, G. (1999) *Social Foundations of Postindustrial Economies*. Oxford: Oxford University Press.

Ganghof, S. (1999) *National Tax Policy Adjustment to Economic Internationalization*. MPIfG Discussion Paper. Köln: Max-Planck-Institut für Gesellschaftsforschung.

Garrett, G. (1998a) *Partisan Politics in the Global Economy*. Cambridge: Cambridge University Press.

Garrett, G. (1998b) Global markets and national politics: collision course or virtuous circle? *International Organization* **52**, 787–824.

Genschel, P. (1999) Tax competition and the welfare state. Manuscript, June 1999. Köln: Max-Planck-Institut für Gesellschaftsforschung.

Gerschuny, J. (1978) *After Industrial Society: The Emerging Self-Servicing Economy*. London: Macmillan.

Green-Pedersen, C. (1999) Welfare-state retrenchment in Denmark and the Netherlands 1982–1998. The role of party competition and party consensus. Paper for the *11th SASE Conference*, Madison, Wisconsin, 8–11 July 1999. Department of Political Science. University of Aarhus, Denmark.

Iversen, T. and Wren, A. (1998) Equality, employment, and budgetary restraint: the trilemma of the service economy, *World Politics* **50**, 507–546.

Miegel, M. and Wahl, S. (1999) *Solidarische Grundsicherung. Private Vorsorge. Der Weg aus der Rentenkrise*. München: Aktuell im Olzog Verlag.

Pierson, P. (1994) *Dismantling the Welfare State: Reagan, Thatcher and the Politics of Retrenchment in Britain and the United States*. Cambridge: Cambridge University Press.

Pierson, P. (1996) The new politics of welfare, *World Politics* **48**, 143–179.

Polanyi, K. (1957) *The Great Transformation*. Beacon Hill: Beacon Press.

Quinn, D. (1997) The correlates of change in international financial regulation, *American Political Science Review* **91**, 531–552.

Scharpf, F. W. (1991) *Crisis and Choice in European Social Democracy*. Ithaca: Cornell University Press.

Schmidt, M. G. (1999) Warum die Gesundheitsausgaben wachsen. Befunde des Vergleichs demokratisch verfasster Länder, *Politische Vierteljahresschrift* **40**, 229–245.

Sinn, H.-W. (1990) Tax harmonization and tax competition in Europe, *European Economic Review* **34**, 489–504.

Soskice, D. and Iversen, T. (1997) *Central Bank – Trade Union Interventions and the Equilibrium of Employment*. Papers FS I 97–308. Berlin: Wissenschaftszentrum für Sozialforschung.

Streeck, W. (1997) German capitalism. Does it exist? Can it survive?, *New Political Economy* **2**, 237–256.

Streeck, W. (1999) *Comparative Solidarity: Rethinking the "European Social Model"*.

MPIfG Working Paper 99/8. Köln: Max Planck Institute for the Study of Societies [http://www.mpi-fg-koeln.mpg.de/publikation/working_papers/wp99–8/index.html].

Swank, D. (1998) Funding the welfare state: globalization and the taxation of business in advanced market economies, *Political Studies* **46**, 671–692.

Visser, J. and Hemerijck, A. (1997) *A Dutch Miracle. Job Growth, Welfare Reform and Corporatism in the Netherlands*. Amsterdam: University of Amsterdam Press.

Vitols, S. (1997) Financial systems and industrial policy in Germany and Great Britain: the limits of convergence. In: D. J. Forsyth and T. Notermans, (eds), *Regime Changes: Macroeconomic Policy and Financial Regulation in Europe from the 1930s to the 1990s*. Providence, RI: Berghahn Books, pp. 221–255

About the Author

Fritz W. Scharpf is Co-Director of the Max-Planck-Institute for the Study of Societies, Cologne. He is a member of the Academia Europaea. He works in the area of comparative political economy with special emphasis on European integration and international economic integration. His most recent books are *Games Real Actors Play* (Westview Press 1997), *Governing in Europe. Effective and Democratic?* (Oxford University Press 1999) and *Welfare and Work in the Open Economy: From Vulnerability to Competitiveness* (co-edited with Vivien A. Schmidt: Oxford University Press, 2000, 2 volumes).

European Review, Vol. 8, No. 3, 427–446 (2000) © Academia Europaea, Printed in the United Kingdom

8 Recasting European welfare states for the 21st Century

MAURIZIO FERRERA*, ANTON HEMERIJCK** and MARTIN RHODES***

This article places Europe's welfare states squarely in the context of the European integration process and takes an optimistic view of the possibility for new 'top-down' EU initiatives. In targeting the needs and concerns of European policy makers, it makes a case for an optimal policy mix, delivered via a new institutional architecture based on 'soft' (as well as 'hard') governance and the diffusion of best practice national policies. The authors argue that the overriding need in welfare reform is to identify new value combinations and institutional arrangements that reconcile solidarity with growth. These are specified with regard to the four families of European welfare states and their differing needs for functional, distributive as well as normative 're-calibration'. Finally the authors outline the different innovations required to reinforce the role of the EU as the guarantor and guardian of the 'European social model'.

Introduction

There is a popular view that West European welfare states are crumbling under pressure from external competition, while the globalisation of production and finance, combined with the policy constraints of EMU, have all reduced the capacity of the state for implementing corrective remedies. Efficiency and equality, growth and redistribution, competitiveness and solidarity are frequently referred to as polar opposites that can only thrive at each other's expenses. Our argument in this article is much more nuanced – and optimistic.

First, we counter the argument that welfare states are crumbling under external and domestically-generated pressures. Although apparently 'in crisis' and subject everywhere to retrenchment, due to the combination of factors mentioned above, welfare states have, in fact,

* Dipartimento di Studi Politici e Sociali, Università degli Studi di Pavia, Corso Strada Nuova 65, 27100 Pavia, Italy. E-mail: ferrera@uni-bocconi.it.
** Leiden University, Department of Public Administration, Wassenaarseweg, 522300 RB Leiden, The Netherlands. E-mail: Hemerijck@fsw.LeidenUniv.nl
*** Department of Social and Political Science,, European University Institute San Domenico di Fiesole, 50016 Florence, Italy. E-mail: rhodes@iue.it

changed relatively little in recent years. According to an OECD investigation of 15 cases of fiscal consolidation involving 11 countries, in all but one (Ireland 1986–1989), governments pursuing consolidation increased revenues as a percentage of GDP in the 1980s and 1990s. In nine of the 15 cases, revenue increases accounted for the majority of fiscal consolidation (see OECD 1996; Pierson 1997). Support for the welfare state remains high amongst publics everywhere and institutional stickiness creates tremendous resilience against pressures for change.

Secondly, we correct the view that national states are increasingly impotent to deal with the range of challenges that confront them. Steering capacity is being constrained by developments beyond national borders; but this does not necessarily mean a loss of state control or 'neo-liberal' convergence, in either institutional change or policy objectives. Indeed, as during much of the postwar era, reforming labour market regulation and recasting welfare states will require that most European countries follow a 'third path' between the state and the market, involving an accommodation of market pressures with the preservation of social protection and consensus.

We argue instead that the overriding need – building on current tendencies in this direction – is to identify new value combinations and institutional arrangements in national systems that are both mixed (in terms of solidarity and growth objectives) and virtuous (capable of producing advances on all the affected fronts).[1] The search for new solutions in diverse member states can be greatly helped by supranational mechanisms of coordination and evaluation, as well as by processes of mutual observation and learning.

We begin with the European Union's social agenda – where the search for new value combinations has been most active – then proceed to the nature of the challenges to adjustment problems confronting Europe's welfare states and their need for 're-calibration' in functional, distributive and normative terms. We then present the core components of an optimal adjustment strategy that could reconcile growth with solidarity objectives before returning to the level of EU policy making and its potential contribution to the preservation of the European social model.

The European Union and the European social policy agenda

In the space of a decade, the mood concerning the nature of Europe's welfare states and the role to be played by European integration in shaping and protecting them has gone from cautiously optimistic to bleak. By the mid-1990s, the failure of a federal – or even quasi-federal – system to emerge to underpin and protect the European social model was widely lamented. For supporters of an integrated European welfare system, it now seemed that European member states would have to face the forces of neo-liberal reform unsupported and would begin to engage themselves in a competitive 'race to the bottom' in social protection and employment standards.

In reality, this pessimism was based on unrealistic expectations of what could be achieved in developing a European 'social dimension' and an unwarranted fear of 'social dumping' in a single European market (see Barnard 2000). Going beyond the raft of measures put in place in the 1970s and 1980s in gender equality, employment protection and minimum standards in labour market regulation was always going to be difficult – even once the British veto of the 1980s had been overcome. In fact, however, a new – albeit loosely – structured supranational regime had already been put in place. The result was less than the harmonisers and European state builders had hoped for and aspired to. But nonetheless, the 1980s and 1990s had witnessed the creation of a multi-tiered policy system and a significant transition from sovereign to *semi*-sovereign welfare states as progress with legislation and institutional reform proceeded (see Pierson and Leibfried 1995, 1998; see also Leibfried and Pierson 2000). As a result, EU social policy-making now displayed the following features:

- joint decision-making in the Council of Ministers, driven by a complex combination of national interest, ideology and practicability, bolstered after Maastricht by an extension of qualified majority voting to health and safety, work conditions and equality at work;
- the creation of a policy network above and beyond the nation-state, involving national and supranational employer and union representatives (and institutionally embedded in the new social dialogue procedures created in the Maastricht Social Protocol and Agreement);
- a reduction of the social policy autonomy of the member states through pan-European regulations, especially in employment rights and protection, backed by European Court of Justice case law;
- a reduction of member state social policy autonomy via market compatibility requirements (i.e. the end of closed welfare borders) with important implications for pensions and health systems.

In sum, member states are now subject to a web of enforceable regulations resulting from EU legislation, and this will help shape if not determine their national approaches to welfare state reform.[2] They are also linked by an institutional architecture with two well-established pillars – European legislation and social dialogue – to which a third (the use of soft law within the Luxembourg process of employment policy coordination) has recently been added (see below).

Much, on the other hand, had not been achieved and, as already indicated, even areas of significant innovation in European social policy had failed to meet the expectations of many. There had even been a growing deadlock in the 1990s after Maastricht and the affirmation of the subsidiarity principle, necessitating new instruments of intervention on the part of the supranational authorities. One should also recognise the importance of the sea change in thinking that occurred in both the Commission and the member states since around 1993 as politicians and policy makers attempted to grapple with the problem of persistent rates of high unemployment. The result was a shift in focus from employment protection towards employment promotion (if necessary, through a more flexible re-regulation of labour market rules), a questioning of cohesion policy priorities and plans to link the structural funds more closely to employment imperatives.[3]

Where once the priority appeared to be a harmonisation, or at least an approximation, of social and employment rights across Europe, given the challenges elaborated below, the priority now lies elsewhere, in reconciling national systems of social solidarity with economic growth while also maintaining the core principles of the European social model. This demands new approaches to social and employment protection in both the EU's member states and at the supranational level.

External and domestic challenges to welfare states

European welfare states face multiple challenges to their sustainability, requiring imaginative new responses across a broad range of policy areas. The external challenges to European welfare are those that frequently grab the headlines and dominate the political discussions, but of all the forces influencing the future of welfare they are probably the least well understood. Thus, the debate on globalisation is often couched in terms of the misleading dichotomy of convergence versus divergence. In fact, since the pressures of economic internationalisation affect different welfare states in varying ways and to differing degrees and at different points of time, such a blunt juxtaposition is not particularly useful. Not only does it fail to capture the full complexities of the economics and politics of national processes of policy adjustment, but it provides little basis for genuine comparative analysis or for policy prescriptions.

Secondly, there are many good reasons for believing that the overall impact of globalisation has been exaggerated, as have its potentially adverse consequences for employment and social standards. Various types of institutional setting and forms of social, social security and labour market policy are equally compatible with competitiveness. There is no need for (or much evidence of) convergence on a 'neo-liberal' value combination and institutional model – despite the conviction in certain political circles that such convergence is required.

Against crude globalisation assumptions, it should be stressed that national economies have neither been wholly absorbed into a new global order or their governments totally incapacitated. Good arguments for the compatibility of large welfare states with internationalisation are regularly rehearsed. Welfare states emerged in line with the growing openness of economies and facilitated the consequent process of socio-economic adjustment. Government consumption appears to play an insulating role in economies subject to external shocks (see Rieger and Leibfried 1996; Rodrik 1997).

Moreover, welfare states have generated many of their own problems and these would have created severe adjustment difficulties even in the absence of greater exposure to flows of capital and goods – and potentially also people with the forthcoming EU enlargement. By helping improve living standards and life spans, welfare states have created new needs that social services were not originally designed to meet. Rising health care costs and pensions provisions have contributed massively to welfare budgets and fiscal strains and these pose the most intractable problems for the politics of welfare adjustment in Europe (see Pierson 1998). At the same time, institutional inertia undermines the capacity of many welfare states to respond to new risks and needs generated by rapid socio-economic change.

Other problems – e.g. the decline in demand for low or unskilled manufacturing workers – stem from the increasingly post-industrial nature of advanced societies. New challenges are being posed by the shift in the advanced economies from an older Fordist 'techno-economic paradigm' – based *on energy-intensive* production systems and services – to a new techno-economic paradigm based on *information-intensive* production systems and services (see Freeman and Soete 1994). The consequence is far-reaching managerial, organisational and distributive changes, including unemployment among particular categories of workers but new opportunities for others. The result has been a shift in labour demand away from non-versatile and poorly educated workers.

But how do these endogenous challenges interact with globalisation and competitive constraints? While such links are more modest, complex and bi-directional than commonly assumed, they do exist and should be taken seriously. Trade competition, the globalisation of finance and constraints on raising taxation all exert potentially important pressures on government capacities for sustaining welfare state commitments. At the same time, post-industrial change is creating a 'service sector trilemma' in which the goals of employment growth, wage equality and budgetary constraint come increasingly into conflict (see Iversen and Wren 1998). As discussed below, in certain countries, funding generous pensions and health care systems can contribute to the problems of employment creation by levying high social charges on employers and making service sector employment too expensive. As we discuss in greater detail below, all welfare states must become 'competitive' to the extent that fiscal, solidarity, employment, productivity and competitiveness objectives are all interrelated components of an optimal policy mix.

However, the impact of those pressures should not be exaggerated. They do not render different national responses or the search for equitable solutions impossible. Nor does the way forward necessarily involve neo-liberal deregulation of labour markets or stringent retrenchment of welfare programmes, whether it be pensions, health or social security. The real task is to find new modes of sustaining and reforming those programmes while building or rebuilding domestic coalitions and arrangements containing trade-offs that make such policies politically 'credible', financially feasible and normatively equitable (see Rhodes 2000a). Responding to this complex set of challenges in political and policy terms involves a complex two-level game in most European countries, incorporating both an electoral arena and a corporatist arena (see Pierson 1998). In addition, as discussed below, a third level – of interaction with the European Union and other member states – is becoming increasingly important. Unilateral, state imposed solutions of a neo-liberal stripe are actually quite inappropriate for these countries. A different solution must be found and existing structures for negotiated but purposeful reform consolidated. We return to this issue below. First, however, it is important to understand the diversity of Europe's welfare states and their problems.

Europe's welfare regimes and adjustment problems

Each of Europe's welfare 'regimes' confronts a different set of adjustment problems depending on its particular characteristics.[4] Four different 'social Europes' can be identified: the Scandinavian, the Anglo-Saxon, the Continental and the South European. These differ – in some respects quite substantially – according to risk coverage and eligibility; the structure of benefits; financing mechanisms and organisational arrangements – and thus also in terms of their adjustment problems and paths to reform.

Scandinavia

Throughout the 1990s the Nordic countries have been grappling with pressures to contain the high and increasing costs of their generous programmes and to re-organise their labour markets, especially to help generate more demand for private employment. Given the high level of popular support for the welfare state, the reform agenda has been shaped by a pragmatic, problem-solving approach. This has mainly centred on the issue of cost containment. The principles of universalism have not been significantly questioned, even if this has meant cuts 'across the board' in replacement rates (e.g. in sickness benefits) or of basic amounts (e.g. family allowance in Sweden). Some significant steps have been taken, however, towards the 'Bismarckian tradition' in pensions: the link between contributions and benefits has been strengthened in both Sweden and Finland. Besides cost-containment, a second important *leitmotiv* of the Scandinavian reform agenda in the 1990s has been the 'activation' of benefits. However, serious problems remain in the labour market of these countries, particularly as regards the growth of private service sector employment.[5]

The United Kingdom

The UK welfare state is characterised by modest levels of protection, tough 'commodification' incentives and targeted provision – with all its adverse effects. It is true that aggregate social spending in the UK is above the EU average, while the NHS caters to the needs of the whole population, and the range of benefits offered (if not their amounts) is comparatively wide. But the institutional logic of the British welfare state is distinct from that of the other 'social Europes'. The flat-rate nature of 'Beveridgean' benefits and their coverage loopholes (based on earnings thresholds) allowed Conservative governments during the 1980s to promote a creeping residualisation of social protection and an expansion of low-pay, low-skill jobs. Universal benefits were left to erode, the middle classes were encouraged to 'opt out' into non-public forms of insurance (e.g. in pensions) and targeted, means-tested benefits increased markedly. Wage subsidies were also introduced to supplement the incomes of low paid workers. The erosion of universal provision has contributed to a solution of the cost problem facing other European countries. Wage subsidisation has fostered an expansion of private – especially service sector – employment. But inequality and poverty levels have also markedly increased – partly in the wake of the perverse effects created by means-testing itself.[6]

Continental Europe

The root of the Continental syndrome lies in the generosity of insurance-based income replacement benefits, their mainly 'passive' or compensatory nature and their contributory financing. Honouring generous insurance entitlements (pension systems) has required high contributory rates on the wages of standard workers in the presence of protective systems of labour laws. This has discouraged firms from continuing to offer traditional 'Fordist' employment, while creating pressures for subsidised early retirement exit, a strategy that reduces labour market participation while increasing social charges – and doing little to promote new employment. In a clear manifestation of the 'service sector trilemma', high wage floors have blocked the expansion of private service employment, while public service employment has been constrained by fiscal overload. The response has been a further expansion of passive income maintenance schemes (unemployment, sickness, disability and early retirement schemes), requiring further increases of social charges. Nor have these systems been effective in promoting arrangements allowing women to combine work and family responsibilities. The result has been an emerging 'bad' equilibrium between low female employment (and high unemployment) and low fertility – with all the ensuing fiscal consequences (see Esping-Andersen 1996).

Southern Europe

South European welfare states suffer from many of the same problems as the Continental family – especially in the labour market – but they also have their own specific traits. In Spain, Portugal, Greece and (to a lesser extent) Italy, the welfare state developed later than in northern Europe and has had to cope with more difficult socio-economic environments. Social protection entered the age of 'permanent austerity' in a state of institutional and financial underdevelopment and was beset by internal unbalances. The social transfer systems of these countries have peaks of generosity for certain occupational groups alongside large gaps of protection for certain others. 'Insiders' and 'outsiders' – both in the labour market and more general access to benefits – are separated by a sharp divide in terms of guarantees and opportunities. The black economy is extensive, posing serious efficiency and equity problems. Public services are still unevenly distributed and, in some cases, insufficient and/or inefficient. These countries have thus been forced into shifting coverage, providing less generous benefits for insiders and – to the extent that budgetary constraints allow it – new benefits and services for the outsiders. The inherent difficulty of doing so is aggravated by a particularly adverse demography: southern European populations (especially those of Italy and Spain) are ageing at one of the fastest rates in the world (see Ferrera 1996 and 2000; Rhodes 1997).

What can be done? Re-calibrating welfare states

The discussion of the problems afflicting Europe's welfare state clusters brings us logically to an examination of the possible solutions. Subsequent sections of this article discuss the scope for optimal policy mixes, lessons from national experience and the potential for a new institutional architecture linking EU member states into Europe-wide guidelines for reform. Here we recast the preceding analysis in more abstract, thematic terms and consider the necessary dimensions of welfare state reform across Europe's welfare states as a process of functional, distributive and normative re-calibration (a fourth dimension – the political-institutional dimension – will be introduced below).

Functional re-calibration relates to the risks around which welfare provision has developed over time. Roughly until the early 1970s, social insurance displayed a good degree of congruence with the population, family and labour market structures of European societies. The traditional catalogue of standard risks tended to reflect quite closely the prevailing pattern of social needs, as shaped by high fertility, a shorter life expectancy than today, growing 'fordist employment', low rates of female employment, a male breadwinner model of the family and a traditional form of gender relations. However, to varying degrees in Europe's different welfare families, the 'goodness of fit' between the welfare state and an evolving socio-economic reality has been eroded. The transition towards a post-industrial, knowledge-based economy is producing an additional mismatch between the supply and demand for institutional 'goods'.

Thus, traditional social insurance schemes still tend to concentrate benefits on risks which no longer – *per se* – generate need, while they increasingly fail in many countries to protect new needs. 'Old' risks continue to receive generous insurance protection, even if, in many instances, they are no longer the source of real need among the prosperous middle classes. Examples include short-term work, absence due to mild sickness, the death of a spouse and even old age – at least in its traditional definition as 'life beyond 60 or 65'. In the wake, however, of social and economic transformation, income insecurity is spreading to earlier phases of the life cycle. In many countries child poverty has been growing, together with other worrying symptoms of 'social dislocation', including crime, teenage pregnancies, homelessness, substance abuse and educational exclusion. In this new context, a re-calibration of social insurance from 'old age protection' to 'societal integration' and 'human capital upgrading' is urgently in order. Completing the pension reform agenda remains the key for solving the allocative dilemmas of the welfare state, especially in Continental Europe.

Distributive re-calibration has to do with social groups. The welfare state has never been evenly extended across the social structure. While this is partly true even in the universalistic systems of Nordic Europe, social differentiation in terms of welfare rights and entitlements have long been the norm in the 'conservative-corporatist' regimes of Continental Europe. In Southern Europe, social rights have never succeeded in crossing certain socio-economic fault lines, most notoriously into the black economy. In many countries there is evidence of an over-accumulation of insurance benefits on the side of 'guaranteed' workers, with quasi-tenured jobs alongside inadequate (if not total) lack of protection for those employed in the outer, weaker sectors of the labour market.

In particular, there seems to be a growing gap between the so-called DINK families (double income, no kids; insider jobs) and the SIMK ones (single income, many kids – or single parent and one child – in an outsider job or unemployed). Although less visible than in the US, an American-style underclass consisting of workless households, lone parents, ethnic minorities or (illegal) immigrants has already formed in some regions of Europe, falling largely outside the reach of social insurance. The emerging skill-based cleavages associated with the new economy will certainly accelerate and reinforce this dynamic.

In certain countries, marked distributive inequalities are evident not only between the insiders and the outsiders, but also among the insiders themselves, i.e. between different categories of insured. Overtime, social insurance systems have come to incorporate – often in implicit forms – increasing doses of interpersonal redistribution, i.e. redistribution across economic sectors, occupational categories or income groups. Many of these transfers, however, have now lost their original rationale and have become a source of growing inequity.

Progress with reform of these imbalances is likely to be slow due the difficult politics of 'entrenched interests and sticky institutions'. But another problem is that progress is hard to define and justify in the first place from a value perspective.

This leads us necessarily into the difficult – and contested area – of normative re-calibration.

On this front too an 'incongruence' can be noted in the European welfare state: the 'goodness of fit' between the broad value premises that inspired its construction and the policies we now observe in practice has been gradually eroding through time, largely as a consequence of institutional inertia. Of course, real world institutions are always imperfect: but there are different degrees of imperfection. If we are correct about the serious functional and distributive shortfalls of the status quo, then the case for re-calibration acquires a normative dimension as well.

The 'service sector trilemma' mentioned offers a good illustration of this point. Given the characteristics of services production and fiscal constraint, solidaristic incomes policies and high wage floors in Continental systems tend to stifle employment creation, especially for the young and low skilled. The policy implication is that these systems must move towards some combination of greater 'flexibility', underpinned by sustained security, under the terms set out in the next section. The normative argument can be presented in Rawlsian terms as follows: it is morally fair to reduce the protection of the insiders and allow for more flexibility and greater earnings dispersion if this delivers greater opportunities to the worst off (Rawls 1971). The security side of the 'positive' argument can itself be bolstered in normative terms: a Rawlsian approach would, in fact, prescribe the consolidation of a floor of equidistributed primary goods, compatible with economic constraints but meant to enable each individual to participate in society. In the present context, this basket of *minima moralia* ought not only to contain a minimum income guarantee and a 'health promotion' guarantee, but also a universal 'human capital guarantee', providing access to high quality education and training. In the latter areas, the Scandinavian and Continental countries do well (although adaptation to the new economy is required), but their UK and Southern counterparts perform much less adequately.

The implications for the wider policy agenda is that European welfare states must place more emphasis within their normative framework on dynamic equality, being primarily attentive to the worst off, more hospitable to incentive-generating differentiation and flexibility, and actively vigilant with regard to the 'openness' of the opportunity structure. More intervention on the mobility – and educational – front is required in most European countries. The literature on social mobility shows that many sectors, trades and occupations remain characterised (in Europe significantly more than in North America) by a high degree of closure and that family backgrounds, rather than 'talent', is still one of the most important determinants of people's work and life chances.

Effective policy mixes

Confronting the problems particular to each of the welfare systems clearly requires solutions tailored to the circumstances of their individual member countries. Yet, as indicated already, one critical problem is common to all of them. As welfare states have become increasingly constrained on the fiscal side they have to increase the efficiency of their welfare programmes if they are not willing to renege on the core commitments of the postwar welfare state and seek to respond to new risks and needs. This effectively means that the sustainability of advanced welfare states requires combined action on several fronts – in health, pensions and labour markets – so as to reconcile the apparent polar opposites of efficiency and equality, growth and redistribution, competitiveness and solidarity. Above all, welfare states must become more employment-friendly – in promoting both the quantity and quality of jobs – as well as more supportive of mobility into them. The central requirements may be summarised as a robust macroeconomic policy, wage moderation and flexibility, employment-friendly and efficient social policy, labour market 'flexicurity', investment in education, training and mobility and new ways of tackling poverty and social exclusion.[7]

Robust macroeconomic policy

Today, moderate rates of inflation and budgetary discipline have become key elements of any sustainable macro-economic policy. Monetary policy has also become more restrictive in the context of liberalised capital markets. First, a stable macro-economic policy is clearly an important precondition for high economic growth and positive employment results. High public deficits and high inflation rates are incompatible in the long run with globalised financial markets. By the same token, if the structural budget deficit is low, on average, there will be some leeway for activating the stabilising function of fiscal policy in periods of low economic growth.

Wage moderation

Wage restraint has become an important requirement for successful adjustment in terms of employment maintenance. As it lowers labour costs, wage restraint can help to boost competitiveness in the exposed sector. It can also serve to create more jobs in domestic services that were previously priced out of the regular labour market. As a second-order effect, it may contribute to a lowering of the costs of social programmes. Finally, by the same token, wage restraint can allow governments to use improved public finances to lower the tax and contribution wedge. Moreover, moderate wage increases allow central banks to pursue a less restrictive monetary policy.

Employment-friendly and efficient tax and social policy

The financing and the benefit structure of the welfare state should allow for an expansion of employment at the lower end of the earnings scale without creating a class of 'working poor' while also stimulating flexible employment patterns (i.e. part-time employment and gradual retirement). A substantial reduction of social contributions for low-paid workers could resolve the dilemma created by social security systems which, being financed from payroll taxes, tend to increase labour costs for low-paid employment above the corresponding productivity levels if wages are sticky downwards.

The continental strategy of labour supply reduction (via early retirement) is a dead-end street, since increasing inactivity rates tend to aggravate the financial burden imposed on the active part of the population. Finally, with respect to pensions, there are reasons to believe that countries with a three-tiered pension system (such as in the Netherlands and Switzerland), combining different modes of financing (a mixture of pay-as-you-go and private and public funding elements) are comparatively robust in their revenue base.

Labour market flexibility and flexicurity

More intense international competition, technological change, shifts in demand and changed family patterns require a greater degree of flexibility in the labour market with respect to working patterns, wages and working time. The challenge for the welfare state lies in reconciling the need for the expansion of non-standard employment patterns, while on the other hand, modifying and eliminating the new social risks of atypical employment. At the same time, a shift away from passive income support to 'activation policies' – a policy trend already well advanced in the UK, Denmark and the Netherlands – would appear necessary to help the unemployed re-enter the labour market. If linked to appropriate tax and social security reforms – as in the Netherlands and Denmark – such policies can promote new employment without increasing the numbers of working poor (see Cox 1998).

Investment in education, training and mobility

As already suggested, in knowledge-intensive economies with increasingly flexible labour markets and more fluid social fabrics, the equality that matters has to do with those resources that allow people to 'keep pace' and cope with change. This means focusing on how effectively (and equitably) such resources are delivered by high quality education and how successfully opportunities for mobility provide escape routes from permanent entrapment in conditions of disadvantage. Even in countries with high quality education and training systems a process of adaptation is underway to align those systems with the rapidly changing demand for skills. In those with less developed systems – in the UK and the South – there is an urgent need for investment at all levels of the education system, linked with new measures for promoting vocational mobility and the transition out of a low-pay/no-pay employment traps.

New ways of fighting poverty and social exclusion

Socio-economic change under new external constraints, and the shift to a knowledge-based economy, creates new opportunities for economic progress and social inclusion, but also new risks of poverty and social exclusion. Recent Eurostat figures, excluding Finland and Sweden, suggest that, in the EU, 18% of the population – approximately 65 million citizens – live in poverty, defined as the percentage of the population under a low income threshold, set at 60% of the median equivalent income per person in each member state (see European Commission 2000).

To confront successfully the problem of poverty requires broad action against social exclusion, which is linked to employment opportunities, education, housing and living conditions, all of which are key determinants of the standard of living and the quality of life. Novel expressions of poverty and social exclusion require a new set of integrated policy measures. Policy strategies must act across a wide variety of areas, including social assistance, housing, education, mobility and culture.

Lessons from national experiences

What, however, is the best way of achieving the above-mentioned objectives? How can European countries reconcile economic growth, employment creation and the preservation – and renewal – of social justice? National experiences suggest that some fundamental interdependencies have to be taken into account.

We argue that successful policy adjustment basically follows a sequential logic, whereby salient policy problems in different policy areas are tackled one at the time. In contrast with the unitary and majoritarian Westminster model of the UK, most continental European economies are, to a greater or lesser degree, 'negotiating systems'. Policy reform in such systems is more likely to be constrained by 'veto power' and, as a consequence, more likely to follow an incremental pattern of policy change.

From a more normative standpoint, we would like to stress that sequential and incremental reforms, as they move at a slower pace than radical change, are also less likely to endanger the overall stability of the economic and political system. As 'big bang' reforms could generate massive uncertainty and undermine trust in the period of transition, this could easily threaten economic performance, at least in the short run, reducing the propensity to take economic risks and increasing social conflict. For reasons of *political* viability, and based on empirical evidence, we advocate a strategy of sequential and coordinated policy change, which allows for temporal learning and incremental adjustment (see Hemerijck and Schludi 2000).

The advantage of this type of temporal policy coordination is best illustrated by the varying degrees to which some countries have been able to organise a smooth interplay between wages, monetary and fiscal policy. Within a framework of tightly coupled systems of social and economic regulation, a successful employment strategy must include a set of coordinated and well-timed measures across various policy areas, aiming to reduce negative spill-over effects from one policy area to another. This type of policy 'concertation' – which experienced a second coming in the 1980s and 1990s – differs from Keynesian corporatist incomes policy of the 1970s, insofar as it is geared towards an improvement of supply-side conditions rather than pure demand management and redistributive policy (see Rhodes 1998b).

Such a coordinated approach is critically dependent on a range of institutional prerequisites. Political actors have to develop a common understanding of both the problem constellation and the policy solutions required, but this cannot be taken for granted. Here, the role of common fora that bring the social partners and state officials together is crucial. Within these fora, linkages between the production problem (the search for 'good' solutions) and the distributive problem (the choice of the solution that is best for each side), if successful, promote mutual trust and commitments.

Policy actors also need the political power to enact their commonly agreed to policies. Wage negotiations are a case in point. In order to generate positive employment results, they have to serve a double function. First, they should prevent wage inflation, secondly they should allow for sufficient flexibility at the micro-level. The second goal definitely requires a high degree of informational resources, which only the social partners can provide and thereby help to unburden the state of its regulatory overload. Thus, in order to realise a combination of wage restraint *and* wage flexibility, the approval of the social partners is essential.

Thus, with respect to the strong coupling between the spheres of labour market regulation and social security, the Dutch and the Danes have pursued conscious strategies of labour market de-segmentation, for which the term '*flexicurity*' has been coined. Labour market de-segmentation is geared towards a negotiated relaxation of employment protection for the stable, full-time, core workforce, which is coupled to increasing protection for peripheral, unstable, part-time and the temporarily employed in the rest of the economy.

This raises the issue of how to implement such coordinated solutions in those countries that do not have the traditional set of organisational prerequisites, including strong and cohesive employer and trade union organisations. Examples of countries that have succeeded in putting new forms of 'concertation' in place in the absence of a corporatist tradition include Italy, Ireland, Portugal and Spain, all of which have been experimenting with various forms of 'social pact'. This has enabled a series of policy innovations in employment, social security and tax policy that are helping to make these welfare states more sustainable and their labour markets more employment-friendly. France and Germany, by contrast, face greater conflict in moving forward with their respective social security, pensions and labour market reforms mostly because coordination currently eludes them.

The logic of the new social pacts in the former group of countries is rather different from traditional forms of social corporatism of the Scandinavian or Austrian varieties. First, they are less routinised. Secondly, and partly as a result, the partners will be institutionally weaker and the exit costs lower. Thirdly, the presence of the state is much more strongly felt, either as a coercive force or provider of incentives. This itself provides important cement for otherwise institutionally fragile bargains. European economic and monetary union has contributed to 'concertation' over macro-economic policy issues via a process of 'hardening' the state – providing a straight-jacket on policy options that allows the state more easily to induce other actors into an accord (see Rhodes 1998b, 2000c).

Thus, not only does the interlocking nature of European social security and employment systems require simultaneous action on multiple fronts, but broadening and deepening the bargain also compensates for the absence of conventional organisational prerequisites. This requires a complex and slow process of coalition building, but one that is essential if countries without a corporatist tradition are to succeed in creating the requisite institutions for a coordinated strategy of adjustment.

The same logic of integration and coordination can be extended to action against poverty and social exclusion. In line with the recognition that the predicament of social exclusion impinges on a wide range of policy areas, successful policy initiatives revolve around integrated approaches embedded in new forms of cooperation and partnerships, with the participation of key stakeholders, i.e. the socially excluded themselves. Both the Irish and Portuguese anti-poverty strategies stand out in terms of their strong partnership approach at various levels of decision making and implementation and the wide usage of targeted policy measures. In addition, in the Netherlands, Belgium and most recently in the United Kingdom, policy makers have launched an integrated approach to social exclusion, to be implemented though specific mechanisms of policy coordination and issue linkage across relevant policy areas.

What role for EU social policy?

What role can the EU play in this era of national welfare innovation and change? The EU has yet to acquire the legitimacy and capacity for intervention beyond certain boundaries, and these have been restricted, rather than extended, since Maastricht. This is not necessarily a tragedy: as already emphasised above, the EU's member states remain the primary level for the achievement, adjustment and defence of trade-offs between equity and efficiency and the complex bargains underpinning them (see Rhodes 1998a).

Of course, a new consensus may emerge on advances in specific areas of EU social policy, with new legislation developed either by the Commission and the Council of Ministers or between the latter and the social partners, as allowed for under the Maastricht Social Protocol and Agreement. Indeed, the Commission and the forthcoming French presidency will emphasise the need for further innovations in social and employment policy using traditional approaches – social action programmes and implementation via directives.

But of equal – if not greater – importance in the long run would be a new EU coordination role, which could influence the range of policies discussed above and seek to develop 'best practice' policy combinations and synergies. This raises the issue of the politico-institutional re-calibration – concerning policy levels and actors – required to consolidate and underpin the European social model. In principle, this could be achieved in two ways.

The first would be to allow differential levels of social protection, linked to varying levels of labour costs and social spending, underpinned by an explicit agreement on a threshold below which welfare expenditure would not fall. However, a differentiated system of social protection faces two predictable obstacles: poorer member states may resist the creation of a two-tier Europe in social policy, and pro-welfare elites in those countries may fear that such a differentiation will consign them permanently to a second-class club.

On the other hand, the idea of an agreed welfare floor is a good one and much more in keeping with EU tradition and practice.[8] This could be bolstered by the supranational reinforcement and encouragement of the national bargains discussed in the preceding section, which tackle existing inequities in welfare cover and extend the natural constituency of the labour movement, as well as introduce new forms of flexible work and social security and tax reform.

One specific area where an EU role is required is in helping ensure that both labour and capital remained linked in national social pacts, given the low exit-costs for these organisations in those countries without a corporatist tradition. At the European level, the Commission and member states should also attempt to forge a link between national pacts and the European social dialogue.

The Commission could also play a role in diffusing notions of 'best-practice' policy sequencing and linkages. In the field of poverty and social exclusion, for example, new integrated approaches, based on cooperation and benchmarking, pursued in many EU member states, has created the potential for Union action in fostering the exchange of national experiences among national policy makers (European Commission 2000). As poverty and social exclusion are increasingly dynamic phenomena, as material needs and social risks change over time, there is a clear need for commonly understood data and analysis that are able to account for the multi-faceted and dynamic understanding of poverty and social exclusion.

Also of central importance will be the development of new 'soft' instruments for European intervention in the member state economies and labour markets. These are essential if the policy blockage encountered by more traditional European instruments (e.g. social and employment policy directives) is to be avoided. They are also critical for areas where our understanding of how successful strategies should be forged is still under-developed. Once again, poverty and social exclusion are areas where monitoring and benchmarking at the level of the Union should take the initiative to make possible this type of problem diagnosis and policy evaluation. The 'openness' of opportunity structures and occupational mobility in the member states also deserves to become the object of systematic cross-national monitoring and benchmarking.

In fact, almost by stealth, during the 1990s the dynamics of European integration have been playing an increasingly important role in shaping social policy developments within the member states. The European Union, acting as a 'semi-sovereign' policy system, seems slowly but surely to be carving out a distinct 'policy space' also as regards social policy.

As far as *gender policy* is concerned, the 1990s have witnessed a real blossoming of EU initiatives addressing gender equality. European law and policy have set new standards for equal treatment in wages, social security and pensions, and a wide array of EU programmes are now available to promote women's integration into the labour market. These encourage an explicit and deliberate connection between the sphere of employment and other social spheres and exposing the relationship between paid and unpaid work (Rees 1998).

In the field of *employment*, the turning point has coincided with the launching of the 'Luxembourg process' in 1997 and the new employment chapter introduced in the new treaty signed at Amsterdam (see Goetschy 2000).[9] This chapter provides for the coordination of national employment policies using a 'management by objectives' approach, whereby EU institutions draw up guidelines and monitor their implementation through an institutionalised procedure. This neither 'binds' the member states in a hard, legal sense, nor foresees possible sanctions as in the case of budgetary policy. The National Action Plans via which this employment strategy is implemented provide a further opportunity for dialogue between the social partners and their involvement in policy design.

Despite its 'softness' this process of coordination is acquiring increasing salience for the shaping of public policy at the supra-national, national and sub-national levels. Although specifically focused on employment issues, the process has crucial implications for other social policies as well. Not surprisingly, many of the employment guidelines drawn up so far in the new institutional framework call for an adjustment of various institutional features of existing welfare arrangements.

Yet, also in the field of social protection, a (very) soft process of coordination seems to be gradually emerging, mainly thanks to efforts by the Commission and the European Parliament. This process started in 1992 with two recommendations on the 'convergence' of social protection objectives. It continued with the establishment of a periodic system of reporting (the *Social Protection in Europe* reports) and the launching of a 'framework initiative' on the future of social protection and its 'modernisation' (a term coined in a 1997 communication). It finally culminated in the recent proposal by the Commission for a 'concerted strategy for modernising social protection'. The latter calls for a new institutionalised process for 'exchanging experience and monitoring developments', based on three elements: (a) the establishment of a group of high level senior officials as a 'focal point' of the process; (b) the improvement of the reporting system and (c) a formal link between this new process and the Luxembourg process itself.

At a more general level, the macro-economic dialogue put in place in Cologne in 1999 begins to address at the European level the more general issue of complex policy interdependencies mentioned above. It specifically promotes relations between European employer and union representatives, the Commission, Ministers of Finance and Employment, the European Central Bank, and governors of national central banks focusing on the interconnections between wages, monetary, budgetary and fiscal policies.

Timid as it may sound, this new concerted strategy could serve as a promising wedge for breaking the institutional traps created by both the logic of asymmetry and the logic of subsidiarity, which isolates social policy from other policy domains and relegates social protection policy inexorably within the preserve of national sovereignty. Thus, in terms of its *de facto* functioning rather than its modest formal 'constitution', Social Europe already appears more integrated and more de-nationalised than is normally assumed. While there remains both a need and opportunity for re-launching a 'hard' agenda, resting on more binding legal instruments and including, among other things, the formal Treaty recognition of fundamental social rights, soft coordination is a promising mechanism for mitigating the undesirable effects of 'negative integration'.

Conclusions

In sum, European welfare states are undergoing a process of recasting and redefinition but thus far not one of retrenchment along the lines of a neo-liberal *pensée unique*. Scope remains for a positive reinterpretation of the philosophy and objectives of European welfare states that simultaneously tackles their most serious problems while also consolidating the core principles of the European social model. Yet the challenges are real, as is the possibility of negative outcomes. If European societies wish to reset themselves on a course of just growth, they will not only have to re-adapt their welfare institutions to the new context, but must increase their adaptability as such, enhancing their social and policy learning capabilities. They must find new ways of combining security with flexibility, competitiveness with solidarity. We present this process as one of functional, distributive, normative and political–institutional re-calibration.

As we have argued, negotiated policy reforms that seek to reconcile competitiveness with solidarity at the national level can be underpinned and encouraged by a new role for the supranational authorities. This could be achieved by extending the new coordination ambitions of the Luxembourg employment strategy and procedures across other social policy domains and integrating them with the parallel Cologne process on macro-economic policies and the Cardiff process on structural policies. The decentralised character of the implementation of the guidelines set by the supranational authorities and the involvement of national bureaucracies (which have margins of manoeuvre, but within these set temporal and substantive limits) could then work in their turn to stimulate an improvement of national policy structures and styles – both in terms of efficiency and effectiveness. If this new process of social policy coordination can be made to operate 'at its best' the whole process can generate an optimal mix of 'Europeanisation' and 'nationalisation' of the policy areas concerned.

In arguing for the utility of soft coordination as a means of guiding the future development of the European social model, it should be stressed that the effects of such a policy are slow to come by. Improvements on two fronts are required if the new institutional architecture is to make an incisive impact on welfare reform across diverse member states. The first is substantive and has to do with the objects of soft coordination. Through the practice of 'mainstreaming', gender and, more generally, anti-discrimination policies have been 'hooked' to the existing processes of supranational guidance. Social exclusion and education and training should be similarly integrated with other EU objectives for reform. These two policy areas are crucial for a 're-calibration' of the European social model in line with the aims and needs of the knowledge-based economy and learning society. A high-level initiative to elevate the salience of these two fields within the EU's emerging coordinative regime is both desirable and legally feasible.

A second front of improvement is more procedural. Precisely because they are soft and open, the coordination mechanisms of the various 'processes' and initiatives launched in recent years are always exposed to the risk of becoming too complex and baroque, leading not only to output inefficiency, but also to actor frustration. This trend is further amplified by the inevitable overlaps (substantive, temporal, personal) between the various processes themselves. Thus, a broad and incisive rationalisation of the overall institutional framework for open coordination is in order. A promising solution could be that of establishing the Cologne process (and especially the Broad Economic Guidelines) as a sort of 'umbrella' framework, under which two distinct but interconnected tracks (with carefully set timetables) would run:

- a track for the coordination of all structural policies, prioritising the objective of a rapid transition to the knowledge-based economy; and
- a track for the coordination of all 'social promotion' policies, prioritising not only the creation of more 'flexicure' employment, but also wider 're-calibration' objectives, broadened to greater inclusion and human capital enhancement for a cohesive 'learning' society.

Hard choices await the European Social Model – choices that concern practices and arrangements that are still taken for granted by social and political majorities in all countries today. However, the institutional reconstruction of the model has already begun with initiatives taken at Luxembourg, Cardiff and Cologne and these are moving mostly in the right direction. At the Lisbon Summit in March 2000, the EU leaders made a commitment to continue along this road. The agenda set at Lisbon needs fine-tuning and some additions, but it is a solid and coherent one. The strains and uncertainties of the current scenario are likely to stay with us for a long time, but our capacities to respond are definitely improving.

Acknowledgements

This chapter derives from work carried out for the Portuguese Presidency of the European Union (January–June 2000). We are grateful to Stephan Leibfried for bringing it into its final shape.

167

Notes

1. For a discussion of the range of possible value combinations and institutional arrangements, see Ferrera and Rhodes (2000).
2. For a fuller discussion see Rhodes (1998a).
3. This new policy approach was most clearly advanced in the Delors White Paper of 1993, see Commission (1993).
4. This categorisation extends Esping-Andersen's 'three worlds' approach to a 'fourth', southern, variety. See Esping-Andersen (1990); see also Ferrera (1996) and F. W. Scharpf in this issue.
5. For useful recent analyses of the Scandinavian countries, see Stephens (1996) and Kuhnle (2000); see also S. Kuhnle's essay in this issue.
6. See Rhodes (2000b); see also G. Bonoli and B. Palier in this issue, contrasting the reform experience of the UK and France.
7. For an extended presentation of the argument which follows, see Hemerijck and Schludi (2000).
8. For a discussion of both the 'welfare club' and 'welfare floor' ideas, see Scharpf (1999).
9. For background and initial evaluations, see Goetschy (1998) and Kenner (1999).

References

Barnard, C. (2000) Social dumping and the race to the bottom: some lessons for the European Union from Delaware?, *European Law Review*, **25**, 57–78.

Commission of the European Communities (1993): *White Paper: Growth Competitiveness and Employment*, 700 Final, Brussels.

Cox, R. H. (1998) From safety net to trampoline: labour market activation in the Netherlands and Denmark, *Governance: An International Journal of Policy and Administration*, **11**(4), 397–414.

Esping-Andersen, G. (1990) *The Three Worlds of Welfare Capitalism*, Cambridge: Polity.

Esping-Andersen, G. (1996) Welfare states without work: the impasse of labour shedding and familialism in continental European social policy, in G. Esping-Andersen (ed), *Welfare States in Transition: National Adaptations in Global Economies*, London: Sage Publications, pp. 66–87.

European Commission (2000) *Building an Inclusive Europe*, Communication from the Commission, Brussels, DGV, Employment and Social Affairs.

Ferrera, M. (1996) The southern model of welfare in social Europe, *Journal of European Social Policy*, **6**(1), 17–37.

Ferrera, M. (2000) Reconstructing the Welfare State in Southern Europe, in S. Kuhnle (ed.), Survival of the European Welfare State, London: Routledge, pp. 166–181.

Ferrera, M. and Rhodes, M. (2000) Building a sustainable welfare state, *West European Politics* **23**(2), 259–283 (special issue on Recasting European Welfare States, edited by M. Ferrera and M. Rhodes).

Freeman, C. and Soete, L. (1994) *Work for All or Mass Unemployment? Computerised Technical Change into the 21st Century*, London, New York: Pinter Publishers.

Goetschy, J. (1998) The European employment strategy: genesis and development, *European Journal of Industrial Relations*, **5**(2), 117–137.

Goetschy, J. (2000) European Union and national social pacts: employment and social protection put to the test of joint regulation. In: G. Fajertag and Ph. Pochet (eds) *Social Pacts in Europe*, European Trade Union Institute.

Hemerijck, A. and Schludi, M. (2000) Sequence of policy failures and effective responses. In: F. W. Scharpf and V. A. Schmidt (eds), *Work and Welfare in the Open Economy*, Oxford: Oxford University Press.

Iversen, T. and Wren, A. (1998) Equality, employment and budgetary restraint: the trilemma of the service economy, *World Politics*, **50**(4), 507–546.

Kenner, J. (1999) The EC employment title and the third way: making soft law work?, *International Journal of Comparative Labour Law and Industrial Relations*, Spring, 33–60.

Kuhnle, S. (2000) The Scandinavian welfare state in the 1990s: challenged but viable, *West European Politics* **23**(2), 210–229 (special issue on Recasting European Welfare States, edited by M. Ferrera and M. Rhodes).

Leibfried, S. and Pierson, P. (2000) Social policy. In: Helen and William Wallace (eds), *Policy–Making in the European Union*, 4th edn, Oxford: Oxford University Press, pp. 267–292.

OECD (1996) The experience with fiscal consolidation in OECD countries, *OECD Economic Outlook*, **59**, June, 33–41.

Pierson, P. (1997) Skeptical reflections on globalization and the welfare state, Paper presented at the *International Conference on Socio–Economics*, Montreal, July.

Pierson, P. (1998) Irresistible forces, immovable objects: post–industrial welfare states confront permanent austerity, *Journal of European Public Policy* **5**(4), 539–560.

Pierson, P. and Leibfried, S. (1995) Multi–tiered institutions and the making of social policy. In: S. Leibfried and P. Pierson (eds), *European Social Policy: Between Fragmentation and Integration*, Washington DC: The Brookings Institution Press, pp. 1–40.

Pierson, P. and Leibfried, S. (1998) Etats providence semi–souverains: élaborer des politiques sociales dans une Europe multi–niveaux. In: S. Leibfried and P. Pierson (eds), *Politiques sociales européennes: entre intégration et fragmentation*, Paris: Editions l'Harmattan, pp. 47–88.

Rawls, J. (1971) *A Theory of Justice*, Cambridge, Belknap Press.

Rees, T. (1998) *Mainstreaming Equality in the European Union: Education, Training and Labour Market Policies*, London: Routledge.

Rhodes, M. (ed) (1997) *Southern European Welfare States: Between Crisis and Reform*, London: Frank Cass.

Rhodes, M. (1998a) Defending the social contract: the EU between global constraints and domestic imperatives. In D. Hine and H. Kassim (eds), *Beyond the Market: the European Union and National Social Policy*, London: Routledge, pp. 36–59.

Rhodes, M. (1998b) Globalisation, labour markets and welfare states: a future of competitive corporatism? In: M. Rhodes and Y. Mény, *The Future of European Welfare: A New Social Contract?* London: Macmillan, pp. 178–203.

Rhodes, M. (2000a) Globalization, welfare states and employment: Is there a European third way? In: N. Bermeo (ed), *Unemployment in the New Europe*, Cambridge: Cambridge University Press.

Rhodes, M. (2000b) Desperately seeking a solution: social democracy, Thatcherism and the third way in British welfare, *West European Politics* **23**(2), 161–187 (special issue on Recasting European Welfare States, edited by M. Ferrera and M. Rhodes).

Rhodes, M. (2000c) The political economy of social pacts: competitive corporatism and European welfare reform. In: P. Pierson (ed) *The New Politics of Welfare*, Oxford: Oxford University Press.

Rieger, E. and Leibfried, S. (1996) Welfare state limits to globalization, *Politics and Society.* **26**(3), 363–390.

Rodrik, D. (1997) *Why Do More Open Economies Have Bigger Governments?* National Bureau of Economic Research (Working Paper No. 5537).

Scharpf, F. W. (1999) *Governing in Europe: Effective and Democratic?,* Oxford: Oxford University Press.

Stephens, J. D. (1996) The Scandinavian welfare states: achievements, crisis and prospects. In: G. Esping-Andersen (ed), *Welfare States in Transition: National Adaptations in Global Economies*, London: Sage Publications, pp. 32–65.

About the Authors

Maurizio Ferrera is Professor of Public Policy and Administration at the University of Pavia and directs the Center for Comparative Political Research at Bocconi University in Milan. His main field of interest is comparative social policy, with a special emphasis on Southern European welfare states. He is the author of several books in Italian. He recently co-edited (with Martin Rhodes) *Recasting European Welfare States* (London: Frank Cass, 2000).

Anton Hemerijck is Senior Lecturer in Public Administration at Leiden University and was a Visiting Fellow at the Max-Planck-Institute for the Study of Societies in Cologne for the past three years. His fields of research are issues of public policy, welfare reform and, more generally, comparative political economy. His book (with Jelle Visser) *A Dutch Miracle. Job Growth, Welfare Reform and Corporatism in the Netherlands* (1997), has also been published in Dutch (1998), Italian (1998), German (1998), and Japanese (2000).

Martin Rhodes is Professor of European Public Policy in the Department of Social and Political Science at the European University Institute in Florence, Italy. His main interest is European integration and globalisation and their effects on governance, labour market regimes and welfare states, comparative public policy, and Southern welfare states. His latest books are (with Maurizio Ferrera, co-editor) *Recasting European Welfare States* (London: Frank Cass, 2000) and (with Yves Meny, co-editor) *The Future of European Welfare: A New Social Contract?* (Basingstoke: Macmillan, 1998).

Kerstin Kurzhals

Resource Recombination in Firms from a Dynamic Capability Perspective

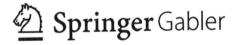 Springer Gabler

Kerstin Kurzhals
Department of Strategic and Applied
Management
Coventry University Business School
Coventry, UK

Dissertation, Coventry University, 2015

ISSN 2731-3220   ISSN 2731-3239   (electronic)
Gabler Theses
ISBN 978-3-658-35665-1   ISBN 978-3-658-35666-8   (eBook)
https://doi.org/10.1007/978-3-658-35666-8

© The Editor(s) (if applicable) and The Author(s), under exclusive license to Springer
Fachmedien Wiesbaden GmbH, part of Springer Nature 2021
This work is subject to copyright. All rights are solely and exclusively licensed by the Publisher,
whether the whole or part of the material is concerned, specifically the rights of translation, reprint-
ing, reuse of illustrations, recitation, broadcasting, reproduction on microfilms or in any other
physical way, and transmission or information storage and retrieval, electronic adaptation, computer
software, or by similar or dissimilar methodology now known or hereafter developed.
The use of general descriptive names, registered names, trademarks, service marks, etc. in this
publication does not imply, even in the absence of a specific statement, that such names are exempt
from the relevant protective laws and regulations and therefore free for general use.
The publisher, the authors and the editors are safe to assume that the advice and information in this
book are believed to be true and accurate at the date of publication. Neither the publisher nor the
authors or the editors give a warranty, expressed or implied, with respect to the material contained
herein or for any errors or omissions that may have been made. The publisher remains neutral with
regard to jurisdictional claims in published maps and institutional affiliations.

Responsible Editor: Anna Pietras
This Springer Gabler imprint is published by the registered company Springer Fachmedien
Wiesbaden GmbH part of Springer Nature.
The registered company address is: Abraham-Lincoln-Str. 46, 65189 Wiesbaden, Germany

Foreword

A fundamental paradigm shift can be observed in the field of innovation research – from innovation being regarded as the result of pure basic research, towards a form of innovation generation, where innovations is seen to create a benefit and as the result of "carrying out new combinations", as originally defined by Joseph Schumpeter.

Also different from the past is the trajectory of an innovation; the innovation process is no longer determined by radical breakthroughs from basic research to the development of new knowledge, but mainly by synthesis, linkage and coupling of existing knowledge, technologies and experience. Therefore, a strong desire exists to understand how companies can successfully recombine their existing resources in new ways and/or integrate new resources within their existing resource base to leverage their innovation potentials. Accordingly, from a research perspective a broader and even different perspective on innovation generation must be taken today than years ago. This can be achieved by focusing less on a rigid innovation process but more on the organisational capacities and capabilities that companies need in order to develop successful innovations.

This book consequently looks at innovation generation in firms from a capacity building perspective and thus makes an important and new contribution to resource- and competence-based research. The focus of the work is on the role of dynamic capabilities in the process of innovation generation through resource recombination. In this context, dynamic capabilities are regarded as organisational capabilities to integrate, build and reconfigure organisational competencies and thus the ability to adapt quickly and dynamically to a constantly changing market environment. By examining the impact of a specific set of dynamic capabilities on the recombination of resources in companies, the research provides concrete answers to the question of which factors explain the competitive differences in value creation between companies.

In this way, existing deficits in management and innovation research are addressed, as there is an urgent need to better understand the interrelationship between dynamic capabilities, the firm's resource base and innovation in the form of resource recombination. The book thus makes an important contribution to clarifying the terminology and concept of dynamic capabilities, their role and impact on the development of new resource recombination in firms.

The dissertation was conducted as part of a cooperative doctoral program between FH Münster University of Applied Sciences (Germany) and Coventry University Business School (UK). The dissertation was submitted to University of Coventry and completed with a disputation (viva voce). For Dr Kurzhals' doctorate, I had the honour of supervising her research on the part of FH Münster University of Applied Sciences – in addition, Dr Gerry Urwin and Prof Tom Donnelly completed the team of supervisors as second supervisor and co-promoter on the part of Coventry University.

Dr Kurzhals achieved excellent results and completed her PhD with high distinction. The theoretical insights gained by this research, which can also be applied in management practice, make a significant contribution to the structuring, concretisation and further development of the research field and provide an excellent basis for the further integration of the dynamic capacity perspective into the wider disciplines of strategic management and innovation management.

Prof. Dr. habil. Thomas Baaken

Münster
August 2021

Acknowledgements

Within the last five years of writing this PhD thesis many individuals have accompanied me, which deserve my sincerely gratitude.

First of all, I would like to express my very great appreciation and thanks to Dr. Gerry Urwin, my first supervisor and director of studies at Coventry University, for his valuable and constructive suggestions and guidance throughout the PhD. Gerry, I always will be grateful for your aspiring supervision, invaluably constructive feedback, and friendly advice during the entire PhD project. I also would like to thank my supervisory team at Coventry University, Dr. Stefania Paladini, for her time and dedication, and especially Professor Tom Donnelly for his valuable comments and feedback in revising the thesis.

Likewise, I would like to thank Professor Thomas Baaken, my supervisor at Münster University of Applied Sciences, for creating manifold opportunities throughout the years for my personal and academic development, for opening countless doors and for removing any obstacles given on the way. Or said differently, with your positive attitude of life – in which barriers simply do not exist as long as the drivers are strong enough – you taught me a way of thinking which shaped me for life. Without your motivating and empowering personality, your unconditional support and trust in my abilities, this PhD thesis simply would not exist. Your mentorship and supervision allowed me to gain the freedom and power to realise this project. Your advice on both research and personal development has been invaluable and I am forever grateful.

I moreover want to acknowledge Dr. Caroline Plewa among my supervisors, as Caroline contributed considerably with her scientific expertise in directing my thesis, acting as external advisor and mentor giving me professional, scientific and methodological advice, reflection, aspiring guidance and valuable feedback whenever needed. I thank you, Carolin, for your selfless dedication to science, your heartsome encouragement and enthusiasm, and at the right point in time also for reminding me that "a good PhD is a done PhD". You have been a tremendous mentor and moreover academic role model for me – both as scientist and lecturer, and as person and friend.

I would also like to thank Professor Mats Magnusson from the KTH Royal Institute of Technology in Stockholm for offering me a visiting researcher position and thereby giving me the opportunity for fruitful discussions, reflections, and refinements of my initial research ideas.

Moreover, as this thesis has been assessed and approved by an outstanding international examination committee, I would like to take this opportunity and thank the members for their important roles they have played. Sincerely thanks to David Morris, Professor of Business Development at the University of Coventry, and Peter van der Sijde, Professor of Organization, Entrepreneurship and Technology at the Vrije Universiteit in Amsterdam.

Besides having the support of such these great faculty members, successfully completing a PhD is built on much more, rather it has been a whole network of people, colleagues, and friends which accompanied me during this PhD trajectory.

First, I would like to thank my dear colleagues and friends at the Science-to-Business-Marketing Research Centre for providing me with a research environment, I could not have imagined better: supportive, trustful, reliable, engaging, open-minded and empowering. It is simply invaluable to know this repository of brilliant minds around you. Seldom I met people like you, you simply are unique. Thank you for being more than colleagues, but trusted friends. I am proud of having had such a great company on my PhD trajectory and I am sure this connection will stay for a lifetime.

I was not expecting to find such an empowering work climate once more, fortunately I found it at noventum consulting: a true "great place to work". I want to thank my colleagues at noventum consulting who accompanied me on the path from research to practice, and especially, I want to thank Uwe Rotermund, who always supported and encouraged me in my research, and truly opened me the path from 'science-to-business'.

In addition, my PhD trajectory builds on a strong foundation of my family: my parents, my husband Reiner, his sons Henry and Louis, and our little daughter Sabeth. This PhD would not have been possible without your continuous support and encouragement.

My wonderful husband: Reiner. It is not possible to find words to describe how thankful I am to know you on my side. You are the person who has been with me through all the ups and downs, side by side, day by day. You accompanied my worries and fears, and celebrated with me my successes and breakthroughs. You were my energy pool, my critical and motivating voice, my balance; especially when I came home after long days at the institute and could no longer grasp a single thought, it was your arms that caught me up. Thank you for keeping me going, for retrieving me out of my 'research tunnel' countless times, but especially for showing me the many more wonderful facets that our life holds besides doing my research.

And there is one more person: my mom, who always has been a role model for me. Together with my dad, early on she has taken me to the mountains and showed me how to climb a hill. It was you, who awoke my love of the mountains. You taught me that no path is straight up, that on the way sometimes there are long valleys in between the mountains, and that the path is sometimes rocky and not always easy. You showed me what it means to never give up, to go on, because the beauty and happiness of having climbed a mountain compensates for all the struggles on the way. But moreover – and this is where I am especially grateful for – you showed me that most often it is the unplanned, and hitherto, untrodden sections of the path, that holds the greatest secrets and beauties of the hike. I thank you for this school of life, for the trust and unconditional love you gave me to find my own way. Your faith in me have built the foundation to define, plan and finally master this hill and to arrive where I am today. I know, if my dad would have the possibility to watch me from one of these hills, he would be proud of his little girl.

Within the last year of my PhD, indeed our little daughter Sabeth was born. She opened a completely new dimension of love, life, and happiness to me, indeed showing me every morning that the most wonderful, most delightful, and sometimes also most challenging paths of my life is yet to come. It was your arrival, Sabeth, that showed me that now is the right time to close this chapter (otherwise I guess I would never have finished!) and to move forward to the next journey of life. There are so many more mountains to discover, and I can't wait to climb the first hill together with you. I therefore dedicate this work to my little daughter Sabeth.

Dr. Kerstin Kurzhals

Münster
March 2015

Abstract of the Thesis

This research elaborates the concept of Resource Recombination in firms from a Dynamic Capability perspective. With the investigation of the role of Dynamic Capabilities in the process of Resource Recombination, this research addresses some existing shortcomings in the Dynamic Capability literature, where there is a crucial need to understand better the interrelationship between Dynamic Capabilities, the firm's resource base, and innovation in the form of Resource Recombinations. Examining the effect of a specific set of Dynamic Capabilities – namely the firm's Sensing Capacity, Learning Capacity, Integrating Capacity and Coordinating Capacity – on Resource Recombination in firms, this research sheds light on what explains the competitive heterogeneity and variance in resource value creation across firms. Addressing this issue, this research contributes to resource and competence-based research by presenting and empirically testing a conceptual model of factors influencing Resource Recombination in firms.

The conceptual model is developed based on a thorough literature review before being further tested, refined and validated using a mixed-method research approach, entailing qualitative and quantitative research steps. Hereto, empirical data from 208 target respondents are analysed applying structural equation modelling (SEM) principles, including structural path analysis and hypothesis testing, model re-specification, as well as mediation and moderation analyses.

In line with the resource-based view (RBV), empirical findings confirm that the firm's resource endowments explain – in part – value creation in firms. But moreover, this study found that the effectiveness of those resource endowments to provide productive performance outcomes depends on the extent to which firms possess specific Dynamic Capabilities: Sensing and Learning capacities are important for building the potential value of resources for Resource Recombination while Integrating and Coordinating capacities are necessary for realising the value creation potential of those resources by developing new Resource Recombinations. Accordingly, regarding their role and effects towards Resource Recombination, two different types of Dynamic Capabilities can be distinguished: Potential Building Dynamic Capabilities and Value Realising Dynamic Capabilities, whereby both capacity modes have complementary roles and are critical to the achievement of superior performance. Moreover, empirical evidence is given that the firm's Entrepreneurial Orientation and Networking Orientation are important antecedents for developing Dynamic Capabilities and consequently, Resource Recombinations.

The principal aim of this research was to bring clarity to the notion of Dynamic Capabilities, their role and effects on building Resource Recombinations in firms. With the Dynamic Capability framework and conceptual model presented, this research offers a more precise definition of the firm's Dynamic Capabilities, shedding light on their role and effects towards developing new Resource Recombinations and separating them from their antecedents and consequences. Therewith, this research not only contributes towards opening up the black box of Resource Recombination in firms but moreover helps to establish Dynamic Capabilities as a theoretically, well-founded and useful construct for strategic management. By explicitly embedding the Dynamic Capability perspective in resource-based explanations for value creation, this research extends the traditional focus of the RBV, working towards a more dynamic interpretation of the RBV. It thereby tries to overcome the identified limitations of past research in this field.

Outline of the Thesis

The following section presents an outline of the thesis and describes the role of each chapter within the thesis in order to lead the reader through the work.

Chapter one provides an introduction of this research, giving an overview of the research and providing the general focus of this PhD thesis. Besides establishing the research scope and context, the research objectives and questions addressed by this research are outlined. Moreover, a brief overview of the research approach and methodology of this research is presented.

Chapter two presents a literature review on the principal parent theories, the resource and competence-based research. In this chapter, first, the concept of *Resource Recombination* (RR) and its importance for economic development is discussed, based on existing literature within the wider disciplines of strategic management and entrepreneurship. Also, the theoretical foundation of this research is established, presenting the evolution and background of the resource and competence-based research, outlining the different streams of literature in this area of research, and demarcating them from related areas. Thereafter, to provide the conceptual foundation for the research, the status quo in literature is described, consolidating current knowledge of the core concepts relevant for this research to develop a mutual understanding. Subsequently, the research gaps derived from the review of current literature and addressed in this research are presented. Importantly, this chapter also identifies and defines the relevant constructs to be included in this study.

Chapter three develops the conceptual model and hypotheses for this research. By investigating the relation between the resource base, *Dynamic Capabilities* (DCs), and its performance outcomes RR, this chapter contributes to establish a better understanding of these interrelations, leading to the development of a conceptual model to be tested, refined, and validated in a following qualitative and subsequent quantitative research step. Starting with an examination of resource value creation in firms, specific characteristics of the resources and their influence for determining the potential value of the resource base for RR are described next, the DC framework is established, and the role of a specific set of DCs in the process of resource value creation is further investigated. Lastly, relevant framework conditions for the development of DCs are discussed. Based on the established understanding of the individual variables and their interrelationships and theoretical linkages, this chapter concludes with the presentation of the conceptual model and the hypotheses for further analysis. This chapter provides the theoretical foundation, the determinants and framework conditions of the RR concept and outlines this research's argument and related hypotheses.

Chapter four describes the overall research design, methodology and focuses on the qualitative findings leading to the model and hypotheses refinement. Starting with a description of the general research design, entailing both research strategy and methods, in the subsequent part, this chapter focuses on describing and justifying the qualitative research methods used in this study and outlines the research findings of the first, qualitative research step. Drawing on the key finding from the qualitative research step, minor adjustments to the conceptual model are presented.

Chapter five subsequently describes the quantitative research methods, questionnaire design, and data collection process applied for empirically testing the conceptual model and hypotheses. A critical examination and justification of the data collection method is followed by a detailed description of the questionnaire design, entailing the levels of measurement, theory and statistical analysis, the operationalisation of the measurement constructs, scales and measurement items, as well as the pre-test of the survey instrument. Furthermore, the data collection process is described, outlining the sampling procedure, frame and size, as well as non-response bias.

Chapter six outlines the individual steps of data analysis and presents the quantitative research results. The conceptual model and thus the proposed interrelationships among the endogenous and exogenous constructs are tested by means of structural path analysis using Structural Equation Modelling (SEM) principles. Starting with the step of data preparation and evaluation of normality assumptions, in the following, as a result of the Exploratory Factor Analyses (EFA) and Confirmatory Factor Analyses (CFA), the *measurement model* is presented, whereby relevant issues, such as construct reliability and validity and model fit, are described. Furthermore, important concerns for SEM are presented, including goodness-of-fit indexes, one-factor congeneric measurement models, model identification, multivariate assumptions, common method bias, measurement model invariance and the calculation of composite variables. Based on the EFA and CFA results, the *structural path model* for analysing the causal relationships between the constructs is presented, and hypotheses are tested. The results are analysed and presented in three steps, namely hypotheses testing, model re-specification and moderation and mediation analysis.

Chapter seven elaborates on the results of this research, discussing and integrating all research findings regarding the role of DCs and the impact of resource endowments in the process of resource value creation through RRs in firms. Based on the discussion of the key findings, managerial implications are derived, contributions to the literature are delineated, and limitations of this research are outlined. Before concluding, suggestions for future research activities are given.

Contents

About the Author

Dr. Kerstin Kurzhals is junior professor for Science-to-Society – Innovation, Engagement und Co-Creation at the Münster School of Business (MSB). Affiliated with the S2BMRC at MUAS in Germany, she researches, lectures and conducts research and industry projects at the intersection of innovation, entrepreneurship and strategic management. As head of the Science-to-Society research group her research activities lies in developing new ways to promote and facilitate the collaboration between academia, society and business.

Next to her academic profile, she has gained several years of experience in industry working as consultant for innovation and change management at an international IT management consultancy. Prior work experience further includes the Fraunhofer Institute for Material Flow and Logistics, the Institute for Management of Innovation and Technology at the KTH Royal Institute of Technology in Stockholm, Proximity Consulting a consulting group of BBDO Germany, as well as Siemens-Business-Services GmbH and Audi AG. Both in her academic as well as industrial career she gained extensive experiences in managing national and international research projects, in inter- and transdisciplinary research contexts.

In 2015, Kerstin Kurzhals successfully completed her doctoral thesis at Coventry University Business School (UK), in which she investigated the role and effect of dynamic capabilities for innovation generation in firms. With a deep enthusiasm for innovation-centred change, she is passionate about exploring, understanding, and initiating transformation and change processes in companies, universities and society. Accordingly, her research interest lies in the field of Digital Transformation, Entrepreneurship, Change Management und Innovation. Her research activities cover a wide range of topics in these fields, have a strong societal focus on responsible research and innovation, and are inspired by schools of thought such as Design Thinking, Lean Startup and Agile Management. In all her doing she convincingly interconnects the latest findings from research and practice, and vice versa.

In her role of educator, Kerstin Kurzhals lectures in the field of Innovation Management (e.g. SME Innovation) and Digital Transformation (e.g. Innovative and Digital Business Models), and Strategic Marketing (e.g. Science-to-Society semester projects) where she designed a variety of new courses and formats implementing Project Based Learning (PBL) and Service Learning (SL) elements to develop digital, leadership, and change management skills to educate the Digital Change Agents of tomorrow. Numerous publications, organisation of international workshops and conferences as well as review activities complete her profile.

Abbreviations

α	Cronbach's coefficient alpha
AGFI	Adjusted Goodness-of-Fit
CAIC	Consistent Akaike Information Criterion
CBV	Competence Based View
CFA	Confirmatory Factor Analyses
CFI	Comparative Fit Index
CMB	Common Method Bias
c.r.	Critical Ratio
CU	Coventry University
DC	Dynamic Capability
DCP	Dynamic Capability Perspective
EFA	Exploratory Factor Analyses
EO	Entrepreneurial Orientation
GFI	Goodness-of-Fit
GLS	Generalised-Least-Squares
ICT	Information and Communications Technology
IT	Information Technology
KBV	Knowledge Based View
KMO	Kaiser-Meyer-Olkin measure
ML	Maximum-Likelihood
NFI	Normed Fit Index
NO	Networking Orientation
NPD	New Product Development
OECD	Organisation for Economic Co-operation and Development
PAF	Principal Axis Factoring
PCA	Principal Component Analysis

ρη	Construct reliability
ρvc (η)	Average Variance Extracted (AVE)
R&D	Research and Development
RBV	Resource Based View
RMR	Root Mean Squared Residual
RMSEA	Root Mean-Square Error of Approximation
RR	Resource Recombination
SD	Standard Deviation
SEM	Structural Equation Modelling
SIC	Standard Industrial Classification
TLI	Tucker-Lewis Index
UK	United Kingdom
B	Beta Value/ Regression Weigth
χ^2	Chi-Square
χ^2/df	Normed Chi-Square
$\Delta\chi^2$	Chi-Square Difference
ζ	Residual (Error Term)

List of Figures

List of Tables

Introduction

1

1.1 Aims and Objectives

> "Indeed, the heart of business management and strategy concerns the creation, evaluation, manipulation, administration, and deployment of unpriced specialized resource combinations" (Lippman and Rumelt, 2003, p. 1085)

In dynamic environments where fierce competition exists, the need to make efficient use of a firm's resources is crucial. The resource based view (RBV) sees a firm's competitive position primarily determined by the special features and quality of firm specific resources (Schreyögg and Conrad, 2006, Barney, 1991). According to the RBV, observable performance differences between firms can primarily be led back to the different resources that are available within the firm at one point in time (Freiling et al., 2006). The RBV proposes that in order to gain sustainable competitive advantage, a firm needs to own or create unique resources which are rare, valuable, difficult to imitate and non-substitutable (VRIN) (e.g. Barney, 1991, Grant, 1991, Miller et al., 1996).

However, while owning or having access to rare, valuable, hardly imitable and non-substitutable resources is necessary for a competitive advantage (Barney, 1991), they must be effectively managed and synchronised *to realise* a competitive advantage (e.g. Hansen et al., 2004, Kor and Mahoney, 2005, Holcomb et al., 2009).

In dynamic environments, where firms continuously strive to find the right match between strategic assets and strategic industry factors (Amit and Schoemaker, 1993), the resources, and the way they are being combined, must be altered if the competitive advantage is to be sustained over time (Barney, 1991, Black and Boal, 1994, Capron et al., 1998). Thus, as stated by Holcomb and

© The Author(s), under exclusive license to Springer Fachmedien Wiesbaden GmbH, part of Springer Nature 2021
K. Kurzhals, *Resource Recombination in Firms from a Dynamic Capability Perspective*, Gabler Theses,
https://doi.org/10.1007/978-3-658-35666-8_1

colleagues (2009): "Efficient production with heterogeneous resources is a result not of having better resources but in knowing more accurately the relative productive performance of those resources" (Holcomb et al., 2009, p. 457, emphasis included in the original by Alchian and Demsetz, 1972, p. 793).

Accordingly in dynamic environments, the firm's **Dynamic Capability**, defined as a "firm's ability to integrate, build and reconfigure internal and external competencies to address rapidly changing environments" (Teece, 1997, p. 516), is crucial in order to develop new innovative **Resource Recombinations**.

Thus, a firm's competitiveness stems from both its access to resources and the Dynamic Capability of the firm to reconfigure their resource base and to integrate the resources into new resource bundles. Correspondingly, the competitiveness of a firm is not only depending on the quality and complementarity of the resource base but also on the firm's Dynamic Capability to manage the process of Resource Recombination, and thereby to extract the value potential of the resources currently owned and to transform it into a realised value (e.g. new innovative resource bundles) (e.g. Barney, 1991, Wiklund and Shepherd, 2009).

Research Problem. While the concept of Resource Recombination to generate continuous innovations has been widely discussed and is recognised as significant in today's knowledge economy (e.g. Henderson and Clark, 1990, Kogut and Zander, 1992, Grant, 1996, Galunic and Rodan, 1998), the insights in the determinants and antecedents that drive Resource Recombinations in firms have still been limited (Zahra and Wiklund, 2002, Galunic and Rodan, 1998). The failure of firms to find systematic ways to identify, evaluate and successfully combine existing resources (e.g. knowledge, intellectual assets, human resources) is well documented in research, stemming from a lack of understanding of how organisations can strategically and practically approach and foster Resource Recombination as a source for continuous innovation generation (Kliewe et al., 2009). Only few publications can be found that have dedicated their work to provide recommendations on how organisations can plan and execute Resource Recombinations and what specific capabilities are needed in order to successfully implement Resource Recombinations (Sirmon et al., 2007).

Despite the high relevance of Resource Recombination and the increasing interest from academia and practice, current publications have not yet elaborated on how a possible framework for Resource Recombination in firms could be designed and established. Although the competence based research and Dynamic Capability perspective have received increasing attention in contemporary research, and Dynamic Capabilities of the firm are—by definition—linked with Resource Recombination in firms, a study that conceptually and empirically applies the Dynamic Capability perspective to the concept of Resource Recombination is lacking. Up to today, little is known about the relationship between the Dynamic Capabilities and one specific, but central organisational performance outcome: Resource Recombination in firms, which implies an urgent need for such a framework to be established.

Research Aims. This research investigates the role of Dynamic Capabilities in the process of Resource Recombination. It thereby elaborates the framework conditions of Resource Recombination in firms from a Dynamic Capability perspective. Hence, the core of this PhD research lies in the concept of Resource Recombination as a source of continuous innovation generation and the Dynamic Capabilities of a firm relevant to develop and implement new innovative Resource Recombinations. With the investigation of the concept of Resource Recombination from a Dynamic Capability perspective, this research addresses some existing shortcomings in the Dynamic Capability literature, where there is a crucial need to better understand the interrelationship between Dynamic Capabilities, the firm's resource base, and innovation in form of Resource Recombinations. Examining the effect of a specific set of Dynamic Capabilities on Resource Recombination in firms, this research aims to shed light on what it is that explains the competitive heterogeneity and variance in value creation across firms. This research proposes that the resources a firm possesses are as important as the firm's Dynamic Capabilities for Resource Recombination. Thus both, the resources as well as the firm's Dynamic Capabilities are important, though not the only, antecedents of Resource Recombination. This argument is grounded in established theories from resources based research (e.g. Barney, 1991, Penrose, 1959, Rumelt, 1987) and competence based research (e.g. Modaschl, 2006, Teece et al., 2007). Addressing this issue, this research aims is to contribute to the academic field by presenting and empirically testing a conceptual model of factors influencing Resource Recombination in firms.

Research Objectives. Therefore, a first empirical investigation of the Dynamic Capability construct and its influence on Resource Recombination will be the object of investigation within this PhD thesis. A number of objectives will be addressed, namely:

(1) to develop a conceptual framework and measurement model of a specific set of Dynamic Capabilities relevant for the process of Resource Recombination,
(2) to empirically investigate the influence of firm's Dynamic Capabilities on Resource Recombinations in firms, and
(3) to examine the factors influencing the development of a firm's Dynamic Capabilities to better understand how organisations can strategically foster the

development of a firm's Dynamic Capability and thus Resource Recombination in firms.

These research objectives and respective questions will be further outlined in Section 1.3 below.

Research Contribution. The contribution this research is expected to make is to develop, apply and empirically test a conceptual model to provide a holistic, integrated picture of the influencing factors of Resource Recombination from a Dynamic Capability perspective, and thereby to open up the black box of Resource Recombination in firms. With the conceptual model presented, this research offers a more precise definition of the firm's Dynamic Capabilities, shedding light on their role and effects towards developing new Resource Recombinations and separating them from their antecedents and consequences.

1.2 Research Scope and Context

For a long time, researchers have highlighted that not only the search for new resources, but also the usage of existing resources in new ways can be seen as an important source of innovation and competitive advantage and thereby future organisational rents (e.g. Schumpeter, 1934, Usher, 1954, Penrose, 1959, Koestler, 1964). Schumpeter was among the first to acknowledge the importance of **Resource Recombination (RR)** for value creation in firms. In his concept of creative destruction, he refers to innovations as a result of "carrying out new combinations" (Schumpeter, 1934, p. 68) pointing out that innovation often "consists to a substantial extent of a recombination of conceptual and physical materials that were previously in existence" (Nelson and Winter, 1982, p. 30). Correspondingly, literature often refers to '*Schumpeterian Innovation*' or '*Resource Recombination*' as "the reconceptualization of an existing system in order to use the resources from which it is built in novel and potentially rent-generating ways" (Galunic and Rodan, 1998, p. 1194, similar in Henderson and Clark, 1990, Kogut and Zander, 1992, Grant, 1996).

Taking up these fundamental thoughts of Schumpeter, current research within the field of entrepreneurship and strategic management acknowledges RRs as crucial source of innovation, by stating: "Through a reconfiguration of existing resources within the firm, or through the integration of new resources into their existing resource base, firms can introduce new products and services or enter into new markets" (Wiklund et al., 2002, p. 152). This notion incorporates that the resources to be bundled into new RRs can either be developed internally and/or sourced externally (Wiklund and Shepherd, 2009). Following Holcomb et al. (2009, p. 458, going back to Peteraf and Barney, 2003, Sirmon et al., 2007), "resource bundles represent unique combinations of resources that enable firms to take advantage of specific market opportunities when effectively deployed".

Over the last decades, studies within the resource and competence based research particularly stressed the crucial importance of RRs as means of creating wealth (Wiklund et al., 2002). A considerable amount of studies have been published within the RBV, which linked RRs to future wealth creation and thereby made a first step to analyse the causalities between RR and firm success (Grant, 1991, Miller and Shamsie, 1996, Rouse and Daellenbach, 1999, Teece et al., 1997). Nowadays there is agreement among researchers that new RRs generate novel products, goods and services (as defined by Majumdar, 1998, Penrose 1959) that give firms competitive advantages (McGrath et al., 1995) and enables to create wealth (Grant, 1991, Teece et al., 1997).

Further research has shown that RRs can be used as an indicator of current entrepreneurial activities within the firm (Brown et al., 2001, Guth and Ginsberg, 1990, Lumpkin and Dess, 1996, Stopford and Baden-Fuller, 1994). Following Grant (1991), the combination of resources itself can be seen as a major source of the competences firms develop and own to reach their goals, particularly in emerging industries. Moreover, since the outcomes of 'Schumpeterian Innovation' are predominantly radical and disruptive in nature, researchers admit the recombination of resources as being an important source of novelty and firm innovation (Galunic and Rodan, 1998). Being innovative by searching and finding out new RRs constitutes the basis for future organisational rents (Galunic and Rodan, 1998) and in consequence can determine market winners and losers (Foster, 1986).

Nowadays in rapidly changing and dynamic markets, it becomes even more essential for firms to be entrepreneurially active by searching for new RR opportunities (Wiklund et al., 2002, Wiklund and Shepherd, 2009). If the competitive advantage is to be sustained over time, resources and the way they are bundled must be changed to adapt to the ever changing, unpredictable environments (Holcomb et al., 2009, Hawass, 2010, Eisenhardt and Brown, 1999). Accordingly, a strong desire exists—within both the resource and competence based research—for understanding how companies can successfully recombine existing resources within the firm in new ways and (or) integrate new resources within their existing resource base to leverage their assets.

Contemporary entrepreneurship and strategic management scholars have indeed shown a strong interest in encouraging firms to innovate by searching out new innovative RRs or new ways of using existing resources (Galunic and Rodan, 1998, Wiklund et al., 2002). However, until recently researchers within the RBV have remained detached from strategic concerns on how these resources are combined, and what factors are influencing the likelihood of RRs in firms. While past research has targeted to catalogue different types of resources and relate them to value and wealth creation (Barney, 1991, Rouse and Daellenbach, 1999), little attention has been given to understand the process on how these resources are recombined into new innovative resource bundles and what capabilities are needed within the firms (Zahra and Wiklund, 2002). Instead, the focus of previous studies within the RBV predominantly were centred in the investigation of the importance of RRs for wealth creation. Until recently, both strategic management and entrepreneurship research remained anchored to a view that sees wealth creation primarily influenced by the resources itself, ignoring the wider aspects of what abilities and competences a company needs to have in order to manage these resources and bundle them into new innovative RRs and thereby leverage the RR opportunities.

To encounter these limitations and to overcome the relatively static perspective of the RBV, which does not consider market dynamisms, a more recent stream within the competence based research has been established, where researchers incorporate a more dynamic perspective of a firm's resources. In contrast to the RBV, the competence based view (CBV) sees competitive advantages not solely deriving "mechanically" from the availability and quality of resources (respectively RRs), but rather from the ability to utilise these resources (Moldaschl, 2006) and adapt them to changing environments (Teece et al., 1997). One important stream in the CBV is the Dynamic Capability literature. Drawing on the CBV, the literature following the Dynamic Capability perspective sees the ability of a firm to reconfigure its resource base—referred to as the **Dynamic Capability (DC)** of the firm—as the key source of competitive advantages in dynamic environments (Eisenhardt and Martin, 2000, Teece et al., 1997, Mathews, 2002). More specifically, Teece et al. (1997, p. 516) refer to a firm's DC as a "firm's ability to integrate, build and reconfigure internal and external competencies to address rapidly changing environments". Eisenhardt and Martin (2000) argue that a firm's DC enables the development of new RRs. The underlying assumption of the DC perspective is that firms that reconfigure their resources faster than their competitors are more likely to receive a competitive advantage and thus superior performance (Isobe et al., 2008). Thus, the emphasis of this stream of research lies especially in the investigation of how firms can sustain their competitive advantage in rapidly changing, dynamic environments.

More recent works proposed by researchers have shown an increased interest in the importance of RR for innovation generation from this DC perspective (e.g. Hawass, 2010, Pavlou and El Sawy, 2011). However, it still is a rather small group of researchers—predominantly coming from the entrepreneurship spectrum—who set out to investigate RRs from this DC perspective. They started to focus on how entrepreneurial RR activities can be stimulated, fostered, and maintained within organisations (Brown et al., 2001, Eisenhardt and Martin, 2000, Galunic and Rodan, 1998, Wiklund et al., 2002). While traditionally research on entrepreneurship has examined, how characteristics of the individual influence strategic management choices and firm performance (Venkataraman, 1997), a few studies (e.g. Wiklund et al., 2002, Hawass, 2010, Galunic and Rodan, 1998) emphasise a shift towards the examination of how characteristics of groups as well as organisational characteristics can influence the development of DC and thus the likelihood of firms to create RRs. Wiklund et al. (2002) for example concentrated their research on how management practices and characteristics influence the likelihood of RRs to occur, suggesting that—independently from the resource base—certain factors such as *Strategic Orientation, Entrepreneurial Culture, Management Structure, Resource Orientation, Growth Orientation and Reward Philosophy* can promote and facilitate entrepreneurial RR activities. Another study presented by Hawass (2010) explored the determinants of the reconfiguration capability from a DC perspective, and concentrated on how the individual, group and organisational level of learning influences the development of the firm's capacity to reconfigure its resources. Also in their qualitative study, Galunic and Rodan (1998) presented valuable propositions on how the properties of knowledge and its social organisation in the firm may influence the likelihood of RR in firms.

A homologue progress can be found in the strategic management literature, where for instance the work by Schreyögg and Kliesch (2003) addressed the organisational competence, referred to as the organisation's ability to implement the process of resource selection and recombination and its importance for making use of its resources. However their investigations remains only on a conceptual level. Similar attempts, though only on a qualitative level, have been made by Sirmon et al. (2007), who investigated different stages in the resource management process in order to effectively bundle resources into valuable RRs.

In consequence, although the competence based research and the DC perspective have received increasing attention in contemporary research, and the concept of DC is—per definition—linked with the process of RR in firms, a study that conceptually and empirically applies the DC perspective to the concept of RR is still lacking. To date, no study of which the author is aware, has investigated

the relationship between the DCs and one specific, but central organisational performance outcome: RR in firms. While first attempts towards an investigation of
certain factors that influence RR has been made, still this stream of research is
in the early stages of development and needs to be further investigated.

Summarising, the above outline has shown that strategic management and
entrepreneurship researchers share a common and strong interest in value and
wealth creation through RR in firms as it is regarded as important source for
continuous innovation generation and sustained competitiveness. Following Hitt
and Ireland (2000) "RC [resource (re)combination—author's note] is an important issue where strategic management and entrepreneurship intersect and where
fruitful integrative research can be carried out" (Zahra and Wiklund, 2002, p. 10).

1.3   Research Objectives and Questions

Research Objectives
In order to address the research gaps defined below in the literature review, and
thereby to lift and fully exploit the potential of the RR approach for innovation
generation, this research sets out to contribute to the academic field by developing
and quantitatively testing a theoretical model of the factors that influence RR in
firms. Since no holistic model is known to be existent thus far that integrates the
factors that influence RR from a DC perspective, this research aims to provide a
comprehensive quantitative model of the influencing factors of RR in firms. Doing
so, the **overall aim** of this research is to investigate the DCs of the firm and their
influence on one specific performance outcome: RR in firms, and thereby to bring
clarity to the notion of DCs, their role and effects towards RRs in firms.

The **overall objective** of this research is to investigate the role of DCs in the
process of RR in firms and thereby to elaborate the framework conditions of RR in
firms from the DC perspective. More precisely, this research investigates the DCs
in relation to the resource base and thereby explores how the two constructs work
together towards developing RRs in firms. The **objectives of this research** are:

(1) to develop a conceptual framework and measurement model of a firm's DCs, by
     (a) identifying and conceptualising a set of DCs relevant for the process of RR,
     (b) describing the underlying activities, processes and routines of the identified
     capabilities, and (c) operationalising and developing a measurement model for
     the DCs to develop a comprehensive understanding of the DC construct.
(2) to empirically investigate the influence of firm's DCs on RR in firms, in partic-
     ular to understand how the specific DCs act upon the resource base by building

and exploiting it, and how both constructs are linked with the organisational outcome of new resource combinations. The aim is to bring clarity to the notion of DCs, and their role and effects towards developing RRs in firms.

(3) to examine the firm and network-level antecedents for the development of a firm's DCs. The aim is to understand to what extend the firm's strategic orientation (observed on the organisational and inter-organisational level) influences the development of DCs and thus RRs.

With the conceptual model presented, this research offers a more precise definition of the firm's DCs, shedding light on their role and effects towards developing new RRs in firms and separating them from their antecedents and consequences. Moreover, a set of hypotheses are presented outlining (1) how the resource base and the DCs are related to one another, (2) how the relationship between the resource base and RRs is moderated by a firm's DCs, (3) how the firm's strategic orientation affects the development and utilisation of DCs for RRs. It is suggested that focusing on specific DCs of the firm, their role and effects, can offer valuable insights into the source of variance in organisational performance outcomes.

Research Questions
Correspondingly to the research objectives, the **research questions** this PhD research aims to answer can be described as the following:

First, in order to address research objective (1), the construct of DC will be subject of investigation. Therefore, a specific set of observable and measurable DCs for the process of resource selection and reconfiguration has to be identified, described, operationalised and measured. Specific research questions originated from the review of literature would be:

(1) How can a Dynamic Capability Framework be described, operationalised and measured?

    (1.1) What specific capacities are needed in firms to integrate, build and reconfigure internal and external resources to address rapidly changing environments? How can the different types of capabilities be described, categorised and aligned? How can a framework be derived with a set of generic types of capacities?

    (1.2) What are the underlying activities, processes and routines of the identified set of capabilities?

    (1.3) How can the identified set of capacities of a firm be operationalised and measured?

Second, in order to address research objective (2), after the first operationalisation of the construct of DC, its influence on the development of RRs in firms will be empirically investigated. For this purpose a conceptual model will be developed and qualitatively validated using expert interviews with industrial representatives. In the second, quantitative research step this model will be empirically tested. Specific research questions are:

(2) What influence have Dynamic Capabilities on RRs in firms?
  (2.1) What is the role and effect of the different DCs in the process of RR? More specifically, are different types of DCs working on different levels (e.g. building and exploiting the resource base)?
  (2.2) Do certain characteristics of the resource base (e.g. quality, diversity, complementarity, transferability, deployment flexibility, renewal) influence the potential value of the resource base for RR in firms?
  (2.3) What is relatively more important for RR in firms, the resources endowment or the DCs of the firm? Or does one not go without the other?

Third, in order to address research objective (3), the influence of specific firm- and network-level antecedents on the development of firm's DCs will be further investigated. More specifically this research addresses, how a firm's Entrepreneurial Orientation (firm-level), and its Networking Orientation (network-level) influence the development of a firm's DC. Specific research questions are:

(3) What is the influence of a firm's Entrepreneurial Orientation and Networking Orientation on the development of the firm's DCs?
  (3.1) Does a higher degree of entrepreneurship in firms positively influence the development of a firm's DCs?
  (3.2) Is there a positive influence of a high Networking Orientation on the development of DCs?
  (3.3) What is relatively more important? Are they complements or substitutes?

Based on the advanced understanding of the specific DCs, their role and effect, and antecedents for building RRs in firms, systematic ways for the development of DCs in order to successfully implement RRs in a firm's innovation strategy can be derived. The aim is to provide practical applicable implications for managers on how to strategically foster RR in firms. The challenge here will be to identify and localise the determining coordinates that constitute the shape of a promising theory, and to connect them in order to draw a clearer and more outlined orientation map.

By doing so, a foundation can be built that fosters RR activities within and between companies.

1.4 Research Approach and Methodology

Based on the resource and competence based research as well as literature from the strategic management and entrepreneurship spectrum, a mixed-method approach research is conducted. The aim is to create research that can be practically applied whilst also robustly defended in a research environment, through a thorough literature review, qualitative and quantitative research methods, and a model validation process.

This study starts with a comprehensive literature review, aiming to establish the research context. Discussing theories as well as empirical findings in the wider field of RR. The literature review will provide the theoretical and conceptual foundation for the development of a conceptual model and delineates the research gaps addressed in this research. Discussing important characteristics of the resource base and providing a detailed elaboration of the DC construct, a DC framework will further be presented, that allows a first operationalisation of the construct of DC, and its influence on RR. Moreover, the antecedents for the development of the DC will be the subject of investigation. Based on the extensive literature review, the conceptual model and hypotheses will be derived.

The second, qualitative research step will be undertaken to further specify the conceptual model (exploratory research). The major research technique for this research step will primarily be in-depth interviews with key informants from industry engaged in RR projects. Based on the newly gained knowledge, the conceptual model and hypotheses will be adjusted and if necessary refined.

In the third, quantitative research step, the theoretical model and respective hypotheses will be tested by conducting empirical research. For this purpose, the model's constructs will be operationalised and included in an online survey, distributed to upper or middle management personnel working in innovation-related functional areas in the UK. The data collected will be analysed statistically based on structural equation modelling (SEM) principles, resulting in an empirically validated model of factors influencing the likelihood of RR. A more detailed description of the research design and the methodology is provided in chapter four.

Literature Review—Theoretical and Conceptual Foundations

2

2.1   Introduction

The following chapter provides a literature review on the resource and competence based research as parent theories for this research. The aim of this literature review chapter is to present an overview on the status quo in literature with respect to the economic relevance of the concept of Resource Recombination (RR) for strategic management and entrepreneurship, the resource and competence based research as parent theories for the concept of RR, together with a view on its background, evolution and demarcation of the research area. Moreover this chapter sets out to introduce a general understanding of the core concepts relevant for this research.

The first section starts with the contextual integration of the RR concept within the wider discipline of strategic management and entrepreneurship, displaying and discussing the economic value and relevance of the concept of RR for future wealth creation, based on existing literature.

The next section provides an overview of the resource and competence based research, recognised as the parent theories for the concept of RR. Therefore, firstly the evolution and historical background of resource and competence based research will be described, thereafter the resource based view (RBV), the competence based view (CBV), as well as the related knowledge based view (KBV) are described, outlining the different streams in literature, and demarcating them

Electronic supplementary material The online version contains supplementary material available at (https://doi.org/10.1007/978-3-658-35666-8_2).

© The Author(s), under exclusive license to Springer Fachmedien Wiesbaden GmbH, part of Springer Nature 2021
K. Kurzhals, *Resource Recombination in Firms from a Dynamic Capability Perspective*, Gabler Theses,
https://doi.org/10.1007/978-3-658-35666-8_2

from related areas. The section closes with an overview of the theoretical bases and approaches of the resource and competence based research.

Having established the theoretical foundation of this research, the subsequent section provides the conceptual foundations of this research. In this section the status quo in literature is described, presenting the current knowledge of the core concepts relevant for this research in order to develop a mutual understanding and deduce the central definitions for this research. This section identifies the relevant constructs to be included into this study.

In the last section, based on the thorough understanding of existing concepts, the research gaps derived from literature that will be further addressed in this research are presented and discussed.

The primary contribution of this chapter is to provide the theoretical and conceptual foundation of the concept of RR and DCs of the firm and embedding it within the wider discipline of strategic management and entrepreneurship.

2.2 The Concept of Resource Recombination in Firms

The concept of RR has drawn significant attention in contemporary research within the strategic management and corporate entrepreneurship spectrum. Research within both these disciplines realise an increasing shift in emphasis from the market based view, more specifically the structure-conduct-performance paradigm that arose from industrial organisation economics, towards theories that rather focus on the management of internal resources of firms being the key determinant in order to gain competitive advantage (Amit and Schoemaker, 1993, Galunic and Rodan, 1998, Teece et al., 1997).

Contemporary research, both from entrepreneurship and strategic management scholars, once more concentrates on entrepreneurial activities as originally defined by Joseph Schumpeter (e.g. Eisenhardt and Martin 2000, Stopford and Baden-Fuller, 1994, Teece et al., 1997), developing towards a 'neo-Schumpeterian theory of the firm' (Teece, 2007). Schumpeter was among the first to acknowledge the importance of RR for value creation, referring to his concept of creative destruction innovations being a result of "carrying out new combinations" (Schumpeter, 1934, p. 68). Schumpeterian innovation, which is used synonymous to 'Resource Recombination', therefore often "consists to a substantial extent of a recombination of conceptual and physical materials that were previously in existence" (Nelson and Winter, 1982, p. 30). Schumpeterian innovation emerges through the re-conceptualisation of an existing system, using the resources from which it is built in new and potentially rent-generating ways (e.g. Grant, 1996,

Henderson and Clark, 1990, Kogut and Zander, 1992). With regard to its outcome, innovation as defined by Joseph Schumpeter is "primarily radical and disruptive in nature" (Galunic and Rodan, 1998, p. 1194). The main point of his definition is the prescribed role of firms as the developer of novel resources. Accordingly, it is essential for firms to be entrepreneurially active by searching for new RR opportunities (Wiklund et al., 2002). Being innovative by searching and finding new RRs constitutes the basis for successful firms (Galunic and Rodan, 1998). These ideas were taken up by researchers, proposing concepts such as architect-ural innovation (Abernathy and Utterback, 1978, Henderson and Clark, 1990), combinative capabilities (Kogut and Zander, 1992), and configuration competence (Henderson and Cockburn, 1994).

Interestingly, a major change of paradigm can be observed within current innovation research, where innovation until recently was primarily seen as the result of basic science (search for new knowledge) or continuous improvement (Kliewe et al., 2009), and nowadays is progressively shifted towards a neo-Schumpeterian view of innovation generated through RR. Hence, in present economy the high relevance of RR for innovation generation has been rediscovered. Matthias Horx, founder of the *Zukunftsinstitut* in Germany, described this ongoing process by the following allegory:

> *"Likewise in a jungle, at some point in time, every colourful butterfly, worm and liana will have been 'invented', the future of technology lies, especially in the variation and recombination"* (Horx, 2011, p. 195).

Basically emphasising, that in today's knowledge economy, firms do not need to reinvent the wheel, but rather have to learn how to innovate by reconfiguring existing resources in new ways in order to create new recombinant innovations through the intelligent (re)combination of existing knowledge. In consequence, according to current research findings, the innovation process is mainly determined by synthesising, coupling and crossing already existing knowledge and experience, rather than being predominantly guided by radical breakthroughs (Horx, 2011, Burnett, 2009).

Taking up the fundamental thoughts of Schumpeter, current research within the field of entrepreneurship and strategic management define RRs as a crucial source of innovation, stating that "through a reconfiguration of existing resources within the firm, or through the integration of new resources into their existing resource base, firms can introduce new products and services or enter into new markets" (Wiklund et al., 2002, p. 152, referring to Schumpeter, 1934). Also, empirical evidence confirming this assumption is given, Gassmann and Enkel

(2006) for example confirmed that 80% of all innovations are based on existing knowledge, technologies, products and service. Hence, innovation mainly occurs through the recombination of resources (Schumpeter, 1934, Kogut and Zander, 1992), which are unevenly distributed among firms (Penrose, 1959).

Thus, researchers acknowledge the value creation potential of RR, admitting that "in achieving new resource recombinations, firms can combine existing skills with new resources, thereby reconfiguring their resource inputs to be more efficient (...) [or] in pursuit of new initiatives such as introducing new products or entering new markets (Wiklund and Shepherd, 2009, p. 196). Accordingly, the efficient and creative use of internal and external resources and capabilities provide various innovation opportunities (Kliewe et al., 2009, Lerdahl, 1999). Following Holcomb et al. (2009) from a firm's perspective, value is created by developing new resource bundles, which allow firms to create novel tasks, services, products or processes, and which are perceived to produce greater value and utility or lower costs of usage. Nowadays, there is agreement among researchers that new RRs generate novel products, goods and services (Majumdar, 1998, Penrose, 1959) that give firms competitive advantages (McGrath et al., 1995) and enable firms to create wealth (Grant, 1991, Teece et al., 1997).

To illustrate the high economic relevance of RRs in today's economy, one of the most frequently mentioned innovations of the last decade, the iPod invented by Apple Inc., can be adduced as a good example of a successfully implemented RR (Van Rijnbach, 2010). Indeed, though the recombination of already existing resources and technologies, namely the MP3 technology[1], the touch screen technology[2], its design and functionality[3], and lastly its business model with iTunes[4], a completely new product was developed and successfully leveraged in the market. Taken the iPod as an example, it emerges that the realised value of this invention only became apparent, after the individual resources have been successfully combined. Given that the process of RR involves uncertainty and great

---

[1] The origin of the MP3 technology goes back to the 1987 when the Fraunhofer Institute in Germany started to research Digital Audio Broadcasting, which resulted in the development of the first, however unsuccessful, MP3 player in the early 1990s. The standard was released by the Moving Picture Expert Group in 1993 (Van Rijnbach, 2010).

[2] The original idea for the touch screen technology was invented by Jason Ford of Elo Touch Systems (formally EloGraphics) in the 1970s (Van Rijnbach, 2010).

[3] Apple confirmed that the design and technology of the iPod was originally invented and patented in 1979 by Kane Kramer, a British inventor. The patent expired in 1988, when the idea fell in public domain (Van Rijnbach, 2010).

[4] The business model of online music stores, for example by MusicNet and Pressplay, already existed before Apple Inc. reinvented it (Van Rijnbach, 2010).

parts of the realised value are observed as being serendipitous and unforeseen a priori (Graebner, 2004), the total value created through RR is often not recognised until the resources have been bundled (Denrell et al., 2003, Moran and Ghoshal, 1999, Wiklund and Shepherd, 2009).

Moreover, studies in strategic management and entrepreneurship research particularly stressed the crucial importance of RRs as a means for wealth creation (Wiklund et al., 2002). Authors of several studies have shown that RR can be used as an indicator of current entrepreneurial activities within firms (Brown et al., 2001, Guth and Ginsberg, 1990, Lumpkin and Dess, 1996, Stopford and Baden-Fuller, 1994). Following Grant (1991), the combination of resources can be seen as a major source of competences that firms develop to reach their goals, particularly in emerging industries. RRs in consequence can determine market winners and losers (Foster, 1986).

Especially worthy of mention are studies from the RBV, which linked RRs to future wealth creation (Grant, 1991, Miller and Shamsie, 1996, Rouse and Daellenbach, 1999a, Teece et al., 1997) and thereby made a first step to analyse the causalities between RR and firm success. Nevertheless, only few empirical research studies applying the RBV have been conducted to date (Miller and Shamsie, 1996, Pavlou and El Sawy, 2011). While past research has targeted to catalogue different types of resources and related them to value and wealth creation (Barney, 1991, Rouse and Daellenbach, 1999), little attention has been given to understand the process on how these resources are combined (Zahra and Wiklund, 2002). Contemporary entrepreneurship and strategic management scholars have indeed shown a strong interest in encouraging firms to innovate by searching out new innovative RRs, or new ways of using existing resources (Galunic and Rodan, 1998, Wiklund et al., 2002). However, apart from a few notable exceptions (e.g. Wiklund et al., 2002, Sirmon et al., 2007), researchers have remained detached from strategic concerns on how these resources are combined, and what factors are influencing the likelihood of RR. Instead, the focus of previous studies within the strategic management and entrepreneurship spectrum predominantly lay in the investigation of the importance of RR. Until recently both strategic management and entrepreneurship research remained anchored to a view that sees wealth creation primarily influenced by the resources themselves, ignoring the wider aspects of what abilities and competences a firm needs to have in order to leverage these RR opportunities.

Recognising the value of RR for future wealth creation, there is a current shift from investigating the importance of RR towards an investigation of how RR can be fostered. Researchers from different scientific disciplines have acknowledged that further research of the abilities and competence a firm needs to have in order to successfully implement RRs is needed to better understand how firms can appropriately carry out the RR process. Therefore, within the last decade researchers started to analyse individual and organisational factors that influence RRs in firms (Galunic and Rodan, 1998, Brown et al., 2001, Eisenhardt and Martin, 2000), addressing (i) *individual competences*, e.g. peoples' absorptive capacity (Cohen and Levinthal, 1990), (ii) *group competences*, e.g. top management team characteristics (Zahra and Wiklund, 2002), or (iii) *organisational competences*, e.g. organisational collaborative capacity (Oelsnitz and Graf, 2006), organisational interpretation capacity (Schreyögg and Kliesch, 2003), or organisational combination skills (Peitz, 2002), that are needed to successfully create RRs.

While traditionally research on entrepreneurship concentrated on how characteristics of the individual influence strategic management choices and firm performance (Venkataraman, 1997), a few studies emphasise a shift towards the examination of how characteristics of groups as well as organisational characteristics influence the likelihood of firms to create RRs. Investigating how entrepreneurial RR activities can be stimulated, fostered, and maintained within organisations and assuming that, independently from the resource base, certain factors can promote and facilitate entrepreneurial RR activities. The study of Wiklund and colleagues (2002) for example concentrated on how management practices and characteristics influence the likelihood of RR to occur. Referring to earlier findings within the entrepreneurship spectrum (e.g. Guth and Ginsberg, 1990, Lumpkin and Dess, 1996, Stopford and Baden-Fuller, 1994, Teece et al., 1997), their findings confirmed that management practices have a significant influence on the likelihood of RR, for instance by making it possible for employees to take entrepreneurial initiatives and by rewarding such efforts (Wiklund et al., 2002). Likewise, the work of Zahra and Wiklund (2002) examined how top management team characteristics influence the likelihood of RR. Their findings suggest that teams, rather than single entrepreneurs, lead most firms (Hitt and Ireland, 2000, Kamm et al., 1990) and confirm that the top management teams' alertness, innovativeness, and growth orientation significantly influence the likelihood of RR.

Other studies suppose that not only the competence of individuals or groups, but rather the competences of a whole organisation are crucial for successful RR. The conceptual work presented by Schreyögg and Kliesch (2003) for instance goes one step further looking at the organisational level and investigating the 'organisational competence', which they define as the complex, systematic selection and recombination capacity, and considers it as elementary for making use of a firm's resources. According to Schreyögg and Kliesch (2003), the three dimensions of organisational competence involve (i) the organisational interpretation capacity, (ii) the organisational cooperation skills and (iii) the organisational combination competence, which in turn is influenced by the determining factors, namely the organisational structure, the organisational learning ability and the organisational culture. However, the work by Schreyögg and Kliesch (2003) only presents a conceptual investigation of the construct of organisational competence. An empirical investigation would be of particular interest.

While a lot of conceptual advancements have been made towards developing a better understanding of RR in firms, it emerges that up to today relatively few studies have connected individual and organisational competences to the concept of RR. Still, this stream of research is in the early stages of development and has to be further investigated. To date no study, of which the author is aware, has empirically applied the DC perspective on the concept of RR. Accordingly, a special emphasis lies in understanding what competences and capabilities are needed to combine resources for value and wealth creation (Galunic and Rodan, 1998, Moran and Ghoshal, 1996, Rumelt, 1987).

Summarising the above findings, both strategic management and entrepreneurship researchers share a common and strong interest in value and wealth creation through RRs. Following Hitt and Ireland (2000) 'RC [resource (re)combination—author's note] is an important issue where strategic management and entrepreneurship intersect and where fruitful integrative research can be carried out' (Zahra and Wiklund, 2002). While the focus of contemporary research within the research field of RR goes apart from the investigation of the resources a firm owns towards an investigation of how these resources can be used in new, rent regarding ways and subsequently what competences are needed. Even within the internally focused resource based research, there is a shift from an observation of which and why resources may be valuable towards an exploration of how these resources (resp. RRs) may be generated (Henderson and Cockburn, 1994, Moran and Ghoshal, 1996, Teece et al., 1997) and therefore especially what competences and capabilities are needed for the process of RR. The focus lies not solely on the resource base anymore (as implied by the RBV), but rather investigates the abilities and competences of a company to make use of its resources (refereeing to the CBV).

2.3   Theoretical Foundation: Resource and Competence Based Research

Being a central part of the strategic management doctrine, the concept of RR significantly contributes to the resource and competence based research. As the basis for a detailed examination of the RR concept, the resource and competence based research will be outlined in the following section as the parent theories for this research. Therefore, first the historical evolution and background of the resource and competence based research will be addressed, furthermore a demarcation of the research area will be given including a detailed description of the resource based view (RBV), the competence based view (CBV), and the knowledge based view (KBV).

2.3.1 Evolution and Background

Traditionally the monographs of Penrose (1959) and Selznick (1957) are considered as being the origin of thoughts in literature, later termed as resource and competence based research (Kor and Mahoney, 2004). Since the early 90's there is a notable change of direction within the strategic management theory. From a broader perspective, a general shift of emphasis from the market based research towards the resource and competence based research of strategic management can be proclaimed (Amit and Schoemaker, 1993, Galunic and Rodan, 1998, Teece et al., 1997). While the focus of the market based view (MBV), as the name implies, promotes the market oriented view of the external environment of the firm, this stream in literature is predominately characterised by the publications of Michael E. Porter, who attributes the success of the competitive strategy of a firm primarily to the industry structure it is active in and to its strategic behaviour (Porter, 1980).

However, as a variety of empirical investigations could not prove the exclusive influence of the industry structure and because of the continual and rising change in the market environment, several research findings inclined towards a rejection of the traditional MBV. One of the main criticism of the MBV thereby is, that the internal structure, resources and capabilities of a firm are mostly neglected. With the aim to overcome this inadequacy, a general orientation towards the resource and competence oriented perspective of the firm emerged and has received growing attention from literature since the early 1990's up to today (Freiling et al., 2006). Within this perspective, the focus shifted from the success of a single product to the success of the whole company. Existing resources and competences within firms thereby have shifted into the centre of attention. Innovation has been identified as the driving factor for growth. Innovative firms are generally directed towards growth, orientated on competences, potentials and resources (Plinke, 2002).

The MBV will not be subject of further investigation within this research, although, especially from an evolutionary perspective, it is deemed valuable to understand the change of direction from a more external towards the internal perspective of the firm. Contrasting the different aspects of the MBV, RBV and CBV, the following table provides a compressed overview of differences between the market oriented approach and the resource and competence oriented approach (Table 2.1).

Table 2.1 Comparison of the Market oriented Approach and the Resource and Competence oriented Approach

	Market oriented approach	**Resource and competence oriented approach**
Perception of the firm	Firm as portfolio of businesses	Firm as reservoir of skills and resources
General objective target	Growth through cash-flow-balance over the course of the lifecycle	Sustainable growth through development, exploitation, transfer of core competences
Place of competition	Business unit against business unit	Firm against firm
Source of innovation	Product centric costs or differentiation advantages	Exploitation of firm wide resources and competences
Character of strategic advantages	Limited in time, business specific, observable	Sustainable, difficult to engage and transfer into other businesses, hidden
Focus of strategy	Rather defensive, exploitation and defence of current business areas, strategy development in response to market changes	Rather offensive through competence transfer, further development of current markets and construction of new markets, formation of market changes
Planning horizon	Rather short- and medium-term	Accentuated long-term
Role of the business unit	Profit centre	Centre of competence
Task of the top management	Allocation of financial resources to-wards the strategic business units	Integration of resources and skills on the basis of an overall business strategy

Source: adopted from Krüger and Homp (1997), p. 63

2.3.2 Demarcation of the Research Area

Being a central part of the strategic management doctrine, the concept of RR significantly contributes to both streams, the resource based view and the competence based view of the firm. The resource and competence oriented research itself can be differentiated within the structural school (e.g. Moran and Ghoshal, 1996, Rumelt, 1987) referring to the original resource based view (RBV) by Grant (1991), and the process school referring to the later competence based view (CBV) by Moldaschl and Fischer (2004). The knowledge based view (KBV) originally founded by Demsetz and Stigler (1973), which leads back to the Chicago Business School, can be integrated and regarded as a more elementary school. Figure 2.1 attempts a generic integration of the concept of RR in the wider disciplines of strategic management and entrepreneurship.

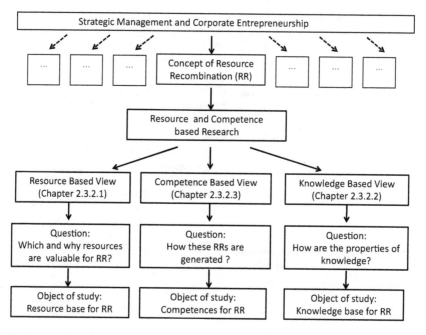

Source: own illustration

Figure 2.1 Theoretical Foundation of this Research

2.3.2.1 The Resource based View

The **resource based view (RBV)** of the firm is a school of thoughts that has its origin in the strategic management literature. The RBV denotes the constitution and orientation phase of the resource and competence based research and can be traced back to the origin approach of Grant (1991), who introduced the 'Resource-based Theory of Competitive Advantages' (Freiling et al., 2006). With the initial publication of Wemerfelt (1984), the RBV as a central approach within the resource and competence oriented research received its name. Later on the 'Resource Advantage Theory' by Hunt and Morgan (1996), the publication 'Firm Resources and sustained Competitive Advantages' by Barney (1991), as well as the more industry economical interspaced 'Resource Dependence Approach' by Pfeffer and Salancik (1978), which has been further developed by Mahoney (1995), significantly contributed to the RBV and can be seen as the constituting publications of the RBV.

In contrast to the MBV, the RBV sees a firm's competitive position primarily determined by the special features and quality of firm specific resource bundles (Schreyögg and Conrad, 2006). Accordingly, the RBV considers a firm as a bundle of resources (Penrose, 1959, Wernerfelt, 1984, Peteraf, 1993, Barney, 1991) and regards the firm's distinctive resources as the direct sources of sustainable competitive advantage (Isobe et al., 2008). According to the RBV, observable performance differences between firms can primarily be led back to the different resources which are available within the firm at one point in time (Freiling et al., 2006). The RBV proposes that in order to gain sustainable competitive advantage, a firm needs to own or create unique resources which are rare, valuable, difficult to imitate and non-substitutable (Barney, 1991).

Later on, the 'Resource Advantage Theory' by Hunt and Morgan (1996) supplemented the initial thoughts by Wemerfelt (1984), proposing that a company's marketplace position and thereby financial performance, results from a comparative advantage (disadvantage) in resources. Hunt and Morgan define resources as tangible entities (e.g. specific machinery) and intangible entities (e.g. skills and knowledge of individual employees) which are available in firms and enable them to produce efficiently and/or effectively market offerings of value for some market segments (Hunt and Morgan, 1997). The 'Resource Advantage Theory' thereby expands the concept of resources (from land, labour, and capital) and includes such resources as organisational culture, knowledge, and specific competences. Competences here are seen as "distinct packages of socially complex, interconnected, tangible and intangible basic resources that fit coherently together in a synergistic manner" (Hunt, 2002, p. 25).

In conclusion, Hunt and Morgan (1996) focus in their 'Resource Advantage Theory' on comparative advantages in resources to explain the performance outcomes, noting that rewards flow to those firms that are able to successfully create new resources. Competition then is seen as "the disequilibrating, ongoing process that consists of the constant struggle among firms for a comparative advantage in resources that will yield marketplace positions of competitive advantage and, thereby, superior financial performance" (Hunt, 2002, p. 9). The general premise of the RBV is that firms which are capable to upgrade their existing resources in a path-dependent manner are suggested to be more likely to achieve superior performance (Isobe et al., 2008).

Looking at the RBV more specifically, it is not the resources itself, but rather RRs that are regarded as the key to success. Accordingly, resources and their (re)combination leads to the development of new or proprietary resource bundles, resulting in a higher degree of heterogeneity in a firm's resource mix, which vice versa makes it more difficult for competitors to copy the firm's strategy (Wemerfelt, 1984). Those unique RRs generate entrepreneurial rents, defined as "the difference between a venture's ex post value (or payment stream) and ex ante cost (or value) of the resources combined to form the venture" (Rumelt, 1987, p. 143). The concept of RR therefore contributes considerably to the RBV (Moran and Ghoshal, 1996, Rumelt, 1987).

There are also certain limitations of the RBV. First, while the RBV sees competitive advantages primarily influenced by the resources (resp. RRs) themselves, still there is ambiguity about what is defined as resources. Hodgson (2000) argues that the 'Resource Advantage Theory' is over-general in its scope and fails to distinguish between different types of resources. While supporting the argument that a firm's portfolio of resources predominantly determines competitive advantages in resources and thus a companies' market position, Hodgson (2000) criticises the missing definition of what resources really are. He argues that the concept of resources as defined by Hunt and Morgan (1997) is too general and accordingly the theory could lose its meaning. Second, the ambiguity of how to define the resource base of a firm can also be seen as one reason for the fact that up to today little empirical research applying the RBV has been conducted (Miller and Shamsie, 1996). According to Rouse and Daellenbach (1999), the scarcity of empirical research can be traced back to the complexity that lies in identifying the core resources a firm owns and can use in order to gain a competitive advantage. Third, while the RBV argues that a firm's portfolio of resources can mean a 'comparative advantage in resources', leading to a higher financial performance, the aspect of how such comparative advantages in resources can be built by firms, is not sufficiently investigated.

2.3.2.2 The Knowledge based View

The **knowledge based view** (**KBV**) on the firm builds upon and extends the RBV in a way that it focusses on *knowledge* as the most strategically significant resource firms possess (Decarolis and Deeds, 1999, Hawass, 2010). Accordingly, the focus of the KBV lies on knowledge, especially the way to handle data, information and knowledge as a generic resource. While the RBV recognises the role of knowledge in firms for archiving competitive advantages, researchers representing the KBV argue that, while treating knowledge as a generic resource, the RBV does not sufficiently elaborate on the specific characteristics of knowledge, and does not distinguish between different types of knowledge based capabilities. Hence, other than the RBV, the KBV views the creation, utilisation and application of knowledge as the principal rationale for a firm's persistence (Nonaka, 1994, Spender, 1996). Following Grant's publication (1996b) "Towards a Knowledge-Based View of the firm", also the organisational capability or competence can be regarded as the result of knowledge integration, whereby "the distinctiveness of a capability depends on the extent to which a firm is able to gain access to and integrate relevant knowledge residing in the minds of employees" (Hawass, 2010, p. 414).

The KBV can be led back to the Chicago School founded by Demsetz and Stigler (1973), which focussed on studying knowledge based approaches for dealing with data, information and knowledge based on the organisational learning theory (e.g. Demsetz, 1988). Whether the KBV of the firm constitutes a theory or not, has been subject of an ongoing debate (for further reading refer to Foss, 1996, Phelan and Lewin, 2000), however, this research follows Grant's (2002, p. 135) perception: "The emerging knowledge-based view of the firm is not a theory of the firm in any formal sense", it rather is seen as a specific sub-category of the RBV of the firm. Nonetheless, the KBV rationale is evident in this study in a similar vein, as it is in many innovation studies, which set out to investigate new product development in firms (Danneels, 2007, Marsh and Stock, 2003, 2006, Hawass, 2010).

2.3.2.3 The Competence based View and Dynamic Capability Perspective

In contrast to the RBV (and the KBV), the **competence based view** (**CBV**) sees competitive advantages not solely deriving "mechanically" from the availability and quality of resources (resp. RRs), but rather from the ability to utilise these resources (Moldaschl, 2006). Underlying this view is the differentiation between resources and their use. As early considered by Edith Penrose (1959), regarded as the founder of the resource oriented research: "It's never resources themselves that are the inputs in the production process, but only the services that the resources can render. (...) The important distinction between resources and services is not the durability; rather it lies in the fact that resources consist of a bundle of potential services and can, for the most part, be defined independently of their use, while services cannot be so defined" (Penrose, 1959, p. 25). In terms of causality, the CBV draws on a different perspective than the RBV. Researchers suggest that a firm needs to hold not only unique resources, but furthermore *specific competences* in order to transform existing resources into actual competitive advantages in the market and thus to realise competitive advantages.

A considerable boost in the strategic competence discussion and the development of an independent CBV took place in the 1990's, with the seminal works on core competences. Short time after, there evolved a second stream of studies, which targeted a dynamisation of the core competence construct, the Dynamic Capability Perspective (DCP). The CBV constituting and most influential publications are 'The Core Competence of the Corporation' by Hamel and Prahalad (1990), the 'Competence-based Strategic Management Approach' by Sanchez and Heene (1997), and the 'Dynamic Capability Approach' by Teece et al. (1997).

With their publication 'The Core Competence of the Corporation', Prahalad and Hamel (1990) notably contributed to the development of the core competence concept. Their fundamental notion was that only those firms that hold specific basic competences, so called core competences, would be sustainable competitive in the long run. According to Hamel (1994), core competences can be defined as a bundle of combined technologies, abilities and knowledge. The latter refers towards technological know-how as well as process know-how (Amponsem, 1996). Following Prahalad and Hamel (1990), core competences are not solely based on one single market or business field, they rather can be described as comprehensive competences that can be successfully implemented or adapted among different business fields. Furthermore, core competences are not the result of strategic plans, they rather develop within an emergent process (Schreyögg and Kliesch, 2003). Essential for the core competence perspective is the concentration on the conscious identification and evolution of a dominating organisational competence and their organisational-wide diffusion.

Following the core competence perspective thus it is not solely the resource base anymore, that determines a company's market position, rather the identification of valuable resources and their reallocation within resource bundles (e.g. bundles of recombined technologies, abilities and knowledge, so called core competences) are essential for competitive advantages. Hence, the core competence approach distinguishes from earlier approaches, considering for the first time the organisational know-how as a crucial competitive factor (Schreyögg and Kliesch, 2003).

Taking a more cognitive, holistic position and abstracting from core competences, Sanchez and Heence (1997) developed the 'Competence-based strategic management approach'. Their theory of competence based strategic management (CbsM) incorporates economical, organisational and behavioural concerns within a dynamic, systemic, cognitive and holistic framework (Sanchez, 2004). This theory defines competence as 'the ability to sustain the coordinated deployment of resources in ways that helps an organisation achieves its goals' (Sanchez, 2004).

However, also the (core) competence based approach has inherent limitations. First, the core competence concept implicitly proceeds on the assumption that bundles of core competences exist in every firm and just have to be identified and subsequently further developed. Second, while there are first indications of the constituting components for theses competence bundles, an explanation on how these bundles are built and combined is notably absent. Especially the aspect of the "mode of bundling", respectively the recombination of resources, would be of particular interest since here is the starting point for business relevant formation and composition. Furthermore, likewise the RBV, the core competence approach forms a relative static perspective. A concentration on once identified core competences can support a firm's competitive position in a stable environment. Yet the assumption of stable conditions may lead to a lack of adaptability within a dynamic environment (Schreyögg and Kliesch, 2003). Firms, on the one hand, have to leverage and develop already existing resources towards stable core competences, meanwhile on the other hand they have to hinder their 'dysfunctional flip' through a permanent change, which requires a permanent replacement of resources (Leonard-Barton, 1992).

In response to this deficiency, an evolving stream of research within the competence based research, began to emerge in the late 1990's and gained growing attention up to today, the **Dynamic Capability Perspective (DCP)**, where researchers set out to incorporate a more dynamic perspective on the core competence idea, aiming to understand how firms sustain their competitive advantages in rapidly changing environments (Teece, 1997). The "Dynamic Capability Approach" published by Teece et al. (1997) is considered as the most influential publication on DCs, together with a more recent framework of DCs (Teece, 2007). With their pioneering article, Teece and colleagues (1997) argue towards a dynamisation of the competence construct, in order to address the need for a permanent advancement and adaptation of existing competences, noting the continuous environmental change and referring to the problem of obsolescence of existing competence.

Hence, essential for the DCP is the assumption that, in order to keep up with the rapidly changing environment, firms have to continuously strive to change their current asset structure and develop new technologies to address new opportunities (Karim and Mitchell, 2000, Isobe et al., 2008). Accordingly, the DCP puts the firm's abilities to reconfigure its internal asset structure, the so called *Dynamic Capabilities (DCs)*, in the centre of interest. Following the DCP the firm's DCs are regarded as central source of sustainable competitive advantage (Eisenhardt and Martin, 2000, Teece et al., 1997, Isobe et al., 2008). The general premise of the DCP is "that firms that reconfigure their resources faster than their rivals to capture newly emerging market opportunities are more likely to achieve superior performance" (Isobe et al., 2008, p. 414). Accordingly, scholars have emphasised the importance of "the processes to integrate, reconfigure, gain and release resources to match and even create market change" (Eisenhardt and Martin, 2000, p. 1107). In a similar vein, Teece et al. (1997, p. 516) defines the firm's DC as "the firm's ability to integrate, build and reconfigure internal and external competences to address rapidly changing environments". As such, DCs are regarded as the organisational processes and routines "by which firms achieve new resources configurations as markets emerge, collide, split, evolve and die" (Eisenhardt and Martin, 2000, p. 1107).

Hence, the DC approach—implicitly and explicitly—analyses the recombination of organisational routines and processes in regard to the continuous development of new RRs (Teece et al., 1997). An organisation's ability or competence to continuously acquire new resources, to eliminate existing ones and moreover to reintegrate and to (re)combine them is in the centre of consideration (Eisenhardt and Martin, 2000).

Thus, in contrast to earlier works, contemporary studies within the fields of competence based research and the wider discipline of organisational learning, concentrate less on specific core competences, but rather on the development of an overall 'organisational competence', or DC to reconfigure its internal asset structure (e.g. Dosi et al., 2000, Schreyögg and Kliesch, 2003). Thereby, the development of the firm's DC is not seen as an integral part, rather it is seen as a continuous development process (Montealegre, 2002). Contemporary scholars following the CBV therefore have emphasised the importance on the microfoundations of DCs (e.g. Teece, 2007, Ambrosini and Bowman, 2009), their determinants (e.g. Hawass, 2010), and perceived role for value creation in firms (e.g. Ambrosini and Bowman, 2009, Barreto, 2010, Pavlou and El Sawy, 2011).

However up to today, in most publications within the context of competence based research (including those following the DCP), competence is usually seen as an amalgam of the resource (as basis for RRs) and their selection and recombination (DCs) (e.g. Prahalad and Hamel, 1990, Turner and Crawford, 1994, Zott, 2003). In most publications within the competence based research the available organisational resources are entirely seen as part of the competence itself. Thus

competence becomes a little selective construct, that in the end includes everything and thus it loses its explanation character (Schreyögg and Kliesch, 2003).
Therefore differentiating between resources and DCs, allows incorporating findings from both, the resource and competence based research, and therewith offers
a fruitful paths for integrative research.

Summarising the above literature review of the resource and competence based
research, the following Figure 2.2 presents the development of the resource and
competence based research from its early formation up to today within a his-
togram (based on the work by Freiling et al., 2006). The graphic shows selected
milestones, which are seen as fundamental contributions to the development of
the researched area. Additionally, Appendix 2.1 in the additional electronic material provides a brief overview of fundamental publications forming the resources
and competence based view, their theoretical foundation and core statements.
Doing so, it presents an overview of elementary theoretical bases and approaches
for this research.

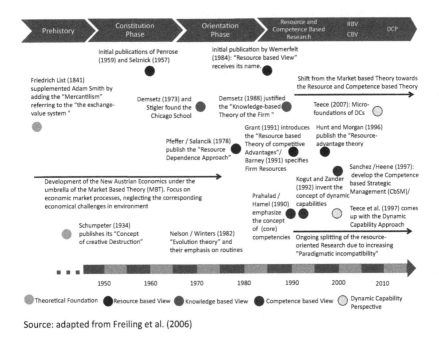

Source: adapted from Freiling et al. (2006)

Figure 2.2 Selective Milestones in the Resource and Competence based Research

To summarise, the review on literature from the resource and competence based research has shown, that the concept of RR and the DC approach is deeply rooted in the intersection of the resource based theory (RBV and KBV) and the competence based theory (CBV). Both theories, the resource and the competence based research, represent two major research streams in the strategy field, which complement each other and contribute to a deeper understanding of the RR concept in firms (Hawass, 2010). The first, resource (and knowledge) based perspective considers firms as a collection of different resources (Wernerfelt, 1984; Penrose, 1959, Wernerfelt, 1984, Peteraf, 1993, Barney, 1991). In this logic, the competitiveness of a firm depends basically on the control of superior resources that allows firms to outperform their competitors (Hawass, 2010). However, in order to sustain the competitive advantages in rapidly changing environments, firms must develop specific competences, DCs, in order to adapt and permanently advance the existing competences to changing market needs, and thus to realise performance potentials. This latter aspect is well addressed within the competence oriented research, which gained great attention and growing popularity in the beginning of the 21th century, and is highly recognised within the strategic management research (Schreyögg, 1999).

2.4   Conceptual Foundations: Resources, Dynamic Capabilities and Resource Recombination

Having established the theoretical foundations of the resource and competence based research, the following section provides the conceptual foundations of this research. In this section the status quo in literature is described, presenting the current knowledge of core concepts relevant for this research in order to develop a mutual understanding and deduce the central definitions for this research. Starting with the general definition of organisational resources, the following section briefly defines this research's understanding of resources and explains the special emphasis given on knowledge based resources. Next, their social organisation within the firm will be investigated, specifically how resources are organised in firms in form of competences, capabilities, and RRs. Lastly, the management of resources will be discussed in detail, outlining the process of RR in firms, and presenting this research's understanding of managerial competences and Dynamic Capabilities relevant for supporting this process.

2.4.1 Organisational Resources

The following section briefly outlines how organisational resources are defined and on what type of resources this research's emphasis is placed. Generally, organisational resources are the basic unit of analysis for the resource based theory of a firm (cf. Burr and Stephan, 2006, Grant, 1991). Therefore, the availability of high qualitative resources builds the basic requirement for the development of organisational competences and competitive advantages. Accordingly, resources can be regarded as 'the soil' for organisational competences (Schreyögg and Kliesch, 2003).

Going back to the original definition by Barney (1991, p. 101), organisational resources in this research include "all assets, capabilities, organisational processes, firm attributes, information, knowledge, etc. controlled by the firm that enable the firm to conceive of and implement strategies that improve its efficiency and effectiveness". In line with Amit and Schoemaker (1993, p. 35) firm's resources are defined in this research "as stocks of available factors that are owned or controlled by the firm." Notably, an important attribute of firm's resources is that a firm does not necessarily need to own a resource or capability to be understood as part of the resource base (Helfat et al., 2007), as for example firms may have access to other resources and capabilities through alliances or networks, which would also be seen as part of the resource base. Following this understanding, resources are regarded as "something an organisation can draw upon to accomplish its aims" (Helfat et al., 2007, p. 4). Moreover, "resources are converted into final products or services by using a wide range of other firm assets and bonding mechanisms such as technology, management information systems, incentive systems, trust between management and labor, and more" (Amit and Schoemaker, 1993, p. 35). Hence, following Wiklund and Shepherd (2003, p. 1307), "resources are inputs into a firm's production process (Barney, 1991)".

Various different classifications of firm resources have been proposed by researchers of the resource based theory, trying to list firm's attributes that enable firms to create value. However, up to today there is no general agreement on how the resources available in the firm can be categorised. Barney (1991, p. 101) classified the numerous firm resources into three different categories of resources, *physical capital resources* (e.g. physical technology, plants and equipment, geographical location and access to raw material), *human capital resources* (e.g. training, experience, judgement, intelligence, relationships and insights), and *organisational capital resources* (e.g. formal and informal planning, controlling, coordinating and reporting systems, informal intra- and inter-organisational relations). Grant (1991, p. 119) extended these three categories by adding another three, namely *technology* (product and process technology), *financial resources*, and *reputation* (firm's reputation and brands). Likewise for Amit and Schoemaker (1993, p. 35) going back to Grant (1991) resources consist, inter alia, of *knowhow* that can be traded (e.g., patents and licenses), *financial and physical assets* (e.g., property, plant and equipment), and *human capital*. In contradiction to most prior classifications proposed by literature, which generally subsume the management team and its skills under *'human capital'*, Gutenberg (1983) explicitly defines the *management team* and *managerial capability* as an additional resource category. Similar to Gutenberg's classification (1983), in the context of this research a differentiation between resources and capabilities is deemed valuable, as the latter decide on the input and combination of resources and therefore possesses a prominent role (Gutenberg, 1983). Hence, this research defines DCs as additional resource category and regards it as integral part of the resource base.

As a result, this research differentiates seven categories of resources that constitute a firm's resource base: (1) *physical capital resources* (machinery, plant, equipment) (2) *human capital resource* (people), (3) *technology* (product and process technology), (4) *financial resource* (financial capital) (5) *dynamic capabilities* (organisational and strategic processes and routines) (6) *market knowledge* (market, customer, industry and competitor intelligence), and (7) *technological knowledge* (operational capabilities, organising principles, operational processes and routines, skills), as illustrated in Figure 2.3:

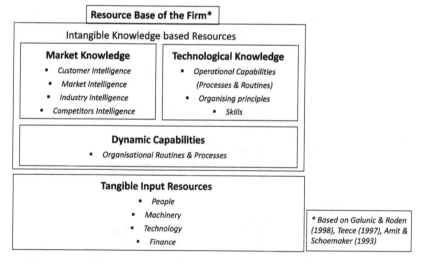

Figure 2.3 The Resource Base of the Firm

Moreover, looking at the firm's resource base and investigating the properties of resources more specifically, agreement is reached among researchers that resources can generally be distinguished into two different types of resources, those that are *knowledge based* and those that are *property based* (e.g. Miller and Shamsie, 1996, Wiklund and Shepherd, 2003, Kogut and Zander, 1992, Nonaka and Takeuchi, 1995, Conner and Prahalad, 1996, Teece et al., 1997). Thereby, literature shares a common understanding that "property based resources typically refer to tangible input resources, whereas knowledge based resources are the ways in which firms combine and transform these tangible input resources" (Wiklund and Shepherd, 2003, p. 1307).

Tangible input resources, or property based resources, in this research refer to those resources that are physical existent in the context of the organisation, e.g. machinery, plants, and equipment, buildings, production and information technologies (Schreyögg and Kliesch, 2003).

Intangible knowledge based resources, in contrast, refer to resources that are not always visible or measurable, but which are of particular importance in the process of value creation in firms (Schreyögg and Kliesch, 2003, Nonaka and Takeuchi, 1995, Galunic and Rodan, 1998). Generally, knowledge based resources refer to "the ways in which the more tangible input resources are manipulated and transformed so as to add value" (Teece et al., 1997, p. 509). Following the definition by Galunic and Rodan (1998, p. 1194), "in essence, they are the organising principles, skills, and processes that direct organisational action (cf. 'know-how')".

Accordingly, in the context of this research also *capabilities* are defined as knowledge based resources and therefore are regarded as 'resources' in the most general sense (cf. Helfat et al., 2007, p. 4, similar refer to Barney, 1991, Ambrosini and Bowman, 2009). At this point, DCs hold a special role as they—per definition—create, modify, or extend the resource base and are part of it themselves. This would imply that they can modify and extend themselves, and indeed many instances can be found where one DC does alter another DC, e.g. Learning capacity may help to modify other DCs and operational capabilities of all types (Helfat et al., 2007). However, it also becomes evident that capabilities and other more tangible resources, should not be regarded on the same level (Schreyögg and Kliesch, 2003). Thus, in this research, even though capabilities are explicitly being defined as part of the resource base, they will be investigated separately to allow having a specific view on the role of DCs and how they are working on towards building and exploiting the resource base.

Looking at **knowledge based resources**, typically literature distinguishes between personalised and person-independent resources. Patents, contracts or licenses, operational capabilities and DCs, for example, are regarded as person-independent intangible resources, whereas individual knowledge, skills, or networks can be attributed to person-related resources (Hall, 1991, Schreyögg and Kliesch, 2003). Moreover, as generally proposed by the strategic management literature, both types of resources, *tangible input resources* and *intangible knowledge based resources* are important for value creation in firms. However, recent work in the RBV place greater emphasis on the intangible knowledge based resources, in comparison to the tangible resources (Schreyögg and Kliesch, 2003, Galunic and Rodan, 1998). This is based on the assumption that tangible resources normally can be easily acquired via strategic factor markets at the respective factor market price (e.g. Hall, 1994), while the latter does not pertain to intangible resources, which generally are more difficultly obtained, especially if they emerged within the company in an evolutionary or path-dependent way. Therefore, in many cases intangible knowledge based resources are suggested to more likely fulfil the criteria of strategic resources as defined by Barney (1991). Thus, following Wiklund and Shepherd (2003, p. 1307): "Knowledge-based resources may be particularly important for providing sustainable competitive advantage, because they are inherently difficult to imitate, thus facilitating sustainable differentiation (McEvily and Chakravarthy, 2002), play an essential role in the firm's ability to be entrepreneurial (Galunic and Eisenhardt, 1994), and improve performance (McGrath et al., 1996)".

For the above reasoning the main focus within this research is placed on the intangible knowledge based resources, without neglecting the importance of tangible resources. Moreover, looking at the knowledge based resources, special emphasis will be given to **Market Knowledge** and **Technological Knowledge**. Market and Technological Knowledge are representing the most important knowledge based resources applicable to a firm's ability to discover and exploit opportunities (Wiklund and Shepherd, 2003, Jansen et al., 2005, De Luca and Atuahene-Gima, 2007, Lichtenthaler, 2009).

2.4.2 Organisation of Resources within the Firm

Having established the general definition of resources for this research, it is important to note that all categories of resources are of no strategic value, unless they are being effectively and efficiently organised and used within the organisation (cf. Sanchez et al., 1996, Burr and Stephan, 2006). Therefore, it is deemed valuable to have a closer look at the social organisation of resources within firms, more specifically, how the resources (intangible knowledge based resources and tangible input resources) are embedded within competence areas (clusters of resources) to form organisational competences and capabilities. Moreover, it will be subject of investigation, how the resources embedded within these competence areas may be (re)combined with other resources in new ways in order to develop new, innovative products or services or enter new markets, defined in this research as Resource Recombinations (RR).

2.4.2.1 Clusters of Resources, Organisational Competences and Capabilities

Generally, knowledge based resources along with their complementary input resources are further organised within firms in the form of **clusters of resources** (Galunic and Rodan, 1998), which basically capture the same concept as what has been referred to in literature as '*competences*' or '*capabilities*' (e.g. Galunic and Rodan, 1998, Prahalad and Hamel, 1990, Leonard-Barton, 1992, Teece et al., 1997). However, given some ambiguity over these terms (Collis, 1994), this research adapts Galunic and Rodan's understanding (1998, p. 1194) and uses the term 'competencies' to describe "combinations of input and knowledge based resources that exist at higher levels in a 'hierarchy of integration'".

Likewise, Teece et al. (1997, p. 516) define **organisational competences** as follows: "When firm-specific assets are assembled in integrated clusters spanning individuals and groups so that they enable distinctive activities to be performed, these activities constitute organisational routines and processes. Examples include quality, miniaturisation, and systems integration. Such competences are typically viable across multiple product lines, and may extend outside the firm to embrace alliance partners". Moreover, they specify those competences which build a firm's fundamental business as **core competences** (Teece at al., 1997, p. 516). Following Teece et al. (1997, p. 516), "the degree to which a core competence is distinctive depends on how well endowed the firm is relative to its com-petitors, and on how difficult it is for competitors to replicate its competences", whereby "the value of core competences can be enhanced by combination with the appropriate complementary assets" (Figure 2.4).

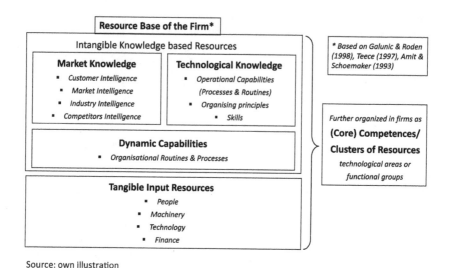

Source: own illustration

Figure 2.4 Organisation of Resources within Firms

Regardless of the fact that competences are much discussed in the literature, it is not yet clearly defined, what defines their boundaries (Galunic and Rodan, 1998). Referring to the example of Canon, describing their competences as fine optics, precision mechanics and electronics (Prahalad and Hamel, 1990), Galunic and Rodan (1998) point out that these competences could be further subdivided into smaller categories, for instance lens design, casting, grinding and others, which they refer to as capabilities. They further suggest that while each element is theoretically independent, these capabilities are typically grouped together into clusters of competence areas in which they are usually being applied. Therefore, capabilities are often established within "functional areas or by combining physical, human, and technological resources at the corporate level" (Amit and Schoemaker, 1993, p. 35). Correspondingly, "organizational capabilities can be built in different fields and on different levels of organizational activity, for instance at departmental, divisional, or corporate level" (Schreyögg and Kliesch, 2007, p. 915). Taking up this example, and therefore accepting that often the boundaries between competences and capabilities are unavoidably blurry (Helfat,

2011), this research adapts Galunic and Roldan's notion (1998, p. 1194), that "at the base are the aforementioned highly specialized capabilities, [... which] are then integrated into some form of higher-order systems or clusters of resources [competences], whether technological areas (e.g., printed circuit board assembly), functional groups (e.g., manufacturing), and so on (cf. Teece et al., 1997: 516)".

Organisational Capabilities   accordingly are defined in this research as a collection of routines (Winter, 2000, 2003), which in term describe how effectively routines are executed relatively to competitors (Nelson and Winter, 1982, Pavlou and El Sawy, 2011). To point out the difference between '*capability*' and '*capacity*', this research adapts the statement by Helfat (2011, p. 1244) that "an organization has a specific '*capability*' to imply that the organization (or its constituent parts) has the *capacity* to perform a particular activity in a reliable and at least minimally satisfactory manner". More generally, capabilities are concerned with putting resources (and other inputs) into action (Dosi et al., 2000, Eisenhardt and Martin, 2000, Winter, 2003, Felin et al., 2012). According to Amit and Schoemaker (1993, p. 35), capabilities "refer to a firm's capacity to deploy resources, usually in combination, using organizational processes, to effect a desired end. They are information-based, tangible or intangible processes that are firm-specific and are developed over time through complex interactions among the firm's resources". As such "they can abstractly be thought of as 'intermediate goods' generated by the firm to provide enhanced productivity of its resources, as well as strategic flexibility and protection for its final product or service" (Amit and Schoemaker, 1993, p. 35).

Contrary to resources, thus, capabilities are based on processes and routines supporting the development, transfer and exchange of information through the firm's human capital and therefore are described as 'invisible assets' (Amit and Schoemaker, 1993). Likewise, Felin et al. (2012) adopting Winter (2003, p. 991) refer to an organisational capability as "a high level routine (or collection of routines) that, together with its implementing input flows, confers upon an organization's management a set of decision options for producing significant outputs of a particular type". Accordingly, this notion regards "learning, experience, resources, and routines as inputs to capabilities" (Felin et al., 2012, p. 5). Thus, when further looking at its microfoundations, capabilities are commonly regarded as combinations of organisational routines (Parmigiani and Howard-Greenville, 2011, Winter, 2000, 2003).

Organisational Routines   are generally accepted as "repetitive, recognizable patterns of inter-dependent actions, carried out by multiple actors" (Feldman and Pentland, 2003, p. 95, Felin et al., 2012, Parmigiani and Howard-Greenville, 2011).

Dosi and colleagues (2000) elaborate this perception by noting that "routines are repetitious organizational activities that, along with other resources and in combination with each other, constitute capabilities, defined as the replicable capacity to bring about an intended action" (Parmigiani and Howard-Greenville, 2011, p. 419). Therefore, capabilities and its underlying routines "enables repeated and reliable performance of an activity, in contrast to *ad hoc* activity that does not reflect practiced or patterned behaviour" (Helfat, 2011, p. 1244, similar cf. Dosi et al., 2000, Winter, 2000, 2003). Moreover, routines are proposed to be "collective rather than individual-level phenomena" (Nelson and Winter, 1982, p. 107, Felin et al., 2012, p. 5), meaning that "the emphasis is placed on the interactions rather than the individuals that are interacting" (Felin et al., 2012, p. 5). Furthermore, routines are regarded as "contextually embedded interactive processes that underpin both stability and change" (Parmigiani and Howard-Greenville, 2011, p. 423). Accordingly, they are collective and socially embedded in nature (Schreyögg and Kliesch, 2007). In consequence, this research suggests that the microfoundations of capabilities can be clustered into three general categories: (1) basic routines, (2) processes and interactions, and (3) activities.

Following Parmigiani and Howard-Greenville (2011), capabilities can further be categorised either as **Ordinary** resp. **Operational Capabilities**, which are associated with typical, day to day operations within the company, or **Dynamic Capabilities (DCs)**, regarded as those that involve creation and change (Helfat et al., 2007, Winter, 2003, Zollo and Winter, 2002). While both types of capabilities are seen as collections of routines, "dynamic capabilities describe the ability to reconfigure and change, whereas operational capabilities denote the ability to "make a daily living""" (Pavlou and El Sawy, 2011, p. 242). Other researchers propose similar schemata, differentiating between 'zero-level' resp. 'zero-order' capabilities and 'higher-level' resp. 'higher-order' capabilities (e.g. Barreto, 2010, Winter, 2003, Collis, 1994), while the former "correspond to ordinary capabilities, (…) that allow a firm to "make a living" in the short term (Winter, 2003), or to substantive capabilities, (…) used to solve a problem (Zahra et al., 2006)" (Barreto, 2010, p. 261), whereby "higher-level" capabilities, in contrast, are consistent with DCs, as they "operate to change ordinary capabilities (Winter, 2003) or substantive capabilities (Zahra et al., 2006)" (Barreto, 2010, p. 261).

Operational Capabilities, as defined in this research, relate to those capabilities "that enable a firm to make a living in the present", and thus "enables a firm to perform an activity on an on-going basis using more or less the same techniques on the same scale to support existing products and services for the same customer population" (Helfat, 2011, p. 1244, Helfat and Winter, 2011). Therefore, operational capabilities are generally regarded to help sustaining the *technical fitness* (e.g. Teece, 2007). To name some examples, following Teece (2007, p. 1345) these operational or technical capabilities (competences) may include basic ones such as order entry, billings, purchasing, financial controls, inventory controls, financial reporting, marketing, and sales.

Dynamic Capabilities, in contrast, relate to "high-level activities that link to management's ability to sense and then seize opportunities, navigate threats, and combine and reconfigure specialised and cospecialised assets to meet changing customer needs" (Teece 2007, p. 1344). Thus, DCs involves the 'capacity of an organization to purposefully create, extend or modify its resource base' (Helfat et al., 2007, p. 4), and in consequence "a firm's product or service offerings, processes for generating and/or delivering a product or service, or customer markets" (Felin et al., 2012). Accordingly, it helps to sustain the *evolutionary fitness* and thereby helps creating value for stakeholders (Teece, 2007).

There is agreement among researchers that competitive advantages can be derived from superior resources and operational capabilities, or what is referred to as *technical fitness* (Teece, 2007, Helfat and Winter, 2011). However, "if an enterprise possesses resources/competences but lacks dynamic capabilities, it has a chance to make a competitive return (and possibly even a supra-competitive return) for a short period; but it cannot sustain supra-competitive returns for the long term except due to chance" (Teece, 2007, p. 1344). Following Teece (2007), this is caused by the fact, that firms possessing resources and operational capabilities but lacking DCs will "earn a living by producing and selling the same product, on the same scale and to the same customer population" (Winter, 2003, p. 992). While those firms might be even be good at invention, they "will likely fail to capitalize on its technological accomplishments" (Teece, 2007, p. 1345), as they lack the ability to adapt their competences to changing environments.

Thus, in order to earn "Schumpeterian rents associated with 'new combinations' and subsequent recombination" (Teece, 2007, p. 1345), firms have to possess DCs. Accordingly, shedding light on "the relationships between these subsystems" (Teece, 2007, going back to Buffa, 1982, p. 2) necessitates to have a closer look on the DCs needed to sense new opportunities, and reconfigure and recombine existing assets and systems as necessary in order to achieve the *evolutionary fitness* and long run competitive success (Teece, 2007).

2.4.2.2 Resource Recombination in Firms

The output of the successful utilisation of resources, organisational competences and capabilities as described above are Resource Recombinations. In other words, "resources are converted into final products or services by using a wide range of other firm assets and bonding mechanisms such as technology, management information systems, incentive systems, trust between management and labor, and more" (Amit and Schoemaker, 1993, p. 35). Hence, the "end products are the final goods and services produced by the firm based on utilizing the competences that it possesses" (Teece, 1997, p. 516). Consequently, their competitive performance (e.g. in terms of price and quality) is dependent upon its competences, more specifically its operational capabilities and DCs.

Resource Recombination (RR) in this research refers to "how the knowledge embedded within a competence may have to be untangled, altered, and integrated with other knowledge bases to create novel business concepts and/or competencies" (Wiklund and Shepherd, 2009, p. 196, as originally defined by Galunic and Rodan, 1998, p. 1195). Therefore, this research proposes the following definition:

> *Resource Recombination, as defined in this research, describes the recombination of resources in new ways in order to develop new, innovative products or services or enter new markets.*

With the above definition, this research adapts Galunic and Roldan's (1998) and Roldan's (2002) view, that creating new products and services depends on innovation, which in turn relies on RR as the source of new ideas.

The theoretical underpinnings and perception of this research, thus, are deeply rooted in the Schumpeterian view of innovation. Schumpeter (1968) proposed that generally innovations are new combinations of existing knowledge and incremental learning (Kogut and Zander, 1992), stating that: "To produce other things, or the same things by a different method, means to combine these materials and forces differently. (…) Development in our sense is then defined by the carrying out of new combinations" (Schumpeter, 1934, p. 65 f). Following Hawass (2010, p. 410), this implies that "an innovation is the product of recombining existing systems, resources and technologies in new ways", meaning that "new-to-the-world products consist of specific components that are already existing but have been creatively connected in an unprecedented manner to solve current problems" (as proposed earlier by Nelson and Winter, 1982, Galunic and Rodan, 1998). Accordingly, going back to Rumelt (1987), Schumpeter (1934) and Penrose (1959), in this research innovation is thought of "as a process of combining existing knowledge in new ways" (Rodan, 2002,

p. 154) to create new, innovative products or services, whereby "this process, as it is applied to a firm's strategic resources, has been termed 'Resource Recombination'" (Rodan, 2002, p. 154). Following Lumpkin and Dess (1996) and Wiklund et al. (2002), this research only considers RRs aiming to develop new products or services or the entering of new markets as entrepreneurial.

According to Rodan (2002, p. 154) "at its heart, resource recombination depends on a cognitive process some psychologists have termed generativity", which describes "the general ability to form multipart representations from elementary canonical parts". They further describe it as a combinatorial mechanism or process of "cognitive integration" and "blending", which "although not fully understood, (...) involves the creation of a new mental space that draws on constituent elements from two completed different mental spaces", and is proposed to lie "at the heart of the creation of novelty" (Rodan, 2002, p. 154).

Although RRs can take many forms (Rumelt, 1987, Galunic and Rodan, 1998), Schumpeter (1934) proposed five principal areas, which include introducing new products or changing the qualitiy of these products, developing new production methods, finding new sources of supply, reorganising industries, and opening new markets (Zahra and Wiklund, 2002, p. 8). To further specify the notion of RR, this research adapts the typology as proposed by Zahra and Wiklund (2002) and Wiklund and Shepherd (2009), who differentiated between **four different types of Resource Recombination** according to their usage of (i) *existing* vs. *new resources*[5] for (ii) *ongoing* vs. *new business initiatives*[6] to create new, innovative products or services (Zahra and Wiklund, 2002). Correspondingly, as presented in Figure 2.5, four different types of RR can be distinguished.

---

[5] The general differentiation of **existing vs. new resources** and its importance have already been extensively discussed in literature (Connor, 1999, Foster, 1986, Hamel and Prahalad, 1994, Wiklund and Shepherd, 2009). For this research's definition, *existing* resources refer to internal resources that have already been existent for a long time in/ or used by the company, while *new* resources refer to external resources that are not previously known in or used by the company, but have recently been acquired from external sources.

[6] Researchers have discussed the deployment of firm's resources for **ongoing vs. new business activities** for a long time (Chandler, 1962, Christensen and Bower, 1996, Majumdar, 1998). *Ongoing* activities in this research are defined as those business activities, with an emphasis on *improving existing* business initiatives, such as adding new features to existing products, expanding or improving service offerings, or enhancing performance in existing business areas. *New* activities refer to business activities, were the emphasis lies on *pursuing new* business initiatives, such as entering a new market, developing (radically) new products or services for new markets, or targeting new market segments.

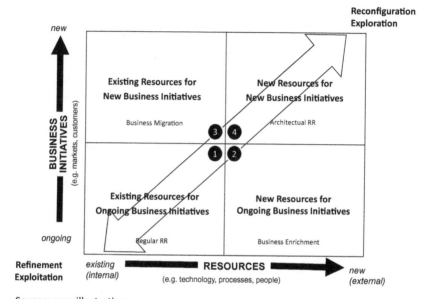

Source: own illustration

Figure 2.5 Four Types of Resource Recombinations in Firms

(1) Existing Resources for Ongoing Business Initiatives (Cell1). Following Zahra and Wiklund (2002, p. 22) the first type of RR is defined as "the reconfiguration of a firm's [existing] resource inputs to make their use more efficient". It covers the re-deployment of the firms current resources to improve existing products, or expand services (Wiklund and Shepherd, 2009, referring to Bell, 1991, Bower, 1970, Markides, 1997), with the aim to achieve objectives more economically and efficiently (Zahra and Wiklund, 2002). It is closely linked to what is referred to as 'resource refinement' in literature, which involves the improvement of the existing asset portfolio (Isobe, 2009) and is directed towards the exploitation of existing resources. Hawass (2010) further proposed a similar mechanism, which he terms 'capability evolution', and that basically captures internal learning processes to modify its current capabilities, aiming to "contribute to the deepening of the firm's current capabilities by creatively reconnecting existing organisational systems to improve capability responsiveness to technological developments" (Hawass, 2010, p. 412). Therefore, this type of RR addresses the recombination of resources in its original meaning.

(2) New Resources for Ongoing Business Initiatives (Cell 2). The second type of RR refers to the "infusion of new [external] resources to improve efficiency, increase product variety, add new features to existing products, and enhance performance in new areas" (Zahra and Wiklund, 2002, p. 23, Wiklund and Shepherd, 2009, p. 200, going back to Grant, 1991). It is closely linked to what has been referred earlier in the literature as strategies for business enrichment (e.g. Baumol, 1993, Chandler, 1962, Day, 1994, Gluck, 1981, Hamel and Prahalad, 1994). Therewith, it encompasses a dynamic learning process that "facilitates business renewal by injecting and incorporating new domains of knowledge to the existing organizational system" (Hawass, 2010, p. 412). Lavie (2006) describes this type of RR to address the same function as the pre-changed capability, however with a clear and noticeable increase in performance and complexity.

(3) Existing Resources for New Business Activities (Cell 3). This third type of RR relates to "changing of the firm's mix of [existing] resource inputs to pursue new initiatives, such as extending the new product line, introducing new products, or entering new markets" (Zahra and Wiklund, 2002, p. 23, Wiklund and Shepherd, 2009, p. 200). It basically describes firm's strategies related to business migration, as noted earlier in literature (e.g., Chandler, 1962, Fombrun and Ginsberg, 1990, Northcraft and Wolf, 1984, Porter, 1980, Leornard-Barton, 1995, Majumdar, 1998).

(4) New Resources for New Business Activities (Cell 4). This fourth type of RR refers to "the acquisition and use of these resource inputs to generate new products, goods or services for new markets" (Zahra and Wiklund, 2002, p. 23), as similarly described earlier in literature (e.g. Acs and Audretsch, 1990, Christensen, 1997, Connor, 1999, Foster, 1986, Rumelt, 1987). Firms might use this strategy to pursue radical innovations and position themselves as pioneer in the market (Acs and Audretsch, 1990, Chistensen, 1997). This type of RR is closely linked to what is referred as 'resource reconfiguration' in literature, which involves the restructuring of the asset portfolio through the integration of new assets (Isobe, 2009) and is directed towards the exploration of new opportunities. A similar concept has also been denoted by Hawass (2011, p. 412), entitled 'capability transformation', which basically captures "combining and connecting a firm's current domains of knowledge with new other domains located elsewhere in the industry". Accordingly the resulting type of RR "is the product of mixing internal knowledge with new external sources of knowledge" (Hawass, p. 412). Moreover, it is closely related to what has been described as "architectural innovation" (Henderson and Clark, 1990), while RR is the general case of which architectural innovation is a special case (Rodan, 2002).

As noted by Galunic and Rodan (1998, p. 1195), "in either case, the realization of resource recombinations depends upon the flow of competency-related knowledge between competence areas", irrespectively of what type of RR. Knowledge flows, as defined here, refer to "the various ways in which information, know-how, understandings, histories, etc., may be exchanged in the firm regarding competencies" (Galunic and Rodan, 1998, p. 1195). The complex and versatile nature of RR in firms becomes obvious as the potential use of resources and capabilities in products is various and "the couplings between different technologies, products, functions, applications, market segments and business areas are typically numerous in complex industrial organizations" (Granstrand and Söjlander, 1988, p. 40). For instance, "the development, production and use of a product usually involve several technologies and each technology can usually be applied in several products" (Granstrand and Söjlander, 1988, p. 40). Accordingly, the number of generic possibilities for new, innovative RR seems to constantly increase, as firms enlarge their stock of knowledge, get access to new technological areas, and extend their fields of knowledge through external networks and alliances. For example, it is suggested by literature that the more knowledge is collectively accumulated, the more opportunities there are for the creation of innovative new RRs (Weitzman, 1996, Moran and Ghoshal, 1999, Rodan, 2002). On the other hand, firm's DCs may also play a major role in these processes of refinement and reconfiguration. The aim of this research therefore is to better understand the combinatorial process of RR, and those factors influencing this process.

2.4.3 Management of Resources within the Firm

After having investigated the social organisation of resources in firms—how resources are organised in firms through clusters of resources, competences and capabilities, leading to the final product of RR in firms—the following section introduces the key constructs and mechanisms concerned with the management of resources within the firm. More specifically, this section introduces the process of RR, thus how resources embedded within a competence may have to be untangled, altered, and integrated with other resources to develop new, innovative products or services or enter new markets (new RRs) (Wiklund and Shepherd, 2009, Galunic and Roden, 1998). It further discusses the managerial capabilities, respectively DCs, which are needed in order to successfully implement the process of RR. Therewith, this research distinguishes between the preconditions of RR, organisational resources, and its actual implementation mechanisms.

2.4.3.1 Process of Resource Recombination

As outlined in the previous section, Resource Recombinations (RR) in this research is defined as the recombination of resources in new ways in order to develop new, innovative products or services or enter new markets, while the process of RR is the outcome of a systematic resource selection and combination task (Schreyögg and Kliesch, 2003). It is important to note that not the cluster of resources as a whole (e.g. competences or capabilities) are the subject of the RR process, but only the single resource elements, which are important to perform a specific task. Hence, the central and often noted task of the firm is its integrating role and problem-specific selection and linking, in order to "bringing together diverse basic inputs and specialized areas of knowledge and bundling them to perform a productive task" (Galunic and Rodan, p. 1194 going back to Grant, 1996).

Except of one notable exception, the recent work presented by Sirmon and colleagues (2007), which integrated managerial processes into the theory of resource management, traditional scholars in the RBV have not "fully explored the actions firms take to create and sustain an advantage or when those actions matter most" (Holcomb et al., 2009, p. 457 f.). The resource management process described by Sirmon and colleagues (2007) outlines a comprehensive framework of the resource management processes to obtain or develop, combine, and leverage resources with the aim to create and maintain competitive advantages, and thus essentially describes, what is referred to as RR process in this research. Components of the resource management process presented by Sirmon et al. (2007) include (1) *structuring* the resource portfolio, (2) *bundling* resources to build new (operational) capabilities, and (3) *leveraging* those capabilities in order to implement new, innovative products or services (RRs) in the market and thereby to provide value to customers, gain a competitive advantage, and create wealth for owners.

The first resource management process step, **structuring** the resource portfolio, refers to the management of the firm's resource portfolio (Sirmon et al., 2007). It comprises specific sub-processes such as *acquiring* (Barney, 1986, Makadok, 2001), *accumulating* (Dierickx and Cool, 1989, Garud and Nayyar, 1994), and *divesting* (Leonard-Barton, 1992), in order to obtain those resources applicable for being used in the subsequent bundling and leveraging resource management stages (see Sirmon et al., 2007, p. 278 ff.). Thereby, *acquiring* refers to purchasing resources from strategic factor markets (Sirmon et al. 2007, p. 278 going back to Barney, 1986), *accumulating* refers to the internal development of resources, which becomes necessary as strategic factor markets are unlikely to provide all resources required (Sirmon et al., 2007, p. 279), and *divesting* refers to the process of shedding firm-controlled resources, necessary for generating the slack and flexibility needed to acquire new resources of higher value (Sirmon et al., 2007, p. 280). However, while structuring the resource portfolio is regarded as an important resource management process step, as the resource portfolio provides the basis for developing new capabilities, and thus new RRs, "this process alone is insufficient to create value for customers and owners" (Sirmon et al., 2007, p. 281).

The second resource management process step, **bundling** resources, refers to combining firm resources to create new operational capabilities (Sirmon et al., 2007) in order to implement new, innovative products or services (RRs) in the market. Bundling involves three different subprocesses, namely *stabilising* (Siggelkow, 2002), *enriching* (Puranam et al., 2003), and *pioneering* (March, 1991). These processes are applied to integrate resources to alter or construct new capabilities for the purpose of developing new innovative products or services (RRs), with "each capability being a unique combination of resources allowing the firm to take specific actions, that are intended to create value for customers" (Sirmon et al., 2007, p. 281). *Stabilising* thereby refers to making "minor incremental improvements to existing capabilities" (Sirmon et al., p. 281). *Enriching* refers to extending and elaborating current capabilities, e.g. by adding complementary resources from the resource base to a current resource bundle (cf. Sirmon et al. 2007, p. 281). *Pioneering* relates to creating new capabilities to address new market opportunities, e.g. by integrating completely new resources, recently acquired from strategic factor markets, and adding them to the existing portfolio to create new resource bundles (cf. Sirmon et al., 2007, p. 282). Accordingly, "while the pioneering bundling process may include the recombination of existing resources, it often involves the integration of new resources with existing ones to create new capabilities" (Sirmon et al. 2007, p. 282). Generally speaking, while structuring is an important step that helps to manage the resource portfolio, "bundling resources into new capabilities is a necessary step in appropriating the potential value embedded in the firm's resource portfolio" (Sirmon et al., p. 281).

The third resource management process step, **leveraging** capabilities, refers to the application of firm's capabilities in order to implement new, innovative products or services (RRs) in the market to create value for the customer and wealth for owner (Simon et al., 2007). It contains a set of subprocesses such as *mobilising* (Hamel and Prahalad, 1994), *coordinating* (Alvarez and Barney, 2002), and *deploying* (Teece, 2007) used to exploit capabilities to address opportunities in the market (see Sirmon et al., 2007, p. 283 ff.). Thereby, *mobilising* refers to identifying the capabilities needed to develop the RRs (e.g. capability configurations, innovative products or services) necessary to exploit opportunities in the market (cf. Sirmon et al., 2007, p. 284), *coordinating* refers to integrating the identified capabilities into effective yet efficient RRs (cf. Sirmon et al., 2007, p. 285), and *deploying* refers to physically using the new resource configurations to support a chosen leveraging strategy. Hence, "the ability of the firm's [operational] capabilities to create value for customers is realised through their successful deployment" (Sirmon et al., 2007, p. 285) in form of new innovative RRs. Summarising, effective leveraging is an important process step because "even when a firm owns or controls resources and has effectively bundled them to develop capabilities with value-creating potential, the firm is unlikely to realise value creation unless it effectively leverages/uses those capabilities in the marketplace" (Sirmon et al., 2007, p. 283).

Notably, while each individual component of the RR process is important to optimise resource value creation in firms, the single resource management steps must be synchronised (Sirmon et al., 2007, 2010). Following Sirmon and colleagues (2007, p. 287), "creating synchronization requires top-level managers to be simultaneously involved in all stages of the resource management process while consistently scanning the external environment for salient cues about important change". Thus, an effective implementation of the RR process steps, as described above, requires firms to possess the necessary competences and capabilities to be able to effectively structure the resource portfolio, to bundle resources to create new capabilities, and to leverage them effectively in the market.

The explication of the RR processes steps in this section gave important insights in explaining, how resources can be managed to create value for the customers and owners. However, it is not defined yet, what capabilities and competences are needed to implement these processes.

2.4.3.2 From Managerial Competences to Dynamic Capabilities

It revealed that the single RR process steps are closely linked to what has been referred to in the literature as '**Managerial Competence**' or '**Managerial Ability**' (e.g. Kraaijenbrink et al., 2010, Sirmon et al., 2010). Research findings reveal multiple reasons to expect that a superior managerial ability to understand and effectively use firm resources would imply higher RR sucess. Thus, to deploy the RR process steps as described above allows firms to exploit the untapped value of their resources, for the following reasoning (Holcomb et al., 2009): First, superior knowledge about the resources is generally proposed to allow managers to be more effective than competitors at the selection and acquisition of new resources at a favourable price by revealing their 'real' value for future use (Makadok, 2003). An explanation may be, that for managers, which have a more precise understanding of the resource value for future activities, it is easier to discover and exploit factor market imperfections (Amit and Schoemaker, 1993, Denrell et al., 2003, Holcomb et al., 2009). Second, managers having superior knowledge of the firm and competitive context are found to be more effective than competitors in adapting strategies that create value for the customers by bundling and leveraging resources in new ways, which allows to exploit the value creation potential of those resources (e.g. Hansen et al., 2004, Lippman and Rumelt, 2003, Holcomb et al., 2009).

For that reason, research finding on resource management reveal that managerial actions determine in large parts the realised value of resources (Sirmon et al., 2007, 2010). It is not surprising that, as firms differ in their ability to manage their resources, the value they extract through RRs varies significantly (Holcomb et al., 2009). Accordingly, in their recent work Wiklund and Sheperd (2009) stressed the crucial importance of RR activities for the effectiveness of alliances and acquisitions, stating that "resource combination activities constitute a broad construct including the acquisition, development, accumulation and usage of resource" and subsequently, that "the greater the capability for conducting such activities, the better firms will be at discovering and exploiting the value of alliances and acquisitions." Following the argument by Wiklund and Shepherd (2009), a sole focus on the value creation potential of resources, as well as on single resource management steps, only provides an incomplete understanding of performance implications for the development of new RRs, unless researchers are looking at the *capabilities of the firm* to recombine these resources.

Consequently, building on the insights of the resource management process as proposed by Sirmon et al. (2007) and translating the single steps of the RR process into firm's capabilities, this research argues that the firm's capability to manage its resources and to bundle them into new RRs, as well as to leverage them on the market, is a critical capability that is necessary to extract the potential value residing in a firm's resource portfolio.

Still, past research from the RBV predominantly concentrated on the managerial competence, referring to the manager's ability to effectively manage the firm's resources (e.g. Sirmon et al., 2010). Barney (1991) for example reasoned that a manager's ability to understand and effectively use the firm's resources, can be regarded as a valuable resource itself, which "has the potential for generating sustained competitive advantages" (Barney, 1991, p. 117). In a most recent attempt, also Holcomb and colleagues (2009) explicated the joint role of manager's ability and resource quality for value creation.

However, demarcating from past research stressing the importance of manager's ability to understand and effectively use firm resources, this research sets out to investigate the firm's capacity on a meta-level. More specifically, this research suggests that the firm's ability to effectively reconfigure its resources is not to be attributed to specific characteristics of individuals, but can be established at an organisational level. Doing so, this research builds on established insights from the DCP and expands the argumentation by Wiklund and Sheperd (2009) and Sirmon et al. (2007) by abstracting from the observed RR processes and activities to a higher-order DC of the firms to recombine its resources. Thereby, it is not solely looking at the RR processes, nor the managerial ability to handle these processes, but moreover sets out to investigate the underlying organisational processes and routines established at an organisational level that build the micro-foundations of a firm's DC. Correspondingly, this research argues that the greater the DCs of the firm relevant for conducting RR activities, the better firms will be at discovering and exploiting the value of their resource base. The following section specifies the notion of DCs for this research.

2.4.3.3 Dynamic Capabilities

The growing body of literature investigating the topic of **Dynamic Capabilities (DCs)** yield to a number of distinct but related definitions of the construct (e.g., Teece et al., 1997, Eisenhardt and Martin, 2000, Zollo and Winter, 2002, Winter, 2003, Zahra et al., 2006, Helfat et al., 2007, Teece, 2007). More recently, with the aim to provide an overview and consolidation of past research, Barreto (2010) reviewed 40 articles on DC in the leading management journals between 1997 and 2007, and found nine different definitions of the concept. As noted by Barreto (2010, p. 257): "such a proliferation of definitions shows the dynamism generated by the topic and is justified by the youth of the approach, but it also produces some confusion that may hinder more effective progress within the field". Accordingly, "despite (or perhaps due to) the large number of theory papers published recently, consistent terminology remains elusive" (Parmigiani and Howard-Greenville, 2011, p. 446).

Since Teece and colleagues' (1997) original contribution, which also builds the principal definition of DC for this research, a variety of authors have contributed own definitions of the concept, however most of them can be traced back to the original definition by Teece et al. (1997), or are adaptations of it (Ambrosini and Bowman, 2009). The most influential definitions are provided in the Table 2.2:

Table 2.2 Main Definitions of Dynamic Capabilities

Author(s)	Definition
Teece et al. 1997 p. 516	„… the firm's ability to integrate, build, and reconfigure internal and external competences to address rapidly changing environments. Dynamic capabilities thus reflect an organization's ability to achieve new and innovative forms of competitive advantage given path dependencies and market positions (Leonard-Barton, 1992)."
Eisenhardt/Martin 2000, p. 1107	„The firm's processes that use resources—specifically the processes to integrate, reconfigure, gain and release resources—to match and even create market change. Dynamic capabilities thus are the organizational and strategic routines by which firms achieve new resources configurations as markets emerge, collide, split, evolve and die."
Zollo/Winter 2002 p. 339–340	„… routinized activities directed to the development and adaptation of operating routines … A dynamic capability is a learned and stable pattern of collective activity through which the organization systematically generates and modifies its operating routines in pursuit of improved effectiveness."
Winter 2003, p. 991	Dynamic capabilities "are those that operate to extend, modify or create ordinary capabilities".
Zahra et al. 2006, p. 918	Dynamic capabilities are "the abilities to reconfigure a firm's resources and routines in the manner envisioned and deemed appropriate by its principal decision-maker"
Teece 2007, p. 1320	"Dynamic capabilities can be disaggregated into the capacity (a) to sense and shape opportunities and threats, (b) to seize opportunities, and (c) to maintain competitiveness through enhancing, combining, protecting, and, when necessary, reconfiguring the business enterprise's intangible and tangible assets. (…) These capabilities can be harnessed to continuously create, extend, upgrade, protect, and keep relevant the enterprise's unique asset base"
Augier/Teece 2007, p. 1190	„Dynamic capabilities refers to the particular (non-imitable) capacity business enterprises possess to shape, reshape, configure, and reconfigure assets so as to respond to changing technologies and markets and escape the zero profit condition. Dynamic capabilities relate to the enterprise's ability to sense, seize, and adapt, in order to generate and exploit internal and external enterprise-specific competences, and to address the enterprise's changing environment."
Helfat et al. 2007, p. 4	A dynamic capability is "the capacity of an organization to purposefully create, extend, or modify its resource base".

(continued)

Table 2.2 (continued)

Author(s)	Definition
Wang/Ahmed 2007, p. 35	Dynamic capabilities as "a firm's behavioural orientation constantly to integrate, reconfigure, renew and recreate its resources and capabilities and, most importantly, upgrade and reconstruct its core capabilities in response to the changing environment to attain and sustain competitive advantage."
Barreto 2010, p. 271	„A dynamic capability is the firm's potential to systematically solve problems, formed by its propensity to sense opportunities and threats, to make timely and market oriented decisions, and to change its resource base."

(Source: based on Barreto, 2010)

Overviewing these definitions shows that from a general viewpoint, consensus is reached among researchers concerning the principal character of the DC construct. However, at some points (e.g. concerning its locus of change, or its environmental context) also contradictory views exist about the concept (Ambrosini and Bowman, 2009), as will be further discussed in the following.

First, regarding the **nature of the concept,** DCs have been defined as *abilities* or *capacities* (capabilities) (e.g., Helfat et al., 2007, Teece, 2000, 2007, Winter, 2003, Zahra et al., 2006), but also as *processes* or *routines* (e.g. Eisenhardt and Martin, 2000, Zollo and Winter, 2002) (for a more detailed analysis, see Barreto, 2010, p. 260). However, given some ambiguity over these terms, they are generally used to describe similar even interchangeable concepts at a different level of granularity, as detailed in Section 2.4.2.1. Hence, this research uses the following conceptualisation of DCs:

(1) *DCs* refer to the firm's *capacities* or *abilities* "to deploy resources, usually in combination, using organizational processes, to effect a desired end" (Amit and Schoemaker, 1993, p. 35). At the same time these capacities are constituted by organizational *processes* and *routines*.

(2) *Routines*, which are "repetitive patterns of interdependent organizational actions" (Parmigiani and Howard-Greenville, 2011, p. 417), build the microfoundations of Dynamic Capabilities (Dosi et al., 2008, Parmigiani and Howard-Greenville, 2011).

(3) Thereby individuals, their skills, and complex processes and activities build the foundation of routines (Parmigiani and Howard-Greenville, 2011).

Second, concerning the **specific role of DCs,** from the above definitions it emerges that the literature is consistent in admitting the central role of DCs in changing the key internal components of the firm. However, the chosen 'locus of change', which describes the specific internal components that are changed, exposes to vary across components such as the *resource base* (e.g., Eisenhardt and Martin, 2000, Helfat et al., 2007, Teece, 2007, Augier and Teece, 2007, Ambrosini and Bowman, 2009, Barreto, 2010) and *capabilities* or *competences* (e.g. Teece et al., 1997, Winter, 2003), operating *routines* (e.g. Zollo and Winter, 2002), and *resources* and *routines* (Zahra et al., 2006) (for a more detailed analysis see Barreto, 2010, p. 261). However, all different attempts correspond in the central perception that they "referred to the concept as a capacity (Helfat et al., 2007) or as the routines (Eisenhardt & Martin, 2000) by which an organization alters its resource base" (Barreto, 2010, p. 261). Bringing it down to a common denominator this research subsumes:

(4) The locus of change where the firm's DCs are working on, is to build and exploit the firm's *resource base.*

While consensus is reached among researchers that the specific role of DCs is to change the resource base, it is not yet clearly defined, how this role is constituted. Therefore, the investigation of how the specific DCs act upon the resource base by building and exploiting it, and how both constructs are linked with the organisational outcome of new RRs, lies in the core of this research. The aim is to bring clarity to the notion of DCs, and their role and effects towards developing RRs in firms.

Third, concerning the **environmental context** relevant for DCs, different views can be found among researchers (refer to Barreto, 2010, p. 261 f.), varying between (1) those attempts that unequivocally attribute the concept to highly *dynamic, volatile,* and *rapidly changing environments* (e.g., Teece et al., 1997, Teece, 2007), (2) those attempts that acknowledge its relevance in highly but *also* in *moderately dynamic environments,* where "change occurs frequently, but along predictable and linear paths" (e.g., Eisenhardt and Martin, 2000, p. 1110) and therefore accept different degrees of environments (e.g., Eisenhardt and Martin, 2000), (3) those attempts proposing that "a volatile or changing environment is not a necessary component of a dynamic capability" (Zahra et al., 2006, p. 922) and thus attribute it to both *stable* and *dynamic environments* (e.g., Zahra et al., 2006, Zollo and Winter, 2002, Helfat et al., 2007), and lastly (4) those attempts that do not explicate the external environmental conditions as relevant, thus implicitly assuming the irrelevance of such conditions for their arguments (e.g., Makadok, 2001). Consistent with this view, this research adapts Zahra and colleagues' (2006) and Zollo and Winter's (2002) argumentation, assuming that:

(5) DCs exist and are also used in environmental contexts characterised by low rates of change. However, at the same time this research suggests, that they may be of higher relevance and value in dynamic markets.

Fourth, concerning the **creation and development mechanisms of DC**, the above definitions show a consistent claim in literature concerning the perceived role of learning mechanisms in the creation and development of DCs (Barreto, 2010). Consistent with literature this research defines:

DCs are regarded as evolutionary organisational learning mechanisms, as such they are:

(6) *path dependent* (Zollo and Winter, 2002),
(7) *built* rather than bought in the market (Makadok, 2001),
(8) *firm specific* and as such embedded in the firm (Eisenhardt and Martin 2000), and
(9) *evolving* over time (Ambrosini and Bowman, 2009).
(10) *learned* and stable pattern of *collective* activity (Zollo and Winter, 2002)

These definitions also delineate what DCs are not. Firstly, they are not ad hoc problem-solving events or spontaneous reaction (Winter, 2003, Helfat et al., 2007, Schreyögg and Kliesch, 2007), hence they must be repeatable or contain some patterned element (Dosi et al., 2000, Winter, 2002, Winter, 2003, Zollo and Helfat, 2011), and secondly, the definitions by Zahra et al. (2006) and Helfat et al. (2007) clearly show that luck does not constitute a DC (Ambrosini and Bowman, 2009).

Fifth, concerning the relationship between DCs and its **performance outcomes,** generally two different types of approaches can be found among the above definitions (cf. Barreto, 2010, p. 274): The first type of approaches assumes a *direct relationship* between DCs and their performance outcomes or competitive advantages (e.g., Teece et al., 1997, Zollo and Winter, 2002), suggesting that DCs are "the sources of enterprise-level competitive advantage over time" (Teece, 2007, p. 1320). In contrast, the second type of approaches reasoned an *indirect relationship* between DCs and performance, presuming that DCs do not necessarily lead to higher performance or competitive advantage (e.g., Eisenhardt and Martin, 2000, Zott, 2003, Helfat et al., 2007), rather that the respective "performance effects may depend on the characteristics of the resulting new resource configuration or on how managers use their dynamic capabilities" (Barreto, 2010, p. 263). For example, Eisenhardt and Martin (2000, p. 1106) argue that "dynamic capabilities are necessary, but not sufficient, conditions for competitive advantage", suggesting that sustainable competitive advantages would not rely on DCs themselves but on the quality of resource configurations (resp. RRs) created by the DCs, e.g. by "using dynamic capabilities sooner, more astutely, more fortuitously than the competition" (Eisenhardt and Martin, 2000, p. 1117). Likewise, Zott (2003) reasoned that DCs are not directly linked to performance outcomes, but in fact are proposed to indirectly influence firm performance through modifying resources bundles (RRs) or routines. Correspondingly, Zahra et al. (2006) postulates the relationship between DCs and performance to be indirectly moderated by the quality of substantive capabilities modified by DCs. Other authors see the proposed causal link between DCs and performance outcomes predominantly determined (mediated) by the availability of the resources on which the DCs act upon (Makadok, 2001). In line with the argument by Barreto (2010) this research subsumes, that the second type of approaches, suggesting an indirect relationship between DCs and performance outcomes, may describe the most promising. Therefore:

(11) DCs are suggested to act on towards changing the resource base.
(12) The availability of high quality resources and the deployment of DCs may influence the development of new, innovative resources combinations RRs, which in turn may affect performance outcomes.
(13) Therefore an *indirect relationship* between DCs and performance outcomes is suggested.

This perception is also consistent with earlier proposals in this field, that presumed DCs as a key antecedent of firm's success and failure, strategic choices and competitive advantage (Teece et al., 1997). However, maybe due to the strong focus initially put on the direct relationship towards performance, up to today those propositions remained mainly unexplored (Barreto, 2010). In recent years, researchers started to conceptually and empirically address the impact of DCs on intermediate outcomes (e.g. Pavlou and El Sawy, 2011), as well as their effect on performance (e.g. Isobe et al., 2008). However, following the call by Barreto (2010, p. 275f) "future research should continue to explore these relationships between DCs and intermediate outcomes, on one hand, and between intermediate outcomes and performance, on the other hand, to better assess which dynamic capabilities and intermediate outcomes deserve more attention".

2.5 Research Gaps derived from the Literature Review

As the first introductory review of current literature has shown, the concept of RR to generate innovation has been widely discussed and is recognised as being significant in today's knowledge economy. Accordingly, the concept of RR has attracted considerable interest in the past with many publications from a variety of academic fields stressing its importance (e.g. Schumpeter, 1934, Usher, 1954, Penrose, 1959, Koestler, 1964, Bouette, 2004). Despite the high relevance of RR and the increasing interest from academia and practice, existing research in the area has not yet elaborated, how a possible framework for RR could be designed and established. Although the DCs of the firm to make use of its resources can be considered as a decisive factor, when it comes to successfully commercialising innovations (Matsumoto et al., 2005), the failure of firms to find systematic ways to identify, evaluate and combine existing resources successfully is well documented in research stemming from a lack of understanding of how organisations can strategically and practically approach and foster RR (Kliewe et al., 2009). Researchers put forward that firms have difficulties in understanding the "black box" involved in "using valuable, rare, inimitable, and non-substitutable resources to gain and maintain a competitive advantage" (Sirmon et al., 2007, p. 288, Priem and Butler, 2001). To date, scarce research exists investigating how organisations can plan and execute RRs and what specific DCs are needed in order to successfully implement RRs (Sirmon et al., 2007).

As the recent increase in the exploration and exploitation of existing resources and capabilities can be seen rather as a trend from practice than a movement initiated by academia (Lichtenthaler, 2007), the insights in the determinants and antecedents of RR in firms have still been limited (Zahra and Wiklund, 2002). Few studies have examined the antecedents necessary for such RR to occur (Galunic and Rodan, 1998), and none have tested them empirically. However, there is a crucial need to understand how firms can effectively structure and manage their resources and bundle them into valuable new RRs in order to leverage their value creation potential (Sirmon et al., 2007). More precisely, the following research gaps could be derived and will be addressed in this thesis:

First, the literature on DCs has often been criticised for a lack of precise definitions, empirical grounding and measurement (e.g. Pavlou and El Sawy, 2011). This is in line with Williamson's tautological criticism of the RBV (Williamson, 1999). While a wide spectrum of different capabilities has been denoted under the "umbrella of Dynamic Capabilities" and an array of different processes and routines has been assumed to provide the microfoundations of DCs (e.g. Teece,

2007, Eisenhardt and Martin, 2000), there still is a lack of a consistent definition of a firm's DCs. Moreover, few attempts have been made to categorise different capabilities and thus to develop a framework incorporating all different types of DCs referred to in literature (e.g. Madsen, 2010, Pavlou and El Sawy, 2011). To date there is still a poor understanding of the DC construct and its existence is often assumed without specifying their exact components (Galunic and Eisenhardt, 2001), which makes it difficult to approach. A clear and precise differentiation of the various capabilities, which are also assumed to be working in different fields (Barreto, 2010), is lacking. Instead, a firm's DCs have rather been described as a "black box" (Pavlou and El Sawy, 2011). Following Felin et al. (2012, p. 1), "while much progress has been made in understanding routines and capabilities the underlying microfoundations or micro-level origins of these constructs have not received adequate attention", accordingly various questions remain regarding the underlying micro-level origins of DCs (Felin and Foss, 2005, Fellin and Foss, 2009, Teece, 2007, Argote and Ren, 2012, Felin et al., 2012, Teece, 2012). Taken together, there is an urgent need for a coherent framework and measurement model for DCs (GAP1). Only if the construct of DC is made observable, and semantically clarified—with an actionable set of specific, measurable DCs and a clarification of their underlying routines, processes and activities—the ambiguity and the inconsistence of the current concept can be overcome and implications for managers can be offered.

Second, while the literature consistently supports the view that RR activities should be particularly important in dynamic environments (Eisenhardt and Martin, 2000, Wiklund and Shepherd, 2009), what influence a firm's DC has on the successful development of RRs has not yet been extensively investigated in the literature (Barreto, 2010), neither has it been measured empirically (Sirmon et al., 2007). Whereas the RBV traditionally concentrates on specific characteristics of the resource base (Barney, 1991), suggesting that the major source for new, innovative RRs in firms can be found in the resources itself, it is neglecting the role of resource management (Holcomb et al., 2009). Hence, previous research on the RBV has not provided sufficient information on how resources are used to create competitive advantages (Priem and Butler, 2001), or, as criticism by Barney and Arikan (2001), simply postulates "that the actions necessary to exploit resources are self-evident when they are not" (Sirmon et al., 2007, p. 274).

On the other side, while important conceptual advancements have been made within the DC perspective concerning the relevance of DCs and how they are developed over time, only an inconsistent picture emerges concerning the effects and locus of where DCs are actually working (Madsen, 2010, Ambrosini and Bowman, 2009). Generally speaking, while the "congruence of a theory is defined by the laws of the relationship among its variables of interest" (Barreto, 2010, p. 274), most of the DC and RBV literature is "characterized by insufficient formulation of clear, a priori statements regarding the relationships among key constructs or variables" (Barreto, 2010, p. 274). More specifically, current literature is either only looking at the DCs and their influence on integrating, building and bundling new RRs, or it is solely concentrating on specific characteristics of resources and their influence on performance outcomes. Doing so, existing literature in the field tends to ignore the synergetic role of resources and DCs in conjunctly achieving RRs in firms. In consequence, "in-between creating access to heterogeneous resources and their ultimate effect on innovation lies unexplored territory, in the learning process between firms that starts when resources are brought together and subsequently combined" (Nooteboom, 2007, p. 4). Hence, there is a crucial need to understand how to effectively build a high valuable resource base, bundle the resources into new RRs, and thereby exploit the value creation potential of the resources through building new RRs (Sirmon et al., 2007). To date, research looking at both, the resource base and the DCs at the same time, is still notably absent. Accordingly, an investigation of the DCs in relation to the resource base is lacking (GAP2). Thus, investigating the relation between the different DCs, the resource base and its performance outcomes (here: RR) would provide an essential step towards establishing a coherent theory by means of governing the relationships between constituting variables and therewith providing a more precise, integrated picture on how RRs in firms are built. Moreover, it would allow to specify the role of DCs in the process of value creation in firms.

Third, there is a growing body of literature looking at the DCs from a slightly different perspective investigating the antecedents that may foster the development of DCs (e.g. Madsen, 2010). Nevertheless existing literature "offers few empirical analyses that explore the processes inside and outside organizations that lead to dynamic capabilities" (Hawass, 2010, p. 414 f.), and only few studies have examined the organisational framework conditions that allow firms to systematically reconfigure its resources to improve innovation (Hawass, 2010, Macher and Mowery, 2009). Recent research has proposed various antecedents of DCs at the individual-, organisational- and network-level (Rothaermel and Hess, 2007). However, far too little attention has been paid to empirically investigating the influencing factors of the development of DCs, especially those that might be grounded in the firm's underlying strategic orientation. Still, it is a quite unspecific picture that has been drawn, concentrating on multiple factors on various different levels and from different perspectives. It is not yet clear which factors influence the development of DCs within firms (GAP 3). Accordingly, this study responds to prior calls for research that explicates firm-related determinants that may explain the development of DCs (Zahra and Wiklund, 2002).

Fourth, to date empirical research from both the RBV and the DC perspective is still in their infancy (Hawass, 2010, Madsen, 2010). Thus, empirical research on the relationships between resources, capabilities and performance outcomes is still lacking. From the DC literature, while a growing number of researchers have taken exploratory research approaches to DC and performance outcomes, leading to a growing amount of normative and conceptual findings (e.g. Teece et al., 1997, Teece, 2007, Eisenhardt and Martin, 2000, Kogut and Zander, 1992), however, apart from a few, notable exceptions (e.g. Pavlou and El Sawy, 2011, Hawass, 2010) empirical research is still remarkably absent. An analogous picture emerges looking at RBV literature, while tremendous conceptual advancements have been made in this area within the last decade, the majority of studies investigating resource endowments and performance outcomes are exploratory in nature (e.g. Barney, 1991, Galunic and Rodan, 1998, Rouse and Daellenbach, 1999). Most of them are based on qualitative studies, and only little quantitative research has been conducted to date. A quantitative validation of the role of DCs and the resource base in the process of value creation in firms is still missing (GAP4). Hence, these propositions should be validated empirically.

In summary, the review of current literature has shown that there is an urgent need for a coherent theory and model of resource value creation in firms through RR. Accordingly, a strong need exists, to examine the DCs relevant for RR to occur (GAP 1), to investigate their role and effect in building and exploiting the resource base for building new RRs (GAP2), and furthermore to investigate the organisational- and interorganisational framework conditions influencing the development of a firm's DCs (GAP 3) within qualitative and quantitative research setting (GAP4). In addition, this research sets out towards incorporating the insights from both the RBV and the DC perspective and applying them to the concept of RR. With the aim to present an integrated picture, this research attempts to weave these streams together, from a conceptual and empirical angle. The following Figure 2.6 shows the knowledge gaps elaborated above, which will be addressed within this PhD work.

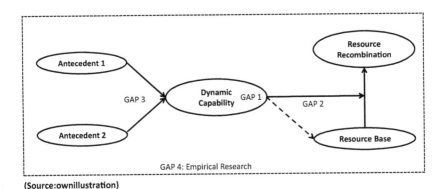

(Source:ownillustration)

Figure 2.6 Research Gaps in the existing RBV and DC Literature

GAP 1: There is a poor understanding of the construct of DC and a lack of a measurable model of a specific set of DCs, which makes it difficult to approach.

GAP2: The influence of the firm's DC on the successful development of RR—specifically its role and effect in building and exploiting the recourse base—has not yet been extensively investigated, neither has it been measure empirically.

GAP3: Far too little attention has been paid to an empirical investigation if the influencing factors for the development if DC in a firm- and network-level.

GAP 4: Empirical research on the relationship between the resource base, DCs and RR is still lacking.

2.6   Chapter Summary

The primary contribution of this chapter was to provide the theoretical and conceptual foundation for this research, embedding the concept of Resource Recombination (RR) and Dynamic Capabilities (DCs) within the wider discipline of strategic management and entrepreneurship, identifying existing knowledge gaps and introducing the core concepts and definitions relevant for the further investigation of this research.

As shown in Section 2.2 both strategic management and entrepreneurship researchers share a common and strong interest in value and wealth creation through RRs. Researchers from both disciplines, the strategic management and entrepreneurship spectrum, have recognised the high relevance of RR for innovation generation and the crucial importance of RRs as a means of creating wealth. It has been shown that RR constitutes an important topic, where different scientific disciplines intersect and where fruitful integrative research can be carried out. Recognising the value of RRs for future wealth creation, there is a current shift in literature from investigating the importance of RRs towards an investigation of how RRs can be fostered. The focus of contemporary research within this research field furthermore goes apart from the investigation of the resources a firm owns (as suggested by the RBV) towards an investigation of how these resources can be used in new, rent regarding ways and subsequently, what competences are needed in order to successfully implement RRs in the strategic management (referring to the CBV).

Section 2.3 further established the theoretical foundation of this research, investigating the resource and competence based research, which could be identified as the principal parent theories of this research. After presenting the evolution and background of both these streams, the resource based view (RBV), the competence based view (CBV), and the knowledge based view (KBV) were further described as relevant streams this research is contributing to.

In Section 2.4 the conceptual foundations of this research could be further established. Based on the status quo in literature, core concepts relevant for this research were defined in order to develop a mutual understanding and deduce the central definitions for this research. Starting with the general introduction of what is meant by organisational resources within this research, its social organisation within firms was delineated, and finally the RR process as well as managerial capabilities and DCs relevant for the management of those resources were discussed. The section closed with a critical review of definitions for the DC construct, leading to a common understanding of the concept as defined for this research.

Finally, Section 2.5 presented the research gaps addressed in this research. Based on the though review of existing literature, the research gaps identified in the literature were outlines and further discussed.

Deriving from the literature review presented in this chapter, several implications for this research can be deduced, summarised in the following working assumptions:

First, Resource Recombinations (RR) will be defined as the recombination of resources in new ways in order to develop new, innovative products or services or enter new markets, while the process of RR is the outcome of a systematic resource selection and combination task, which is substantially influenced by the firm's DCs.

Second, based on the review of resource and competence based research, this research differentiates between 'Resources' and 'Dynamic Capabilities', referred to as the firm's ability to manage, renew and recombine the resource base in new ways to develop new innovative products and services (RRs). With the differentiation between 'Resources' and 'Dynamic Capabilities', this approach demarcates from most publications within the context of competence based research, where usually organisational competence is seen as an amalgam of the resource (as raw material for RRs) and their selection and recombination (represented by its DCs) (e.g. Prahalad and Hamel 1990, Turner and Crawford 1994, Zott 2003, Schreyögg and Kliesch, 2003). Thus, in most publications within the competence based research, the available organisational resources are entirely seen as part of the organisational competence itself, the consequence being that competence becomes a little selective construct, that in the end includes everything and thus it loses its explanatory character (Schreyögg and Kliesch, 2003).

Third, the fundamental requirements for the development of RRs are (i) the availability of valuable resources and (ii) the firm's DC, regarded as the firm's ability to manage, renew and recombine the resource base in new ways. Resources thus are seen as the "raw material" or "building blocks" for the RRs. They are considered as the "soil", without those RR and in turn competitive advantages cannot be derived (Schreyögg and Kliesch, 2003). However, the focus of this research lies on the DC, respectively the intersection between the resource base and the DC in archiving RRs. Hence, the examination of construct of DC, its characteristics and influencing factors, will be the central subject of investigation within this research, as the DC defined as "the firm's ability to integrate, build, and reconfigure internal and external competences to address rapidly changing environments" (Teece, 1997, p. 516) is suggested to determine the situational, organisational selection and combination of organisational resources.

For the above reasoning, this research assumes that a substantial proportion of variance in resources productivity across firms can be explained by the differences attributed to the firm's DCs for the selection and recombination of resources. The availability of (high quality) resources in contrast is rather seen as a precondition for the development of RRs. Further specifying these preliminary assumptions, the following chapter presents a detailed discussion of the conceptual model.

Development of the Conceptual Model and Hypotheses 3

3.1 Introduction

To provide a basis for the conceptual development and empirical investigation of RR in firms from a DC point of view, this chapter outlines the theoretical framework, the determinants and framework conditions of the RR concept and outlines the research's arguments and related hypotheses. By investigating the relation between the resource base, DCs, and its performance outcomes RR, this chapter contributes to establish a better understanding of these interrelations, leading to the development of a conceptual model to be tested, refined, and validated in a following qualitative and subsequent quantitative research step. Doing so, this research addresses some existing shortcomings in the DC literature, where there is a crucial need to understand better the interrelationship between DCs, the resource base of the firm, and innovation in the form of RRs. The aim is to bring clarity to the notion of DCs, their role and effects towards RRs in firms. Hence, with the conceptual model presented in this chapter, a more precise understanding of the firm's DCs will be given, shedding light on their role and effects towards developing new RRs in firms. Doing so, this chapter opens up the black box of RR in firms and offers strategic pathways on how firms can strategically foster the recombination of existing resources as an important source for continuous innovation generation.

The conceptual model presented within this chapter is based on a comprehensive literature review in the fields of resources and competence-based research,

Electronic supplementary material The online version contains supplementary material available at (https://doi.org/10.1007/978-3-658-35666-8_3).

© The Author(s), under exclusive license to Springer Fachmedien Wiesbaden GmbH, part of Springer Nature 2021
K. Kurzhals, *Resource Recombination in Firms from a Dynamic Capability Perspective*, Gabler Theses, https://doi.org/10.1007/978-3-658-35666-8_3

drawing on existing theories from the entrepreneurship and strategic management spectrum. Reviewing and aligning current theories as well as existing empirical studies in the wider field of RR, this research develops a conceptual model for RRs in firms.

First, this chapter begins with an examination of resource value creation in firms, integrating the RBV and DC perspective to form the model's theoretical base. With the differentiation of potential and realised value of resources, the preliminary considerations of this research are outlined.

Second, based on these preliminary considerations, the following section investigates the potential value of the resources base of the firm for RR, comprising the introduction of a set of characteristics of resources suggested as relevant for determining the potential value of the resource base, namely *resource diversity, resource quality, resource complementarity, resource transferability, resource deployment flexibility,* and *resource renewal.* The discussion is followed by a presentation of theoretical linkages between these selected characteristics of the resource base and RR, culminating in a subset of the study's hypotheses.

Third, the subsequent section elaborates on the DCs of the firm, presenting the *Dynamic Capability Framework* and investigating the role of DCs in the process of RR. The DC framework builds the conceptual foundation of the firm's DCs, introducing the four DCs relevant for the process of RR, namely *Sensing Capacity, Learning Capacity, Integrating Capacity* and *Coordinating Capacity,* describing their underlying activities, processes and routines, and outlining their general relation towards RR with the aim to provide a general understanding of the construct of DC. Based on the DC framework and the conceptualisation of the four DCs, their role in the process of resource value creation is further elaborated and hypotheses are derived clarifying their role and effects towards building RR.

Fourth, the subsequent section investigates the framework conditions for the development of the four DCs. Investigating the effect of the firm's strategic orientation on the development of a firm's DCs, specifically its *Networking Orientation* and *Entrepreneurial Orientation,* the aim is to elaborate the extent to which the firm's strategic orientation (directed towards internal and external entities) influences the development of DCs and thus RRs. Also this section closes with a subset of hypotheses to be tested in this research.

Aligning the research findings, the last section outlines the conceptual model and summarises the studies' hypotheses to be further analysed in the subsequent qualitative and quantitative research steps.

3.2 Preliminary Considerations: Resource Value Creation through Resource Recombination

The following discussion refers to a large degree to Linnemann (2012) due to a thorough discussion of the conceptual foundation and framework in this article.

3.2.1 Potential and Realised Value of the Resources

Scholars from both the resource based and competence-based tradition often ask 'how value is created in firms' and 'what it is that explains the competitive heterogeneity and variance in value creation across firms'. According to the RBV, the competitiveness of a firm can be primarily lead back to its access to resources that are valuable, rare, inimitable and non-substitutable (VRIN) (e.g., Barney, 1991), while the CBV sees the competitive advantages rather influenced by a firm's ability to utilise these resources by devising and implementing strategies to extract the value potential of resources (e.g. Moldaschl, 2006). Consequently, when studying the concept of RR in firms, an investigation of resource value creation in firms is deemed valuable.

Looking at resource value creation in firms, literature generally distinguishes between the '**potential value**' and the '**realised value**' of resources (e.g. Madhok and Tallman, 1998). Applied to the concept of RR in firms, this research differentiates between the potential value of resources *for* RR and the realised value generated *through* new RRs.

The **potential value of resources <u>for</u> RR** describes the value of resources a firm possesses for their use in new, synergetic RRs, and therefore is also referred to as the *value creation potential* of resources. The value creation potential is determined by the quality and diversity of the resources itself in such a way that the resource portfolio establishes the upper bounds of the firm's value creation potential (Makadok, 2003) and thus builds the basis for value creation in firms (Sirmon et al., 2007, Holcomb et al., 2009, Barney, 1991). In the context of this research, the resources thus can be regarded as the "raw material" for the development of new RRs, and the more valuable resources are the higher their value creation potential of those resources is suggested to be. This is in line with the RBV's perception of value creation in firms.

However, under the premises that a 'strategic factor market', as defined by Barney (1986) exist, "where firms buy and sell the resources necessary to implement their strategies" (p. 1232), and thus assuming that all required resources or assets can be bought and sold for a given price, in such markets, following Barney (1986, p. 1231) "the cost of acquiring strategic resources will approximately be equal to the economic value of those resources". In consequence, presuming "the absence of imperfections in [those] strategic factor markets, buyers will not be able to extract superior economic performance from any factor" (Diericks and Cool, 1989, p. 1504). In other words, the value of any resource would on average equal the factor market price, and yet no value would be created simply through owing resources.

Accordingly, scholars following the resource-based tradition often ask "what it is about resources that give them inherent potential for value creation" (Holcomb et al. 2009, p. 461), aiming to identify important characteristics of resources that allow explaining differences in resource productivity and value creation performance (e.g. Peteraf, 1993, Peteraf and Barney, 2003). It is suggested that the value creation potential of the resource base is influenced by certain characteristics of the resources (contextual or contingency factors) that determine its utility for RR (e.g. Noteboom et al., 2006, Birkinshaw et al., 2002).

However, solely possessing or having access to high valuable resources does not guarantee that the value creation potential of those resources becomes realised and new value is created (Barney and Arikan, 2001, Priem and Butler, 2001, Sirmon and Hitt, 2009). Therefore, extending the focus of the RBV, scholars following the CBV have added "that while owning or having access to valuable and rare resources is necessary for competitive advantage, they must be effectively managed and synchronised to *realise* a competitive advantage" (Holcomb et al., 2009, p. 457, going back to Hansen et al., 2004, Kor and Mahoney, 2005). Accordingly, possessing valuable, rare, in-imitable and non-substitutable (VRIN) resources (Barney, 1986) is regarded as a necessary but insufficient condition for resource value creation (Sirmon et al., 2007). De facto, value is rather created when resources are evaluated, manipulated and deployed in new, synergetic RRs (Lippman and Rumelt, 2003, Sirmon et al., 2007). Moreover, research highlights that the synergetic use of existing and new resources can lead to a higher total (realised) value than the use of resources independently from each other (Chi, 1994, Hitt et al., 1991, Larsson and Finkelstein, 1999, Madhok and Tallmann, 1998).

Indeed, as important as the investigation of the resources, and how specific characteristics of the resources determine the value creation potential, is it to explore the extent to which firms exploit that potential (Holcomb et al., 2009). Less research, however, investigates that question, and even though, most RBV scholars agree that "what a firm does with its resources is as important as which resources it possesses" (Holcomb et al., 2009, p. 461), the RBV is often criticised for underestimating the question of resource utilisation. Barney and Arikan (2001, p. 174) for example state that the "resource-based theory has a very simple view about how resources are connected to the strategies the firm pursues". Subsequently, more research is required as "the processes by which firms obtain or develop, combine, and leverage resources to create and maintain competitive advantages are not well understood" (Sirmon et al., 2007, p. 274).

The **realised value of resources <u>through</u> RR,** also termed *value realisation,* refers to the total value created in firms through the efficient usage of resources in form of new, innovative RRs. According to Holcomb et al. (2009, p. 461), an indicator for the realised value created from resources is the "level of resource productivity", which they describe as the net benefits achieved from resource management through successful RR activities. In this research, RR is regarded as an indicator for the realised value of resources, seen as net benefits achieved from resource management, through the "firm's ability to integrate, build and reconfigure internal and external competencies to address rapidly changing environments" (Teece, 1997). New, synergetic RRs are a proxy for measuring the performance outcome of the firm's DCs through efficiently managing resources.

Accordingly, differences in value realisation performance across firms can either be attributed to resources possessing different levels of latent (e.g. unrealised) efficiency, thus referring to the potential value of resources for RR, or the firm's usage of the available resources in different ways (Holcomb et al. 2009). This reflects Penrose's (1959, p. 25) early notion that "the services yielded by resources are a function of the way in which they are used—exactly the same resource when used for different purposes or in different ways and in combination with different types or amounts of other resources provides a different service or set of services". Following this perception of value creation in firms, the realised value increases when firms produce greater utility with the same inputs (resp. the same utility with fewer inputs) through effective management and redeployment of resources in superior RRs (Peteraf and Barney, 2003, Bowman and Ambrosini, 2000, Holcomb et al. 2009). This is based on the assumption that most often it is not the individual resources that are proposed to be VRIN, rather more it is the unique, in-imitable and non-substitutable combinations of those resources, the RRs that give them inherent value. However, given that the process of RR involves uncertainty and great parts of the realised value are observed as being serendipitous and unforeseen a priori (Graebner, 2004), the total value created is often not recognised until the resources have been bundled (Denrell et al., 2003, Moran and Ghoshal, 1999, Wiklund and Shepherd, 2009)[1].

These reasoning suggests that firms—in order to realise the total value creation potential of their resources—should foster the ability to combine their resources in predictable and in novel ways to create both expected and serendipitous value. The findings further imply that firms with superior DCs to manage their resources, can realise a performance advantage (Adner and Helfat, 2003, Sirmon et al., 2007, Teece, 2007). It reveals that achieving synergetic RRs is not simply a matter of adding high quality and complementary resource to the existing resource portfolio (Wiklund and Shepherd, 2009). Over time, the set of resources the firm possesses must be altered and the way they are bundled must be changed if the competitive advantage of the firm is to be sustained (Barney, 1991, Black and Boal, 1994, Capron et al., 1998). Thus, in order to untangle the value creation potential these resources must be effectively managed. To realise the value creation, firms must accumulate, combine and exploit its resources (Grant, 1991, Sirmon and Hitt, 2003).

To summarise, when speaking of the potential value of resources in this research, it comprises (only) the *value creation potential* of the resources *for* the development of new, synergetic RRs, while the *realised value* is the actual measurable value of those new generated RRs. The potential value of resources is related to resource acquisition and exploration, while the realised value of resources refers to combination activities and exploitation (Denrell et al., 2003, Penrose, 1959, Zahra and George, 2002, Wiklund and Shepherd, 2009). Hence, for this research it is important to look at both, the resources a firm possess, which determine the *potential value for RR*, as well as the DCs of the firm that influences the *realised value through* building new, synergetic *RRs*.

---

[1] For this reasoning, the realised value of resources can be further differentiated in *expected* and *serendipitous value*, whereby the former refers to resource benefits that were predictable a priori (e.g. at the time of the acquisition), while the later refers to value creation that was not anticipated a priori but rather emerged from opportunities to discover new paths to create value (Graeber, 2004). Investigating value creation within technological mergers and acquisitions, Graebner (2004) revealed that the most successful acquisitions involved the creation of such serendipitous value, and moreover, that firms varied significantly in their ability to realise appropriate serendipitous value. On the downside, firms are found to enforce constraints as "many value-creating resource combinations fail to occur because managers have neither the ability to recognize the opportunity nor the means to exploit it" (Holcomb et al., 2009, p. 461), resulting in considerable differences that exist among firms in their ability to realise value from the resources they possess (Holcomb et al., 2009).

3.2.2 Resource Endowments and Dynamic Capabilities

Comprising the conceptual considerations about resource value creation in firms as outlined above, and integrating the RBV and DC perspective, the following chapter further specifies the model's theoretical base, delineating the three core propositions for this study.

The RBV suggests that a firm's resource base can be regarded as a set of resources (e.g. technologies, knowledge, competences, skills) that is available at one point in time. In the context of this research, the resource base is seen as the "raw material" or "building blocks" for the development of new RRs. Hence, the resource portfolio establishes the upper bounds of the firm's **value creation potential** (Makadok, 2003). Accordingly, the resource base builds the basis for value creation through new RRs (Sirmon et al., 2007). At the same time it is assumed that the extent to which the firm's resources determine the potential value of the resource base for RR depends on certain **characteristics of the resource base**, that might influence the value creation potential of the resources for RR. Thus it is suggested that certain characteristics of the resources forming each resource bundle may have a measurable effect on the realised value through RR. Accordingly, investigating RR in firms needs to take into account the nature of the firm's knowledge base (e.g., Birkinshaw et al., 2002, Germain and Dröge, 1997). Together, these arguments suggest that the value creation potential of the resource base for RR is influenced by certain characteristics of resources, its resource endowments. In other words, it is the resource endowments that determine the **potential value** of resources for RR. Hence, it is suggested that the more valuable the resources the higher their potential value for RR and thus, the higher the likelihood of new RRs in firms. This leads us to our first proposition:

Proposition 1: A high valuable resource base is positively associated with RR in firms. The potential value of the resource base for RR thereby is influenced by certain characteristics of the resources.

On the other hand, as the preliminary considerations have shown, solely possessing or having access to resources that are valuable, however, does not guarantee that the value creation potential becomes realised and new value is created through new RRs (Barney and Arikan, 2001, Priem and Butler, 2001, Sirmon and Hitt, 2009). Likewise in dynamic environments, the availability of high valuable resources alone does not guarantee a competitive advantage over time. Indeed, in dynamic environments the resources and the way they are bundled have to be changed. As stated by Lippman and Rumelt (2003, p. 1085) "the heart of business management and strategy concerns the creation, evaluation, manipulation, administration, and deployment of unpriced specialized resource combinations". Thus, value is realised only when the resources available are recombined and managed appropriately to the environmental context (Sirmon et al., 2007). Research findings further revealed that the synergetic use of existing and new resources, can lead to a higher total, realised value than the use of the resources independently from each other (Chi, 1994, Hitt et al. 1991, Larsson and Finkelstein, 1999, Madhok and Tallmann, 1998). Accordingly to stay competitive in dynamic environments firms have to develop DCs to manage, renew and recombine the resource base (the "raw material") in new ways to develop new innovative products and services (RRs).

This research assumes that firms differ in their DCs to manage and recombine their resources in ways that enhance performance. Accordingly, the extent to which the value potential of the resource base becomes *realised* (in form of new innovative RRs) depends on the ability of the firm to integrate and coordinate those resources in order to discover and conduct new RRs. Thus, this research postulates that the firm's DCs to manage resources and to bundle them into new RRs is a critical capability that is necessary to extract the potential value residing in a firm's resource portfolio, and transform it into a **realised value**. Hence, firms that have developed higher DCs are more likely to build and exploit the potential value of their resource base, and therefore are more likely to successfully develop new RRs. This means, that owing the "right" resource brings limited benefits to firms unless deliberate effort is devoted towards developing the DCs necessary for resource combination. Thus, DCs help both creating and realising value by enhancing resource productivity through efficient usage of resources, leading to the second proposition:

Proposition 2: A firm's overall DC is positively associated with the amount of RRs in firms due to both building and exploiting the potential value of the resources base.

Finally, this research postulates that the firm's strategic orientation, specifically its Entrepreneurial Orientation and Networking Orientation, play a major role in developing DCs in firms. The underlying assumption is, that while DCs reside in the organisational processes and routines, they are regarded to being impacted by the organisational framework conditions (at firm- and network-level) that the organisation has created to manage it business activities (Teece 2007). Current literature shows growing interest in investigating the antecedents that are suggested to influence the development of DCs (e.g. Madsen 2010, Hawass, 2010). While a wide range of different antecedents residing at individual-, firm- and network-levels have been proposed in the literature (Rothaermel and Hess, 2007) and discussed as relevant determinants for the development of DCs (e.g. Teece, 2007, Zollo and Winter, 2002, Eisenhardt and Martin, 2000), this research is focussing on firm- and network-level antecedents, leading to the third proposition:

Proposition 3: Entrepreneurial Orientation and Networking Orientation act as antecedents for the development of a firm's DCs.

Summarising the above findings, when investigating RR in firms—it would be insufficient only to look at certain characteristics of the resource base and how they are influencing the development of RRs in firms. Instead, the aim is to look at the DCs in relation to the resource base, especially how the DCs are working towards building and exploiting the resource base, and what the framework conditions are for the development of such capabilities in firms.

Assuming that firm's resources vary in their potential to create value (depending on certain characteristics of those resources, as e.g. quality and diversity) and that firms vary in their DCs to build and extract this value creation potential and transfer it into a realised value, this research makes a contribution towards exploring how the two phenomena work together. By explicitly embedding the DC perspective in resource-based explanations for value creation, the aim is to specify the **joint role of the firm's DCs** and the **resources endowments** in conjunctly achieving **new RR** by building and exploiting the potential value of resources.

3.3 The Potential Value of the Resource Base and Resource Recombination

The following section starts with a specification of the above Proposition 1 in order to specify the interrelationship between the potential value of the resource base and RR in firms, while controlling for the influence of specific characteristics of the resource base on its potential value. The aim is to better understand how **specific characteristics of the resource base** influence the **potential value of the resources for RR**.

Proposition 1: A high valuable resource base is positively associated with RR in firms. The <u>potential value of the resource base</u> for RR thereby is influenced by certain characteristics of the resources.

While scholars following the resource-based tradition often ask "what it is about resources that give them inherent potential for value creation" (Holcomb et al. 2009, p. 461), aiming to identify important characteristics of resources that allow explaining the differences in resource productivity and value creation performance (e.g. Peteraf, 1993, Peteraf and Barney, 2003), little research has empirically measured their influence on RR in firms. Hence, further research is required to clarify the influence of specific characteristics of the resource base for value creation in firms.

Literature suggests that the firm's existing resource base plays an essential role in the process of resource value creation (Cohen and Levinthal, 1990, Isobe et al., 2008). The notion underlying this perception is that the firm's future recombinant innovation depends on the existing resource base, essentially saying that the amount and level of the firm's current resources are the primarily prerequisite to the successful reconfiguration of these resources (Isobe, 2008). This is in line with the view that firm's assets evolve in a path dependent manner (Teece et al., 1997).

As outlined in section 2.4.1 this research focusses on the firm's knowledge-based resources, specifically its Market Knowledge and Technology Knowledge, as both are referred to in literature as representing important knowledge-based resources applicable to a firm's ability to discover and exploit opportunities (Wiklund and Shepherd, 2003, Jansen et al., 2005, De Luca and Atuahene-Gima, 2007, Lichtenthaler, 2009). **Market Knowledge** refers to the firm's understanding of the market environment, particularly of customers and competitors (e.g. De Luca and Atuahene-Gima, 2007), while **Technological Knowledge** refers to the firm's technological expertise, R&D as well as engineering skills and competences (e.g. De Luca and Atuahene-Gima, 2007). Technological and Market Knowledge complement each other, and their availability likely enhances innovation and performance (Lane et al., 2006, Song et al., 2005). Dierickx and Cool (1989) emphasised that the amount and level of the firm's knowledge-based resources are the primary determinants defining the firm's asset position. Generally, when investigating the value creation potential of the resource base, literature predominantly refers to *resource quality* (e.g. Holcomb et al., 2009) and *diversity* (e.g. Granstrand and Sjölander, 1990, Peteraf, 1993) as important determinants for the value creation potential of the firm's resource base. Thus, the potential value of the resource base in this study is, in the first place, determined to the availability and quality of Market and Technological Knowledge.

There is a consistent claim in literature that a high degree of **Technological Knowledge** is positively associated with RR in firms. Firms having a high degree of Technological Knowledge have developed an advanced understanding of technologies, products and processes, R&D expertise and skills. Thus, Technological Knowledge can foster the firm's ability to effectively address market opportunities by providing the necessary technological skills, e.g. for developing an optimal design of products or for redesigning technical processes to optimise functionality, costs, and reliability (Rosenberg, 1994, Wiklund and Shepherd, 2003). Hence, a high degree of Technological Knowledge is proposed to advance firm's innovation performance (Zahra et al., 2000). This implies that the potential value of the resource base for RRs will predominantly depend on the amount and quality of Technological Knowledge the firm possess. Accordingly, this research suggests the following hypothesis:

H1: Technological Knowledge has a direct, positive effect on RR.

Likewise Technological Knowledge, **Market Knowledge** is proposed to positively affect RR in firms. A high degree of Market Knowledge provides firms with information about the market, specifically about customers and competitors, is a source for stimulating the firm's Technological Knowledge (Day, 1994, Nonaka, 1994) and is a driver for high market and customer orientation (De Luca and Atuahene-Gima, 2007). Following De Luca and Atuahene-Gima (2007, p. 97), "a firm that correctly identifies, collects, and uses information about customer and competitor conditions is deemed to be knowledgeable about the market". Therefore, it is proposed to be positively associated with RR in firms. Literature commonly agrees that a high degree of Market Knowledge (in terms of breadth and depth) is positively associated with RR in firms. However the relationship will only be indirectly through Technological Knowledge. This is based on the argument by Lichtenthaler (2009, p. 823), who argues that the role of Market Knowledge is to provide "a firm with insights into the functions that Technological Knowledge may fulfil", thus the "technological knowledge is the knowledge that a firm actually explores, transforms, and exploits" through its RR activities. Accordingly, this research suggests the following hypothesis:

H1(1): Market Knowledge has an indirect, positive effect on RR, through Technological Knowledge.

Based on these more general assumptions that both Market and Technological Knowledge are proposed to have a positive effect on RR in firms, the following sections sets out to elaborate **specific characteristics of knowledge based resources** that might have an influence on value creation potential of the resource base for RR. Based on an extensive review of existing RBV literature, six characteristics of the Market and Technological Resources could be derived, and are proposed as relevant characteristics for determining the potential value of the resources for RR, these are namely: (1) **resource diversity** (e.g. Granstand and Sjölander, 1988, 1990, Galunic and Rodan, 1998, De Luca and Atuahene-Gima, 2007), (2) **resource quality** (e.g. Zahra et al., 2000, De Luca and Atuahene-Gima, 2007, Wiklund and Shepherd, 2003), (3) **resource complementarity** (e.g. Wiklund and Shepherd, 2009, Chi, 1994, Hitt et al., 1991, Larsson and Finkelstein, 1999, Madhok and Tallmann, 1998), (4) **resource transferability** (e.g. Nonaka, 1994, Galunic and Rodan, 1998, Szulanski, 1996), (5) **resource deployment flexibility** (e.g. Sanchez, 1995, Sanchez, 2004, 1995; Holcomb et al., 2009; Sanchez and Mahoney, 1996), and (6) **resource renewal** (e.g. Connor, 1999, Foster, 1986, Hamel and Prahalad, 1994, Wiklund and Shepherd, 2009). In the following sections each characteristic will be discussed and elaborated in detail and hypotheses will be derived.

Doing so, this research contributes to an enhanced understanding of value creation in firms by addressing how specific characteristics of the knowledge-based resources may influence a firm's ability to recognise and exploit the resources through building new RRs (Lane et al., 2006). The aim is to provide further insights by investigating where heterogeneity of resource positions comes from and how the characteristics of knowledge-based resources influence the firm's innovation performance (Noteboom, 2003). Doing so, this research addresses existing shortcomings in the RBV literature, where there is a lack of empirical evidence on the influence of knowledge characteristics on the firm's ability to utilise it for new RRs (Lane et al., 2006). This is especially relevant as "the majority of studies fail to adequately explain the underlying factors driving performance differences across firms" (Noteboom et al., 2003, p. 2). Next, we explore the effect of resource diversity on resource value creation.

3.3.1 Resources Diversity: Market and Technological Knowledge Breadth

Resource Diversity in this research is addressed by means of **Market and Technological Knowledge Breadth**, which refers to the number or range of different knowledge areas the firm is familiar with (De Luca and Atuahene-Gima, 2007, Bierly and Chakrabarti, 1996). This is in line with Prabhu et al. (2005, p. 116) referring to knowledge breadth as "the range of fields over which the firm has knowledge". Following De Luca and Atuahene-Gima (2007), thereby **Market**

Knowledge Breadth refers "to the firm's understanding of a wide range of diverse customer and competitor types and factors that describe them". Accordingly, a firm is regarded to possess a high Market Knowledge breadth if it holds broad knowledge of current and potential customers and competitors and uses a variety of parameters to describe and evaluate them (Zahra et al., 2000, De Luca and Atuahene-Gima, 2007). Consistently, **Technological Knowledge Breadth** refers to the firms understanding of a wide variety of knowledge and expertise in various technical areas and different technological environments, thus it denotes the range of areas in which a venture learns new technological skills (Teece et al., 1994, Zahra et al. 2000).

There is a consistent claim in the literature that firms with a broad knowledge base have a greater potential to recombine different elements of that knowledge and thus generate more possibilities for new RRs by improving opportunity recognition and creative potential (Kogut and Zander 1992, Reed and DeFillippi, 1990, Granstand and Sjölander, 1988, 1990, Galunic and Rodan, 1998, De Luca and Atuahene-Gima, 2007). Thus, Market and Technological Knowledge breadth positively affect the potential value of the resource base for RR. Accordingly, in recent literature increasing consensus is reached that resource diversity or heterogeneity provide a significant potential for knowledge creation and innovation because it yields opportunities for novel combinations of complementary resources (Noteboom et al., 2006). Viewed differently, reducing the heterogeneity of activities taking place in the organisation will reduce the variety of knowledge held in the organisation and thus lowers the potential for new combinations (Galunic and Rodan, 1998). Accordingly, drawing on existing theory in innovation, creativity and knowledge management, a predominant view is that broad Market Knowledge is suggested to enhance product innovation by means of increasing the firm's ability to draw linkages among disparate market information, ideas, and concepts to develop new perspectives (Reed and DeFillippi, 1990). While in a similar vein broad Technological Knowledge suggested to positively affect innovation performance as it provides access to diverse technological areas that can be used to design and offer a greater variety of innovative products (Zahra et al., 2000). Related arguments are put forward in organisational learning theory, admitting knowledge diversity to have a positive effect on learning and innovation, as it provides a robust basis for assimilating new and related knowledge-based on what is already known, and moreover facilitates the innovative process by enabling novel connections and linkages to be made (Cohen and Levinthal, 1990). Also empirical evidence to these findings is given, Van Wijk et al. (2001) for instance confirm that breadth and depth of knowledge is positively associated with a firm's propensity to explore new and related knowledge

(Zahra and George, 2001). This view is supplemented by research findings look-ing at ideation processes within firms, showing that groups possessing a larger knowledge base formed by different knowledge areas are shown to develop bet-ter innovations than homogenous groups (Björk and Magnusson, 2008). This is corresponding to Nonaka (1994) who argues that one prerequisite for knowledge creation and innovation is resource diversity (Björk and Magnusson, 2008).

However, also a number of articles exist in the innovation literature contrast-ing this view, stating that too much heterogeneity may also negatively affect RR in firms. For example Wiklund et al. (2002, p. 5) propose that "the accu-mulation of too many resources may restrict the searching for new innovative resource recombination". Thus, it is suggested by several authors that a too high knowledge breadth might hinder recombination activities as a high degree of diversity of knowledge leads to an enhanced complexity of knowledge transfer across functional units caused by communication difficulties, misunderstand-ings and unproductive conflicts (e.g. Galunic and Rodan 1998, De Luca and Atuahene-Gima, 2007, Tushman and Romanelli, 1996, Teece et al. 1997, Björk and Magnusson, 2008). This is especially true as broad Market and Technologi-cal knowledge may require regular and numerous changes, which further enhance the complexity of knowledge transfer. As a consequence, increased difficulties in transferring and sharing broad knowledge requires firm's to develop necessary capacities for integrating and coordinating diverse resources in order to discover and conduct new RRs (De Luca and Atuahene-Gima, 2007, Bhidé, 2000).

Summarising the above arguments, the discussion has shown that the diversity of knowledge-based resources, specifically the Market and Technological Knowl-edge breath, plays an important role in building the potential value of the resource base for RR. Consistent with these research findings, this research generally sug-gests a positive relation between Market and Technological Knowledge breadth and RR in firms, proposing that the more diverse the resource base, the more possibilities for RR exists and thus the higher the amount of RRs in firms. How-ever, this relationship is suggested to be influenced by the firm's Integrating and Coordinating capacities (refer to section 3.4.2.2.), in a way that the broader the Market and Technological Knowledge, the greater the use of knowledge integra-tion and coordination mechanisms (De Luca and Atuahene-Gima, 2007). This leads to the following hypothesis:

H1a (Resource Diversity): A high Market and Technological Knowledge breadth is positively associated with RR in firms.

3.3.2 Resource Quality: Market and Technological Knowledge Depth

Resource Quality in this research is addressed by means of **Market and Technological Knowledge Depth**, which is defined in this study as the level of sophistication and complexity of the firm's knowledge in a specific area (De Luca and Atuahene-Gima, 2007), referring to the depth and quality of learning (Zahra et al., 2000). Thus, while Market and Technological Knowledge breadth denote the horizontal dimension of knowledge, knowledge depth captures its vertical dimension (De Luca and Atuahene-Gima, 2007). Thereby, following Prabhu and colleagues (2005), **Technological Knowledge Depth** captures "the amount of within-field knowledge the firm possesses" (De Luca and Atuahene-Gima, 2007, p. 98) and refers to the quality and complexity of knowledge in technical areas and understanding of its different, interdependent and unique elements (McEvily and Chakravarthy, 2002). Whereas **Market Knowledge Depth** on the other hand refers to the level of sophistication and quality of the firm's knowledge of its customers and competitors, comprising in-depth understanding about the interdependencies of customer needs, behaviours, and desires, as well as competitor's products and strategies (De Luca and Atuahene-Gima, 2007).

Likewise knowledge breadth, the depth of knowledge is regarded as essential determinant influencing the potential value of the resource base for RR. In recent years, consensus is reached among researchers, that deep Market and Technological Knowledge is positively associated with innovation performance (e.g. Zahra et al., 2000, De Luca and Atuahene-Gima, 2007, Wiklund and Shepherd, 2003). The literature claims, that firms possessing a thorough understanding and deep expertise of markets and technologies will have a higher potential to efficiently combine different elements of that knowledge and in consequence come up with new innovations (De Luca and Atuahene-Gima, 2007). Thus, Market and Technological Knowledge depth is proposed to positively affect the potential value of the resource base for RR. Vice versa, it can be assumed that firms, which are exposed to hold Market and Technological Knowledge only at an elementary or basic level and have not yet learned or mastered to develop new skills, indicated by a low depth or quality of learning, will have a reduced quality of stock of knowledge available for RR (De Luca and Atuahene-Gima, 2007), and therefore are proposed to have an inferior position for developing new, innovative RRs. More specifically, Market Knowledge depth is suggested to positively affect innovation performance as it fosters the firm's ability to adapt its products and services to changing market needs, capitalise on market dynamics and identify emerging technological changes, that may influence firm performance (Zahra et al., 2000). In a similar vein, Technological Knowledge depth is proposed to advance firms innovation performance (Zahra et al., 2000) by fostering the firm's ability to address market opportunities, for instance by redesigning its products for ease of use, optimising functionality, cost or reliability (Rosenberg, 1994). In consequence, a high quality of available resources, captured by the firm's Market and Technological Knowledge depth, can be seen as a necessary precondition for developing new RRs.

There are also publications, however, stating that deep knowledge may also cause problems for recombination (e.g. Galunic and Rodan, 1998). As deep Market and Technological Knowledge implicate complex interdependences among the different elements of knowledge (McEvily and Chakravarthy, 2002), the transfer of deep knowledge comprises a high risk of misconception and misapplication in new RRs (Galunic and Rodan, 1998, De Luca and Atuahene-Gima, 2007). Therefore, knowledge depth may bound the firm's rationale for drawing new conclusions and finding new linkages among different elements of knowledge (De Luca and Atuahene-Gima, 2007). Moreover, by means of comprising expertise in different functional areas, deep knowledge may also lead to "strong local identities" and different "thought worlds" (Leonard-Barton, 1992, Dougherty, 1992), which is suggested to further hamper the ease of knowledge transfer, as it hinders the firm's ability to assimilate new knowledge from other functional areas (Szulanski, 1996, De Luca and Atuahene-Gima, 2007). This is due to the fact that "as the stock of within-competence knowledge and meaning grows, and becomes more complex relative to the stock of knowledge about other competencies, people's absorptive capacity for within-competence knowledge will rise compared to their intercompetence absorptive capacity (Cohen and Levinthal, 1990)" (Galunic and Rodan, 1998, p. 1199). Therefore according to Galunic and Rodan (1998), the social and institutional packaging of firm's knowledge will also impact RR in firms.

Summarising the above arguments, this research generally suggests that deep Market and Technological Knowledge positively affect the potential value of the resources for RR. However, as outlined above, the availability of deep Market and Technological Knowledge alone does not automatically lead to realised value of the resources, indicated by the amount of RR (McGrath et al., 1995, Zahra et al., 2003). For deep Market and Technological Knowledge to yield a competitive advantage, it must be captured, integrated, and deployed effectively (Grant, 1991, 1996). Therefore it is proposed that the deeper the within-competence knowledge the greater the use of knowledge integration and coordination mechanisms (De Luca and Atuahene-Gima, 2007). Accordingly, the relationship

between Market and Technological Knowledge depth and RR in firms is suggested to be influenced by firm's Integrating and Coordinating capacities (refer
to section 3.4.2.2.).

*H1b (Resource Quality): A high Market and Technological Knowledge depth is
positively associated with RR in firms.*

3.3.3 Resource Complementarity: Knowledge Complementarity

Resource Complementarity refers to the level to which different areas of knowledge available to the firm complement each other, and is captured in this research
by means of **complementarity of Market and Technological Knowledge**. Complementarity in this context refers to firm's resources that are complementary to
each other, meaning that they can be effectively combined with other resources
the firm possess (Hitt et al., 2001, Song et al., 2005). Moreover, it can be con-
tradistinguished from supplementary resources, which describe resources that
serve the same functions than other resources (Wernerfelt, 1984, Song et al.,
2005). To illustrate this, when a firm has strong R&D capabilities for example, it may easily detect the potential for research-based synergy by acquiring
another firm with similar (supplementary) resource strengths through pursuing
economies of scale and scope, or increased market power (Ansoff, 1965, Montgomery, 1985). However if the same firm acquires a firm with weaker R&D
capabilities, yet strong (complementary) market-related capabilities (e.g. strong
marketing and distribution capabilities), the potential synergy from the combination of those complementary resources may lead to a higher total value
and competitive advantage, as it is more likely to realise serendipitous value,
which is difficult for competitors to detect and to assess a priori (Harrison et al.,
2001). Hence, integrating different, yet complementary Market and Technological Knowledge opens new opportunities for synergetic RRs (Song et al. 2005),
reduces the resource deficiency, and generates new applications of those resources
(Kogut and Zander, 1992, Teece et al., 1997).

Resource complementarity, thus, is proposed as a relevant determinant that
may influence the potential value of the resource base for RR. Support for
this assumption emerges predominantly from research investigating resource
value creation in alliances and acquisitions, where recent research findings point
towards complementarity of resources, rather than its similarity as proposed by
earlier works (e.g. Kusewitt, 1985, Singh and Montgomery, 1987), creates the

potential for higher synergy among resources, and therefore would lead to a higher long-term firm performance (Harrison et al., 1991, Harrison et al., 2001). Hence, it is suggested that valuable, unique, and inimitable, synergetic RRs are more likely to be realised by integrating complementary resources. This is especially relevant in the light of research findings following the RBV, giving evidence that the synergetic and complementary use of existing and new resources can lead to a higher total, realised value than the use of the resources independently from each other (Chi, 1994, Hitt et al. 1991, Larsson and Finkelstein, 1999, Madhok and Tallmann, 1998). Consistent with the general perceptions of the RBV, Wiklund and Shepherd (2009) argue that the potential value of the resource base would increase when the resources acquired are complementary to the existing ones. Accordingly, a high complementarity of resources is suggested to lead to a higher value creation potential of resources for RR. For the difficulties in measurement, however, empirical evidence is still scare, and only few studies exist that could empirically confirm the proposed relation. A notable exception is the work by Song and colleagues (2005), who could empirically verify the positive effect of the complementarity of market and technological resources on firm performance.

Based on the above arguments, this research assumes a positive effect of *resource complementarity* on RR, in a way that the higher the complementarity of the Market and Technological Knowledge within the resource base, the higher the amount of RRs in firms. However, at the same time it must be noted, that the existence of complementary resources is regarded as necessary, yet insufficient condition for realising synergetic RRs, as following Harrison (2001, p. 679) "the resources must be effectively integrated and managed to realise the synergy". In consequence, the positive effect is proposed to be enhanced with higher integrating and coordinating mechanisms.

H1c (Resource Complementarity): Complementary Market and Technological Knowledge is positively related to RR in firms.

3.3.4 Resource Transferability: Knowledge Tacitness

Resource Transferability refers to the degree to which resources within the firm can easily be transferred and articulated across disciplines. It is regarded as relevant resources characteristic that might influence the potential value of the resource base for RR, as recombination is based on competence-related knowledge flows (Galunic and Rodan, 1998) and existing and new knowledge may not always be easily understood, replicated and transferred to new contexts (Leonard-Barton, 1995, Szulanski, 1996). Resource transferability was captured in this research by means of **Knowledge Tacitness,** which describes "the extent to which market knowledge is not explicit but rather is difficult to codify and communicate" (De Luca and Atuahene-Gima, 2007, p. 98), prostrating that a high tacitness of knowledge is negatively related to its observability, and thus transferability. Knowledge is described as tacit, when people perceive difficulties in making explicit what they know, thus when "the knowledge consists of implicit and non-codifiable skills or 'know-how'" (Lane et al., 2006, 846). This underlies the assumption, that knowledge, which does not become explicit, cannot easily be leveraged by the organisation as a whole (Nonaka, 1991), as tacit knowledge can only be transferred from one individual to another through a complex process of articulation and apprenticeship (Galunic and Rodan, 1998, Szulanski, 1996, Nonaka, 1991).

Literature commonly agrees that "tacitness slows the internal transfer of (market) knowledge because tacit knowledge cannot be fully codified and articulated even by an expert" (De Luca and Atuahene-Gima, 2007). Generally the effectiveness of knowledge codification as a common method for making knowledge accessible across disciplines will more decrease, the greater the tacit component of knowledge (Galunic and Rodan, 1998). In consequence, following the argument by Galunic and Rodan (1998), this research suggests that the likelihood of RR will be diminished, the higher the tacitness of the knowledge base, both due to both lower detection probability and higher costs of resource exchange. Reasons supporting this assumption are the following: First, the detection probability for new, valuable RRs will be reduced, the more tacit the knowledge, as it is more difficult to identify tacit knowledge available in the firm and envision novel ways for its application. Therefore "knowledge that is difficult to codify is likely to be difficult to detect" (Galunic and Rodan, 1998, p. 1196). Second, even if the RR opportunity was being identified, the cost of exchange will be increased, as "knowledge that is difficult to codify will be difficult to transfer in order to combine it with other knowledge in the firm (Teece, 1981)" (Galunic and Rodan, 1998, p. 1196). As a result, both factors will reduce the competence-related knowledge flows across disciplines, which is a prerequisite for stimulating and supporting the creation of novel RRs in firms (Galunic and Rodan, 1998). Accordingly, the extent to which the firm's knowledge is not formally documented, codified and communicated through written reports, and therefore difficult to transfer and absorb (Szulanski, 1996, Lane et al., 2007), is suggested to affect its transfer and consequently RR in firms.

Based on these arguments, this research postulates that the likelihood of RR will be diminished, the more tacit the knowledge involved, meaning the higher the tacitness of the knowledge within the resource base, the lower the amount of RRs in firms. At the same time this research suggests that the more tacit the knowledge, the more important the firm's Integration and Coordination capacity (refer to section 3.4.2.2.) to unearth the potential value of resources (Madhavan and Grover 1998, De Luca and Atuahene-Gima, 2007) and transfer it into realised value through new RRs.

H1d *(Resource Transferability): Tacit knowledge is negatively related to RR.*

3.3.5 Resource Deployment Flexibility: Knowledge Context-Specificity

Resource Deployment Flexibility refers to the degree to which the resources available in a firm are generalisable and flexible for being deployed in other areas or applied in other courses of action. Resource deployment flexibility is "the ability of the resources in an organisation's resource chains to be used in alternative ways, (…)[and] can be described by the range of uses that the resources can be applied to, by the time that it takes an organisation to change the use of a resource and by the costs the organisation incurs to change the use of a resource" (Sanchez, 2004, p. 526). Resource deployment flexibility, thus "depends jointly on the inherent flexibilities of the resources available to the firm and on the firm's flexibilities in applying those resources to alternative courses of action" (Sanchez, 1995, p. 138). In this research, resource deployment flexibility is captured by the **Context-Specificity of the Knowledge,** which describes "the extent to which the firm's knowledge is tailored to the requirements of specific contexts, in which it is maximally effective but loses its value in other contexts" (De Luca, 2007, p. 98). In a similar vein, Galunic and Rodan (1998, p. 1194) define knowledge context-specificity as "the extent to which knowledge is highly contextualised and codependent on unidentified aspects of the local environment". Accordingly, as knowledge is often found to be highly contextualised, the context in which it is embedded is also an important factor influencing its flow (Galunic and Rodan, 1998).

Notwithstanding that generally knowledge may have multiple uses (Prahalad and Hamel, 1990), for the purpose of specialisation advantages it is often found to be highly customised to a specific use, which diminishes its flexibility for flowing elsewhere (Galunic and Rodan, 1998). De Luca and Atuahene-Gima (2007) for instance propose, that firm's Market Knowledge can be highly related to a specific customer segment, particular product or market strategy, or behaviour of a specific competitor, and therefore is difficult to being applied to other contexts. Similar examples can be found for Technological Knowledge, where e.g. highly specialised machines may only be of limited use in alternate contexts, depending on their upgradability, scalability, and extendability to modify existing functionalities or add new functionalities (Sanchez, 1995). In both cases, the knowledge acquired is valuable only in the specific context of the focal firm. Thus, highly specialised and valuable resources may turn out to be of little use outside a relatively narrow context for which they were developed (Galunic and Rodan, 1998). Indeed, while this imperfect mobility of context-specific resources may be desirable at the interfirm level, it is regarded as disadvantageous to intrafirm RR (Galunic and Rodan), mainly for the reasoning, that RR requires firm's to redeploy resources into new resource bundles, with the aim to address deployment strategies that more effectively match resources to the competitive context (Holcombs and Holmes, 2009). Doing so necessitates the transfer of resources to serve new tasks (Sanchez, 1995). The resource deployment flexibility, respectively its context-specificity, therefore is proposed to play a major role for RR in firms.

Accordingly, following the argument by Galunic and Rodan (1998), this research suggests, that the likelihood of RR increases, the higher the deployment flexibility of the resources the firm possesses. Formulated differently, it is suggested that the lower the context specificity (respectively the higher the deployment flexibility) of the resources within the resource base, the higher its potential value for RR, and the higher the amount of RR in firms. Also here, it has to be noted that the relationship of context specific knowledge and the amount of RRs in firm suggested to be influenced by the firms integrating and coordination capacities (refer to section 3.4.2.2.)

H1e (Resource Deployment Flexibility): Context-specific knowledge is negatively related to RR.

3.3.6 Resource Renewal: Knowledge Origin

Resource Renewal refers to the degree to which the resources available within the firm's resource base consists of newly acquired resources, and therefore basically addresses the **Knowledge Origin**. In other words, it captures how much of the knowledge is internally based '*existing*' and how much is externally acquired '*new*'. The general differentiation between *existing* and *new* resources and its importance has extensively been discussed in the literature (Connor,

1999; Foster, 1986; Hamel and Prahalad, 1994, Wiklund and Shepherd, 2009). For this research's definition, *existing* resources refer to <u>internal</u> resources that have already been existent for a long time in/ or used by the company, while *new* resources refer to <u>external</u> resources that are not previously known in or used by the company but have recently been acquired from external sources. This definition is based on the idea that organisational boundaries matter: *'existing'* knowledge is already owned by the firm, while *'new'* knowledge must be imported by the firm from beyond its boundaries (Rosenkopf and Nerkar, 2001). The rate of renewal is determined by the ratio of *new* resources relatively to the *existing* resources.

Notwithstanding that existing resources may provide an inherent potential for RR in firms (Galunic and Rodan, 1998), following the argument by Wiklund and Shepherd (2009, p. 195) "there are limitations with reliance solely on resources internal to the firm for generating new productive resource combinations because it is unlikely that the exact same set of resources can be used to develop new and more valuable combinations over and over again". The general perception in literature is that a high internal renewal rate of the resources may lead to a respectively greater amount of new components within the resource base, which in turn build the raw material for RRs, and thus is suggested to provide a greater potential to recombine different elements of that knowledge through building new RRs (e.g. Galunic and Roden, 1998, Wiklund and Shepherd, 2009). A higher internal renewal of the resource base through adding new external resources, thus, may lead to a greater amount of RRs in firms. However, other authors add for consideration that resource renewal per se does not necessarily enhance the potential value of the resource base for RRs, because adding new resources to the existing ones does not ensure the creation of VRIN resources. For instance, a new set of resources may only provide competitive parity or turn out to be irrelevant in terms of creating value for customers (Helfat et al., 2007, Ambrosini and Bowman, 2009). Therefore, the overall quality and diversity of newly accessed resources may play a considerably larger role than its origin. Yet to control for the potential influence of the knowledge origin on RR, this research suggests that the higher the proportion of new, external resources among the firm's resources, the higher its potential value for RR, as it may facilitate firms to detect new possibilities for building RRs. However, for the same reasons as outlined before, the effect of newly acquired knowledge on RRs will be moderated by the firm's Integration and Coordination capacities (refer to section 3.4.2.2.).

H1f (Resource Renewal): New, external knowledge is positively related to RR.

3.4   Dynamic Capabilities and Resource Recombination

After having outlined and discussed how specific characteristics of the resources may influence the potential value of the resources base for RR, based on these preliminary considerations, the following section specifies Proposition 2 and further elaborates the relationship between DCs and RR in firms.

Proposition 2: A firm's overall DC is positively associated with the amount of RRs in firms due to both building and exploiting the potential value of the resources base.

The aim is to better understand how the DCs act upon the resource base by building and/ or exploiting the potential value of the resource base and how both constructs (the resource base and the DCs) are linked with the organisational outcome of new, synergetic RRs. In order to investigate the role and effects of DCs in the process of RR in firms, first a framework will be established, describing a specific set of DCs relevant for RR and their suggested interrelations towards RR, where in a subsequent research step based on the conceptualisation of the specific DCs, their role in the process of resource value creation will be investigated in more detail and hypotheses will be derived.

3.4.1 Dynamic Capability Framework

The DC framework builds the conceptual foundation of the firm's DCs, introducing the four DCs relevant for the process of RR, namely Sensing, Learning, Integrating and Coordinating Capacities, investigating their underlying activities, processes and routines, and outlining their general relation towards RR. Hence the DC framework outlines the microfoundations of DCs with the aim to develop a general understanding of the construct of DC and its underlying dimensions.

A strong motivation for unpacking the microfoundations of DCs is to thereby contribute towards an enhanced understanding and explanation of what drives differences in firm's behaviour and performance in regard to RR (Felin and Foss, 2005, Gavetti, 2005, Teece, 2007, Abell et al., 2008, Argote and Ren, 2012, Felin et al., 2012).

First, by investigating the microfoundations of DCs, within the DC framework this research will enhance the understanding of the primary components, processes and mechanism, underlying each capacity. Based on a review and categorisation of the multi-faceted capabilities proposed in the literature, the framework will allow defining a set of relevant DCs, specifying its routines and processes, which results in the development of a consistent and precise definition of its exact components. Thus by making the DCs observable and semantically clarified, it addresses the current lack of precise definitions, empirical grounding and measurement (e.g. Pavlou and El Sawy, 2011).

Second, having established an enhanced understanding of the firm's DCs, this will allow to investigate their role in the process of resource value creation in firms, and thus helps clarifying the sources of heterogeneity in firm's performance. Investigating the relation between the different types of DCs, the resource base and its performance outcomes allows a more precise understanding of RR in firms and will shed light on how differences in routines and capabilities may contribute towards explaining differences in innovation performance among firms.

The development of the DC framework comprises the following steps. Starting with a review, syntheses and re-conceptualisation of existing approaches of DCs found in the literature, a proposed set of specific DCs relevant for the process of RR will be identified. In a subsequent step, the four identified DCs—Sensing, Learning, Integrating and Coordinating capacity –, their underlying activities, organisational routines and processes will be investigated in more detail. Based on the conceptualisation of the specific DCs, hypotheses are drawn regarding their relationship towards RR. In a last section the suggested interrelations of the DCs among each other are specified. The chapter closes with the presentation of the DC framework, building the conception foundation for the subsequent research steps.

3.4.1.1 Conceptualising Dynamic Capabilities and Organisational Routines

Generally two different approaches towards conceptualising DCs can be found in the literature (Madsen, 2010). The first type of approaches considers DCs as an **evolutionary process** consistent of different stages, basically comprising a variety of decision-making and problem-solving activities undertaken by firms. Representative for this type of approaches, Zollo and Winter (2002) and Zott (2003) describe organisational knowledge to evolve through a series of three stages of: (1) **searching (variation)**, where firms search for new ideas based on the combination of external stimuli and internal resources in response to changing market environments, (2) **selection (evaluation),** where proposed ideas are evaluated based on experience, tested and critically analysed and the most promising ones are selected, (3) **routinisation (retention/ enactment)**, where the selected ideas are implemented through establishing routines (Madsen, 2010). All of which are regarded as evolving learning mechanisms, through which firm's develop DCs, or in other words the DCs are proposed to be "shaped by the co-evolution of these learning mechanisms" (Zollo and Winter, 2002, p. 2).

A similar concept is presented by Hargadon (2002), who delineates four different knowledge brokering stages: (1) **Access**, (2) **Bridging and Learning**, (3) **Linking**, and (4) **Building**. The first stage *Access* describes a firm's ability to access information and knowledge, e.g. to predict emerging technologies and future trends and adapt the firm's capabilities to them. Thus by describing the external conditions that "create the potential for innovation (...) by importing useful yet unvalued knowledge" (Hargadon, 2002, p. 57), it rather describes the structural precondition for the RR process. The second stage *Bridging and Learning* refer to the firm's ability to connect the isolated, otherwise disconnected domains of knowledge and to develop a comprehensive understanding of the business field (Hargadon, 2002). Both stages, *Bridging* different domains of knowledge and thereby *Learning* and transferring new knowledge to existing problems are regarded as essential capacities because "recombinant innovation occur when ideas in one domain are valuable but unknown in others" (Hargadon, 2002, p. 55). The third stage, *Linking* refers to the firm's ability to link "existing problem definitions and solutions to current situations through a process of analogical reasoning" and thereby to "recognise how past learning can apply to the current situation" (Hargadon, 2002, p. 63). Fourth, *Building* lastly refers to "the activities that individuals and teams use to connect new networks around those new combinations in order to ensure their success" (p. 68 f). Altogether, the four stages as proposed by Hargadon (2002) are closely related to the three steps **Structuring, Bundling**, and **Leveraging**, underpinning the resource management process as proposed by Sirmon et al. (2007) and described in section 2.4.3.1. These approaches have in common that DCs are regarded as evolving through a series of evolutionary process stages.

The second type of approaches, which also the conceptualisation of this research is in line with, regards DCs as **organisational capacities and mechanisms** (Madsen, 2010) to integrate, build, and reconfigure internal and external resources to address changing environments (Teece, 2007, Eisenhardt and Martin, 2000). In their early works Teece and Pisano (1994) and Teece et al. (1997) propose three organisational and managerial processes as essential elements of DC, namely (1) **coordination and integrating** of internal and external activities and resources (2) **learning**, referring to repetition and experimentation activities, that enable firms to improve existing functions, and (3) **reconfiguring and restructuring** of resources and the firm's asset structure to enable internal and external transformation (Madsen, 2010).

Later in Teece (2007) these processes are further specified and defined as "a subset of the processes that support sensing, seizing and managing threats" (Teece, 2007, p. 1341). Correspondingly, according to Teece (2007) the DC of the firm can be disaggregated into three different capacities: (1) **Sensing Capacities**, (2) **Seizing Capacities**, and (3) **Transformational (Reconfiguring) Capacities.** The first, *sensing capacity* relates to identifying and shaping new opportunities in the environment, accordingly "sensing (and shaping) new opportunities is very much a scanning, creation, learning, and interpretive activity" (Teece, 2007, p. 1322). Secondly, *seizing capacity* refers to addressing those new opportunities through new products, processes or services. Thirdly, *transformational capacity* relates to maintaining competitiveness through reconfiguring and recombining a firm's resources. Altogether, sensing, seizing and transformational capacities are suggested to build a firm's overall DC and thus enable managers to find new value enhancing resource combinations by means of asset orchestration processes (Helfat and Peteraf, 2009, Teece, 2007). This disaggregation is consistent with (e.g. Marsh and Stock, 2006, Verona and Revasi, 2003), or adapted by other research (e.g. Lichtenthaler, 2012), which based their work in Teece (2007).

A corresponding conceptualisation is presented by Eisenhardt and Martin (2000), who proposes the firm's DC to be consistent of three related capacities: (1) DCs for **acquiring and releasing** resources, which is constituted by alliance and acquisition routines, internal knowledge creation routines, as well as routines for knowledge retention and release, (2) DCs for **integrating** resources, which comprise strategic decision making and product development routines, and (3) DCs for **reconfiguring** internal resources, which regard resource placement, adaption and allocation routines, as well as management cooperation routines (Eisenhardt and Martin, 2000).

Coming from a different stream in literature, however also building upon the DC perspective and capturing related constructs, Zahra and George (2001, p. 186) refer to the **Absorptive Capacity** (ACAP) of the firm "as the firm's ability to value, assimilate, and apply new knowledge" to be formed by four different dimensions: (1) the **Knowledge Acquisition Capability** defined as "a firm's capability to identify and acquire externally generated knowledge that is critical to its operations" (Zahra and George, p. 189), (2) the **Assimilation Capability** referring to "the firm's routines and processes that allow it to analyse, process, interpret and understand the information obtained from external sources" (Zahra and George, p. 189), (3) the **Transformation Capability** representing "a firm's capability to develop and refine the routines that facilitate combining existing knowledge and the newly acquired and assimilated knowledge" (Zahra and George, p. 190), and lastly (4) the **Exploitation Capability** which is "based on the routines that allow firms to refine, extend, and leverage existing competencies or to create new ones by incorporating acquired" (Zahra and George, p. 190). While the former two dimensions are supposed to form the *Potential Absorptive Capacity (PACAP)* accountable for incorporating new knowledge, however not being concerned with its exploitation, the latter two dimensions are proposed to denote the *Realised Absorptive Capacity (RACAP)* responsible for leveraging and exploiting the knowledge that has been absorbed.

In a similar vein, the classification by Madsen (2010) differentiates between external and internal processes and propose a firm's DC to be delineated through four sub-processes: (1) **External observation and evaluation**, which comprise "dynamic capabilities which monitor the environment, provide impulse to new ideas, discover new possibilities and evaluate these" (Madsen, 2010, p. 230), (2) **External resource acquisition**, incorporating DCs relevant for acquiring new, external resources, (3) **Internal resource renewal**, which denotes DCs that "integrate new resources in original and effective resource configurations" (Madsen, 2010, p. 231) and (4) **Internal resource reconfiguration,** relating to DCs concerned with reconfiguring or restructuring internal resources (Madsen, 2010).

Lastly, an important step towards a conceptualisation of the DC construct has been done by Pavlou and El Sawy (2011) by presenting a generic framework and moreover, first measurement model of a set of identifiable and specific DCs for resource reconfiguration. Based on the work by Teece et al. (1997, 2007), Pavlou and El Sawy (2011) distinguish between four related but distinct types of DCs facilitating organisations to integrate, build and reconfigure internal and external resources to address rapidly changing environments, namely (1) **Sensing Capacity**, defined as "the ability to spot, interpret, and pursue opportunities in the environment" (Pavlou and El Sawy, 2011, p. 243), (2) **Learning Capacity**, which refers to the "ability to revamp existing operational capabilities with new knowledge" (Pavlou and El Sawy, 2011, p. 244), (3) **Integrating Capacity**, relating to the "ability to embed new knowledge into the new operational capabilities by creating a shared understanding and collective sense-making" (Pavlou and El Sawy, 2011, p. 245), and (4) **Coordinating Capacity**, describing the "ability to orchestrate and deploy tasks, resources, and activities in the new operational capabilities" (Pavlou and El Sawy, 2011, p. 246).

As the above review has shown different conceptualisations of the DC construct exist in the literature, whereby "different labels have been used in the literature to refer to similar capabilities, or similar labels for different capabilities" (Pavlou and El Sawy, 2011, p. 242). The diversity and complexity of the concept can also be seen in the various definitions that exist in the literature describing DCs (Madsen, 2010), refer to section 2.4.3.3. Hence, in order to sort out and bring clarity to the construct of DC, the various labels and meanings used

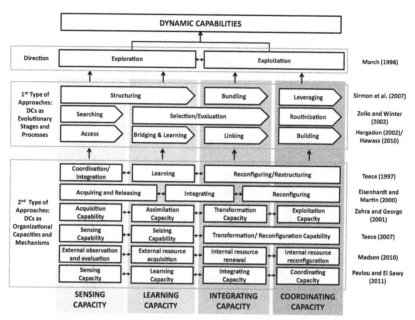

Source: own illustration

Figure 3.1 Framework comprising the different Conceptualisations of DCs found in the Literature

to refer to similar concepts were converted into a framework that comprises the firm's DC at three levels as suggested by Madsen (2010). Figure 3.1 presents the framework aligning the different concepts found in the literature.

First, at the top level, DCs are developed along two main dimensions *exploration and exploitation,* which relates to the balancing act firms have to accomplish between the two diverging directions of the firm: (1) the exploration of new opportunities on the one hand side, which is directed towards innovation and search, and (2) the exploitation of existing resources, which is more efficiency oriented, on the other (March, 1991). The second level comprises the *evolutionary processes* as such DCs are conceptualised by the first group of approaches (e.g. Zollo and Winter, 2002, Zott, 2003), all of which refer to DCs as something that best can be captured by the different stages, that describe how the process of RR in firms is carried out (Madsen, 2010). Complementing, and thus closely related to these evolutionary processes are the *organisational capacities and mechanism*, which are captured at the third level in the framework, describing the capabilities, capacities or activities relevant for accomplishing the evolutionary processes. As conceptualised by the second group of approaches (e.g. Teece, 2007, Eisenhardt and Martin, 2000, Pavlou and El Sway, 2011), taken together these different *organisational capacities and mechanisms* are suggested to form the firm's overall DC.

Summarising, the framework as presented in Figure 3.1 allows the different manifestations of DCs described or utilised in the literature to be placed into a holistic frame. Doing so, this framework aligns the different evolutionary processes found in the literature, e.g. searching/ access/ structuring as exploration processes and e.g. routinisation/ building/ leveraging as exploitation processes, with its respective capabilities, capacities and activities (e.g. sensing, seizing and transformation capacities) and thus integrates the varying approaches suggested by different authors. This is valuable as "dynamic capabilities actually consist of identifiable and specific routines that often have been the subject of extensive empirical research in their own right" (Eisenhardt and Martin, 2000, p. 1107). Moreover it emerges, that as different as they seem to be a priori, all of them describe similar, yet related concepts. Accordingly, with the synthesis of the different concepts, the framework allows aggregating the diverse notions found in the literature into **four generic types of DCs**, which—in line with the conceptualisation by Pavlou and El Sawy (2011)—can best be described as **Sensing capacity, Learning capacity, Integrating capacity**, and **Coordinating capacity**.

The following Figure 3.2 presents the generic framework of the proposed set of DCs as presented by Pavlou and El Sawy (2011), briefly describing each capacity and the logical sequence of how each capabilities contributes in the process of RR in order to reconfigure existing resources into new ones that better fit the environmental conditions. Notably, the logical sequence as shown in Figure 3.2 only gives a simplified representation of the interaction effects, which will be further detailed in section 3.4.1.6. The generic framework hence gives emphasis that the DC of the firm should be conceptualises as a multidimensional construct, including four very different dimensions of DCs.

While drawing on the conceptualisation of the four generic types of DCs as presented by Pavlou and El Sawy (2011), this research further elaborates the conceptual specifications of the four DCs by aligning them with the conceptual works presented by Sirmon et al. (2007), Zollo and Winter (2002), Hargadon (2002), Hawass (2010), Teece (2007), Teece et al. (1997), Eisenhardt and Martin (2000), Madsen (2010), resulting in a re-conceptualisation of the four DCs, that is more detailed and that allows us to have specific constructs that can be operationalised and measured.

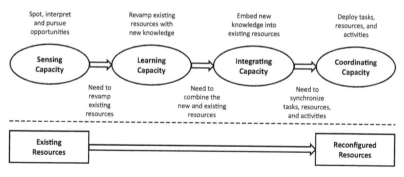

Source: adapted from Pavlou and El Sawy (2011)

Figure 3.2 Generic Framework representing the proposed Set of Dynamic Capabilities

The four generic types of DCs, as presented in Figure 3.2 and defined as relevant for this research, are outlined and discussed in the following section.

3.4.1.2 Sensing Capacity

The firm's Sensing capacity refers to the identification and development of new opportunities in the environment by means of scanning, screening and interpreting activities. In line with the definition presented by Pavlou and El Sawy (2011) and corresponding to Teece's (2007) conceptualisation of 'Sensing' as a firm's capacity responsible for identifying and shaping new opportunities in the environment, this research proposes the following definition:

Sensing capacity is defined as the firm's ability to spot, interpret and pursue opportunities in the internal and external environment.

Accordingly, this research's definition of Sensing capacity is corresponding with Teece (2007, p. 1322) stating: "Sensing (and shaping) new opportunities is very much a scanning, creation, learning, and interpretive activity". Comparable definitions can be found in the literature, Lichtenthaler (2012) for example refers to 'Sensing' as developing new opportunity through environmental scanning, learning, and investments in research and related activities, while Madsen refers to *'External observation and evaluation',* a similar concept with different labelling, which "comprise dynamic capabilities which monitor the environment, provide impulse to new ideas, discover new possibilities and evaluate these" (Madsen, 2010, p. 230).

Sensing new opportunities in the environment fosters RR in firms. For recombinant innovation to occur, firms have to sense the environment to explore technologies and markets to discover and identify new opportunities (Day, 1994, McGrath, 2001). In other words, "Reconfiguration requires a surveillance of market trends and new technologies to sense and seize opportunities" (Pavlou and El Sawy, 2011, p. 243). This is closely related to Armit and Schoemaker's (1993) perception of identifying *Strategic Industry Factors* at the market side, which they refer to as "a set of Resources and Capabilities that has become the prime determinant of economic rents for industry participants" (Armit and Schoemaker, 1993, p. 93), and which are "determined at the market-level through complex interactions among the firm's competitors, customers, regulators, innovators external to the industry, and other stakeholders" (Armit and Schoemaker, 1993, p. 93). According to Armit and Schoemaker (1993), the rationale deciding about competitive advantages and rent generation in firms is finding the right match between these *Strategic Industry Factors* at the industry level and *Strategic Assets* at the firm level. In this regard, a strong Sensing capacity highly contributes to identifying *Strategic Industry Factors,* which consequently needs to be attended through the development of appropriate internal resources and capabilities (*Strategic Assets*).

In support of this view, as market needs, technological opportunities, and competitor activity are constantly changing especially in today's dynamic environment, according to Teece (1997, p. 521) "there is obviously value in the ability to sense the need to reconfigure the firm's asset structure, and to accomplish the necessary internal and external transformation". On the downside, "if enterprises fail to engage in such activities, they won't be able to assess market and technological developments and spot opportunities. As a consequence, they will likely miss opportunities visible to others" (Teece, 2007, p. 1323).

Thus, in order to raise the potential to identify new opportunities for reconfiguration, firms must continuously sense the environment to generate market intelligence by capturing market needs, competitor action, new technologies and market trends (Teece, 2007, Pavlou and El Sawy, 2011, Day, 1994, McGrath, 2001). Establishing the view Teece et al. (1997, p. 521) proposed that "the ability to calibrate the requirements for change and to effectuate the necessary adjustments (...) depend[s] on the ability to scan the environment, to evaluate markets and competitors, and to quickly accomplish reconfiguration ahead of competition." A strong Sensing capacity hence is regarded as a critical capability of the firm, as it enables a dynamic co-evolvement of the firm's capacities and competences and its market-related environment (Teece, 2007, Lichtenthaler, 2012).

Specifically, 'Sensing' is regarded as an essential capacity as is extends the firm's resource base with new Market Knowledge (Lichtenthaler, 2012).

According to Teece (2007), the identification of new opportunities requires both, the access to information as well as the ability to recognise, sense and shape developments. The relatedness to the knowledge brokering stage '*Access*' as proposed by Hargadon (2002), referring to the firm's ability to access information and knowledge, e.g. for predicting emerging technologies and future trends and adapt the firm's capabilities to them, becomes obvious. In line with what literature suggests, Teece (2007) further delineates that opportunity discovery and creation may either be originated in the cognitive and creative capacity of individuals ('right brain') or can be grounded in organisational processes and routines. Accordingly, following Teece (2007, p. 1323) in order to anchor a firm's Sensing capacity "organizational processes can be put in place inside the enterprise to garner new technical information, tap developments in exogenous science, monitor customer needs and competitor activity, and shape new products and processes opportunities". Subsequently, establishing processes for embedding scanning, interpretive and creative processes inside the firm, would be the more desirable approach for long term economic growth, rather than solely building firm's future prospects on the creative or cognitive skills of individuals (Teece, 2007).

In spite of these knowledge, researchers found the ability to identify new opportunities to vary significantly among firms (Teece, 2007). While some firms have already established specific processes and routines supporting the environmental scanning for new opportunities, others are still underemphasised (Lichtenthaler, 2012). Thus, in order to better understand the microfoundations of the firm's Sensing capacity, it is important to investigate the organisational processes that can be put in place inside the firm and are constituting a firm's Sensing capacity (Ambrosini and Bowman, 2009).

Sensing capacity, as defined here, comprises the identification of innovation-related assets (Lichtenthaler, 2012), specifically knowledge on market needs (market intelligence), customer needs and competitor moves (customer and competitor intelligence), and new technologies (technological intelligence) in order to identify and shape opportunities (Teece, 2007). Accordingly, the **three basic routines underlying Sensing capacity** involve: (1) **Generating Market Intelligence**, (2) **Generating Customer and Competitor Intelligence**, and (3) **Generating Technological Intelligence**. These routines are related to kindred processes and activities in the DC literature (Pavlou and El Sawy, 2011).

Firstly, *Generating Market Intelligence* relates identifying market opportunities (Day, 1994), being responsive to market trends (Amit and Schoemaker,

1993), recognising rigidities (Sinkula, 1994), and identifying and recognising new business opportunities (Pavlou and El Sawy, 2011, Galunic and Rodan, 1998). Secondly, *Generating Customer and Competitor Intelligence* relates to identifying customer needs (Teece, 2007, Pavlou and El Sawy, 2011), monitoring competitor activity (Teece, 2007), allocating resources to search and discovery activities (Teece, 2007). Thirdly, *Generating Technological Intelligence* relates to identifying technological developments and opportunities (Teece, 2007), gathering new technical information, data, and statistics (Teece, 2007), and taping developments in exogenous science (Teece, 2007).

While generating market, customer and technological intelligence describe the underlying routines, defined as repetitious organisational activities that constituting a firm's Sensing capacity, following the conceptualisation by Pavlou and El Sawy (2011), each routine can be further described by three **sub-processes.** These are **gathering market** (customer and competitor) **intelligence** (Galunic and Rodan, 1998), **disseminating market** (customer and competitor) **intelligence** (Kogut and Zander, 1996) and **responding to market** (customer and competitor) **intelligence** (Teece, 2007). More specifically, these three processes can be further delineated by the following **basic activities** underlying these processes:

(1) Gathering new market (customer and technological) intelligence refers to **spotting, scanning and monitoring the environment** and entails activities, such as (i) to *scan, search,* and *explore* technologies and markets, both 'local' and 'distant' (Teece, 2007, Nelson and Winter, 1982), (ii) to *scan* and *monitor* technological developments and opportunities, both internal and external (Teece 2007), (iii) to *identify* and *recognise* new business opportunities (Pavlou and El Sawy, 2011), (iv) to *understand* customer decision making processes (Nonaka and Toyama, 2007), (v) to *assess* customer an market needs, both those that are expressed and those that are latent (Teece 2007), (vi) to *identify* market and industry trends (Amit and Schoemaker, 1993), and (vii) to *recognise* and *monitor* supplier and competitor moves (Pavlou and El Sawy, 2011, Teece 2007).

(2) Disseminating market (customer and technological) intelligence refers to **accumulating, filtering and interpreting available information** and refers to activities, and captures activities, such as (i) to *accumulate, filter* and *making sense* of information, gained internally and externally (Teece 2007), (ii) to *evaluate* markets and competitors (Teece 2007), (iii) to *build* scenarios about the likely evolution of technology developments, customer needs, suppliers and competitor moves and changing market and technological reality (Teece 2007), (iv) to *understand* customer decision making (Nonaka and Toyama, 2007), (v) to *execute* learning, interpretation, and creative activity (Teece, 2007).

(3) Responding to market (customer and technological) intelligence refers to **valuing, identifying and shaping opportunities** in order to correspond to new developments in the environment, specifically (i) to *assess* for instance, how to interpret new technological and market developments, how technologies will evolve and which technologies to pursue, which market and customer segments to target, or how and when competitors, suppliers, and customers will respond (Teece 2007, p. 1322), and (ii) to *initiate* plans on how to capitalise on the new knowledge (D'Aveni, 1994).

The delineation of the key elements of Sensing capacity shows, while Sensing capacity includes the *screening* for external resource acquisition opportunities, it does not capture the acquisition itself, which is part of the Learning capacity. As opposed to Lichtenthaler (2012), who sees external and internal opportunity exploitation as being part of 'Sensing', the Sensing capacity as conceptualised here only captures the external opportunity identification. The internal opportunity generation is rather seen as part of the firm's Learning capacity. Hence, in line with Pavlou and El Sawy (2011, p. 244), this research notes "Sensing and learning capabilities are distinct capabilities because sensing focuses on gathering new market intelligence [external opportunity identification], and learning focuses on using market intelligence [internal opportunity generation] to create new knowledge".

Hypotheses Development

Having established the conceptualisation of Sensing capacity, its underlying routines, processes and activities, allows hypotheses to be derived regarding its relationship towards RR. A firm's Sensing capacity is proposed to enable reconfiguration of the firm's resources through its three basic routines and processes (Pavlou and El Sawy, 2011). First, *generating market intelligence* raises the potential to identify new market opportunities for reconfiguration (Zahra and George, 2002, Pavlou and El Sawy, 2011). Second, *generating customer and competitor intelligence* helps to achieve responsiveness to customer needs and competitor moves (Day, 1994, Pavlou and El Sawy, 2011). Third, *generating technological intelligence* helps to identify technological opportunities and developments in the environment (Teece, 2007), which is important to raise the potential for discovering new RR opportunities in the environment.

A strong Sensing capacity thus is found to enhances strategic flexibility, innovativeness, and responsiveness to market trends and customer needs and therefore is proposed to be positively associated with the development of **Market Knowledge**, which refers to the firm's understanding of the market environment, particularly of customers and competitors (Lichtenthaler, 2012, Ramaswami et al., 2009, Teece,

2007). Likewise, an enhanced understanding of the market environment also facilitates taping new developments in the exogenous science, monitoring technological developments and opportunities, which facilitates the identification of technological opportunities (Generating Technological Intelligence). Therefore, in addition, Sensing capacity is proposed to indirectly and positively influence the development of new **Technological Knowledge**[2], which refers to the firm's technological expertise, R&D as well as engineering skills and competences (Teece, 2007, Thomas et al., 1993, Lichtenthaler, 2012). Given that, a strong Sensing capacity contributes to developing valuable market-related assets (Market Knowledge and subsequently Technological Knowledge), it is an essential capacity for extending a firm's resource base (Lichtenthaler, 2012). As a result, a high Sensing capacity is suggested to positively affect the potential value of the resource base, as it is leading to a higher Market Knowledge (and subsequently Technological Knowledge) breadth and depth.

On this basis, a high Sensing capacity helps to guide the firms RR activities based on the development of a thorough market understanding (Atuahene-Gima et al., 2005, Helfat et al., 2007). In particular, grounded in the market-related assets gained through Sensing, firms can generate additional opportunities for innovation (Ramaswami et al., 2009, Pavlou and El Sawy, 2011). Moreover, by identifying the *Strategic Industry Factors* (Amit and Schoemaker, 1993), the firm's Sensing capacity contributes to a high market orientation, and as such is regarded as a critical capacity to ensure market-orientated innovation (Lichtenthaler, 2012). Consistent with this view, a high Sensing capacity of firms is proposed to facilitate RR in firms (Pavlou and El Sawy, 2011), as it enables firms to explore external opportunities for new products and services that better meet customer needs (Jaworski and Kohli, 1993). However, a high Sensing capacity *per se* does not ensure a successful realisation of these opportunities, rather it enables identifying *Strategic Industry Factors* and shaping new opportunities in the business environment by means of developing superior understanding of the market environment, which subsequently is likely to be employed and leveraged in form of new RRs (Lichtenthaler, 2012). As such, a high Sensing capacity does not necessary directly link to a higher amount of RR in firms, instead Sensing acts as enabler, identifying new opportunities and providing the market-related knowledge for subsequently seizing these innovation opportunities (Helfat and Peteraf, 2009, Lichtenthaler, 2012).

---

[2] Generating *Technological Intelligence* is not to be used equivalent to generating *Technological Knowledge*. *Technological Intelligence* is generated through 'Sensing' and as such only concerns the pre-screening and identification of relevant Technological Knowledge, while its acquisition and assimilation would be part of 'Learning'. Therefore 'Sensing' predominantly contributes to generating Market Knowledge and only indirectly affects Technological Knowledge, while Learning contributes to generating Market and Technological Knowledge.

Consistent with these theoretical research findings, arguments therefore suggest a positive relation between Sensing capacity and RR in firms, through its positive effect on Market and Technological Knowledge. However, this relationship may be influenced by the firm's Integrating and Coordinating capacities (refer to section 3.4.2.2.). This leads to the following hypothesis:

H2: *A high Sensing capacity is positively associated with RR, through Market and Technological Knowledge.*

3.4.1.3 Learning Capacity

Learning capacity refers to the firm's ability to learn and create new knowledge inside the firm's boundaries. After sensing new opportunities in the environment, firms have to learn and integrate new knowledge into their own resource base to ensure the availability of relevant internal knowledge for addressing these opportunities (Lavie, 2006, Lichtenthaler, 2012). While Sensing capacity was rather externally oriented towards identifying the *Strategic Industry Factors* at the market side (Armit and Schoemaker, 1993), as it captured the analysis of the external environment and was directed towards external opportunity generation, 'Learning' is rather internally oriented towards building the respective *Strategic Assets* at the firm level. *Strategic Assets* refer to "the set of firm specific Resources and Capabilities developed by management as the basis for creating and protecting their firm's competitive advantage" (Armit and Schoemaker, 1993). In this regard, the firm's Learning capacity is concerned with the assimilation and accumulation of knowledge in order to build a rich and diverse resource base, the "raw" material for innovation (Hargadon, 2002).

Learning and internally creating new knowledge hence is a critical capacity for RR in firms. It is essential for building a valuable resource base for RR. Based on the stock of available resources, firms can engage in subsequent, integrative activities, by means of matching *Strategic Assets* developed through Learning, which basically captures the technological-side knowledge (e.g. technologies, resources and capabilities), with *Strategic Industry Factors* identified through Sensing, which refers to the market-side knowledge (e.g. customer needs, market opportunities, etc.) (refer to Figure 3.3). Hence, for firms to take advantage of RR opportunities, they must engage in learning processes (Pavlou and El Sawy, 2011). Likewise, Zollo and Winter (2002) underscore the importance of deliberating learning mechanisms, in the development of internal assets for reconfiguration.

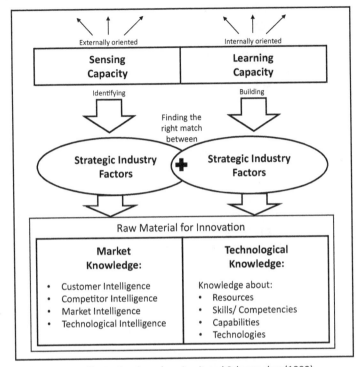

Source: own illustration based on Armit and Schoemaker (1993)

Figure 3.3 Matching Strategic Industry Factors and Strategic Assets

Correspondingly, the firm's Learning capacity as defined by Pavlou and El Sawy (2011, p. 244) refers to "the ability to revamp existing operational capabilities with new knowledge". This requires the organisations to continuously learn new knowledge and skills, and to renew and maintain existing knowledge to be at the cutting edge for ensuring market orientation (Teece, 2007).

When operationalising the underlying routines of Learning capacity, however, Pavlou and El Sawy (2011) further regard Learning capacity to be equal to the Absorptive Capacity (ACAP) construct as conceptualised by Zahra and George (2002). Hence, the four underlying routines of Learning capacity, as suggested by Pavlou and El Sawy (2011), are proposed to be acquiring, assimilating, transforming, and exploiting knowledge, and in the conceptualisation by Pavlou and El Sawy (2011) capture both the Potential Absorptive Capacity (PACAP) and the Realised Absorptive Capacity (RACAP) dimensions. This research however establishes a different understanding of the firm's Learning capacity for the following reasoning.

Firstly, the conceptualisation of 'Learning' as presented by Pavlou and El Sawy (2011) considers the ACAP of the firm, which by definition exclusively regards utilising external knowledge within the firm (Cohen and Levinthal, 1990, Lane et al., 2006), and as such neglects the internal learning part (Lane et al., 2006, Zahra and George, 2002). Indeed, internal knowledge generation processes are found to provide substantial input to a firm's Learning capacity and RR in firms (Khilji et al., 2006, Smith et al., 2005, Hargadon, 2002). Respectively, this research puts forward an integrative picture of how firm's revamp their knowledge base by managing both internal and external knowledge (Lichtenthaler and Lichtenthaler, 2009), and in consequence conceptualises Learning capacity as capturing both external knowledge exploration (ACAP) and internal knowledge exploration processes (Knowledge Creation).

Secondly, while seeing ACAP as an essential element of Learning, this research refers to ACAP in its original meaning as formerly proposed by Cohen and Levinthal (1990), when the concept was restricted to the two basic activities of *acquiring* and *assimilating* external knowledge. Accordingly ACAP, as defined for this research, only refers to Knowledge acquisition and assimilation, i.e. the PACAP dimensions conceptualised by Zahra and George (2002). Hence, in distinction from the conceptualisation by Pavlou and El Sawy (2011), while including the PACAP dimensions—covering the firm's *Knowledge Acquisition Capability* and *Assimilation Capability*—this research refrains from including the RACAP dimensions, compromising *Transformation* and *Exploitation Capability*, for the reason that due to their focus on knowledge exploitation processes the latter two were attributed to Integrating and Coordinating Capacity, respectively.

Thus, by including internal knowledge creation and at the same time excluding the RACAP dimensions within the conceptualisation of Learning capacity, an integrative perspective is adapted for this study. Consequently, Pavlou and El Sawy's (2011) and Zahra and George's (2002) definitions have been modified into the following definition of Learning capacity for this study:

Learning capacity refers to the firm's ability to assimilate, accumulate, retain, and create (new) knowledge to revamp the firm's resource base with substantial knowledge, developed internally or obtained externally.

Given this definition, Learning capacity captures two basic components of learning: (1) **external knowledge absorption**, which comprises *knowledge acquisition* and *knowledge assimilation (PACAP)* of external knowledge, and (2) **internal knowledge renewal**, which is seen as a complement to *ACAP* and relates to *knowledge accumulation and retention* of existing, internal knowledge as well as the *internal creation of new knowledge*. This is in line with the perception that resources to be bundled into new RRs can either be developed internally or obtained externally (Wiklund and Shepherd, 2009).

Similar in character, a vast variety of approaches can be found in organisational learning theory elaborating on processes and routines for organisational learning (e.g. Zahra and George, 2002, Sirmon et al., 2007, Pavlou an El Sawy, 2011). Based on the delineation of the concept as defined above, and consistent with earlier research findings from organisational learning theory, **three underlying routines of Learning capacity**, its constituting processes and underlying activities, could be identified: (1) **Acquiring and Assimilating external knowledge**, (2) **Creating new internal knowledge**, and (3) **Accumulating and Retaining internal knowledge**.

(1) Acquiring and Assimilating external knowledge relates to the external knowledge absorption, i.e. PACAP, and captures the processes of *Knowledge Acquisition* and *Knowledge Assimilation*.

Knowledge Acquisition refers to obtaining and integrating new resources from external sources by means of purchasing resources from strategic factor market (Barney, 1986), or alternatively by adapting interorganisational mechanisms for resource exchange, such as strategic alliances, mergers and acquisitions (Capron et al., 1998, Wiklund and Shepherd, 2009), licensing or contractual agreements (Granstrand and Sjolander, 1990). Accordingly, firms acquire knowledge from diverse external sources, whereby the diversity of these sources is suggested to significantly affect the firm's acquisition and assimilation capabilities (Zahra and George, 2002). This is especially relevant as "the fast changes in consumers' preferences, the increased complexity and costs of developing truly new products, and advances in new technology often require the firm to look beyond its boundaries to access knowledge" (Mu and Di Benedetto, 2012, p. 8). While the internal resources are crucial for a firm's competitive position over time, "there are limitations with reliance solely on resources internal to the firm for generating new productive resource combinations because it is unlikely that the exact same set of resources can be used to develop new and more valuable combinations over and over again" (Wiklund and Shepherd, 2009, p. 195). Thus, firms increasingly rely on interorganisational knowledge transactions to extend their internal knowledge base (Lichtenthaler and Lichtenthaler, 2009, Argote et al., 2003, Gulati, 1999). Knowledge Acquisition Capability is defined as "a firm's capability to identify and acquire externally generated knowledge that is critical to its operations" (Zahra and George, 2002, p. 189). Thus, for generating new opportunities to improve performance, external resources must be acquired and integrated with those resources the firm already possesses (Wiklund and Shepherd, 2009, p. 195). This is in line with Cohen and Levinthal's (1990) description of a firm's capacity to value and acquire external knowledge.

Knowledge Assimilation on the other hand refers to understanding the newly acquired knowledge and developing problem-solving skills by means of incorporating them into the firm's knowledge base (Lane et al., 2006, Zahra and George, 2002). It concerns the interpretation, comprehension, and learning of new knowledge (Eisenhardt and Martin, 2000, Zahra and George, 2002), as for instance due to its context specificy, institutionalisation, dispersion, or tacitness, newly acquired knowledge may not always be easily understood, replicated and transferred to new contexts (Leonard-Barton, 1995, Szulanski, 1996, Galunic and Rodan, 1998). The notion that prior knowledge thereby facilitates the learning of new knowledge is well established in literature (Cohen and Levinthal, 1990, Jansen et al., 2005), suggesting that learning builds upon what is already known by the firm because the memory or stock of knowledge is developed through associative learning (e.g. Cohen and Levinthal, 1990). On the downside, previous activities and resource usage may also limit the probability for learning new knowledge outside those areas the firm already is familiar with, leading to organisational rigidities and structural inertia (Cohen and Levinthal, 1990, Teece, 1987, Leonhard-Barton, 1995). Prior knowledge thus (positively or negatively) influences the comprehension of new knowledge, which in turn is requisite to knowledge assimilation and allows firms to internalise the newly acquires knowledge (Zahra and Geoge, 2002, Lane and Lubatkin, 1998). Knowledge Assimilation Capability refers to "the firm's routines and processes that allow it to analyse, process, interpret and understand the information obtained from external sources" (Zahra and George, 2002, p. 189). Correspondingly, assimilating new knowledge is regarded as an essential part of a firm's Learning capacity (Pavlou and El Sawy, 2011).

(2) Creating new internal knowledge refers to the internal knowledge exploration and the creation of new knowledge (Rothaermel and Hess, 2007), thus it complements the ACAP dimensions which relates to the external exploration of new knowledge. Prior research has emphasised the importance of firm's internal inventive and knowledge generation activities (Khilji et al., 2006, Smith et al., 2005). Accordingly, *Internal Knowledge Creation* routine is necessary as "strategic factor markets are unlikely to provide a firm with all its required resources, especially when environmental munificence is low" (Sirmon et al., 2002). Following Nonaka (1991, p. 2), "successful companies are those that continuously create new knowledge, disseminate it widely throughout the company and quickly embody it in new technologies and services". Generating new knowledge inside the firm is also referred to in the literature as internal knowledge exploration (Smith et al., 2005) or inventive capacity (Lichtenthaler and Lichtenthaler, 2009). *Internal knowledge creation* comprises the process stages of internally generating new knowledge (e.g. through inventions resulting from internal R&D), and integrating the newly created knowledge into the firm's knowledge base (Nonaka, 1994, Smith et al., 2005, Lichtenthaler and Lichtenthaler, 2009). Investigating the underlying processes of Internal Knowledge Creation that drive the knowledge-creating company, Nonaka (1991) defines the two critical process steps for creating new knowledge being (1) *Articulation*, which refers to converting tacit knowledge into explicit knowledge, and (2) *Internalisation*, which denotes using the explicit knowledge to extend one's own tacit knowledge.

Looking at the organisational activities underlying these processes, the *Articulation* of knowledge (from tacit to explicit knowledge) refers to the organisational activity of making the tacit knowledge ('know-how') of individuals available to others, by sharing and thus learning the tacit knowledge through articulating the insights and intuitions, and translating it into explicit knowledge, that can be easily communicated and shared with others (Nonaka, 1991). Thus, by sharing their individual opinions, experiences and beliefs and comparing their viewpoints with others, individuals can achieve an improved level of comprehension and draw causal linkages between actions and performance outcomes, which in term foster collective learning (Zollo and Winter, 2002).

Respectively, the *Internalisation* of knowledge (from explicit to tacit knowledge) relates to the organisational activity of sharing the new explicit knowledge throughout the company, which allows others in the company to internalise that knowledge, and thus to broaden, understand and re-frame their own tacit knowledge base (Nonaka, 1991). While kindest activities can be established in firms fostering the articulation and internalisation of knowledge, both processes effort the active involvement of individuals and their personal commitment (Nonaka, 1991). Hence learning "new knowledge always begins with the individual" (Nonaka, 1994, p. 3).

(3) Knowledge Accumulation and Retention refers to the organisational routine of internally managing and retaining knowledge over time (Garud and Nayyar, 1994, Dierickx and Cool, 1989). In a similar vein Lichtenthaler (2009 p. 1315) denotes the 'Knowledge management capacity' as a dynamic capability, which refers "to a firm's ability to successfully manage its knowledge base over time".

Knowledge Accumulation and Retention is a basic routine of Learning capacity, as the internal knowledge needs to be actively managed and retained to keep the knowledge 'alive' (Lichtenthaler and Lichtenthaler, 2009, Lane et al., 2006). Otherwise, when employees change their positions or leave the companies, or when skills and routines are not used anymore or become obsolete, their firms sustain a loss of knowledge (Szulanski, 1996). To avoid this, firms need to accumulate and retain the knowledge about the extant resources, capabilities and organisational skills in ways that enables them to become the raw material for innovation (Hargadon, 2002). Knowledge accumulation and retention captures the processes of *Knowledge Codification* (Coombs and Hill, 1998) and *Unlearning* (Leonhard-Barton, 1995).

Knowledge Codification regards the internal storage of knowledge through formal procedures, knowledge management systems or databases that are employed in order to enhance the sustainability of knowledge and allow knowledge to be maintained, captured and diffused throughout the organisation (Zollo and Winter, 2002, Coombs and Hill, 1998). Knowledge codification is the process by which firms "document understanding of the effectiveness of specific practices" (Macher and Mowery, 2009, p. 45) through codifying information into formats more suitable for data analysis, e.g. in written tools, such as manuals, blueprints, spreadsheets, decision support systems, project management software, or IT systems (Zollo and Winter, 2002, Coombs and Hill, 1998). Hence, codifiability refers "to the ability of the firm to structure knowledge into a set of identifiable rules and relationships that can be easily communicated" (Kogut and Zander, 1992). *Knowledge Codification* involves actively converting implicit into explicit knowledge, thus helps the process of *Knowledge Articulation* by transferring the knowledge gained into a shared knowledge repository (Macher and Mowery, 2009, Albino and Garavelli, 2001). Accordingly, *Knowledge Codification* facilitates Learning as it supports the identification of causal linkages through mapping knowledge relationships and enables the systematic management, replication and diffusion of existing knowledge throughout the organisation (Zollo and Winter, 2002, Zander and Kogut, 1995, Nonaka, 1994, Macher and Mowery, 2009). By providing a 'blueprint' of the firm's current knowledge, it also helps organisations to capture the internal knowledge available in the firm and keep track of "knowing what we know", a necessary precondition for RR. In summary, with the codification of otherwise tacit knowledge, it contributes to the firm's Learning capacity through improved problem solving skills, coordination of available knowledge, knowledge administration and management, knowledge sharing and dissemination (Macher and Mowery, 2009). However, research also suggest that efforts to capture and codify knowledge in centralised databases cannot substitute the social interactions between individuals working in different areas, rather it is regarded as a supportive process for knowledge management (Hargadon, 1998).

'Unlearning' refers to the process of divesting valuable resources or resources that have become obsolete over time (Sirmon et al. 2007, Leonard-Barton, 1992) and removing them from the firm's resource base. Evidence is given by research that not seldom once functional routines become dysfunctional over time and act as rigidities that keep firms from adapting and acting in ways to improve performance (Leonard-Barton, 1992, 1995, Rumelt, 1987). As firm's have limited resources, the evaluation of firm-controlled resources and the divestment of less valuable resources is required to generate the slack and flexibility that allows to acquire and accumulate new resources of higher value (Sirmon and Hitt, 2003, Sirmon et al., 2007). As noted by Teece (2007, p. 1333): "By jettisoning 'dead' or dying assets, the enterprise is no longer shackled with an asset base that can be a crutch". Hence, through divesting obsolete assets, firms disentangle oneself of organisational constraints inside its boundaries (Teece, 2007) and create space for resources of higher value.

Looking at the overall concept of Learning capacity as defined here, reveals that it is closely related to the RR process step of 'Bridging and Learning' as defined by Hargadon (2002), were individuals by *bridging* otherwise disconnected domains of knowledge and moving resources from one domain to another, and *learning* new knowledge (be it from external or internal sources) by putting resources in different contexts. According to Hargadon (2002. p. 62) "learning activities of knowledge brokers entail more than just acquiring knowledge of existing resources within a particular domain", moreover 'Learning' encompasses four activities: (i) learning about the existing resources of each new domain; (ii) learning the related problems in that domain; (iii) learning what others in their own firm know; and (iv) learning how to learn (Hargadon, 2002, p. 58). Thus, learning "describes the set of activities that individuals and groups in organisations engage in to extend their ability to comprehend and act within their environment". (Hargadon, 2002, p. 57).

Hypotheses Development

Given the conceptualisation of Learning capacity, its underlying routines and processes allows hypotheses to be derived regarding its relationship towards RR. A firm's Learning capacity is proposed to facilitate RR in firms through its three basic routines. First, *acquiring and assimilating external knowledge* helps to obtaining and incorporating new knowledge from external sources and making it available for the firm's business by integrating it into the firm's knowledge base (Lane et al.,

2006, Zahra and George, 2002). Second, as new knowledge does not only emerge externally but also within the firm's boundaries, *internal knowledge creation* helps to enhance the current stock of knowledge by internally generating new knowledge through articulation and internalisation (Nonaka, 1994, Smith et al., 2005). Third, *knowledge accumulation and retention* endeavour a continuous retention and maintenance of the internal knowledge available in the firm, thus ensuring a constant renewal of the firm's resource base and keep the knowledge 'alive' (Lichtenthaler and Lichtenthaler, 2009, Lane et al., 2006).

It emerges that Learning is predominantly directed towards developing a valuable stock of knowledge from internal and external sources. The new knowledge gained through Learning hence comprises both **Technological Knowledge** and **Market Knowledge**, as well as the knowledge about the (internal) resources and capabilities. Subsequently, firms can apply the newly created knowledge to refine further and improve existing products and processes (Mu and Di Benedetto, 2012). Accordingly, "Learning builds a rich and diverse knowledge base into these organizations, yet past problems and solutions enter entangled in their original context and often end up in different comers of the organization" (Hargadon, 2002, p. 63). As a result, a high Learning capacity is suggested to positively affect the potential value of the resource base for RR, as it is leading to a higher Market and Technological Knowledge breadth and depth.

On this basis, by developing a rich and diverse knowledge base, Learning capacity is proposed as an enabler of reconfiguration in firms. Supporting this view, Cohen and Levinthal (1990) put forward that the diversity and quality of knowledge available in firms facilitates the innovative process by enabling the individual to make novel associations and linkages. In a similar vein, van den Bosch et al. (1999) argue that 'Learning' facilitates reconfiguration and innovation. Thus, the firm's Learning capacity is suggested to help firms to accumulate and retain a stock of valuable knowledge about the extant resources, capabilities and organisational skills, in ways that enable it to become the 'raw material' for recombinant innovation (Hargadon, 2002). Likewise Sensing capacity, the firm's Learning capacity is not assumed to be directly linked to the amount of RR in firms, instead Learning is proposed to act as an enabler of RR, providing the relevant internal knowledge, i.e. the *Strategic Assets*, which have to be matched with the *Strategic Industry Factors* in a subsequent integrating RR step in order to build synergetic RRs and thereby to address the opportunities created by the firm's Sensing capacity (Helfat and Peteraf, 2009, Lichtenthaler, 2012). Therefore, a higher Learning capacity is suggested to enhance RR in firms, but only if firms possess the necessary Integrating and Coordinating capacities to bundle these resources into new synergetic RRs.

Taken together, these arguments suggest a positive relation between Learning capacity and RR in firms, through its positive effect on Market and Technological Knowledge as it builds the raw material for recombinant innovation. However, this relationship may be further influenced by the firm's Integrating and Coordinating capacities (therefore refer to section 3.4.2.2.). This leads to the following hypothesis:

H3: A high Learning capacity is positively associated with RR, through Market and Technological Knowledge.

3.4.1.4 Integrating Capacity

Integrating capacity relates to integrating resources into new, innovative resource bundles. Pavlou and El Sawy (2011, p. 247) define the firm's **Integrating capacity** as the firm's "ability to embed new knowledge into the new operational capabilities by creating a shared understanding and collective sense-making" and therewith relate to the firm's "ability to combine [embed and transfer] individual knowledge into the unit's new operational capabilities" (Pavlou and El Sawy, 2011, p. 245). However, while embedding new knowledge by transferring individual knowledge to create collective, organisational knowledge (Nonaka, 1991) is a mandatory process step towards knowledge brokering, it may not be sufficient for new reconfigurations being created (Hawass, 2010). Indeed, the definition, as presented by Pavlou and El Sawy (2011), remains imprecise about how the new operational capabilities are actually being created. The collective and creative activities of bundling, reconfiguring, transforming the resources to build the new operational capabilities are not captured, however needs to be included in the concept.

Bundling thereby refers to "the combining of firm resources to construct or alter [new] capabilities" as described by Sirmon et al. (2007, p. 281), accordingly "resources within the firm's resource portfolio are integrated (i.e., bundled) to create capabilities, with each capability being a unique combination of resources allowing the firm to take specific actions (e.g., marketing, R&D, etc.) that are intended to create value for customers." Hence, the integration of resources into new resource bundles, e.g. operational capabilities, is regarded as a necessary step in exploiting the value creation potential embedded in the firm's resource base (Sirmon et al., 2007), and therefore represents an important aspect of Integrating capacity.

This is basically what is addressed by the '*Transformational/Reconfigurational Capability*' as proposed by Teece (2007, p. 1335), who sees the ability to recombine and to reconfigure assets and organisational structures as a key function to sustained profitability and growth in changing environments. He therefore proposes "achieving semi-continuous asset orchestration and corporate renewal, including the redesign of routines" as an essential task of the firm. In a similar vein, Hawass (2010, p. 410) refers to *'Reconfiguration Capability'* as "the organizational art of combining variant domains of knowledge for the purpose of creating new products and technologies". Although solely focussing on the integration of knowledge-based assets from *external* sources, similar aspects are entailed in the conceptualisation of *'Transformation Capability'* (as part of the RACAP), referring to "a firm's capability to develop and refines the routines that facilitate combining existing knowledge and the newly acquired and assimilated knowledge [e.g. through analogical reasoning]" (Zahra and George, 2002, p. 190). Similar concepts have been proposed in the DC literature spanning *'Integrative Capabilities'* (e.g. Brown and Eisenhardt, 1997, Henderson, 1994), *'Integration Capability'* (e.g. Iansiti and Clark, 1994), or *'Architectural Competence*[3]' (Henderson and Cockburn, 1994), *'Combinative Capacity*[4]' (Kogut and Zander, 1992).

Combining these different aspects outlined above, Integrating capacity in the context of this research is defined as follows:

> **Integrating capacity** *refers to the firm's ability to creatively combine, integrate and transform diverse knowledge-based resources in new ways to construct or alter new operational capabilities for the purpose of developing new innovative products or services.*

Integration, as defined here, thus comprises two aspects and will be achieved by, firstly, transferring individual knowledge to the group (resp. organisation) and therewith creating a shared understandding and collective sense making, that allows, secondly, to establish new linkages across different domains of knowledge, which result in the creation of new resource bundles (e.g. configurations of existing capabilities in order to develop new products and services). "Integration competencies enable the firm to combine the wide-ranging capabilities, information, and perspectives necessary to develop products that succeed in the marketplace" (Fowler et al., 2000, p. 363, going back to Grant, 1996). Integration,

---

[3] Henderson and Cockburn (1994, p. 66) define *Architectural Competence* as "the ability to access new knowledge from outside the boundaries of the organization and the ability to integrate knowledge flexibly across disciplinary (...) boundaries within the organization."

[4] *Combinative Capabilities* refers to "the intersection of the capability of the firm to exploit its knowledge and the unexplored potential of the technology, or what Scherer (1965) originally called the degree of "technological opportunity" (Kogut and Zander, 1992, p. 391)

thus, refers to horizontal communication, as opposed to hierarchical communication (Germain and Dröge, 1997). Thus according to Germain and Dröge (1997, p. 621) "as knowledge is developed within more decentralised or specialised units, managers may increasingly view integration as a necessary mechanism to combat excessive compartmentalisation of that knowledge". Integrating capacity as defined here is closely related to the resource management process step of 'Linking' (Hargadon, 2002) were "Individuals and groups, in this stage, exert analogical thinking efforts to handle current problems by extracting new solutions from previously learned domains of knowledge" (Hawass, p. 410).

Also, empirical evidence is giving support to this assumption, for instance Hendersen and Chockburn (1994) found a firm's *Architectural Competence* to be positively associated with research productivity, as measured by number of patents (Hendersen and Chockburn, 1994). Similar results were revealed by Iansiti and Clark (1994), who found that the firm's Integrating capacity was to be positively related to firm's performance outcome. Both studies give emphasise on the importance of knowledge integration skills (Teece, 2007).

Looking towards the micro-level origins of Integrating capacity, Hendersen and Chockburn (1994) propose two major aspects of integrating competence relevant for appointing it as sources of enduring competitive advantage: (1) the ability to access new knowledge (resources) from outside the boundaries of the organisation and (2) the ability to integrate knowledge (resources) flexible across disciplines within the organisation. The access to new internal and external knowledge is already provided by Sensing and Learning capacities of the firm, accountable for establishing a high valuable resource base. Given this, it depends on the firm's Integrating capacity to exploit that knowledge by developing a shared understanding and interrelating different knowledge areas ("bringing the different parts of the puzzle together") for the purpose of developing new resource configurations.

While diverse processes and mechanisms supporting the integration of resources have been denoted in literature (e.g. Henderson and Clark, 1990, Felin et al., 2012, Hawass, 2010), there still is a lack of consistent definition of its underlying routines. Based on, but at the same time slightly extending the conceptualisation of Integrating capacity as proposed by Pavlou and El Sawy (2011), that captures the *contribution, representation* and *interrelation* of individual input to the entire business unit, this research proposes the following **three underlying routines of Integrating capacity**, its constituting processes and underlying activities, as referred to in the DC literature:

(1) Transforming individual to collective knowledge refers to the processes of *contribution* and *representation* of individual and group knowledge as proposed by Pavlou and El Sawy (2011). *Contribution* relates to disseminating individual knowledge to the group or business unit (Okhuysen and Eisenhardt, 2002), while *representation* refers to the understanding of peoples' tasks and responsibilities, as well as knowledge and skills (Crowston and Kammerer, 1998). This is important "because the reconfiguration of existing operational capabilities requires a collective logic and shared interaction patterns" (Pavlou and El Sawy, 2011, p. 245). As the new knowledge created by Learning is usually held by individuals, it has to be transferred to a collective level (Teece, 1982, Pavlou and El Sawy, 2011, Argote and Ren, 2012). This is especially relevant in the context of this research as firm's capabilities and competences are supra-individual, meaning they do not reside in an individual person but on the organisational level (Pavlou and El Sawy, 2011). Accordingly, both processes *contribution* and *representation* are regarded as essential processes in order to create a shared understanding and collective sense making, and thus a common ground (Argote and Ren, 2012, Weick and Roberts, 1993). Relating to these processes, kindest fundamental knowledge exchange and communication activities can be found in the literature, such as (i) to contribute individual knowledge to the business unit (Okhuysen and Eisenhardt,2002), (ii) to make personal knowledge available to others in the firm (Nonaka, 1991) (iii) to facilitate communication flows, internal networks, technology and personal interaction (Sirmon et al., 2007), (iv) to execute collective, intradepartmental activities (e.g. regular team meetings, knowledge exchange, jour fixe) (Conway, 1995), (v) to encourage informal communication and social relationships between employees (Homburg, 2000), (vi) to interrelate actions to each other to meet changing conditions (Pavlou and El Sawy, 2011), (vii) to establish gatekeeping or boundary-spanning roles who monitors the environment and translates the technical information into a form understandable to the research group (Cohen and Levinthal, 1990).

(2) Interrelating different knowledge domains refers to the processes of *interrelation* of diverse knowledge inputs to the collective system (Grant, 1996) and the *execution* of collective activities (Helfat and Peteraf, 2003), which is suggested to harvest the benefits from analogical reasoning by enabling individuals to spot "hidden similarities" between otherwise isolated domains of knowledge and technologies and successfully transfer their principles to new contexts (Hawass, 2010, Hargadon, 1998). It thus facilitates the creative and effective recombinant search for innovation (Helfat and Peteraf, 2003). Both processes thus enable firms to reconfigure their resources "by gaining access to a wide range of industries, learning the diverse knowledge that resides within these different industries, linking this past knowledge to solutions for current problems, and finally, implementing these new solutions into forms of new products or processes" (Hargadon, 1998, p. 225). This is in line with this research's underlying perception that "the realization of resource recombinations depends upon the flow of competency-related knowledge between competence areas" (Galunic and Rodan, 1998, p. 1195), and thus concerns the intra- and interdepartmental, as well as the interorganisational knowledge exchange. Accordingly, effectively interrelation of different knowledge domains is seen as an essential element of successful reconfiguration, as "reconfiguration requires collective efforts to relink various 'webs of collaborations' across organizational borders to generate creative combination of existing capabilities" (Hawass, 2010, p. 410, with reference to Eisenhardt and Martin, 2000).

Kindest activities underlying these processes can be found in the DC literature, such as (i) to *foster* competence-related knowledge flows among isolated competence areas (e.g. Nonaka and Takeuchi, 1995, Galunic and Rodan, 1998), (ii) to *establish* regular patterns of interactions and information-sharing, that enable the transfer, recombination, and use of knowledge from different functions within the firm (De Luca and Atuahene-Gima, 2007), (iii) to *integrate* different functional areas by building cross-functional teams (Sirmon et al., 2008), (iv) to *foster* interdepartmental information exchange, interaction and connectedness (Menon, 1997, Jaworski and Kohli, 1993), (v) to *exchange* and *adopt* knowledge and technologies between individuals working in various industry sectors, organisations and domains to foster innovation (Lerdahl, 1999), (vi) to *move* people possessing tacit knowledge to different areas in the firm and thereby to *allow* socialisation to inspire new combination.

(3) Reconfiguration and refinement lastly capture the internal integration and transformation processes. Following the definition by Galunic and Rodan (1998, p. 1195): "Resource recombination concerns itself with how the knowledge embedded within a competence may have to be untangled, altered, and integrated with other knowledge bases to create novel business concepts and/or competencies." Accordingly the routine of reconfiguration and refinement lies in the heart of RR. It captures the processes of *capability transformation* and *capability evolution* as proposed by Lavie (2006). Both are processes undertaken in order to change the firm's current capabilities and are concerned with the actual reconfiguration and refinement of its current resources.

Capability transformation refers to modification and improvement of existing capabilities through the integration of new knowledge domains to existing ones (reconfiguration), thus it aims "to inject and incorporate new domains of knowledge to the existing organizational system" (Hawass, 2010, p. 412). The transformed capability hence is the outcome of combining internal knowledge with new externally acquired knowledge and comprises the modification and improvement of existing capabilities through the integration of new knowledge domains to existing ones (Hawass, 2010). Capability transformation thus basically depends on the firm's ability to integrate the newly acquired knowledge to form new resource bundles.

Capability evolution instead refers to the integration and synthesis of the existing resources in new ways (refinement). In other words, it refines existing capabilities "by creatively reconnecting existing organizational systems" (Hawass, 2010, p. 412) with the aims to detect and view "potentially new interrelationships among its existing domains of knowledge" (Hawass, 2010, p. 412). This is in line with Galunic and Rodan (1998, p. 1195) stating that RR may be generated through "the synthesis of existing competencies" or through "reconfiguring the ways in which competencies are linked to jointly achieve some broader purpose". Capability evolution thus predominantly depends "on the firm's internal sources of knowledge and the extent to which it views potentially new interrelationships among its existing domains of knowledge" (Hawass, p. 412). Focusing on the modification and extension of existing capabilities the process of capability evolution is directed towards exploitation (March, 1991).

Both *capability evolution* and *transformation* relate to innovative problemsolving (Iansiti and Clark, 1994), brainstorming (Pisano, 1994), and creative new thinking (Henderson and Cockburn, 1994), and also here kindest activities can be found in the DC literature, such as (i) to *creatively combine* and *connect* a firm's current domains of knowledge with new other domains located elsewhere in the industry (Hawass, 2010), (ii) to *integrate* capabilities into comprehensive sets of value-creating organisational skills (Hamel and Prahalad, 1990), (iii) to *identify* two apparently incongruous sets of information and then combine them to arrive at a new schema (Zahra and George, 2002), (iv) to *recognise* non-obvious similarities through building analogies to previously known problems (Hawass, 2010, Hargadon, 1998), (v) to *create* innovative solutions by *linking* past experiences to the current situations they face (Sirmon et al., 2008), (v) to *adapt* and *interconnect* knowledge and technologies from different industry sectors and knowledge domains (Lerdahl, 1999).

Hypotheses Development

The conceptualisation of Integrating capacity allows hypotheses to be drawn concerning its effects towards RR. As delineated above, the firm's efforts on developing a high Integrating capacity is intended to result in integrating resources into new resource bundles. This is consistent with the view that in its heart reconfiguration bears on integrating new resources, knowledge, and assets and the reconfiguration of existing resources (Pavlou and El Sawy, 2011, Galunic and Eisenhardt, 2001).

Hence, not surprisingly the firm's Integrating capacity is proposed to facilitate RR in firms through its three basic routines. First, *transforming individual to collective knowledge* through *representation* and *contribution* of individual and group knowledge helps to create a shared understanding and collective sense making. Second, because RR depends upon competency-related knowledge flows between competence areas (Galunic and Rodan, 1998), *interrelating different knowledge domains* allows firms, once through the *interrelation* of various knowledge areas and at the same time through the *execution* of collective activities, to discover untapped linkages between otherwise isolated knowledge areas and technologies, and thus facilitates the creative and effective search for recombinant innovation. Third, *reconfiguration and refinement* of its resources allow firms to actually change current capabilities, both through the reconfiguration of existing capabilities with new, external knowledge (capability transformation) or the refinement and synthesis of the existing capabilities and resources in new ways (capability evolution), in order to develop new, synergetic RRs.

Taken together, these theoretical arguments suggest a positive relationship between a firm's Integrating capacity and RR in firms. Accordingly, it can be proposed that the higher the firm's Integrating capacity, the more likely it is for firms to be able to realise novel RRs. Therefore, this research develops the following hypothesis:

H4: A high Integrating capacity is positively associated with RR.

3.4.1.5 Coordinating Capacity

Coordinating capacity refers to the firm's ability to orchestrate and deploy tasks, resources, and activities in new operational capabilities in order to implement new, innovative products or services (RRs) in the market.

This definition goes back to Pavlou and El Sawy (2011) and is based on the assumption that any new synergetic RR to be realised and implemented in the market, requires a change of existing operational routines and therefore necessitates an effective coordination of tasks and resources, as well as the synchronisation of activities (Iansiti and Clark, 1994, Helfat and Peteraf, 2003, Pavlou an El Sawy, 2011). The firm's Coordinating capacity thus enables reconfiguration being put into place "by administering tasks, activities, and resources to deploy the reconfigured operational capabilities" (Pavlou and El Sawy, 2011). This is in line with Teece et al. (1997), who argue "[the firm's dynamic] capability is embedded in distinct ways of coordinating" (p. 519).

Coordinating capacity is regarded as a necessary capacity to exploit the value creation potential of the resources by implementing and exploiting new products and services. Hence, the conceptualisation of Coordinating capacity is closely related to the resource management process step *'Leveraging'* as proposed by Sirmon et al. (2007), which focuses on the exploitation of market opportunities. Following Sirmon et al. (2007, p. 283), "effective leveraging is important, in that even when a firm owns or controls resources and has effectively bundled them to develop capabilities with value-creating potential, the firm is unlikely to realise value creation unless it effectively leverages/uses those capabilities in the marketplace". The implementations of new combinations in the market goes along with the resource management process step *'Building'* as described by Hargadon (2002, p. 69), which refers to "the activities that individuals and teams use to connect new networks around those new combinations in order to ensure their success." Another related concept is the *'Exploitation capability'* suggested as sub-component of the realised absorptive capacity (RACAP), referring to "the routines that allow firms to refine, extend, and leverage existing competences or to create new ones by incorporating acquired and transformed knowledge into its operations" (Zahra and George, 2002, p. 190). Therefore, the results of those systematic exploitation routines are the sustainable creation of new goods, systems, processes, knowledge, or new organisational forms (Spender, 1996). Accordingly, a firm's Coordinating capacity is an essential capacity for value realisation supporting the leveraging process as it enables the configurations to be coordinated and deployed in appropriate ways to create value for the customers (e.g. Pavlou and El Sawy, 2011, Sirmon et al., 2007).

Likewise other DCs, Coordinating capacity is suggested to be constituted by specific organisational routines. Hence, a variety of established processes used by firms to systematically build or support a firm's Coordinating capacity can be found in the literature. Pavlou and El Sawy (2011, p. 246) refer to four **basic routines underlying the Coordinating capacity**, comprising (1) assigning resources to tasks (Helfat and Peteraf, 2003) (2) appointing the right person to the right task (Eisenhardt and Brown, 1999), (3) identifying complementarities and synergies among tasks and resources (Eisenhardt and Galunic, 2000), and (4) orchestrating collective activities (Henderson, 1994). Extending the conceptualisation by Pavlou and El Sawy (2011) and aligning it with the three leveraging routines, *mobilising, coordinating* and *deploying,* as presented by Sirmon et al. (2007), a more detailed description of the routines underlying the firm's Coordinating capacity is presented. Coordinating capacity, thus, can be described by the following three basic routines and corporate-level processes that form the capacity, and its underlying activities:

(1) **Allocating and Mobilising Resources** describes the routine, resp. processes of identifying the resources, capabilities, and skills needed to design the capability configurations necessary to exploit opportunities in the market (Sirmon et al., 2007). Thus it helps to provide a plan or vision of those resources, capabilities, and skills needed to form the requisite capability configurations (Sirmon et al., 2010) and comprises activities such as: (i) to *understand* the market and customer needs to guide the design of capability configurations (Sirmon et al., 2007), (ii) to *recognise, assemble,* and *allocate* resources (Collis, 1994, Pavlou and El Sawy, 2011), (iii) to *appoint* the right person to the right task (Eisenhardt and Brown, 1999, Pavlou and El Sawy, 2011), (iv) to *assign* resources to tasks (Helfat and Peteraf, 2003, Pavlou and El Sawy, 2011), and (v) to continuously *orchestrate* assets, involving the alignment, coalignment, realignment, and redeployment of assets (Teece, 2007). The effective allocation of resources, thus, is seen as an essential element of successful reconfiguration, as it increases firm's flexibility by enabling them to appoint the right people to the right tasks (Eisenhardt and Brown, 1999, Pavlou and El Sawy, 2011),

(2) **Coordinating and Orchestrating Resources** describes the routine resp. processes of coordination and orchestration of identified resources, capabilities and skills for being deployed into effective yet efficient capability configurations (Sirmon et al., 2007, 2010). It involves activities such as: (i) to *possess* knowledge about the value of individual capabilities, resources and skills (Sirmon et al., 2007), (ii) to *orchestrate* individual tasks and collective activities (Henderson, 1994, Pavlou and El Sawy, 2011), (iii) to *synchronise* tasks and activities (Helfat and Peteraf, 2003), (iv) to *identify* complementarities and synergies among tasks and resources (Eisenhardt and Galunic, 2000, Pavlou and El Sawy, 2011), and (v) to *redeploy* and *reconfigure* resources (Capron et al., 1998). The efficient coordination and orchestration of resources is regarded as essential element for reconfiguration as it helps to manage the resources in efficient and appropriate manners.

(3) **Implementing and Deploying new configurations** lastly describes the routine resp. processes of the physical implementation and deployment of new configurations in the market to leverage and exploit resource opportunities formed by the prior activities and sub-processes (Sirmon et al., 2007, 2010). It involves activities such as: (i) to *implement* and *deploy* the reconfigured operational capabilities (Pavlou and El Sawy, 2011), (ii) to *leverage* resources and knowledge to *exploit* new product ideas (Teece, 2007), (iii) to *realise* the leveraging strategy to create value for customers (Alvarez and Barney, 2002), (iv) to *recombine* and *(re)deploy* resources in reconfigured combinations (Teece, 2007). The physical implementation and deployment of resources in new configurations is regarded as necessary element for reconfiguration as it finally puts them into operation.

Hypotheses Development

Given the conceptualisation of Coordinating capacity, effective coordination results in the leveraging of existing and new resources by implementing them in new effective configurations (Pavlou and El Sawy, 2011). Hence, Coordinating capacity is proposed to facilitate RRs to be successfully implemented in the market through its three basic routines. First, it enables firms to effectively allocate and mobilise resources (Collis, 1994, Pavlou and El Sawy, 2011) by identifying and assigning the resources, capabilities, and skills needed to design the capability configurations necessary in order to exploit opportunities in the market opportunities (Sirmon et al., 2007). Second, through a systematic coordination and orchestration of tasks and resources (Henderson, 1994, Pavlou and El Sawy, 2011), as well as the synchronisation of activities (Helfat and Peteraf, 2003), it enables the reconfiguration and redeployment of resources in the form of new RRs (Capron et al., 1998). Third, Coordinating capacity further helps to efficiently leverage the firm's resources and knowledge by deploying them in reconfigured operational capabilities that allow to implement and exploit new product ideas. Overall, Coordinating capacity is regarded as essential element for reconfiguration as resources must be coordinated and implemented in appropriate ways to create value. Thus, Coordinating capacity helps to implement and to deploy RR in firms through orchestrating individual tasks and activities.

Summarising the above arguments, this research suggests a positive relation between Coordinating capacity and RR to be in place, as the firm's Coordinating capacity helps to exploit the value creation potential of the resources by implementing and exploiting new products in the market. These arguments lead to the following hypothesis:

H5: A high Coordinating capacity is positively associated with RR.

3.4.1.6 Interrelationships between Sensing, Learning, Integrating and Coordinating Capacity

While the proposed framework (refer to Figure 3.2 in section 3.4.1) presents the four DCs as interacting in a sequential logic to reconfigure existing operational capabilities, it only represents a simplified image of reality where interrelations exist between Sensing, Learning, Integrating and Coordinating capacity. Thus, although the four DCs are distinct capacities, there are reciprocal relationships among these capabilities, as already partially theorised in the description of the proposed DCs. This implies that the four capacities are not mutually exclusive, in fact high levels of capacities can coexist, leading to potential interdependencies (Helfat et al. 2007).

While both, Sensing and Learning capacity are regarded as distinct capacities, in line with Pavlou and El Sawy (2011), a reciprocal two-way relationship between Sensing and Learning is proposed to be existent. While Sensing focuses on the identification of new opportunities in the external environment, Learning focuses on internal opportunity generation. Therefore, a strong Sensing capacity is suggested to facilitate the firm's ability to address external opportunities through learning new and utilising existing knowledge (Pavlou and El Sawy, 2011). Moreover, a high Sensing capacity is suggested to further comprise potential constraints enforced by the scarcity of internal resources as it enhances the identification of opportunities for external resources acquisition (Katila and Ahuja, 2002, Lichtenthaler, 2012). On the other side, the firm's Learning capacity may also enhance the firm's ability to detect new opportunities in the environment, this is suggested as prior knowledge facilitates the detection of new knowledge (Cohen and Levinthal, 1990, Zahra and George, 2002).

Additionally, a high Sensing capacity determines the innovation opportunities that may be seized by integrating resources in new ways to construct or alter new operational capabilities, therefore a high Sensing capacity is proposed to also positively affect the firm's Integrating capacity (Helfat et al., 2007, Lichtenthaler, 2012).

In a similar vein, Integrating and Coordinating capacity are conceptualised as distinct capacities, whereby Integrating focuses on interrelating different knowledge areas and building a shared understanding (Galunic and Eisenhardt, 2001), while Coordinating focuses on orchestrating tasks and activities for deploying new RRs (Pavlou and El Sawy, 2011). Nonetheless, a strong Integrating capacity is proposed to positively affect the firm's Coordinating capacity, as coordination is facilitated through a shared understanding and collective sense making (Galunic and Eisenhardt, 2001, Pavlou and El Sawy, 2011).

Besides Integrating, also the firms Learning capacity is suggested to positively affect the firm's Coordinating capacity, as 'Learning' not only contributes towards developing new knowledge, but also adds to comprehensive knowledge about the internal resources and capabilities available for the firm (Hargadon, 1998), which is an essential condition for effective coordination and allocation of resources, tasks and activities (Sirmon et al., 2010).

Notably, even though the four DCs are theoretical distinct capacities with each single capacity offering a unique component to the overall DC (Pavlou and El Sawy, 2011), there are reciprocal relationships among these capabilities, and these interrelations are a constituent part of the conceptual model and hence need to be considered in the measurement model.

3.4.1.7 The Dynamic Capability Framework

Summarising the research findings so far, this section presents the DC framework and gives an overview of the proposed set of DCs as discussed and re-conceptualised in the previous sections. The DC framework builds the conceptual basis for this research. In this chapter one major aim was to unpack the microfoundations of DCs and to develop a general understanding of the construct of DC and its underlying dimensions. The study has gone some way towards enhancing our understanding of the primary components underlying each capacity. These findings, in turn, allow in a subsequent research step to explore how these components interact with their environment and what role they have in value creation in firms, and hence will shed light on how differences in routines and capabilities may contribute towards explaining heterogeneity in innovation performance among firms.

Table 3.1 presents the DC framework and gives an overview of (1) the *definitions* of the four DCs relevant for RR, (2) the *related step in the resource management process* by Hargadon (2002), (3) the *core activities* related to each capacity, as well as (4) the *underlying routines* and *processes* constituting each capacity. The framework allows a synthesis of most of the processes and routines found in the DC literature and allows their categorisation under each capacity (Pavlou and El Sawy, 2011). This ensures that the framework presented is closely linked to the processes and routines found in the DC literature.

Table 3.1 Dynamic Capability Framework

Sensing Capacity: Sensing new opportunities in the environment

Definition: The ability to spot, interpret and pursue opportunities in the internal and external environment. (Pavlou and El Sawy, 2011)

Related Resource Management Process Step: Access knowledge (Hargadon, 2002)

Core Activities: Scanning, Identifying & Recognising

Basic Routines and Processes:
(1) Generating Market Intelligence
  • Generating market intelligence (Galunic and Rodan, 1998);
  • Identifying market opportunities (Day, 1994)
  • Being responsive to market trends (Amit and Schoemaker, 1993)
(2) Generating Customer and Competitor Intelligence
  • Monitoring customer needs (Teece, 2007, Pavlou and El Sawy, 2011)
  • Observing competitor activity (Teece, 2007)
  • Allocating resources to search and discovery activities (Teece, 2007)
(3) Generating Technological Intelligence
  • Identifying technological developments and opportunities (Teece, 2007)
  • Gathering new technical information, data, statistics (Teece 2007)
  • Taping developments in exogenous science (Teece, 2007)

Intention: to raise the potential to identify new market opportunities for configuration

---

Integrating Capacity: Integrating resources into new innovative resource bundles

Definition: The ability to creatively combine, integrate and transform diverse knowledge based resources in new ways to construct or alter new operational capabilities for the purpose of developing new innovative products or services

Related Resource Management Process Step: Linking (Hargadon, 2002)

Core Activities: Communicate, Integrate & Bundle

Basic Routines and Processes:
(1) Transforming individual to collective knowledge
  • *Contribution* of individual knowledge to the unit (Okhuysen and Eisenhardt,2002)
  • *Representation* of individual and group knowledge (Crowston and Kammerer, 1998)
(2) Interrelating different knowledge domains
  • *Interrelation* of diverse knowledge inputs to the collective system (Grant,1996)
  • *Execution* of collective activities (Helfat and Peteraf, 2003).
(3) Reconfiguration and refinement of resources
  • *Capability evolution*: refinement and synthesis of existing capabilities in new ways (Lavie, 2006, Hawass, 2010, Galunic and Rodan, 1998)
  • *Capability transformation*: reconfiguration of existing capabilities with new knowledge (Lavie, 2006, Hawass, 2010, Galunic and Rodan, 1998)

Intention: to exploit the value creation potential of the resources by creating new innovative products and services

---

Learning Capacity: Absorptive Capacity & Knowledge Creation

Definition: The ability to assimilate, transform and create (new) knowledge to revamp the existing resource base with new knowledge, created internally or obtained externally (Pavlou and El Sawy, 2011)

Related Resource Management Process Step: Bridging and learning (Hargadon, 2002)

Core Activities: Acquiring, Transforming & Creating new knowledge

Basic Routines and Processes:
(1) Acquiring and Assimilating external knowledge
  = External Knowledge Absorption (Cohen and Levinthal, 1990)
  • *Knowledge acquisition* of external resources (Cohen and Levinthal, 1990)
  • *Knowledge assimilation* of external resources (Eisenhardt and Martin, 2000)
(2) Creating new internal knowledge
  = Internal knowledge creation (Rothaermel and Hess, 2007)
  • *Articulation*, converting tacit knowledge into explicit knowledge (Nonaka, 1991)
  • *Internalisation*, using the explicit knowledge to extend tacit knowledge (Nonaka, 1991)
(3) Accumulating and Retaining internal knowledge
  = Internal Knowledge Management and Retention
  • *Knowledge codification* and maintenance (Zollo and Winter, 2002)
  • *Knowledge 'unlearning'* (Leonard-Barton, 1992, 1995)

Intention: to build a rich and diverse resource base, the "raw" material for innovation

---

Coordinating Capacity: Coordinating and deploying tasks and allocating resources

Definition: The ability to orchestrate and deploy tasks, resources, and activities in the new operational capabilities in order to develop new, innovative products or services (based on Pavlou and El Sawy, 2011)

Related Resource Management Process Step: Building (Hargadon, 2002)

Core Activities: Allocate, Coordinate & Implement

Basic Routines and Processes:
(1) Allocating and Mobilising Resources
  • *understand* market needs for designing capability configurations (Sirmon et al., 2007)
  • *recognise, assemble,* and *allocate* resources (Collis, 1994, Pavlou and El Sawy, 2011)
(2) Coordinating and Orchestrating Resources
  • *possess* knowledge about capabilities, resources and skills (Sirmon et al., 2007)
  • *orchestrate* individual tasks and collective activities (Henderson, 1994, Pavlou, 2011)
(3) Implementing and Deploying new configurations
  • *implement and deploy* the reconfigured operational capabilities (Pavlou and El Sawy, 2011)
  • *leverage* resources and knowledge to *exploit* new product ideas (Teece, 2007)
  • *realise* the leveraging strategy to create value for customers (Alvarez and Barney, 2002)
  • *recombine and (re)deploy* resources in reconfigured combinations (Teece, 2007)

Intention: to exploit the value creation potential of the resources by implementing and exploiting new products and services

The framework shows that Sensing, Learning, Integrating and Coordinating Capacities are conceptualised as distinct sub-components of the firm's overall DC, all of them have different functions in managing a firm's RR activities over time (Pavlou and El Sawy, 2011). While the proposed set of DCs are neither intended to be exhaustive, nor sufficient for reconfiguration to take place, they are considered as being essential capacities in the process of RR (Pavlou and El Sawy, 2011).

In line with Pavlou and El Sawy (2011) this research suggests that the four DCs—Sensing capacity, Learning capacity, Integrating capacity and Coordinating capacity—intersect with each other and all together build a firm's overall DC. The framework is based on the perception that regards the overall DC of the firm as a multidimensional construct, formed by four very different sub-dimension. This is in accordance with Brown and Eisenhardt (1997), who consider the firm's overall DC as complex combinations of simpler routines (Pavlou and El Sawy, 2011). However, when operationalising the DC construct, the few empirical studies that exist in the DC literature, predominantly applied composite (aggregate) approaches to investigate the firm's DC (e.g. Pavlou and El Sawy, 2011, Madsen, 2010) and hence tend to lump all sub-capabilities together under the 'umbrella of an overall DC'. Therefore, prior works often sustained a loss of explanatory power.

Thus, in distinction to previous research rather than choosing an aggregate approach, this research purposefully distinguishes between the subset of the four different DC, which in turn are suggested to have different effects and 'working modes' towards the resource base and RR. Accordingly, the DC framework established here with its differentiation of the four related but distinct DCs, allows in a subsequent research step to have a more detailed look at the role and effects of each specific DC. Hence, the DC framework presented assists in building a deeper understanding of the role of DCs in the process of RR and allows examining the relationships between the DCs, the resource base and RR in firms, which have been highlighted as an important research area in prior research (Ambrosini and Bowman, 2009, Helfat et al., 2007, Wiklund and Shepherd, 2009).

3.4.2 Role of Dynamic Capabilities in the Process of Resource Value Creation

The research findings so far suggest that DCs can be a source of value creation as it allows superior 'Sensing', 'Learning', 'Integrating' and 'Coordinating' of resources. Moreover, findings suggest that the higher the firm's DCs—its **Sensing, Learning, Integrating** and **Coordinating capacities**—the higher the amount of new RRs. Accordingly, firms that have developed higher Sensing, Learning, Integrating and Coordinating capacities, are more likely to successfully develop new RRs. However, it was not yet clearly specified what the specific role of DCs is in this process of resource value creation.

Based on the DC framework and the conceptualisation of the four DCs, this chapter elaborates on their specific role in the process of resource value creation. Doing so, the following chapter aims to specify the above hypotheses H2, H3, H4, and H5, in order to explain the interrelations between DCs and RR in firms in more detail, clarifying the role of DCs in the development of RRs in firms. Following Ambrosini and Bowman's (2009) call for research investigating how DCs operate towards performance outcomes, the aim is to specify the role and effect of each single capacity in relation to their relevant performance and contextual factors. Therewith, this chapter aims to clarify the linkage between building the resource base for RR (potential value) and new RRs in firms (realised value).

3.4.2.1 Sensing and Learning as Potential Building Dynamic Capabilities

Following Sanchez and Heene (1997, p. 307) competence building is "any process by which a firm achieves qualitative changes in its existing stocks of assets", while competence leveraging is "a process through which a firm applies its existing competences to current or new market opportunities in ways that do not require qualitative changes in the firm's assets or capabilities."

Taking up these conceptual thoughts, this research assumes that the firm's Sensing and Learning capacities work on towards **building the potential value** of a firm's resources (in terms of its quality and diversity) by continuously renewing and reconfiguring the firm's resource base with new resources and knowledge. Accordingly, it is especially the Sensing and Learning capacity that "enables the firm continually to refresh the resource stock so that the firm can continue to 'hit a moving target'" (Ambrosini and Bowman 2009, p. 48). Thus, a firm's Sensing capacity and Learning capacity is suggested to contribute to build a rich and diverse resource base, the "raw material" for RR. More specifically, Sensing and Learning capacities are positively related to **resource diversity**, leading to a higher accumulation of new Market and Technological Knowledge (*knowledge breadth*). Sensing and Learning capacity are also positively related to **resource quality**, leading to a higher Market and Technological Knowledge depth. In other words, a high Sensing and Learning capacity is positively associated with a high diversity and quality of the resource base in regard to Market and Technological Knowledge (H2a/H3a), which in term is positively associated with RR in firms (H2c/H3c).

More precisely, while a high Sensing capacity is positively associated with a high diversity and quality of the Market Knowledge, as it is leading to a higher Market Knowledge breadth and depth, a high Learning capacity is positively related to both, broad and deep Market <u>and</u> Technological Knowledge. Thus, Sensing and Learning capacity are positively related to a high potential value of the resource base for RR.

➜ Mediating Role of the Resource Base between Sensing and Learning capacity and RR
Viewed differently, Sensing and Learning capacity leads to increased performance in regard to RR. However, as not all firms that have developed high DCs are subsequently high performing in achieving RR, this relation is expected to be fully and positively mediated by Market and Technological Knowledge. Rather more it is theorised that "some other variable is needed to explain the reason for the inconsistent relationship between IV [independent variable] and DV [dependent variable]" (Gaskin, 2012d). It is suggested that Market and Technological Knowledge act as such a mediator and are regarded as key variables that fully and positively mediates the relationship between Sensing and Learning capacity and RR. The relationship between Sensing and Learning capabilities and RRs in firms is fully mediated by the (resulting) quality of resource base (the potential value of the resource base). Hence H2 and H3 can be formulated more precisely through the following hypotheses:

H2a/H2b/H2c: The effect of Sensing capacity on RR <u>is positively and fully mediated</u> by the diversity and quality of Market and Technology Knowledge.

H3a/H3b/H3c: The effect of Learning capacity on RR <u>is positively and fully mediated</u> by the diversity and quality of Market and Technology Knowledge.

3.4.2.2 Integrating and Coordinating as Value Realising Dynamic Capabilities
On the other hand, it is expected that the Integrating and Coordinating capacity work towards *exploiting the value potential* of the resource base by transforming it into new RRs and thus help to realise the value potential through RRs. The underlying assumption is, that Sensing and Learning *per se* cannot ensure superior innovation performance (Lichtenthaler, 2012, Helfat and Peteraf, 2009). Only when firms possess the necessary capabilities to integrate and reconfigure the resources into new innovative resource bundles, and to coordinate and deploy tasks, activities and resources in these newly developed resource bundles, value

is created. Hence, while Sensing and Learning provide the basis, the resource leveraging process is established through a firm's Integrating and Coordinating capacities.

Thus, the Integrating and Coordinating capabilities help to *realise* the value creation potential of the resource base through the development of new RRs. In other words, given the same assessment of the potential value of a firm's resources base for RR (in terms of its quality and diversity), firms that have developed a higher Integrating and Coordinating capacity are more likely to develop new RRs, and therefore are able to realise more of the value potential of the resource base than firms that have fewer capacities.

→ **Moderating Role of Integrating and Coordinating capacity between Resource Base and RR**

In other words, Integrating and Coordinating capacities moderate the relationship between Technological Knowledge (breadth and depth) and RR. Said differently, Integrating and Coordinating capacity strengthens the positive relationship between Technological Knowledge and RR. A high Integrating and Coordinating capacity is positively associated with RR in firms as it is moderating the relationship between the resource base and RR in firms. The effect of the knowledge base on RR is moderated by the Integrating and Coordinating capacity, in such a way that a low Integrating and Coordinating capacity decreases the amount of new RR while a high Integrating and Coordinating capacity increases the amount of new RR in firms. The higher a firm's Integrating and Coordinating capacity, the more positive the relationship between (i) the resource base and (ii) the amount of new RRs in firms. In other words Integrating and Coordinating capacity (positively) moderates the positive effect of Technological Knowledge on RR, such that if firms have low Integrating and Coordinating capacity the effect is weaker. Hence, it is suggested that both these effects will affect the ability to develop new RRs.

H4a: A high Integrating capacity is positively associated with RR in firms as it is moderating the relationship between Technological Knowledge and RR in firms.

H5a: A high Coordinating capacity is positively associated with RR in firms as it is moderating the relationship between Technological Knowledge and RR in firms.

3.4.2.3 Potential Building and Value Realising Dynamic Capabilities and their Role in the Process of Resource Value Creation

Summarising the above findings, regarding their relationship to the performance outcome of new RRs, it is assumed that two different types of DCs can be distinguished: **Potential Building** and **Value Realising DCs**[5], both components have different effects and "working modes" towards RR in firms:

- The Sensing and Learning capacities are necessary for building the potential value of the resources for RR, and thus can be referred to as *Potential Building DCs*. They are directed towards *exploration* of new opportunities in the environment and the building of a rich and diverse resource base.
- The Integrating and Coordinating capacities are necessary for the value potential of the resource base to become realised by creating, implementing and exploiting new innovative RRs, and thus can be referred to as *Value Realising DCs*. They are directed towards the *exploitation* of the existing resources through the development of new RRs.

Figure 3.4 gives a graphical illustration of the proposed causal relationships as outlined above.

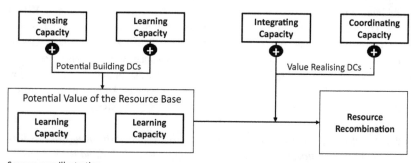

Source: own illustration

Figure 3.4 Potential Building and Value Realising Dynamic Capabilities.

---

[5] This differentiation is related to Zahra and George's (2006) re-conceptualisation of the ACAP construct, just as the ACAP construct can be distinguished in two sub-sets, namely PACAP and RACAP, the DC construct can be differentiated into two main types of DCs in regard to RR.

Taken as a whole, this research proposes that the higher the firm's DCs—its **Sensing, Learning, Integrating and Coordinating capacities**—the better the firm will be at *building* and *exploiting* the value potential of the resource base, resulting in a higher amount of new RRs. The detailed view showed that firms having developed higher Sensing and Learning capacities are more likely to *build* the potential value of the resource base, while firm's having developed higher Integrating and Coordinating capacities are more likely to *exploit* and *thus realise* the potential value of their resource base, and therefore are more likely to develop new RRs successfully.

3.5 Framework Conditions for the Development of Dynamic Capabilities

Having specified the DC framework allows in a subsequent step to have a closer look on the framework conditions for the development of DCs, in order to examine how DCs can be enhanced by identifying their antecedents. The underlying assumption is, that while DCs reside in the organisational processes and routines (as described in depth and detail in the DC framework presented previously), they are supposed to being impacted by the organisational framework conditions, which the organisation has created to manage its business activities (Teece, 2007). Hence, it is suggested that the evolution of DCs is influenced by a range of organisational factors. Based on these preliminary considerations, the following section specifies Proposition 3 and further elaborates the framework conditions for the development of DCs.

Proposition 3: Entrepreneurial Orientation and Networking Orientation act as antecedents for the development of a firm's DCs.

Current literature shows growing interest in investigating the antecedents that are suggested to influence the development of DCs (e.g. Madsen, 2010, Hawass, 2010). Accordingly, a wide range of different antecedents residing at individual-, firm- and network-levels (Rothaermel and Hess, 2007) have been proposed in the literature and are being discussed as relevant determinants for the development of DCs (e.g. Teece, 2007, Zollo and Winter, 2002, Eisenhardt and Martin, 2000). However, up to today only scarce empirical research exists exploring the conditions and processes inside and outside the organisations that lead to DCs (Hawass, 2010). Still it is a quite unspecific picture that has been drawn, concentrating on multiple factors of various different levels and from different perspectives. Hence, far too little attention has been paid to empirical investigate of the influencing factors for the development of DCs (Ambrosini and Bowman, 2009), especially those that might reside in the underlying strategic orientation of the firm.

To address this research gap, the following section set out to examine the determinants of the firm's DC from a multilevel organisational perspective. While this research agrees with previous research suggesting that antecedents to DCs can be found at individual-, firm-, and network-levels (e.g. Zollo and Winter, 2002, Rothearmel and Hess, 2007, Eisenhardt and Martin, 2000, Hawass, 2010), and that firms can draw on antecedents across different levels to build DCs (Rothearmel and Hess, 2007), this study refrains from investigating the individual-level antecedents of DCs. Instead, the following chapter specifies the framework conditions for the development of DCs, looking at **Entrepreneurial Orientation** and **Networking Orientation** identified as important antecedents for DCs, and thus focussing on firm- and network-level antecedents. While a wide range of literature exists concerning firm's strategic orientation, based on a thorough review of literature from the strategic management and entrepreneurship spectrum, Entrepreneurial Orientation and Networking Orientation could be identified as the two antecedents relevant for this study.

By focusing on Entrepreneurial Orientation and Networking Orientation as antecedents of DCs, this study responds to prior calls for research that explicates firm-related determinants that may explain the development of DCs (Zahra and Wiklund, 2002). Therewith findings add to theory by improving the understanding of the antecedents necessary for DCs and respectively RR in firms to occur.

3.5.1 Entrepreneurial Orientation

Entrepreneurial Orientation (EO) refers to a firm's strategic orientation, which characterises the firm's entrepreneurial behaviour by capturing specific entrepreneurial aspects of decision-making styles, methods, and practices (Lumpkin and Dess, 1996, Wiklund and Shepherd, 2003), and commonly is regarded as a combination of *Innovativeness*, *Proactiveness*, and *Risk-taking* (e.g., Miller, 1983, Covin and Selvin, 1989, Zahra 1991, Wiklund, 1999, Baker and Sinkula, 2009). This research adopts Lunpkin and Dess's (1996) definitions of the three dimensions of EO:

First, *Innovativeness* refers to the firm's tendency or willingness to engage in and support new ideas, novelty, experimentation, and creative processes, which may result in new products, services, or technological processes (Lumkin and Dess, 1996). Thus, it is regarded to "reflect a basic willingness to diverge from the status quo and embrace new ideas" (Baker and Sinkula, 2009, p. 447). Second,

Proactiveness refers to the firm's attitude towards taking initiatives by anticipating and pursuing new opportunities and by participating in emerging markets (Lumkin and Dess, 1996). Third, *Risk-taking* is reflected by "the willingness of managers to commit a large percentage of a firm's resources to new projects and to incur heavy debt in the pursuit of opportunity" (Baker and Sinkula, 2009, p. 447, referring to Lumpkin and Dess 1996).

There is a consistent claim in literature that management practice and entrepreneurial activities can facilitate RRs in firms (e.g. Brown and Eisenhardt, 1998, Eisenhardt and Martin, 2000, Zahra and Wiklund, 2002, Wiklund et al., 2002). Besides DCs, hence, the firm's EO is regarded as important determinant for the creation of new combinations of resources (Penrose, 1959, Brown and Eisenhardt, 1998, Eisenhardt and Martin, 2000, Zahra and Wiklund, 2002, Madsen, 2010), as a result "this provides a clear and close association between entrepreneurship and resource-based theory, especially dynamic capabilities" (Madsen, 2010, p. 233).

Theory and empirical findings reveal that entrepreneurial flexibility of combining existing resources in new ways in order to find innovative RRs, will consequently lead to new products and services in the market (Wiklund et al., 2002). Thus entrepreneurial management practices are proposed to result in organisational change activities, as they are leading to an increased understanding of the establishment and utilisation of firm's resources (Madsen, 2010). Consistent with this view, a variety of studies gave evidence to the perceived role of EO as key factor for improving a firm's performance outcomes (Covin and Slevin, 1989, Lumpkin and Dess, 1996, Wiklund, 1999, Madsen, 2007, 2010). Investigating the effect of entrepreneurship in management practice on RR in firms, Wiklund et al. (2002) confirmed a positive, direct effect of entrepreneurial management practices (specifically entrepreneurial culture, growth orientation, and strategic orientation, all representing over-arching aspects of EO) on RR, however their findings also revealed entrepreneurial management practices to only have modest explanatory power with respect to RR (Adj. $R^2 = 0.16$, resp. 0.17) (Wiklund et al., 2002, p. 1515). Following Wiklund et al. (2002, p. 1510), one explanation could be that "the specific vehicles through which a vision and culture of entrepreneurship are translated into effective resource recombination" have not been investigated, neither been measured empirically.

Interestingly, while a vast variety of studies assume a direct linkage between EO and RR, resp. firm performance, there is a scarcity of literature investigating the association between EO and DCs (e.g. Madsen, 2010). Those theoretical works that were found suggest a positive relationship (Madsen, 2010), while empirical evidence is still lacking. Assuming that both concepts EO and DCs are somewhat attached to how the firm builds and exploits internal and external resources and thus creates new RRs, the aim of this research is to elaborate the relationship between EO, DCs and RR.

Based on the original thoughts by Madsen (2010) this research assumes that while the EO primarily reflects the *willingness* or *attitude* of the firm concerning the engagement in entrepreneurial behaviour (Wiklund, 1998), the *DCs* refer to the *activities* itself which build, develop, integrate and reconfigure internal and external resources. Accordingly, EO and DCs emerge at different levels. While EO refers to "a firm's willingness to be innovative, proactive and engage in risk-taking behaviour in order to achieve its strategic goal" (Madsen, 2010, p. 236), it is proposed to operate on a more superior strategic level than DCs, which in turn are proposed to "include operational activities which are essentially concerned with the development of the organisation and carrying out diverse operations (for example, product development, alliance building, strategic decision-making, etc.)" (Madsen, 2010, p. 236).

Given this delineation of the two concepts, it emerges that while both concepts have a number of common denominators, they are theoretically and empirically distinct (Madsen, 2010). Thus a firm's EO, hence a culture of change and transformation, can be regarded as a necessary framework condition and "should be embedded within the social fabric of organization" (Hawass, 2010, p. 410) to facilitate the actual recombinant activities (implemented through Sensing, Learning, Coordinating and Integrating Capacities) for RR. Subsequently EO is proposed to support the development of the firm's DCs, in such a way that firms having established a higher EO are more likely to have a certain tendency to develop higher DCs over time. Therefore EO is suggested to act as antecedent of DC. Consequently, it can be argued that there is a positive association between EO and DCs, leading to the following hypothesis:

H6: *A higher degree of Entrepreneurial Orientation is positively associated with the development of the firm's DCs.*

More specifically, the firm's EO is proposed to affect the firms Sensing, Learning, Integrating and Coordinating capacities in ways as described in the following.

A high EO is proposed to positively affect the firm's **Sensing capacity** as it promotes an outward focus on new opportunities in the environment (Wiklund et al., 2002), which is suggested to be positively associated with the firm's Sensing capacity. According to Shane and Venkataraman (2000), the firm's EO reveals the priority that firms place on the process of identifying and exploiting new opportunities in the market environment, as a result it becomes evident that firms with a higher EO, will most likely develop a high Sensing capacity over time. The firm's Sensing capacity comprises activities such as monitoring the environment, providing impulse to new ideas and discover new possibilities (Madsen, 2010), and will be positively affected by the firm's willingness and attitude to be innovative, proactive, and to take risks (Miller, 1983) in the following ways:

First, high *innovativeness*, regarded as the firm's orientation towards innovation and its general openness to new ideas, will facilitate the search and perception of new technologies, changing customer requirements and new developments in the market, and therefore positively affects the firm's Sensing capacity (Hitt and Ireland, 2000). Second, a high *proactiveness* facilitated the firm's ability to identify new opportunities in the environment, as it describes the firm's general posture of anticipating and acting on future market needs and creating a first-mover advantage vis-a-vis competitors (Lumkin and Dess, 1996). Third, a positive attitude towards *risk-taking* moreover will foster the firm's ability to spot, interpret and pursue opportunities in the internal and external environment through its inclination to handle uncertainty affiliated with addressing new opportunities in the environment (Teece et al., 1997). Consequently, a firm's EO is proposed to positively influence the development of the firm's Sensing capacity, leading to the following hypothesis:

H6a: *A high degree of Entrepreneurial Orientation is positively associated with the development of the firm's Sensing capacity.*

A high EO is further proposed to positively affect the firm's **Learning capacity** as the firm's tendency or willingness to engage in, and support new ideas, novelty, experimentation will be positively associated with the adaption and creation of new knowledge, which basically constitutes a firm's Learning capacity. Covin and Miles (2006) suggest in order to address new opportunities in the environment, firm's with a high EO will be more prospective towards analysing and changing its own operational capacities in order to facilitate utilising and exploiting market opportunities. Accumulating and learning new knowledge hence is positively affected by the firm's willingness to be innovative, proactive and engage in risk-taking behaviour (Lumkin and Dess, 1996).

First, *innovativeness*, as it captures the firm's willingness and attitude to engage in, and support new ideas, novelty, experimentation, and creative processes, also concerns the adoption of new technology and knowledge, and revamp internal processes and procedures (Lumpkin and Dess, 1996), and thus will be positively associated to developing higher Learning capacity. Second, *proactiveness* is encouraging 'Learning', as individuals engaged in learning activities need to be open for internalising new knowledge and be proactive in articulating and sharing insights, intuitions, and tacit knowledge (Zollo and Winter, 2002). Third, *risk-taking* encompasses a positive attitude towards committing sufficiently time and resources to projects with uncertain outcomes. As such typically activities concerning the acquisition, assimilating and creation of new knowledge can be regarded, hence a positive attitude towards risk-taking, is suggested to be positively related to Learning.

Taken together, EO—regarded as a combination of innovativeness, proactiveness, and risk-taking—supports the development of Learning capacity, leading to the following hypothesis:

H6b: *A high degree of Entrepreneurial Orientation is positively associated with the development of the firm's Learning capacity.*

Besides its influence on Sensing and Learning capacity, a high EO is proposed to positively affect the firm's **Integrating capacity.** This can be deduced to the perception that as a high EO promotes thinking new ways and restraining from the old, it is suggested to be positively associated with the firm's Integrating capacity. Following Wiklund and Shepherd (2003), the firm's EO will be positively associated with how firms integrate new bundles of knowledge-based resources to develop new products and services. Similarly, Wiklund et al. (2002) confirmed that by encouraging new ideas, experimentation and creativity in firms (e.g. Covin and Slevin, 1991), firms that have created an entrepreneurial culture are more likely to come up with creative ideas for how to best reconfigure and refine their resources in order to adjust its resource base to new opportunities in the environment. A firm's EO, its willingness to be innovative, proactive and engage in risk-taking behaviour, thus is suggested to be positively associated with the development of the firm's Integrating capacity in the following ways:

First, *innovativeness* is closely linked to creativity (Scott, 1965) and represents a strong tendency to introduce novel, innovative or creative solutions (Whiting, 1988). A firms EO thus encourages firms to connect divergent ideas (Leonard and Sensiper, 1998), see new connections of existing resources (Zahra and Wiklund, 2002), and envisioning new combinations (Zahra and Wiklund, 2002). Second, equipped with a high *proactiveness* entrepreneurial firms will foster the intention to develop and explore ideas for innovative RCs, promote a cooperative spirit, and encourage a greater understanding among team members (Zahra and Wiklund, 2002). For this reasoning, a high proactiveness is positively associated with the firm's Integrating capacity. Third, as the combination of resources into new bundles generally involves uncertainty and the value of the resources is typically not recognised until they are being integrated (Denrell et al., 2003, Moran and Ghoshal, 1999, Wiklund and Shepherd, 2009), the firm's willingness to take risks is positively related to Integrating capacity. Hence, a firm's EO supports the development of Integrating capacity, leading to the following hypothesis:

H6c: *A high degree of Entrepreneurial Orientation is positively associated with the development of the firm's Integrating capacity.*

Lastly, a high EO is proposed to positively affect the firm's **Coordinating capacity**, because a high EO promotes a culture within the organisation where entrepreneurial activities are fostered (e.g. Brown et al., 2001, Covin and Slevin, 1991). A firm's EO, thus its willingness to be innovative, proactive and engage in risk-taking behaviour, is suggested to be positively associated with the development of the firm's Coordinating capacity in the following ways:

First, following Hamel and Prahalad (1994) within entrepreneurial oriented firms special emphasis is given on stretching the use of available resources over a wide range of areas and leveraging resources in new ways to develop new applications and create new products and services (Zahra and Wiklund, 2002). Second, following Stevenson (1983) entrepreneurial firms are typically organised with multiple informal networks, hence an entrepreneurial oriented management structure allows to easily access resources within the firm or through informal collaborative network relationships (Wiklund et al. 2002), which in turn facilitates the coordination and orchestration of resources into new productive resource bundles. This is in line with Teece et al. (2007, p. 1323) proposing that "more decentralized organizations with greater local autonomy are less likely to be blindsided by market and technological developments" and therefore are more likely to allocate the resources in appropriate ways to create value (e.g. Pavlou and El Sawy, 2011, Sirmon et al., 2007). Third, given such an environment where people have the flexibility to pursue new opportunities and can easily access resources to address new opportunities, is suggested to positively enhance the firm's ability to orchestrate and deploy tasks, resources, and activities in the new operational capabilities in order to implement the new, innovative products or services (RRs) in the market. Consequently, a firm's EO is proposed to support the development of the firm's Coordinating capacity, leading to the following hypothesis:

H6d: *A high degree of Entrepreneurial Orientation is positively associated with the development of the firm's Coordinating capacity.*

3.5.2 Networking Orientation

Networking Orientation (NO) in this research is conceptualised as "the extent to which a firm's business strategy stresses effective and efficient location of network partners, management of network relationships, and improvement of network performance" (Mu and Di Benedetto, 2011, p. 341). A firm's NO thus captures the firm's strategic orientation towards collaborating with external entities, i.e. its suppliers, customers, universities or research institutions, and can be described as the firm's openness to external sources through alliances, networks, and partnerships (Dahlander and Gann, 2010). The construct is based on the perception that firms, which are accessible for and open to external partners, are suggested to be more capable of drawing new ideas and resources from these exogenous sources to enlarge their own pool of market opportunities, complementary assets, and external resources available to the firm (Mu and Di Benedetto, 2011). Thus, "the importance of networking orientation lies in that firms can employ networking as a means to exploit knowledge, take advantage of established and new technologies and products, and pool resources through their relationships with various partners" (Mu and Di Benedetto, 2011, p. 352).

There is a consistent claim in literature that interorganisational collaboration can serve as significant source of competitive advantages by bringing in new opportunities and resources (McEvily and Zaheer, 1999, Gulati, 1999, Phan and Peridis, 2000, Peng and Delios, 2006, Mathews, 2002, Isobe et al., 2008). Accordingly, a variety of empirical studies confirmed a positive relationship between inter-organisational linkages, technological development and firm performance (Powell et al., 1996, Henderson and Cockburn, 1994, Baum et al., 2000, Isobe et al., 2008). Whilst it is generally agreed that "inter-firm collaborations are not simply a means to compensate for the lack of internal skills, nor should they be viewed as a series of discrete transactions" (Powell et al., 1996, p. 119), to a greater degree strong network ties are suggested to allow firms strengthen and develop their internal competence and resource position through collaboration (Isobe et al., 2008). Consistently, Isobe et al. (2008) found interfirm collaboration to play an essential role for the development of the firm's reconfiguration capability by means of allowing external learning, which supplements previous research findings emphasising the crucial role of interorganisational networks for interorganisational learning and firm performance (Lane and Lubatkin, 1998, Lee et al., 2001, Rothaermel, 2001).

Given these research findings, a firm's NO, which captures the firm's tendency to embed close interactions with external entities in their core business, is regarded as an important determinant for resource value creation in firms.

This is due to the fact that firms with high NO assign value to "purposefully create and improve the ability to orchestrate its networks to tap into complementary resources that are beneficial to new product commercialization" (Mu and Di Benedetto, 2011, p. 341). Also, findings from product innovation, marketing and network relationship management give evidence that firms with a higher NO attach superior value at searching, managing, and leveraging network relationships (Mu and Di Benedetto, 2012). Likewise EO, which described the firm's *willingness* or *attitude* to engage in entrepreneurial activities, the firm's NO thus describes the firm's *willingness* or *attitude* towards engaging in interfirm collaborations.

Research from different disciplines showed evidence for networking activities and inter-organisational linkages to act as a means for creating value in firms (Isobe et al., 2008, Lorenzoni and Lipparini, 1999, Lee et al., 2001, Rothaermel, 2001). Traditionally, researchers assume a direct effect of NO and firm performance, without asking how an enhanced NO is leading to superior performance. However, literature also claims that firm's must have the ability to orchestrate their networks to extract value (Mu and Di Benedetto, 2012). Despite this awareness, literature on network theory focuses on network structure and outcomes rather than examining the internal processes and capabilities a firm needs for managing, building and leveraging the benefits from its networks to create competitive advantages (Mu and Di Benedetto, 2012). Therefore this research sets out to investigate the relationship between NO and DCs towards building new RR, as both concepts are somewhat attached to how the firm builds and exploits internal and external resources and thus creates new RRs.

It is assumed that firms with an increased NO should have an increased ability to purposefully create, extend and modify its resource configurations (Mu and Di Benedetto, 2012) by improving its Sensing, Learning and Integrating and Coordinating capacities. Hence, this study does not only investigate the direct effect of NO on RR, but moreover sets out to investigate if a high Sensing, Learning, Integrating and Coordinating capacity respectively mediates the effect of NO on RR in firms.

H7: *A high degree of Networking Orientation is positively associated with the development of a firm's DCs.*

More specifically, the firm's NO is proposed to affect the firms Sensing, Learning, Integrating and Coordinating capacities in ways as described in the following.

A high NO is suggested to be positively associated with the firm's **Sensing capacity** as the firm's openness towards collaborating with external partners is found to positively affect the firm's awareness of external opportunities (Isobe et al., 2008). This is corresponding with Teece (2007, p. 1322) who notes that "to identify and shape opportunities, enterprises must constantly scan, search, and explore across technologies and markets, both 'local' and 'distant'". Accordingly, a high degree of NO can help firms to identify new, external opportunities for the following reasoning:

First, by induced collaboration with external partners firms can obtain unique sources of information about untapped opportunities in the environment (Mu and Di Benedetto, 2012). Second, increased interaction with external partners enhances the firm's opportunity-sharing facilities and information-processing channels, enabling firms to be more perceptive and responsive to dynamic changing environments and emergent opportunities (Mu and Di Benedetto, 2012). Third, the exploration of existing and new network ties, allows firms to develop a mutual understanding and awareness of resources available at different prices in the market and also to discover new, yet unknown resources (Mu and Di Benedetto, 2012). Hence, having information about the accessibility of appropriate resources at appropriate prices will enhance the firm's ability to exploit these new opportunities (Shane and Venkataraman, 2000).

Summarising, the above arguments imply that highly developed external network ties can help to provide firms with useful information about technological breakthroughs and trajectories, capture new insights to existing problems, expose failure and success of current research activities, and thus can help firms to validate their prognoses about future technological and market trends and purposefully adapt the current business activities to these newly discovered opportunities (Mu and Di Benedetto, 2012). Consequently, a firm's NO is supporting the development of a high Sensing capacity, leading to the following hypothesis:

H7a: *A higher degree of Networking Orientation is positively associated with the development of a firm's Sensing capacity.*

Furthermore, a high NO is proposed to positively affect the firm's **Learning capacity** as the firm's tendency to collaborate with external network partners will be positively associated with the adaption and creation of new knowledge, which basically constitutes firm's Learning capacity. Accordingly, if a firm is open to find, build and coordinate new network relationships, it generally facilitates the absorption of external knowledge (Cohen and Levinthal, 1990) and the generation of new knowledge (Rothaermel and Hess, 2007) for the following reasoning:

First, for the *absorption of external knowledge* firms are constrained to interact with network partners to obtain access to the necessary external resources to be acquired in a subsequent step and used in order to develop new products or services (Lee et al., 2001). Accordingly, by drawing on the benefits of their network relations, firms are found to have information advantages by knowing whom to ask for obtaining the appropriate resources, but also by possessing superior knowledge about new resources ex ante, which allows a more accurate differentiation of those value-enhancing against value-destroying resources. This permits a correct evaluation of resources of interest and is subsequently leading to the acquisition of the 'winning' resources from the networks (Mu and Di Benedetto, 2012). Accordingly, a high NO is suggested to facilitate the acquisition of new knowledge by connecting network resources and activities. Moreover researchers have argued for transactional intensive firms to have a higher ability to integrate and learn knowledge that resides both inside and outside the firm's boundaries (Lorenzoni and Lipparini, 1999). In their empirical study Mu and Di Benedetto (2002) moreover confirmed that resource acquisition (part of Learning capacity) partially mediates the positive relationship between networking capability and NPD performance.

Second, the *creation of new knowledge*, which comprises the routines of knowledge articulation and internalisation, is positively affected by the firm's NO. As the reciprocal exchange, interaction and knowledge transfer among network partners not only enhances the firm's ability to obtain, articulate, and exchange rich, fine-grained and tacit knowledge (Gulati, 1999, McEvily and Zaheer, 1999), which would be more expensive or not even accessible at all for firm's lacking external network ties (Uzzi, 1997), it moreover ensures a high level of accuracy, reliability and quality of the knowledge exchanged, which in term allows generating a deeper understanding of technologies, innovations, and markets and thus facilitates the *internalisation* of knowledge gained from external sources (Mu and Di Benedetto, 2012). Confirming these arguments, Mu and Di Benedetto (2012) could give empirical evidence that both Market Knowledge generation and Technological Knowledge generation mediate the positive relationship between networking capability and NPD performance. Consistent with these findings, Powell et al. (1996) confirmed that knowledge creation processes incorporating external linkages by means of interfirm collaborations lead to superior technological development and thus firm performance (Isobe et al., 2008).

Based on these arguments, NO can help firms to access external knowledge sources, which are important for the adoption and generation of new knowledge. Consequently, a firm's NO is regarded to support the development of a firm's Learning capacity, leading to the following hypothesis:

H7b: *A higher degree of Networking Orientation is positively associated with the development of a firm's Learning capacity.*

Besides its influence on the firm's Sensing and Learning capacity, a high NO is proposed to positively affect the firm's **Integrating capacity** as the firm's openness to external entities will be positively associated with the firm's ability to creatively combine, integrate and transform disparate resources to form new operational capabilities. Hence, a high NO is proposed to facilitate the three underlying routines of Integrating capacity, namely (1) *transforming individual to collective knowledge*, (2) *interrelating different knowledge domains*, and (3) *reconfiguration and refinement*, in the following ways:

First, a critical and regular feedback and knowledge exchange process throughout the network is supposed to provide the firm with a more comprehensive, rigorous, and unbiased appraisal of opportunities and thus facilitates the development of a collective knowledge (Mu and Di Benedetto, 2012). This can best be explained as "the scope and quality of information enables the firm in the network to process information in composite chunks rather than disparate pieces, elevating its cognitive capacity from those of bounded rationality to expert rationality" (Mu and Di Benedetto, 2012, p. 8).

Second, as the development of new RRs is found to be more effective when people from different disciplines interact (De Luca and Atuahene-Gima, 2007) and when otherwise isolated domains of knowledge are interrelated (Hawass, 2010, Hargadon, 1998), these processes require heterogeneity of knowledge inputs, and as such also require heterogeneity of actors (Mu and Di Benedetto, 2012). A high NO enables firms to search for, manage, and coordinate multiple network ties with external partners, which can provide access to specialised knowledge widely dispersed throughout the network members (Galunic and Rodan, 1998), and therewith facilitates to establish linkages between otherwise disconnected domains of knowledge, which in turn are supposed to facilitate firms to create more integrative solutions.

Third, because diverse inflows of new knowledge are proposed to strengthen assimilative abilities (Cohen and Levinthal, 1990) and analogical reasoning (Hawass, 2010, Hargadon, 1998), this facilitates the creative and effective recombinant search for novel associations (Helfat and Peteraf, 2003). This assumption is consistent with previous research finding confirming a strong positive effect of external learning through interfirm collaboration on reconfiguration and refinement capability (Isobe et al., 2008, Rothaermel, 2001, Lane and Lubatkin, 1998, Lee et al., 2001).

Hence, a strong NO is suggested to facilitate the firm's ability to integrate and combine the diverse and multi-faceted knowledge inputs from external sources (Mu and Di Benedetto, 2012). Based on the above arguments, this research implies that a high NO is regarded to support the development of a firm's Integrating capacity, leading to the following hypothesis:

H7c: *A higher degree of Networking Orientation is positively associated with the development of a firm's Integrating capacity.*

Lastly, a high NO is proposed to positively affect the firm's **Coordinating capacity**, as it facilitates the development of relevant skills for the internal orchestration of resources, which is suggested to be positively associated with the firm's Coordinating capacity.

First, in accordance with Mu and Di Benedetto (2012, p. 8), this research suggests that "networking with other partners can enable the firm within a network to make sense of information and to classify it into perceptual categories, which help the firm to determine in what context the acquired information and knowledge can be put into use". Accordingly, it is suggested that firms, which are successful in finding, managing and coordinating its complex network relationships, will also develop the relevant skills for internally coordinating the resources more effective than its competitors (Nelson and Winter, 1982).

Second, NO warrants a high level of connectivity necessary for assembling resources in order to leverage the opportunities discovered by allowing the firm to mobilise and exploit the divergent resources of its network partners (Dyer and Singh, 1998, Mu and Di Benedetto, 2012). Consequently, if firms have the ability to identify and evaluate the value of appropriate knowledge residing at different points in the network and can orchestrate its transfer to where it is needed, then it can successfully promote knowledge creation and innovation (Gulati, 1998, Mu and Di Benedetto, 2012).

Third, research finding moreover revealed that, if firms are solely focussing on developing strong internal network ties without giving emphasis on the development of external network ties for accessing complementary knowledge and external sources of information, this can have a negative impact on innovation performance (e.g. Uzzi, 1997, Mu et al., 2008, Mu and Di Benedetto, 2011). This is due to the fact that firm's with a high NO can easily access resources from the network in which it is embedded, and therefore can address possible constraints and prevent it from resource dependencies (Mu and Di Benedetto, 2012).

Hence, external resource orientation through networks is suggested to positively affect the internal coordination of knowledge and resources as it avoids giving an overemphasis on internal resources. On the other hand, it may be proposed that a too strong orientation towards external resources by means of placing emphasis on developing external network ties may also negatively affect the coordination of internal abilities, as it may overshadow internal network ties. Nonetheless, as the previous arguments revealed, this research suggests a positive effect of NO on the development of the firm's Coordinating capacity:

H7d: *A higher degree of Networking Orientation is positively associated with the development of a firm's Coordinating capacity*

The hypotheses, as outlined above, add to theory by improving the understanding of the antecedents of DCs, necessary for RR to occur, and therewith contribute to conceptualise the influencing factors of RRs within a model. The conceptual model, summarising and representing the proposed relationships discussed in this chapter, is presented in the following.

3.6   The Preliminary Conceptual Model and Hypotheses

3.6.1 The Preliminary Conceptual Model

Comprising this research's arguments and presenting the theoretical arguments of this research the preliminary conceptual model and its respective hypotheses are presented in the following. Figure 3.5 gives a graphical illustration of the conceptual model and expected causal relationships between the constructs relevant for this study to be tested empirically in a subsequent research step.

In brief, the conceptual model presented in Figure 3.5 shows the expected causal dependencies between the DCs, the resource base, and the outcome variable of RR. The conceptual model shows the four DCs, their interrelationships and impacts on performance outcome variable (RRs), as well as their effects on the resource base.

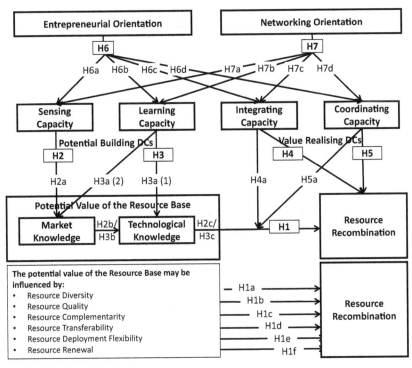

Source: own illustration

Figure 3.5 Conceptual Model based on the Literature Review

Doing so, the model illustrates the role of DCs in the process of RR in firms. While the Sensing and Learning capacity are expected to work towards *building* the resource base relevant for RRs, the Integrating and Coordinating capacity are working towards *exploiting* the resources base by building new innovative RRs, and therefore act as a moderator between the resource base (endogenous variable ξ) and RR in firms as outcome (the exogenous variables η).

Thus, it is suggested that the **realised value through RRs** is a function of the **potential value of the resource base** (measured by means of Market and Technology Knowledge breadth and depth) and **the DCs** (Sensing, Learning, Integrating, Coordinating capacity) relevant for the process of RR.

Hence, the greater emphasis the firm puts on the development of these specific DCs the more it first *builds*, and second *realises* the potential value of the resource base by successfully developing new RRs. Hence, both the resource base and the DCs of the firm are seen as important factors that influence RR in firms. A logical effect of this would be that the relative importance and value of the firm's resource and DCs, respectively, is very different in various environments, depending on the dynamics.

Moreover, the conceptual model shows the expected causal relationships between Entrepreneurial and Networking Orientation and the firm's DCs. Both EO and NO are regarded as important antecedents (at the firm- and network-level) for the development of DCs. While EO (respectively NO), reflects the *willingness* or *attitude* of the firm concerning the engagement in entrepreneurial behaviour (networking activities, respectively), the DCs refer to the *activities* (processes and routines) itself which build, develop, integrate and reconfigure internal and external resources. A summary of the corresponding hypotheses, discussed in depth and detail in this chapter, is presented in the following section.

3.6.2 Hypotheses

The conceptual model and hypotheses presented in this chapter provide the conceptual foundation of RR in firms and opens paths for the subsequent qualitative and quantitative analyses in order to test the developed theory regarding the effects of a firm's DCs and resource endowments on RR, respectively value creation in firms. For further analysis, the hypotheses developed in this chapter based on the literature review are summarised in Table 3.2 to 3.7. The hypotheses are further tested by means of qualitative and quantitative research undertaken and described in the following chapter 4 and 5, respectively.

A) Interrelations between the Resource Base and RR

Table 3.2 Interrelations between the Resource Base and RR

Hyp.	Independent Variable	Dependent Variable	Predicted Relationship
	Potential Value of the Resource Base	RR	positive
H1	Technological Knowledge (Techno. Knowl. Breadth and Depth)	RR	Positive
H1(1)	Market Knowledge (Market Knowl. Breadth and Depth)	RR (through Technological Knowledge)	positive (indirect)

While controlling for: Characteristics of the Resource Base and RR

H1a	Knowledge Breadth	RR	Positive
H1b	Knowledge Depth	RR	Positive
H1c	Knowledge Complementarity	RR	Positive
H1d	Knowledge Tacitness	RR	Negative
H1e	Knowledge Context Specificy	RR	Negative
H1f	Knowledge Origin	RR	Positive

B) Interrelations between DCs and RR (through the Resource Base)

Table 3.3 Interrelations between DCs and RR (through the Resource Base)

Hyp.	Independent Variable	Dependent Variable	Predicted Relationship
	Overall DC	RR	Positive
H2	Sensing Capacity	RR (through Market and Technological Knowledge)	positive (indirect)
H3	Learning Capacity	RR (through Market and Technological Knowledge)	positive (indirect)
H4	Integrating Capacity	RR	Positive
H5	Coordinating Capacity	RR	Positive

C) Role of DCs in the Process of Resource Value Creation

(I) Sensing and Learning as Potential Building DCs in the process of Resource Value Creation

Table 3.4 Mediating Role of the Resource Base between Potential Building DCs and RR

Hyp.	Independent Variable	Mediator	Dependent Variable	Predicted Relationship
	Potential Building DCs	Potential Value of the RB	RR	positively mediating
H2a H2b H2c	Sensing Capacity	Market Knowledge and Technological Knowledge	RR	positively mediating
H3a H3b H3c	Learning Capacity	Market Knowledge and/or Technological Knowledge	RR	positively mediating

(II) Integrating and Coordinating as Value Realising DCs in the process of Resource Value Creation

Table 3.5 Moderating Role of Value Realising DCs between the Resource Base and RR

Hyp.	Independent Variable	Moderator	Dependent Variable	Predicted Relationship
	Potential Value of Resource Base	Value Realising DCs	RR	positively moderating
H4a	Technological Knowledge	Integrating Capacity	RR	positively moderating
H5a	Technological Knowledge	Coordinating Capacity	RR	positively moderating

D) Entrepreneurial and Networking Orientation as Antecedents for DCs

Table 3.6 Entrepreneurial Orientation as Antecedent for DCs

Hyp.	Independent Variable	Dependent Variable	Predicted Relationship
H6	Entrepreneurial Orientation	Dynamic Capabilities	positive
H6a	Entrepreneurial Orientation	Sensing Capacity	positive
H6b	Entrepreneurial Orientation	Learning Capacity	positive
H6c	Entrepreneurial Orientation	Integrating Capacity	positive
H6d	Entrepreneurial Orientation	Coordinating Capacity	positive

Table 3.7 Networking Orientation as Antecedent for DCs

Hyp.	Independent Variable	Dependent Variable	Predicted Relationship
H7	Networking Orientation	Dynamic Capabilities	positive
H7a	Networking Orientation	Sensing Capacity	positive
H7b	Networking Orientation	Learning Capacity	positive
H7c	Networking Orientation	Integrating Capacity	positive
H7d	Networking Orientation	Coordinating Capacity	positive

3.7   Chapter Summary

To provide a basis for the conceptual development and empirical investigation of RR in firms from a DC perspective, this chapter examined the theoretical framework, the determinants and framework conditions of the concept of RR and outlined the research's arguments and related hypotheses. The aim was to bring clarity to the notion of DCs, their role and effects towards RRs in firms.

Starting with an introduction of the current knowledge of resource value creation in firms from the DC perspective, including the differentiation of the *potential* and *realised value* of the resources, the preliminary considerations of this research were presented, forming the theoretical base of this study. Based on these preliminary considerations, first the characteristics of the resource base were discussed in respect to their perceived role in forming the potential value of the resource base for RR. This was followed by the presentation of the DC framework, providing a detailed elaboration of the four DCs: *Sensing capacity, Learning capacity, Integrating capacity* and *Coordinating capacity*, their underlying processes and activities. Based on the delineation of the four DCs, moreover, their role in the process of resource value creation was further specified. This was followed by an investigation of the framework conditions for the development of DCs, whereby based on existing literature from the resource and competence-based theory the firm's *Entrepreneurial Orientation* and *Networking Orientation* could be identified and were discussed as important antecedents of DCs. The chapter concluded with the presentation of the conceptual model for this research, presenting the theoretical linkages between the studies' constructs of interest and culminating into a subset of studies' hypotheses, which have to be tested empirically in the subsequent qualitative and quantitative research steps.

By doing so, this chapter merged the understanding of the RBV and DC perspective, outlining the concept of RRs by investigating the relation between the resource base, DCs, and its performance outcomes RR. Therewith this chapter addressed existing shortcomings in the DC literature, where there is a crucial need to understand better the interrelationship between capabilities, the resource base of the firm, and innovation in the form of RRs. With the presentation of the DC framework, this chapter allowed a clarification of the DC constructs, extending the focus of current literature by investigating the organisational processes and activities underlying each DCs. The DC framework thereby brings clarity to the notion of DCs, moreover, it opens avenues for empirical research. Additionally, given the enhanced understanding of the four DCs, the conceptual model presented here allowed to delineate key differences in their role and effects towards building RRs. One result is that regarding their relationship to performance outcome of new RRs, two different types of DCs are proposed to be distinguished: *Potential Building* and *Value Realising DCs*.

Thus, with the conceptual model presented in this chapter, a more precise understanding of the firm's DCs has been given, shedding light on their role and effects towards developing new RRs in firms and investigating their antecedents. Therewith, this chapter opens the black box of RR in firms and offers strategic pathways of how firms can strategically foster the recombination of existing resources as an important source for continuous innovation generation.

The conceptual model and the hypotheses presented in this chapter have provided the conceptual foundation for a subsequent empirical investigation, where the conceptual model has to be tested, refined, and validated. The subsequent research step thus is to qualitatively and quantitatively test the model and hypotheses presented here in order to empirically validate the conceptual model and establish it as a theoretical robust and validated concept for strategic management and thereby to contribute to an advanced understanding of DCs and RR in firms. Thereby this research addresses Ambrosini and Bowman's (2009, p. 45 f.) directions to further research, firstly to "clarify some of the concepts that seem to be open to differing interpretations", second "establishing dynamic capabilities as a theoretical well-founded construct", and third "to embark on appropriate empirical research". Correspondingly, the following chapter first presents the research design and qualitative research step undertaken to refine the theoretical model for further quantitative testing in the subsequent research step, where the conceptual model and hypotheses are tested empirically.

Qualitative Research: Model and Hypotheses Refinement

4

4.1 Introduction

Despite the active discussion of firms policies to foster innovation generation, few researchers have engaged in analysing RRs, their characteristics and key drivers, be it from a management or a research perspective. On the other hand, conceptual elaborations have been made within the DC literature, and "the dynamic capability framework is drawing support and increased validity by researchers, empirical studies of dynamic capabilities remain relatively rare" (Pablo et al. 2007, p. 690). Scattered research has emerged in recent years stating the increased relevance of DCs in firms and conceptually investigating the notion of DCs, hitherto "we have little theoretical or empirical evidence on which to base any suggestions as to how dynamic capabilities can be deliberately built" (Ambrosini and Bowman, 2009, p. 44). Today there emerges an increasing array of conceptual elaborations about DCs, however empirical support is still limited (Ambrosini and Bowman, 2009).

To provide a basis for the conceptual development and empirical investigation of RR in firms from a DC perspective, the previous chapter examined the theoretical framework of the RR concept, investigated the DC of the firm and established their antecedents and interrelationships towards building RR. Hence, this chapter allowed a clarification of the constructs and provided an outline of the preliminary conceptual model based on literature, therewith the basis for an empirical investigation.

Electronic supplementary material The online version contains supplementary material available at (https://doi.org/10.1007/978-3-658-35666-8_4).

© The Author(s), under exclusive license to Springer Fachmedien Wiesbaden GmbH, part of Springer Nature 2021
K. Kurzhals, *Resource Recombination in Firms from a Dynamic Capability Perspective*, Gabler Theses, https://doi.org/10.1007/978-3-658-35666-8_4

In order to elaborate on these theoretical and conceptual findings and to transfer the preliminary conceptual framework into a generic model—one that is not only theoretically well founded but also empirically tested—this research conducted a mixed method research strategy, entailing both a qualitative and quantitative research steps. In a first step, exploratory qualitative research was conducted in order to further specify the preliminary conceptual model and the hypotheses derived from the literature review. The refined conceptual model and the related hypotheses were thereafter empirically tested in the second, quantitative research step.

This chapter describes and justifies the *research design* and *methodology* and outlines the research findings of the first, qualitative research step. The first section of this chapter starts with an elaboration of the research design. It involves an introduction and discussion of the mixed-method research strategy and further illustrates the research methods applied in this research.

Following the introduction and discussion of the general research design, the second section of this chapter addresses the research methods applied for the first, qualitative research step in more detail. Within this section, the two qualitative research methods applied, namely a *discussion forum* and *participant observation* as part of an intercultural innovation workshop, and a subsequent *series of in-depth interviews* with industrial representatives, are outlined and discussed.

Thereafter, in the last section of this chapter, based on a structured content analysis of the *discussion forum* and the *in-depth interviews*, the results from the qualitative research are presented and discussed. Drawing on the key finding from the qualitative research step, minor adjustments of the conceptual model, that shows the 4 DCs, their interrelationships and impacts on performance outcome variable (RRs), as well as their effects on the resource base, are presented.

4.2   Research Design

The following section outlines the **research design**, which describes "the plan or proposal to conduct research" (Creswell, 2009, p. 5) and involves the intersection of philosophical worldview, research strategies and specific methods of data collection, analyses, and interpretation. In order to test the developed theory and to contribute to the establishment of the concepts of RR and DCs as a well-founded and robustly defendable area of research, the research strategy and methods applied for this research were based on previous studies in the related fields (e.g. Plewa, 2010). The following sections elaborate on the **research strategies** and subsequently the **research methods** used in this research, which guides the procedures of data collection and analysis.

4.2.1 Research Strategy

Integrating both qualitative and quantitative research methods, this research adapted a **mixed-method research strategy**. More precisely, a two-stage approach was applied, where a first phase of qualitative data collection and analysis was followed by a second phase of quantitative data collection and analysis. The mixed-method approach is also referred to in literature as a **sequential exploratory strategy** (Creswell, 2009, p. 211). Hence, the research strategy applied follows Carson and Coviello's (1996) call for multi-method approaches to achieve highly valuable findings. Following Plewa (2010) this goes in line with Edmonson and McManus' (2007) review on methodological fit in management field research, where they propose that qualitative and quantitative methods should be combined when the aim is either to increase validity of new measures trough triangulation or to generate greater understanding of the methods underlying quantitative results in at least partially new territory. The research strategy applied in this study can be further classified according to the different research types that are referred to in literature as *exploratory, descriptive,* and *explanatory* research (Kinnear et al., 1993). As outlined in the following, this PhD research combines all three of these research types.

Exploratory research is generally applied to investigate unknown and complex phenomena (e.g. Plewa, 2010). As a means for exploring and understanding these phenomena, exploratory research builds the basis for further research, which often is found to be applied subsequently in order to provide evidence of the exploratory findings (Zikmund, 2003). In light of the novelty of the denotation of DCs and the perception of RR as a source of wealth creation in strategic management research, exploratory qualitative research was conducted to refine the conceptual model and related hypotheses derived from the literature review before conducting any further quantitative analysis.

The first exploratory research step was justified based on the following aspects: First, while the concept of RR has been recognised in literature as source for wealth creation, still little is known about the process how firms recombine their resources (Galunic and Rodan, 1998). The introduction of the DC perspective on the concept of RR in firms is new. This research goes beyond traditional approaches to understand competitive advantages. Furthermore, little is known about how a possible framework to measure RR in firms could be designed.

Second, while a wide spectrum of different capabilities has been denoted under the "umbrella of DCs" and an array of different processes and routines has been assumed to provide the microfoundations of DCs (e.g. Teece, 2007; Eisenhardt and Martin, 2000), there is still a lack of a consistent definition of a firm's DCs. At the same time, as existing studies mainly describe DCs as "broad organizational processes", they "do not delve into the detailed, micro mechanisms of how these capabilities are deployed and 'work'" (Ambrosini and Bowman 2009, p. 37). To date there is still a poor understanding of the construct of DC and its existence is often assumed without specifying their exact components (Galunic and Eisenhardt, 2001, Ambrosini and Bowman, 2009), what makes it difficult to quantitatively approach the concept without a first exploratory investigation. Hence, one further aim of the exploratory research step was to first "identify discrete processes inside the firm that can be unambiguously causally linked to resource creation" (Ambrosini and Bowman 2009, p. 44), and therewith to establish DCs as a theoretically well-founded construct before any further quantitative research was undertaken. Doing so, this research followed Lockett and Thompson (2001, p. 743) suggestion to use a plurality of methods, as "it may be necessary to sacrifice some of the generality of quantitative investigations for a more qualitative attention to the detail".

Third, despite an increasing acknowledgement of DCs in the literature, the sparse knowledge that existent in the area of how these capabilities can be build and what influence they have on specific performance outcomes (e.g. RR), is limited to single case studies, focused only on one level of analysis, or is limited to a specific business segment or industry (Rothaermel and Hess, 2007).

In summary, given the complex research context of RRs in firms, coupled with very limited understanding of the DCs, its role and effects, explorative research methods were deemed most valuable for the investigation of RRs in firms from a DC perspective, as they allowed the development of an in-depth understanding of concepts, situations and behaviours (Flint et al., 2002). Hence, as the DC construct, its antecedents and the RR outcomes to be tested in this study are of a complex and versatile nature, an exploratory investigation of these constructs was considered crucial for the validity of findings deriving from quantitative research.

Based on the exploratory findings of the first, qualitative research step, descriptive and explanatory research was conducted in a second, quantitative research step in order to empirically test the conceptual model. **Descriptive research** is generally used to describe and determine characteristics and frequencies of a phenomenon involved in a study (Zikmund, 2003). While descriptive research can be used to predict associations between variables, it is not appropriate to explain patterns within data (Ticehurst and Veal, 1999, Kinnear et al., 1993). Thus **explanatory research,** also referred to as confirmatory or causal research, in addition was used in this study to test the predicted causal relationships in data (Kinnear et al., 1993, Zikmund, 2003).

This second, quantitative research step was justified based on the following aspects:
While a number of researchers have taken exploratory research approaches to DCs and RR, leading to a growing amount of normative and conceptual findings (Teece at al., 1997, Teece 2007, Eisenhardt and Martin 2000, Kogut and Zander 1992), these findings have to be aligned, operationalised and tested empirically. Extant empirical research is either limited only to specific industry sectors or approaches only a partial picture of the multilevel effects associated with the various mechanisms firms use to recombine their resources. A large number of authors thus have emphasised the importance of empirical research on DCs to foster the comprehensive understanding and theory development of DC perspective as well as to offer a greater generalisability of findings (Hawass 2010, Rothaermel and Hess 2007). Ambrosini and Bowman (2009, p. 30) for instance conclude that "a dynamic capabilities perspective provides a valuable focus on change processes within the firm. However, owing to a lack of empirical work and problems in deriving managerial prescriptions from the perspective, it currently has limited utility". Hence, in order to establish DC as a theoretically well founded construct, one that is measurable against its outcome (RR in firms) and also one that is managerial relevant, the exploratory research findings and conceptual enhancement made so far, suggested a strong need for empirical, explanatory research in this area.

In summary, exploratory qualitative research was carried out in the first step of this research, providing the theoretical and conceptual foundation for the descriptive and explanatory (confirmatory) research of the second, quantitative research step. As revealed by the data the latter research step was followed by a further exploratory investigation of the quantitative data by means of model re-specification. The following section further outlines the research methods conducted to complement the research strategy.

4.2.2 Research Methods

In order to implement the research strategy described above, the following section further details the specific research methods applied in this study. Through the application of a mixed method research strategy, which includes a literature review, qualitative and quantitative research methods, and a model validation process, the aim was to create research that can be practically applied whilst also robustly defended in a research environment.

This study intended to start with a **comprehensive literature review** aiming to establish the research context and demarcate it from related fields. Being a central part of the strategic management doctrine, the concept of RR significantly contributes to the resource and competence based research. As the basis for a detailed examination of the concept of RR the resource and competence based research has been outlined as the parent theories for this research. Discussing theories as well as existing empirical studies in the wider field of RR, the literature review provided the theoretical and conceptual base for the development of the conceptual model, leading to a first conceptualisation of the construct of DC and its influence on the likelihood of RR. Furthermore, the antecedents for the development of the DC were subject of investigation.

The literature review thus offered the theoretical foundation for the first, exploratory research step, where **qualitative research methods** were applied subsequently to further specify the preliminary conceptual model and the hypotheses derived. Qualitative research is a means to focus on people's perceptions and meanings in order to explore and understand unknown and complex phenomena in depth and detail (Ticehurst and Veal, 1999, Creswell, 2009). Hence, it has been considered as particularly valuable for the exploration of situations, behaviours or activities (Carson et al., 2001) and the in-depth understanding of new concepts and their interrelationships (Bendapudi and Leone, 2002, Flint et al., 2002). A range of qualitative research methods can be found in literature, including in-depth interviews, group interviews and focus groups, participant observation and ethnography (Ticehurst and Veal, 1999).

Those methods, that have been identified as appropriate for this study, are first, an inductive, **informal discussion forum** and **participant observation** conducted, and second, a subsequent **series of in-depth interviews** with key informants from industry environment engaged in RR projects. As both *informal discussion forums* as well as *participant observations* generally help to develop an understanding of the research area and problem and stimulate the creative process (Plewa, 2010), in past research both instruments have frequently been used as qualitative, exploratory research method (Kinnear et al., 1993, Zikmund, 2003). Researchers refer to one key advantage of these methods being their potential to generate new ideas, topics or areas, which might not have been revealed in one-to-one interviews (Plewa, 2010 referring to Kinnear et al., 1993, Zikmund, 2003).

Accordingly, these two qualitative research steps served as a pilot study for the subsequent **series of in-depth interviews**, which have been conducted with industrial representatives. An in-depth interview is defined as a "personal interview, which uses extensive probing to get a single partner respondent to talk freely and to express detailed believes and feelings on a topic" (Kinnear et al.,

1993, p. 240). For a qualitative, explanatory research study talking to experts in the area is deemed as an extremely valuable research method in order to gain a comprehensive understanding of a topic prior to a quantitative study (Saunders et al., 2003, p. 97, Ticehurst and Veal, 1999, Plewa, 2010). Hence in-depth interviews are generally regarded as valuable to gain deeper insights or a list of ideas to a complex concept (Fern, 1982), especially when the anticipated information is expected to vary notably across respondents (Ticehurst and Veal, 1999). Based on the newly gained knowledge from this qualitative research step, the conceptual model could be specified and the hypotheses could be qualitatively confirmed. The following section 4.3 provides a more detailed description of the qualitative research methods applied, the sampling method, data collection and data analysis procedure, while section 4.4 further details the findings from this qualitative research step.

In the second, quantitative research step both descriptive and explanatory research was conducted. Therefore **quantitative research methods** were applied in order to empirically test the conceptual model and the respective hypotheses derived from the literature review and the qualitative research step. For data collection a **self-administered online survey** was carried out. In order to enable the accurate application of statistical procedures and analyses, quantitative research requires the careful planning and structuring of research in advance to ensure accuracy of the research findings (Kinnear et al., 1993), accordingly, standard questionnaire development procedures, a pre-specified sample strategy, and structured data collection methods were conducted (as detailed in chapter 5). In a first step the conceptual model and its constructs were operationalised, whereby whenever suitable measurement items were adopted from existing scales; in case new scales had to be developed standard scale development procedures were applied. After being pre-tested and validated, the developed questionnaire was converted into an online survey using the online survey tool *Unipark*. The study was carried out in companies currently acting in innovation-intensive industries and targeted upper and middle management personnel in the UK. After the data was being collected, in a subsequent confirmatory research step the data was statistically analysed using causal analysis. More specifically structural paths analysis was applied to the data, which enables hypotheses testing, based on **Structural Equation Modelling (SEM)** principles. Accordingly, the conceptual model and related hypotheses were tested using the software *SPSS AMOS 20* for SEM. As revealed by the data, the conceptual model was further re-specified. Such model re-specifications procedures generally aim to achieve a more parsimonious model and are again exploratory in nature (Byrne, 2001, Diamantopoulos, 1994). A description of the quantitative research methods applied, the data collection and sampling, will be provided in chapter 5, while chapter 6 elaborates the quantitative research findings in depth.

4.3   Qualitative Research Methods

As the above chapter illustrated, this research contains a qualitative and a quantitative research part. The following chapter further details the **qualitative research methods** applied in this research to further specify the relevant concepts and interrelations to refine the conceptual framework before being further tested empirically. The different methods used are described in the following chapter.

4.3.1 Informal Discussion Forum and Participant Observation

As a first qualitative, exploratory research step, an informal discussion forum and a participant observation was carried out during the *4th Intercultural Innovation Workshop* in Istanbul, Turkey, organised by noventum consulting GmbH[1] in May 2012. The workshop format was designed as a management workshop directed towards upper and middle management personal and addressed topics such as future and innovation management, with a specific focus on cross innovation and RR. In total 34 managers from different functional areas (amongst them innovation managers, future managers, strategy consultants, CIOs, and IT managers) from diverse industry sectors (e.g. IT, Finance, Consultancy, and Automotive) and intercultural background (Germany, Turkey, India, UK) took part in the workshop.

As part of the *4th Intercultural Innovation Workshop,* an inductive, **informal discussion forum** was conducted in order to gain an in-depth understanding of the research topic, the process of RR and DCs in firms, resources and their interrelationships. Therefore, a one-hour presentation was held by the researcher covering an introduction of the research topic in general, findings derived from the literature review as well as the research gaps as perceived by the researcher. The presentation closed with an outline of the preliminary conceptual model

---

[1] noventum consulting GmbH is an international IT management consulting group, founded 1996 in Germany. The group is represented in Turkey, Luxembourg and Southafrica. The consulting approach combines strategic and procedural issues with technical solutions. The focus of noventum's service offering lies in the definition, optimisation and implementation of commercial and IT processes, beside this noventum is active in the field of innovation and future management, where service offerings cover the development of future concepts, future management workshops, innovation and ideas management (source: www.noventum.de)

based on the literature review. After the presentation, time was disposed for a group discussion of the concept, related topics and experiences from praxis. The discussion between the participants was moderated by the researcher, however its role was clearly defined as the role of a facilitator of the discussion rather than a discussion leader. This was important in order to ensure that the discussion was kept free flowing and flexible (Ticehurst and Veal, 1999), which facilitated new topics to emerge in the forum (Kinnear et al., 1993, Zikmund, 2003). At the same time special emphasis was given to the manager's perceptions and interpretation of the concept in order to explore the complex phenomena of RR and DCs in firms in depth and detail, to gain a comprehensive understanding (Ticehurst and Veal, 1999, Creswell, 2009).

Moreover, the developed survey instrument for the DC framework was pre-tested within the workshop following standard scale development procedures to examine the statistical properties of the measurement constructs. Therefore, a **self-evaluation questionnaire** was handed out to the participants (refer to Appendix 4.1 in the additional electronic material). Within the questionnaire, the participants were asked to evaluate their company regarding the four DCs: Sensing, Learning, Integrating and Coordinating Capacities. After being collected and analysed, the anonymised results were discussed with the workshop participants. Therefore, the groups' means for each of the four DCs were graphically illustrated within a spider-matrix and benchmarked against individual anonymised company results. By means of a gap analysis, implications could be derived and were discussed within the group.

As a last element supporting the qualitative research, **a participant observation** was undertaken by the researcher. To enable a playful access to innovation through RR, the *Zukunftsinstitut* in Germany developed the so called *Cross Innovation Game*, which promotes the combination of different industry sectors, market and consumer trends through specific playing cards, in order to trigger the cognitive process of building cross-analogies with the aim to development new innovative products and services (RRs). According to the *Zukunftsinstitut,* the cross innovation approach fosters innovation generation through interdisciplinary combination and linkage of products, services and trends within various industry sectors by means of analogical thinking and cooperation (Steinle et al., 2009, p. 28). Given the task to develop new, innovative RRs by means of playing the *Cross Innovation Game,* the workshop participants were divided into six intercultural groups. The idea generation process was followed by the researcher. This observation based approach was developed as a playful experience directed towards innovation generation stimulating the creative process. For all involved parties, this approach provided access and understanding of a complex and abstract research topic, and therewith a good basis for a subsequent research step, the series of in-depth interviews, where the participants inter alia were asked for their experience during this process.

To conclude, in order to develop a comprehensive understanding of the research topic, and delve into the detailed, micro mechanisms of value creation through RR, while clarifying the notion, role and framework conditions of DCs, an informal discussion forum and participant observation was conducted as first part of the exploratory qualitative research step. Hence, this research step basically served as a pilot study for the subsequent series of in-depth interviews with industrial representatives, further discussed in the following section.

4.3.2 In-Depth Interviews

A series of in-depth interviews were regarded as valuable instrument to further elaborate the conceptual model, discuss the most relevant variables, their conceptualisation and interrelation-ships with respect to the subsequent quantitative part of this research. The following section elaborates on the sampling frame, size and procedure, data collection and data analysis procedure used for the in-depth interviews.

Sampling Frame, Size and Procedure

Following Plewa (2010, p. 91) referring to Kinnear et al. (1993), "a sampling frame is the list of sampling units from which the final sample will be reached". As the concept of RR is relevant in almost all industries regardless of company size, not every company is involved in RR activities. Hence, for the qualitative interviews this research abstained from concentrating on a specific industry sector in order to not limit the potential sampling frame (Plewa, 2012), but targeted key informants on the basis of their experience. Participants were identified as eligible experts on the basis of their involvement and decision-making role in RR activities. The target group for the qualitative interviews were key informants from industry engaged in RR activities, predominantly middle and upper management personnel working in the related fields of innovation, new product development (NPD), business development and strategic management from industry sectors operating in dynamic environments.

A necessary precondition for the selection of the interview partners was, that the interviewees needed to possess an extensive knowledge and experience regarding RR, compromising experience with a minimum of one RR-related activity and experience and knowledge in both, decision-making and day-to-day practice and routines (e.g. Plewa, 2010). Accordingly, the following **four selection criteria** were defined and used to identify eligible interviewees for the sample. First, the interviewee needed to hold one of the following or comparable positions: Innovation manager, R&D manager, NPD managers, future manager, capability manager, business development manager, change manager, strategy consultant. Second, the interviewee needed to be involved in at least one RR related activity (e.g. R&D projects, NPD projects, cross innovation activities, resource allocation processes, business development activities, strategy change projects, transformation projects, capability management and transformation activities, resource planning activities, enterprise architecture management, mergers and acquisitions, business process management). Third, the interviewee were requested to have a minimum of 3 years of experience working with industry. Fourth, the interviewee needed to be formally related to an industry acting in dynamic environments. Following Capron et al. (1998) dynamic environments are characterised by the following criteria: (1) a high frequency of technical and regulatory change, (2) market globalisation, (3) product-market redefinition, (4) and competitive entry.

In accordance with the above predefined selection criteria, four interviewees were chosen from the participants of the *4th Intercultural Innovation Workshop* for an exploratory in-depth interview. Additionally, as previous research regarded snowball sampling as valuable method under the premise that no database of the overall target group is available, identified members of the target group were requested to indicate other experts in the field of research (Plewa, 2010). Additionally, two experts in the area of DC and RR were identified by means of referrals as judged by the researcher. In total six interviews were conducted with eligible partners.

To encounter the likely effect of an industry-specific bias (Patton, 2002) and to capture potential differences in view (Plewa et al., 2013), interviewees were chosen to represent a broad sample of different industry sectors (including IT Service Provider, I(C)T Management Consultancy, Strategy Consultancy, Engineering and Product Development), different company sizes (small, medium and large companies), different countries (Germany and Ireland), diverse positions and responsibilities for different focus areas. A detailed list of interview partners is presented in Appendix 4.2 in the additional electronic material, entailing their level of experience[2] in RR activities, position, industry sector, focus area, country(s) the company is active in, interviewee's nationality (underlined), and company size.

---

[2] All interviewees were categorised based on their self-rated level of experience in RR activities, leading to an equal number of interviewees with a high and moderate level of experience in RR activities.

Data Collection

The in-depth interviews were semi-structured in nature and followed an interview guide (see Appendix 4.3 in the additional electronic material). The interview guide consists of a range of different themes, that emerged from the literature review as well as the knowledge gained from the informal discussion round and participant observations. Following common research practice, whilst attention was paid towards a comprehensive discussion of all themes, there was no pre-defined order of the themes to be discussed during the interviews (e.g. Plewa, 2010, Plewa et al., 2013). Less flexibility however was given regarding homogeneity of content. Thus it was ensured that the interview guide and the visualisation material used during the interviews were equal in each case. All items considered, the interview guide method allowed a systematic approach to a series of in-depth interviews, as it ensures that the same themes were covered within each interview, without limiting the opportunity for emerging topics to arise, that have not yet been included in the interview guide (Plewa, 2010; Plewa et al., 2013). Moreover, it also allowed identifying similarities or differences in the views of the different interview partners on certain themes (Plewa, 2010).

All interviews were conducted face-to-face, with one exception where the interview was conducted via phone. The interviews lasted between one and two hours. All of them were tape recorded and transcribed afterwards. While tape recording is criticised for the inclination to limit open communication, which might restrain the disclosure of industry or personal information (Carson et al. 2001), at the same time it allows higher flexibility for the data gathering process and greater data comprehensiveness. Therefore, the advantages of this method are argued by many authors to outweigh their limitations (Carson et al., 2001, Patton, 2002, Plewa, 2010), especially as the interview themes are not being regarded as sensitive.

The interviews were conducted to gain a better understanding of the role of DCs in the process of RR. Hence, the interviews concentrated on topics such as RR in the interviewee's firm with a special focus on the firm's DCs, processes and routines relevant for RR to occur. Special emphasis was given to the topics on (1) how RRs are developed in firms and how this process can be stimulated and fostered, (2) the notion of DCs, their role and effects towards RR in firms, and (3) the influence of EO and NO on the development of DCs.

First, RR in general was discussed from a broader perspective in order to understanding the role, activities and experience of each interviewee in regard to RR activities, as well as the process of value creation through RR activities. Therefore, the interviewees were questioned about their involvement and general experiences with RR activities in their business area. Thereafter, they were asked to choose one or more successful RR activities they have been engaged in, which then were discussed in more detail in order to identify good practice examples of RR in firms. Furthermore the discussions aimed for a deeper understanding of the relevance and evaluation of RR activities in practice.

Second, to investigate the role of DCs in the process of RR, the DCs of the firm were discussed in order to understand the factors that drive RR in firms and to generate a deeper understanding of the microfoundations of these complex and multifaceted phenomena in practice. Interviewees were asked to outline firm-specific processes and routines underlying the firm's DCs, their key success drivers and perceived importance for the overall process. The target was to gain knowledge of the fine-grained structure of the firm's DCs and its influence on building and exploiting the resource base. Moreover, the role and effect of the identified DCs and specific characteristics of the resource bases on the development of new RRs were investigated.

Third, the framework conditions for the development of DCs were discussed in more detail. The aim was to elaborate on factors found in literature, namely EO and NO, which are considered as being relevant for the development of a firm's DC and thus RR, but at the same time to leave the window open to disclose and identify other antecedents of DCs, which have not been considered in literature.

In a final step, the preliminary conceptual model derived from literature was shown to each interviewee. With that model a set of propositions was discussed outlining (1) how the resource base and the DCs are related to one another, (2) how the relationship between the resource base and RRs is moderated by a firm's Integrating and Coordinating capacity, (3) how EO and NO might affect the development and utilisation of DCs for RRs. This merging step was conducted to discuss and validate the preliminary conceptual model and the hypotheses derived from the literature review and align it with the experience reported from praxis as unveiled by the interviewees. The visualisation of the conceptual model allowed an illustration of the constructs discussed, facilitated a judgment regarding the relevance of the single items compared to others, and enabled a clarification of their interdependencies and linkages. In line with previous research findings using a similar methodological approach (e.g. Plewa, 2010), this final step was considered extremely valuable for the development and refinement of the conceptual model on the basis of the most relevant constructs and their interrelations. Interviews lasted until consensus was reached on the relevant constructs to be included in the quantitative study.

Data Analysis

Based on the full transcription of tape records, the in-depth interviews were analysed using the digital coding software *NVivo 8* (QSR). *NVivo* is a software package supporting the qualitative data analysis, especially when rich text-based information is subject of investigation, as it helps researchers to classify, sort and arrange information and analyse relationships and tendencies in qualitative data. For the content analysis so called 'nodes' were build based on the literature review results and the themes covered in the interview guide as common in research practice (e.g. Huberman and Miles, 1994, Plewa, 2010, Plewa et al., 2013). *NVivo* therewith supports the iterative process of structuring the qualitative data and allows a systematic review and analysis of the interview data until a thorough understanding of the research topic, the relevant constructs and relevant measures was deduced (Carson et al., 2001). This approach offered valuable insights and emerging themes, which were used to conceptualise RR in firms from a DC perspective. The findings derived from the qualitative data analysis, utilised to refine the conceptual model and hypotheses for the subsequent, quantitative research step, are presented in the following section.

4.4   Results from the Qualitative Research

The following section briefly discusses the results of the qualitative research step to further refine the conceptual model and the respective hypotheses derived from the literature review and convert it into a qualitatively proven conceptual model. Therefore, the discussion below refers to the preliminary conceptual model, including the most relevant variables, their conceptualisations and interrelationships in the model, with respect to refine the model to be empirically tested in the subsequent quantitative part of this research.[3]

4.4.1 Resource Recombination: Performance Outcomes and Value Creation

Confirming the importance of RR in firms, the data reflects the highly complex nature of value creation in firms through RR and the variety of benefits that might determine the perceived value of RR in firms. The purpose of RR as described in the innovation literature is to build unique and innovative bundles of resources and thereby to achieve competitive advantages (Galunic and Rodan, 1998). The

---

[3] Note from the author: The quotes from the interviews display the original and transcribed outcome of the interviews, which is that often interviewees interrupted sentences, switched their thoughts within the same sentence, and used a rough wording. Nonetheless, to avoid any change of meaning, the quotes were included in its original wording without any grammatical or language corrections.

relevance of the concept of RR for building new innovative products and services was confirmed clearly by the interviewees, for instance interviewee #1 stated:

> *"Often single components [...] build common services, easily to access and to imitate, but through combination it becomes a service that is unique and new. Hence, for us the particular aim was to develop something inimitable through the combination of resources [...] and it emerged, that this gave us a new profile. The core interest certainly was to obtain and to retain future fitness for the company. Doing so, we want to make sure to develop solutions that meet the future demands of the customers."* *(Interviewee #1)*

Whereby special emphasis was placed by those interviewees coming from small and medium sized companies towards *interorganisational* RR activities through external networks and partnerships, as illustrated by the following quote:

> *"For our company, resource recombination is extremely important. I personally think, that as a medium sized enterprise we do not have the vast variety of different resources to adequately correspond to all customer needs. For this reasoning, an intelligent network consistent of complementary skills of different partners or organisations is extremely important to stay competitive in the long run."* *(Interviewee #4)*

Moreover, RR was supported by the interviewees as appropriate measure of innovation in firms and therefore was confirmed as valuable indicator of current entrepreneurial activities within the firm (Brown et al., 2001, Lumpkin and Dess, 1996, Stopford and Baden-Fuller, 1994). Aiming at the determination of value creation in firms through RR, however, findings reveal that the vast majority of companies surveyed did not perform a direct evaluation of RR success. One reason may be, that for most interviewees it emerged as difficult to define appropriate KPI's for measuring RR success. Interviewees appeared indifferent on whether to apply hard figures, such as turnover and profit, or additionally to incorporate soft figures, such as innovativeness, brand reputation and image. The statement of one interviewee may best describe the trade-off: *"Often as important as making profit with our RR products, is the benefit to attract awareness of our customers"* *(Interviewee #1)*

As a result, findings revealed that involved parties perceived different outcomes of RR as beneficial, confirming the appropriateness of employing RR as an overall outcome measure, and rather focusing on the extent to which firms engage in distinct RR activities, than measuring performance outcomes.

4.4.2 Dynamic Capabilities: Their Notions, Interrelationships and Impact on Outcome Variables

Capabilities in general. Looking at capabilities from a more general perspective, findings confirmed the relevance of the concept and its complex nature. At the same time interviewees presented a highly differentiated view of capabilities in firms, distinguishing between different subsets of capabilities—*Operational* and *Dynamic Capabilities*—even though in practice different notions for describing related concepts as proposed in literature were used, as the following quote illustrates:

> *"The concept of capabilities exists. (...) One is* **business capability** *and the other is* **technical capability**. *(...) So it is very important to understand that you have two sets of capabilities: One is what the business is trying to do (business capability), and then the other is really how it is actually doing it (technical capability)." (Interviewee #3)*

The perception of capabilities as described in this quote is consistent with literature (e.g. Helfat et al., 2007, Winter, 2003, Zollo and Winter, 2002), describing **Operational Capabilities**, as those that are associated with typical, day to day operations within the company, and **Dynamic Capabilities**, referring to those that involve creation and change.

Dynamic Capabilities. Investigating the role of DCs in the process of RR, first the relevance and notion of DCs were discussed. Data revealed a growing relevance of DCs, as it becomes ever more important in today's business environment to develop unique combinations of resources, considering that in an increasingly interconnected business environment, resources, technologies, even operational capabilities are becoming increasingly uniform across industries (e.g. as they can be easily applied via strategic factor markets, networks or alliances), and therefore seldom meet the criteria of being VRIN (Barney, 1991). This progress is well described by interviewee #3:

> *"If we take matured industries, you will find that the companies have evolved and in many ways do all very similar things. So you need to look then at the capabilities, to say, which capabilities are the ones that make me different, which are the ones that I believe are gonna make me even more successful in the future, and which are the ones that are commodities; and the commodities are the ones that can be outsourced. (...) the real thing is to determine, not just what you are doing today, and what you are doing well, but somehow trying to say, how to concentrate the company to find new capabilities or prioritise the existing capabilities, which will make a difference to go forward. So it's all about differentiation and ongoing performance." (Interviewee #3)*

Accordingly, the DCs of the firm, defined as a "firm's ability to integrate, build and reconfigure internal and external competences to address rapidly changing environments" (Teece, 1997, p. 516), is regarded as crucial in order to develop new innovative RRs. Moreover, at the same time data confirmed the perceived role of DCs lying in the heart of business strategy and management, as stated by one of the interviewees:

"I see business strategy being about deciding (1) which capabilities they want, (2) how should they be adjusted, (3) how should they be managed, and (4) how should they be evolved over time." Associated are questions, such as: *"What changes do we want to make? How do we manage the transition from the technical capabilities we have today, and the people associated with those capabilities, or the people who are managing those capabilities? How to adjust that from what we have to today, to where we want to be? And this goes back then to the stage, where you need to start looking at resources."* (Interviewee #3).

Hence, for managing this transition phase, the DCs of the firm—especially the Sensing and Learning capacity—are important as these capabilities allow firms to change the existing resource base, or existing skills and develop them into new skills. Thus, while data confirmed that the concept of capabilities is commonly known and widely accepted also from a business perspective, considerable ambiguity existed among interviewees concerning their exact definition, or what was noted by Galunic and Rodan (1998) as the question of what defines their boundaries. Not seldom interviewees referred to different levels of granularity of the concept, a point well captured by interviewee #3:

*"And below these **high level capabilities** we would have a hierarchy, so there would be second level, third level or maybe even more levels of capabilities. (...) And what you will find is that these capabilities eventually start to become very like **processes**. So once you go far enough down the hierarchy, capabilities should almost correspond to processes. [However] (...) companies confused business capabilities with processes (...) Every process can cover more than one capability, but maybe more than one process is required for a capability. I think this relationship is complicated."* (Interviewee #3)

For the operationalisation of the constructs in the conceptual model, therefore, this research stays on a higher level of granularity investigating specific routines and processes, but at the same time abstains from investigating the fine-grained sub-processes and activities constituting each capability. Notwithstanding, it is clearly stated that the **microfoundations of capabilities** are processes and activities (Parmigiani and Howard-Greenville, 2011), which in terms are performed by people, and use resources; a perception which was also supported by the interviewees:

> *"And of course every capability (...) would also have to have a certain **skill set** associated with it, in terms of people. **People** will need to automatically manage these **processes** (...), so there will be people associated with (...) actually managing those capabilities and they would need to have **technical skills**." (Interviewee #3)*

> *"According to our understanding, capabilities always have at least three dimensions, these are the **people**, the **processes** and the **resources** (including IT, etc). From my point of view, one could additionally bring in the product level, which also can be seen as the result of a capability." (Interviewee #6)*

In the following section, the specific DCs of the firm will be investigated in more detail in order to understand factors that drive RR and to generate a deeper understanding of the microfoundations of these complex and multifaceted phenomena in practice and discuss the proposed interrelationships and their impact on RR outcomes.

Sensing Capacity. Sensing capacity, defined as the firm's ability to spot, interpret and pursue opportunities in the internal and external environment (Teece, 2007, Pavlou and El Sawy, 2011), was confirmed by the data as an essential sub-capability of the firms DC, with all interviewees describing its critical role for identifying and shaping new opportunities. The following statement, given by one of the interviewees, well captures the organisational challenges affiliated to business development, which requires the development of a firm's Sensing capacity:

> *"There are certain things that are externally defined (...), so this is the **content** that feeds to the strategy of a company. So the challenge for the management is to look at these [content], e.g. best practice and challenges, to try and relate them to their own particular company, and somehow customise them and map them back onto the actual work that is happening within the company. With that, they will develop new projects." (Interviewee #3)*

Moreover, while qualitative findings showed, that Sensing capacity is rather externally oriented towards identifying and seizing opportunities in the external environment, interview data revealed, that the demand for addressing new opportunities can either be externally or internally initiated:

> *"What we tend to call these new challenges would be, we term them as being a **demand**. (...) The demand could be coming from a new strategy (e.g. innovation, or to combat competition, or to create growth), it could be coming from some outside regulations (like there are maybe some new laws or new standards), or it could be coming from your existing business, whereby you have existing products or services that are going on and people are requesting changes." (Interviewee #3)*

Correspondingly, the critical role of developing a high Sensing capacity in the context of RRs, was confirmed clearly by the interviews for example, interviewee #4 stated that:

> *"A crucial task is to identify market trends, to evaluate what may become relevant for the company in the future, but moreover drawing conclusions for the core business of the company, e.g. how people will behave in the future, what influence future developments will have on our employees, customers etc. Moreover it is important to focus on technological developments in the environment, for example what IT trends are arising. This is especially important for our company, as normally, the IT-industry is characterised by cycles of five years, and when you are missing one or another important trends then it could have tremendous effects for the company." (Interviewee #4)*

As described in this quote, the conceptualisation of Sensing capacity developed on the basis of the literature review, which captures the three basic routines, namely (1) *Generating Market Intelligence* (e.g. Amit and Schoemaker, 1993, Pavlou and El Sawy, 2011), (2) *Generating Customer and Competitor Intelligence* (e.g. Teece, 2007, Pavlou and El Sawy, 2011), and (3) *Generating Technological Intelligence* (e.g. Teece, 2007), could be confirmed.

Moreover, investigating the microfoundations of Sensing capacity, the three underlying processes and activities constituting a firms Sensing capacity that emerged from the literature review, namely (1) *spotting, scanning and monitoring the environment* (e.g. Teece, 2007, Nelson and Winter, 1982), (2) *accumulating, filtering and interpreting available information* (e.g. Teece, 2007), and (3) *valuing, identifying and shaping opportunities* (e.g. Teece, 2007), were confirmed by the qualitative findings.

While special emphasis was placed by the interviewees on the first, identifying process step, a general awareness of the relevance of the subsequent process steps of evaluating information ('accumulating, filtering and interpreting available information') and seizing new opportunities ('valuing, identifying and shaping opportunities'), were expressed by the majority of interviewees, as outlined by the following quotes:

*"Cloud computing, for example, is a highly recognised topic at the moment, but in order to **evaluate** its relevance (what does this mean for our company specifically?), it is not enough only to point out that cloud computing is an interesting topic for the future. Moreover, we also have to ask ourselves how to address this market, whether we have got the required resources, and what we as a company could do to participate successfully in the market."* (Interviewee #4).

"And the other thing is to actually say, do we even want to do the demand? So again, we could have a demand for something, but it is not really part of our strategy and therefore we might want to reject that project." (Interviewee #3).

*"And then after all of that, you have a list of **qualified** or **approved** demands and you somehow need to **prioritise** them to say, which ones are the most important and which ones are the least important. And there is a whole lot of measurements that you could apply to that in terms of KPIs or even things like."* (Interviewee #3)

Notwithstanding its relevance, however findings also revealed that firms often described problems in finding systematically ways of filtering and seizing new opportunities:

"The next step would be, that the identified, relevant information is processed further. This is partially methodical, but not yet consistent" (Interviewee #1).

Hence, given the importance of Sensing capacity, the data reflected the highly complex nature of the concept. Moreover, consistent with research findings derived from the literature review, qualitative data could confirm the suggested positive relation between Sensing capacity and RR in firms, through its positive effect on Market and Technological Knowledge. Thus interview findings substantiated a proposed positive impact on RR in firms.

Learning Capacity. Learning capacity is described as the firm's ability to assimilate, accumulate, retain, and create (new) knowledge to revamp the firm's resource base with substantial knowledge, developed internally or obtained externally (Pavlou and El Sawy, 2011, Zahra and George, 2002). Interviewees ascribed high recognition to the construct of Learning capacity:

"Learning is important for a lot of business processes, especially for RR, as this is a special type of business development. Here, learning is especially important as we enter a lot of unknown territory." (Interviewee #1)

Hence, Learning capacity was confirmed by the data as an important sub-capability of the firms DC, with interviewees approving its central role in renewing the firm's existing resource base with new knowledge. For instance, interviewee #4 stated:

"First, you need to be aware of the existing knowledge, second, you need to be aware of the missing knowledge and then, finally, you need to be willing to invest [e.g. time and money] in that missing knowledge by learning new knowledge (on the basis of knowing what might be important in the future) in order to eliminate or minimise the existing knowledge gaps. And this final step can either be realised with the help of internal resources [e.g. re-skilling, training, internal R&D] or through partnering by means of acquiring or bundling external resources." (Interviewee #4)

Investigating the microfoundations of Learning capacity, qualitative findings moreover confirmed the three underlying routines of Learning capacity: (1) *Acquiring and Assimilating of external knowledge*, which captures the processes of *Knowledge Acquisition* and *Knowledge Assimilation* (e.g. Zahra and George, 2002, Sirmon et al., 2007, Pavlou an El Sawy, 2011), (2) *Creating new internal knowledge*, which refers to the internal knowledge exploration and creation of new knowledge (Rothaermel and Hess, 2007), and (3) *Accumulating and Retaining internal knowledge*, which refers to internally managing and retaining knowledge over time (Garud and Nayyar, 1994, Dierickx and Cool, 1989). At the same time it became apparent that most often, learning new knowledge entails acquiring knowledge from external sources, as for instance stated by one interviewee:

"Normally firms cannot randomly expand and enlarge their existing competences as they would like to in the required depth, they necessarily need to acquire external competencies to complement their internal resources" (Interviewee #1).

Accordingly, interviewees confirmed the argument propound by researchers (e.g. Lichtenthaler and Lichtenthaler, 2009, Argote et al., 2003, Gulati, 1999, Wiklund and Shepherd, 2009), that firms increasingly rely on interorganisational knowledge transactions to extend their internal knowledge base. Moreover special emphasis was placed on the third routine *Knowledge Accumulation and Retention*, as the following statement shows:

*"Companies don't really understand what they have. So one of the big challenges is to understand first of all, what we actually have today, what technologies we are supporting, etc. Once we know what technologies we are supporting, we need to find out what people and expertise are required in order to support these technologies (...) All these are decisions that need to be made—unless **you know what exists** and unless you have some **way of categorising resources**, it's just meaningless. You have to have a baseline" (Interviewee #3).*

While interview data generally confirmed the high relevance of *Knowledge Accumulation and Retention* being an important routine underlying the Learning capacity, interviewees especially pointed towards the processes of *Knowledge Articulation* and *Unlearning* as important sub-processes constituting this routine.

First, *Knowledge Articulation* describes the process of actively converting implicit into explicit knowledge by communicating and interacting throughout the organisation. Its relevance for assuring sustainable learning mechanisms within the firm is well described by the following statement:

> *"If I have a knowledge management system, where I insert all the relevant knowledge and information, I have not yet gained quite a lot. (...) Instead, in order to be used in the right context, it must be put into the right place within the organisation and therefore first and foremost requires a basic understanding of the area of knowledge. I have not yet found a solution for this challenge, how best to bring the knowledge relevant for our business into real action." (Interviewee #1)*

Second, *Unlearning* refers to the process of divesting valuable resources or resources that have become obsolete over time (Sirmon et al. 2007, Leonard-Barton, 1992). Interviewees emphasised the ongoing challenge of renewing the existing knowledge base, not only by acquiring new knowledge, but also by releasing outdated knowledge. The statement of one interviewee may best describe the complex and versatile nature of this organisational learning mechanism:

> *"Companies spend an awful lot of time just supporting and maintaining things, 80% of their budget, just maintaining what they have. (...) So each year the amount of maintenance cost for operational capabilities gets bigger and bigger. So you have to kill some things in order to free up money to spend on new things. (...) Somehow you need to phase out the old technology and to place in the new technology, and therefore the skills." (Interviewee #3)*

Taken together, in accordance to the conceptual findings revealed from the literature review, Learning capacity was confirmed by the interviews to positively influence RR in firms by renewing and retaining the firms knowledge base, specifically its Market and Technological Knowledge, in ways that enable it to become the 'raw material' for recombinant innovation.

Integrating Capacity. Besides Sensing and Learning capacities, also Integrating and Coordinating capacities were confirmed by the qualitative data as highly important for RR success, confirming the conceptual framework developed on the basis of the literature review. Integrating capacity, which describes the firm's ability to creatively combine, integrate and transform knowledge based resources in new ways to construct or alter new operational capabilities for the purpose of developing new innovative products or services (e.g. Pavlou and El Sawy, 2011, Zahra and George, 2002), was confirmed by the data as important capability in the RR process in firms.

"Integration often it is just a linkage of interpersonal communication." (Interviewee #1)

The qualitative data analysis emphasised the importance of integration, with interviewees describing communication as extremely important, but often not interactive enough to successfully link diverse domains of knowledge within the company to create new, innovative RRs.

"Over and over again I notice that often it's during the informal talks with my colleagues from different operational areas, (e.g. during lunch breaks), when we discuss current business problems, and when the most promising ideas and new solutions are coming up, those that have been very helpful. If we were able to institutionalise and systematise these informal talks in our company, then this would result in a great success. I am pretty sure about this." (Interviewee #4)

While the construct of Integration capacity involves bilateral communication, it goes further by including frequent interactions, participation and involvement of parties in the overall process. Hence, integration, rather than communication, was incorporated into the final path model.

*"For us 'Integration' can basically be seen at two levels: First there is the **internal integration**, meaning that we have different business areas which can practice what we refer to as cross innovation [RR]. This is supported by our internal knowledge development process, (...) a central process that takes into consideration how different products internally to the firm can be bundled in new combinations. (...) So we possess the capability to integrate two things, which in sum solves a specific customer problem. Second, there is the **external integration**, basically the same processes, with the only difference that we internally possess one component A, which is combined with an external component B." (Interviewee #1)*

Accordingly, the three underlying routines of Integrating capacity, its constituting processes and underlying activities, namely (1) *Transforming individual to collective knowledge*, which refers to the processes of *contribution* and *representation* of individual and group knowledge (Pavlou and El Sawy, 2011), (2) *Interrelating different knowledge domains*, which refers to the processes of *Interrelation* of diverse knowledge inputs to the collective system (Grant, 1996) and the *Execution* of collective activities (Helfat and Peteraf, 2003), (3) *Reconfiguration and Refinement*, which captures the internal integration and transformation processes (Lavie, 2006, Hawass, 2010, Galunic and Rodan, 1998), could be confirmed by the interviewees.

In our data, Integrating capacity was linked to RR outcomes and was also described as influencing the relationship between firm's resource base and RR (e.g. interviewees #1, #4), supporting literature findings (Sirmon et al., 2007, Pavlou and El Sawy, 2011). In sum, in accordance with the theoretical arguments synthesised from the literature review, the proposed positive relationship between Integrating capacity and RR in firms could be confirmed by the qualitative data. Accordingly, it can be proposed that the higher the firm's Integrating capacity, the more likely it is for firms to be able to realise novel RRs.

Coordinating Capacity. In a similar vein, Coordinating capacity, which describes the firm´s ability to orchestrate and deploy tasks, resources, and activities in new operational capabilities in order to implement new, innovative products or services (RRs) in the market, emerged from the qualitative data as essential sub-capability of the firms DC, with interviewees referring to its critical role for leveraging the value creation potential of the resources by implementing and exploiting new products and services. Likewise for Integrating capacity, support was found for the importance of Coordinating capacity for the successful deployment of RRs.

In line with what the findings from the literature review suggested (e.g. Sirmon et al., 2010), interviewees described the necessity of having a vision or plan of those resources, capabilities, and skills needed to form the new operational capabilities to implement new RRs as an essential element of the firm's Coordination capacity, allowing an efficient *Allocation* and *Mobilisation* of resources. For example, interviewee #1 stated:

> *"There are definitely certain challenges concerned with 'Coordination', one important for instance is, that I have to take care of developing people according to those skills types presumably needed in the future. (...) This would also involve a kind of capability model, where I have to allocate resources available (...) in order to answer the questions: Do I have the right resources to address the requested demand? And vice versa, can every resource be assigned to address a specific demand in the future, or do I have resources where I have to divest, as the skills in that specific area are not*

needed in the future anymore? (...) This is not an automated system, rather more it is implicit knowledge." (Interviewee #1)

Moreover, interviewees highlighted the ongoing challenge of *Coordinating* and *Orchestrating* of resources, capabilities and skills for being deployed into new capability configurations (Sirmon et al., 2007, 2010), while special emphasise was given by the respondents on the complexity of finding systematic ways of mapping those resources available in the firms:

*"Once we have made all those distinctions, we essentially have a plan in terms of what we want to do. And the next thing then is that we need to somehow **map my resources** onto that: what resources are available and how can they be somehow assigned to the master plan that we have created." (Interviewee #3)*

Notwithstanding its relevance, however findings also revealed that firms often experience problems in finding systematically ways for synchronising tasks and activities (Helfat and Peteraf, 2003), and identifying complementarities and synergies among tasks and resources (Eisenhardt and Galunic, 2000, Pavlou and El Sawy, 2011), as not always systematic ways exists within the firms that allow to precisely describe and capture the different skills and capabilities available within the firm. This is well expressed by the following statement:

"The problem is that as a scientific measure it [a capability map] is not very reliable. The top people have multiple skills and if you put them into two different skill type buckets, e.g. as a programmer and as a project manager, then you have to be careful as you need to make sure that they don't double count. So how companies manage that is really on them to decide." (Interviewee #3)

Overall, qualitative data confirmed the three **basic routines underlying Coordinating capacity,** namely (1) *Allocating and Mobilising Resources* needed to address the demand (Sirmon et al., 2007), (2) *Coordinating and Orchestrating Resources* for being deployed into effective yet efficient capability configurations (Sirmon et al., 2007, 2010), and (3) *Implementing and Deploying new configurations* in the market to leverage and exploit resource opportunities (Sirmon et al., 2007, 2010). Moreover interview findings approved the proposition deduced from the literature review, suggesting that a high Coordinating capacity would be positively associated with RR in firms, as the effective coordination of resources is proposed to result in implementing and exploiting new products in the market by leveraging the value creation potential of the resources.

Taken together, Sensing, Learning, Integrating and Coordinating capacities were confirmed during qualitative data analysis as key drivers of RR in firms, and their microfoundations could be affirmed. The following section details the verification of the proposed characteristics of the resource base that are suggested to influence the potential value of resources for RR.

4.4.3 Characteristics of the Resource Base: Relevance for Resource Recombination

While interviews primarily focused on the discussion of *resource diversity, resource quality, resource complementarity, resource deployment flexibility, and resource transferability* as relevant characteristics of the resource base highlighted in the resource based literature, interviewees were also encouraged to freely discuss other relevant characteristics in order to not only confirm and refine the conceptual framework, but also to avoid the potential failure of disregarding relevant influencing factors. Interview findings clearly substantiated the importance of the given resource characteristics in a given RR context.

Resource Diversity. Resource diversity, captured by Market and Technological Knowledge *Breadth*, and defined as the number or range of different knowledge areas the firm is familiar with (De Luca and Atuahene-Gima, 2007, Bierly and Chakrabarti, 1996), was confirmed by the interviews as relevant characteristic of the resource base influencing its potential value for RR. Interviewees were consistent in their perception that the heterogeneity of resources may have an influence on RR in firms. While the majority of literature proposes that firms with a broad knowledge base have a greater potential to recombine different elements of that knowledge and thus generate more possibilities for new RRs by improving opportunity recognition and creative potential (Kogut and Zander 1992, Reed and DeFillippi, 1990, Granstand and Sjölander, 1988, 1990, Galunic and Rodan, 1998, De Luca and Atuahene-Gima, 2007), interview findings revealed that too much diversity may also hinder the development of RR, as stated by one of the interviewees:

> *"Maybe you can manage up to a hundred of different skill types within a company. I don't know. But it is not an endless number. Otherwise it can't be managed anymore. And therefore it can't be at that individual level anymore. (...) If there are too many skill types it becomes too difficult to manage and also it becomes expensive." (Interviewee #3)*

This finding is consistent with Galunic and Rodan (1998), De Luca and Atuahene-Gima (2007), Tushman and Romanelli (1996), Teece et al. (1997), Björk and Magnusson (2008), who found that a high degree of resource diversity may also lead to an enhanced complexity of knowledge transfer across functional units. Hence, findings suggest that there might be an optimum of different skill types within a firm, meaning that up to a certain degree it might be good to have diverse skill types but at a certain point resource diversity becomes too high to effectively being managed, unless firms possess the needed integration and coordination mechanisms.

Resource Quality. Besides resource diversity, the quality of resources, captured by Market and Technological Knowledge *Depth*, and defined in this study as the level of sophistication and complexity of the firm's knowledge in a specific area (De Luca and Atuahene-Gima, 2007), was also confirmed by the interviewees as a decisive characteristic influencing the value creation potential of resources. However, findings also revealed that possessing high qualitative resources alone would not automatically lead to competitive advantages over time:

> *"I would rather doubt the proposition, that if you have a lot of high quality individual players it also works out collectively. Concerning the quality, I would rather say, that you need to have the right mix [of resources]" (Interviewee #1)*

Notably, qualitative findings already indicated, what also emerged later from the quantitative data, that respondents had difficulties in differentiating between knowledge *breadth* and *depth*. For reducing complexity of the study, and as both categories appeared to be closely related to each other, breadth and depth of knowledge were merged to a single construct in the quantitative analysis, used to measure the quality and diversity of Market Knowledge (breadth and depth) and Technological Knowledge (breadth and depth).

Resource Complementarity. The complementarity of resources, specifically Market and Technological Knowledge (Hitt et al., 2001, Song et al., 2005), was also supported by the interviewees as important factor, as already indicated by the previous quote by interviewee (#1). Resource complementarity, rather than resource modularity, was included in the model as the term caused less ambiguity in respondent's understanding.

Resource Transferability. In comparison to resource quality, diversity and complementarity, interviewees appeared to assign less recognition and significance to resource transferability, which referred to the degree to which resources within the firm are transferred and articulated easily across disciplines (De Luca and Atuahene-Gima, 2007). Still support was found among interviewees that the tacitness of resources might have a negative effect on the exchange and absorption of knowledge across competence areas.

Resource Deployment Flexibility. The flexibility of resources available in firms refers to the degree to which the resources available in a firm are generalisable and flexible for being deployed in different areas apart from their original context. In this research resource deployment flexibility is captured by the context-specificity of knowledge, which describes "the extent to which the firm's knowledge is tailored to the requirements of specific contexts" (De Luca, 2007, p. 98). Interviews generally acknowledge the importance of resource flexibility for their deployment in new RRs:

> *"Some people [resources] indeed have the ability to be applicable in various different project prototypes [RRs], meaning that for both from skills [resources] to project prototypes [RRs] as well as from the prototypes [RRs] to customer demands are certain flexibilities. This allows, that these resources can be put together modularly [in new RRs]." (Interviewee #1)*

Moreover, while profound arguments can be found that support a high degree of specialisation in firms, consistent with the argument by Galunic and Rodan (1998), interview findings revealed that in the context of RR in firms a high level of specialisation and context-specificity may hinder resources from being applied elsewhere, a point well captured by interviewee #3 describing two scenarios:

> *"[One scenario is that you have] people and some of them are very specialised, they are focused only on a very small part of their business. You might have a whole team of people, who are very expensive and very highly skilled people, but they are only supporting something that contributes only 1% to your overall business. (...)*
>
> *The other scenario is that the company has somehow evolved and became quite mature and it has a small number of technologies that are common right across the business. (...) Say, you have a big team of people with Microsoft skills, because this technology is used in 50% of our business, these people can be moved very easy, they are more flexible because they have a common skill set, that can easily be applied to the major technologies that the business uses. And that major technologies support a lot of the business capabilities. This means that they are more flexible in terms of mobility and how they can be used." (Interviewee #3)*

Accordingly, findings support the proposition, that the lower the context specificity and thus the higher the resource deployment flexibility of the resources, the higher its potential value for RR.

Resource Renewal. Addressing the origin of firm's resources, resource renewal was mentioned by the interviewees as additional characteristic that may influence RR in firms. Findings emerged that the degree to which the firm's resources consist of 'newly acquired' or 'already existing' resources (e.g. Wiklund and Shepherd, 2009) may have an effect on RR in firms. However, respondents were indifferent whether the origin of resources may persist as decisive characteristic influencing the value creation potential of resources, as long as integration is given.

To conclude, interviews clearly substantiated the relevance of certain characteristics of the resource base for determining the value creation potential of resources for RR. In particular, *resource diversity, resource quality, resource complementarity, resource transferability, resource deployment flexibility* and *resource renewal* were confirmed by the interviews as relevant characteristics and are consequently included in the conceptual model. However, for reducing complexity of the model, the results indicated the relevance of merging in the final model the quality and diversity of Market Knowledge (breadth and depth), and Technological Knowledge (breadth and depth), respectively, instead of measuring knowledge breadth and depth separately, as respondents had difficulties in differentiating between the two constructs. Based on the discussion of the DC constructs and their interrelationships, the two proposed antecedents, Entrepreneurial Orientation and Networking Orientation, and their proposed interrelationships and impact on DCs are discussed in the subsequent section.

4.4.4 Entrepreneurial and Networking Orientation: Antecedents to Dynamic Capabilities

Respondents agreed that organisations differ in their strategic orientation, for instance the *willingness* or *attitude* of the firms concerning the engagement in entrepreneurial behaviour (Wiklund, 1998) or interfirm collaborations (Mu and Di Benedetto, 2012). Qualitative findings supported the conceptual framework, stressing the importance of organisational framework conditions, relevant for the development of DCs and thus RRs (Hawass, 2010).

Entrepreneurial Orientation. Entrepreneurial Orientation (EO), which characterises the firm's entrepreneurial behaviour, commonly regarded as a combination of *innovativeness, proactiveness,* and *risk-taking* (Lumpkin and Dess, 1996, Wiklund and Shepherd, 2003), was confirmed by the interviewees as decisive factor relevant for the development of DCs, and consequently RR. Its relevance is well described by the following statement given by one of the interviewees:

> *"A crucial factor that needs to be in place is the attitude, always to enjoy pursuing something new, instead of being satisfied with the old, hence never to stay still and to rest. However, the common attitude in firms is 'what performed well in the past, will be performing well in the future', and certainly it might be that a lot of things will still perform well in the future, but the initiative and desire to continuously strive to find things that can be improved in the future to become even better, is a crucial precondition that this even happens. Otherwise one only concentrates on the core competences and loses everything else".(Interviewee #1)*

Interviewee #1 further specified the importance of EO for RR in firms as follows:

> *"Innovation is demanding, even more demanding are RRs. And in the end over 80% of all projects fail, what might be seen as proof for 'would we rather have done it the old way, than we wouldn't have wasted all the money', but in the end it is the 20% that actually makes the difference." (Interviewee #1)*

Networking Orientation. Besides EO, also Networking Orientation (NO), which captures the firm's strategic orientation towards collaborating with external entities (Mu and Di Benedetto, 2011), emerged from the qualitative data as important antecedent for DCs, with interviewees highlighting the increasing relevance of collaborating with external partners for extending their own competences. Interviewee #1 for instance stated:

> *"Knowing that on the one hand side I have my core competence, but on the other hand side the customer will become more and more demanding in the future, and consequently will require more than I can offer as I cannot randomly expand or enlarge my competences within the desired depth, I necessarily need to acquire external competencies." (Interviewee #1)*

Being asked for important framework conditions driving RR in firms, interviewee #1 further stated:

> *"This certainly is **openness** and the **ability to communicate** with partners. This comprises a form of **external trust culture**, meaning that you are open towards your partner, instead of thinking, how can I demarcate my own products and services offerings from my partner's activities. (...) Once you have the motivation to establish this*

[RR in firms], openness is the necessary precondition that actually makes it functioning. It is especially necessary for the efficiency [of the RR process], because if you do not collaborate with partners you will permanently run against walls, which costs you a lot of energy. Openness, instead, enables you to run through open doors."
(Interviewee #1)

Accordingly, as qualitative findings reveal, both EO and NO were described by the respondents as important organisational framework conditions for the development of DCs, confirming the conceptual findings that emerged from the literature review.

4.5   Chapter Summary

This chapter started with an outline of the research design, entailing the research strategy and general research methods applied in this research. Subsequently the qualitative research methods used were outlined, including a description of the *informal discussion forum* and *participant observation* and the subsequent *in-depth interviews* conducted. In the second part of this chapter the results from the qualitative research steps were presented. The main purpose of the qualitative research step was to validate and refine the model before the quantitative research was conducted. Based on a structured content analysis of the qualitative data, the preliminary conceptual model could be confirmed, while minor adjustments were discussed and justified, leading to the qualitatively proven conceptual model, illustrated in Figure 4.1.

The qualitative proven conceptual model shows the four DCs, their interrelationships and impacts on performance outcome variable (RRs), as well as their effects on the resource base. All proposed relationships between the constructs could be confirmed by the qualitative data. In distinction from the initial model, the (refined) conceptual model presented in Figure 4.1 does not explicitly specify the variables of resource quality and resource diversity anymore, as interviewees had difficulties in differentiating between knowledge breadth and depth. Hence, in order to reduce complexity of the model, but at the same time not to lose any substance of content, both knowledge breadth and depth are applied in the quantitative research to evaluate the quality and diversity of Market Knowledge and Technological Knowledge, respectively, but are not assessed as separate constructs. The original hypotheses H1a and H1b were therefore omitted from the model and are not being tested separately anymore, as they where (already) included in H1 and H1 (1) (refer to section 3.6.2, Table 3.2).

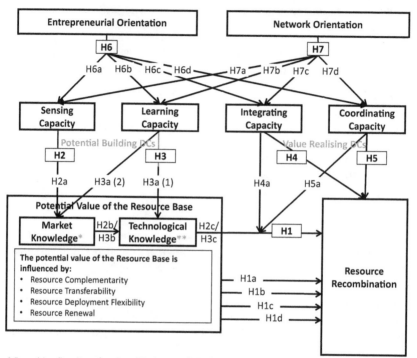

* Comprising diversity _and_ quality of Market Knowledge (measured by Market Knowledge breadth and depth)
** Comprising diversity _and_ quality of Technology Knowledge (measured by Technological Knowledge breadth and depth)

Source: own illustration

Figure 4.1 Qualitatively proven Conceptual Model

   As a result, the qualitative data analyses contributed to a specification of the conceptual model, which could be confirmed by the interviewees and subsequently will be tested in the quantitative research step. Therefore the propositions developed based on the literature review and confirmed by the qualitative research will be tested in the quantitative research step. The following chapter 5 first describes the quantitative research methods applied, while chapter 6 presents the results of the quantitative analyses.

Quantitative Research: Questionnaire Design and Data Collection

5

5.1   Introduction

Following the introduction and discussion of the general research design and the presentation of the results from the qualitative research, this chapter specifies the quantitative research method applied for testing the conceptual model and hypotheses. The chapter starts with a critical examination of the data collection method, a self-administered online survey, chosen for the quantitative research part, and justifies its use. This is followed by a discussion of the questionnaire design, which incorporates the levels of measurement, theory and statistical analysis, an operationalisation of the measurement constructs and scales used, as well as the pre-test of the survey instrument. The last section describes the data collection process outlining the sampling procedure, frame and size, as well as nonresponse bias.

5.2   Quantitative Research Method

As briefly introduced in section 4.2.2., a survey was chosen as appropriate data collection method for the quantitative analysis of the model and hypotheses. The decision was made based on the following considerations. Generally, surveys are seen as valuable instrument, commonly used in research practice, when the aim is to collect quantitative data for statistical analysis from a variety of different

Electronic supplementary material The online version contains supplementary material available at (https://doi.org/10.1007/978-3-658-35666-8_5).

© The Author(s), under exclusive license to Springer Fachmedien Wiesbaden GmbH, part of Springer Nature 2021
K. Kurzhals, *Resource Recombination in Firms from a Dynamic Capability Perspective*, Gabler Theses, https://doi.org/10.1007/978-3-658-35666-8_5

respondents in a cost- and time-efficient manner (Kinnear et al., 1993, Veal and Ticehurst, 2005, Zikmund, 2003, Lukas et al., 2004, Page and Meyer, 2000). This is faced by the critics of a lack of control over the respondent and lack of knowledge whether the answers given are reliable and faithful, generally rather low response rates, and a high reliance on the survey design (Plewa, 2010 referring to Lukas et al., 2004). Moreover while different survey channels exists, including personal (face-to-face), phone, fax, mail or online surveys, "the appropriateness of one type or channel for a particular study may be based on several factors, such as the versatility, cost, time, sample control, quantity of data, quality of data and response rate" (Plewa, 2010, p. 81, referring to Klassen and Jacobs, 2001).

For this research a self-administered online survey was deemed the most appropriate instrument due to the following weighting of advantages and disadvantages. It is commonly agreed that one disadvantage of web-based surveys is the potential misconception of questions by the respondents, as the respondents are not in direct communication with the researcher (Lukas et al., 2004). Although the possibility is given to all respondents to contact the researcher in case any questions occur, not always are the respondents aware of a misconception, and in case they are it is more likely for them to leave the question unanswered (Plewa, 2010). This generally leads to lower item completion rates in online surveys (Klassen and Jacobs, 2001).

As opposed to this, common advantages of online surveys are, first, the low costs for the online survey to be set up, as no printing or postage of the questionnaires arises (Aaker et al., 2004, Lukas et al., 2004). Second, online surveys allow a high degree of flexibility in responding, as the participant can answer the questions at their own time (Plewa, 2010), thus leading to a high level of accuracy of measurement (Aaker et al., 2004, Zikmund, 2003). This was regarded as especially relevant for this study as the target respondents, being industrial representatives in middle and upper management positions, are often impaired by time constraints. Third, online surveys are regarded as preferable instrument when concerned with sensitive topics (Aaker et al., 2004). Entailing questions regarding the firm's capabilities and resources, this also includes aspects such as the evaluation of internal capabilities against competitors, hence the topic in this survey are likely to be viewed as sensitive by respondents. Fourth, although the response rate of online surveys is found to be lower than in face-to-face surveys (Lukas et al., 2004), a comparatively high response rate was ensured through a specific targeting in the sampling procedure supported by an professional panel service provider.

Hence, an email-distributed online survey was assessed as most appropriate method for this study, considering the costs and target sample pool available for this research. Moreover, using the online survey tool *Unipark*, the data gathered by the respondents could be directly exported into the statistical software *SPSS*, which ensured accuracy of data processing. Besides, by means of controlling for the IP address, respondents that had already completed the survey could be disclosed from entering a second time.

5.3   Questionnaire Design

The following section elaborates on the questionnaire design, which has to be based on a deep understanding of the research topic and questions to be addressed in the study (Veal and Ticehurst, 2005). The conceptual model and hypotheses, developed in chapter 3 and specified in chapter 4, already indicated the relevant constructs for this study and the proposed associations between those constructs. Based on these findings a questionnaire was developed for the data gathering phase. Adapting a step-by-step procedure (Veal and Ticehurst, 2005, Plewa, 2010), first the levels of measurement, theory and statistical analysis were defined, second a specification of the nature of constructs (whether they were formative or reflective) was provided, thereafter the constructs were operationalised and measurement scales determined. Finally, the questionnaire was pre-tested and revised, as described in the following section.

5.3.1 The Levels of Measurement, Theory and Statistical Analysis

Prior to the development of the questionnaire the unit of analysis has to be defined (Zikmund, 2003) and the levels of measurement, theory and statistical analysis have to be clarified (Currall and Inkpen, 2002).

First, the **level of measurement** defines the sampling unit, that is to say the source of the data. For this study a key informant approach was utilised (Patterson and Spreng, 1997), collecting data on a personal measurement level, with upper and middle managers being the key respondent. While there is an ongoing debate on its appropriateness, previous research showed that "a single key informant can provide reliable and valid information on a personal level as well as higher levels of theory" (Plewa, 2010, p. 79).

Second, the **level of theory** determines the unit that the study intends to examine and generalises on (Klein et al., 1994). In this study DCs, Resources, and RR are measured at the firm level, hence the study´s unit of analysis is the firm. A review of publications showed that DCs and knowledge based resource are often operationalised on the individual level (Hawass, 2010) or the group level (Pavlou and El Sawy, 2011[1]), namely research group and business unit, whereby only few publications exist, that assess them on the firm level. This study aims to examine interrelations between capabilities, resources and RR at the firm level, therefore not an individual research group or business unit is examined, but the DCs are measured for the whole company.

Third, the **level of analysis** describes the statistical treatment of data (Klein et al., 1994). The firm level was also regarded as the appropriate level of analysis for all constructs. Respondents hence were asked to report on their firm's level of DCs, resources and RR success.

Briefly it can be said, that the level of analysis is aligned with the level of theory. The prevalent level of theory and analysis in this research is the firm level, hence only one level of measurement, theory and analysis is incorporated in the model and utilised in this study.

5.3.2 Formative vs. Reflective Measurement Models

Prior the development of the measurement scales a specification of the nature of constructs used in the study, whether they are formative or reflective in nature, is needed. Latent variables are theoretical constructs which a priori cannot be directly measured and thus have to be assessed by indicator variables, also called manifest variables, which in term are observable (Diamantpopoulos et al., 2008). To display the causal relationships between the latent constructs in a structural path model, previously they need to be operationalised in a measurement model, which describes the causal relationships between the latent constructs and its indicator variables (Eberl, 2004). Hereto, latent constructs are usually operationalised through multiple observable indicator variables to prevent them from being biased by single measures (Homburg and Dobratz, 1991). Generally two different forms of operationalisation of measurement models regarding the causality (direction) of the relationships between construct and indicators can be distinguished: *reflective* measurement models (from construct to indicators) and *formative* measurement models (from indicators to construct) (e.g. Edwards and Bagozzi 2000, Dimantpopoulos et al., 2008). While the distinction is not new, it received increased attention in the last years, where a debate raised on the correct operationalisation

---

[1] In their study Pavlou and El Sawy (2011) focus on the group level, explicitly the NPD unit's attributes, not the firm's attributes are addressed.

of latent constructs, especially as still deficits exist regarding the use of formative indicators for construct measurement (Albers and Hildebrandt 2006, Jarvis et al., 2003, Diamantpopoulos et al., 2008). Hence in recent years, formative models receive increasing attention, however its use in empirical studies is still scarce, and despite its appropriateness for operationalisation of specific constructs, its applications is still neglected in many cases in favor of reflective models, leading to high rates of misspecifications (Jarvis et al., 2003, Fassot and Eggert, 2005, Podsakoff et al., 2006).

Reflective measurement models have a long tradition in social science, its fundamental characteristic is that the latent construct 'causes' or 'reflects' its indicator, hence "a change in the latent variable causes variation in all measures simultaneously [..., and] all measures in a reflective measurement model must be positively intercorrelated" (Dimantpopoulos et al., 2008, p. 1240). Accordingly measurement items represent manifestations of an underlying latent construct (Bollen and Lennox, 1991). Due to the required high correlations among the indicator items, the items are interchangeable, meaning that the elimination of one item would not change the nature of the underlying construct (Bollen and Lennox, 1991, Diamantpopoulos and Winklhofer, 2001). This implies that the quality of measurement is not necessarily affected by the elimination of single items, as all facets of the latent construct might be represented by the remaining indicators (Jarvis et al. 2003).

Formative measurement models by contrast, assume that the latent construct is 'caused' or 'formed' by its indicators, hence "the indicators determine the latent variable which receives its meaning from the former" (Dimantpopoulos et al., 2008, p. 1241). The latent construct hence is defined as a linear sum of a set of measurement items that build the construct (Bagozzi, 1994). Given this causal direction each indicator captures a specific aspect of the latent construct. Hence formative indicators can be regarded as a 'set of distinct causes' (Jarvis et al. 2003), whereby each indicator represents a unique input, therefore indicators are not interchangeable, and thus allowed to be (positively, negatively or not at all) correlated among each other (for a detailed discussion see Bollen, 1984). For this reasoning and opposed to reflective models, internal consistency of the constructs is not presumed for formative models (Bollen, 1984), likewise it is difficult to assess reliability and construct validity for formative constructs (Bagozzi, 1994, Bollen and Lennox, 1991, Jarvis et al., 2003). Hence, for the operationalisation of formative models more important than achieving commonly used quality criteria for validity and reliability of the measurement, is to capture the entire range of distinct inputs to build the latent variable (Diamantopoulos and Winklhofer,

2001). On the other hand an elimination of a single item in a formative model would lead to a sacrifice of content validity.

To avoid misspecification prior any empirical investigation, the nature of the indicator variables and thus constructs needs to be specified a priori as it needs to be aligned with the questionnaire design (Jahn, 2007). To determine the nature of constructs, decision rules were followed as presented by Jarvis et al. (2003), which were based on the characteristic of formative and reflective models as outlined above. The results lead to the majority of constructs used in this research being conceptualised as reflective constructs, implying that the specific constructs (e.g. DCs) are reflected through its measurement items. Only RR was conceptualised as a second-order formative model, formed by different distinct types of RR. As detailed below, in this case a formative model was more appropriate than a reflective one. The operationalisation of the constructs is detailed in the following.

5.3.3 Operationalisation of Constructs

The operationalisation of the constructs used in this research required the identification or development of appropriate measurement instruments. This comprises, the decisions about whether existing scales can be used for this study, moreover whether an adaptation of these scales is required to suit this research context, or whether measurement instruments needed to be newly developed following standard scale development procedures (Page and Meyer, 2000). Whenever suitable, measurement items were adapted from existing, validated scales identified in the available literature. All scales used were adapted to the studies level of analysis (the firm level), and phrased relative to competitors. Based on a discussion and justification of the operationalisation of constructs, the measurement scales used in this study are presented in the following sections. The final questionnaire and the individual measurement items applied to measure each construct are provided in Appendix 5.1, section A-G, in the additional electronic material. Items followed by [R] are reverse coded.

Dynamic Capabilities
Due to the lack of empirical research on the DC construct, only few studies exist that discussed differrent ways for the operationalisation of DCs (Pavlou and El Sawy, 2011, Barreto, 2010), all of them have conceptualised the construct as a "second-order formative" or "aggregated multi-dimensional construct" that is formed out of its individual dimensions. As this research aims to shed light on the individual

dimensions of DC, as Sensing, Learning, Integrating and Coordinating capacity are proposed to take different roles and effects in the process of resource value creation in firms, however this study refrains from regarding DCs as a simple "sum of its dimensions", forming an overall DC out of the single dimensions. Thus, in this study DCs are not conceptualised as a multi-dimensional (second-order formative) construct, but rather measured as individual first-order reflective constructs.

Given this conceptual understanding of DCs as distinct constructs, the scales developed by Pavlou and El Sawy (2011) to measure Sensing, Learning, Integrating and Coordinating capacity were used in this research. However the original scales needed to be adapted to this research's understanding of the firm's DCs as developed in chapter 3, hereto most of the measurement items were adapted from the original scale, some items were partially modified and contextually respecified, while other were added to the scale. Following standard scale development procedures, the modified scales were tested in a separate pre-test (refer to section 4.3.1 and Appendix 4.1 in the additional electronic material) before being used in the quantitative survey. All DCs were measured at the firm level. Respondents were asked to rate their firm's capacities in different areas relative to their major competitors. Using a seven-point likert scale (1 = I strongly disagree, 7 = I strongly agree) respondents were asked to indicate for each statement the extent to which it describes their firm (refer to Appendix 5.1, section A).

Sensing Capacity refers to the generation of market intelligence, customer and competitor intelligence, and technological intelligence and was measured based on the work by Pavlou and El Sawy (2011). Sensing capacity was operationalised by six reflective items as presented in Appendix 5.1, section A, whereby the first three items were taken from the original scale by Pavlou and El Sawy, while V0804, V0805 and V0806 were added to the original scale to further address technological orientation, responsiveness to industry trends and competitor activity. The new items were based on Teece (2007).

Learning Capacity captures the acquisition, assimilation, creation and retention of (new) knowledge. The operationalisation of the construct was based on the scale developed by Pavlou and El Sawy (2011), whereby three items (V0901, V0903, V0906) were taken from the original five-item scale, while the other two items used to capture Realised Absorptive Capacity (RACAP) were disclosed for the reason that Learning capacity as defined in this research comprises Potential Absorptive Capacity (PACAP) and Knowledge Creation, but not RACAP (referring to Zahra and George, 2002). Instead three items were added to the original scale that addressed the extent to which a firm uses processes and routines for Knowledge Acquisition (V0902), Knowledge Codification (V0904) and Knowledge Retention

(V0905) to acquire, capture and renew knowledge (refer to Appendix 5.1, section A). The conceptualisation of these new items was informed by the Exploratory and Transformative Learning scales developed by Lichtenthaler (2009).

Integrating Capacity captures the contribution, representation, and interrelation of individual input to the entire business following Pavlou and El Sawy (2011). Seven items were used to measure Integrating capacity. Two items (V1001, V1002) were taken from the original scale developed by Pavlou and El Sawy (2011), while four items were added to the original scale (see Appendix 5.1, section A). The new items were informed by previous studies by Menon et al. (1997), Jaworski and Kohli (1993), Morgan and Piercy (1998) and De Luca and Atuahene-Gima (2007), used to capture firm's routines and processes directed towards intra- and interdepartmental integration as well as cross-functional integration. Hence the items incorporated the level of interorganisational integration during the entire process, the frequency of interaction between groups and departments and the level of cross-functional team effort.

Coordinating Capacity captures resource allocation, task assignment, and synchronisation referring to Pavlou and El Sawy (2011). Therefore all items were taken from the original five-item scale by Pavlou and El Sawy (2011) and extended by one additional item (V1105), which was added to ensure the correct and comprehensive measurement of efficiency of resource and knowledge exploitation routines to incorporate the original thoughts by Teece (2007) (refer to Appendix 5.1, section A).

As DCs are abstract, intangible, not directly observable, thus latent constructs, it was deemed valuable to use these multiple reflective indicator items to measure each dimension-related construct (Pavlou and El Sawy, 2011, Barretto, 2010). As can be seen from the conceptualisation of the items, the constructs are reflective in nature as each construct (e.g. Sensing capacity) causes its items (e.g. we frequently scan the environment to identify new business opportunities). Accordingly, the items are regarded as manifestations of the construct. It should be noted however, that while the DCs are being conceptualised as distinct constructs, they may still be weakly correlated, and interdependences may exist (Pavlou and El Sawy, 2011) (as outlined in section 3.4.1.6).

Characteristics of the Resource Base
To evaluate the potential value of the resource base, different characteristics of the resources base were assessed. This research differentiates between Market and Technology Knowledge. **Market Knowledge** refers to the firm's understanding of the market environment, particularly of customers and competitors (e.g. De Luca

and Atuahene-Gima, 2007), while **Technological Knowledge** refers to the firm's technological expertise, R&D as well as engineering skills and competences (e.g. De Luca and Atuahene-Gima, 2007). In line with De Luca and Atuahene-Gima (2007) and opposed to other studies (e.g. Atuahene-Gima, 2005, Li and Calantone, 1998, Narver and Slater, 1990, Danneels, 2007, Wiklund and Shepherd, 2003) that differentiate between different sub-types of Market Knowledge (e.g. customer and competitor knowledge) and Technological Knowledge (e.g. technical, R&D, engineering knowledge), for this study a holistic measurement approach to the concept of Market and Technological Knowledge was chosen as appropriate means in order to reduce the complexity of the measurement model for the informants. This approach was justified following the argument by De Luca and Atuahene-Gima (2007) stating, that the characteristics of knowledge are the same for customers and competitor knowledge, respectively for technical, R&D, engineering knowledge, and therefore no theoretical rationale is given to expect differential effects of the different sub-types of Market and Technological Knowledge on RR (see De Luca and Atuahene-Gima, 2007, p. 101). For this reason an aggregated measure of Market Knowledge and Technological Knowledge was chosen. However, to ensure a consistent understanding of Market and Technological Knowledge in the survey their definitions were included in the questionnaire. Given a common understanding of the terminology, respondents were asked to refer to the different characteristics of their firm's Market and Technological Knowledge, hereto they were asked to evaluate their Market and Technological Knowledge *breadth and depth*, thereafter *knowledge tacitness, knowledge specifity, knowledge complementarity* and *knowledge origin*.

Market and Technological Knowledge Breadth is defined as the number or range of different knowledge areas the firm is familiar with (De Luca and Atuahene-Gima, 2007, Bierly and Chakrabarti, 1996). Different measures can be found in the literature for the knowledge breadth. Based on the work by Gupta and Govindarajan (2000), Wiklund and Shepherd (2003) present a comprehensive measurement scale of the firm's procedural knowledge by means of evaluating 11 different knowledge domains measuring a firm's knowledge position compared to companies in the industry. While the scale is highly comprehensive in terms of its scope, however, it does not offer a clear differentiation between the Market and Technological Knowledge areas. Other more objective measures for knowledge breath exists, as to name total number of patents (Henderson and Cockburn, 1994), number of technologies (Pavitt, 1985), multi-technologicalness (Granstand and Sjölander, 1988), technical diversification (Granstand and Sjölander, 1988), knowledge heterogeneity (Rodan and Galunic, 2004), however a big penalty of all those measures is, that an exact assessment of knowledge by numbers is highly dependent on the level of abstraction and granularity used, hence comparability between firms is difficult to reach (Granstand and Sjölander, 1988). Accordingly Rouse and Daellenback (1999) claim that the "major reason for the scarcity of empirical studies lies in the difficulty of identifying the core resources that firms can use to gain a competitive advantage" (Zahra and Wiklund, 2002, p. 33). To overcome these restrains, in this research the scale originally developed by Zahra et al. (2000) and adapted by De Luca and Atuahene-Gima (2007) was used, for its benefits of its simplicity and coherence, reliability and validity, and suitability for measuring both Market Knowledge breadth (De Luca, 2007) and Technological Knowledge breadth (Zahra et al., 2000). Respondents were asked to evaluate their firm's Market and Technological Knowledge on a continuum from "limited" to "wide ranging" and "narrow" to "broad" (refer to Appendix 5.1, section B).

Market and Technological Knowledge Depth is defined in this study as the level of sophistication and complexity of the firm's knowledge in a specific area (De Luca and Atuahene-Gima, 2007), referring to the depth and quality of learning (Zahra et al., 2000). Likewise knowledge breadth different measures can be found in the literature for knowledge depth. Danneels (2007) for example provides a good measurement example of the propensity to change the resource base, looking at market resource accumulation and technology resource accumulation, and asking to what extend a company build or developed new resources that it did not have three years ago. However, this scale only measures the extent or quality of new knowledge-based resources, independently of the existing knowledge base in the company. For the same reasons as mentioned above (simplicity, reliability and validity of the scale), Market and Technology Knowledge depth was measured using the scale developed by Zahra and colleagues (2000) and adapted by De Luca and Atuahene-Gima (2007). Accordingly Market Knowledge depth was measured on a semantic-differential scale asking the respondents to evaluate their firm's Market and Technology Knowledge on a continuum form "basic" to "advanced", and "shallow" vs. "deep" (refer to Appendix 5.1, section B).

Knowledge Tacitness is nowadays a familiar category for knowledge and an established construct in organisation theory, and was included as a further characteristic of the resource base. Knowledge Tacitness, as conceptualised in this research, focuses on the transferability and codification of knowledge. Hence, items by De Luca and Atuahene-Gima (2007) going back to Szulanski (1996) were deemed suitable for this research and used to operationalise knowledge tacitness. Knowledge tacitness thus was measured with four items (refer to Appendix 5.1, section B), capturing the extent to which the firm's knowledge is formally documented, codified and communicated through written reports, and hence transferable (Szulanski, 1996). This measurement reflects the embedded nature of knowledge in firms.

Knowledge Specificy refers to "the extent to which the firm's knowledge is tailored to the requirements of specific contexts in which it is maximally effective but loses its value in other contexts" (De Luca, 2007, p. 98). This study operationalised knowledge specificy based on the scale developed by De Luca and Atuahene-Gima (2007), going back to Reed and De Fillippi (1990). Their three items reflect the extent to which the Market and Technological Knowledge is tailored to the firm's environment. One additional item (V1604) was added measuring knowledge specific from a different perspectives capturing the generalisability of knowledge, hence this item was conceptualised as reverse coded (refer to Appendix 5.1, section B).

Knowledge Complementarity refers to the level to which the areas of knowledge available in the firm complement each other. The requirement for a generic knowledge complementarity measure as well as the peculiarity of the research field limited the usability of existing scales for this research. A range of scales are available in literature, most of them were found as too specific in terms of measurement, focusing primarily on the specific characteristics of products and their complementarity, resource modularity (Sanchez, 1995, Sanchez and Mahoney, 1996), or complementarity of alliance partners (Lin et al., 2009). The study by Song et al. (2005) is the only study, that empirically investigated resource complementarity in regard to Market and Technological resources, however, in this study resource complementarity was not directly measured, rather it was conceptualised as a simple interaction term build through Market and Technological Knowledge. Other studies were found as too restrictive due to the specificity of dimensions regarding the research area or field. Hence, due to the lack of existing scales, an own scale comprising three items was developed and pre-tested (refer to Appendix 5.1, section B).

Knowledge Origin in this study refers to the degree to which the resources available within the firm's resource base consist of externally acquired resources or have already been internally existent. Knowledge origin was conceptualised as a one-item measure, asking respondents to rate on a scale from 0% to 100%, how much of their knowledge is internally based (existing) and how much is externally acquired (new). To ensure a consistent understanding of the terminology, a definition was enclosed in the survey. All constructs measuring the characteristics of the resource base were operationalised as reflective constructs, an overview of all items is given in Appendix 5.1, section B.

Outcome Variable: Resource Recombination

RR was conceptualised as a multidimensional formative construct that is a composite variable formed by four different types of RR. The conceptualisation of multidimensional constructs necessitates a distinction between two levels of analysis, the first level relates the indicator variables to the (first-order) dimensions, while the second level relates the individual dimensions to the (second-order) latent construct (Diamantpopoulos et al. 2008).

Thus, in contrast to all other constructs used in this research which are conceptualised as first-order reflective constructs, RR is formed by the four different types of RR and thus conceptualised as a second-order formative construct. Following Lee and Cardogan (2013) alternatively to building multiple independent first-order reflective constructs (refer to Model A in Figure 5.1), researchers can compute a higher-order constructs by using the first-order (reflective) constructs $\xi 1$, $\xi 2$, $\xi 3$ to build the formative latent construct $\eta 1$ (refer to Model B in Figure 5.1). Figure 5.1 gives a graphical notation of first-order reflective models and its alternative use in a second-order formative construct.

Model A) Three independent first-order reflective constructs	Model B) Second-order formative construct
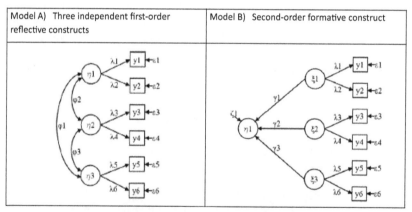	

Source: Lee and Cardogan, 2013, p. 245

Figure 5.1   A first-order reflective Measurement Model and its alternative Specification

Modelling RR as a formative, aggregated measure is justified in this research following the argument by Cenfetelli and Bassellier (2009, p. 690), stating that "formative measurement simplifies what might otherwise be multiple paths in a structural model into a more concise single path (…) [between the exogenous construct and the endogenous] formatively measured construct. Such bundling of indicators enhances parsimony through the substitution of a single construct in place of multiple indicators within a theoretical model." While there is an ongoing discussion of the appropriate usage of formative models in SEM (e.g. Diamantopoulos et al., 2008, Diamantopoulos and Siguaw, 2006), being conscious of its constraints as detailed discussed by Lee and Cardogan (2013), for this research its usage is regarded as a sufficient way of aggregating first-order constructs into higher-order constructs in regard to reduce the complexity of the research model.

The operationalisation of multidimensional constructs involves both the conceptualisation of the second order formative construct as well as the measurement of the dimension-related first order reflective constructs (each of the four types of RR) (Barreto, 2010). The formative model was build consistent with the guidelines presented by Diamantpopoulos and Winklhofer (2001): (i) specifying the content domain of the second- and first-order constructs, (ii) proposing the effects of the first-order on the second-order construct, (iii) specifying the relationships and distinctions among the first-order constructs, and (iv) proposing the role of the second-order construct on the study's dependent variables (Pavlou and El Sawy, 2011, p. 252).

Other than a second-order *reflective* model would assume, the construction of second-order *formative* models as presented in Figure 5.1 does not require the **first-order (reflective) constructs** to be conceptually identical (Lee and Cardogan, 2013). Rather more, the first-order reflective models can be theoretical distinct entities that represent different facets of the overall construct. In this research, as explained earlier, each of the four types of RR is distinct from each other, with every type of RR offering a unique component to the overall RR in firms. The resulting formative model of RR thus represents a measurable model that can be used to capture RR through the four underlying components. Therefore a formative multidimensional construct revealed appropriate for the construction of RR in this research.

In line with the conceptualisation of RR provided in section 2.4.2.2, the RR measures applied in this study focus on the deployment of *existing* versus *new resources* for *ongoing* versus *new business initiatives* to create new products or services, as defined by Zahra and Wiklund (2002). The first-order reflective constructs, used to measure the four different types of RR, were conceptualised based on the scale developed by Zahra and Wiklund (2002) and applied by Wiklund and Shepherd (2009), and were adopted to this research's context, due to the lack of alternative reliable and valid measures for RR in literature. The measures were conceptualised to focus on the extent to which firms are engaged in distinct RR activities. For all four types, respondents were asked to indicate their agreement with different statements with respect to the four different types of RR (refer to Appendix 5.1, section C). In all cases, instruction reads as follows: "Often innovation is seen as the recombination of resources in new ways to create new, innovative products or services. We differentiate between 4 types of Resource Recombination according to their usage of EXISTING vs. NEW RESOURCES for ONGOING vs. NEW BUSI- NESS INITIATIVES (definitions were provided). The following questions ask you to what extent your company focused on different types of Resource Recombination over the past 3 years and compared to the common practice in your industry."

Type 1 RR: Existing Resources for Ongoing Business Initiatives
Following Zahra and Wiklund (2002, p. 22) this type of RR is defined as "the recon- figuration of a firm's [existing] resource inputs to make their use more efficient". It was measured by four items developed by Zahra and Wiklund (2002), capturing the "re-deployment of a business' current resources to add features to existing prod- ucts, or expand service offerings" (Wiklund and Shepherd, 2009, p. 200) in order to achieve objectives more economically or more efficiently (Zahra and Wiklund, 2002). Minor specifications in the wording were made to avoid ambiguity. A high score in this index would give evidence that the firm places great emphasis on this type of RR.

Type 2 RR: New Resources for Ongoing Business Initiatives
Following the definition by Zahra and Wiklund (2002, p. 23) and Wiklund and Shepherd (2009, p. 200) type 2 of RR refers to the "infusion of new resources to improve efficiency, increase product variety, add new features to existing products, and enhance performance in new arenas". Type 2 RR was measured by four items based in the original scale developed by Zahra and Wiklund (2002) whereby small adaptions of the wording were made. According to the measures a high score in this index would give evidence that the firm places great emphasis on this type of RR.

Type 3 RR: Existing Resources for New Business Activities
In line with Zahra and Wiklund (2002, p. 23) and Wiklund and Shepherd (2009, p. 200), this type of RR refers to "changing of the firm's mix of resource inputs to pursue new initiatives such as extending the new product line, introducing new products, or entering new markets". Type 3 of RR was conceptualised based on the scale developed by Zahra and Wiklund (2002). Their four items reflect the emphasis given by the firm to this type of RR.

Type 4 RR: New Resources for New Business Activities
Following the definition presented by Zahra and Wiklund (2002, p. 23) this type of RR refers to "the acquisition and use of these resource inputs to generate new products, goods or services for new markets." In line with the other measures type

4 of RR was conceptualised based on the six-item-scale developed by Zahra and Wiklund (2002), however to reduce complexity only four items were applied in this research, reflecting the firm's emphasis given to this type of RR.

The scales used to measure each single type of RR (as first-order reflective construct) are presented in Appendix 5.1, section C. Having built the first-order reflective constructs, these models were used in a second step to form the **second-order formative** construct of RR. The aggregation heuristic used for the calculation of the second-order construct is detailed in the data analysis section 6.4.7. Additionally for identification purposes, an overall measure of RR was developed and included in the questionnaire, assessing RR through four (direct) indicator items (see Appendix 5.1, section C). The reason for additionally measuring second-order constructs with these (direct) indicator items is to cross-validate that the indirect measurement through the first-order dimensions (Types of RR) is also consistent with their (direct) indicator items (e.g. Pavlou and El Sawy, 2011).

Antecedents: Networking Orientation and Entrepreneurial Orientation
Networking Orientation and Entrepreneurial Orientation were included as antecedents to DCs in the model (refer to Appendix 5.1, section D and G).

Networking Orientation in this research is conceptualised as "the extent to which a firm's business strategy stresses effective and efficient location of network partners, management of network relationships, and improvement of network performance" (Mu and Di Benedetto, 2011, p. 341). The construct was measured using the original scale developed by Mu and Di Benedetto (2011), which based their scale on an extensive theoretical review on social network and new product development literature (e.g. Dyer and Singh, 1998, Ahuja, 2000, Gulati et al., 2000, Moran, 2005). Respondents were asked to indicate for each statement the extent to which it describes the firm's orientation towards collaborating with external partners (i.e. suppliers, customers, institutions) on a seven-point likert scale (1 = I strongly disagree to 7 = I strongly agree).

Entrepreneurial Orientation, regarded as a combination of *innovativeness, proactiveness*, and *risk-taking* (e.g., Wiklund, 1999), reflects the extent to which firms establish the identification and exploitation of untapped opportunities (Lumpkin and Dess, 1996, Baker and Sinkula, 2009). EO was measured applying the established scale developed by Baker and Sinkula (2009) going back to Covin and Slevin (1989) and refined by Naman and Stevin (1993). The scale is widely accepted and used in research practice (e.g. Wiklund and Shepherd, 2003), as items are regarded as good conceptualisation of the three key-dimensions of EO. Pairs of statements were given to the respondents, which represent opposite ends. They were asked to mark on a semantic differential scale the number which best represents the view of their firm. To avoid response bias and control for correctness of answer the last three items were reverse coded.

Control variables

The study also controlled for a number of variables, which deemed to be important determinants that might affect the hypothesised relationships, including *environmental turbulence, company size, company age, position, functional area,* and *industry sector* (whether the company was acting in an industry or service sector), and *R&D intensity*. The measures were drawn from related research on value creation in firms (e.g. Isobe et al., 2008, Pavlou and El Sawy, 2011, Wiklund et al. 2002). The individual items used to measure the control variables are provided in Appendix 5.1.

Environmental Turbulence was measured with the five-item-scale as developed by Atuahene-Gima (2005) (see Appendix 5.1, section E) to capture the pace of change and uncertainty in the environment that arises through changing customer needs and technological volatility (Isobe et al., 2008). The variable was included in the model to control for the likely effect of uncertain and unpredictable environments on the development of DCs and RR in firms as suggested by the DC perspective (e.g. Teece et al., 1997, Brown and Eisenhardt, 1997).

Company Size was assessed by the firm's total number of employees (e.g. Isobe et al., 2008, Pavlou and El Sawy, 2011, Wiklund et al. 2002). The variable was included to test for the potential effect of company size on RR in firms, as a variety of studies indicate that well-established, big companies might possess advantages in terms of availability of resources, while at the same time smaller companies might possess a higher flexibility to refine their asset structure (e.g. Isobe et al., 2008), both of which might influence RR in firms. The central view represented in the literature is that older and larger firms are less adaptive or flexible and therefore less capable to change their resource base (Danneels, 2008).

Company Age was measured by the number of years a venture had been in existence (Zahra et al. 2000) and assessed by asking respondents to report the year in which the company was founded (e.g. Isobe et al., 2008, Zahra et al. 2000). Age might influence a firm's technological learning (Zahra et al. 2000), as resource accumulation is the result of a variety of path-dependent processes of investment, sensing, learning and decision-making (e.g. Teece et al. 2007), thus processes that firms adopt over time (Dierickx and Cool, 1989). Hence, following Isobe et al. (2008, p. 416), it might be suggested that "as a result of this path dependence, firms tend to confine themselves to a limited set of technological domains and lose flexibility in their ability to respond to environmental change". Thus company age might have an influence on RR, in a way that older firms are less flexible and effective in developing new RRs than younger.

Functional Area was controlled for by asking respondents to specify their core functional area, whether it is (1) General Management, (2) Innovation Management, (3) Product Development Management, (4) Business Development Management, (5) R&D, or (6) Others (whereby the latter group of respondents were screened out as they were not in the target sample, refer to 5.4). This variable was included to test if the right target sample was reached and moreover to control if different evaluations of the studies' constructs dependent on the functional area of the respondent (e.g. whether the respondent yield a general management function or a specialist function). The same accounts for the **current position** of the respondent. Here the respondents were asked to indicate their current position (e.g. whether the respondent was in the upper or middle management). The responses were coded as a dichotomous variable, with 0 for upper management and 1 for middle management.

Industry Segment was controlled for based on the UK Standard Industrial Classification (SIC) Scheme (2007). Respondents were asked to refer to the industry sector their firm is working in (defined in the survey as the one from which the company generates most of its turn-over) based on a 2-diget SIC code (whereby relevant information on the UK SIC Scheme was provided in a separate pdf-document). As industries vary in their technological opportunities and ability to induce learning (Li, 1995), R&D expenditure (OECD, 2011), and resource profitability (Brown and Garten, 1994), the variable was included to test for the potential effect of different industry sectors (e.g. high tech vs. low tech industries, manufacturing vs. service sector) on RR in firms.

Ownership Structure was assessed by asking respondents, whether their firms was a (1) public company (listed on stock exchange), (2) private company (ownerships by CEO and family), (3) family-owned company (ownerships by family), or (4) others, which they were asked to specify (similar to Zahra and Wiklund, 2002, Zahra et al. 2002). Differences between independent and corporate-owned companies were reported in regard to their strategic choices and technological strategies (e.g. Zahra, 1996). The variable was included in order to test the likely effect that private or family-owned businesses might have different control-mechanisms in respect to decision making processes than corporate-owned companies (Bell, 1991). This is as "managers of corporate-owned ventures often have limited discretion to initiate strategic changes such as revising the mix of their companies' resources or the way these resources are combined. Such changes often require corporate approval, which can induce conservatism" (Zahra and Wiklund, 2002, p. 26). Hence a positive relationship is expected between a private or family owned company and RR. The responses were coded as a dichotomous variable, with 0 for independent firms and 1 for corporate units.

R&D Intensity defines the R&D expenditures as a percentage of sales, and was employed in this study as commonly accepted indicator for technology-intensiveness and thus innovation-activeness of firms, respectively industry sectors (OECD, 2011). The logic behind is that, "firms which are technology-intensive innovate more, win new markets, use available resources more productively and generally offer higher remuneration to the people that they employ" (Hatzichronoglou, 1997, p. 4). Therefore, the OECD uses R&D intensity as indicator to classify manufacturing industries in „high", „medium-high", „medium-low" and „low" technology industries (OECD, 2011). In line with previous studies (e.g. Pavlou and El Sawy, 2011), in this research R&D intensity was measured by the percentage of sales spent on R&D. The variable was included to control for the likely effect of R&D intensity on RR. Beside it was used to test if the right target sample was reached and to cross-validate the data by correlating it with the industry segment data. Strong approval between the two information sources and data provided by the respondents obtained. Notably, as R&D intensity as an indicator for technology-intensiveness allows inferences about the firm's innovation-activeness of the industry, however, it is not always suitable for service industries. Instead, for service industries other indicators as skill intensity or indirect R&D measures, such as technology embodied in investment or investment in ICT goods are more suitable (OECD, 2011). Due to the lack of readily accessible scales to gather that information, the percentage of R&D expenditure was taken as a proxy.

Innovation Performance was additionally included in the questionnaire to allow testing the established effect of RR on innovation performance. Innovation performance as conceptualised in this research entails both strategic performance (product effectiveness) and operational efficiency (process efficiency) (e.g. Isobe, 2008, Pavlou and El Sawy, 2011), and was measured based on the scale developed by March and Stock (2006). As March and Stock's scale was originally developed in the context of new product development, their items were adapted to this studies' context (product and service innovation). To complement the strategic performance measures, the scale was further extended by two additional items used to measuring operational efficiency as developed by Isobe et al. (2008). Hence, overall innovation performance was measured with six items that asked respondents to indicate the extent to which the firm has achieved its objectives regarding innovation performance formed by strategic performance and operational efficiency (see Appendix 5.1, section F). Consistent with Pavlou and El Sawy (2011), this operationalisation places weights on both dimensions of innovation performance, and thereby captures that firms are encouraged to handle both efficiency and effectively, rather than focusing on one dimension over the other (Sethi, 2000).

In summary, the overall questionnaire entailed 98 items to measure the exogenous and endogenous constructs used in the measurement model, among those 24 items for measuring the DCs, 20 items for measuring the characteristics of the resource base, 22 items measuring for the RR construct, 14 items for measuring the antecedents, and another 18 items for measuring the controls. Details of the individual items that were used to measure each construct are provided in Appendix 5.1.

5.3.4 Measurement Scales

Closely linked with the operationalisation of the constructs is the decision about the appropriate measurement scales, used to measure the differentiating values of the respondent's answers. Generally a distinction can be made between four different types of measurement scales, namely *nominal, ordinal, interval* and *ratio* scales (Kinnear et al., 1993, Zikmund, 2003).

Nominal scales are regarded as the simplest scales solely, used to label specific characteristics of the addressed subject (Zikmund, 2003, Weis and Steinmetz, 2002), while ordinal scales already indicate a predefined order of the measured values (Kinnear et al., 1993). Similar to ordinal scales, interval scales are also used to present an order of the measured objects, but moreover they allow measuring the distance between the variables in equal intervals whereby no zero point exists (Zikmund, 2003, Page and Meyer, 2000). Ratio scales are analogous to interval scales, however, including a definite zero point (Kinnear at al., 2003). In marketing research interval scales are merely used for assessing attitudes, opinions and predispositions (Kinnear et al., 1993).

In this study, nominal scales are used solely for categorising different manifestations of specific control variables, such as current position, functional area, or industry type. Other control variables, such as R&D intensity firm's size, or firm's age were measured using interval or ratio scales. For the majority of items in this questionnaire respondents were asked to report their responses on a seven-point likert scale, anchored with the statements *'I strongly agree'* and *'I strongly disagree'*. Strictly regarded likert scales are ordinal in nature (Zikmund, 2003), however they are generally treated as interval or "ordinal interval" scale in research (Lukas et al., 2004, p. 334). This reasoning is justified as respondents are observed to treat the distance between the different options statements *'I strongly agree'* and *'I strongly disagree'* as equal. Therefore the use of likert scales as quasi-interval scales is widely accepted in research practice (Kinnear et al., 1993). All DC dimensions, their antecedent NO, most characteristics of the resource base, as well as the outcome variable RR were measured on a seven-point likert scale and threated as interval scale for the data analysis. Exclusively, knowledge breadth and depth and EO were measured on a semantic differential scale, where pairs of statements were given, which represent opposite ends and a seven-point scale divided the two ends. In line with the above argumentation this scale is also considered an interval scale in this research.

Beside the specification of the type of scale used, a definition of an appropriate number of measurement points was needed. The seven-point scale was regarded as appropriate in this research for the following reasoning: First, the scales used in this study were constructed with an odd number of measurement points to provide a focal point and thus allow the respondents to take a 'neutral' position in the middle of the scale (between the positive and negative labelled ends of the scale). This was deemed reasonable in avoidance of forcing undecided respondents to decide for one or another position. Moreover, seven points were evaluated as a sufficient level of differentiation for measurement, rather than five points, which emerged to be to imprecise, and nine points, which turned out to be too differentiated and overexerted the respondents as emerged from the discussion with experts.

Moreover, given the lack of archival data or external objective scales available for measuring the constructs of this study, this research was obliged to rely on self-reported assessments of the respondents. Thus for the majority of constructs perceptual, subjective scales were used. The study hence is limited to this point. This proceeding was justified as objective scales often are incident to lower levels of specificity in terms of industry, economic condition and time horizon and do not allow meaningful comparisons across companies (Song and Parry, 1997, Pavlou and El Sawy, 2011). Moreover to counterbalance the likely effect of overestimating of the firm's own position when using perceptive scales, respondents were asked to assess their own firm's position (in terms of capacities, resource endowments, RR success) relative to their major competitors respectively compared to the common practice in industry.

To sum up, measurement scales used in this study were described and their appropriateness for this research justified. A pre-test of the questionnaire however was deemed valuable to ensure accurate and consistent measurement and to test the operationalisation of the constructs and measurement scales in the context of this study. The pre-testing of the questionnaire is briefly described in the following section.

5.3.5 Pre-Test

The questionnaire was developed in accordance with general principles of good research in regard to content, wording, format and sequence to ensure accurate and consistent measurement (Kinnear et al., 1993, Veal and Ticehurst, 2005). To reduce measurement error and avoid ambiguity, special objective emphasis was given to a clear, easy to understand, and precise wording (Zikmund, 2003). A pre-test of the questionnaire was carried out during February 2013 among a group of experts, consistent of seven key informants from the university with focus on empirical research in innovation and marketing related fields and five key informants with industry background in the area of interest. The participants were asked to fill out the questionnaire and to give comments on potential biased, confusing or ambiguous questions or other perceived difficulties regarding the terms used in the questionnaire (Page and Meyer, 2000, Zikmund, 2003). Moreover feedback on the structure and sequence of the questions, as well as the appropriateness of survey instrument was asked for. Additionally, respondents were requested to document the time they needed to complete the questionnaire in order to assess and, if necessary, alter a feasible length of the questionnaire (Plewa, 2010). While no changes regarding the length were needed, minor changes were made regarding the wording, whereby special emphasis was given towards phrasing the terms in the professional language used by the respondents. For this purpose, informants were asked to re-phrase those questions they regarded as problematic to understand. The information gained was valuable to see, firstly if informants understood the content correctly and secondly to determine a more accurate wording (Plewa, 2010). The results of the pre-test supported that the data gained from the questionnaire would ensure an accurate and consistent measurement compliant with the research objectives. The final questionnaire is provided in Appendix 5.2 in the additional electronic material.

Additionally to pre-testing the questionnaire in order to examine the statistical properties, it was deemed valuable to test the survey instrument in a small-scale study. Thereto the survey link was initially sent out to 10% of the sample to examine the statistical properties of the single measures (Pavlou and El Sawy, 2011). Given the good reliability and validity values achieved for all measures, the survey was approved to be send out to the whole sample.

To sum up, the questionnaire design was described in detail, compromising the levels of measurement, theory and statistical analysis, the operationalisation of constructs, measurement scales and pre-testing of the questionnaire. The following section outlines data collection and sampling issues.

5.4   Data Collection

This section describes the data collection process outlining the target population, the sampling procedure, sample size and structure. Empirical studies require the definition of the relevant population to be studied, as well as the determination of the target sample on which basis research findings may be generalised outside the collected set of research data (Zikmund, 2003). Vice versa it also sets the boundaries for the generalisation of the research finding (Page and Meyer, 2000). The following section provides a definition of the target population, further elaborates the sampling frame and procedure utilised to gain the final sample for this research, which is subsequently described in regard to its characteristics and tested for potential nonresponse bias.

5.4.1 Target Population

The target population is regarded as a collection of elements that share a specific set of characteristics, e.g. geographical and personal characteristics (Zikmund, 2003), which are considered as relevant to contribute the required information to achieve the research objectives (Lukas et al., 2004). The population for this research included UK business representatives engaged in innovation activities. The target population can be described more precisely through a specific set of characteristics: (1) personal characteristics as position, function and company size, (2) industrial characteristics namely industry sector and type, and (3) geographical characteristics as the target country.

Personal characteristics. Target respondents for this research were defined as individuals (i) holding an upper or middle management positions (e.g. CEO, Managing Director, General Manager, C-level Executive, Owner or Partner, Senior Manager, Middle Manager), (ii) working in an innovation-related functional area, defined for this research as including General Management, Innovation Management, Product Development Management, Business Development, R&D, and (iii) working in a small, medium or large companies, with a minimum of 10 employees. The reasoning behind this specific targeting is that these individuals are assumed to be typically involved in innovation and resource recombination activities in the company and therefore likely to have a good understanding of the firm's resource endowments, processes and capabilities and their impact on firm's innovation performance, which gives reasons to expect a high accuracy of the responses. Moreover, they are high enough in the hierarchy to possess an aerial view of the processes and routines to see a comprehensive picture, while at the same time still being sufficiently involved in the operational activities, enabling the evaluation of their own firm's capacities and resources against competitors. Screening questions were included at the beginning of the questionnaire and only those respondents that possessed the defined characteristics were allowed to take part in the survey.

Industrial characteristics. This study is cross-sectional in nature, covering both manufacturing and service industries. However, only those industry sectors were included which are seen as innovation-active industries. As described earlier, R&D expenditure is generally accepted as an appropriate indicator for innovation in firms (OECD, 2011), and therefore was employed for identifying the relevant target industries for this research. While high R&D expenditure is often associated with high-tech firms aiming to develop new technologies, also established consumer goods companies are found to have high expenditures on a systematic basis to improve their existing products (Office for National Statistics, 2011). Hence R&D expenditure is regarded as a valuable indicator for measuring the industries' emphasis given to innovation, covering both innovation directed towards the development of new products and services, as well as the improvement of established products and services. To identify the most innovation-active industries in UK a statistic of the British Office for National Statistics (2011, p. 57) on R&D expenditures per industry sector performed in UK in 2011 was used. Out of 61 listed industries or groups of industries as defined by SIC codes, the TOP 15 industries in regard to R&D expenditures were identified and defined as relevant for this research, as those 15 industries account for more than 90% of the total R&D expenditures of 17.408 Mio £ in UK in 2011 (for a detailed description of sectors and numbers, see Appendix 5.3 in the additional electronic material). Accordingly, the 2-diget SIC codes of those industries were matched against the internal coding scheme used by CINT[2] for the

---

[2] CINT is a professional panel data provider that was conducted for target sampling as described in 5.4.2.

panel profiling, whereby only those firms were included in the target sample that could be assigned to one of the selected innovation-active industries.

Moreover, a further screen-out question was included in the questionnaire, where all 21 industry sections as defined by the SIC Code were listed and only those six defined as relevant for this research, namely (C) Manufacturing (SIC 10–33), (G) Wholesale and trade (SIC 45–47), (J) Information and Communication (SIC 58–63), (K) Financial and Insurance activities (SIC 64–66), (M) Professional scientific and technical activities (SIC 69–75) as well as (N) Administrative and support service activities (SIC 77–82), were allowed to take part in the survey. Consequently, the main focus of this research lied on the six industries which again were deliberately selected to capture those 15 sub-industries responsible for more than 90% of the overall R&D expenditure in UK. Additionally, as a control variable used to test if the right target sample was reached, respondents were asked to indicate the percentage of sales spend on R&D expenditures. With the integration of several industry types, this research did not concentrate on a specific industry segment (e.g. high-tech manufacturing), but rather concentrated on both manufacturing and service industries in order not to limit the potential sampling frame and at the same time to keep the cross-sectional nature and relevance of the concept of study.

Geographical characteristics. The geographical focus of this study was restricted to United Kingdom (UK), meaning that only respondents working in companies resident in UK were targeted. This was deemed valuable to prevent the results from being biased by national culture issues (Plewa, 2010). The CINT UK panel list (as described below) was used providing a representative sample of the UK population, regarded as the basic population used in this research. Given this definition of the general population, the sampling frame was further specified in a step-wise sampling procedure applied to ensure the access to the target population as defined above.

5.4.2 Sampling Procedure and Sample Size

Different procedures can be used by researchers to select samples for their research (Kinnear et al., 1993). As no contact lists of the target population as described as relevant for this research exists, the help of CINT a professional panel data provider was conducted. CINT provides access to contacts of industrial representatives through their representative UK online panel, with a total of 564.867 listed panelists in UK. During the whole process it was ensured that the participation within the panel was genuinely voluntary. The following section outlines the four steps of the sampling procedure used in this research to attain the final sample.

Framing the sample. The invitation email to take part in the survey was distributed to a total number of 30.712 people (*invited sample*) drawn from the representative UK online panel with 564.867 listed panelists (*general population*) based on age, gender, company age, industry sector, and position. In the period from 15th March 2013 till 3rd April 2013, 21 daily batches were released in total. Additionally, two days apart from the initial invite, reminders were send. The respondents were asked to click on a link in the email message, which directed them to the CINT landing page. Of these potential candidates for the survey, a total number of 7.581 respondents clicked on the link to take part in the study and entered the CINT landing page, resulting in a response rate of 24.5%. CINT uses a reward system for their panelists, for a 20 minutes survey the respondents are incentivised by marketplace points equivalent to a value between £1.20 to £1.52. The incentive have been set to encourage long-term participation, but also to discourage professional respondents who seek to take surveys only to obtain payment. Furthermore, as the target respondents are industrial representatives in middle and upper management positions in the UK, which can be considered as well-paid, cash payment can be seen rather as a representation allowance for the participants. Therefore, the incentive might affect their intention to take part in the study, but it would not cause any industrial representative to consent to risks that they might not otherwise find acceptable. In addition, the respondents were offered a customised report summarising the results of the study to increase the response rate.

Panel Profiling. To ensure the right target sampling and guarantee quality standards, in a first pre-screening step executed by CINT, 6.996 respondents were screened out from the sample due to either not fitting predefined selection criteria defining the target group (company age, respondent's position, industry sector, company size) or not fulfilling security criteria (e.g. the respondent did not have a unique IP address, the survey was already taken by the respondent, the survey was already closed), leading to an effective target sample of 617 people (*target sample 1*) that qualified and hence were allowed to take part in the survey. This profiling step aimed at developing a database of key informant engaged in leading positions in industries where innovation takes place. Individuals acting in those positions and industry sectors were likely to fit the requirements of this study. Of the 617 people in the target sample, 585 target respondents actually entered the survey in UNIPARK, were the first page was used to explain the purpose of the research and strict confidentiality of the results was ensured (for a screenshot of the invitation page, see Appendix 5.2 in the additional electronic material).

Target Sampling. In a second pre-screening step, which was executed by the researcher to cross-validate the validity of sampling and further sharpen the target group, additional screening questions were included on the second page of the survey. As a result of this step from the 585 respondents that entered the survey another 243 respondents did not qualify for the target group, and thus were not allowed to continue the survey and were redirected, as key informants either did not work in one of the selected functional areas (152) or target industry sectors (86) for this research, worked in a company below 10 employees (2), or did not possess one of the target positions (3) defined as relevant for this research. This step was conducted in addition to the first pre-screening step, as the panel profiling by CINT allowed only the selection of pre-defined categories and might not always be up to date as people change their company and position. Moreover, the pre-screening aimed to reduce the potential risk of addressing people that might not be knowledgeable regarding RR. Finally, 342 respondents qualified for taking part in the survey (*target sample 2*), as they fulfilled all criteria of the target group, and filled out the questionnaire.

Validating. After eliminating those responses which did not complete the questionnaire and entailed systematically missing values (20), a total of 322 fully completed questionnaires were returned. From those 322 completed questionnaires another 114 respondents were identified as 'unengaged respondents' and therefore were further eliminated from the data set. The identification of those cases based on quality control variables that were included in the questionnaire, and gave indications that either the time to complete the questionnaire was regarded as to low to ensure the high quality of answers (71), or that the responses entailed systematic error and invalid answers (43). This final validation step resulted in a final sample of 208 quality proven completes, that were used for the data analysis to test the conceptual model (n = 208).

Table 5.1 gives an overview of how the final sample was drawn, entailing the single steps that led to the final sample used for the quantitative analysis.

Table 5.1 Sampling Procedure and Sample Size

Total number of panelist in UK: *= General Population*	**575.126**
Total number of people invited to the panel: *= those that received the invitation email = candidates = Invited Sample*	**30.712**
Total number of respondents: *= those that clicked on the link and entered the CINT landing page*	**7.581**
Total number of screen outs after stage 1 – CINT, amongst those: *- due to security termination[17]* *- due to full quotas* *- used as test cases* *- due to the survey was already closed* *- based on the CINT Pre-Screener 1: Company Age* *- based on the CINT Pre-Screener 2: Position* *- based on the CINT Pre-Screener 3: Industry Sector* *- based on the CINT Pre-Screener 4: Company Size*	**- 6.996** 1.026 59 2 291 103 4.067 1.271 145
Target sample 1 (qualified respondents after first screen out – CINT): *= those that qualified for entering the online survey*	**= 617**
Target respondents 1 *= those that entered the online survey*	**585**
Total number of screen outs after stage 2 – RESEARCHER, amongst those: *- based on the INTERNAL Pre-Screener 1: Function (added)* *- based on the INTERNAL Pre-Screener 2: Position (double check)* *- based on the INTERNAL Pre-Screener 3: Industry Sector (double check)* *- based on the INTERNAL Pre-Screener 4: Company Size (double check)*	**- 243** 152 3 86 2
Target sample 2 (qualified respondents after second screen out – RESEACHER): *= those that entered and qualified for the survey*	**= 342**
Total number drop outs: *= those that dropped out during the survey*	**- 20**
Full Completes: *= those that fully completed the survey*	**= 322**
Total number of screen outs for quality reasons, amongst those: *- based on Quality Control Variable 1: Duration <300 sec* *- based on Quality Control Variable 2-4: invalid answers*	**- 114** 71 43
Quality checked Completes: *= those that qualified for data analysis*	**= 208**
Completion rate: *= Full Completes / Target sample 1*	**55%**
Drop-out rate: *= Total number of drop-outs/ Target sample 2*	**6 %**
Response rate: *= Number of respondents / Number of people invited*	**24,6 %**

5.4.3 Sample Structure

As a result of the sampling procedure, 208 key informants from different companies contributed to the survey, providing the data set on which the conceptual model was empirically tested. In the following, a detailed description of the specific characteristics and attributes of the final respondents is given. An overview of the characteristics of the final respondents is provided in Table 5.2.

In accordance with the target sample, responses were collected from six different **industry types**, including manufacturing (20%), professional, scientific and technical activities (22%), wholesale and retail trade (21%), financial and insurance activities (16%), information and communication (15%), and administrative and support activities (7%). Interestingly, when looking at those firms working in manufacturing industries, they could be further specified as manufacturer of computer, electronic and optical products (17%), machinery and equipment (10%), pharmaceutical products (7%), rubber and plastic products (7%) and furniture (7%), metal products (5%), motor vehicles, trailers, transporttation equipment (5%), paper products (5%), and food products (5%), or other manufacturing products (29%) as indicated by the respondents classification according to the SIC Codes. Given that all of the TOP 15 most innovative industry types measured by R&D expenditure as reported by the British Office for National Statistics (refer to Appendix 5.3 in the additional electronic material) are well represented in the sample, the strong focus of this research onto innovation-active industries is reflected by the sample structure.

This is also supported by the figures about **R&D intensity** as reported by the respondents, were the vast majority of companies in the sample (59%) exhibited R&D expenditures of more than 3% of sales, and therewith laid considerably above the OECD average of 2.3% in 2011 (OECD, 2011). Moreover, 39 of the companies (equals 22%) spend more than 10% of sales on R%D, and therefore can be classified as high-tech manufacturing firms, thus regarded as highly innovation-active companies according to the OECD (2011) segmentation. Notably, 31 respondents did not know the percentage of sales spend on R&D and therefore were not included in the statistics.

From the final responses 79% were in middle and 21% in upper management **positions.** Of the final respondents 108 respondents were working as middle manager and 61 respondents as senior manager, while another 20 respondents were employed as C-level executive (CFO, CIO, COO) and 14 respondents as CEO, managing director or general manager of the company. Only 9 respondents acted as owner or partner of the company. The **functional areas** of the interviewees ranged from General Management (63%) to more specialised functions as Business Development Management (13%), Research and Development (10%), Product Development Management (10%) and Innovation Management (4%). In regard to **company size**, 50% of the respondents worked in big companies (with more than 250 employees), 29% were engaged in medium-sized companies (with a number of employees between 51 and 250), and only 21% worked in smaller companies (with 10 to 50 employees). In terms of the companies' **ownership structure**, nearly two-thirds of the respondents were working for private companies that were either family-owned (9%) or owned by the CEO and family (57%). On the other hand 26% worked for public companies listed on the stock exchange, while 8% indicated to work in a company with another ownership structure. The **age of the companies** differed considerably, from 1 year to 331 years, with the median age of 27.5 years. Only 8 companies were 5 years and younger and thus regarded as new companies.

The following Table 5.2 gives an overview of the characteristics of the final respondents, which were further considered for the data analysis and discussion.

Table 5.2 Characteristics of Final Respondents

Current Position	CEO	C-level Executive	Owner/ Partner	Senior Manager	Middle Manager	Total
N	14	20	9	61	104	208
%	7%	10%	4%	29%	50%	100%
Functional Area	General Mgmnt	Innovation Mgmnt	Product Developm. Mgmnt	Business Developm. Mngmt	R&D	Total
N	131	9	20	27	21	208
%	63%	4%	10%	13%	10%	100%
Respond. Age	14-22		23-35	36-55	56-80	Total
N	0		56	115	37	208
%	0%		27%	55%	18%	100%
Gender		Males			Females	Total
N		129			79	208
%		62%			38%	100%
Company Size	10-50 employees		51-250 employees		> 250 employees	Total
N	44		59		105	208
%	21%		29%		50%	100%
Company Age	Minimum =	Lower Quartile =	Median =	Upper Quartile =	Maximum =	
	1 year	17 years	27.5 years	57 years	331 years	
Ownership Structure	Public Company (listed on stock exchange)		Private Company (CEO and family)	Family-Owned Company	Other	Total
N	54		119	19	16	208
%	26%		57%	9%	8%	74%
R&D Intensity	< 1%	1-3%	3,01-10%	>10%	Missing data	Total
N	29	43	66	39	31	177
%	16%	24%	37%	22%	--	100%
Industry Type	Manufac- turing	Wholesale and retail trade	Information and Communication	Financial and insurance activities	Professional, scientific and technical Activities	Administrative and support service activities
N	41	43	31	34	46	13
%	20%	21%	15%	16%	22%	6%

Industry Type: Manufacturing	N	%
... of computer, electronic and optical products	7	17
... of machinery and equipment n.e.c.	4	10
... of basic pharmaceutical products and pharmaceutical	3	7
... of rubber and plastic products	3	7
... of furniture	3	7
... of fabricated metals or metal products	2	5
... of motor vehicles, trailers, transportation equipment	2	5
... of paper and paper products	2	5
... of food products	2	5
... of other manufacturing	12	29
Missing	1	2
Total	41	100 %

The outline of the final sample showed that the target group as defined in section 5.4.1 was reached. Following the discussion and outline of the final sample structure the following section elaborates on the potential nonresponse bias in the data.

5.4.4 Nonresponse Bias

Nonresponse bias addresses a potential problem while using survey instrument, concerned with the number of people not responding to the questionnaire, and the risk that the answers of these nonrespondents would have differed considerably from the respondents (Pearl and Fairley, 1995). Firstly, efforts were taken to maximise the response rate leading principally to a reduction of nonresponse bias (Armstrong and Overton, 1977). The attained response rate of 24,6% was regarded as reasonable and compared well with similar studies among the target group, considering the time-consuming nature of middle- and upper management jobs, moreover a group of people that tend to be over-surveyed by researchers, and paired with potential concerns about confidentiality.

Secondly, following the approach by Armstrong and Overton (1977), early and late respondents in the sample were compared across selected key variables to estimate nonresponse bias. The procedure was used to verify that early and late respondents did not differ in their responses. Those respondents that answered in the first (two) week were considered as earlier respondents (163), while all others regarded as late respondents (45). Levene's test for the equality of variances was conducted to test for potential differences in variances (Brosius, 2004), followed by a t-test for assessing the equality of means (Coakes and Steed, 2003) between the two groups. The results showed no significant differences between the two groups for any of the variables, neither in terms of demographics nor in terms of parameter values ($p < 0.05$ level). The results are presented in Appendix 5.4 in the additional electronic material, showing the 2-tailed significance level for demographics, including current position, company size, company age, industry sector, as well as for the selected key variables, including *Sensing, Learning, Integrating, Coordinating capacity, Technological and Market Knowledge* and *RR, Entrepreneurial Orientation* and *Networking Orientation*. Given that no significant differences in variance and in means between early and late respondents emerged, it could be assumed that nonresponse bias is not a serious problem and that the sample was adequate for further analysis.

Besides nonresponse bias, common method bias was tested, which is a potential bias in the data caused by a systematic external measurement error and hence attributed to the measurement method used. The approach by Podsakoff et al. (2003) was used to calculate the likelihood of common method variance being present in the data, the procedure and results are detailed in section 6.4.4.

5.5   Chapter Summary

This chapter described the methodology chosen for the quantitative research study. First, the reasons for choosing a self-administered online survey as appropriate data collection method for the quantitative analysis of the model and hypotheses were detailed and discussed.

Subsequently, the questionnaire design was outlined, describing the levels of measurement, theory and statistical analysis, and the operationalisation of constructs. In the core of this section a detailed description of the measurement items and scales used to capture each construct was provided, resulting in the final questionnaire, which qualified after being pre-tested as appropriate measurement instrument and was used for the quantitative study.

The last section of the chapter elaborated on sampling issues. Starting with a detailed description of the target population and its specific characteristics, the step-wise sampling procedure used to reach the target respondents was outlined. With the help of a professional panel data provider, the invitation email to take part in the survey was distributed to a total number of 30.712 people, of which a total of 7.581 people responded, resulting in a response rate of 24.5%. A first panel profiling step led to an effective target sample of 617 respondents, 585 entered the survey, and after a second screen out stage a total of 322 fully completed questionnaires were returned. After a final validation step, 208 responses qualified for being included in the further data analysis to test the conceptual model (n = 208). Screening questions were used for the panel profiling and at the beginning of the questionnaire to ensure that the right target respondents were reached.

The chapter closed with a detailed description of the final sample, which showed to represent a good cross-selection of the target group as defined before, and thus allows a generalisation of the research findings outside the collected set of data.

Results

6

6.1 Introduction

This chapter outlines the individual steps of data analysis and presents the results of the quantitative research step. The data was analysed applying structural equation modelling (SEM) principles using the statistical software *SPSS AMOS 20*. SEM serves purposes akin to a regression-analytical approach (Schreiber et al., 2006), however is regarded as "a more powerful alternative to multiple regression, path analysis, factor analysis, time series analysis and analysis of covariance" (Gaskin, 2012a, Gason, 2012) and is utilised in this research for several reasons. First, the central advantage of SEM lies in its potential to evaluate entire models proposed on the basis of previous research steps (Steenkamp and Baumgartner, 2000). Second, by accounting for measurement and structural error, and modelling of interactions, nonlinearities or correlations across the models' independent variables, SEM is regarded to offer a more accurate analysis than other multivariate methods (Diamantopoulos and Siguaw, 2000, Gaskin, 2012a). Third, an additional advantage SEM has over other multivariate methods is its ability to integrate latent or unobservable constructs measured by multiple indicators which are often to be found in marketing literature (Parasuraman et al., 1988, Gaskin, 2012d) and are also existent in this research study. For this reasoning and by conducting a confirmatory rather than exploratory approach to data analysis (Byrne, 2001), in recent years SEM is achieving a high popularity among researchers from different disciplines (Kline, 2005, Garson, 2012). Consequently, SEM was identified as a valuable and appropriate method of data analysis for this research.

Electronic supplementary material The online version contains supplementary material available at (https://doi.org/10.1007/978-3-658-35666-8_6).

© The Author(s), under exclusive license to Springer Fachmedien Wiesbaden GmbH, part of Springer Nature 2021
K. Kurzhals, *Resource Recombination in Firms from a Dynamic Capability Perspective*, Gabler Theses, https://doi.org/10.1007/978-3-658-35666-8_6

This chapter elaborates the quantitative research steps undertaken in depth and detail.

After a brief introduction and overview presented in this section, the data preparation steps and evaluation of normality of the data are described. A description of the **Exploratory Factor Analysis (EFA)** follows, whereby the factoring method and rotation type leading to the resulting factor structure are presented first, moreover an outline of analyses relating to construct reliability and validity is given.

The fourth section outlines the results of the **Confirmatory Factor Analysis (CFA)**. In this section the criteria for the evaluation of the model fit, the so called goodness-of-fit indices, are presented first. Subsequently, the one-factor congeneric **measurement models**, used for the calculation of the composite scores for the latent constructs, along with their factor score weights and respective model fit indices are presented. In addition to this, and analogous to the procedure applied during the EFA, an assessment of the constructs validity and reliability is conducted and the results are reported. Additionally common method bias (CMB) and measurement model invariance is tested. Finally to this section the procedures used for the calculation of the composite scores for the reflective measurement models as well as the formative construct used to measure RR, are described and their use is justified.

The fifth section of this chapter finally outlines the **structural path model** for analysing the causal relationship between the constructs, including hypotheses testing. Prior to any analyses important concerns for a stable application of the SEM procedure are described, comprising the model identifycation as well as a variety of multivariate assumptions, namely linearity, (absence of) multicollinearity and heteroscedasticity. Having ensured a stable application, the structural path model is analysed. First, the conceptual model and proposed interrelationships among the endogenous and exogenous constructs (as conceptualised in chapter 3 and 4, respectively) is tested by means of structural path analysis using AMOS. Second, the conceptual structural path model is re-specified with the aim to achieve a more parsimonious, well-fitting model. Given the achieved good overall model fit, the re-specified structural path model qualifies for the subsequent hypotheses testing.

The subsequent sections present a more detailed investigation of the theorised **mediation effect** (section 6.6) by means of mediation analysis, and **moderation effects** (section 6.7) by means of multi-group moderation and interaction effect analyses. This is followed by a discussion of the **competing models** (section 6.8).

The last section of this chapter summarises the results of the quantitative research and hypotheses support. While the results are presented and analysed in this chapter, a detailed discussion of the research findings is provided in chapter 7. Based on the research cycle presented by Gaskin and Lyytinen (2011), Figure 6.1 gives an overview of the individual analysis steps conducted for this research while embedding it in the overall research process.

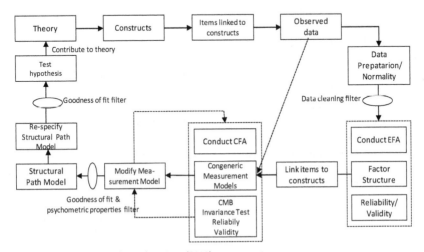

Source: adapted from Gaskin and Lyytinen (2011)

Figure 6.1   Research Cycle

6.2   Data Preparation and Normality

6.2.1 Data Preparation

To ensure that the observed data is clean, thus useful for testing causal relationships the data needs to be prepared before conducting any statistical analysis (Gaskin, 2012a). Hence for this research the data was prepared in a four step procedure, including (1) **re-codification** of reverse-codes variables, (2) screen out of **unengaged responses**, (3) **clearing of missing data** and (4) **detection of outliers.**

First, in a **re-codification** step all reverse-coded variables (V1604_KnowSpeci, V2201_InnoPerf, V2306_EntreOrient, 2307_EntreOrient, V23078 EntreOrient) were re-coded.

Second, **unengaged responses,** referring to respondents that answered with systematic error (e.g. a single value for each question, a constant row of numbers etc.), were screened out as described previously, both by calculating the standard deviation (SD) per row, whereby a SD < 0.5 implies an insufficient amount of variance in the responses, and by means of visual screening (Gaskin, 2012a). The latter was supported by inserting four quality control variables: *Q1_duration, Q2_knowledge specificy*[1], *Q3_innovation performance*[2], *Q4_entrepreneurial orientation*[3]. Variable Q1 captured the time each respondent took for answering the questionnaire. Those cases, where respondents took below five minutes, were screened out. The other three variables were used to test the consistency of answers given by the respondents for the respective constructs. Cases that did not show a logical consistency were additionally screened out.

Third, **missing data** in the sample was analysed utilising SPSS 20. All respondents with more than 5% of missing data were screened out from the sample to preserve the data from being biased. In the remaining two cases, missing values were replaced with the maximum likelihood (ML) estimation. The ML estimation was chosen as appropriate method as it has shown to be the least biased method for the replacement of missing data (Hair et al., 2010) and was approved as valuable method by previous research (Byrne, 2001, Plewa, 2010). From 322 completed questionnaires, based on the quality control variables described above, 43 respondents were identified as unengaged respondents based on poor quality (in regard to Q2,Q3,Q4) and another 71 respondents were disclosed based on

---

[1] **Q2_knowledge specificy:** V1604 was used as control variable, after being re-codified it should show similar values as V1601/V1602/V1603. Comparing the values of V1604 with V1601/V1602/V1603, the responses were classified into three groups: 0 = V1604 and V1601/V1602/V1603 show opponent values, 1 = V1604 and V1601/V1602/V1603 show equal (or only slightly different) values, 2 = V1604 and V1601/V1602/V1603 differ for more than 3 points)

[2] **Q3_innovation performance:** V2201 was used as control variable, after being re-codified it should show similar values as the remaining items used to measure innovation performance and V2301. The responses were classified into three groups following the same procedure as described above.

[3] **Q4_entrepreneurial orientation:** V2306, V2307 and V2308, were used as control variable, after being re-codified they should show similar values as the remaining items used to measure EO. The responses were classified into three groups following the same procedure as described above.

duration (in regard to Q1). In sum, 208 quality proven respondents qualified for the further analyses (n = 208).

Fourth, data was tested for **outliers** (Kline, 2005), as they can bias the results, pulling away the mean from the median (Gaskin, 2012a). Two types of outliers are differentiated: *univariate outliers* for the individual variables and *bivariate outliers* for the model (Gaskin, 2012a). As in this research all latent variables were measured on a likert scale, only continuous variables as company age were eligible for detecting univariate outliers. By means of calculating boxplots in SPSS, those variables being identified as outliers were replaced by the mean. Testing for bivariate outliers Mahalanobis d-squared was calculated in AMOS (Gaskin, 2012a), the results did not show influential multivariate outliers.

6.2.2 Check for Normality

A necessary precondition for the stable application of SEM procedures is the assumption of multivariate normality in the data (Hair et al., 2010). Following Gaskin (2012a) normality refers to the distribution of the data for a particular parameter. To ensure univariate and multivariate normality, skewness and kurtosis were analysed (DeCarlo, 1997).

Skewness refers to whether the responses are distributed towards one end of the scale, implying that data is not normally distributed. Values for skewness ranged between 0.057 and −0.925 (see Table 6.1). As only values above 1 are referred to as being positive (right) skewed and values below −1 are regarded as being negative (left) skewed (Gaskin, 2012a), all variables met the required criteria.

Kurtosis on the other hand refers to the peakedness respectively flatness of data distribution (Gaskin, 2012a). With values for kurtosis lying between −0.656 and 1.075 only the value for Market Knowledge slightly exceeded the recommended threshold of +/−1 indicating to slight non-normality, while all other values indicated that univariate normality was established (Lei and Lomax, 2005) (see Table 6.1 below). Also the c.r.-values for kurtosis showed acceptable results, again only the value for Market Knowledge lied above the critical threshold of 2.57 (Backhaus et al., 2010).

Table 6.1   Assessment of Normality

Variable	min	max	skew	c.r.	kurtosis	c.r.
NetwOrientFact	1	7	−0.740	−4.359	0.345	1.015
EntreOrientFact	1	7	−0.133	−0.781	−0.656	−1.931
SensingFact	1	7	−0.871	−5.131	0.853	2.51
IntegratingFact	1	7	−0.713	−4.198	−0.038	−0.111
LearningFact	1.97	7	−0.416	−2.448	−0.402	−1.183
MarketKnowlFact	1.55	7	−0.925	−5.444	1.075	3.164
TechnoKnowlFact	2	7	−0.648	−3.813	−0.311	−0.916
CoordinatingFact	1	7	−0.739	−4.352	0.705	2.075
RR_singleitem_Composit	2.5	7	0.057	0.338	−0.146	−0.43
Multivariate					**19.493**	**9.99**

Looking at *multivariate normality* according to Kline (2005) only values for skewness higher than 3 and values for kurtosis higher than 10, may be regarded as problematic. With a multivariate value for kurtosis of 19.493, multivariate non-normality may be suggested, however considering the common lack of multivariate normality in research practice (Byrne, 2001, Gaskin, 2011), this is regarded as acceptable.

However, to restrict the impact of multivariate non-normality on the data analysis results, a range of procedures was established. First, as the principal goodness-of-fit index (the Chi-Square χ^2) is rather sensitive to non-normality, a range of alternative fit indices was employed for analysing model fit, e.g. the Normed Fit Index (NFI) and Comparative Fit Index (CFI) as detailed in section 6.4.1 (Lei and Lomax, 2005). Second, the **Bollen-Stine bootstrapping technique** was applied to reduce the reliance on normality assumptions regarding the distribution of the parameters (Hair et al., 2010). The Bollen-Stine bootstrapping (Bollen and Long, 1991) is a statistical re-sampling technique by which multiple sub-samples are created out of the original sample from which the confidence estimates are derived (Byrne, 2001). While using this method, a sample is seen as a "pseudo-population that represents the broader population from which the sample was derived" (Preacher et al., 2007, p. 190). By computing the statistics that are of interest in multiple re-samples of the data set, the sampling distribution of any statistic can be reproduced (Preacher et al., 2007). Hence, bootstrapping was applied for the data analyses, as it allows testing the theorised model and its hypotheses by offering an alternative, "modified bootstrap method for the Chi-Square goodness of- fit statistic" (Byrne, 2001, p. 284). Subsequent to the outline of data preparation and normality, the following section details the Exploratory Factor Analysis, as a first SEM step. Further multivariate assumptions as linearity, multicollinearity and homoscedasticity will be discussed in section 6.5.2.

6.3   Exploratory Factor Analysis (EFA)

Exploratory Factor Analysis (EFA) is a multivariate statistical method used to identify the underlying factor structure of a set of observed variables without imposing a preconceived structure on the outcome (Child, 1990). The EFA is exploratory in nature, and therefore often builds the first step in a SEM procedure. Based on these results, a Confirmatory Factor Analysis (CFA) is applied in a subsequent research step (refer to section 6.4). The CFA aims to confirm the predicted relationships and to set up the final measurement model for the latent constructs to be included in the structural path model.

On the basis of correlations among the observed variables (measurement items) in the data set, the EFA identifies a smaller number of underlying factors (latent constructs) that comprise all substantial information about the linear interrelations between the variables in the data set (Backhaus et al., 2008). Accordingly, the aim of the EFA procedure is the reduction of the data structure with the help of a minimal number of factors (Backhaus et al., 2008). As a result, an EFA aims to achieve distinct constructs (discriminant validity), that each measures a single thing (convergent validity), and that are reliable (reliability) (Gaskin, 2012b). In total 61 observed variables from the questionnaire were included in the EFA. Being conceptualised as a formative construct, however, the indicators for RR could not be included in the EFA (and CFA as well) as this would have been an obstacle to the EFA's (and CFA's) underlying assumption of reflective constructs (Backhaus et al., 2008) (the formative constructs are considered separately in section 6.4.6). The measurement items applied in the questionnaire already indicate the expected factor structure. However, despite of usage of established scales, some items might not capture what they were thought to measure. Therefore, it was deemed valuable to first test in an exploratory research step using EFA, which items belong to which constructs as it helps identifying what the factor structure looks like according to the participants' responses. Vice versa, an EFA is also useful to discover variables that are in spite of theoretical considerations not fitting well to the constructs. Therefore, EFA is considered as a valuable instrument to prepare the variables in order to provide a cleaner factor structure to be used in a CFA as a subsequent SEM step (Gaskin, 2012b). Factor analysis thus is regarded a fundamental component of SEM (Gaskin and Lyytinen, 2011).

6.3.1 Factoring Method and Rotation Type

Beside the specification of variables included in the EFA the selection of (a) the method for factor extraction, (b) an adequate rotation method, as well as (c) the criteria for the extraction of factors were important considerations, outlined in the following section.

In general there are two main **methods for factor extraction**: Principal Component Analysis (PCA) and Principal Axis Factoring (PAF)[4]. The main difference between the two methods lies in the way the communalities are used. Generally researchers pointed out that the decision whether to make use of the PCA or the PAF procedure should solely be made on the basis of content based considerations (Backhaus et al., 2008). For this research the use of the PCA was justified, as it is the most commonly used technique for identifying important dimensions in multivariate datasets (Cooley and Lohnes, 1971, Hildebrandt and Temme, 2006) and widely accepted by different scientific disciplines (Abdi and Williams, 2010). While some restrictions exist for a PCA, as the algorithms do not consider the errors in the measurement of the variance as well as the specific variance of the indicators (Hildebrandt and Temme, 2006), many authors agree on the benefits of the PCA in comparison to other factor extraction methods, especially in the SEM context (e.g. Fabrigar et al., 1999). Thus, generally leading to a clearer factor structure the PCA method is preferred over the PAF, where the resulting factor structure often suffers from score indeterminacy (Arrindell and van der Ende, 1985). Furthermore the "solutions generated from principal component analyses differ little from those derived from factor analyses techniques" (Field, 2000, p. 434), hence the algebraic differences between the two methods are found to be minimal (Velicer and Jackson, 1990) and even decreases as the number of variables and the magnitudes of the factor loadings increases.

Another decision that had to be made is the choice of an adequate **rotation method**. Due to the fact that direct (unrotated) extraction methods gain the factor matrix directly from the correlation matrix, most often the resulting factor solutions are not sufficient for interpretation. By reducing some of the ambiguities associated with the direct extraction method, rotation methods cause factor loadings to be more clearly differentiated and thereby facilitate interpretation of the factor loadings (Child, 1990, Gaskin, 2012b). Simply said, the aim of rotation is to simplify the data structure. Generally two rotation types can be differentiated: *orthogonal* and *oblique* rotation types (Costello and Osborne, 2005). While the

---

[4] Other extraction methods exist in literature, however PCA and PAF are the most commonly used (Field, 2000).

Varimax rotation, as an orthogonal rotation method, is the most commonly used, it contains the underlying assumption of uncorrelated factors and often result in an inexplicit factor structure, where it is not easy to assign indicators to factors. Due to the fact that factors in empirical studies often exhibit small and moderate correlations, which violates the assumption of the Varimax rotation, Hildebrandt and Temme (2006) regard this method as inappropriate in an SEM context and suggest instead making use of an oblique rotation type, such as Promax. Oblique rotation types consider a moderate correlation between the factors being analysed (Costello and Osborne, 2005). As detailed in section 3.4.1.6, the constructs used in this research are expected to be weakly correlated with each other. Thus, given that "there is substantial theoretical and empirical basis for expecting the constructs to be correlated with each other (...) oblique rotations provide a more accurate and realistic representation of how constructs are likely to be related to one another" (Fabrigar et al., 1999, p.282). In addition, oblique solutions provide more information than orthogonal rotations, because orthogonal rotations require factors to be oriented in 90° angles in the multidimensional space whereas oblique rotations allow orientations of less than 90°. As a result, orthogonal rotations usually lead to solutions that have a more simple structure when the interrelation of the factors is based on correlated factors (Fabrigar et al., 1999). For this reasoning, Promax rotation was selected as appropriate for this survey.

With the aim of keeping factors in the analysis that account for most of the variance in the data set, determining the right number of factors in the final solution is a critical step. Therefore different statistical **criteria for the extraction** of factors exist. Beside the Kaiser criterion that considers those factors with an eigenvalue greater than 1 as common factors (Nunnally, 1978), Cattell's scree test, also named "elbow criterion", is another commonly used method. However, to solely base the decision on statistical criteria seldom leads to the correct number of factors (Hildebrandt and Temme, 2006). Hence the extraction of factors should also be based on content and interpretability criteria (DeCoster, 1998). Consequently, a 12 factor solution (eigenvalue = 0,875) was chosen in favor of a 10 factor solution suggested by the Kaiser criterion (eigenvalue > 1) and Cattell's scree test. As for the 12 factor solution all extracted factors measure different constructs and contain at least three item per factor with sufficiently high loadings on the respective factor (> 0.40), that beside share a conceptual meaning, and no cross-loadings (Gaskin, 2012b).

6.3.2 Factor Structure

Before presenting the resulting factor structure of the EFA, relevant quality measures are controlled for, namely the Kaiser-Meyer-Olkin (KMO) measure of sampling adequacy, the Bartlett's test of sphericity, the off-diagonal elements of the anti-image covariance matrix, and the commonalities of the factor solution.

First, the **Kaiser-Meyer-Olkin measure** of sampling adequacy, which determines whether a dataset is appropriate for an EFA, was tested (Kaiser et al., 1974). While a minimum for the KMO value is reported at 0.50, values over 0.80 are considered as very good (Frohlich and Westbrook, 2001). With a KMO value of 0.898 an excellent selection of variables for factor analysis was confirmed. Second, the **Bartlett test of sphericity** showed a significant and positive result (p < 0.001), which indicates that the matrix is not an identity matrix, meaning that the variables are appropriate for EFA (Frohlich and Westbrook, 2001). Third, the inspection of the off-diagonal elements of the **anti-image covariance matrix** gave further evidence that the sample is adequate for an EFA, because all variables are above a critical value of 0.5 (Field, 2000). Fourth, the **communalities** of the factor analysis, indicating the degree to which one item correlates with all other items, were checked. Higher communalities are appreciated as low communalities (< 0.4) indicate that a variable will not significantly load on any factor (Gaskin, 2012b). In this model the smallest communality is at 0.69, which proves all variables as being useful for further analyses. The results are provided in Appendix 6.1 in the additional electronic material.

As all quality criteria displayed adequate values, the **resulting factor structure** of the EFA, which shows the loadings for each variable on each factor, is presented in Appendix 6.2 in the additional electronic material. The factor structure refers to the intercorrelations among the variables being tested in the EFA (Gaskin, 2012b). Using an iterative process of withdrawing those items showing low loading on the respective factor or loadings across different factors, the aim was to achieve a suitable factor structure used for further analyses. The result of the EFA was a rotated pattern matrix consistent of 12 factors that account for 79.46 % of the variance in the data. As the results indicate, an ideal factor structure could be derived in which convergent and discriminant validity are evident as all variables show high factor loadings on each respective factor and no cross-loadings exist (Gaskin, 2012b). While single items had to be withdrawn within the process of clarification, the results show that all remaining variables ideally loaded on the respective factors, which confirms the theoretical considerations. Notably, as already indicated by the qualitative research findings (refer to section 4.4.3), respondents had difficulties in differentiating between knowledge *breadth* and *depth*, the respective items were also statistically loading on a single factor in the quantitative analysis, used to measure the quality and diversity of Market Knowledge and Technological Knowledge, respectively.

6.3.3 Construct Reliability and Validity (from EFA)

Even though the clean factor structure presented points towards an adequate solution, a more detailed assessment of validity and reliability of the factors is required. This is to ensure that the measuring variables are consistent and accurate, and capture what they are intended to measure (Hair et al., 2010).

Content validity comprises the subjective expert opinion on the appropriateness, meaningfulness and usefulness of a measurement and evaluates if it represents all facets of the given construct (Kinnear et al., 1993, Zikmund, 2003). Content validity was already considered during the questionnaire design phase (by founding the scales used on previous research findings), tested during the pre-test of the questionnaire and lastly approved through the exploratory research step, as the resulting factor structure reproduces what theory suggested (e.g. each variable loads on the respective factor, and those that are similar in nature load on the same factor).

Convergent validity is given when the variables <u>within</u> a single factor are highly correlated (Kinnear et al., 1993, Zikmund, 2003), as indicated by sufficiently high factor loadings. Sufficient loadings are determined by the sample size, as regularly smaller samples require higher loadings. For a sample size of 200 loadings above 0.40 are recommended (Gaskin, 2012b). As can be seen from the pattern matrix (Appendix 6.2 in the additional electronic material), all items achieve sufficient loadings on each factor (> 0.40).

Discriminant validity on the other hand refers to the extent, to which the single factors are distinct and uncorrelated <u>among</u> each other and thus can be regarded as complement of convergent validity (Page and Meyer, 2000). When discriminant validity is given, this means that the factors are theoretically different, as the rule is that the variables should relate more strongly to their own, respective factor than to any other factor (Gaskin, 2012b). As presented in the pattern matrix, discriminant validity is ensured as all variables load solely on one factor and no significant cross-loadings[5] exist. Additionally, correlations between

---

[5] Cross loadings refer to variables loading on multiple factors. When cross-loadings are present they should differ more than 0.20, as recommended by Gaskin (2011). For reasons of clarity and comprehensibility all factor loadings smaller than 0.30 are suppressed in the pattern matrix as being insignificant.

factors should not exceed 0.70, as correlations greater than 0.70 point toward a majority of shared variance (0.7 *0.7 means 49% shared variance), explained by the two factors (Gaskin, 2012b). As can be seen from the factor correlation matrix presented in Table 6.2 below, none of the factor correlations exceeds the 0.70 threshold.

Table 6.2 Factor Correlation Matrix

Component	Netw Orient	Coord.	Tech Knowl	Market Knowl	Integr.	Knowl Tacit	Entre Orient	Env Turb	Knowl Compl	Sens.	Learn.	Knowl Speci
NetwOrient	1.000											
Coordinating	.426	1.000										
TechnoKnowl	.403	.508	1.000									
MarketKnowl	.271	.440	.449	1.000								
Integrating	.418	.545	.422	.195	1.000							
KnowlTacit	-.062	-.140	.026	-.146	.014	1.000						
EntreOrient	.241	.273	.402	.317	.275	-.046	1.000					
EnvTurb	.167	.039	.065	.002	.058	.258	.016	1.000				
KnowlCompl	.433	.630	.575	.434	.432	-.078	.313	.030	1.000			
Sensing	.467	.504	.343	.360	.302	-.208	.252	.145	.426	1.000		
Learning	.445	.536	.557	.359	.480	-.074	.400	.115	.470	.449	1.000	
KnowlSpeci	.219	.094	.242	.073	.194	.297	.080	.036	.127	-.061	.223	1.000

Extraction method: PCA; Rotation method: Promax with Kaiser Normalisation

Reliability relates to the absence of random errors within the measurement (Kinnear et al., 1993, Zikmund, 2003). Therewith, the reliability of the measurement accounts for accurate, consistent and predictable results (Kinnear et al., 1993), as a "reliable" measurement constantly loads on one factor (Gaskin, 2012b). By means of calculating Cronbach's alpha (α) for each individual factor, reliability can be assessed during an EFA. Cronbach's alpha has been widely accepted as a measure for the internal consistency of the factors (Cortina, 1993, Kline, 2005, Streiner, 2003), values above 0.7 are commonly regarded as adequate, enhancing the closer the value gets to 1 (Hair et al., 2010, Kline, 2005). As the value generally increases with the number of measurement items per factor, a minimum of three factors is recommended (Gaskin, 2012b). With the exception of Knowledge Specificy, internal consistency was achieved for all factors with Cronbach alpha values ranging between 0.762 and 0.941. The respectively low value (α = 0.606) for Knowledge Specificy however indicates low internal consistency of this factor, leading to an elimination of the item V1602 during the CFA (refer to section 6.4.2).

In summary, an EFA was conducted first in order to identify the underlying factor structure of the observed variables. The results of the EFA showed an ideal loading pattern, with convergent, discriminant and content validity, as well as reliability ensured by high and constant loadings without any cross-loading problems. Given that the exploratory research step resulted in a very clear factor structure, the subsequent research step aims to confirm the factor structure and set up the measurement models for the latent constructs to be included in the final structural model.

6.4   Confirmatory Factor Analysis (CFA)

Confirmatory Factor Analysis (CFA) is a multivariate statistical method used to validate the factor structure of a set of observed variables. Contrary to the EFA, a preconceived structure on the outcome already exists, and hence the CFA is used for testing whether the predicted relationships between observed variables and their underlying latent constructs statistically exist, exposing its confirmatory character. Usually, researchers build on knowledge that emerged from theoretical or empirical findings or both in order to postulate a suggested factor structure a priori, which is then tested statistically a posteriori using confirmatory research methods (Backhaus et al., 2010). Hence, the CFA concerns the determination whether the number and composition of factors is "conform" to what is expected by theoretical considerations (Gaskin, 2012c). At the same time, by presenting the measurement models for the latent variables, the CFA represents the basis for the formulation of the structural equations and the analysis of the relationships between the latent variables with the help of SEM (Backhaus et al., 2010). Accordingly, SEM models always consist of two inter-related models: (a) the measurement model (resulting from the CFA) and (b) the structural path model (as presented in section 6.5) (Gefen et al., 2000).

The **measurement model** first and foremost determines the latent constructs that are used in the structural model, specifying the relationship between constructs and measures (Diamantopoulos et al., 2008), and ascertains which observed variables belong to each construct. During the factor analytical procedure, the exact loadings of each observed variable on the respective latent construct are estimated and the preconceived factor structure is tested (Gefen et al., 2000). Thus, the CFA aims to confirm the predicted relationships and sets up the final measurement model for the latent constructs to be included in the structural path model.

Based on the CFA results, the **structural path model** consequently tests the causal relationships between the latent variables. With that, the supposed causal and covariance relationships among the endogenous and exogenous latent constructs are estimated. At the same time the structural model includes the shared measurement error of these constructs in the calculation (Gefen et al., 2000).

The **Maximum-Likelihood (ML)-method** was used in this research, as it is the most commonly used technique for the estimation of both, testing the theoretical factor structure in the measurement model, as well as for testing the causal relationships in the structural model (Backhaus, 2010). One reason for its popularity is that the ML-method maximises the likelihood that the theoretical estimated correlation is represented by the observed correlation (Backhaus, 2010), as the method uses an iterative process to minimise the difference between the estimated and observed correlation matrix (Backhaus, 2010). However, there are also some restraints concerned with the use of the ML-method. A methodologically precondition for the application of the ML-method is the assumption of multivariate normality (Reinecke, 1999). As described in section 6.2.2, slight to moderate univariate and multivariate non-normality might be suggested in the obtained data. However, as a variety of recent simulation studies shows, the ML-method and its parameter estimates demonstrate to be relatively robust and stable against violations of normality as long as the sample size is large enough (n > 200) (Anderson and Gerbing, 1984, Hair et al., 2010, Hoogland and Boomsma, 1998, Hoyle and Panter, 1995). For this reason, the use of the ML-method was justified for the estimation process for both the measurement and structural models.

6.4.1 Goodness-of-Fit Indices

Prior to presenting the measurement models, criteria for the evaluation of the model fit will be presented and discussed in this following chapter. Model fit relates to how well the postulated model "fits" the observed or estimated model. Good model fit is given, when the postulated model accounts for all major correlations and covariances between the variables in the dataset. In contrast if there is a significant discrepancy between the implied and obtained correlation or covariance matrices, then poor model fit is evident (Gaskin, 2012c). Beside the principal goodness of fit index (Chi-Square), a variety of alternate **goodness-of-fit indices** has been developed in the literature and can be calculated in AMOS to determine goodness of fit.

However, as there is a constant debate and change of knowledge about the appropriateness of individual indicators (Kline, 2005, Hu and Bentler, 1998, Marsh et al., 2004), and as the strength and weaknesses of different indices are still not sufficiently studied (Fan and Sivo, 2005, Jahn, 2007), researchers agree that there is not the one "best" index. Instead, the consideration of different, alternative indices is recommended (Hair et al., 2010, Bollen and Long, 1993, Marsh et al., 1996, Jahn, 2007). Hence, in order to ensure a thorough assessment and comprehensive reflection of the overall model fit, it was deemed valuable to employ a variety of different indices in this research. Commonly researchers distinguish between **absolute, incremental** and **parsimony fit indices** (Hu and Bentler, 1995), all of which supplement the principal Chi-Square (χ^2) statistic for model fit (e.g. Jahn, 2007). An overview of the fit indices applied for this research, their abbreviation along with their acceptable thresholds, is presented in Table 6.3, and will be discussed in more detail below.

As model fit is inversely related to sample size and the number of variables included in the model, the thresholds below should rather be seen as guidelines emerged from literature (Gaskin, 2012c). Notably, the calculation of the values also differs depending on the method applied, Maximum-Likelihood (ML) or Generalised-Least-Squares (GLS), while the GLS-method usually leads to higher values (Hu and Bentler, 1999). Being more adequate for model evaluation, the

Table 6.3 Summary of Fit Indices Used to Assess Model Fit

Name	Abbreviation	Type	Acceptable level
Chi-Square	χ^2	Model Fit	$p > 0.05$
Normed Chi-Square	χ^2/df	Absolute Fit Model Parsimony	$1.0 < \chi^2/df > 3.0$
Goodness-of-Fit	GFI	Absolute Fit	GFI > 0.90
Adjusted Goodness-of-Fit	AGFI	Absolute Fit	AGFI > 0.90
Tucker-Lewis Index	TLI	Incremental Fit	TLI > 0.95
Comparative Fit Index	CFI	Incremental Fit	CFI > 0.95
Normed Fit Index	NFI	Incremental Fit	NFI > 0.95
Root Mean-Square Error of Approximation	RMSEA	Absolute Fit	RMSEA < 0.08 (not > 1)
Root Mean Squared Residual	RMR	Absolute Fit	RMR < 0.08 (not > 1)
Consistent Akaike Information Criterion	CAIC	Model Parsimony	No defined level

Sources: Byrne, 2001, Diamantopoulos and Siguaw, 2000, Hair et al., 2010, Hu and Bentler, 1998, Kline, 2005, Marsh et al., 1996

ML-method is applied in this research (Hu and Bentler, 1999), thus the thresholds reported below are based on the ML-method.

Absolute fit indices

Absolute fit indices calculate how good an a-priori-model is reproduced by the data set (derived from the fit of the implied and obtained covariance matrices) and do not use an alternative model for comparison reasons (Jahn, 2007).

The **Chi-Square** (χ^2) statistic of the model fit is the only statistical measure for the model fit (Hair et al., 2010). The p-value of the χ^2 is required to be non-significant (p > 0.05), only then evidence is given that "the actual and predicted input matrices are not statistically different" (Hair et al., 1998, p. 654) and hence that the proposed model fits the observed one. Due to the fact that the Chi-Square statistic is sensitive to sample size, a sample size of 100 to 200 is recommended by literature (Hair et al., 2010). Because non-normality and sample size impact the χ^2 statistic (Hair et al., 2010, Hu and Bentler, 1995, Marsh et al., 1996), additional indices were employed.

The **Normed Chi-Square** (χ^2/**df**) calculates the Chi-Square (χ^2) adjusted by the degrees of freedom (df) (Hair et al., 2010). There is no consensus in the literature when a 'good' fit is reached, yet recommended values ranging between 1 and 3 (Bollen 1989, p. 278) up to 5 (Arbuckle and Wothke, 1999, p. 399 f.), with values below 1 representing an overfit of the model (Hair et al., 2010).

Another commonly used absolute fit index is the **Goodness of Fit Index (GFI)**, as well as the **Adjusted Goodness of Fit-Index (AGFI)** corrected by the degrees of freedom (df). Values for both the GFI and AGFI range between 0 and 1, while contrary to the Chi-Square statistics values close to 1 indicate a good model fit. As a rule of thumb, values greater than 0.9 indicate an acceptable model fit (Hair et al., 2010, Hoyle and Panter, 1995, Jahn, 2007). However Hu and Bentler (1998) point out that both GFI und AGFI are very sensitive to sample size. Moreover their values generally decrease in complex models, potentially leading to an unjustified rejection of the model (Anderson and Gerbing, 1984).

The **Root Mean-Square Error of Approximation (RMSEA)** is also given much attention as a measure of the misfit of a model. Accordingly, the RMSEA is also called "badness-of-fit index" (Kline, 2005). The RMSEA calculates the discrepancy between the postulated and the observed model divided by the degrees of freedom. Due to that, the RMSEA accounts for the parsimony of a model (as a complement to complexity) and therewith does not place a disadvantage on the simple and easy to interpret models (Jahn, 2007). While values for the RMSEA between 0.05 and 0.08 have been described as acceptable (Hair et al., 2010), good fit is given with values smaller than 0.05, with zero indicating the best fit. By contrast, values above 0.1 speak against the model (Browne and Cudeck, 1993).

Likewise the **Root Mean Squared Residual-Index (RMR)** informs about the "badness-of-fit" of a model. The RMR calculates the square root of the difference between the residuals of the observed and the hypothesised covariance matrix (Fan and Sivo, 2005). Thereby it is equivalent to the standard error calculated in a regression analysis (Jahn, 2007). Similar to the RMSEA, values for the RMR range from 0 to 1 with smaller values indicating better model fit. Models are regarded as showing good fit when values less than 0.05 are exhibited (Byrne, 2001, Diamantopoulos and Siguaw, 2000). However, values below 0.08 are still considered as acceptable (Hu and Bentler, 1999).

Incremental fit Indices

Incremental fit indices on the other hand derive from the comparison of the chi-square difference between a postulated model and a so called "baseline" model, which is more strongly restricted, as its variables are not allowed to correlate with each other (Hu and Bentler, 1998, Jahn, 2007). The **Tucker-Lewis Index (TLI)**, also called Non-normed fit index, accounts for the comparison between the model of interest and the baseline or null model (Diamantopoulos and Siguaw, 2000, Hair et al., 2010). In comparison to other incremental measures, such as the **Comparative Fit Index (CFI)** and the **Normed Fit Index (NFI)**, that both are "normed", meaning that their values range between 0 and 1, the TLI can also show values greater than 1 (Diamantopoulos and Siguaw, 2000). Values above 0.95 are reported as acceptable, improving the closer the value comes to 1. Marsh et al. (1996) recommend the application of TLI and CFI as a result of their analyses of different incremental fit indices. The NFI, even though it is commonly used in research practice, tends to arrive at biased results, caused by its sensibility to sample size (Jahn, 2007). In this research all three indices were employed, with particular importance placed on the TLI and CFI, given their respective strengths, such as their appropriateness for research with smaller sample sizes and non-normality conditions (Hair et al., 2010, Lei and Lomax, 2005, Plewa, 2010).

Parsimony fit indices

Parsimony fit indices are relative fit indices that calculate the goodness of fit in proportion to the number of estimated parameters, in a way that simpler models are favored over more complex ones and thereby take parsimony of the model into account. Hence, parsimony fit indices address the problem that nearly saturated, highly complex models often depend to a high degree on the sample data, resulting paradoxically in better fit indices but less rigorous theoretical models (Mulaik et al., 1989, Crowley and Fan, 1997).

The **Akaike Information Criterion (AIC)** or the **Consistent** version of **Akaike Information Criterion (CAIC)** adjusted by sample size, is a frequently used measure for model parsimony (Akaike, 1974). As it accounts for the effects of sample size (Diamantopoulos and Siguaw, 2000, Kline, 2005), the CAIC was chosen for this research. Generally used as a comparative measure between different models estimated with the same data, the CAIC is also known as 'information criteria' index as it enables information about which of the suggested models is the most parsimonious (Hooper et al., 2007). Model parsimony increases with decreasing CAIC values (Diamantopoulos and Siguaw, 2000, Hair et al., 2010). Accordingly, the closer its value comes to zero, the more parsimonious is the model (Hair et al., 2010). However, as the indices are not normed a specific value range is not given and thus literature does not provide a threshold level other than that "the model that produces the lowest value is the most superior" (Hooper et al., 2007, p. 56). Notably, a minimum sample size of 200 is recommended by literature to ensure reliable measures for these indices (Diamantopoulos and Siguaw, 2000).

To summarise, a comprehensive overview and discussion of different indices applied in this research for the assessment of model fit were given in this section. By balancing out absolute and incremental fit indices with the parsimony of the model, a thorough assessment and comprehensive reflection of the model fit is ensured for the next research steps, when all indices are applied for the assessment of one-factor congeneric models (refer to the following section 6.4.2), the structural path model (section 6.5.3), as well as its re-specification (section 6.5.4).

6.4.2 One-Factor Congeneric Measurement Models

The one-factor congeneric measurement models, which represent the simplest form of measurement models, are presented in this chapter, along with the full measurement model used for the calculation of the composite scores for the latent constructs. These models were developed based on the suggested factor structure indicated by the EFA. In this confirmatory research step, both theoretical as well as empirical factors were considered, with the aim to achieve highly fitted, yet parsimonious measurement models (Kline, 2005), and therewith suitable composites for further analysis.

The individual one-factor congeneric measurement models were calculated using AMOS with goodness-of-fit and parsimony indices (refer to section 6.4.1) applied for the assessment of model fit. To identify whether all items load high on their respective construct, the variance of the latent construct was set to 1. A mandatory precondition for computing the measurement models is, that the degrees of freedom are above zero, which requires a higher number of observations than free parameters (Kline, 2005). Hence, to allow the computation of measurement models with only three items, based on a pair-wise parameter comparisons the variance of two residuals was set equal, as it is common practice in research (e.g. Plewa, 2010). Notably, the Bollen-Stine bootstrap technique with bootstrap samples set to 500 (as described in section 6.2.2) was performed and the respective p-value is provided.

In case the fit indices did not show acceptable fit, models were re-specified. Re-specification primarily concerned the elimination of items with small factor loadings, whereby a minimum of 0.5 is recommended by literature to ensure convergent validity (Steenkamp and van Trijp, 1991). Besides, in order to achieve more parsimonious models, modification indices for covariances were further consulted in some cases and provided suggestions for covarying error terms that are part of the same factor (Gaskin, 2012c). The resulting one-factor congeneric measurement models for each latent construct are presented in Appendix 6.3 in the additional electronic material, along with their factor score weights and respective model fit indices.

In accordance to the acceptable threshold as described in section 6.4.1., all models show a good model fit. Moreover, all items show sufficiently high loadings on their respective constructs, with all beta values exceeding the recommended threshold of 0.5 (Steenkamp and van Trijp, 1991). Notably, while all values of the Normed Chi-Square (χ^2/df) are well situated below the critical value of 3 (Bollen, 1989), several values even lie below the value of 1, indicating a model overfit (Hair et al., 2010). As often seen in similar studies, a slight overfit in the congeneric measurement models is common (e.g. Plewa, 2010) and was deemed acceptable for this research due to the known effect of sample size on the χ^2 statistics (Hair et al., 2010, Hoyle and Panter, 1995). The consideration of parsimony in tandem with other goodness-of-fit indices was valuable for the assessment of the one-factor congeneric models and the determination of the number of indicators used for computing each construct. In sum, the overall goodness of fit, measured by means of a variety of absolute, incremental and parsimony fit indices, gave evidence that all models qualified for the calculation of composite scores and hypotheses testing in the final structural model.

The Full Measurement Model

After all one-factor congeneric measurement models were built and assed for quality, in a next step they were included in a **complete measurement model**, whereby covariances were drawn between all constructs, showing the following fit indices: While the χ^2/df (= 1.514) and RMSEA (= 0.050) indicated good model fit, the GFI (= 0.826), TLI (= 0.936), and CFI (= 0.945) were close to, although did not meet their acceptable thresholds, whereby the AGFI (= 0.788) and NFI (= 0.855) indicated poor fit. However, given the good model fit obtained for the congeneric measurement models, a good fit for *all* indices computed for the full measurement model is neither assumed nor necessarily being achieved. The major purpose of the model evaluation rather is to test the measurement model for reliability and validity of measurement (Backhaus, 2008), by means of examining the extent of interrelationships and covariations among the latent construct (Schreiber et al., 2006). The measurement model is rather used to test for common method bias and measurement model invariance, as presented in the following sections 6.4.4 and 6.4.5.

6.4.3 Construct Reliability and Validity (from CFA)

Similar to the procedure during the EFA, an assessment of the validity and reliability of constructs emerged from the CFA is required. Without having convergent and discriminant validity, as well as reliability established, moving forward to test the causal model would lead to useless results (Gaskin, 2012c). As already referred to in section 6.3.3, an assessment of the **validity** of the latent constructs, more specifically the convergent, discriminant and content validity (Lukas et al., 2004, Page and Meyer, 2000) is deemed crucial in order to approve that the measurement items "measure what they are supposed to measure, but also not measure what they are not supposed to measure" (Kline, 2005, p. 60).

Convergent validity refers to the correlation between the measurement items for the same construct (refer to section 6.3.3). Given that all factor loadings of the one-factor congeneric measurement models exceed the recommended threshold of 0.5, convergent validity was further assessed by means of the Average Variance Extracted (AVE). The AVE (pvc) for the construct η, with λ representing the ith factor loading on the respective construct, is computed based on the following formula (Fornell and Larcker, 1981):

$$p_{vc(\eta)} = \frac{\sum_{i=1}^{p} \lambda_{yi}^{2}}{\sum_{i=1}^{p} \lambda_{yi}^{2} + \sum_{i=1}^{p} Var(\varepsilon_i)} \qquad (6.1)$$

An acceptable level of convergent validity is given when the values for pvc (η) are higher than 0.5 (Hair et al., 2010) meaning, that the measurement items account for a larger degree of variance than the measurement error (Diamantopoulos and Siguaw, 2000). Convergent validity is given for all constructs as all pvc (η) values meet the respective criteria (as reported below in Table 6.5). Convergent validity confirms that the theoretically anticipated correlations between the individual measurement items and the respective construct are present.

Discriminant Validity in turn accounts for the distinctiveness between constructs (refer to section 6.3.3), revealing that the constructs are theoretically different and sufficiently uncorrelated. Given the context of this research, where theoretical considerations as well as empirical findings suggest the presence of moderate correlations among constructs (e.g. Pavlou and El Sawy, 2011), potential multicollinearity issues caused by inter-correlations among the DC constructs might be a problem. Therefore it was deemed extremely important to demonstrate discriminant validity among constructs in order to secure validity of the findings. As shown in the correlation matrix presented in Table 6.4, as expected moderate to high correlations appeared between Sensing, Learning, Coordinating and Integrating capacity.

Table 6.4 Correlation Matrix of Final Constructs

Component	Knowl Speci	Knowl Compl	Knowl Tacit	Techno Knowl	Market Knowl	Entre Orient	Env Turb	Netw Orient	Coord.	Integr.	Learn.	Sens.
KnowlSpeci	1.000											
KnowlCompl	0.475	1.000										
KnowlTacit	0.252	-0.048	1.000									
TechnoKnowl	0.266	0.682	-0.062	1.000								
MarketKnowl	0.304	0.422	-0.088	0.604	1.000							
EntreOrient	0.117	0.372	-0.084	0.41	0.371	1.000						
EnvTurb	0.031	0.114	0.28	0.107	0.107	0.04	1.000					
NetwOrient	0.351	0.526	-0.037	0.383	0.332	0.276	0.248	1.000				
Coordinating	0.37	**0.726**	-0.094	0.614	0.494	0.395	0.053	0.52	1.000			
Integrating	0.242	0.584	-0.085	0.418	0.331	0.316	0.097	0.479	**0.776**	1.000		
Learning	0.215	0.663	-0.207	0.609	0.51	0.433	0.167	0.566	**0.762**	0.531	1.000	
Sensing	0.139	0.48	-0.182	0.434	0.463	0.345	0.209	0.584	0.56	0.482	**0.712**	1.000

Given these high correlations, a further assessment of discriminant validity was deemed valuable. Following the Fornell/Larcker criterium, discriminant validity is given when the highest squared correlation between two constructs, and thus the squared variance (λ^2), is smaller than the Average Variance Extracted (AVE), calculated earlier by the pvc score (Fornell and Larcker, 1981, Straub et al., 2004, Hair et al., 2010). The following Table 6.5 presents the highest shared variance (λ^2) and the AVE (pvc) values for each construct.

Table 6.5 Convergent and Discriminant Validity Scores

Construct	Pvc (η)		highest λ^2
Sensing capacity	0.524	>	0.507
Learning capacity	0.736	>	0.581
Integrating capacity	0.688	>	0.602
Coordinating capacity	0.703	>	0.602
Market Knowledge	0.826	>	0.365
Technological Knowledge	0.672	>	0.465
Knowledge Tacitness	0.822	>	0.078
Knowledge Specificy	0.548	>	0.227
Knowledge Complementarity	0.736	>	0.527
Networking Orientation	0.746	>	0.341
Environmental Turbulence	0.603	>	0.078
Entrepreneurial Orientation	0.603	>	0.187

As all AVE (pvc) values reported in Table 6.5 exceed the values for the highest shared variance (λ^2), discriminant validity is established for all constructs (Fornell and Larcker, 1981, Rokkan et al., 2003).

Content validity, as already explained in detail in section 6.3.3., was yet approved during the exploratory research step. Similar findings revealed during the CFA, whereby the theoretical anticipated correlations could also be empirically confirmed. For example, a high degree of Integrating capacity was expected and shown as being associated with a higher level of Learning and Coordinating capacity (Pavlou and El Sawy, 2011).

Reliability, as already addressed in section 6.3.3, accounts for the internal consistency of the measurement, and is closely related to the absence of random errors within the measurement (Kinnear et al., 1993, Zikmund, 2003). During a CFA the internal consistency can either be assessed by means of computing **Cronbach's alpha (α)** (see section 6.3.3) or calculating **Construct Reliability (pη)** (Hair et al., 2010). The latter is estimated using information on factor loadings and error variances (Diamantopoulos and Siguaw, 2000) and is regarded as being more precise than Cronbach's alpha as it is not sensitive to the number of constructs (Hair et al., 2010). The formula for estimating the construct reliability p for the construct η(with λ representing the ith factor loading on its respective construct) is (Fornell and Larcker, 1981):

$$p_\eta = \frac{(\sum\limits_{i=1}^{p} \lambda_{yi})^2}{(\sum\limits_{i=1}^{p} \lambda_{yi})^2 + \sum\limits_{i=1}^{p} Var(\varepsilon_i)} \qquad (6.2)$$

An acceptable level of construct reliability is given when pη exhibit values higher than 0.70 (Fornell and Larcker, 1981, Hair et al., 2010). As shown by the respective values of Cronbach's alpha (α) and Construct reliability presented in Table 6.6, all constructs show a high degree of internal consistency and construct reliability, especially considering the small number of items used for each construct.

Table 6.6 Reliability Measures

Construct	No. items	α	pη
Sensing capacity	3	0.762	0.767
Learning capacity	3	0.889	0.897
Integrating capacity	4	0.895	0.898
Coordinating capacity	4	0.903	0.904
Market Knowledge	3	0.866	0.934
Technological Knowledge	3	0.919	0.858
Knowledge Tacitness	3	0.931	0.932
Knowledge Specificy	2	0.707	0.708
Knowledge Complementarity	3	0.892	0.893
Networking Orientation	4	0.921	0.922
Environmental Turbulence	3	0.813	0.819
Entrepreneurial Orientation	3	0.818	0.820

With reliability and validity confirmed, the following section tests the presence of common method bias, before calculating the composite scores.

6.4.4 Common Method Bias (CMB)

Common method bias (CMB) is a potential bias in the dataset caused due to a systematic (external) measurement error that is influencing the correct measurement of the relationships between the constructs (Chang et al., 2010). CMB arises because of common method variance, which is the "variance that is attributable to the measurement method rather than to the constructs the measures represent" (Podsakoff et al., 2003, p. 879). Simply said, when the majority of the variance can be explained by a single factor, CMB is present (Gaskin, 2012c).

Researchers agree that CMB may be a concern, when a single source (e.g. self-report questionnaires within an online survey) is used for collecting data from the same participants, at the same time interval (Podsakoff and Organ, 1986, Chang et al., 2010). However, there is a constant debate on the likelihood and nature of CMB in self-reported data (Richardson et al., 2009), while some authors regard CMB as a common problem researchers are required to control for (e.g. Podsakoff et al., 2003), others refer to it as an 'urban legend' and consider any attempts made to control for CMB as "exaggeration and oversimplification of the true state of affairs" (Spector, 2006, p. 230).

The most widely and traditionally used technique for testing common method variance is the **Harman's single-factor test**, which controls if the majority of variance in the data can be attributed to a single factor (Podsakoff et al., 2003, Chang et al., 2010). The basic assumption of the method is, if a substantial amount of common method variance exists, the variance extracted by the one single factor accounts for more than 50% of the variance in the model, this would indicate that CMB is an issue (Podsakoff et al., 2003). For using this method, all 38 items from each of the studies' constructs were included into an EFA, while the number of factors extracted was constrained to one (Gaskin, 2012c). The results of the unrotated one-factor solution were then examined and gave hints whether CMB is an issue or not. The results of the Harman's single factor test show that only 38.57% of variance extracted is explained by the single factor, claiming that CMB is not a pervasive issue.

Despite its wide usage and apparent appeal, there are also several limitations reported for this method. First, it is criticised for being insensitive due to the fact that it is rather unlikely that a one-factor model will fit the data (Podsakoff et al., 2003, Chang et al., 2011). Furthermore, its explanatory power is restricted, as it only gives an indication of the existence of a CMB and does not statistically control for or partial out the common variance effects (Podsakoff et al., 2003). Hence, the method should be used rather as a "diagnostic technique" for "assessing the extent to which common method variance may be a problem" (Podsakoff et al., 2003, p. 879).

Besides a variety of other post hoc statistical methods—such as the correlational marker approach (Lindell and Whitney, 2001), the CFA marker approach (Williams et al., 2010), and the unmeasured latent method construct (ULMC) (William et al., 1989)—for testing CMB have been proposed, that allow the detection and correction of common method variance. However, there is a constant debate and change of knowledge among scholars on their appropriateness and efficiency. In a recent and comprehensive study about the appropriateness of those post hoc statistical methods, Richardson et al. (2009) revealed that there is hardly any benefit for any of the suggested methods as "all techniques produced highly inaccurate corrected correlations" (Richardson et al., 2009, p. 798). They conclude, that using any of those methods will "be no better than 'throwing darts in the dark'", while "leading researchers to falsely conclude CMV [common method variance] is not present and biasing their data or vice versa" (Richardson et al., 2009, p. 798). As findings revealed the potential risks associated with using these techniques, they were not used in this research.

6.4.5 Measurement Model Invariance

Before creating composite variables for being used in the structural path model, configural and metric invariance of the measurement model is tested during the CFA. **Measurement model invariance** ensures that the factor structure and loadings (refer to Appendix 6.3 in the additional electronic material) that were previously tested on a single sample (using the complete dataset), are also sufficiently equivalent across different sub-sample groups (Vandenberg and Lance, 2000, Gaskin, 2012c). If measurement model invariance is not given, creating composite variables would be error-prone and may hinder meaningful interpretations, as the underlying factor structure does not account for the different groups (Gaskin, 2012c). Beside this, establishing measurement model invariance is crucial when a multi-group moderation test for the structural model is conducted in a subsequent analysis (Plewa, 2010). Thus, to test configural and metric invariance was deemed valuable in order to identify whether the final measurement model replicates well for each sub-sample group. A detailed description of the procedure used to test for configural and metric invariance is provided in Appendix 6.4 in the additional electronic material.

As the results presented in Appendix 6.4 in the additional electronic material show, both, configural and metric invariance was established. While the chi-square difference test gave evidence that groups are different *at the model level*, metric invariance could be confirmed *at the path level*, meaning that groups are equivalent with regard to the overall factor structure. Hence measurement model invariance was supported, as the relationships between manifest indicator variables and the latent construct show to be the same across groups. These findings allow the computation of composite variables from the factor scores.

6.4.6 Composite Variables

Having construct reliability and validity as well as measurement invariance established for the one-factor congeneric measurement models, this chapter describes the procedure used for the calculation of the composite variables and justifies its use.

To ensure stable parameter estimation, in comparison to other multivariate methods SEM necessitates relatively large sample sizes, that should at least exceed 100 to 150 with reference to statistical stability (Anders and Gerbing, 1988, Lei and Lomax, 2005), with recommended sample sizes of 200 or higher (Hair et al., 2010). A general rule of thumb is that the ratio of sample size compared to the number of model parameters should be at least 5:1, preferably 10:1 (Hair et al., 2010, Kline, 2005). Under conditions of multivariate non-normality, as it is common in research practice (Byrne, 2001), an even higher ratio is recommended (Hair et al., 2010).

Although the sample size of 208 for this research would exceed the recommended 200, instead of a 'true' structural equation model with latent and observed variables included in the final model, composite variables are used in this research for two reasons. First, due to the fact that multiple items were used to measure each latent construct, the application and analysis of a 'true' structural model would involve a highly complex model if the latent constructs and observed variables were to be included, the sample size is not sufficiently large enough to make use of a 'true' structural equation model. Second, with the application of composite variables, which are mathematically calculated artefacts (Farris et al., 1992) usually calculated as a means of data reduction (Rowe, 2002), the number of analysed parameters could be decreased for the benefit of statistical stability, as they limit the conceivable effect of idiosyncrasies of individual components (Hulin et al., 2001). Hence, the usage of composite variables promotes the evaluation of complex models as well as stable parameter estimations, even when the sample size is relatively small (Hewett et al., 2002).

Correspondingly, composite variables were calculated for each latent construct based on the one-factor congeneric measurement models. Following Plewa (2009), the calculation of the composite variables followed a three step approach. In a first step, the one factor congeneric measurement models were created for every construct (as presented in section 6.4.2). Due to the fact that all measures loaded high on their respective factor and showed good model fit according to the calculation of the goodness-of-fit indices, the one-factor congeneric models were approved, and the measurement instrument was verified as valid (Hau, 1995). Furthermore, to ensure that substantial and meaningful composite variables were obtained, convergent and discriminant validity and reliability was determined (as reported in section 6.4.3). Common method bias (section 6.4.4) and measurement model invariance (section 6.4.5) were tested thereafter for the same reason.

In a second step, factor score regression weights for all one-factor-congeneric models were calculated in AMOS and used for the calculation of composite scores (Jöreskog and Sörbom, 1989). While in accordance to Rowe (2002), different procedures can be applied for the calculation of composite variables, e.g. simple, unweighted, additive indices or factor scores, the latter was used in this research for the benefit of taking random measurement error as well as different factor loadings into account, instead of simply averaging the item scores. As a result, different indicators are allowed to contribute in different manners, which leads to a more realistic representation of the original data (Fleishman and Benson, 1987). Hence, to derive the proportional weighted scale scores, the factor score of each individual item was divided by the sum of factor score weights of the respective construct (Plewa, 2010).

In the third step, a new variable was computed in SPSS to lastly calculate the final composite score. First, the proportional weighted scales scores for each individual item were multiplied by the original value of the respective item (Rowe, 2002). The resulting scores for those items that related to the same construct, were then added up in order to derive the final composite scores for each construct (Plewa, 2010). To summarise, with the composite variables calculated as the final result of the CFA, they represent the basis for the formulation of the structural path model for analysing the causal relationship between the constructs.

6.4.7 Second-Order Formative Construct

Prior formulating the structural path model, in a last pre-processing step this section outlines a different procedure used for the calculation of the formative construct, that was employed to measure the outcome variable RR. Thus, in contrast to all other constructs used in this research which are conceptualised as first-order reflective constructs, RR is formed by the four different types of RR and thus conceptualised as a second-order formative construct (refer to section 5.3.2 and 5.3.3).

For its computation first, one-factor congeneric measurement models were calculated for the first-order reflective measurement models, following the procedure as described in section 6.4.2. The RR measures, however, revealed problematic in regard to discriminant validity (as rather strong correlations emerged between the items measuring the four different types of RR), leading to the elimination of several items. Consequently, only two items remained for the first-order constructs used to measure Type 2, 3 and 4, while three items remained for the measurement model for Type 1. Those measurement difficulties of the RR constructs may be related to the research field, especially as both interviews as well as the questionnaire pre-test indicated that respondents were not familiar with the nomenclature of RR and the respective items. Despite changes in the wording of the individual items, this unfamiliarity may cause measurement difficulties as already indicated by previous works in this field (e.g. Zahra and Wiklund, 2002). However the strong reliability scores for the two-item constructs suggest their suitability for further analysis. Moreover, as all remaining items for each individual construct relate to similar activities (while addressing different resources and outcomes) they qualified for being used to form the second-order formative model of RR. Notably, by means of calculating the first-order constructs "the indicators of the construct can still be individually evaluated based on their specific contributions to the construct by evaluating their path weights" (Cenfetelli and Bassellier, 2009, p. 690).

Having built the first-order reflective constructs, these models were used in a second step to form the **second-order formative** construct. Therefore an aggregation heuristic was used. As suggested by Lee and Cardogan (2013) for the weighting of formative constructs, researchers can either estimate weights by means of statistical algorithms (e.g. PLS) or by fixing the relative weightings of the formative dimensions to its "true value" using the aggregation heuristic that is part of the construct definition (Hardin et al., 2011). Therefore, each dimension forming the multidimensional construct and its respective weightings should be specified a priori, given that the theory concerning the construct provides sufficient theoretical rationale to "prescribe the exact algebraic relation between the multidimensional construct and its dimensions" (Law et al., 1998, p. 751). According to this research's definition of RR, each Type (1, 2, 3 and 4) is regarded to be similar important for building the overall construct. Therefore, RR is constituted as a simple equally-weighted linear composite of its constituent dimensions. Unlike statistical weighting procedures, the aggregation heuristic used here is recommended in the literature as a more appropriate method allowing the estimation based on theoretical considerations and giving more transparency to the computation of multidimensional constructs and thus comparability of research findings (see Lee and Cardogan, 2013). Figure 6.2 illustrates the measurement model used to measure RR along with its respective path weights.

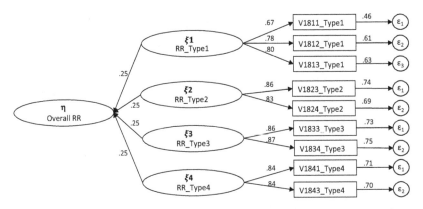

Figure 6.2   Second order-formative Construct – Measurement Model Resource Recombination

Having both the composite variables (6.4.6) as well as the formative construct (6.4.7) calculated, in a subsequent research step they were included in the structural path model in order to finally test the causal relationship between constructs. This research step is regarded as the core of SEM and will be outlined in the following section.

6.5   The Structural Path Model

This section outlines the structural path model, including hypotheses testing and model re-specification. The **structural path model**, comprises the second core component in SEM, where the causal relationships between the constructs are tested. The structural model displays the interrelationships among the endogenous and exogenous constructs in the proposed model as a succession of structural equations, akin to a regression-analytical approach (Schreiber et al., 2006), but at the same time including the shared measurement error of these constructs into the calculation (Gefen et al., 2000).

6.5.1 Model Identification

Before testing the proposed structural path model, the model has to be identified. A model is said to be identified if a value can be estimated for every parameter in the model (Backhaus, 2010). An imperative for model identification therefore is, that the overall model has got a unique solution (Breckler, 1990, Diamantopoulos and Siguaw, 2000), which requires two conditions to be fulfilled: (1) the number of observations is equal or more than free model parameters, and (2) every unobserved construct is assigned a scale (Kline, 2005).

Different forms of identification exist: a model may be empirically *under-identified*, *just-identified* or *over-identified* (Kline, 2005). A model is regarded as under-identified or not identified, if condition (1) is not fulfilled, because this makes a unique solution theoretical impossible. At the same time, while models that are just-identified or over-identified are regarded as identified models and therefore fulfilling condition (1), whereas the just-identified model is constituted by an equal number of parameters and observations, while in contrast the over-identified model is characterised by more observations than parameters (Kline, 2005). All models used in this research meet the fundamental conditions of identification. Moreover, due to the fact that the models are over-identified and thus positive degrees of freedom exist, the scientific use of the models is given (Kline, 2001).

6.5.2 Multivariate Assumptions

The stable application of structural path models depends on a range of multivariate assumptions (Hair et al., 2010). Beside multivariate normality as already discussed in section 6.2.2, linearity of all relationships, the absence of multicollinearity and homoscedasticity of data are important assumptions for the application of SEM.

Linearity refers to "the consistent slope of change" that illustrates the relationship between the independent (endogenous) variable and the dependent (exogenous) variable (Gaskin, 2012a). Being a covariance-based SEM algorithm, the ML-method applied in this research postulates linear relationships among variables (Reinecke, 1999). Hence, if the relationships between the dependent and independent variables were radically inconsistent, this would hinder the application of SEM analyses (Gaskin, 2012a). To test the assumption of linearity, curve estimation was conducted for all proposed relationships in the proposed model to determine, if all relationships could be assumed to be linear in order to be tested using a covariance based SEM algorithm (Gaskin, 2012a). The results showed all proposed relations to be linear, with the exception of the relation between Knowledge Tacitness ➔ RR, as well as Knowledge Origin ➔ RR, both being used to control for specific characteristics of the resource base in the model. For the former the relationship between the variables indicated to be a cubic or quadratic function rather than linear, while the latter appeared inconsistent throughout. As already outlined before there are many reasons for a non-linear relationship to be suggested (e.g. interaction effects between the controls and RR as outlined in section 3.3). Therefore and for the reason that both variables (Tacitness and Origin) were solely used as controls in the model, the violation of the linearity assumption was not regarded as problematic.

Multicollinearity is given when two or more independent (endogenous) variables are highly correlated among themselves, meaning that one variable can be linearly predicted from the other (Backhhaus, 2011). While small and moderate degrees of multicollinearity are reported as common in research practice (Backhhaus, 2011), a high degree of multicollinearity is undesirable as in consequence the impact of the individual variables on the dependent variable tends to be less precise (Hair et al., 2010, O'Brien, 2007) A widely used method for determining whether multicollinearity is an issue or not, is the calculation of the variance inflation factor (VIF) for multicollinearity (Backhaus, 2011). Different thresholds are reported in the literature, with VIF values higher than 5 up to 10 (O'Brien, 2007, Backhaus, 2010) indicating a multicollinearity problem. As all VIF values for this research lie below 3, the critical thresholds alluding multicollinearity are not exceeded for this research (O'Brien, 2007, Hair et al., 2010), giving evidence that multicollinearity is not an issue.

Homoscedasticity of the data is a further pre-assumption for the application of SEM. Homoscedasticity is given when the variable's residuals (or errors) have a constant variance among the dataset (Backhaus, 2010), meaning that the variance exhibits consistently across different levels of the variable (Hair et al., 2010). By contrast, heteroscedasticity exists if the errors or residuals do not have a constant variance among the data set (Backhaus, 2010). Given that interaction (moderation) effects between the variables are expected in this research model, homoscedasticity of the data is not assumed for this research. This is capped by research praxis, where heteroscedastic data is often found when the data is moderated by different groups (Gaskin, 2012a).

   In brief, prior to testing the structural model a variety of multivariate assumptions as linearity, (the absence of) multicollinearity and heteroscedasticity were discussed and tested using the data, whereby the results indicated towards a stable application of the SEM methods.

6.5.3 The Structural Path Model

After the identification of the model and the test of all multivariate assumptions, finally the structural path model is presented and its overall model fit assessed. For this purpose, the conceptual model and the proposed interrelationships among the endogenous and exogenous constructs as developed based on the literature review and the preliminary qualitative research step were tested using AMOS.

Figure 6.3 presents the structural path model detailing hypotheses H1 to H7 and shows the estimated model fit indices for the model. Prior to testing the hypotheses however, an assessment of the overall model fit was conducted. A

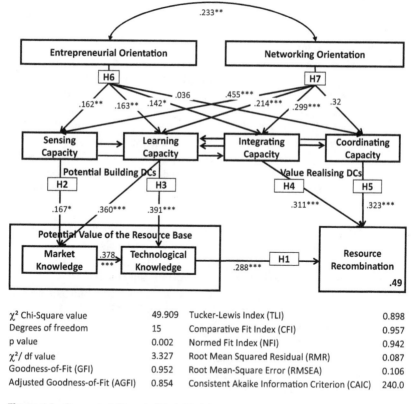

χ^2 Chi-Square value	49.909	Tucker-Lewis Index (TLI)	0.898
Degrees of freedom	15	Comparative Fit Index (CFI)	0.957
p value	0.002	Normed Fit Index (NFI)	0.942
χ^2/ df value	3.327	Root Mean Squared Residual (RMR)	0.087
Goodness-of-Fit (GFI)	0.952	Root Mean-Square Error (RMSEA)	0.106
Adjusted Goodness-of-Fit (AGFI)	0.854	Consistent Akaike Information Criterion (CAIC)	240.0

Figure 6.3 Conceptual Structural Path Model

thorough assessment and comprehensive reflection of the model fit is ensured by the employment of a variety of different goodness-of-fit indices. The indices along with their acceptable thresholds were presented in section 6.4.1 and have already been employed for the assessment of the one-factor measurement models.

Even though the conceptual model was based on a thorough literature review of the resource- and competence based literature and the causal relations were additionally confirmed by qualitative research findings, not all goodness-of-fit indices showed an acceptable model fit as shown in Figure 6.3. While the GFI ($= 0.952$) and CFI ($= 0.957$) indicated a good fit, the χ^2/df ($= 3.327$), AGFI ($= 0.854$), TLI ($= 0.898$), and NFI ($= 0.942$) were close to, however did not meet the acceptable thresholds, and this was not supported by a significant χ^2 (p < 0.05) and an RMSEA value of 0.106. In particular the RMSEA is notably higher than the accepted level for this research (0.08), reflecting a poor fit for all values above 0.10 (Byrne, 2001).

The proposed model explains 49% of the variance in RR performance. Hence, despite the fact that some indicators point to a good model fit, an investigation of potential modification indices was deemed valuable to achieve a better fitting and more parsimonious model.

6.5.4 The Re-specified Structural Path Model

The conceptual structural path model was re-specified with the aim of achieving a more parsimonious, well-fitting model. Many authors have argued that it is unlikely for the conceptual model to reveal the best or most parsimonious representation of the logical structure of the data, and therefore often it requires a modification of the model (Anderson and Gerbing, 1988, Baumgartner and Homburg, 1996, Hoyle and Panter, 1995, Plewa, 2010). Hence, it was legitimated that, when different causal relationships are conceivable, an evaluation of alternatives is an established mean to further improve a structural model (Jahn, 2007). Thus, for this research a stepwise approach for model re-specification was chosen in order to achieve a more parsimonious model (Kaplan, 1990, Medlin, 2001, Plewa, 2010).

Modification indices were consulted as they offered "suggested remedies to discrepancies between the proposed and estimated model" (Gaskin, 2012c). A modification index for a parameter is referred to as "an estimate of the amount by which the discrepancy function would decrease if the analysis were repeated with the constraints on that parameter removed" (Jöreskog and Sörbom, 1989), in other words, it "shows the minimum decrease in the model's Chi-squared value if a previously fixed parameter is set free" (Diamantopoulos and Siguaw, 2000, p. 108). Therefore, the higher the value of a modification index for a specific path to be included in the model, the higher the potential of improvement in regard to the model fit (Kline, 2005). Modification indices were consulted, along with their expected estimate for parameter change, which accounts for the amount by which a parameter would positively or negatively change in the model if the constraints on it were removed (Byrne, 2001, Jöreskog and Sörbom, 1989, 1996).

Following the assessment of the conceptual structural model, the analyses of modification indices and parameter changes displayed the value of adding two additional paths, namely one between Entrepreneurial Orientation ➜ Market Knowledge, and the other between Networking Orientation ➜ RR. At the same time it was deemed essential to base any decision concerning the re-specification of the model not solely on statistical considerations, but also on theoretical and content-wise considerations (Anderson and Gerbing, 1988, Diamantopoulos and Siguaw, 2000, Plewa, 2010). Notably, as the aim was not to find the "best" fitting model, not all modifications indices were addressed, but only those that were theoretically grounded, were revised (Gaskin, 2012d). The statistically significant direct effect Entrepreneurial Orientation has on Market Knowledge ($p < 0.05$) as well as Networking Orientation has on RR ($p < 0.001$), and the potential integration of the two paths in the re-specified model were thus assessed based on existing theory and logical content.

First, investigating the identified path between **Entrepreneurial Orientation and Market Knowledge**, EO as defined in this research is regarded as a combination of *proactiveness, innovativeness* and *risk-taking* (e.g. Wiklund, 1999), which promotes the firm's willingness to capitalise on new opportunities by engaging in entrepreneurial activities (e.g. Wiklund, 1999, Wiklund and Shepherd, 2000). A high EO thus is positively associated with the *ability* to sense and seize new opportunities and revamp the existing resource base with new knowledge (Sensing and Learning capacity), meanwhile it will also proactively contribute to the development of knowledge about markets and customers itself. Not surprisingly, there is also a significant direct effect between EO and Market Knowledge to be found in the data. Hence, the additional direct path helps specifying that EO not only *indirectly* influences the development of Market Knowledge through Sensing and Learning capacity, but also *directly* affects the development of Market Knowledge. While being logically consistent, it is also consistent with literature, where support can be found by empirical research confirming the contingent relation between EO and knowledge based resources and performance (Wiklund and Shepherd, 2000). These findings are complemented by the argument by

Chockburn and colleagues (2000), who propose that EO can help to explain the managerial processes on the one hand and provides firms the ability to utilise their knowledge based resources on the other hand (Wiklund and Shepherd, 2000).

Likewise the identified path between **Networking Orientation and RR** can be explained by its conceptualisation and measurement. As NO is defined in this research as "the extent to which a firm's business strategy stresses effective and efficient location of network partners, management of network relationships, and improvement of network performance" (Mu and Di Benedetto, 2011, p. 341), it is embedded in a firm's interactions with external partners and serves as significant source for new external knowledge and resources (Isobe et al., 2008, Peng and Delios, 2006, Mathews, 2002). Thus, while NO is rather orientated towards the external resources, Coordinating capacity is primarily directed towards the coordination of internal resources. Given these different directions, a high Networking capacity does not automatically lead to a higher internal Coordinating capacity, but can foster RR in firms by bringing in new resources. Moreover recent research findings suggest that "if firms are overembedded with strong [internal] network ties without building external network ties with divergent knowledge and information sources, networking can have a negative impact on innovation performance" (Mu and Di Benedetto, 2011, p. 342). Thus, emphasis should be given to the firm's capabilities to also orchestrate their networks and external sources (Mu and Di Benedetto, 2012), e.g. through the development of a high Integrating capability to extract value. This is especially relevant as research findings suggest that "as a firm's networking capability increases, it should be able to increase its ability to purposefully create, extend, modify its resource configurations, and ultimately improve its marketing and technological capabilities for effective commercialisation of new products" (Mu and Di Benedetto, 2012, p. 7). Given these theoretical underpinnings the strong and positive direct effect NO has on RR supports the emphasis given by network theory and its underlying idea, that firms which are accessible to external sources through networks, alliances and partnerships are being more capable of external resources to enlarge their existing pool of resources available to extract value. Hence the direct link between NO and RR can be justified.

Based on these content-wise considerations, the two additional paths were added to the final model. Following the call for more transparency in reporting re-specification in regard to predicted and "discovered" paths (Hoyle and Panter, 1995), Figure 6.4 presents the final re-specified model with its original and added paths. The parameter estimates and model fit indices, thus enable a comparison to the conceptual model.

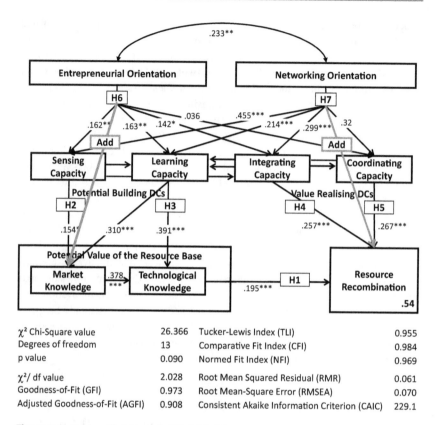

Figure 6.4 Re-specified Structural Path Model

χ² Chi-Square value	26.366	Tucker-Lewis Index (TLI)	0.955
Degrees of freedom	13	Comparative Fit Index (CFI)	0.984
p value	0.090	Normed Fit Index (NFI)	0.969
χ²/ df value	2.028	Root Mean Squared Residual (RMR)	0.061
Goodness-of-Fit (GFI)	0.973	Root Mean-Square Error (RMSEA)	0.070
Adjusted Goodness-of-Fit (AGFI)	0.908	Consistent Akaike Information Criterion (CAIC)	229.1

As the goodness-of-fit indices show, a good overall model fit as well as a high level of parsimony could be established based on only slight modifications of the model, leading to a non-significant χ^2 of 26.366 (p = 0.09), and a RMSEA value (= 0.070) within the acceptable range. Similarly, all other fit indices indicate a high degree of goodness-of-fit (χ^2/df =2.028, GFI = 0.973, AGFI = 0.908) or respectively no badness-of-fit (RMR = 0.051), while also the incremental fit indices (TLI = 0.955, CFI = 0.984, NFI = 0.969) showed excellent values for the model fit. Even the CAIC value improved from 240.036 for the conceptual model to 229.167 for the re-specified model, indicating a higher level of parsimony for the re-specified model, despite of two additional paths. The proposed (re-specified) model explains 54% of the variance in RR performance.

In brief, with the aim of achieving a more parsimonious, well-fitting model, the structural path model was re-specified by means of statistical and theoretical considerations as it is common in research practice (e.g. Plewa, 2010). The re-specification of the conceptual model led to the addition of two paths, the first was added between EO and Market Knowledge, and the second between NO and RR. Worth noting, as opposed the principal nature of SEM, the procedure of model re-specification is not confirmatory but exploratory in nature (Byrne, 2001, Diamantopoulos, 1994). Whereas only slight modifications were made, the re-specified path model should be validated with a further, independent sample in the future (Diamantopoulos, 1994, Hoyle and Panter, 1995, Plewa and Quester, 2007, Plewa, 2009). Given the achieved good overall model fit, the model qualified for being used for hypotheses testing in the further analyses. The findings regarding the path coefficients and hypotheses support are detailed in the next chapter.

6.5.5 Hypotheses Support

As the local and global fit indices revealed a good model fit, hypotheses could finally be tested. When the relationship between two constructs is significantly different from zero and shows the expected direction (positive or negative relationship), the proposed hypothesis is regarded as being confirmed (Jahn, 2007). The proposed causal and covariance relationships among the endogenous and exogenous constructs were estimated using AMOS. Findings regarding standardised effects and the support of hypotheses are provided in Table 6.7.

The table incorporates the **standardised direct effect,** also referred to as path coefficient or beta coefficient and presented in the structural path model (Figure 6.4), as well as the **standardised indirect effect**. Furthermore, the aggregate of both effects builds the **standardised total effect**, which comprises the complete influence one variable has on another variable, throughout all conceivable relationships with additional constructs (mediating variables). A consideration of standardised total effects is regarded as valuable as it enables a better understanding of the causal relationships in holistic and complex models (Jahn, 2007). Furthermore, the **critical ratio** and the **level of significance** of the direct effect are presented in Table 6.7. In case that there was no direct relationship theorised between two constructs, only the indirect effect is reported, the respective hypotheses H1(1), H2 and H3, and their levels of significance will be subject of further investigation in the mediation analysis (section 6.6). For reasons of transparency the respective results for the original conceptual model are provided in Appendix 6.5 in the additional electronic material.

Table 6.7   Standardised Effects, Critical Ratios and Hypotheses Tests

Hyp.	Independent (endogenous) Variable	Dependent (exogenous) Variable	Standardised Effects			Critical Ratio	Support
			Direct	Indirect	Total		
H1	Techno. Knowledge	RR	0.195	0.000	0.195	3.387***	YES
H1(1)	Market Knowledge	RR	n.p.	0.063	0.063	*refer to chapter 6.6*	
H2	Sensing capacity	RR	n.p.	0.185	0.185	*refer to chapter 6.6*	
H2a	Sensing capacity	Market Knowledge	0.154	0.127	0.281	2.056*	YES
H3	Learning capacity	RR	n.p.	0.225	0.225	*refer to chapter 6.6*	
H3a(1)	Learning capacity	Techno. Knowledge	0.391	0.117	0.508	6.614***	YES
H3a(2)	Learning capacity	Market Knowledge	0.310	0.000	0.310	4.000***	YES
H2b/3b	Market Knowledge	Techno. Knowledge	0.378	0.000	0.378	6.393***	YES
H4	Integrating capacity	RR	0.257	0.171	0.428	3.816***	YES
H5	Coordinating capacity	RR	0.267	0.000	0.267	3.568***	YES
H6a	EO	Sensing capacity	0.162	0.000	0.162	2.653**	YES
H6b	EO	Learning capacity	0.163	0.095	0.258	3.081**	YES
H6c	EO	Integrating capacity	0.142	0.036	0.178	2.278*	YES
H6d	EO	Coordinating capa.	0.036	0.193	0.229	0.799	NO
H7a	NO	Sensing capacity	0.455	0.000	0.455	7.430***	YES
H7b	NO	Learning capacity	0.214	0.246	0.459	3.545***	YES
H7c	NO	Integrating capacity	0.299	0.100	0.399	4.319***	YES
H7d	NO	Coordinating capa.	0.032	0.382	0.414	0.645	NO
Add	NO	RR	0.237	0.259	0.496	4.302***	YES
Add	EO	Market Knowledge	0.157	0.105	0.262	2.429*	YES

*** $p<0.001$; ** $p<0.01$; * $p<0.05$; Results are based on Bootstrap = 500; 95% confidence level
n.p.: not proposed, only an indirect effect was proposed and tested (refer to chapter 6.6.)

As presented in Table 6.7, the results of the structural path analysis provide support for the majority of hypotheses, while only two hypotheses had to be rejected due to non-significant relationships. Hence the vast majority of proposed causal relationships between DCs, their antecedents, the resource base and the outcome variable of RR could be confirmed. The specific hypotheses, their path coefficients and significance levels are discussed in more detail in the following.

Hypotheses relating to the Interrelationship between the Resource Base and RR

Proposition 1: A high valuable resource base (Market and Technological Knowledge) is positively associated with RR in firms.

H1: Technological Knowledge has a direct, positive effect on RR.

Strong support emerged for the impact of a high valuable resource base in terms of Market and Technological Knowledge on the development of RR in firms. **Technological Knowledge** (breadth and depth) has a strong, positive and direct effect on RR with a beta coefficient of 0.195 (p < 0.001), thus supporting H1.

H1(1): Market Knowledge has an indirect, positive effect on RR, through Technological Knowledge.

The association between Market Knowledge and Technological Knowledge was confirmed highly significant (p < 0.001) with a beta coefficient of 0.387. Furthermore, in line with what theory suggested **Market Knowledge** (breadth and depth) does not have a direct effect on RR, instead the results indicate that Market Knowledge has a weak positive, indirect effect on RR through Technological Knowledge (ß = 0.063). The results in Table 6.7, however, do not yet give indications about the type and significance of this indirect effect, thus a more detailed investigation of H1(1) is provided by means of mediation analysis in section 6.6.

Hypotheses relating to the Interrelationship between DCs and RR

Proposition 2: A firm's overall DC is positively associated with the amount of RRs in firms due to both building and exploiting the potential value of the resources base.

H2: A high Sensing capacity is positively associated with RR, through Market and Technological Knowledge.

H3: A high Learning capacity is positively associated with RR, through Market and Technological Knowledge.

Sensing capacity and Learning capacity were both found to be positively associated with the development of high Market and Technological Knowledge, and thus RR, supporting H2 and H3. The results show that **Sensing capacity** directly contributes towards building Market Knowledge (ß = 0.154), significant at a 0.05 level. Notably, this relatively weak, yet significant direct effect of Sensing capacity on Market Knowledge increases considerably to a beta coefficient of 0.281, when taking indirect effects through Learning into account. At the same time, and in line with the theoretical considerations as presented in section 3.4.1.2, no direct effect between Sensing capacity and Technological Knowledge could be found. Instead, evidence is given for an indirect contribution of Sensing capacity on Technological Knowledge through building Market Knowledge and through enhancing the firm's Learning capacity.

Learning capacity on the other hand, was found to positively and directly con-
tribute towards both, building Market Knowledge (ß = 0.310) and Technological
Knowledge (ß = 0. 391), and through that indirectly RR (as confirmed by H1 and
H1 (1)). Both effects are significant at a 0.001 level.

Moreover, as the results in Table 6.7 show, the suggested indirect effects of
Sensing capacity (ß = 0.185) and Leaning capacity (ß = 0.225) on RR through the
resource base emerged relatively strong and positive, confirming H2 and H3. These
findings give already indications towards a proposed mediating role of Market and
Technological Knowledge on the relationship between both, Sensing and Learning
capacities and RR. However, to give evidence to the type and level of significance of
these indirect effects, a more detailed investigation of these causal sequences (H2a,
H2b, H2c) and (H3a, H3b, H3c) is deemed necessary and will be provided in the
following section 6.6.

H4: A high Integrating capacity is positively associated with RR.

H5: A high Coordinating capacity is positively associated with RR.

In accordance with theoretical considerations as presented in section 3.4.1.4 and
3.4.1.5 both, Integrating and Coordinating capacity were found to be positively
associated with RR, supporting H4 and H5. The results show a strong and positive direct effect of **Integrating capacity** on RR with a beta coefficient of 0.257
(p < 0.001). Notably, this direct effect was enhanced considerably when taking indirect effects of Integrating capacity into account, to a strong total effect of 0.428,
supporting H4.

Likewise, **Coordinating capacity** is positively and directly associated with RR
with at beta coefficient of 0.267 (p < 0.001), supporting H5. For a further investigation of the moderation effect of Integrating and Coordinating capacity on the
relation between Technological Knowledge and RR (as suggested in H4a and H5a),
a more detailed analysis is required and will be presented in section 6.7.

Important note: In this research DCs were operationalised as distinct but related
constructs. Therefore it was suggested that also interrelations between the four DCs
are to be found (refer to section 3.4.1.6). As these interrelations are constituent part of
the structural model the interrelations between Sensing, Learning, Integrating, and
Coordinating capacities are detailed and discussed in Appendix 6.6 in the additional
electronic material.

Hypotheses relating to Entrepreneurial and Networking Orientation as Antecedents for DCs

Proposition 3: Entrepreneurial Orientation and Networking Orientation act as antecedents for the development of a firm's DCs.

H6: *A high degree of Entrepreneurial Orientation is positively associated with the development of a firm's DCs.*

H7: *A high degree of Networking Orientation is positively associated with the development of a firm's DCs.*

The support for hypotheses regarding the impact of Entrepreneurial Orientation as well as Networking Orientation on the DC was mixed. As presented in Table 6.7, the results show that **Networking Orientation** has strong direct and total effects on Sensing, Learning and Integrating capacity (with positive and significant beta coefficients 0.455, 0.214 and 0.299, respectively) supporting H7a, H7b and H7c. However, no direct effect emerged on Coordinating capacity ($p > 0.05$), leading to the rejection of H7d.

Likewise, **Entrepreneurial Orientation** showed an admittedly weaker, yet significant direct link to Sensing ($\beta = 0.162$), Learning ($\beta = 0.163$) and Integrating capacity ($\beta = 0.142$), supporting H6a, H6b, H6c. Also no support was established for the direct paths between Entrepreneurial Orientation and Coordinating capacity ($p > 0.005$), rejecting H6d.

Hence, while neither Entrepreneurial Orientation nor Networking Orientation directly affect Coordinating capacity, interestingly the data revealed that for both, Networking Orientation and Entrepreneurial Orientation an indirect effect exists through the other DCs. As the above findings can only give indications on the type and significance level of the indirect effect, a more detailed analysis will additionally be provided in section 6.6.

Hypotheses relating to the potential Effect of specific Control Variables on RR

Two different groups of control variables were included in the analysis to reduce the possibility of alternate explanations. As illustrated in Figure 6.5 first the first group of controls looks at the potential effect of **specific characteristics of the resource base on RR**, while the second group includes **company and business related variables** and controls for their effect on RR.

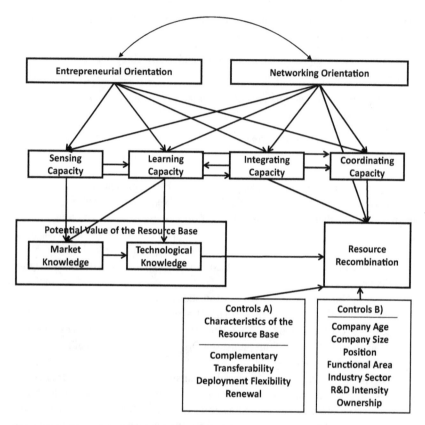

Figure 6.5 Control Variables tested in the Model

Controls A: Specific Characteristics of the Resources Base

Proposition 1: The <u>potential value of the resource base</u> for RR is proposed to be influenced by certain characteristics of the resources.

H1a (Resource Complementarity): Complementary Market and Technological Knowledge is positively related to RR in firms.

H1b (Resource Transferability): Tacit knowledge is negatively related to RR.

H1c *(Resource Deployment Flexibility): Context-specific knowledge is negatively related to RR.*

H1d *(Resource Renewal): New, external knowledge is positively related to RR.*

As part of the analysis it was controlled for a potential effect of **specific characteristics of the resource base** on RR, as proposed in section 3.3. Prior to the structural path model a regression analysis was conducted, where the results showed, that no significant correlations between *Knowledge Tacitness, Knowledge Context Specificy, Knowledge Origin* and RR were established in this study. The only significant correlation emerged between *Knowledge Complementarity* and RR (p < .05).

Similar results were shown when including the controls in the structural path model, where no significant direct effects emerged between Knowledge Tacitness, Knowledge Specificy, Knowledge Origin and RR, and moreover also Knowledge Complementarity did not show to have a significant effect on RR, as the results presented in Table 6.8 show. The results hence lead to a rejection of H1a, H1b, H1c, H1d, implying that regardless of its characteristics—in terms of knowledge complementarity, tacitness, context specificy, origin—an increase in Market and Technological Knowledge significantly increases RR in firms.

Table 6.8   Standardised Effects, Critical Ratios and Hypotheses Tests

Hyp.	Independent Variable	Dependent Variable	Standardised Effects			Critical Ratio	Support
			Direct	Indirect	Total		
H1	Techno. Knowledge	RR	0.182	0.000	0.182	2.877**	YES
H4	Integrating Capacity	RR	0.264	0.155	0.419	3.863***	YES
H5	Coordinating Capacity	RR	0.241	0.000	0.241	3.089**	YES
Add	Networking Orientation	RR	0.226	0.248	0.474	3.940***	YES
H1a	Knowl. Complementarity	RR	0.032	0.000	0.032	0.658 (ns)	NO
H1b	Knowl. Tacitness	RR	- 0.027	0.000	- 0.027	0.584 (ns)	NO
H1c	Knowl. Specificy	RR	0.080	0.000	0.080	0.140 (ns)	NO
H1d	Knowl. Origin	RR	- 0.042	0.000	- 0.042	0.390 (ns)	NO

*** p<0.001; ** p<0.01; * p<0.05; Results are based on Bootstrap = 500; 95% confidence level

Controls B: Company and Business Related Control Variables

Additionally a number of **company and business related variables** were included in the analysis to test for confounding variables. Confounding variables are variables that do not drive theory, however might have an influence on the outcome variables, and thus need to be controlled for (Gaskin, 2011). Thus it was controlled for a potential effect of *company size, company age, position* (whether the respondent was in the upper or middle management), *functional area* (whether the respondent yield a general management function or a specialist function), and *industry sector* (whether the company was acting industry or service sector), and *R&D intensity* on RR. The results presented in Table 6.9 show that none of the control variables emerged significant, thus this research findings are stable also when controls were included. Said differently, regardless of company size, age, position, functional area, industry sector and R&D intensity findings revealed that DCs and the Market and Technology Knowledge have a positive effect on RR in firms.

Table 6.9   Standardised Effects, Critical Ratios and Hypotheses Tests

Hyp.	Independent Variable	Dependent Variable	Standardised Effects			Critical Ratio	Support
			Direct	Indirect	Total		
H1	Techno. Knowledge	RR	0.184	0.000	0.184	3.021**	YES
H4	Integrating Capacity	RR	0.250	0.174	0.324	3.645***	YES
H5	Coordinating Capacity	RR	0.272	0.000	0.272	3.000***	YES
Add	Networking Orientation	RR	0.245	0.258	0.503	4.346***	YES
Control	Company Size	RR	0.036	0.000	0.036	0.701(ns)	NO
Control	Company Age	RR	- 0.059	0.000	- 0.059	-1.167(ns)	NO
Control	Position	RR	- 0.23	0.000	- 0.23	-0.437(ns)	NO
Control	Functional Area	RR	- 0.62	0.000	- 0.62	-1.274(ns)	NO
Control	Industry Sector	RR	0.034	0.000	0.034	0.691(ns)	NO
Control	R&D Intensity	RR	- 0.037	0.000	- 0.037	-0.726(ns)	NO

*** $p<0.001$; ** $p<0.01$; * $p<0.05$; Results are based on Bootstrap = 500; 95% confidence level

Having tested the potential effect of specific control variables on RR, the following sections further elaborate on research findings, showing support, or lack thereof, for individual **hypotheses regarding the role of DCs in the process of resource value creation**. The proposed mediating role the resource base has in the relationship between Sensing (H2a, H2b, and H2c) and Learning (H3a, H3b, H3c) and RR will be further tested in the section **mediation analysis**. While the moderating role of Integrating (H4a) and Coordinating capacity (H5a) in the relationship between Technological Knowledge and RR will be in the core of section 6.7 **moderation analysis**.

6.6   Mediation Analysis

This section outlines the results of the mediations analysis applied to further test the hypotheses relating to the mediating role of the resource base between Sensing and Leaning capacity and RR. **Mediation analysis** is used to describe a causal chain X➜M➜Y in order to provide a more precise explanation for the effect the independent variable (X) has on the dependent variable (Y), as transmitted through a mediation variable (M). Hence, by including a mediator "mediational models advance an X➜M➜Y causal sequence, and seek to illustrate the mechanisms through which X and Y are related" (Mathieu and Taylor, 2006, p. 1032) and thus help to explain more of the observed behaviour in the sample (Gaskin, 2012d).

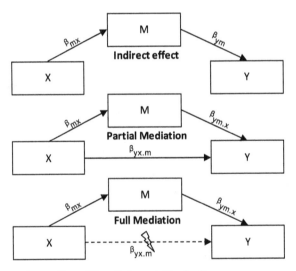

Indirect effect of X on Y through M = $\beta_{mx}\,\beta_{ym.x}$
Direct effect of X on Y = $\beta_{yx.m}$

Source: adapted from Gaskin (2012d), Hair et al. (2010), and Hayes (2013)

Figure 6.6 Types of Mediation – Statistical Diagram

Three different types of mediation exist: (1) *indirect effect*[6], (2) *partial mediation*[7] and (3) *full mediation*[8] and, as illustrated in Figure 6.6.

Hypotheses relating to the Mediating Role of the Resource Base between Sensing and Leaning Capacity and RR
As formulated in **H2** and **H3** and already indicated by the preliminary results from the structural path analysis presented in the previous section the results confirm that a high Sensing and Learning capacity leads to an increased performance in regard to RR. However, as not all firms that have developed high DCs are subsequently high performing in achieving RR, this relation was expected to be fully and positively mediated by Market and Technological Knowledge, thus leading to a more precise formulation H2 and H3 through the following hypotheses:

---

[6] An **indirect effect** implies that the independent variable (X) has a direct effect on the mediator (M), and the mediator has a direct effect on the dependent variable (Y), while at the same time there is no significant direct effect from X to Y. Thus X is said to have an indirect effect on Y. This hypothesis, however, can only be supported if the direct effect from X on Y is insignificant when the mediator is not included in the model, prior testing for an indirect effect (when the mediator is included) (Mathieu and Taylor, 2006).

[7] **Partial mediation** refers to the situation when both the direct and indirect effects from the independent variable (X) to the dependent variable (Y) are significant. This means that the unmediated X→Y relationship is significant, as well as the X→M and M→Y relationship. In order to avoid concluding that the partially mediating effect is significant, when in fact only the three independent partial effects are individually significant a significance test for mediation must be performed. Statistically speaking, in simple partial mediation βmx is the path coefficient for X predicting M, and βym.x and βyx.m are the path coefficients for M, respectively X predicting Y. The latter (βyx.m) accounts the direct effect of X on Y, while the product βmx*βym.x describes the indirect effect X has on Y through M. Hence, if all variables are observed then the total effect βyx equals βyx.m + βmx*βym.x (Lyytinen and Gaskin, 2011, Mathieu and Taylor, 2006).

[8] **Full mediation** means that the direct effect of X on Y is only significant if the mediator is absent. When the mediator is present this direct effect becomes insignificant, while the indirect effect remains significant. Statistically, full mediation requires that βyx.m to be close to zero. In case βyx.m does not drop close to zero and remains significant when the mediator is included, evidence is given for partial mediation instead. Notably, likewise partial mediation also for full mediation both path βmx and βym.x have to be significant, otherwise if the X→M or M→Y relationship prove to be insignificant no mediation is existent (Lyytinen and Gaskin, 2011, Mathieu and Taylor, 2006).

H2a/H2b/H2c: *The effect of Sensing capacity on RR <u>is positively and fully mediated</u>by Market and Technology Knowledge.*

H3a/H3b/H3c: *The effect of Learning capacity on RR <u>is positively and fully mediated</u>by Market and Technology Knowledge.*

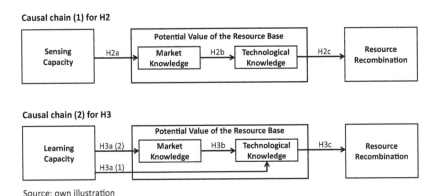

Source: own illustration

Figure 6.7 Mediation Analysis – Causal Chains

The causal sequences as graphically presented in Figure 6.7, are tested in the following using mediation analysis. Mediation analysis usually "requires researchers to make a priori hypotheses concerning full or partial mediation and transforms confirmatory tests to exploratory data mining" (Lyytinen and Gaskin, 2011, p.24). To test the causal chains as described above a two step approach was conducted.

In a first step the structural path model was tested *without* mediators in AMOS as presented in Figure 6.8, where a direct path was drawn from Sensing capacity to RR (refer to model A1), respectively from Learning capacity to RR (refer to model A2), with everything else ceteris paribus. That means, the indirect path from the independent variable to the dependent variable through the mediating variables was deleted, while instead a direct effect was established.

Step 1: Models without Mediators

Model A1 – Sensing capacity

Step 2: Models with Mediators

Model B1 – Sensing capacity

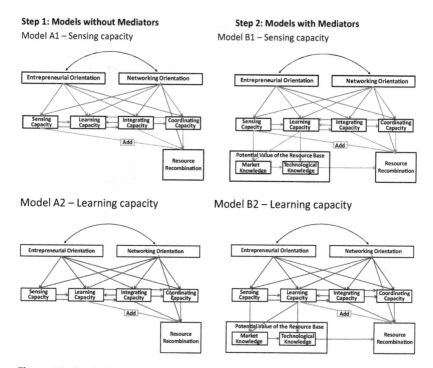

Model A2 – Learning capacity

Model B2 – Learning capacity

Figure 6.8 Mediation Analysis – Models with and without Mediation

In a second step the mediating variables were again included in the model (refer to model B1 for Sensing capacity, and model B2 for Learning capacity, respectively). Finally, comparing the direct effect models *without* mediation A1 (resp. A2) and the model *with* mediation B1 (resp. B2) a change in path coefficients gives evidence whether the proposed mediation effect is existent and what type of mediation is observed. The results are presented in Table 6.10.

Table 6.10 Results of the Mediation Analysis: Sensing and Learning Capacity on RR

Hyp	Causal Chain	Model without Mediators (A)	Model with Mediators (B)		Mediation type observed	Support
		Direct βyx w/o med (p-values)	Direct βyx.m w/ med (p-values)	Indirect βmx* βym.x w/med (p-values)		
H2a H2b H2c	(1) Sens ➔ Mknowl ➔ Tknowl➔RR	.126* (.030)	.106 (.066 – ns)	.012*(.028)	**full mediation,** with moderate and signifi-cant indirect effect	YES
H3a H3b H3c	(2) Learn ➔ Mknowl ➔ Tknowl➔RR	.186** (.006)	.123 (.087 – ns)	.101**(.002)	**full mediation,** with strong and significant indirect effect	YES

*** p < 0.001; ** p < 0.01; * p < 0.05; Results are based on Bootstrap = 500; 95% confidence level

As the results presented in Table 6.10 show, an initial significant direct effect for Sensing on RR (p < 0.05) and Learning on RR (p < 0.01) could be established for both causal chains (1) and (2), which is a necessary precondition for a mediation effect being in place (Lyytinen and Gaskin, 2011). Furthermore, as shown in the fourth column this direct effect (between Sensing capacity and RR, as well as Learning capacity and RR) does not remain significant when the mediator was included in the model, which implies full mediation following Baron and Kenny (1986). According to Barron and Kenney (1986), the reason for the reduction in the path coefficients is due to the mediating variable, explaining some of the variance in the dependent variable that had previously been explained by the dependent variables but is more appropriately being explained through the mediator.

However, in order to determine and prove the significance of the suggested mediated relationship, it is suggested by several authors to further examine the significance of the indirect effects by using the bootstrapping technique (Preacher and Hayes, 2004, Gaskin 2011d). Looking at the two-tailed significance levels for the standardised indirect effects as presented in column 5, both indirect effects were significant (p < 0.05 for Sensing on RR, p < 0.01 for Learning on RR, respectively) with the bias-corrected confidence interval set up to 0.95 and a bootstrap with m = 500. The results give statistical support to H2a/H2b/H2c and

H3a/H3b/H3c, that Market and Technological Knowledge fully mediate the effect of Sensing and Learning capacity on RR in firms (p < 0.05).

H1(1): Market Knowledge has an indirect, positive effect on RR, through Technological Knowledge.

Additionally, while being integral part of the causal sequence as described above, a more detailed investigation of the causal relationship between Market Knowledge, Technological Knowledge and RR was deemed valuable. The results as presented in Table 6.11, confirm that Market Knowledge only indirectly affects RR, through Technological Knowledge, as both direct effects are not significant, but the indirect effect is significant (p < 0.01). Hence, additional support is given to H1(1) that Market Knowledge has an indirect, positive effect on RR, through Technological Knowledge.

Table 6.11   Results of the mediation analysis: Market Knowledge on RR

Hyp	Causal Chain	Model without Mediators (A)	Model with Mediators (B)		Mediation type observed	Support
		Direct Beta w/o med (p-values)	Direct Beta w/ med (p-values)	Indirect Beta (p-values)		
H1(1)	(3) Mknowl → Tknowl →RR	.070 (.195-ns)	-.003 (.954- ns)	.074** (.007)	indirect effect (no mediation), as both direct effects are insignificant, but indirect effect is significant	YES

*** p<0.001; ** p<0.01; * p<0.05; Results are based on Bootstrap = 500; 95% confidence level

Beside it was deemed valuable to further analyse the **mediating role that DCs** have in the relationship between EO, respectively NO, and RR. As already indicated by the results presented in section 6.5.5, support was given to H6a, H6b, H6c and H7a, H7b, H7c, confirming that both EO and NO positively influence the development of Sensing, Learning and Integrating capacities. On the other hand, no significant direct association emerged between EO (NO, respectively) and Coordinating capacity, leading to a rejection of H6d (and H7d). To further elaborate on these findings, it was deemed valuable to investigate the relation EO and NO have on RR though the DCs in more detail, specifying the direct and indirect relations, and in case mediation is in place, what type of mediation (full or partial). The results are presented in Appendix 6.7 in the additional electronic material.

6.7   Moderation Analysis

This section outlines the results of the moderation analysis to further test the hypotheses relating to the moderating role of Integrating and Coordinating capacity between the resource base and RR. Moderation analysis is used as a method to provide a more precise explanation of a causal relationship between a dependent variable (X) and an independent variable (Y), as it considers "not only how X effects Y, but also under what circumstances the effect of X changes depending on the moderating variable (W)" (Gaskin, 2002d). To illustrate this causal effect, the conceptual model for moderation is presented in Figure 6.9. According to Preacher et al. (2007), moderation also referred to as conditional effect, is present "when the strength of the relationship between two variables is dependent on a third [moderating] variable" (Preacher et al., 2007, p.191). Similar to mediation, moderation analysis enables a more precise investigation of the causal effects between two variables and helps explaining more of the observed behaviour in the sample. Moderating variables must be chosen with strong theoretical support (Hair et al., 2010).

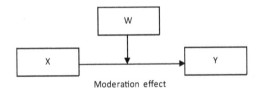

Moderation effect

Source: adapted from Gaskin (2012d) and Hayes (2013)

Figure 6.9 Conceptual Diagram of the Moderation Effect

Hypotheses relating to the Moderating Role of Integrating and Coordinating capacity between Resource Base and RR

H4a:A high Integrating capacity is positively associated with RR in firms as it is moderating the relationship between Technological Knowledge and RR in firms.

H5a:A high Coordinating capacity is positively associated with RR in firms as it is moderating the relationship between Technological Knowledge and RR in firms.

As formulated in **H4a** and **H5a** it was to be expected that Integrating and Coordinating capacity of the firm moderate the relation between the resource base and RR. The results from the path analysis in section 6.5.5 already confirmed the positive relation between Technological Knowledge and RR, the following section sets out to test if this relation is moderated by Integrating and Coordinating capacity. Hence it is suggested that a high Integrating and Coordinating capacity (W) is positively associated with RR in firms as it is moderating the relationship between the resource base (X) and RR (Y) in firms[9]. The following chapter aims to test these causal relations as describes above using a moderation analysis technique.

Kenny und Judd (1984) have presented a method for statistical assessment of moderation effects which explicitly considers latent moderation variables through the calculation of a manifest product variable (Reinecke, 1999). Based on Kenny and Judd's (1984) considerations a moderation effect is typically addressed with the regression equation:

$$Y = \alpha + \beta_{yx} X + \beta_{yw} W + \beta_{yxw} XW + \zeta; \qquad (6.3)$$

whereby X represents the independent and Y the dependent variable, W is considered as the moderator, and XW represents the interaction variable formed by the product of W and X. Furthermore α represents the vectors for the intercept term, while the regression weights β describe the main direct effects βyx between X and Y, βyw between W and Y, and βyxw between XW and Y, respectively. ζ represents the residual (or error term) of Y. Hence the moderator M interacts with X in predicting Y, as the regression weight of X on Y (βyx) varies as a function of W. Basically the regression equation specifies that the slope of the regression weight relating X

---

[9] Given the suggested causal chain in this research's model, more correctly it is to speak about **moderated mediation**. As described by Preacher et al. (2007), moderated mediation is given "when the strength of an indirect effect depends on the level of some variable, or in other words, when mediation relations are contingent on the level of a moderator" (Preacher et al., 2007, p.193). In other words, the strength of an indirect or mediation effect may depend linearly upon the value of the moderation variable. Therefore, in the literature moderated mediation is also referred to as conditional indirect effect (Preacher et al., 2007). As for this research model, the mediation effect of Market/ Technological Knowledge on the relation between Sensing/Learning and RR (as presented in the previous chapter) might only occur for those firms having high Integrating or Coordinating capacities, but not for firms having low Integrating and Coordinating capacities. Hence, moderated mediation models enable a more precise explanation of 'how' and 'when' a suggested indirect effect occurs (Preacher et al., 2007). In this regard, it is of interest whether or not a suggested mediating effect remains constant across different contexts, groups or values of the moderating variable (Gaskin, 2011d). It is expected that the effect of Sensing and Leaning on RR is mediated by Market and Technological Knowledge, and moreover that this mediation differs across firms with high and low Integrating and Coordinating capacities. Preacher et al. (2007) claim that moderated mediation can take many forms, for some of which they provide examples. This research concentrates on the type of moderated mediation illustrated in model 3 presented by Preacher et al. (2007).

to Y changes at different levels of W (Preacher et al., 2007, Reinecke, 1999). The graphical notation of the model by Kenny and Judd is presented in Figure 6.10.

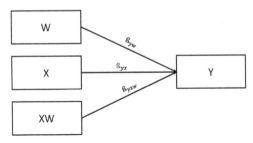

Source: adapted from and Hayes (2013)

Figure 6.10   Statistical Diagram of the Moderation Effect

For testing moderation models, generally two categorical different methods exist: (1) **Multi-group moderation analysis,** e.g. using Chi-square difference test or Critical Ratios for differences test and (2) **Interaction effect methods,** e.g. using SEM techniques with interaction terms or traditional non SEM-methods for interaction effects.

Main differences between the two methods are that while *multi-group moderation analysis* generally use categorical variables, whereby the dataset is split into two categorical different groups and paths are constrained across groups, the *interaction effect method* uses continuous variables, applies the whole dataset, and integrates an interaction variable (the product term X*W, as illustrated in Figure 6.10 above) (Gaskin, 2011d). In spite of these elementary differences, the literature makes little distinction between multi-group and interaction effect methods. One reason might be due to the fact that also in interaction effect models continuous interaction effect variables are often approached as categorical variables, similar to those used for multi-group analysis[10] (e.g. Preacher et al., 2007), which in consequence leads to a similar interpretation of results although different methods were applied (Gaskin, 2011d).

To encounter the indifference in use, and thereby to enable a comparison of each method's results while at the same time making use of each method's merits, both methods are applied for this research, whereby categorical variables are used both for the multi-group analysis, and categorical variables are used for the interaction effect method. Correspondingly, in a first step *multi-group analysis* will be applied in the

---

[10] Preacher et al. (2007) themselves, while makings use of interaction effect methods, ended up treating their continuous interaction variables as categorical variables at the end.

following section in order to provide evidence whether the underlying measurement models are valid and whether meaningful and statistically significant interaction effects are likely to be expected (Reinecke, 1999). In a second step the *interaction effect method* will be applied in section 6.7.2 for calculating the path coefficient of the interaction term and thus getting indications about the actual strength of the moderation effect (Preacher et al., 2007).

6.7.1 Multi-Group Moderation Analysis

A multi-group moderation analysis was deemed valuable to test whether high or low levels of Coordinating and Integrating capacities have different effects on the relation between Technological Knowledge and the outcome variable RR. Multi-group moderation analysis is a specific form of moderation, whereby the given dataset is grouped along values of a categorical variable, and in a subsequent step the model is separately tested among these two groups in order to determine whether the suggested relationships in the model are contingent on the value of the moderator (Gaskin, 2011d).

In order to test the variance in the regression coefficient (βyx) for the different groups, the data set was split using the variables Integrating and Coordinating capacity into two separate groups for each variable. Through mediatisation of the indices by means of calculating the grouping variable's mean $+/-$ 0.5 standard deviations (sd), two categorical different groups were built, one containing those firms with high Integrating capacities (values between 5.961–7), respectively high Coordinating capacity (values between 5.823–7), and the other comprising those firms with low Integrating capacity (values between 0–4.673), respectively Coordinating capacity (values between 0–4.629).

Table 6.12 Mean, Standard Deviation and N for the Grouping Variables

Grouping Variable	mean	sd	mean $+$ ½ sd	mean$-$½ sd	N	
					High	Low
Integrating capacity	5.317	1.288	5.961	4.673	85	63
Coordinating capacity	5.226	1.194	5.823	4.629	72	61

In order to test for statistical differences among those groups, two multi-group analysis per construct were performed, where the relationship between Technological Knowledge and RR was once tested for the group with high and simultaneously for the group with low Integrating capacity. Thereafter the same procedure was adapted for the two groups "high Coordinating capacity" vs. "low Coordinating capacity".

For testing multi-group moderation the regression equation (3) as presented above, usually is transformed as follows:

$$Y = (\alpha + \beta_{yw} W) + (\beta_{yx} + \beta_{yxw} W)^* X + \zeta \qquad (6.4)$$

Equation 4 shows the regression of the independent construct Technological Knowledge (X) on RR (Y) as a function of Integrating resp. Coordinating capacity (W). In case interaction effects exist, βyxw is higher than βyx for those firms with a value for W above the mean plus 0.5 sd, and lower for those firms with values for W below the mean minus 0.5 sd (Reinecke 1999).

Two statistical methods for the analysis of mediation effects my means of multiple-group analysis exists: (1) a (stepwise) Chi-square difference test or (2) a Critical Ratio for differences test, both methods leading to similar results in order to determine whether meaningful significant interaction effects exist (Gaskin, 2011d). To test the proposed effect, both methods were applied in this research resulting in comparable results. While the method and results of the Chi-Square-Difference test is described in detail below, the results of the Critical Ratio for differences test can be found in the Appendix 6.8 in the additional electronic material.

A **chi-square difference test** was used to determine, if the difference in the strength and direction of the regression weights between the two groups is significant. A $\Delta\chi^2$-test was conducted simultaneously for the two groups, following the three step standard procedure, as detailed in Appendix 6.4 in the additional electronic material, including the estimation of (1) the unconstrained multi-group model, (2) the constrained multi-group model, and (3) the comparison of the difference of $\Delta\chi^2$ and Δdf between the constrained and unconstrained model. The results are provided in Table 6.13 for those firms with high and low Integrating capacity (Model A). Table 6.14 provides the corresponding results for firms with high and low Coordinating capacity (Model B).

Table 6.13 $\Delta\chi 2$Test—Model A: Integrating Capacity high and low

Model A: Integrating	χ^2	df	$\Delta\chi^2$	Δdf	P
unconstrained model	60.266	30	–		
fully constrained model	96.14	50	35.943	20	**0.016**

Table 6.14 $\Delta\chi2$Test—Model B: Coordinating Capacity high and low

Model B: Coordinating	χ^2	Df	$\Delta\chi^2$	Δdf	P
unconstrained model	48	30	–		
fully constrained model	88.822	50	40.822	20	**0.004**

The result shows that the $\Delta\chi^2$ is significant at the 0.05 level, when comparing firms with high vs. low Integrating capacity. In a similar vein, significant differences (p > 0.01) could be established at the model level when comparing firms with high vs. low Coordinating capacity. The results lead to the conclusion that not all regression weights are equal across groups (Kline, 2005), and that there are significant differences in strength and direction of the regression weights between the two groups.

Given these results, a stepwise estimation of the model was deemed valuable for a more detailed investigation of which specific paths are different across groups. This is done by constraining one path at a time and comparing the χ^2 of the (path-wise) constrained model with the χ^2 of the unconstrained model (Plewa, 2010). The results of the path by path model estimation are presented in Table 6.15 for Integrating capacity, and in Table 6.16 for Coordinating capacity high vs. low, respectively.

Table 6.15 Stepwise $\Delta\chi2$Test—Model A: Integrating Capacity high and low

Model A: Integrating Capacity	χ^2	df	$\Delta\chi^2$	Δdf	P
unconstrained model	60.266	30	-		
constrained path: EO --> Sensing	61.727	31	1.461	1	0.227
constrained path: EO --> Learning	60.33	31	0.064	1	0.800
constrained path: EO --> Integrating	60.803	31	0.537	1	0.464
constrained path: NO --> Sensing	61.18	31	0.914	1	0.339
constrained path: NO --> Learning	60.377	31	0.111	1	0.739
constrained path: NO --> Integrating	62.371	31	2.105	1	0.147
constrained path: Sensing --> Market Knowledge	60.494	31	0.228	1	0.633
constrained path: Learning --> Market Knowledge	61.074	31	0.808	1	0.369
constrained path: Market Knowledge--> TechnoKnowl	60.642	31	0.376	1	0.540
constrained path: Learning --> Technological Knowledge	60.538	31	0.272	1	0.602
constrained path: Technological Knowledge --> RR	**63.664**	31	3.398	1	**0.065**
constrained path: Integrating --> RR	60.524	31	0.258	1	0.611
constrained path: Coordinating --> RR	**64.04**	31	3.774	1	**0.052**
constrained path: EO --> Market Knowledge	60.817	31	0.551	1	0.458
constrained path: NO --> RR	60.503	31	0.237	1	0.626

A χ^2 above the threshold of 62.97 (90% confidence), 64.11 (95% confidence) or 66.90 (99% confidence) indicates variance at the specific path.

Table 6.16 Stepwise $\Delta\chi$2Test—Model B: Coordinating high and low

Model B: Coordinating Capacity	χ^2	df	$\Delta\chi^2$	Δdf	P
unconstrained model	48	30	-		
constrained path: EO --> Sensing	48.911	31	0.911	1	0.340
constrained path: EO --> Learning	48.201	31	0.201	1	0.654
constrained path: EO --> Integrating	50.538	31	2.538	1	0.111
constrained path: NO --> Sensing	48.963	31	0.963	1	0.326
constrained path: NO --> Learning	48.35	31	0.35	1	0.554
constrained path: NO --> Integrating	48.55	31	0.55	1	0.458
constrained path: Sensing --> Market Knowledge	49.618	31	1.618	1	0.203
constrained path: Learning --> Market Knowledge	48.241	31	0.241	1	0.623
constrained path: Market Knowledge--> TechnoKnowl	49.247	31	1.247	1	0.264
constrained path: Learning --> Technological Knowledge	50.144	31	2.144	1	0.143
constrained path: Technological Knowledge --> RR	**50.905**	31	2.905	1	**0.088**
constrained path: Integrating --> RR	**53.922**	31	5.922	1	**0.015**
constrained path: Coordinating --> RR	48.207	31	0.207	1	0.649
constrained path: EO--> Market Knowledge	48.206	31	0.206	1	0.650
constrained path: NO --> RR	48.201	31	0.201	1	0.654

A χ^2 above the threshold of 50.91 (90% confidence), 52.04 (95% confidence) or 54.84 (99% confidence) indicates variance at the specific path.

Two sources of variance on the path level were identified in each model A (Integrating) and model B (Coordinating). The results confirm a moderating role of Integrating and Coordinating capacity as the path between Technological Knowledge and RR ($p < 0.10$) showed a significant $\Delta\chi^2$ in both models meaning that this path is different across groups. The difference in the regression weights between the two groups indicates a non-linear relations between Technological Knowledge and RR (Reinecke, 1999). Furthermore, the path between Coordinating capacity and RR ($p < 0.10$) and the path between Integrating capacity and RR ($p < 0.05$) also showed a significant $\Delta\chi^2$ in the respective model[11].

Thus, it can be said with 90% confidence that Integrating and Coordinating capacity, both moderate the relationship between Technological Knowledge and RR, as for the two groups both these relationships are significantly different across groups. Furthermore, the finding suggests that while Integrating capacity moderates the path between Coordinating capacity and RR at a 90% confidence level, Coordinating capacity moderates the path between Integrating capacity and

---

[11] The Chi-square difference test usually regards the 90% confidence level for significant differences; therefore also p-values < 0.10 are regarded as significant for this kind of analyses (Gaskin, 2012d).

RR at a 95% confidence level. At the same time, all other paths are invariant across groups, meaning that invariance is established at the paths level for all other relationships. As mentioned before, similar results could be found by means of the Critical Ratio for difference test, the results can be found in Appendix 6.8 in the additional electronic material.

Given that there is variance established at the path-level, to further elaborate the differences across groups for the specific paths identified above, a more detailed investigation of the direction and strength of variance are worthwhile. Therefore in a last step the model was calculated separately for each of the groups (Integrating high, Integrating low, Coordinating high, Coordinating low) and the respective regression weights (β) for the non invariant paths were compared (Plewa, 2010). The findings are presented in Table 6.17. However, considering the small sample size of the single groups (refer to Table 6.12), the statistical power of the results should be treated with caution (Diamantopoulos and Siguaw, 2000) unless the findings are being confirmed by an independent, preferably larger sample (Plewa, 2010).

Table 6.17 Comparison of Regression Weights—Integrating Capacity high and low

Paths	Integrating_low		Integrating_high		Coordinating_low		Coordinating_high	
	Stand. Regr. weights	P	Stand. Regr. weights	P	Stand. Regr. weights	P	Stand. Regr. weights	P
TechnoKnowl --> RR	0.139	0.275	0.364	0.001	0.204	0.091	0.327	0.000
Coordinating --> RR	0.228	0.091	0.380	0.000	--	--	--	--
Integrating--> RR	--	--	--	--	0.163	0.224	0.466	0.000

The coefficients show that for firms with high Integrating and Coordinating capacity the relationship between Technological Knowledge und RR is stronger than for firms with low Integrating and Coordinating capacity. More specifically, the differences in the regression weights indicate that the positive influence Technological Knowledge has on RR is 2.6 times as strong when Integration is high ($\beta_{lowI} = 0.139$ vs. $\beta_{highI} = 0.364$) and 1.6 times as strong when Coordination is high ($\beta_{lowC} = 0.204$ vs. $\beta_{highC} = 0.327$). With respect to p-values, Technological Knowledge only influenced RR significantly when high Integrating and Coordinating capacity is established in firms. In both cases the relation between Technological Knowledge and RR became insignificant ($p > 0.05$) when Integrating and Coordinating capacity was low. In consequence, even if the Technological Knowledge a firm possesses is high, it does not affect RR in firms, if the firm does not possess a high capacity to integrate and coordinate that knowledge in order to achieve RR.

Results from the mediation analysis (see section 6.6) showed that Technological Knowledge mediates the relationship between Sensing/Learning capacity and RR. However the above findings indicate that this mediating effect is further moderated by the firm's level of Integrating and Coordinating capacity, in a way that Technological Knowledge mediates the relation between Sensing/ Learning capacity and RR only for those firms possessing a high Integrating and Coordinating capacity. This is when research also speaks about moderated mediation (for a similar investigation see Ng et al., 2008). Elaborating the moderated mediation effects, an analysis of the differences in size, direction and significance of the indirect (mediating) effects for each group were additionally conducted, the results are presented in Appendix 6.9 in the additional electronic material.

In sum, to capture the conception of causal relations between the DCs, the Resource Base and RR more closely, a multi-group moderation analysis was conducted. The regression weights in the final structural path model were compared across groups and differentiated based on their levels of sophistication in firms and their intentions to recombine new resources. The results give statistical **support for H4a and H5a**, confirming that both Integrating and Coordinating capacity moderate the relationship between Market and Technological Knowledge and RR. Said differently, Integrating and Coordinating capacity is found to strengthen the positive relationship between Technological Knowledge and RR.

However, several restrictions exist for the multi-group moderation analysis. First, for the multiple-group comparison the applied grouping method (unweighted mediatisation of the indices) is rather chosen ad hoc, and thus a different grouping procedure for the same variables might lead to different results for the multi-group analysis (Reinecke, 1998). Second, multi-group analysis does not consider a random measurement error of the grouping variable (Reinecke, 1998). Third, in multi-group moderation analysis the strength and significance of the moderation (interaction) effect can only be investigated *indirectly* through the differences in parameters between the two groups. The calculation of the structural regression weight (β_{yxw} in equation 4), which indicates the strength and significance of the effect the moderating variable has on the dependent latent variable, is not provided (Reinecke, 1998). The later restriction of the multi-group analysis is probably the most important argument for the construction of a latent interaction effect variable, whereby a value for βyxw can be estimated.

6.7.2 Interaction Effect Method

As the results of the multi-group analysis gave evidence that significant interaction effects exist, it was deemed valuable to analyse these interaction effects in a subsequently research step in regard to their strength by means of interaction effect method as provided in the following.

Although the approach by Kenny and Judd (1984) of modelling interaction as a simple product term by using all cross products as indicators of the latent variables, is widely used in research practice (e.g. Pavlou and El Sawy, 2011), there is still an ongoing debate on the appropriate modelling of interaction effects especially in the context of SEM (e.g. Van den Putte and Hoogstraaten, 1997). While most methodologists agree that the product term builds a 'proper quantification' of the interaction effect and hence is regarded as the most accurate statistical representation and method available (MacKinnon et al., 2004), up to today modelling moderated mediation is still a methodological dispute as "clear methods have not yet been articulated in the literature for investigating whether (and, if so, how) an indirect effect varies systematically as a function of another variable" (Preacher et al., 2007, p. 187). Preacher et al. (2007) made a first attempt towards overcoming this issue, however, they used only traditional non SEM-techniques to test for conditional indirect effects, while likewise stating that moderated mediation is best tested in SEM software like AMOS, where all paths can be tested simultaneously and continuous variables can be used. Subsequently, this research takes up the conceptual thoughts as presented by Preacher at al. (2007) by applying the interaction effect method in a more complex SEM context.

Thus, in this research the interaction effects of Integrating and Coordinating capacity were tested following Preacher at al. (2007, 2005), Ping (1995) and Van den Putte and Hoogstraaten (1997), whereby first all variables in the model were Z-transformed (standardised) in SPSS to avoid identification problems (Cortina et al., 2001). Secondly, a new interaction effect variable X*Y was computed by calculating X and Y: $X*Y = \sum X_i * \sum Y_i$, with the loadings of the interaction variable X*Y being $\lambda_{X,Y} = \sum \lambda_{Xi} * \sum \lambda_{Yi}$ (as proposed by Ping, 1995 and Pavlou and El Sawy, 2011), and thirdly the new interaction variable was included in the model in order to estimate the strength and significance of the regression weight β_{yxw} (Gaskin, 2011d)[12].

---

[12] The integration of interaction effect terms in SEM-based models involves the consideration of non-linear restrictions when building the model, which gives potential rise to constraints in regard to the model estimation procedure (Reineke, 1998): First, while the ML-method applied here generally suggests the assumption of multivariate normality (Reinecke, 1999), this condition is hurt when using product terms (even though the single measured constructs

In a first estimation step, the models were calculated for each interaction variable separately. The results are presented in Figure 6.11 for Integrating capacity and in Figure 6.12 for Coordinating capacity. For both models a good model fit was achieved. All model fit indices for the **Interaction effect model A: Integrating capacity** indicated excellent fit with a χ^2/df (= 1.756), GFI (= 0.966), AGFI (= 0.910), TLI (= 0.960), CFI (= 0.981) and NFI (= 0.958), this was supported by a non-significant χ^2 (p > 0.05) and an RMSEA value of 0.060 and RMR of 0.072. Similar good model fit results were obtained for the **Interaction effect model B: Coordinating capacity** with a non-significant χ^2/df (= 1.937), GFI (= 0.963), AGFI (= 0.902), TLI (= 0.950), CFI (= 0.977), NFI (= 0.954) and RMSEA (= 0.067), all indicating to an excellent fit, solely the RMR (= 0.094) was slightly above the acceptable threshold for this research. Given this good model fit, both models qualified for further hypotheses testing.

---

are normal distributed, their products are not). Irrespectivly, recent simulation studies could approve the ML-method to be relatively robust and stable against violation of the normal distribution as long as the sample size is higher than 200 (e.g. Hoogland and Boomsma, 1998). Second, although there is an ongoing debate on the appropriateness of the standard error of measurement for inferential statistical evaluations when using product variables (see Jonnson, 1997), the use of standard errors is commonly accepted among researchers also when applying non-linear components (Jaccard and Wan, 1996, Reineke, 1999). Third, when using product terms often the violation of multivariate normality leads to high χ^2 values, especially when applying the ML-method, where the statistical precondition are worst affected due to the use of product terms (Reineke, 1999).

Notably, aside from the deterioration of the model fit indices, a comparative study applying three different estimation methods (the ML, GLS and WLS method) revealed no substantial difference in the interpretation of the latent interaction models. Instead, the comparison of the estimates in terms of significance levels (p-value) and the strength of effects, lead to the same interpretations regarding the content for the three different procedures applied (see Reineke, 1999). For this reasoning, the use of interaction effects in the model was justified for the estimation process. Additionally, against expectations, an excellent model fit was achieved for all three models (as presented below), therefore the appropriateness of the applied interaction effect method was further ratified.

Morover, as an integration of each additional interaction effect leads to a growing number of non-linear restrictions (Reineke, 1998), this poses the risk of convergence problems during model estimation, as for example presented and discussed in Jonsson (1997) and Reineke (1999). Hence, to avoid convergence problems, this research abstained from including all potential mediation effects, instead only those moderation effects are included, that were theoretically considered before. For that reasoning the proposed moderation effect of Integrating capacity on Coordinating capacity ➜ RR, and Coordinating capacity on Integrating capacity ➜ RR, as indicated by the results of the multi-group moderation analysis, were not considered.

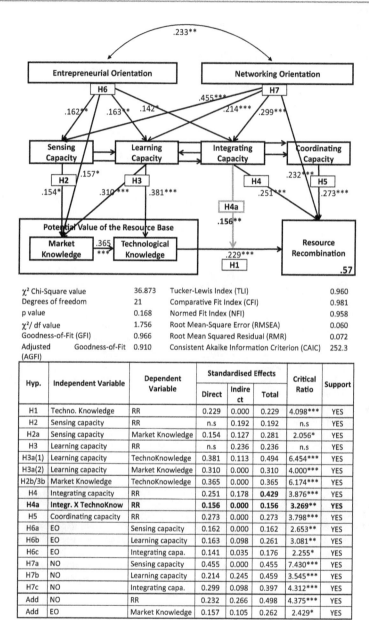

Hyp.	Independent Variable	Dependent Variable	Standardised Effects			Critical Ratio	Support
			Direct	Indirect	Total		
H1	Techno. Knowledge	RR	0.229	0.000	0.229	4.098***	YES
H2	Sensing capacity	RR	n.s	0.192	0.192	n.s	YES
H2a	Sensing capacity	Market Knowledge	0.154	0.127	0.281	2.056*	YES
H3	Learning capacity	RR	n.s	0.236	0.236	n.s	YES
H3a(1)	Learning capacity	TechnoKnowledge	0.381	0.113	0.494	6.454***	YES
H3a(2)	Learning capacity	Market Knowledge	0.310	0.000	0.310	4.000***	YES
H2b/3b	Market Knowledge	TechnoKnowledge	0.365	0.000	0.365	6.174***	YES
H4	Integrating capacity	RR	0.251	0.178	0.429	3.876***	YES
H4a	Integr. X TechnoKnow	RR	0.156	0.000	0.156	3.269**	YES
H5	Coordinating capacity	RR	0.273	0.000	0.273	3.798***	YES
H6a	EO	Sensing capacity	0.162	0.000	0.162	2.653**	YES
H6b	EO	Learning capacity	0.163	0.098	0.261	3.081**	YES
H6c	EO	Integrating capa.	0.141	0.035	0.176	2.255*	YES
H7a	NO	Sensing capacity	0.455	0.000	0.455	7.430***	YES
H7b	NO	Learning capacity	0.214	0.245	0.459	3.545***	YES
H7c	NO	Integrating capa.	0.299	0.098	0.397	4.312***	YES
Add	NO	RR	0.232	0.266	0.498	4.375***	YES
Add	EO	Market Knowledge	0.157	0.105	0.262	2.429*	YES

*** p<0.001; ** p<0.01; *p<0.05; Results are based on Bootstrap = 500; 95% confidence level

Figure 6.11 Interaction Effect Model A – Integrating Capacity

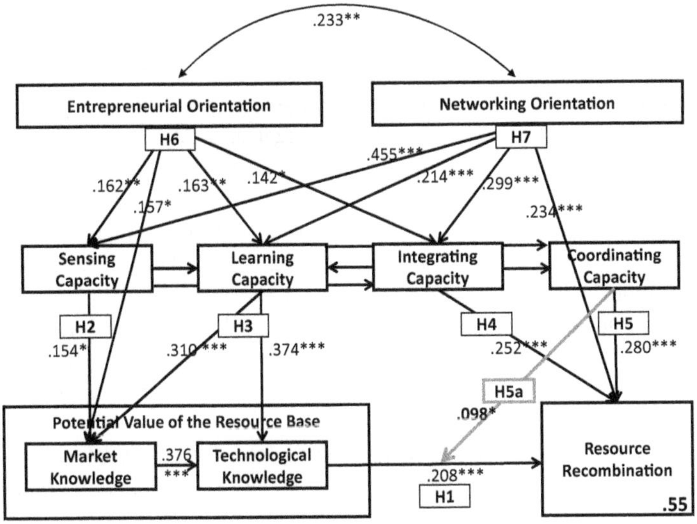

χ² Chi-Square value	40.678	Tucker-Lewis Index (TLI)	0.950
Degrees of freedom	21	Comparative Fit Index (CFI)	0.977
p value	0.108	Normed Fit Index (NFI)	0.954
χ²/ df value	1.937	Root Mean-Square Error (RMSEA)	0.067
Goodness-of-Fit (GFI)	0.963	Root Mean Squared Residual (RMR)	0.094
Adjusted Goodness-of-Fit (AGFI)	0.902	Consistent Akaike Information Criterion (CAIC)	256.2

Hyp.	Independent Variable	Dependent Variable	Direct	Indirect	Total	Critical Ratio	Support
H1	Techno. Knowledge	RR	0.208	0.000	0.208	3.692***	YES
H2	Sensing capacity	RR	n.s	0.189	0.189	n.s	YES
H2a	Sensing capacity	Market Knowledge	0.154	0.127	0.281	2.056*	YES
H3	Learning capacity	RR	n.s	0.226	0.226	n.s	YES
H3a(1)	Learning capacity	Techno.Knowledge	0.374	0.117	0.491	6.202***	YES
H3a(2)	Learning capacity	Market Knowledge	0.310	0.000	0.310	4.000***	YES
H2b/3b	Market Knowledge	Techno.Knowledge	0.376	0.000	0.376	6.318***	YES
H4	Integrating capacity	RR	0.252	0.180	0.432	3.801***	YES
H5	Coordinating capacity	RR	0.280	0.000	0.280	3.839***	YES
H5a	Coord. X TechnoKnow.	RR	0.098	0.000	0.098	1.990*	YES
H6a	EO	Sensing capacity	0.162	0.000	0.162	2.653**	YES
H6b	EO	Learning capacity	0.163	0.095	0.258	3.081**	YES
H6c	EO	Integrating capa.	0.142	0.036	0.178	2.278*	YES
H7a	NO	Sensing capacity	0.455	0.000	0.455	7.430***	YES
H7b	NO	Learning capacity	0.214	0.246	0.460	3.545***	YES
H7c	NO	Integrating capa.	0.299	0.100	0.399	4.319***	YES
Add	NO	RR	0.234	0.263	0.497	4.325***	YES
Add	EO	Market Knowledge	0.157	0.105	0.262	2.429*	YES

*** p<0.001; ** p<0.01; * p<0.05; Results are based on Bootstrap = 500; 95% confidence level

Figure 6.12 Interaction Effect Model B – Coordinating Capacity

H4a: *A high Integrating Capacity is positively associated with RR in firms as it is moderating the relationship between Technological Knowledge and RR in firms.*

The results presented in Figure 6.11 indicate a strong and positive influence of the interaction effect variable on RR, significant at a 0.01 level. The value of the structural regression weight (β_{yxw}) shows a significant direct effect of 0.156 the moderating variable Integrating capacity has on the relation between Technological Knowledge and RR. This positive association gives support to H4a and confirms the moderating role of Integrating capacity as a key driver for resource value creation in firms, supporting hypothesis H4a. Besides, its already established strong and positive direct effect of 0.251 on RR in firms, with a total effect rising to 0.429, Integrating capacity thus was additionally proven to enhancing the relation between the resources available in firms and their recombinations.

H5a: *A high Coordinating Capacity is positively associated with RR in firms as it is moderating the relationship between Technological Knowledge and RR in firms.*

Support was also found for hypothesis 5a, as the results shown in Figure 6.12 confirm a significant positive impact of the interaction variable (Integrating*Technological Knowledge) on RR. In relation to Integrating capacity a relatively weak interaction effect of 0.098 was established, however the effect was still found to be significant at a 0.05 level. Notably, while the moderating role of Coordinating capacity could be confirmed, it does not show to be as strong as for Integrating capacity. This result is somewhat surprising, given the strong direct effect of 0.280 from Coordinating capacity to RR.

Following the call for a proper integration of the interaction terms, which are most often calculated separately for each interaction effect model in statistical analyses (Reineke, 1999), in a last analysis step the interaction terms for Integrating and Coordinating capacity have both been included simultaneously in the model. Following Reineke (1999), by linking the integrated interaction effect terms with the linear part of the theoretical model, iteratively an adequate statistical representation of the holistic model can be obtained, whereby the modelling is not only restricted on linear relationships anymore. The results are presented in Figure 6.13 below.

As the results show, good model fit was also achieved for the holistic model, with all model fit indices indicated excellent fit with a χ^2/df (= 1.510), GFI (= 0.962), AGFI (= 0.908), TLI (= 0.963), CFI (= 0.982) and NFI (= 0.956), this was supported by a non-significant χ^2 (p > 0.05) and an RMSEA value of 0.056, again solely the RMR (= 0.105) was slightly above the acceptable threshold for this research. Given these good results the model qualified for hypotheses testing.

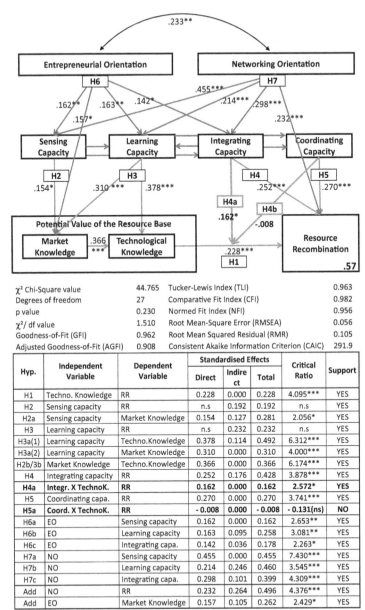

Hyp.	Independent Variable	Dependent Variable	Standardised Effects			Critical Ratio	Support
			Direct	Indirect	Total		
H1	Techno. Knowledge	RR	0.228	0.000	0.228	4.095***	YES
H2	Sensing capacity	RR	n.s	0.192	0.192	n.s	YES
H2a	Sensing capacity	Market Knowledge	0.154	0.127	0.281	2.056*	YES
H3	Learning capacity	RR	n.s	0.232	0.232	n.s	YES
H3a(1)	Learning capacity	Techno.Knowledge	0.378	0.114	0.492	6.312***	YES
H3a(2)	Learning capacity	Market Knowledge	0.310	0.000	0.310	4.000***	YES
H2b/3b	Market Knowledge	Techno.Knowledge	0.366	0.000	0.366	6.174***	YES
H4	Integrating capacity	RR	0.252	0.176	0.428	3.878***	YES
H4a	Integr. X TechnoK.	RR	0.162	0.000	0.162	2.572*	YES
H5	Coordinating capa.	RR	0.270	0.000	0.270	3.741***	YES
H5a	Coord. X TechnoK.	RR	- 0.008	0.000	- 0.008	- 0.131(ns)	NO
H6a	EO	Sensing capacity	0.162	0.000	0.162	2.653**	YES
H6b	EO	Learning capacity	0.163	0.095	0.258	3.081**	YES
H6c	EO	Integrating capa.	0.142	0.036	0.178	2.263*	YES
H7a	NO	Sensing capacity	0.455	0.000	0.455	7.430***	YES
H7b	NO	Learning capacity	0.214	0.246	0.460	3.545***	YES
H7c	NO	Integrating capa.	0.298	0.101	0.399	4.309***	YES
Add	NO	RR	0.232	0.264	0.496	4.376***	YES
Add	EO	Market Knowledge	0.157	0.105	0.262	2.429*	YES

*** p<0.001; ** p<0.01; * p<0.05; Results are based on Bootstrap = 500; 95% confidence level

Figure 6.13 Interaction Effect Model A and B – Integrating and Coordinating Capacity

As the results from the path analysis presented in Figure 6.13 further show, interestingly, the moderation (interaction) effect Integrating capacity has on the relation between Technological Knowledge and RR was found to be stronger (exhibiting coefficients of 0.162) when the interaction effect variable Coordinating*Technological Knowledge was included in the model. At the same time the moderation (interaction) effect Coordinating capacity has on the relationship between Technological Knowledge and RR emerged as insignificant (exhibiting coefficients of −0.008) when the interaction effect variable Integrating*Technological Knowledge was included in the model. These results may indicate that the moderating role of Coordinating capacity on the relation between Technological Knowledge and RR may be restricted as long as Integration is given, suggesting the need for a greater consideration of Integrating capacity as an accelerator for RR in firms. Notably, Coordinating capacity is shown to directly influence the outcome measure of RR (with a strong, direct effect of 0.270), but did not significantly affect the relation between Technological Knowledge and RR (as long as Integration is provided).

In conclusion, for each suggested mediation effect an interaction effect model was formulated in accordance to equation (3) $Y = \alpha + \beta_{yx}X + \beta_{yw}W + \beta_{yxw}XW + \zeta$. In a first research step, these models were tested by means of multi-group moderation analysis. The multi-group comparisons showed the moderation effect of Integrating and Coordinating capacity on the relation between Technological Knowledge and RR to be present and considerable meaningful. The results gave statistical support for H4a and H5a, confirming that both Integrating and Coordinating capacity strengthen the positive relationship between Technological Knowledge and RR. In a second step the significance of this interaction effect could be confirmed by means of interaction effect method due to non-linear SEM, which also gave support to H4a and H5a. Hence, the analysis strategy as suggested by Jonsson (1997), to first applying multi-group analysis, before testing the more complex model formulation for the non-linear interaction effect model, has proved to be reliable: For both models, A) Integrating capacity and B) Coordinating capacity, moderation effects were confirmed by means of multi-group analysis and confirmed when including interaction effect variables separately in the non-linear structural models. Interestingly, and this could only be shown by means of interaction effect method, when both interaction effect variables, Integrating and Coordinating capacity, were simultaneously included in the model, the significant moderation effect of Coordinating capacity turned insignificant, connecting the support for H5a on the presence (resp. absence) of Integrating capacity.

6.8   Competing Models

After all hypotheses have been tested and different models have been presented in this chapter, the following section conclusively offers a comparison of the models presented in this research against competing models. Following Jahn (2007), when different causal relationships between the variables are conceivable, a comparison of the alternative, competing models is deemed valuable.

For the comparison of competing models, a variety of different statistical criteria are referred to in the literature, all aiming to give indications on which model is the most parsimonious (Hooper et al., 2008). The model fit indices, as presented for each model, especially the CFI and CAIC, can give indications for such a comparison. However, to ensure comparability between models (and hence its indices), the models should be similar in the level of complexity (Jahn, 2007). For this research model, fit indices were evaluated independently from parsimony considerations, to avoid placing a disadvantage on models that are having more parameters, but at the same time—in case simpler alternative models exist and show similar good results—taking simplicity of the models into account. Nested models are regarded as useful, as here only the relationships between constructs are changed, meaning that specific paths are added to or removed from the model (Jahn, 2007).

As recommended by Morgan and Hunt (1994) the proposed models with its competing models are compared based on the following criteria:

(1) the **overall model fit**, as implied by the fit of the postulated and observed covariance matrices, and measured by the goodness-of-fit indices (especially the comparative fit index (CFI), where higher values of the CFI indicate towards the better alternative);
(2) the **percentage of hypotheses supported** in the model, measured by the relation between those parameters that showed statistically significant results and all others;
(3) the **explanatory power** of the model, as described by the variance explained in the outcome variable, and measured by its squared multiple correlation; and

(4) the **models' parsimony,** as measured by the parsimony fit indices (especially the CAIC, whereby the model, that displays the lowest value for the CAIC is regarded the most superior[13]).

For a comparative investigation Table 6.18 below confronts the criteria for the three competing models for this research: (A) the re-specified model as outlined in section 6.5.4 (and presented in Figure 6.4), (B) a simple direct effect model, were only direct effects from the DCs to RR were allowed, and (C) the inter-action effect model as presented in the previous section 6.7.2 (and shown in Figure 6.13). The arrows indicate a deterioration ↓, improvement ↑, or constancy ↔ of the obtained value compared to the re-specified model.

Re-specified Model vs. Direct Effect Model
In line with what RBV literature suggests the results of the re-specified structural model revealed a strong and positive effect of a firm's knowledge based resources (Market and Technological Knowledge) on RR performance in firms ($\beta = 0.195$, $p < 0.001$). Furthermore, it was supported that the firm's resources mediate the performance effects *Potential Building DCs* (Sensing and Learning capacity) have on resource value creation through RR. In order to further analyse and test this mediating role of the firm's resources, an alternative model was tested where the path between *Potential Building DCs* and Market/Technological Resources was omitted, and instead only direct paths between DCs and RR were allowed (direct effect model).

Looking at criterion (1) the **overall model fit** the results showed, that while the CFI for this competing, direct effect model remained at the same level (CFI = .981 versus .984), except of the GFI = .981 and NFI = .977 which slightly improved, a substantial deterioration of all other model fit indices was obtained (given a significant X^2 ($p < 0.05$), $\chi 2/df = 4.888$, AGFI = .821, TLI=0.870, RMSEA = .137).

Concerning criterion (2) the **percentage of hypotheses supported,** the results show that only 14 of 17 (82.35%) hypothesised paths are supported at the $p < 0.05$ level for the competing, direct effect model. In contrast, 20 of 22 hypothesised paths (90.1%) are supported at the $p < 0.05$ level in the original, re-specified model. Importantly, only three of the four direct effects of the DCs on RR were significant

---

[13] As the absolute and incremental fit indices do not account for differences in parsimony, the CAIC was used as a comparative measure for model's parsimony. Beside the AIC and CAIC, Jöreskog (1993) and Brown and Cudeck (1993) describe alternative measures as the CVI and ECVI used for the cross-validation of a single model as well as for the comparison of competing models.

Table 6.18 Analyses of the Competing Structural Models

No.	Criterion	(A) Re-specified Model*	(B) Direct Effect Model**	(C) Interaction Effect Model***
	Graphical Representation			
	Characteristics	mediators included, no moderators	no mediators, no moderators	mediators included, moderators included
(1)	χ^2 Chi-Square value	26.366	14.644	44.765
	Degrees of freedom	13	3	27
	p value	0.090	0.012 ↓	0.230 ↑
	χ^2/ df value	2.028	4.888 ↓	1.510 ↑
	Goodness-of-Fit (GFI)	0.973	0.981 ↑	0.962 ↓
	Adjusted Goodness-of-Fit (AGFI)	0.908	0.821 ↓	0.908 ↔
	Tucker-Lewis Index (TLI)	0.955	0.870 ↓	0.963 ↑
	Comparative Fit Index (CFI)	0.984	0.981 ↔	0.982 ↔
	Normed Fit Index (NFI)	0.969	0.977 ↑	0.956 ↓
	Root Mean-Square Error (RMSEA)	0.070	0.137 ↓	0.056 ↑
(2)	% of Hypotheses supported	20/22 (90%)	14/17 (82%) ↓	21/22 (95%) ↑
(3)	Squared Multiple Correlation	53.6	51.00 ↓	57.0 ↑
(4)	Consistent Akaike Info. Criterion (CAIC)	229.2	173.1 ↑	291.9 ↓

in the rival model, while all four DCs have significant direct or indirect effects on RR in the proposed, re-specified model for this research.

In regard to the criterion (3) the **explanatory power** of the model, it is shown that for the competing direct effect model the squared multiple correlation of RR furthermore decreased to 51% of variance explained, thus leading to an inferiority of explanation power. Hence, substantial higher explanatory power is gained through the additional paths included in the re-specified model, compared to the direct effect model.

Lastly, looking at criterion (4) the **models' parsimony**, as expected the decreasing complexity (17 versus 22 paths) of the direct effect model against the re-specified model led to a difference in parsimony. The re-specified model's CAIC of 229.2 exceeded the competing model's CAIC of 173.1. Hence for this criterion, the competing model showed better results, as model parsimony increased with decreasing CAIC values (Diamantopoulos and Siguaw, 2000). However, as no guidelines exist for determining what a significant difference in model parsimony values is, and for the reason that all other criteria showed inferior results for the competing, direct effect model, an increment of 32.4% in CAIC was justified (see Morgan and Hunt, 1994).

In sum, comparing the two models, three out of four criteria revealed a deterioration of model fit for the competing, direct effect model. Therefore, the re-specified model chosen for this research could sustain the comparison against the direct effect model. The results thus support the RBV literature and this research's argumentation, that the proposed impact of *Potential building DC* on per-formance is mediated by the resource base.

Re-specified Model vs. Interaction Effect Model

Given that the re-specified model outperformed the direct effect model, in a last step the results of the re-specified model and the interaction effect model were compared against each other. This was deemed valuable in order to additionally test if the moderating role of the *Value Realising DCs* (Integrating and Coordinating capacity) actually resulted in a perceivable better model-fit, from a more holistic viewpoint. Confirming the conceptual model developed on the basis of the literature review, the comparison of the two models revealed the following results:

Regarding criterion (1) the **overall model fit**, for the majority of model fit indices notwithstanding its complexity, the interaction effect model showed improved model fit compared to the re-specified model. In detail, improved values were shown for the $\chi 2/df = 1.510$, TLI $= 0.963$, and RMSEA $= 0.056$; while the CFI $= .982$ and AGFI $= .908$ remained at the same level; only the GFI $= .962$ and NFI $= .956$, while remaining on a high level, did not show an improvement in comparison to the model without interaction effect.

Looking at criterion (2) the **percentage of hypotheses supported,** for the interaction effect model, 21 of 22 (95.45%) of hypothesised paths were supported at the $p < 0.05$ level. In contrast, only 20 of 22 hypothesised paths (90.1%) were supported at the $p < 0.05$ level for the in re-specified model.

Criterion (3) the **explanatory power** of the model showed that the squared multiple correlation for RR increased from 53% of variance explained in the dependent variable by the re-specified model to 57% of variance explained by the interaction effect model, meaning that additional explanatory power is gained from the additional paths in the interaction effect model.

Lastly as expected, looking at criterion (4) the **models' parsimony**, the results showed a deterioration of the CAIC value form 229.2 for the re-specified model to 291.9 for the interaction effect model, where the two moderating effects were added in the model. For the same reasoning as described above, an increment of 27.4 % in CAIC was scarified by the higher explanatory power gained for the interaction effect model.

In brief, the comparison of the two models revealed an improvement in three out of four criteria for the interaction effect model, in comparison with the re-specified model. As a result of the comparison of competing models, the interaction effect model conceptualised in this research, not only proved to be the most adequate model when reflecting the theoretical considerations behind this research, but moreover sustained the comparison against competing models based on reliable statistical criteria, and hence could be confirmed as being the adequate model for representing and testing the causal relationships suggested in this research.

6.9   Chapter Summary

This chapter outlined the results of the quantitative research step using SEM principles. First, the process of data preparation and analysis was outlined. This was followed by a description and discussion of the results from the EFA and CFA, undertaken to build the one-factor congeneric **measurement models** used for the computation of the latent constructs in the structural model. Goodness-of-fit indexes were specified and one-factor congeneric measurement models presented for each multi-item construct, including the assessment of construct reliability and validity, common method bias (CMB) and measurement model invariance. Given excellent values for construct validity and reliability, the results further indicated that CMB was not a pervasive issue and that configural and metric invariance was established as the model parameters replicated well across group. Thus the one-factor congeneric measurement models qualified for the calculation of composite variables, which were calculated for all multi-item constructs and used in the structural path model. Moreover the procedure used for the computation of the formative construct RR was detailed and justified.

The subsequent section of the chapter finally outlined the results of the **structural path model**. Therefore the conceptual model as descried in chapter 3 (and specified in chapter 4) and its proposed hypotheses were tested by means of structural path analysis used to test the causal relationship between the constructs. Following the investigation of the model fit indices, based on empirical and theoretical considerations the conceptual model was re-specified with the aim to achieve a more parsimonious, well-fitting model. Given the achieved good overall model fit for the re-specified model, the individual path coefficients were presented and hypotheses were tested. The results of the **structural path analysis provide support the majority of hypotheses**, while only two hypotheses had to be rejected due to non-significant p-values. Table 6.19 provides an overview of all hypotheses tested in this empirical research and summarises the results from the quantitative research step.

Finally the **mediation and moderation effects** were further analysed by means of mediation, multi-group moderation and interaction effect analysis. The results gave evidence to the mediating role of Sensing and Learning capacity and the moderating role of Integrating and Coordinating capacity. In a final analysis step, the structural (interaction effect) model used in this research was conclusively assessed against competing models, confirming its superiority against alternative measurement models and thus its adequacy for measuring and testing the causal relations in this research. While the results are presented and partly discussed in this chapter, a detailed discussion of the findings is provided in the following chapter.

Table 6.19 Hypotheses Support

Hypo.	Independent variable	Dependent variable	Predicted Relationship	Support
	Potential Value of the Resource Base	**RR**	**Positive**	
H1	Technological Knowledge	RR	Positive	Confirmed
H1 (1)	Market Knowledge	RR	positive (indirect)	Confirmed
	Controls	**RR**		
H1a	Knowledge Complementarity	RR	Positive	No influence
H1b	Knowledge Tacitness	RR	Negative	No influence
H1c	Knowledge Context Specificy	RR	Negative	No influence
H1d	Knowledge Origin	RR	Positive	No influence
	Overall DC	**RR**	**positive (indirect)**	
H2	Sensing capacity	RR	positive (indirect)	Confirmed
H3	Learning capacity	RR	positive (indirect)	Confirmed
H4	Integrating capacity	RR	positive	Confirmed
H5	Coordinating capacity	RR	positive	Confirmed
	Potential Building DCs on RR		**mediating**	
H2a	Sensing capacity	Market Knowledge	Positive	Confirmed
H3a (1)	Learning capacity	Technological Knowledge	Positive	Confirmed
H3a (2)	Learning capacity	Market Knowledge	Positive	Confirmed
H2b / H3b	Market Knowledge	Technological Knowledge	Positive	Confirmed
H2c / H3c	Technological Knowledge	RR	Positive	Confirmed
	Value Realising DCs	**Potential Value of the RB and RR**	**moderating**	
H4a	Integrating capacity	Technological Knowledge on RR	moderating	Confirmed
H5a	Coordinating capacity	Technological Knowledge on RR	moderating	**Partly confirmed**
	Entrepreneurial Orientation	**Dynamic Capabilities**	**Positive**	
H6a	Entrepreneurial Orientation	Sensing capacity	Positive	Confirmed
H6b	Entrepreneurial Orientation	Learning capacity	Positive	Confirmed
H6c	Entrepreneurial Orientation	Integrating capacity	Positive	Confirmed
H6d	Entrepreneurial Orientation	Coordinating capacity	Positive	**Rejected**
	Networking Orientation	**Dynamic Capabilities**	**Positive**	
H7a	Networking Orientation	Sensing capacity	Positive	Confirmed
H7b	Networking Orientation	Learning capacity	Positive	Confirmed
H7c	Networking Orientation	Integrating capacity	Positive	Confirmed
H7d	Networking Orientation	Coordinating capacity	Positive	**Rejected**

Discussion, Managerial Implications and Directions for Future Research

7

7.1   Introduction

The RBV and DC literature has highlighted the importance of the firm's resources and DCs for value creation trough the recombination of resources. By explicitly embedding the DC perspective in resource based explanations for value creation, the principal aim of this research was to bring clarity to the notion of DCs, their role and effects towards building RRs in firms. Accordingly, the overall objective of this study was to better understand the role of DCs in the process of RR, and thereby to elaborate the framework conditions of RR from the DC perspective.

Therefore, a number of objectives have been addressed, namely (1) to develop a conceptual framework and measurement model of a specific set of DCs relevant for the process of RR, (2) to empirically investigate the influence of a firm's DCs on RRs, and (3) to examine the factors influencing the development of a firm's DC to better understand how organisations can strategically foster the development of a firm's DC, and thus RR in firms.

In order to approach these objectives, a first empirical investigation of the DC construct and its influence on RR was conducted. Based on a thorough literature review of the resource and competence based literature, several research gaps were identified and a conceptual model, including a number of respective propositions and hypotheses, was developed. In a subsequent step, first qualitative research was conducted to explore the accuracy of the conceptual model and to refine it for the second, quantitative research step. The results of the quantitative research step, the structural path analysis, model re-specification, as well as moderation and mediation analyses, were presented in the previous chapter.

© The Author(s), under exclusive license to Springer Fachmedien Wiesbaden GmbH, part of Springer Nature 2021
K. Kurzhals, *Resource Recombination in Firms from a Dynamic Capability Perspective*, Gabler Theses, https://doi.org/10.1007/978-3-658-35666-8_7

In this chapter, the research findings are discussed in more detail. Based on the discussion of the findings, managerial implications are derived. Thereafter limitations of the study are pointed out and contributions to theory and practice are outlined. Before concluding, the chapter closes with directions for future research. Finally a summary of the last chapter is provided.

7.2   Discussion of the Findings: Key Drivers of Resource Recombination

The quantitative data offered considerably support for the research model. Besides examining the role and effects of Sensing, Learning, Integrating and Coordinating capacities in the process of RR, the influence of organisational resources in the relationships was further studied. Additionally, Entrepreneurial Orientation (EO) and Networking Orientation (NO) were identified as antecedents for the development of DCs, and their influence was empirically tested in this research. The individual findings of the quantitative research step are discussed in the following section.

The discussion of the findings thereby is divided into three sections, picking up the three originally formulated propositions, which guided through this research, and based on which the studies' hypotheses were derived and tested. The discussion of the research findings provides important insights into how theories of resource and competence based research, strategic management and entrepreneurship can be integrated and extended, what managerial implications can be derived, and what future studies should explore.

7.2.1 The Influence of the Resource Endowments on Resource Recombination

The following section discusses the findings regarding the influence of resource endowments on building the potential value of the resource base for RR. It thereby addresses Proposition 1.

Proposition 1: A high valuable resource base is positively associated with RR in firms. The <u>potential value of the resource base</u> for RR thereby is influenced by certain characteristics of the resources.

Investigating if certain characteristics of the resource base—its quality, diversity, complementarity, transferability, deployment flexibility, and renewal—influence the potential value of the resources for RR in firms, several hypotheses were derived in order to address Proposition 1. The advanced understanding of the potential influence of specific characteristics of the resources on RR offers important insight into resource value creation in firms. Moreover it allows answering the questions, what is relatively more important for RR in firms, the resources or the DCs of the firm, and how the interplay between both factors is organised in practice. Regarding the influence of resource endowment on RR, the empirical results as outlined in chapter 6 yield two key findings, which will be further discussed in the following:

(1) The overall quality and diversity of the resources play a considerably larger role in resource value creation than its origin, tacitness, context specificy, or complementarity.
(2) Resources are important for building the potential value for RR and are a key driver of RR, but even more important are the firm's DCs.

First, the influence of specific characteristics of the resources on RR was tested. Thereby, most interestingly, the results showed the potential value of the resource base for RR to be predominantly influenced by the **Quality and Diversity of Market and Technological Knowledge,** measured by its knowledge depth and breadth, while surprisingly, no significant effects were found in this study between **Knowledge Complementarity, Knowledge Tacitness, Knowledge Context Specificy, Knowledge Origin** and RR. The results therefore led to a rejection of H1a, H1b, H1c, H1d, implying that regardless of specific characteristics of resources—their complementarity, tacitness, context specificy, and origin—an increase in Market and Technological Knowledge depth and breadth significantly increases RR in firms. In other words, findings imply that as long as firms hold a considerably amount of qualitative and diverse Market and Technological Knowledge, any further characteristic of that knowledge does not play a major role for resource value creation. A possible explanation of this might be that as long as firms possess the necessary DCs, especially Integrating and Coordinating capacities, they do have the necessary abilities to integrate, build and reconfigure those resources into new bundles and thereby to unearth the potential value of those resources (Madhavan and Grover, 1998, De Luca and Atuahene-Gima, 2007), irrespectively of their characteristics. In consequence, the characteristics of resources, be it its complementarity, tacitness, context specificy, or origin, become irrelevant in regard to performance outcomes. As a result, evidence is given by the research findings that the overall quality and diversity of resources play a considerably larger role in resource value creation than its origin, tacitness, context specificy, or complementarity.

Second, another key finding is that regarding their impact on RR, the resources a firm possess (measured by its Market and Technological Knowledge breadth and depth) emerge to be a key driver of RR, but data reveals that even more important are the firm's DCs. Looking at the standardised total effects, which comprise the complete influence one variable has on another variable throughout all conceivable relationships with additional constructs, **Technological Knowledge** (breadth and depth) was confirmed to have a strong, positive effect on RR, with coefficients ranging from 0.195 in the generic (re-specified) model to 0.228 in the final interaction effect model. Also **Market Knowledge** (breadth and depth) revealed an admittedly weaker, yet significant positive, indirect effect on RR through Technological Knowledge ($ß = 0.063$). Thus, the fundamental influence Technological and Market Knowledge has on RR was clearly established, confirming H1 and H1 (1). In line with the RBV's perception of value creation in firms, findings hence approved that a high valuable resource base was found to significantly influence RR. At the same time, and this is probably the more notably finding, the influence of the DCs on RR is shown to be relatively more important, with strong and positive standardised total effects revealed for Sensing capacity ($ß = 0.185^*/ 0.192^{**}$[1]), Learning capacity ($ß = 0.225^*/ 0.232^{**}$), Integrating capacity ($ß = 0.428^*/ 0.428^{**}$), Coordinating capacity ($ß = 0.267^*/ 0.270^{**}$) on RR. According to these findings, resources certainly are confirmed to be an important element and inherent for value creation in firms, as they establish the potential value of the resource base for RR, but even more important as possessing valuable resources are the DCs to build and translate them into realised value. In consequence both, the resources as well as the firm's DCs, emerged as key drivers of RR.

The results thus validate the significant focus of the DC literature on developing the necessary capabilities to reconfigure its resource base, as the key source of competitive advantages in dynamic environments (Eisenhardt and Martin, 2000, Teece et al., 1997, Mathews, 2002). While being consistent with previous findings in the DC literature, claiming that considerably emphasise should be placed on the development of DCs in firms (Pavlou and El Sawy, 2011, Hawass, 2010), at the same time the results contradict, or one could also say extend the traditional focus of the RBV, which sees a firm's competitive position primarily determined by the specific characteristics of firm resources (Schreyögg and Conrad, 2006, Barney, 1991, Grant, 1991). Instead, findings support the idea of an interplay between the resources and DCs as major source for new, innovative RRs in firms.

---

[1] For reasons of comparison values are reported for the *generic (re-specified) model and the **final interaction effect model.

Therewith, this study produced results that corroborate the findings of previous work in the DC field (e.g. Hansen et al., 2004, Kor and Mahoney, 2005, Holcomb et al., 2009), which found that while owning or having access to high valuable resources is necessary for a competitive advantage, they must be effectively managed and synchronised *to realise* a competitive advantage. As a result, evidence is given by the research findings that a substantial proportion of variance in resource productivity across firms can be explained by the differences attributed to the firm's DCs relevant for the selection and recombination of resources, while the availability of resources only builds the basis for the development of RRs.

One of the issues that emerges from these findings is that firms should leave their traditional focus on merely possessing the "right" resources to take on a more holistic approach towards developing the necessary capabilities to manage those resources. Thus, rather than solely focusing on specific characteristics of the resource base, which—except for resource quality and diversity—proved to be irrelevant in regard to performance outcome of RR anyway, special emphasis should be given by managers on the development of DCs. These findings have important implications for resource value creation in firms, which will be discussed in section 7.3.

7.2.2 The Role of Dynamic Capabilities in the Process of Resource Value Creation

The conceptual model, hypotheses and findings presented help to delineate key differences in regard to the role of DCs in the process of resource value creation. The following section discusses these findings, addressing Proposition 2.

Proposition 2: A firm's overall DC is positively associated with the amount of RRs in firms due to both building and exploiting the potential value of the resources base.

The principal aim of this research was to bring clarity to the notion of DCs, their role and effects towards RRs by *building* and *exploiting* the resource base. Investigating what the role and effect of different DCs in the process of RR is, and whether different types of DCs are work on different levels, several hypotheses were derived to test the proposed mediation effect of the resource base between Sensing/Learning capacities and RR, and the proposed moderation effect of Integrating/ Coordinating capacities on the link between the resource base and RR. Instead of addressing a firm's overall DC, the study thereby investigated the way in which specific dimensions of the DC construct, independently and jointly influence RR in firms. Due to the complexity of analyses applied for testing moderation and mediation effects, the findings regarding the proposed mediation and mediation effects have already been presented and discussed in detail in the previous chapter (refer to section 6.6. and 6.7). For this reason, this section provides merely a brief review and integration of the previous discussion.

Findings give evidence that regarding the role and effect of the specific DCs in the process of resource value creation, two different types of DCs can be distinguished: *Potential Building DCs* and *Value Realising DCs*, whereby both components have different effects and 'working modes' towards RR. Correspondingly, the study has three key findings, which are discussed in the following:

(1) The Sensing and Learning capacities are necessary for building the potential value of resources for RR, and thus can be referred to as *Potential Building DCs*.

(2) The Integrating and Coordinating capacities are necessary for the value potential of the resource base to become realised by creating, implementing and exploiting new innovative RRs, and thus can be referred to as *Value Realising DCs*.

(3) Both the *Potential Building DCs* and the *Value Realising DCs* are critical to the achievement of superior performance in the long run. *Potential Building DCs* and *Value Realising DCs* thereby have separate but complementary roles.

First, as the results of the structural path analysis and mediation analysis in particular showed, high **Sensing and Learning capacities** generally lead to an increased performance in regard to RR. However, as not all firms that have developed high Sensing and Learning capacities are subsequently high performing in achieving RRs, this relation was expected to be fully and positively mediated by the resource base (Market and Technological Knowledge). Literature therefore suggested that Sensing and Learning capacities per se do not result in superior innovation performance, rather they help to provide the basis for subsequently leveraging innovation opportunities (Helfat and Peteraf, 2009, Lichtenthaler, 2012). Confirming what theory suggested, statistical support was given by the quantitative data analysis, manifesting that Market and Technological Knowledge fully mediate the effect of Sensing and Learning capacity on RR in firms ($p < 0.05$), thus confirming H2a/H2b/H2c and H3a/H3b/H3c. In other words, evidence was given by the data that the direct relationship between Sensing capacity, respectively Learning capacity and RR is better explained through the mediator variables of Market and Technological Knowledge.

Notably, while Learning capacity emerged to have a strong positive, and direct effect on building the potential value of Market Knowledge (ß = 0.310) and Technological Knowledge (ß = 0. 391), Sensing capacity, while still significant, showed to have a relatively low *direct* influence on Market Knowledge (ß = 0.154), though yet a strong *indirect* effect on both Market Knowledge (ß = 0.281) and Technological Knowledge (ß = 0.408) through Learning capacity. This allows the conclusion that, besides its direct effect on Market Knowledge, Sensing capacity finds its expression through Learning. It therewith supports the argumentation by several researchers (e.g. Pavlou and El Sawy, 2011, Lichtenthaler, 2012) that a high Sensing capacity, which focuses on the identification of new opportunities in the external environment [external opportunity generation], also acts as enabler of a strong Learning capacity, as it is suggested to facilitate the firm's ability to address external opportunities through creating new and utilising existing knowledge [internal opportunity generation]. Taken together, it can be said with statistical certainty that both, Sensing and Learning capacities, significantly contribute towards building the potential value of the resource base.

As an important result, research findings thus confirm the suggested role of Sensing and Learning capacities as *Potential Building DCs* in the process of RR, as they help to build the relevant resources for RR. While results imply that firms with a higher Sensing and Learning capacity tend to recombine their resources more effective, data also indicate that even if firms have high Sensing and Learning capacities, this will not necessarily lead to higher RR performance, unless they use these capacities to build a valuable knowledge base, the 'raw material' for RR. Most notably, the results of this study statistically confirm and specify the argument proposed earlier by Ambrosini and colleagues (2009), that it is the DCs—more specifically the *Potential Building DCs*—that directly impact the firm's resource base by continuously refreshing the stock of resources, and thereby enable firms to 'hit a moving target', seen as the source of firm's competitive advantage.

Second, the results of the moderation analysis furthermore gave support to the perceived role of **Integrating and Coordinating capacities** as *Value Realising DCs*. As formulated in H4a and H5a, Integrating and Coordinating capacities were expected to moderate the relation between the resource base and RR. Hence, moderation analysis techniques were applied to test whether high or low levels of Coordinating and Integrating capacities have different effects on the relation between Technological Knowledge and RR. Besides its strong direct effect on RR, the results of the multi-group comparison confirmed the moderating role of Integrating and Coordinating capacity. The positive influence Technological Knowledge has on RR was proved to be 2.6 times as strong when Integration capacity was high, and 1.6 times as strong when Coordinating capacity was high. Moreover, the relation between Technological Knowledge and RR became insignificant ($p > 0.05$) when Integrating and Coordinating capacity were low, which denotes that only if firms possess high Integration and Coordination capacities, will the resources a firm holds, lead to higher success in RR. In consequence this means, that even if a firm has high levels of Market and Technological Knowledge, it does not necessary lead to the desired performance outcome if the firm does not possess the relevant capacities to integrate and coordinate that knowledge in order to achieve new RRs. The results thus gave statistical support for H4a and H5a, confirming that both Integrating and Coordinating capacity strengthen the positive relationship between Technological Knowledge and RR.

The significance of this moderation effect was further validated by means of interaction effect method. Notably, while the interaction effect of Coordinating capacity was confirmed as significant ($ß = 0.098$, $p < 0.05$), it did not show to be as strong as it revealed for Integrating capacity ($ß = 0.156$, $p < 0.05$). This result is somewhat surprising, given the strong direct effect of 0.280 from Coordinating capacity to RR. Interestingly, in a further analysis when both interaction effect variables—Integrating and Coordinating capacity—were simultaneously included in the model, the significant interaction effect of Coordinating capacity turned insignificant ($p > 0.05$), connecting the support for H5a on the presence (respectively absence) of Integrating capacity. These results may indicate that the strong focus on coordination mechanisms as moderating variable may be restricted as long as integration is given, suggesting the need for a greater consideration of processes and routines supporting interaction and communication. Findings therefore sustain the assumption that different DCs will be working in very different ways, according to the situation in which the firm is found at any given time (Madsen, 2010). Future research should set out to further analyse and confirm these findings. Notably, given the strong direct effect Coordinating capacity has on RR (which remains similar strong across models), its influence on resource value creation remains unaffected. From the four DCs, Coordinating capacity emerged to have the strongest direct effect on RR, while Integrating capacity exhibited to have the strongest total effect throughout the models. These results validate the significant focus of the DC literature on the concept of integration and coordination for value creation.

Briefly said, these results confirm the suggested role of Integrating and Coordinating capacities as *Value Realising DCs* in the process of RR, as they help to leverage the value potential of the resource base by creating, implementing and exploiting new innovative RRs. These findings are consistent with qualitative research results and corroborate results of previous studies in this field, which has often highlighted the role of Integrating and Coordinating capacity as critical in the process of resource value creation in firms (e.g. Pavlou and El Sawy, 2011, Galunic and Eisenhardt, 2001, Galunic and Rodan, 1998), due to its influence on the realised value of RR in firms (e.g. Grant, 1991, Sirmon and Hitt, 2003). In total, quantitative data revealed that the effort and investment provided by firms to build and renew their resources has a similar strong influence on resource value creation in form of new RRs, as their efforts in building and maintaining strong Integrating and Coordinating capacities. Consequently, high Integration and Coordination capacity appears desirable for firms.

Taken these findings together, they suggest that both the *Potential Building DCs* and the *Value Realising DCs* are critical to the achievement of superior performance in the long run. Hence, evidence is given by the research findings that much of the variation in firm's performance is explained by the variation in their level of DCs. Important implications for resource management therefore are that in order to stay competitive in dynamic environments firms have to develop both *Potential Building DCs* and *Value Realising DCs*. The findings suggest that firms lacking *Potential Building DCs* will not generate a rich and diverse knowledge base, the 'raw material' for innovation, while firms lacking *Value Realising DCs* might indeed have a valuable resource base, however at the same time will not be able to exploit the value creation potential of the resources.

Third, findings clearly reveal that *Potential Building DCs* and *Value Realising DCs* have separate but complementary roles. As the firm's ability to successfully create value through RR depends on having adequate strength in both complementary capacity modes, meaning that each single capacity (Sensing, Learning, Integrating and Coordinating capacity) can act as a potential 'bottleneck', limiting a firm's overall ability to strategically develop RRs. For example, the utility of strengthening Sensing and Learning capacities may reveal relatively limited if a firm lacks Integrating and Coordinating capacities (see Lichtenthaler, 2012). Although a firm's Integrating and Coordinating capacity is not easy to develop, managers ought to recognise that the mere accumulation of resource assets does not guarantee a sustainable competitive advantage over time (Isobe et al., 2008). This implies that having strong *Potential Building DCs* may be a necessary but insufficient condition for improved value creation performance in firms. Instead, "in a rapidly changing environment, firms need to continuously search for new competence bases and reconfigure their existing portfolio of competences" (Isobe et al., 2008, p. 424). On the other hand, firms cannot possibly leverage the value creation potential of its resources without first having built the relevant stock of knowledge through acquisition and assimilation activities.

In order to avoid theses trade-offs, firms have to develop systematic approaches to find and maintain a strategic balance between a *Potential Buildings* and *Value Realising DCs,* its underlying routines and processes. Hence, the results are consistent with Sanchez (2004, p. 531) noting that "organizational competence does not depend simply on achieving excellence in one or two key success factors, but rather on developing an interrelated and balanced set of success factors". Accordingly an important implication in turn is that firms have to strive to achieve a proper balance and alignment among these two distinct subsets of DCs. While the existing literature tends to ignore the effects of DCs on performance outcomes, this study demonstrated that different capabilities have different effects and 'working modes' and therefore should be treated separately in future research.

From a broader perspective, these findings also complement March's (1991) seminal paper on exploration and exploitation, where he discussed the difficulty of finding and maintaining this balance, and as such research findings give support to the initial idea that "routines [that are constituting a DC—author's note] could provide the microfoundations and the key mechanisms by which firms both explore and exploit" (Parmigiani and Howard-Greenville 2010, p. 442). Thus, with the DC framework presented here, this research presents one possible approach that could help managers to find the right balance between exploration and exploitation, by simultaneously developing both *Potential Building* and *Value Realising DCs*.

7.2.3 The Antecedents for the Development of Dynamic Capabilities

The development of firm's DCs was suggested to be influenced by a variety of firm- and network-level antecedents. Addressing the last Proposition 3, the following section discusses the findings regarding a firm's Entrepreneurial Orientation (EO) and Networking Orientation (NO), which were proposed to positively influence the development of a firm's DCs.

Proposition 3: Entrepreneurial Orientation and Networking Orientation act as antecedents for the development of a firm's DCs.

Investigating what the influence of a firm's EO and NO on the development of the firm's DCs is, several hypotheses were derived to address Proposition 3. This research set out to investigate, whether a high degree of EO, respectively NO, has a positive influence on the development of a firm's DCs, and consequently RR. Moreover, the relatively importance of the proposed antecedents was tested, and in addition whether NO and EO act as complements or rather as substitutes.

Evidence is given by the research findings that (besides possessing the necessary DCs) achieving RR success to a great extend depends on a firm's organisational structure and culture supportive of interorganisational and entrepreneurial activities, which positively affect the development and utilisation of DCs for resource value creation. Regarding the antecedents of DCs, two key findings can be deduced, which are further discussed in the following:

(1) Entrepreneurial Orientation and Networking Orientation act as antecedents for the development of DCs.
(2) While Networking Orientation emerged as relatively more important than Entrepreneurial Orientation for resource value creation, both are complementing each other in their perceived role of developing Sensing, Learning and Integrating capacities.

First, the firm's **Entrepreneurial Orientation** was confirmed by the data to be positively associated with the development of the firm's DCs, and consequently RR. While a vast variety of studies assumed a direct linkage between EO and RR, respectively firm performance (e.g. Wiklund et al., 2002, Zahra and Wiklund, 2002, Covin and Slevin, 1991, Zahra, 1991), no study could be found that further investigated the activities or 'vehicles'—suggested in this research as firm's DCs—through which a firm's entrepreneurial culture is transformed into effective RRs (Wiklund et al., 2002). This research therefore set out to examining the relationship between EO, DCs and RR in more detail.

Empirical findings confirmed the *indirect* effect EO has on RR through developing DCs. Indeed, EO emerged to only have a moderate direct impact on RR, where no significant *direct* effect was shown to be existent when being tested in the generic model. Instead, it revealed by the data that the relationship between EO and RR is better explained by its positive effect on DCs, through which EO is translated into new RRs. Hereof, EO was shown to act as significant and relatively strong direct predictor for Sensing capacity ($\beta = 0.162$, $p < 0.01$), Learning capacity ($\beta = 0.163$, $p < 0.01$), and Integrating capacity ($\beta = 0.142$, $p < 0.05$), confirming H6a, H6b, H6c, proposing that EO is a necessary precondition for DCs to develop over time. Moreover, its direct effect on Market Knowledge emerged in the data analysis as comparable strong ($\beta = 0.157$, $p < 0.05$), approving literature that proposes a direct effect of EO to the stock of available knowledge (Wiklund and Shepherd, 2000, Chockburn et al., 2000). Interestingly, less support was found for its effect on Coordinating capacity, leading to a rejection of H6d.

The overall results, yet demonstrated the importance of EO as an important antecedent for the development of DCs, which in consequence positively affects RR in firms. This research therefore elaborated previous research and established a more detailed explanation of the interrelationship between EO on performance outcomes, such as RR.

Second, findings clearly showed that **Networking Orientation,** which captures the firm's tendency to embed close interactions with external entities in their business, moreover is an important antecedent for resource value creation in firms. The firm's NO already emerged in the qualitative research as extremely relevant for value creation in firms and was confirmed by the quantitative data to be strongly related to RR, in two different ways, *indirectly* through the development of DCs, and most interestingly also *directly*.

Implied by the modification indices but also well-grounded in theory, NO revealed by the data to have a strong direct effect on RR in firms ($ß = 0.237$, $p < 0.001$). The high support for NO as a critical factor for RR is in line with previous findings from network theory (Mu and Di Benedetto, 2011, Mu and Di Benedetto, 2012) and DC literature (Isobe et al., 2008, Chi, 1994, Harrison et al., 2001, Larsson and Finkelstein, 1999, Madhok and Tallman, 1998), proposing that firms with strong network ties are more accessible to external resources and thereby enlarge their stock of available resources and opportunities to extract value through RRs. Accordingly, the high level of new (external) knowledge and its constant exchange inherent to value creation in firms may explain the significance of NO as a key driver of RRs. Besides its strong *direct* effect on RR, NO was moreover confirmed to influence RR *indirectly* through its substantial contribution to the development of the firm's Sensing capacity ($ß = 0.455$, $p < 0.001$), Learning capacity ($ß = 0.214$, $p < 0.001$), and Integrating capacity ($ß = 0.299$, $p < 0.001$), confirming H7a, H7b, H7c. Notably, likewise for EO, no direct effect was found between NO and Coordinating capacity, leading to a rejection of H7d. Accordingly, both NO and EO only indirectly affect Coordinating capacity through the other DCs. One possible explanation may be found in the rationale that a higher tendency and openness to entrepreneurial and interorganisational activities may negatively affect the ease of coordination, as it provides considerably more opportunities for value creation and in consequence raises the complexity of implementation. Future research should further investigate those findings.

In sum, evidence was given by the findings that interfirm collaboration is a very effective means of enhancing DCs, and thus RRs. In other words, findings confirmed that firms with a higher NO will develop an increased ability to purposefully create, extend and modify its resource configurations (Mu and Di Benedetto, 2012) by improving its Sensing, Learning, and Integrating capacities. In line with what literature suggested (e.g. Isobe et al., 2008), especially for small and medium-sized firms with limited resources, a high level of NO thus strengthens its resource position and enhances their DCs for RR by providing new external resources bases through the creation of networks of collaboration.

Finally, looking at the relative importance of the proposed antecedents and whether they act as complements or substitutes, two important implications can be made. First, the overall results demonstrate the importance of both, NO and EO as relevant antecedents for developing DCs and for resource value creation. Remarkably, in the model NO emerged to be the overall strongest predictor for RR in firms (ß = 0.496, p < 0.001, total effect). Given the strong direct impact NO has on the outcome variable of RR, the lack of a direct link between EO and RR may appear somewhat surprising at the first glance but can be well explained by its indirect effect on the DCs. As a result, even so the influence EO has on DCs is admittedly lower compared to NO, it should not be underestimated for its perceived role in developing the firm's Sensing, Learning, and Integrating capacities. Second, findings clearly indicate that EO and NO complement each other in terms of their impact and effect. While both constructs describe the firm's *willingness* or *attitude* to engage in entrepreneurial and networking activities, findings indicate that they act as complements rather than substitutes, because EO captures firm's attributes such as *innovativeness, proactiveness*, and *risk-taking*, describing the degree to which firm's growth objectives are driven by initiatives rather coming from inside the firm (*endogenous*), while NO reflects its tendency to engage in interorganisational initiatives, thus their triggers are rather coming from outside the firm (*exogenous*).

Taken together and interpreting these findings from a more holistic viewpoint, quantitative data clearly confirmed what was suggested by literature: While a firm's NO and EO primarily reflect the *willingness* or *attitude* of the firm concerning the engagement in interfirm collaborations, and entrepreneurial activities respectively, the DCs refer to the *activities* itself which build, develop, integrate and reconfigure internal and external resources. Thereby the DCs of the firm indeed build the decisive factor for resource value creation, however, if firms do not possess a supportive strategic orientation, often these capabilities would remain untapped. In other words, if the organisational framework conditions would not be put into place, in consequence the firm's capacities would not take their full effect. For this reasoning and revealed by the quantitative data, the firm's NO and EO were confirmed by this research to act as important antecedents for the development of the firm's DCs, and thus RR, and can be regarded as necessary pre-condition for an efficient and effective resource value creation in firms.

As presented above, with respect to three originally formulated propositions, overall seven key findings regarding (i) the influence of the resource endowments on RR (section 7.2.1), (ii) the role of DCs in the process of resources value creation (section 7.2.2), (iii) and the antecedents for the development of DCs (section 7.2.3) could be derived and were discussed in this section. The discussion of the key findings offered insights into the key drivers of RR in firms, and thus helped to better understand the interrelationship between DCs, the resource base of the firm, and innovation in the form of RR. Respectively the aim and objectives of this research were met to a large degree. On the basis of these findings and the related discussion, important managerial implications for resource management could be derived, and will be discussed in the following.

7.3   Managerial Implications

A number of managerial implications arose from the discussion of key drivers and antecedents. Based on the advanced understanding of the specific DCs, their role and effect in building RRs in firms, as well as their antecedents, systematic ways for the development of DCs to successfully implement RRs in a firm's innovation strategy can be derived. Moreover, with the DC framework presented this research offers a measurement model of DCs, while at the same time exploring the underlying processes and activities of each capacity to be strategically implemented for resource management (Pavlou and El Sway, 2011). Doing so, this research counteracts the criticism that DCs cannot be measured, and that they are born, not made (Winter, 2003). In practical terms, based on the key findings discussed above three main implications for managers can be derived.

First, findings have shown that possessing high valuable resources is important for building the potential value for RR. At the same time findings revealed that as important as the resources themselves, are the DCs to leverage those resources. Accordingly, before outlining any individual implications for managers derived from the discussion of the key drivers and antecedents, first of all a broad understanding of the interplay between resources and capabilities should be established in firms to successfully implement the concept of RR and to enable a holistic, integrated view of resource management in firms. Establishing this multi-faceted view is especially important, when considering that until recently academia and practice predominantly focussed on possessing the 'right' resources as being the imperative for value creation in firms (e.g. Peteraf, 1993, Peteraf and Barney, 2003). However, in times where firm's boundaries are becoming more and more indistinct and open (e.g. Chesbrough, 2003, 2006), and interorganisational collaboration becomes common practice (e.g. Isobe et al., 2008, Rothaermel, 2001, Lane and Lubatkin, 1998, Lee et al., 2001), solely having access to resources is not the decisive factor anymore. Rather it is the intelligent management of those resources available, which comes in the centre of interest (Holcomb et al., 2009, Hansen et al., 2004, Kor and Mahoney, 2005). For firm's management aiming at strategically fostering RR, this means that it is not possible if the senior management opposes the idea of internal capacity building, and instead continuous a strategy, that is solely concentrating on the resources. In practical terms, referring to the literature on continuous innovation, a senior management initiative is recommended to ensure an overall understanding and application of those principles (Boer, 2004). Accordingly, management should be conscious of their willingness and abilities towards building both, the required resources and internal capacities (as well as framework conditions) with respect to RR. To enable this, expectations, goals and objectives should be clearly debated, and potential obstacles resolved internally to ensure a mutual understanding and to enhance commitment before any organisational actions are initiated. Additionally, incentive systems that foster rather than restrict capacity development should be implemented. Employees from all levels, but first and foremost the top management level, should manifest a shared belief in value creation through RR and support the RR process through the allocation of time, money, training, and other resources, so that everyone can participate by being actively involved.

Second, the research findings further gave evidence that both the *Potential Building DCs* and the *Value Realising DCs* are critical for the achievement of superior performance in the long run. As *Potential Building DCs* and *Value Realising DCs* fulfil separate but complementary roles, and RR success depends on having adequate strength in both complementary capacity modes, managers are required to develop systematic approaches to find and maintain a strategic balance between both complementary capacity modes. With the DC framework and respective measurement model presented here, this research offers a valuable instrument and actionable guidance for managers to (1) identify and understand internal DCs, (2) measure and assess the status quo of each capacities for resource management, (3) evaluate their strength and weaknesses and benchmark them against competitors, and finally (4) define targeted strategies for purposefully developing and enhancing those capacities identified as bottlenecks. Thus, by presenting an actionable set of DCs and at the same time an instrument for assessing strength and weaknesses, the DC framework allows managers, to systematically outbalance existing shortcomings in order to find and maintain the right balance between *Potential Building* and *Value Realising DCs*. This is given, as the DC framework details and explains DCs as managerially amenable processes and routines that decision-makers can readily act upon (Pavlou an El Sawy, 2011). Doing so it helps managers to implement the relevant routines and processes in order to support each respective capacity mode (for a detailed description of those processes and routines refer the DC framework, Table 3.1, section 3.4.1.7). Looking at the individual implications for managers this means, they should install this instrument to regularly (re-) assess the development of firm´s DCs over time in order to constantly monitor and maintain the continuous process of resource management. This is especially relevant, as DCs develop over time, and thus managers need to adopt a long-term strategy, such as to set up pre-defined milestones and establish clear responsibilities and process owners. Notably, although DCs have been viewed and measured at the firm level manifesting their relevance for managers at the top level, their implementation in day-to-day routines and processes impacts all organisational levels, and therefore also demands the involvement of lower level managers (Pavlou and El Sawy, 2011).

Third, evidence was given by the findings that the firm's Entrepreneurial Orientation (EO) and Networking Orientation (NO) are important antecedents for the development of DCs and RR, and thus can be regarded as a necessary framework condition, crucial for the efficient and effective resource value creation in firms. Accordingly, to facilitate the actual recombinant activities implemented through Sensing, Learning, Coordinating and Integrating capacities for RR, findings imply that both, a firm's NO as well as a firm's EO, should be embedded within "the social fabric of organization" (Hawass, 2010, p. 410). To put this into action, managers are encouraged to actively promote and stress the firm's willingness to embed close interactions with external entities, and at the same time develop a positive attitude towards being engaged in entrepreneurial activities, in order to act towards creating and maintaining an organisational structure and culture supportive of interorganisational and entrepreneurial activities. Notably, findings advice that the firm's activities intended to orchestrate multiple types of network ties and to engage in entrepreneurial activities should come with strategic intent, rather than being the result of relatively unforeseen actions (Mu and Di Benedetto, 2012).

For managers this means, in order to systematically foster a firm's EO, which stands for a culture of change and transformation, that they have to actively contribute towards developing an organisational culture open for entrepreneurial actions by enabling and encouraging staff to engage in dialogues, becoming involved in entrepreneurial activities, and participating in the process of experimentation (Shane and Venkataraman, 2000). Moreover managers are encouraged to value, and actively contribute to the development of new ideas, support novelty, experimentation, and creative processes in order to achieve continuity (Lumkin and Dess, 1996, Wiklund and Shepherd, 2003). Also it is important to offer staff trainings, mentoring programs, support and appropriate incentive systems and hire people passionate about, and experienced in entrepreneurship (Zahra and Wiklund, 2002, Wiklund et al., 2002).

Correspondingly, related implications can be given for managers in respect to developing and strategically fostering a firm's NO, which was revealed by the data to have an even stronger effect on developing DCs and RR. Accordingly, managers first of all need to be aware that a firm's NO represents a key element by which recombinant innovation can be leveraged. Especially when striving to collaborative RR efforts, managers will need to actively encourage their employees to learn new knowledge by incorporating knowledge from external network partners, which also enables them to critically revise their own processes, products and services, technologies, and resources, and thereby enhance their capacity to conjointly create and develop products that meet the market demand (Mu and di Benedetto, 2011). Rather than being reluctant to new network ties, managers thus are encouraged to adopt a business strategy that stresses effective and efficient location of network partners, management of network relationships, and improvement of network performance. This should come along with managerial actions directed towards developing new network ties to access new resources, expose new opportunities and obtain new knowledge (Mu and Di Benedetto, 2012). It may include hiring people from different industries and disciplines to orchestrate strong network ties in various industries and business areas. Another aspect is to develop corporate strategies empowering groups to contribute to interorganisational activities and maintain relationships the organisation wants to retain. Associated with those actions are regular staff trainings, mentoring programs, support and appropriate incentive systems.

Table 7.1 outlines the managerial implications for resource value creation through RR, developed based on the key findings and discussion of the research results presented in the previous chapter. Besides giving important implications for managers, this study has also some potential limitations, which are presented and discussed next.

Table 7.1 Managerial Implications for Resource Management

Findings	Managerial Implications	... at the Top Management Level	... at Lower Management Levels
I. Resources are important for building the potential value for RR and thus are a key driver of RR, but even more important as the resources are the DCs to leverage those resources	I. Establish a mutual understanding of the interplay between resources and capabilities at all management levels	Develop a holistic, integrated view and strategy of resource management to ensure an overall understanding and application of those principles	o Manifest a shared belief in value creation through RR, so that everyone can participate, by being actively involved. o Discuss expectations, goals, and objectives and resolve potential obstacles and to ensure a mutual understanding and commitment o Allow an extensive amount of time, money, training and rewards to overcome unfamiliarity and potential prejudices o Offer staff training, mentoring, support and appropriate incentive systems that foster rather than restrict capacity development o Hold not only formal discussions but also informal events to develop a common understanding and shared experiences o Implement corporate strategies empowering groups towards building both, the required resources and internal capacities for RR
II. Potential Building DCs and Value Realising DCs fulfil separate but complementary roles. Both capacity modes are critical for the achievement of superior performance	II. Find and maintain the strategic balance between Potential Building and Value Realising Capacities	Understand and regularly (re-)assess internal DCs to systematically outbalance existing shortcomings by developing and enhancing ... a) a firm's Sensing Capacity b) a firm's Learning Capacity c) a firm's Integrating Capacity d) a firm's Coordinating Capacity, respectively.	(1) Identify and understand internal DCs (2) Measure and assess the status quo of DCs for resource management (3) Evaluate their strength and weaknesses and benchmark them against competitors (4) Define targeted strategies for purposefully developing and enhancing those capacities identified as bottlenecks (5) Implement those processes and activities for the respective capacity, defined in the DC framework (6) Set up pre-defined milestones and establish clear responsibilities and process owners (7) Regularly (re-)assess the development of firm´s DCs over time to constantly monitor and maintain the continuous process
III. Entrepreneurial Orientation and Networking Orientation are important antecedents for the development of DCs and RR	III. Implement an organisational structure and culture supportive for entrepreneurial and networking activities	Develop a high Networking Orientation by actively promoting and stressing the firm's willingness to embed close interactions with external entities Develop a high Entrepreneurial Orientation by supporting a positive attitude towards being engaged in entrepreneurial activities	o Implement an organisational culture and group mechanisms that enable staff to engage in dialogues and become involved in entrepreneurial activities. o Foster informal communication, staff exchange and mixed teams, personal networking, and empower groups to contribute to inter-organisational activities o Hire people from different industries and disciplines to orchestrate strong network ties in various business areas o Encourage personal to engage in dialogues, becoming involved in entrepreneurial activities, and participating in the process o Value, and actively contribute to the development of new ideas, support novelty, experimentation, and creative processes o Offer staff training, mentoring programs, support and appropriate incentive systems and hire people passionate about, and experienced in entrepreneurship

7.4   Limitations of the Research

While this research considerably contributes to the resource and competence based research and all aims and objectives as formulated were fully met, it also has some limitations. Consequently research results should be interpreted in the knowledge of its limitations.

First, notwithstanding that a sufficiently large sample size was achieved for the calculation of the structural measurement model, few analyses, namely the multi-group moderation analysis and the measurement model invariance test, necessitated to divide the sample into two sub-groups. Considering the smaller sample size of these sub-groups, the statistical power of the results should be treated with caution (Diamantopoulos and Siguaw, 2000), unless the findings are being confirmed by an independent, preferably larger sample (Plewa, 2010).

Second, one further limitation of this study is also related to the research's approach of obtaining the data. Given the lack of archival data or external objective scales available for measuring the constructs of this study, this research was obliged to rely on self-reported assessments of the respondents. Thus, for the majority of constructs perceptual scales were used. The study hence is limited to this point. To prevent the data from being potentially biased by the subjective evaluation of single respondents, future studies might not only rely on one response from the focal firm's management, but moreover interview a second respondent, or even third parties (Barreto, 2010) in order to gain dyadic data. Alternatively, objective proxies may be consulted, for example, King and Tucci (2002) employed experience measures, which might be appropriate for use in future studies to assess some of the propensities composing the DC construct (Barreto, 2010).

Third, as noted earlier, opposed to the principal nature of SEM, the procedure of model re-specification is not confirmatory but exploratory in nature (Byrne, 2001, Diamantopoulos, 1994, Diamantopoulos and Siguaw, 2000). Even though only slight modifications were made to improve model parsimony (only two additional paths were added), and the changes were justified based on literature, the re-specification may be built on specific peculiarities of the given sample. The re-specified path model is thus limited to the given sample and should therefore be verified by means of an independent sample in the future (Diamantopoulos, 1994, Hoyle and Panter, 1995, Plewa, 2010).

Fourth, the final measurement of the RR construct may encompass further limitations of this study. Due to the lack of alternative, reliable and valid scales for measuring RR in the literature, the construct of RR was conceptualised as a second-order formative construct formed by the four different types of RR, and adopted the scale as originally developed by Zahra and Wiklund (2002). The lack of discriminant validity among the measures intended to capture the four different types of RR, however, led to the elimination of several items for the one-factor congeneric models, and resulted in the use of two-item measures for Type 2, 3, and 4 of RR, and a three-item measure used to measure Type 1 of RR in the final analysis. While the remaining items were assumed to appropriately reflect the nature of the different types of RR as defined and conceptualised for this research, nonetheless the difficulties with the measurement of the RR construct may be related to the unfamiliarity of industrial representatives with the nomenclature and the respective items. Given that RRs can take many forms (Zahra and Wiklund, 2002) alternative proxis for RR, e.g. innovation or creation of new business as applied in past research (Rumelt, 1987), may also be appropriate for assessing single aspects of RR in firms, and may be easier to access by industry. Future researchers therefore should investigate and validate alternative RR measures.

Lastly, as this research focused on resource management practices in UK companies to avoid the impact of national culture issues, the generalisability of the findings to other countries may be limited (Plewa, 2010). Despite the limitations of this research, its contribution to theory and practice is apparent and will be further specified in the following section.

7.5   Contributions of the Research

The overall contribution this research is expected to make is to develop a better understanding of RR in firms from a DC perspective, by exploring the relationships between DCs, the resource base of the firm, and innovation in the form of RR. By means of developing and quantitatively testing a conceptual model of factors that influence RR in firms, this research provided a first empirical investigation of the concept of RR and the construct of DC, presenting a holistic, integrated picture of influencing factors of RR from a DC perspective. With the conceptual model presented, this research offered a more precise definition of the firm's DCs, shedding light on their role and effects towards developing new RRs and separating them from their antecedents and consequences.

With the investigation of the concept of RR from a DC perspective, this PhD research significantly contributes to the resource and competence based research. The primary contributions this research is expected to make, is inherently related to five characteristics of this research, namely (1) the conceptual elaboration of the DC framework, their microfoundations and underlying routines, (2) the empirical investigation of influence of firm's resource endowments and DCs on RR in firms, (3) the empirical analysis of firm- and network-level antecedents for the development of DCs, (4) the qualitative and quantitative research setting, and (5) the integration of the established RBV and the emerging DC literature.

Doing so, the findings contribute to theory and practice by improving the understanding of organisational factors influencing the likelihood of RR to occur. At the same time, by investigating the DCs of the firm and their influence on resource value creation, this research further extends the resource and competence based theory by explicating the role of DCs in the process of RR, which allows to gain insights about the extent to which DC actually account for the variance in firm's performance outcomes. Therewith, this research not only contributes towards opening up the black box of RR in firms, but moreover helps to establish DC as a theoretically, well-founded and useful construct in strategic management theory. Overall, this research makes several contributions to both, theory and practice as outlined below.

7.5.1 Contribution to Theory

The **contribution to theory** this thesis is expected to make can be regarded as follows:

First, by explicitly embedding the DC perspective in resource based explanations for value creation, this research specifies the joint role of (i) a specific set of *DCs of the firm*, and (ii) its *resource endowments* in conjunctly achieving new RR by building and exploiting the potential value of the resources. By explicating how this interrelation affects RR in firms, this research extends resource and competence based theory, as it integrates the DC perspective and the RBV and thus replaces the relative static approaches used in most of the previous research on the RBV. Doing so, this approach contrasts the majority of RBV literature, according to which observable performance differences between firms can primarily be led back to the different resources that are available within the firm at one point in time (Barney, 1991, Grant, 1991, Miller et al., 1996, Freiling et al., 2006). Considering the variety of benefits organisations seek from effectively structuring and managing their resources and bundle them into valuable new RRs in order to leverage their value creation potential (Sirmon et al., 2007), a narrow focus on the availability of valuable resources was deemed overly restrictive. Hence, with the integration of the DC perspectives in the resource based explanations for value creation, specifically looking at the capabilities firm's need to develop to reconfigure and change their current resources, this research works towards the dynamisation of the RBV, and thereby tries to overcome the limitations of past research in this field.

Second, the conceptual model, hypotheses, and discussion presented within this research help to delineate key differences in the role and effects of the specific DCs. With the DC framework established in this research, which explicates a specific set of DCs necessary for the process of RR and enhances the understanding of the microfoundations underlying each capacity, this research established the basis for exploring how these components interact with their environment and what role they have in value creation in firms. By specifically focusing on how DCs build and exploit the firm's resource endowments by leveraging the potential value of those resources through building new RRs, this study expands previous studies of the RBV and DC literature. Hence, explicating that different DCs have different roles and effects on the resource base—Sensing and Learning capacities are working towards building the resource base (*Potential Building DCs*), while Integrating and Coordinating capacities are working towards exploiting the resource base (*Value Realising DCs*)—this research helps to develop an enhanced understanding of DCs and how they operate. Shedding light on how differences in capabilities contribute towards explaining heterogeneity in innovation performance among firms, this research represents a clear extension of the DC literature and contributes to research on its efficiency. Thereby, this research brings clarity in the notion of DCs and offers valuable insights into the source of variance in organisational performance outcomes.

Third, by differentiating specific capabilities and their different effect on different levels in the process of RR, this research extends the DC literature, where most of the previous research studies bunches all DCs together and only provides a quite imprecise picture. Moreover, it goes beyond traditional research by not only looking at the DC constructs but also by investigating the underlying strategic orientation—Entrepreneurial Orientation and Networking Orientation—and its influence on the development of DCs. Hence, with the integration of environmental contingency factors (Entrepreneurial and Networking Orientation) at the same time, it enhances knowledge about the RBV, which has often been criticised for "being insular and overly focused on internal firm attributes" (Sirmon et al., 2007, p.289).

Finally, while some authors have argued that "it is difficult for researchers to fully explain how firms use resources and capabilities to create competitive advantage" (Helfat and Peteraf, 2003, p.997), the conceptual model presented here opens up the black box of RR in firms. This study is one of the few studies in the resource and competence based research adopting SEM method for incorporating the multifaceted effects of resource endowments, DCs, and their antecedents, into the model of RR in firms. Therewith, unlike traditional regression analytical approaches, this research allows to quantitatively test the systematic linkages among these variables (Isobe et al., 2008) and to explain associations between the antecedents to and consequences of DCs in the process of resource value creation in firms. Therewith, this research offers a theoretical and empirical base for new research integrating the DC perspective and RBV, and thus helps to further develop an important area of research, where strategic management and entrepreneurship intersect. Besides, this research has shown that traditional research methodology can be fruitfully applied to RBV (Miller and Shamsie, 1996, Zahra and Wiklund, 2002). Enhancing current knowledge of managing the process of RR in dynamic environments, this research creates a learning opportunity for theorists and practitioners and provides an important contribution to the innovation theory and practice. These results contribute to our understanding of resource management and provide empirical evidence for the importance of a firm's DCs in the RBV.

Summarising, while the impact of resources endowments and DCs on resource value creation in firms has been considered in isolation, their joint interaction effect has never been examined. Integrating knowledge from the established RBV and the emerging DC literature, this research investigated the relation between the different DCs, the resource base and its performance outcomes RR, and thereby provided an essential step towards establishing a coherent theory by means of governing the relationships between constituting variables and therewith providing a more precise, integrated picture on how RRs in firms are build.

7.5.2 Contribution to Practice

Besides its contribution to theory, this research also offers a variety of practical contributions, as the range of managerial implications presented previously has already shown. Earlier research findings have already pointed out, that well-known companies often embark on a 'resource-based strategy', however that this strategy often is not enough to sustain a competitive advantage over time in dynamic environments (Teece et al., 1997, Teece, 2007). Instead findings indicate, that "winners in the global marketplace have been firms that can demonstrate timely responsiveness and rapid and flexible product innovation, coupled with the management capability to effectively coordinate and redeploy internal and external competences" (Teece et al., 1997, p. 515). However up to today, observations of current management practice have shown that the concept of DCs is still not well known, neither sufficiently applied in strategic management. Accordingly, by elaborating on the source of variance in firm performance, this research contributes to establish a better understanding of RR in firms from a DC perspective, and thereby establishes important knowledge for resource management practice, highlighting that as important as the resources themselves are the DCs to build and exploit the value creation potential of the resources.

Therefore, the **contribution to practice** this paper is expected to make, can best be described in the words of Ambrosini et al. (2009, p. 44): "For dynamic capabilities to be a <u>useful</u> construct [for strategic management] it must be feasible to identify discrete processes inside the firm that can be unambiguously causally linked to resource creation." Correspondingly, by investigating a set of specific, measurable DCs, addressing (i) what their underlying processes and routines are, (ii) how certain types of DCs work onto the resource base, and (iii) what their role and effects are in establishing RR in firms, this research offers a detailed elaboration of the DC concept and links it to resource value creation in firms. Doing so, this research delves into the micro mechanisms of DCs, how they are developed, and how they work. Moreover, with the DC framework presented this research offers a simple method for managers to conceptualise, operationalise, and measure DCs in firms and thereby makes a first step towards establishing DC as a theoretically well-founded construct, in order to become one that is also managerial relevant.

The results of this research thus can help managers, (1) to better understand the impact of resource endowments and DCs on everyday resource management practice, (2) to improve organisational efforts for developing DCs, and (3) thereby to create new opportunities for RR in firms. As a result, resource value creation in firms will be better understood by industry and a framework can be built to systematically develop DC in order to utilise the exploitation of the potential lying in RR. In doing so this research addressed Ambrosini and Bowman's direction to further research, who emphasised that generating a deep understanding of "how, in practice, dynamic capabilities are created, (...) would allow us to start developing guidance for managers about how they can deliberately develop dynamic capabilities" (Ambrosini and Bowman, 2009, p. 45).

In brief, the contribution to practice this research is expected to make is first and foremost to establish an enhanced understanding of how resource value is created in firms. With the DC framework presented and the conceptual model applied, this research offers a procedure of practical use that enables firms to develop and evaluate a common RR strategy. Doing so, this research aims to contribute to the business field by providing practically usable results. The desirable function of this methodology would be that the process of RR in firms would not be left to chance—as it is mostly the case in today's businesses—but a framework is provided that can be utilised for the systematic initialisation and exploitation of the value creation potential lying in RR. The intended results are that by strategically developing DCs and applying them to RR management practice, single companies or networks of collaborating 'RR clusters' can create new innovations based on RR principles, define new markets or exploit existing market potentials more sustainable and with less effort in terms of time and financial resources.

7.6   Directions for Future Research

Besides its contributions to theory and practice presented in the previous section, this research provides several directions for future research. While this research significantly contributed to develop a better understanding of RR in firms from a DC perspective, more research on the topic needs to be undertaken before the association between resources, DCs and RR, as well as their antecedents is fully understood and a coherent theory of resource value creation in firms is established. Several important issues emerge, that should be investigated in future research.

First, the relationship between RRs and different levels or kinds of **firm's performance outcomes** (e.g. growth and profitability) deserve empirical investigation in future studies. While there is a consistent claim in literature that RRs acts as a means for creating wealth (Wiklund et al., 2002, Kogut and Zander, 1992, Grant, 1996, Galunic and Rodan, 1998, Wiklund and Shepherd, 2009), only few empirical studies applying RR to firm performance outcomes have been conducted up to date. Further investigating this relationship is of special interest, particularly as researchers have argued, that probably not all RRs may consequently lead to wealth creation in the long run, given that there are also costs associated with their development (Zahra and Wiklund, 2002). Moreover, it might be suggested that different types of RRs may lead to different types of performance outcomes, e.g. Type 1 and 3 might contribute more to operational efficiency, while Type 2 and 4 might rather contribute to strategic performance. Therefore the effect of RRs on different levels or kinds of firm performance merit further examination (Isobe, 2008). Elaborating this relationship will require future studies to gather longitudinal data and also to find adequate ways of taking the costs into account. In the end the results will allow researchers to draw stronger conclusions about the importance of RR activities (Wiklund and Zahra, 2002).

Second, further research should be done to investigate the effect of **environmental dynamics** in the proposed model. While this study controlled for the likely effect of a variety of internal and external factors (e.g. environmental turbulence, company size, company age, etc.) on the development of RR in firms, it did not take the likely effect of environmental dynamics on the development of DCs into account, as suggested by literature (e.g. Teece et al., 1997, Brown and Eisenhardt, 1997). Madsen (2010) for example proposed, that different types of DCs may be working in very different ways, depending on the situation in which the firm founds itself. He further argues, that some capabilities might be more relevant under conditions of major changes in the firm (e.g. Sensing and Learning capacities, as they are associated with *exploration* of new external opportunities and internal knowledge creation), while others might be of greater importance in periods of internal pressure and cost efficiency (e.g. Integrating and Coordinating capacities as they are directed towards the *exploitation* of the existing resources and the development of new reconfigurations) (Madsen, 2010). This would imply that different DCs not only have different, and complementary working modes towards developing RRs, and moreover that internal resources as well as a firm's strategic orientations (its EO and NO) have different effects on the development of DCs, as this research has shown, but moreover that various other situational firm factors may have an effect on how the DCs develop and unfold in practice. A logical effect of this would be that the relative importance and value of the resources and DCs, respectively, is very different across different environments, depending on the dynamics. Taken this research as a basis, future research may therefore evaluate the different environmental contexts that necessitates the possession of different DCs. Moreover, it would be of interest, for example, to study the use and development of DCs in young vs. established firms, or if the use of different types of DCs is different across industries (Ambrosini at al., 2009). On the basis of the theoretical and empirical foundation established in this research, further studies, which take these variables into account, will need to be undertaken.

Third, this research has emphasised the effect of organisational framework conditions on the development of DCs, thereby, however, it only concentrated on firm- and network-level antecedents grounded in the firm's underlying strategic orientation (its EO and NO). While a wide range of different antecedents residing at individual-, firm-, and network-levels have been proposed in the literature (Rothaermel and Hess, 2007, Teece, 2007, Zollo and Winter, 2002, Eisenhardt and Martin, 2000), with some notable exception (e.g. Hawass, 2010, Rothaermel and Hess, 2007), little empirical research can be found, that set out to investigate the antecedent of the development of DCs. More quantitative research is needed on investigating other types of antecedents of the specific DCs, especially on the group, or individual levels. From an organisational behaviour perspective, Hawass (2010) for instance proposes that future research should investigate patterns of **managerial leadership styles** supportive for reconfiguration. Accordingly, a more participative leadership style, which is suggested to motivate individuals to actively contribute in decision making and idea generation, may be argued to build the basis for a structure and culture of transformation and change, and hence stimulate the development of DCs and RRs in firms (Hawass, 2010). On the basis of the proposed measurement model of DC and RR, future research should investigate these linkages. Besides empirically investigating the suggested relationships, future research could also conduct case studies on successful leaders, which have managed to successfully reconfigure their firm's assets.

As outlined above, various directions for future research emerge from this research. While a number of questions remain for future research, the above outlined are only those regarded as most relevant for being addressed from the author's view. In any case, with the DC framework and structural model presented, this research provides a theoretical and empirical base and opens avenues for new, integrative research in an area, which finds itsselves at the forefront of research agendas of many scholars (Zahra et al., 2006, Ambrosini at al., 2009). On this basis, future research should now set out to establish and extend this research's understanding of resource value creation in firms from a DC perspective, its constituting variables, their key drivers, and antecedents. This would be the subsequent step in transforming the DC framework and model presented here into a coherent resource and competence based theory of value creation in firms.

7.7 Chapter Summary

The last chapter elaborated on the research results presented in the previous chapter. Therefore a detailed discussion of the findings that derived from the qualitative and quantitative data analysis, with the latter including model respecification, hypotheses testing, as well as moderation and mediation analyses, was presented. First the findings regarding the influence of the resource endowments for resource value creation in firms were discussed in detail, were thereafter the specific role of DCs in the process of resource value creation and their interrelationships were analysed. This was followed by an in-depth discussion of EO and NO as the antecedents of DCs and RR outcomes. Based on the discussion of research findings, managerial implications were derived, providing recommendations for management, how to strategically foster the development of DCs and the process of RR in firms. Before concluding, limitations of this research were outlined and the contributions this research makes to theory and practice were presented. Finally some directions for future research were given.

Bibliography

Aaker, D. A., Kumar, V., Day, G. S., and Leone, R. (2009) *Marketing Research.* New York: John Wiley & Sons.

Abdi, J. and Williams, L. (2010) 'Principal Component Analysis'. *Wiley Interdisciplinary Reviews: Computational Statistics* 2 (4), 433–459.

Abell, P., Felin, T., and Foss, N. (2008) 'Building micro-foundations for the routines, capabilities, and performance links'. *Managerial and Decision Economics* 29 (6), 489–502.

Abernathy, W. and Utterback, J. (1978) 'Patterns of Industrial Innovation'. *Technological Review* 80 (7), 40–47.

Acs, Z. J. and Audretsch, D. B. (1990) *Innovation and Small Firms.* Cambridge, MA: MIT Press.

Adner, R. and Helfat, C. E. (2003) 'Corporate effects and dynamic managerial capabilities'. *Strategic Management Journal* 24 (10), October Special Issue, 1011–1025.

Ahuja, G. (2000) 'Collaboration networks, structural holes and innovation: a longitudinal study'. *Administrative Science Quarterly* 45 (3), 425–455.

Akaike, H. (1974) 'A New Look at the Statistical Model Identification'. *IEE Transactions on Automatic Control* 19 (6), 716–723.

Albers, S. and Hildebrandt, L. (2006) 'Methodische Probleme bei der Erfolgsfaktorenforschung: Messfehler, formative versus reflective Indikatoren und die Wahl des Strukturgleichungs-Modells'. *Zeitschrift für betriebswirtschaftliche Forschung* 58 (1), 22–33.

Alchian, A. A. and Demsetz, H. (1972) 'Production, Information Costs, and Economic Organization'. *American Sociological Review* 62 (5), 777–795.

Albino, V. and Garavelli, A. (2001) 'A Metric for Measuring Knowledge Codification in Organisation Learning'. *Technovation* 21 (7), 413–422.

Alvarez, S. and Barney, J. B. (2002) 'Resource-based theory and the entrepreneurial firm'. in *Strategic entrepreneurship: Creating a new mindset.* ed. by Hitt, M. A., Ireland, R. D., Camp, S. M. and Sexton, D. L. Oxford: Blackwell, 89–105.

© The Editor(s) (if applicable) and The Author(s), under exclusive license to Springer Fachmedien Wiesbaden GmbH, part of Springer Nature 2021
K. Kurzhals, *Resource Recombination in Firms from a Dynamic Capability Perspective*, Gabler Theses,
https://doi.org/10.1007/978-3-658-35666-8

Ambrosini, V. and Bowman, C. (2009) 'What are dynamic capabilities and are they a useful constructs in strategic management'. *International Journal of Management Reviews* 11 (1), 29–49.

Ambrosini, V., Bowman, C., and Collier, N. (2009) 'Dynamic Capabilities: An Exploration of how Firms Renew their Resource Base'. *British Journal of Management* 20 (S1), 9–24.

Amit, R. and Schoemaker, P. J. H. (1993) 'Strategic Assets and Organizational Rent'. *Strategic Management Journal* 14 (1), 33–46.

Anderson, J. and Gerbing, D. (1984) 'The Effect of Sampling Error on Convergence, Improper Solutions, and Goodness-of-Fit Indices for Maximum Likelihood in Confirmatory Factor Analysis'. *Psychometrika* 49 (2), 155–173.

Arbuckle, J. and Wothke, W. (1999) *AMOS 4.0 User's Guide*. Chicago: Small Waters.

Argote, L. and Ren, Y. (2012) 'Transactive memory systems: a micro foundation of dynamic capabilities'. *Journal of Management Studies* 49 (8), p. 1375–1382.

Argote, L., McEvily, B., and Reagans, R. (2003) 'Managing knowledge in organizations: an integrative framework and review of emerging themes'. *Management Science* 49 (1), 571–582.

Armstrong, J. S. and Overton, T. S. (1977) 'Estimating Nonresponse Bias in Mail Surveys'. *Journal of Marketing Research* 14 (3), 396–402.

Arrindell, W. and van der Ende, J. (1985) 'An Empirical Test of the Utilities of the Observations-to-Variables Ratio in Factor and Component Analysis'. *Applied Psychological Measurement* 2 (9), 165–178.

Atuahene-Gima, K. (2005) 'Resolving the Capability—Rigidity Paradox in New Product Innovation'. *Journal of Marketing* 69 (4), 61–83.

Atuahene-Gima, K., Slater, S. F. and Olson, E. M. (2005) 'The contingent value of responsive and proactive market orientations for new product program performance'. *Journal of Product Innovation Management* 22 (6), 464–82.

Augier, M. and Teece, D. (2007) 'Dynamic Capabilities and Multinational Enterprise. Penrosean Insights and Omissions'. *Management International Review* 47 (2), 175–192.

Backhaus, K., Erichson, B., and Weiber, R. (2010) *Fortgeschrittene Multivariate Analysemethoden: Eine Anwendungsorientierte Einführung*. 2nd edn. Berlin: Springer.

Backhaus, K., Erichson, B., Plinke, W., and Weiber, R. (2008) *Multivariate Analysemethoden: Eine Anwendungsorientierte Einführung*. 12th edn. Berlin: Springer.

Bagozzi, R. P. (1994) 'Structural equation models in marketing research: basic principles'. in *Principles of marketing research*. ed. by Bagozzi, R. P. Oxford: Blackwell, 317–385.

Baker, W. E. and Sinkula, J. M. (2009) 'The Complementary Effects of Market Orientation and Entrepreneurial Orientation on Profitability in Small Businesses'. *Journal of Small Business Management* 47 (4), 443–464.

Barney, J. B. (1986) 'Strategic factor markets: Expectations, luck and business strategy'. *Management Science* 32 (10), 1231–1241.

Barney, J. B. (1991) 'Firm Resources and Sustained Competitive Advantage'. *Journal of Management* 17 (1), 99–120.

Barney, J. B. and Arikan, A. M. (2001) 'The resource-based view: origins and implications'. in *The Blackwell Handbook of Strategic Management*, ed. by Hitt, M. A., Freeman, R. E. and Harrison, J. S. Malden, MA: Blackwell Publishers, 124–188.

Baron, R. M. and Kenny, D. A. (1986) 'The moderator-mediator variable distinction in social psychological research: Conceptual, strategic and statistical considerations'. *Journal of Personality and Social Psychology* 51 (6), 1173–1182.

Barreto, I. (2010) 'Dynamic Capabilities: A Review of Past Research and an Agenda for the Future'. *Journal of Management* 36 (1), 256–280.

Baum, J. A. C., Calabrese, T., and Silverman, B. S. (2000) 'Don't go it alone: Alliance network composition and startups' performance in Canadian biotechnology'. *Strategic Management Journal* 21 (3), 267–294.

Baumgartner, H. and Homburg, C. (1996) 'Applications of Structural Equation Modelling in Marketing and Consumer Research: A Review'. *International Journal of Research in Marketing* 13 (2), 139–161.

Baumol, W. J. (1993) *Entrepreneurship, Management and the Structure of Payoffs.* Cambridge, MA: MIT Press.

Bell, C. (1991) *High-Tech Ventures: The Guide for Entrepreneurial Success.* Reading, MA: Addison-Wesley.

Bendapudi, N. and Leone, R. P. (2002) 'Managing Business-to-Business Customer Relationships Following Key Contact Employee Turnover in a Vendor Firm'. *Journal of Marketing* 66 (2), 83–101.

Bidhé, A. V. (2000) *The origin and evolution of New Business.* Oxford University Press.

Bierly, P. and Chakrabarti, A. (1996) 'Generic Knowledge Strategies in the U.S. Pharmaceutical Industry' *Strategic Management Journal* 17 (Winter Special Issue), 123–135.

Birkinshaw, J., Nobel, R., and Ridderstråle, J. (2002) 'Knowledge as a Contingency Variable: Do the Characteristics of Knowledge Predict Organizational Structure?'. *Organization Science* 13 (3), 274–289.

Björk, J., and Magnusson, M. (2008) 'Heterogeneity and performance in innovation idea networks', Proceedings of the 9th CINet Conference, September 6–9 , Valencia, Spain.

Black, J. A. and Boal, K. B. (1994) 'Strategic Resources: Traits, Configurations and Paths to Sustainable Competitive Advantage'. *Strategic Management Journal* 15 (1), 131–148.

Boer, H. (2004) 'Organising for continuous innovation'. in *Fremtidens produktion i Denmark.* ed. by Johansen, J. and Riis, J. O. Copenhagen: Dansk Industri, 77–99.

Bollen, K. (1984) 'Multiple Indicators: Internal Consistency Or no Necessary Relationship?'. *Quality and Quantity* 18 (4), 377–385.

Bollen, K. (1989) *Structural Equations with Latent Variables.* New York: Wiley.

Bollen, K. and Lennox, R. (1991) 'Conventional Wisdom on Measurement: A Structural Equation Perspective'. *Psychological Bulletin* 110 (2), 305–314.

Bollen, K. and Long, J. (1993) *Testing Structural Equation Models.* Newburry Park: Sage Publications.

Borch, O. J. and Madsen, E. L. (2007) 'Dynamic capabilities facilitating innovative strategies in SMEs', *International Journal of Technoentrepreneurship* 1 (1), 109–125.

Bouette, R. D. (2004) *Creative Coupling Programme.* Melbourne: Ingara Technology Strategies Pty Ltd.

Bower, J. L. (1970) *Managing the resource allocation process: A study of corporate planning and investment.* Cambridge, MA: Harvard University Press.

Bowman, C. and Ambrosini, V. (2000) 'Value Creation Versus Value Capture: Towards a Coherent Definition of Value in Strategy'. *British Journal of Management* 11 (1), 1–15.

Breckler, S. (1990) 'Applications of Covariances Structure Modelling in Psychology: Cause for Concern?'. *Psychological Bulletin* 107 (2), 260–273.

Brosius, F. (2004) *SPSS 12*. Bonn: mitp-Verlag.

Brown, R. H. and Garten, J. E. (1994). U.S. industrial outlook: An almanac of industry, technology and services (35th ed.). Austin, Texas: Reference Press.

Brown, S. L., and Eisenhardt, K. M. (1997) 'The art of continuous change: Linking complexity theory and time-paced evolution in relentlessly shifting organizations'. *Administrative Science Quarterly* 42 (1), 1–34.

Brown, T. E., Davidsson, P., and Wiklund, J. (2001) 'An Operationalization of Stevenson's Conceptualization of Entrepreneurship as Opportunity-Based Firm Behavior'. *Strategic Management Journal* 22 (10), 953–968.

Browne, M. and Cudeck, R. (1993) 'Alternative Ways of Assessing Model Fit'. in *Testing Structural Equation Models*. ed. by Bollen, K. and Long, J. Newbury Park: Sage, 136–161.

Buffa, E. (1982) 'Research in operations management'. *Journal of Operations Management* 1 (1), 1–7.

Burnett, B. (2009) 'Building New Knowledge and the Role of Synthesis in Innovation'. *International Journal of Innovation Science* 1 (1), 13–27.

Burr, W. and Stephan, M. (2006) *Dienstleistungsmanagement: Innovative Wertschöpfungskonzepte Im Dienstleistungssektor*. Stuttgart: Kohlhammer.

Byrne, B. M. (2001) *Structural Equation Modelling with Amos: Basic Concepts, Applications and Programming*. Mahwah, New Jersey: Lawrence Erlbaum Associates.

Cadogan, J. W. and Lee, N. (2013) 'Improper use of Endogenous Formative Variables'. *Journal of Business Research* 66 (2), 233–241.

Capron, L., Dussauge, P., and Mitchell, W. (1998) 'Resource Redeployment Following Horizontal Acquisitions in Europe and North America, 1988–1992'. *Strategic Management Journal* 19 (7), 631–661

Carson, D. and Coviello, N. (1996) 'Qualitative Research Issues at the Marketing/ Entrepreneurship Interface'. *Marketing Intelligence & Planning* 14 (6), 51–58.

Carson, D., Gilmore, A., Perry, C., and Gronhaug, K. (2001) *Qualitative Marketing Research*. 1st edn. London: Sage Publications.

Cenfetelli, R. T. and Bassellier, G. (2009) 'Interpretation of formative measurement in information systems research'. *MIS Quarterly*, 33 (4), 689–707.

Chandler, A. D., Jr. (1962) *Strategy and Structure: Chapters in the History of the American Industrial Enterprise*. Cambridge, MA: Harvard University Press.

Chang, S., van Witteloostuijn, A., and Eden, L. (2010) 'From the Editors: Common Method Variance in International Business Research'. *Journal of International Business Studies* 41 (2), 178–184.

Chesbrough, H. W. (2003). *Open Innovation: The new imperative for creating and profiting from technology*. Boston, MA: Harvard Business School Press.

Chesbrough, H. W. (2006). *Open business models: How to thrive in the new innovation landscape*. Boston, MA: Harvard Business School Press.

Child, D. (1990) The Essentials of Factor Analysis. 2nd edn. London: Cassel Educational Limited.

Chockburn, I.M., Henderson, R.M., Stern, S. (2000) 'Untangling the origins of competitive advantage'. *Strategic Management Journal* 21 (10–11), Special Issue, 1123–1145.

Christensen, C. (1997) *The Innovator's Dilemma: When New Technologies Cause Great Firms to Fail*. Cambridge, MA: Harvard Business School Press.

Christensen, C. and Bower, J. (1996) 'Customer power, strategic investment, and the failure of leading firms'. *Strategic Management Journal*, 17(3), 197–218.

Coakes, S .J. and Steed, L. G. (2003) *SPSS: Analysis without Anguish*. Milton, QLD: John Wiley & Sons Australia Ltd.

Cohen, W. M. and Levinthal, D. A. (1990) 'Absorptive Capacity: A New Perspective on Learning and Innovation'. *Administrative Science Quarterly* 35 (1), 128–152.

Collis, D. J. (1994) 'Research note: how valuable are organizational capabilities?' *Strategic Management Journal* 15, Winter Special Issue, 143–152.

Conner, K. R. and Prahalad, C. K. (1996) 'A Resource-Based Theory of the Firm: Knowledge Versus Opportunism'. *Organization Science* 7 (5), 477–501.

Connor, T. (1999) 'Customer-led and market-oriented: A matter of balance'. *Strategic Management Journal* 20 (12), 1157–1163.

Conway, S. (1995) 'Informal boundary-spanning communication in the innovation process: an empirical study'. *Technology Analysis and Strategic Management* 7 (3), 327–342.

Cooley, W. and Lohnes, P. (1971) Multivariate Data Analysis.: John Wiley & Sons Inc.

Coombs, R. and Hull, R. (1998) 'Knowledge Management Practices' and Path-Dependency in Innovation'. *Research Policy* 27 (3), 237–253.

Cortina, J. (1993) 'What is Coefficient Alpha? an Examination of Theory and Applications'. *Journal of Applied Psychology* 78 (1), 98–104.

Costello, A. and Osborne, J. (2005) 'Best Practices in Exploratory Factor Analysis: Four Recommendations for Getting the most from Your Analysis'. *Practical Assessment Research & Evaluation* 10 (7), 1–9.

Covin, J. and Miles, M. (1999) 'Corporate Entrepreneurship and the Pursuit of Competitive Advantage'. *Entrepreneurship: Theory and Practice* 23 (3), 47–63.

Covin, J. G. and Slevin, D. P (1991) 'A conceptual model of entrepreneurship as firm behavior'. *Entrepreneurship Theory and Practice* 16 (1), 7–26.

Covin, J. G. and Slevin, D. P. (1989) 'Strategic Management of Small Firms in Hostile and Benign Environments'. *Strategic Management Journal* 10 (1), 75–98.

Creswell, J. W. (2009) *Research Design: Qualitative, Quantitative and Mixed Methods Approaches*. 3rd edn. Thousand Oaks: Sage.

Crowston, K. and Kammerer, E. E. (1998) 'Coordination and collective mind in software requirements development'. *IBM Systems Journal* 37 (2), 227–245.

Currall, C. C. and Inkpen, A. C. (2002) 'A Multilevel Approach to Trust in Joint Ventures'. *Journal of International Business Studies* 33 (3) 479–495.

D'Aveni, R. (1994) *Hypercompetition: Managing the dynamics of strategic maneuvering*. New York: Free Press.

Dahlander, L. and Gann, D. M (2010). 'How open is innovation?'. *Research Policy* 39 (6), 699–709.

Danneels, E. (2007) 'The Process of Technological Competence Leveraging'. *Strategic Management Journal* 28 (5), 511–533.

Danneels, E. (2008) 'Organizational Antecedents of Second-Order Competences'. *Strategic Management Journal* 29 (5), 519–543.

Day, G. (1994) 'The Capabilities of Market-Driven Organizations'. *Journal of Marketing* 58 (4), 37–52.

De Luca, L. M. and Atuahene-Gima, K. (2007) 'Market Knowledge Dimensions and Cross-Functional Collaboration: Examining the Different Routes to Product Innovation Performance'. *Journal of Marketing* 71 (1), 95–112.

DeCarlo, L. (1997) 'On the Meaning and use of Kurtosis'. *Psychological Methods* 2 (3), 292–307.

Decarolis, D. M. and Deeds, D. L. (1999) 'The impact of stocks and flows of organizational knowledge on firm performance: an empirical investigation of the biotechnology industry', *Strategic Management Journal* 20 (10), 953–968.

DeCoster, J. (1998) Overview of Factor Analysis [online] available from <http://www.stat-help.com/notes.html> [07/2013].

Demsetz, H. (1988) 'The theory of the firm revisited'. *Journal of Law, Economics, and Organization* 4 (1), 141–161.

Denrell, J., Fang, C. and Winter, S. G. (2003) 'The economics of strategic opportunity'. *Strategic Management Journal* 24 (10), October Special Issue, 977–990.

Diamantopoulos, A. (1994) 'Modelling with LISREL: A Guide for the Uninitiated'. *Journal of Marketing Management* 10 (1–3), 105–136.

Diamantopoulos, A. and Riefler, P., and Roth, K. P. (2008) 'Advancing Formative Measurement Models'. *Journal of Business Research* 61 (12), 1203–1218.

Diamantopoulos, A. and Siguaw, J. A. (2000) *Introducing Lisrel: A Guide for the Uninitiated.* London: Sage Publications.

Diamantopoulos, A. and Siguaw, J. A. (2006) 'Formative versus reflective indicators in organizational measure development: a comparison and empirical illustration'. *British Journal of Management* 17 (4), 263–82.

Diamantopoulos, A. and Winklhofer, H. M. (2001) 'Index Construction with Formative Indicators: An Alternative to Scale Development'. *Journal of Marketing Research* 38 (2), 269–277.

Dierickx, I. and Cool, K. (1989) 'Asset stock accumulation and sustainability of competitive advantage'. *Management Science* 35 (12), 1504–1510.

Dosi, G., Faillo, M., and Marengo, L. (2008) 'Organizational capabilities, patterns of knowledge accumulation and governance structures in business firms: An introduction'. *Organization Studies* 29 (8–9), 1165–1185.

Dosi, G., Nelson, R., and Winter, S. (2000) 'Introduction: The Nature and Dynamics of Organizational Capabilities'. in *The Nature and Dynamics of Organizational Capabilities,* ed. by Dosi, G., Nelson, R., and Winter, S., New York.

Dougherty, D. (1992) 'Interpretive barriers to successful product innovation in large firms'. *Organization Science* 3 (2), 179–202.

Dyer, J. H. and Singh, H. (1998) 'The relational view: Cooperative strategy and sources of inter-organizational competitive advantage'. *Academy of Management Review* 23 (4), 660–679.

Eberl, M. (2004) *Formative und reflektive Indikatoren im Forschungsprozess: Entscheidungsregeln und die Dominanz des refelektiven Modells.* München: Institut für Marktorientierte Unternehmensführung.

Edmondson, A. C. and McManus, S. E. (2007) 'Methodological Fit in Management Field Research'. *Academy of Management Review* 32 (4), 1155–1179.

Edwards, J. R. and Bagozzi R. P. (2000) 'On the nature and direction of relationships between constructs and measures'. *Psychological Methods* 5 (2), 155–174.

Eisenhardt, K. M. and Brown, S. (1999). 'Patching: Restitching business portfolios in dynamic markets'. *Harvard Business Review* 77 (1), 72–82.

Eisenhardt, K. M. and Galunic, D. C. (2000) 'Coevolving: at last, a way to make synergies work'. *Harvard Business Review* 78 (1), 91–101.

Eisenhardt, K. M. and Martin, J. A. (2000) 'Dynamic Capabilities: What are they?'. *Strategic Management Journal* 21 (10/11), Special Issue: The Evolution of Firm Capabilities, 1105–1121.

Fabrigar, L., Wegener, D., MacCallum, R., and Strahan, E. (1999) 'Evaluating the use of Exploratory Factor Analysis in Psychological Research'. *Psychological Methods* 4 (3), 272–299.

Fan, X. and Sivo, S. (2005) 'Sensitivity of Fit Indexes to Misspecified Structural Or Measurement Model Components: Rationale of Two-Index Strategy Revisited'. *Structural Equation Modeling* 12 (3), 343–367.

Farris, P., Parry, M., and Ailawadi, K. (1992) 'Structural Analysis of Models with Composite Dependent Variables'. *Marketing Science* 11 (1), 76–94.

Fassot, G. and Eggert, A. (2005) 'Zur Verwendung formativer und reflektiver Indikatoren in Strukturgleichungsmodellen: Bestandaufnahme und Anwendungsempfehlung'. in *Handbuch PLS-Modellierung, Methode, Anwendung, Praxisbeispiele*. ed. by Bliemel, F. W., Eggert, A., Fassot, G., and Henseler, J. Stuttgart: Schaeffer-Poeschel, 31–47.

Felin, T. and Foss, N. J. (2005) 'Strategic organization: A field in search of micro-foundations'. *Strategic Organization* 3 (4), 441–455.

Felin, T., Foss, N. J., Heimeriks, K. H., and Madsen, T. L. (2012) 'Microfoundations of Routines and Capabilities: Individuals, Processes, and Structure'. *Journal of Management Studies* 49 (8), 1351–1374.

Fern, E. F. (1982) 'The use of Focus Groups for Idea Generation: The Effects of Group Size, Acquaintanceship, and Moderator on Response Quantity and Quality'. *Journal of Marketing Research* 19 (1), 1–13.

Field, A. (2000) *Discovering Statistics using SPSS for Windows*. New Delhi: Sage Publications.

Fleishman, J. and Benson, J. (1987) 'Using LISREL to Evaluate Measurement Models and Scale Reliability'. *Educational and Psychological Measurement* 47 (4), 925–939.

Flint, D. J., Woodruff, R. B., and Gardial, S. F. (2002) 'Exploring the Phenomenon of Customers' Desired Value Change in a Business-to-Business Context'. *Journal of Marketing* 66 (4), 102–117.

Fombrun, C. J. and Ginsberg, A. (1990) 'Shifting gears: Enabling change in corporate aggressiveness'. *Strategic Management Journal* 11 (4), 297–308.

Fornell, C. and Larcker, D. (1981) 'Evaluating Structural Equation Models with Unobservable Variables and Measurement Error'. *Journal of Marketing Research* 18 (1), 39–50.

Foss, N. J. (1996) 'More Critical Comments on Knowledge-Based Theories of the Firm'. *Organization Science* 7 (5), 519–523.

Foster, R. (1986) *The Attacker's Advantage*. New York, NY: Summit Books.

Fowler, S. W., King, A. W., Marsh, S. J. and Victor, B. (2000) 'Beyond products: new strategic imperatives for developing competencies in dynamic environments'. *Journal of Engineering and Technology Management* 17 (3–4), 357–377.

Freiling, J., Gersch, M., and Goeke, C. (2006) 'Eine "Competence-Based Theory of the Firm" als Marktprozesstheoretischer Ansatz'. in *Management von Kompetenz*. ed. by Schreyögg, G. and Conrad, P. Wiesbaden: Gabler, 37–82.

Frohlich, M. and Westbrook, R. (2001) 'Arcs of Integration: An International Study of Supply Chain Strategies'. *Journal of Opertaions Management* 19 (2), 185–200.

Galunic, D. C. and Eisenhardt, K. M. (1994) 'Renewing the strategy–structure–performance Paradigm'. in *Reserch in Organizational Behavior. ed. by* Cummings, L. and Staw, B. Greenwich: JAI Press, 215–255.

Galunic, D. C. and Eisenhardt, K. M. (2001) 'Architectural Innovation and Modular Corporate Forms'. *Academy of Management Journal* 44 (6), 1229–1249.

Galunic, D. C. and Rodan, S. (1998) 'Resource Recombinations in the Firm: Knowledge Structures and the Potential for Schumpeterian Innovation'. *Strategic Management Journal* 19 (12), 1193–1201.

Garson, G. D. (2012) *Structural Equation Modeling*. Asheboro, NC: Statistical Associates Publishers.

Garud, R. and Nayyar, P. (1994) 'Transformative Capacity: Continual Structuring by Intertemporal Technology Transfer'. *Strategic Management Journal* 15 (5), 365–385.

Gaskin, J. (2012a) Data Screening, Gaskination's StatWiki. [online] available from <http://statwiki.kolobkreations.com> [07/2013].

Gaskin, J. (2012b) Exploratory Factor Analysis, Gaskination's StatWiki [online] available from <http://statwiki.kolobkreations.com> [07/2013].

Gaskin, J. (2012c) Confirmatory Factor Analysis, Gaskination's StatWiki. [online] available from <http://statwiki.kolobkreations.com> [07/2013].

Gaskin, J. (2012d) Structural Equation Modeling, Gaskination's StatWiki. [online] available from <http://statwiki.kolobkreations.com> [07/2013].

Gaskin, J. and Lyytinen, K. (2011) Explorative Factor Analysis (EFA) [online] available from <http://www.kolobkreations.com/Factor%20Analysis.pptx> [07/2013].

Gavetti, G. (2005) 'Cognition and hierarchy: rethinking the microfoundations of capabilities' development'. *Organization Science* 16 (6), 599–617.

Gefen, D., Straub, D., and Boudreau, M. (2000) 'Structural Equation Modeling and Regression: Guidelines for the Research Practice'. *Communications of the Association for Information Systems* 4 (7), 1–78.

Germain, R. and Dröge, C. (1997) 'An Empirical Study of the Impact of Just-in-Time Task Scope Versus Just-in-Time Workflow Integration on Organizational Design'. *Decision Sciences* 28 (3), 615–635.

Gluck, F. (1981) 'The dilemmas of resource allocation' *The Journal of Business Strategy* 2 (2), 67–71.

Graebner, M. (2004) 'Momentum and Serendipity: How Acuired Leaders Create Value in the Integration of Technology Firms'. *Strategic Management Journal* 25 (8), 751–777.

Grandstrand, O. and Sjölander, S. (1990) 'Managing Innovation in Multi-Technology Corporations'. *Research Policy* 19 (1), 35–60.

Grant, R. M. (1991) 'The Resource-Based Theory of Competitive Advantage: Implications for Strategy Formulation'. *California Management Review* 33 (3), 114–135.

Grant, R. M. (1996) 'Toward a Knowledge-Based Theory of the Firm' *Strategic Management Journal* 17 (Winter Special Issue), 109–122.

Gulati, R. (1998) 'Alliances and networks'. *Strategic Management Journal* 19 (4), 293–317.

Gulati, R. (1999) 'Network location and learning: The influence of network resources and firm capabilities on alliance formation'. *Strategic Management Journal* 20 (5), 397–420.

Gulati, R., Nohria, N., and Zaheer, A. (2000) 'Strategic networks'. *Strategic Management Journal* 21 (3), 103–215.

Gupta, A. K. and Govindarajan, V. (2000) 'Knowledge Flows within Multinational Corporations'. *Strategic Management Journal* 21 (4), 473–496.

Guth, W. D. and Ginsberg, A. (1990) 'Guest Editors' Introduction: Corporate Entrepreneurship'. *Strategic Management Journal* 11 (4), 5–15.

Hair, J., Anderson, R., Tatham, R., and Black, W. (1998) *Multivariate Data Analysis*. Upper Saddle River, New Jersey: Prentice-Hall Inc.

Hair, J., Black, W., Babin, B., and Anderson, R. (2010) *Multivariate Data Analysis*. 7th edn. Upper Saddle River, New Jersey: Prentice-Hall Inc.

Hall, R. (1991) 'The Contribution of Intangible Resources to Business Success'. *Journal of General Management* 6 (4), 41–52.

Hall, R. (1994) 'A Framework for Identifying the Intangible Sources of Sustainable Competitive Advantage'. in *Competence-Based Competition*. ed. by Hamel, G. and Heene, A. New York.

Hamel, G. and Prahalad, C. K. (1994) *Competing for the Future*. Boston, MA: Harvard Business School Press.

Hansen, M. H., Perry, L. T., and Reese, C. S. (2004) 'A Bayesian Operationalization of the Resource-Based View'. *Strategic Management Journal* 25 (13), 1279–1295.

Hardin, A. M., Chang, J. C., Fuller, M. A., and Torkzadeh, G. (2010). 'Formative Measurement and Academic Research'. *Educational and Psychological Measurement* 71 (2), 281–305.

Hargadon, A. (2002) 'Brokering knowledge: Linking learning and innovation'. *Research in Organizational Behavior* 24 (1), 41–85.

Harrison, J. S., Hitt, M. A., Hoskisson, R. E., and Ireland, R. D. (1991) 'Synergies and post-acquisition performance: Differences versus similarities in resource allocations'. *Journal of Management* 17 (1), 173–190.

Harrison, J. S., Hitt, M. A., Hoskisson, R. E., and Ireland, R. D. (2001) 'Resource complementarity in business combinations: Extending the logic to organizational alliances', *Journal of Management* 27 (6), 679–690.

Hatzichronoglou, T. (1997) 'Revision of the High-Technology Sector and Product Classification'. Technology and Industry Working Paper, Paris: OECD Science.

Hau, K. (1995) 'Confirmatory Factor Analyses of Seven Locus of Control Measures'. *Journal of Personality Assessment* 65 (1), 117–132.

Hawass, H. H. (2010) 'Exploring the Determinants of the Reconfiguration Capability: A Dynamic Capability Perspective'. *European Journal of Innovation Management* 13 (4), 409–438.

Hayes, A. and Matthes, J. (2009) 'Computational Procedures for Probing Interactions in OLS and Logistic Regression: SPSS and SAS Implementations'. *Behavioral Research Methods* 41 (3), 924–936.

Helfat, C. E. and Peteraf, M. A. (2003) 'The Dynamic Resource-Based View: Capability Lifecycles'. *Strategic Management Journal* 24 (4), 997–1010.

Helfat, C. E. and Winter, S. G. (2011) 'Untangling Dynamic and Operational Capabilities: Strategy for the (N)ever-Changing World'. *Strategic Management Journal* 32 (11), 1243–1250.

Helfat, C. E., and Peteraf, M. A. (2009) 'Understanding dynamic capabilities: Progress along a developmental path'. *Strategic Organization* 7 (1), 91–102.

Helfat, C. E., Finkelstein, S., Mitchell, W., Peteraf, M., Singh, H., Teece, D., and Winter, S. (2007) *Dynamic Capabilities: Understanding Strategic Change in Organizations*. Malden, MA [u. a.]: Blackwell.

Henderson, R. M. (1994) 'The evolution of integrative capability: Innovation in cardiovascular drug discovery'. *Industrial and Corporate Change* 3 (3), 607–630.

Henderson, R. M. and Clark, K. B. (1990) 'Architectural Innovation: The Reconfiguration of Existing Product Technologies and the Failure of Established Firms'. *Administrative Science Quarterly* 35 (1), 9–30.

Henderson, R. M. and Cockburn, I. (1994) 'Measuring Competence? Exploring Firm Effects in Pharmaceutical Research'. *Strategic Management Journal* 15 (1), 63–84.

Hewett, K., Money, R., and Sharma, S. (2002) 'An Exploration of the Moderating Role of Buyer Corporate Culture in Industrial Buyer-Seller Relationships'. *Journal of the Academy of Marketing Science* 30 (3), 229–239.

Hildebrandt, L. and Temme, D. (2006) 'Probleme der Validierung mit Strukturgleichungsmodellen '. SFB 649 Discussion Paper, Berlin: Humboldt-Universität zu Berlin.

Hitt, M. A. and Ireland, R. D. (2000) 'The Intersection of Entrepreneurship and Strategic Management Research'. in *The Blackwell Handbook of Entrepreneurship*. ed. by Sexton, D. L. and Landström, H. Oxford, U.K.: Blackwell Business, 45–63.

Hitt, M. A., Harrison, J. S., and Ireland, R. D. (2001) *Mergers and acquisitions: A guide to creating value for shareholders*. New York: Oxford University Press.

Hitt, M. A., Hoskisson R. E., Ireland R. D., and Harrison, J. S. (1991) 'Effects of acquisitions on R&D inputs and outputs'. *Academy of Management Journal* 34 (3), 693–706.

Holcomb, T. R., Holmes, Jr., R. M., and Connelly, B. L. (2009) 'Making the most of what You have: Managerial Ability as a Source of Resource Value Creation'. *Strategic Management Journal* 30 (5), 457–485.

Homburg, C. and Dobratz, A. (1991) 'Iterative Modellselektion in der Kausalanalyse'. *Zeitschrift für betriebswirtschaftliche Forschung* 43 (3), 213–237.

Hoogland, J. and Boomsma, A. (1998) 'Robustness Studies in Covariance Structure Modeling'. *Sociological Methods & Research* 26 (3), 329–367.

Hooper, D., Coughlan, J., and Mullen, M. (2007) 'Structural Equation Modelling: Guidelines for Determining Model Fit'. *Electronic Journal of Business Research Methods* 6 (1), 53–60.

Horx, M. (2011) *Das Megatrend-Prinzip: Wie die Welt von morgen entsteh*. Frankfurt: Deutsche Verlags-Anstalt.

Hoyle, R. and Panter, A. (1995) 'Writing about Structural Equation Models'. in *Structural Equation Modelling: Concepts, Issues, and Applications, Thousand*. ed. by Hoyle, R. Thousand Oaks: Sage Publications, 158–179.

Hu, L. and Bentler, P. (1995) 'Evaluating Model Fit'. in *Structural Equation Modelling: Concepts, Issues, and Applications*. ed. by Hoyle, R. Thousand Oaks: Sage Publications, 76–99.

Hu, L. and Bentler, P. (1998) 'Fit Indices in Covariance Structure Modeling: Sensi-Tivity to Underparameterized Model Misspecification'. *Psychological Methods* 3 (4), 424–453.

Huberman, M.A. and Miles, M.B. (1994) 'Data Management and Analysis Methods', in Handbook of Qualitatve Research. ed. by.. Denzin N.K and Lincoln Y.S.: Thousand Oaks: Sage Publications, 428–445.

Hulin, C., Cudeck, R., Netemeyer, R., Dillon, W., McDonald, R., and Bearden, W. (2001) 'Measurement'. *Journal of Consumer Psychology* 10 (1–2), 55–69.

Iansiti, M. and Clark, K. (1994) 'Integration and dynamic capability: Evidence from product development in automobiles and mainframe computers'. *Industrial and Corporate Change* 3 (3), 557–605

Mathews, T., Makino, S., and Montgomery, D. B. (2008) 'Technological Capabilities and Firm Performance: The Case of Small Manufacturing Firms in Japan'. *Asia Pacific Journal of Management* 25 (3), 413–428.

Jaccard, J. and Wan, C. (1996) *LISREL Approaches to Interaction Effects in Multiple Regression*. Newbury Park: Sage.

Jahn, S. (2007) *Strukturgleichungsmodellierung mit LISREL, AMOS Und SmartPLS—Eine Einführung*. Chemnitz: Technische Universität Chemnitz.

Jansen, J. J. P., van den Bosch, F. A. J. and Volberda, H. W. (2005) 'Managing potential and realized absorptive capacity: how do organizational antecedents matter?'. *Academy of Management Journal* 48 (1), 999–1015.

Jarvis, C. B., MacKenzie, S. B., and Podsakoff, P. M. (2003) 'A Critical Review of Construct Indicators and Measurement Model Misspecification in Marketing and Consumer Research'. *Journal of Consumer Research* 30 (2), 199–218.

Jaworski, B. J. and Kohli, A. K. (1993) 'Market Orientation: Antecedents and Consequences'. *Journal of Marketing* 57 (2), 53–71.

Jekel, J., Katz, D., Wild, D., and Elmore, J. (2007) *Epidemiology, Biostatistics and Preventive Medicine*. 3rd edn. Philadelphia: Saunders Elsevier Inc.

Jöreskog, K. (1993) 'Testing Structural Equation Models'. in *Testing Structural Equation Models*. ed. by Bollen, K. and Long, J. Newbury Park: Sage Publications, 294–316.

Jöreskog, K. and Sörbom, D. (1989) *LISREL 7: User's Reference Guide*. Mooresville: Scientific Software Iternational.

Jöreskog, K. and Sörbom, D. (1996) *LISREL 8: Structural Equation Modeling with the SIMPLIS Command Language*. Chicago: Scientific Software International.

Jöreskog, K. and Yang, F. (1996) 'Non-Linear Structural Equation Models: The Kenny—Judd Model with Interaction Effects'. in *Advanced Structural Equation Modeling. Issues and Techniques*. ed. by Macoulides, G. and Schumacker, R. Hillside: Erlbaum, 57–88.

Kaiser, H. (1974) 'An Index of Factorial Simplicity'. *Psychometrika* 39 (1), 31–36.

Kaplan, D. (1990) 'Evaluating and Modifying Covariance Structure Models: A Review and Recommendations'. *Multivariate Behavioural Research* 25 (2), 137–155.

Karim, S. and Mitchell, W. (2000) 'Path-dependent and path-breaking changes: Configuring business resources following acquisitions in the U.S. medical sector, 1978–1995'. *Strategic Management Journal* 21 (10–11), 1061–1081.

Katila, R. and Ahuja, G. (2002) 'Something old, something new: A longitudinal study of search behavior and new product introduction'. *Academy of Management Journal* 45 (6), 1183–1194.

Khilji, S. E., Mroczkowski, T. and Bernstein, B. (2006) 'From invention to innovation: toward developing an integrated innovation model for biotech firms'. *Journal of Product Innovation Management* 23 (6), 528–540.

King, A. A. and Tucci, C. L. (2002) 'Incumbent entry into new market niches: The role of experience and managerial choice in the creation of dynamic capabilities'. *Management Science* 48, 171–186.

Kinnear, T. C., Taylor, J. R., Johnson, L., and Armstrong, R. (1993) *Australian Marketing Research*, Roseville: McGraw-Hill.

Kirzner, I. M. (1997) 'Entrepreneurial discovery and the competitive market process: An Austrian approach'. *Journal of Economic Literature* 35 (1), 60–85.

Klassen, R. D. and Jacobs, J. (2001) 'Experimental Comparison of Web, Electronic and Mail Survey Technologies in Operations Management'. *Journal of Operations Management* 19 (6), 713–728.

Klein, K. J., Dansereau, F., and Hall, R. J. (1994) 'Levels Issues in Theory Development, Data Collection, and Analysis'. *Academy of Management Review* 19 (2), 195–229.

Kliewe, T., Marquardt, P., and Baaken, T. (2009) 'Leveraging Organizational Resources by Creative Coupling: An Evaluation of Methods for Intellectual Asset Identification'. *Journal of Knowledge Globalisation* 2 (2), 1–23.

Kline, R. B. (2005) *Principles and Practice of Structural Equation Modelling*. 2nd edn. New York: The Guilford Press.

Koestler, A. (1964) *The Act of Creation*. New York: Macmillan.

Kogut, B. and Zander, U. (1992) 'Knowledge of the Firm, Combinative Capabilities, and the Replication of Technology'. *Organization Science* 3 (3), 383–397.

Kogut, B. and Zander, U. (1996) 'What Firms do? Coordination, Identity, and Learning'. *Organization Science* 7 (5), 502–518.

Kor, Y. Y. and Mahoney, J. T. (2005) 'How Dynamics, Management, and Governance of Resource Deployments Influence Firm-Level Performance'. *Strategic Management Journal* 26 (5), 489–496.

Koruna, S. (2004) 'Leveraging Knowledge Assets: Combinative Capabilities—Theory and Practice'. *R&D Management* 34 (5), 505–516.

Kraaijenbrink, J., Spender J. C., and Groen, A. J. (2010). 'The resource-based view: A review and assessment of its critiques'. *Journal of Management* 36 (1), 349–372.

Kusewitt, J. B. (1985) 'An exploratory study of the strategic acquisition factors relating to performance'. *Strategic Management Journal* 6 (2), 151–169.

Lane, P. J., and Lubatkin, M. (1998). 'Relative absorptive capacity and interorganizational learning'. *Strategic Management Journal* 19 (5), 461–477.

Lane, P. J., Koka, B. R., and Pathak, S. (2006) 'The reification of absorptive capacity: a critical review and rejuvenation of the construct'. *Academy of Management Review* 31 (4), 833–863.

Larsson, R. and Finkelstein, S. (1999) 'Strategic, organizational, and human resource perspectives on mergers and acquisitions: A case survey of synergy realization'. *Organization Science* 10 (1), 1–26.

Laursen, K. and Salter, A. (2006) 'Open for innovation: the role of openness in explaining innovation performance among U.K. manufacturing firms'. *Strategic Management Journal* 27 (2), 131–150.

Lavie, D. (2006) 'Capability reconfiguration: an analysis of incumbent responses to technological changes'. *Academy of Management Review* 31 (1), 153–174.

Law, K. S., Wong, C. S., and Mobley, W. H. (1998) 'Toward a taxonomy of multidimensional constructs'. *Academy of Management Review* 23 (1), 741–755

Lee, C., Lee, K., and Pennings, J. M. (2001) 'Internal capabilities, external networks, and performance: A study on technology-based ventures'. *Strategic Management Journal* 22 (6), 615–640.

Lee, N. and Cadogan, J. W. (2013) 'Problems with Formative and Higher-Order Reflective Variables'. *Journal of Business Research* 66 (2), 242–247.

Lei, M. and Lomax, R. (2005) 'The Effect of Varying Degrees of Nonnormality in Structural Equation Modelling'. *Structual Equation Modelling* 12 (1), 1–27.

Leonard-Barton, D. (1990) 'The Intraorganisational Environment: Point-to-Point Diffusion'. In *Technology Transfer: A Communication Perspective*. ed. by Williams, F. and Gibson, D. Newbury Park: Sage Publications, 43–62.

Leonard-Barton, D. (1992) 'Core Capabilities Und Core Rigidities: A Paradox in Managing New Product Development'. *Strategic Management Journal* 13 (S1), 111–125.

Leonard-Barton, D. (1995) *Wellsprings of Knowledge-Building and Sustaining the Sources of Innovation*. Boston, MA: Harvard Business School Press.

Lerdahl, E. (1999). 'A Conceptual Model for Creative Coupling of Expert Knowledge'. Proceedings of the International Conference on Engineering Design, August 24–26, Munich, Germany.

Li, T. and Calantone, R. J. (1998) 'The Impact of Market- Knowledge Competence on New Product Advantage: Conceptualization and Empirical Examination'. *Journal of Marketing* 62 (4), 13–29.

Li. J. (1995) 'Foreign entry and survival: The effects of strategic choices on performance in international markets'. *Strategic Management Journal* 16 (5), 333–351.

Lichtenthaler, U. (2007) 'Open for Innovation: Understanding the Determinants of External Technology Commercialization'. *Zeitschrift für Betriebswirtschaft* 77 (4), 21–45.

Lichtenthaler, U. (2009) 'Absorptive Capacity, Environmental Turbulence, and the Complementarity of Organizational Learning Processes'. *Academy of Management Journal* 52 (4), 822–846.

Lichtenthaler, U. (2012) 'The Performance Implications of Dynamic Capabilities: The Case of Product Innovation'. *Journal of Product Innovation Management*, n/a-n/a Retracted.

Lichtenthaler, U. and Lichtenthaler, E. (2009) 'A Capability-Based Framework for Open Innovation: Complementing Absorptive Capacity'. *Journal of Management Studies* 46 (8), 1315–1338.

Lindell, M. and Whitney, D. (2001) 'Accounting for Common Method Variance in Cross Sectional Research Designs'. *Journal of Applied Psychology* 86 (1), 114–121.

Linnemann, K. (2012) 'Exploring the Role of Dynamic Capabilities in the Process of Resource Recombination in Firms'. Proceedings of the 13th International CINet Conference "Continuous Innovation Across Boundaries", September 16–18, Rome, Italy.

Lippman, S. A. and Rumelt, R. P. (2003) 'A Bargaining Perspective on Resource Advantage'. *Strategic Management Journal* 24 (11), 1069–1086.

Lockett, A. and Thompson, S. (2001) 'The resource-based view and economics'. *Journal of Management* 27 (6), 723–754.

Lorenzoni, G. and Lipparini, A. (1999) 'The leveraging of interfirm relationships as a distinctive organizational capability: A longitudinal study'. *Strategic Management Journal* 20 (4), 317–338.

Lukas, B., Hair, J., Bush, R., and Ortinau, D. (2004) *Marketing Research*. North Ryde: McGraw-Hill Australia.

Lumpkin, G. T. and Dess, G. (1996) 'Clarifying the Entrepreneurial Orientation Construct and Linking it to Performance'. *Academy of Management Review* 21 (1), 135–173.

Macher, J. T. and Mowery, D. C. (2009) 'Measuring Dynamic Capabilities: Practices and Performance in Semiconductor Manufacturing'. *British Journal of Management* 20 (1), 41–62.

MacKenzie, S., Podsakoff, N., and Podsakoff, P. (2011) 'Construct Measurement and Validation Procedures in MIS and Behavioral Research'. *MIS Quarterly* 35 (2), 293–334.

Madhavan, R. and Grover, R. (1998) 'From Embedded Knowledge to Embodied Knowledge: New Product Development as Knowledge Management'. *Journal of Marketing* 62 (10), 1–12.

Madhok, A. and Tallman, S. B. (1998) 'Resources, transactions and rents: Managing value through interfirm collaborative relationships'. *Organization Science* 9 (3), 326–339.

Madsen, E. L. (2007) 'The significance of sustained entrepreneurial orientation on performance of firms—A longitudinal analysis'. *Entrepreneurship & Regional Development* 19 (2), 185–204.

Madsen, E. L. (2010) 'A Dynamic Capability Framework- Generic dimensions of Dynamic Capabilities and Their Relationship to Entrepreneurship'. in *Strategic Reconfigurations: Building Dynamic Capabilities in Rapid-Innovation-Based Industries, ed. by* Wall, S., Zimmermann, C., Klingebiel, R. and Lange, D. Chaltenham: Edward Elgar

Majumdar, S. K. (1998) 'On the Utilization of Resources: Perspectives from the U.S. Telecommunications Industry'. *Strategic Management Journal* 19 (9), 809–831.

Makadok, R. (2001) 'Toward a synthesis of the resource-based and dynamic-capability views of rent creation'. *Strategic Management Journal* 22 (5), 387–401.

Makadok, R. (2003) 'Doing the right thing and knowing the right thing to do: why the whole is greater than the sum of the parts'. *Strategic Management Journal* 24 (10), 1043–1055.

March, J. G. (1991) 'Exploration and Exploitation in Organizational Learning'. *Organization Science* 2 (1), 71–87.

Markides, C. (1997) 'Strategic innovation'. *Sloan Management Review* 38 (3), 9–23.

Marsh, H., Balla, J., and Hau, K. (1996) 'An Evaluation of Incremental Fit Indices: A Clarification of Mathematical and Empirical Properties'. in *Advanced Structural Equation Modeling.* ed. by Marcoulides, G. and Schuhmacker, R. Mahwah: Lawrence Erlbaum Associates, 315–353.

Marsh, H., Hu, K., and Wen, Z. (2004) 'Search of Golden Rules: Comment on Hypothesis-Testing Approaches to Setting Cutoff Values for Fit Indexes and Dangers in Overgeneralizing Hu and Bentler's Findings'. *Structural Equation Modeling* 11 (3), 320–34.

Marsh, S. J. and Stock, G. N. (2006) 'Creating dynamic capability: The role of intertemporal integration, knowledge retention, and interpretation'. *Journal of Product Innovation Management* 23 (5), 422–36.

Mathews, J. A. (2002) 'Competitive advantages of the latecomer firm: A resource-based account of industrial catch-up strategies'. *Asia Pacific Journal of Management* 19 (4), 467–488

Matsumoto, I. T., Stapleton, J., Glass, J., and Thorpe, T. (2005) 'A Knowledge-Capture Report for Multidisciplinary Design Environments'. *Journal of Knowledge Management* 9 (3), 83–92.

McEvily, B. and Zaheer, A. (1999) 'Bridging ties: A source of firm heterogeneity in competitive capabilities'. *Strategic Management Journal* 20 (12), 1133–1156.

McEvily, S. K. and Chakravarthy, B. (2002) 'The Persistence of Knowledge-Based Advantage: An Empirical Test for Product Performance and Technological Knowledge' *Strategic Management Journal* 23 (4), 285–305.

McGrath, R. G. (2001) 'Exploratory learning, innovative capacity, and managerial oversight'. *Academy of Management Journal* 44 (1), 118–131.

McGrath, R. G., Macmillan, I. C., and Venkataraman, S. (1995) 'Defining and Developing Competence: A Strategic Process Paradigm'. *Strategic Management Journal* 16 (4), 251–275.

McGrath, R. G., Tsai, M. H., Venkataraman, S., and MacMillan, I. C. (1996) 'Innovation, Competitive Advantage and Rent: A Model and a Test'. *Management Science* 42 (3), 389–403.

Medlin, C. (2001) *Relational Norms and Relationship Classes: From Independent Actors to Dyadic Interdependence, Unpublished Doctoral Dissertation.* Adelaide: Adelaide University.

Menon, A., Jaworski, B. J., and Kohli, A. K. (1997) 'Product Quality: Impact of Interdepartmental Interactions'. *Journal of the Academy of Marketing Science* 25 (3), 187–200.

Miller, D. (1983) 'The correlates of entrepreneurship in three types of firm)', *Management Science* 29 (7), 770–791.

Miller, D. and Shamsie, J. (1996) 'The Resource-Based View of the Firm in Two Environments: The Hollywood Film Studios from 1936 to 1965'. *Academy of Management Journal* 39 (3), 519–543.

Moldaschl, M. (2006) 'Innovationsfähigkeit, Zukunftsfähigkeit, Dynamic Capabilities: Moderne Fähigkeitsmystik Und Eine Alternative'. in *Management Von Kompetenz—Managementforschung.* ed. by Schreyögg, G. and Conrad, P. Wiesbaden: Gabler, 1–36.

Moran, P. (2005) 'Structural vs. relational embeddedness: social capital and managerial performance'. *Strategic Management Journal* 26 (12), 1129–1151.

Moran, P. and Ghoshal, S. (1996) 'Value Creation by Firms'. Academy of Management Best Paper Proceedings, 56th Annual Meetings, 41–45.

Morgan, N. A. and Piercy, N. F. (1998) 'Interactions between Marketing and Quality at the SBU Level: Influences and Outcomes'. *Journal of the Academy of Marketing Science* 26 (3), 190–208.

Morgan, R. and Hunt, S. (1994) 'The Commitment-Trust Theory of Relationship Marketing'. *Journal of Marketing* 58 (3), 20–38.

Mu, J. and Di Benedetto, A. (2012) 'Networking Capability and New Product Development'. Engineering Management, *IEEE Transactions on Engineering Management* 59 (1), 4–19.

Mu, J. and Di Benedetto, C. A. (2011) 'Strategic Orientations and New Product Commercialization: Mediator, Moderator, and Interplay'. *R&D Management* 41 (4), 337–359.

Mulaik, S., James, L., Van Alstine, J., Bennet, N., Ling, S., and Stilwell, C. (1989) 'Evaluation of Goodness-of-Fit Indices for Structural Equation Models'. *Psychological Bulletin* 105 (3), 430–345.

Naman, J. L. and Slevin, D. P. (1993) 'Entrepreneurship and the Concept of Fit: A Model and Empirical Tests'. *Strategic Management Journal* 14 (2), 137–153.

Narver, J. C. and Slater, F.S. (1990) 'The Effect of a Market Orientation on Business Performance' *Journal of Marketing*, 54 (8), 20–35.

Nelson, R. R. and Winter, S. G. (1982) *An Evolutionary Theory of Economic Change.* Cambridge, MA: Harvard University Press.

Nonaka, I. (1991) 'The Knowledge Creating Company'. *Harvard Business Review* 69 (6), 96–104.

Nonaka, I. (1994) 'A Dynamic Theory of Organiational Knowledge Creation'. *Organization Science* 5 (1), 14–37.

Nonaka, I. and Takeuchi, H. (1995) *The Knowledge Creating Company: How Japanese Companies Create the Dynamics of Innovation.* New York [u.a.]: Oxford University Press.

Nonaka, I., Toyama, R. (2007) 'Strategic management as distributed practical wisdom (phronesis)'. *Industrial and Corporate Change* 16 (3), 371–394.

Nooteboom, B., Vanhaverbeke, W. P. M., Duijsters, G. M., Gilsing, V. A., and Oord, A. J. (2007) 'Optimal cognitive distance and absorptive capacity'. *Research Policy* 36 (7), 1016–1034.

Northcraft, G. B. and Wolf, G. (1984) 'Dollars, sense, and sunk costs: A life cycle model of resource allocation decisions'. *Academy of Management Review* 9 (2), 225–234.

O'Brien, R. (2007) 'A Caution regarding Rules of Thumb for Variance Inflation Factors'. *Quality & Quantity* 41 (5), 673–690.

OECD (2011) 'ISIC Rev. 3: Technology intensity definition—Classification of manufacturing industries into categories based on R&D intensities', Directorate for Science, Technology and Industry Economic Analysis and Statistics Division, [online] available from < http://www.oecd.org/science/inno/48350231.pdf > [01/2013].

Office for National Statistics (2012) 'Business Enterprise Research and Development, 2011– Statistical Bulletin', 20 November 2012, [online] available from <http://www.ons.gov.uk/ons/dcp171778_287868.pdf > [07/2013].

Okhuysen, G. A. and Eisenhardt, K. M. (2002) 'Integrating knowledge in groups: How formal interventions enable flexibility'. *Organizational Science* 13 (4), 370–386.

Pablo, A. L., Reay, T., Dewald, J. R., and Casebeer, A. L. (2007) 'Identifying, Enabling and Managing Dynamic Capabilities in the Public Sector'. *Journal of Management Studies* 44 (5), 687–708.

Page, C. and Meyer, D. (2000) *Applied Research Design for Business and Management.* Sydney: McGraw-Hill Companies Inc.

Parasuraman, A., Zeithaml, V. A., and Berry, L. L. (1988) 'SERVQUAL: A Multiple-Item Scale for Measuring Consumer Perceptions of Service Quality'. *Journal of Retailing* 64 (1), 5–6.

Parmigiani, A. and Howard-Grenville, J. (2011) 'Routines Revisited: Exploring the Capabilities and Practice Perspectives', *The Academy of Management Annals* 5 (1), 413–453.

Patterson, P. G. and Spreng, R.A. (1997) 'Modelling the Relationship between Perceived Value, Satisfaction and Repurchase Intentions in a Business-to-Business, Services Context: An Empirical Examination'. *International Journal of Service Industry Management* 8 (5), 414–434.

Patton, M.Q. (2002) *Qualitative Evaluation and Research Methods.* Newbury Park: Sage Publications.

Pavitt, K. (1985) 'Patent Statistics as Indicators of Innovative Activities: Possibilities and Problems'. *Scientometrics* 7 (1–2), 77–99.

Pavlou, P. A. and El Sawy, O. A. (2011) 'Understanding the Elusive Black Box of Dynamic Capabilities'. *Decision Sciences* 42 (1), 239–273.

Pearl, D. K., and Fairley, D. (1985) 'Testing for the Potential for Nonresponse Bias in Sample Surveys' *Public Opinion Quarterly* 49 (4), 553–560.

Peng, M. W. and Delios, A. (2006) 'What determines the scope of the firm over time and around the world? An Asia Pacific perspective'. *Asia Pacific Journal of Management* 23 (4), 385–405.

Penrose, E. (1959) *The Theory of the Growth of the Firm*. New York: Wiley.

Peteraf, M. A. (1993) 'The cornerstones of competitive advantage: a resource-based view'. *Strategic Management Journal* 14 (3), 179–191.

Peteraf, M. A. and Barney, J. B. (2003) 'Unraveling the Resource-Based Tangle'. *Managerial and Decision Economics* 24 (4), 309–323.

Phan, P. H. and Peridis, T. (2000) 'Knowledge creation in strategic alliances: Another look at organizational learning'. *Asia Pacific Journal of Management* 17 (2), 201–222.

Phelan, S. E. and Lewin, P. (2000) 'Arriving at a strategic theory of the firm', *International Journal of Management Reviews* 2 (4), 305–323.

Pisano, G. (1994) 'Knowledge, integration, and the locus of learning: An empirical analysis of process development'. *Strategic Management Journal* 15 (1), 85–100.

Plewa, C. (2009) 'Exploring Organizational Culture Difference in Relationship Dyads'. *Australasian Marketing Journal* 17 (1), 49–57.

Plewa, C. (2010) *Key Drivers of University-Industry Relationships—and the Impact of Organisational Culture Difference*. Saarbrücken: VDM Verlag Dr. Müller.

Plewa, C. and Quester, P. (2007) 'Key Drivers of University-Industry Relationships: Organisational Compatibility and Personal Experience'. *Journal of Service Marketing* 21 (5), 370–382.

Plewa, C., Korff, N., Johnson, C., Macpherson, G., Baaken, T., and Rampersad, G. C. (2013) 'The Evolution of university–industry linkages—A Framework'. *Journal of Engineering and Technology Management* 30 (1), 21–44.

Podsakoff, N. P., Shen, W., and Podsakoff, P. M. (2006) 'The Role of Formative Measurement Models: Review, Critique, and Implications for Future Research'. *Strategic Management Research* 3 (1), 197–252.

Podsakoff, P. M. and Organ, D. (1986) 'Self-Reports in Organizational Research: Problems and Prospects'. *Journal of Management* 12 (4), 69–82.

Podsakoff, P. M., MacKenzie, S. B. and Podsakoff, N. P. (2003): 'Common Method Biases in Behavioral Research: A Critical Review of the Literature and Recommended Remedies'. *Journal of Applied Psychology* 88 (5), 879–903.

Porter, M. E. (1980) *Competitive strategy*. New York: Free Press.

Powell, W. W., Koput, K. W. and Smith-Doerr, L. (1996) 'Interorganizational collaboration and the locus of innovation'. *Administrative Science Quarterly* 41 (1), 116–145.

Prabhu, J. C., Rajesh, K. C., and Mark, E. E. (2005) 'The Impact of Acquisitions on Innovation: Poison Pill, Placebo, or Tonic?' *Journal of Marketing* 69 (1), 114–130.

Prahalad, C. K. and Hamel, G. (1990) 'The Core Competence of the Corporation'. *Harvard Business Review* 68 (3), 79–91.

Preacher, K. and Hayes, A. (2004) 'SPSS and SAS procedures for estimating indirect effects in simple mediation models'. *Behavior Research Methods, Instruments, & Computers* 36 (1), 717–731.

Preacher, K., Curran, P., and Bauer, D. (2005) 'Computational Tools for Probing Interaction Effects in Multiple Linear Regression, Multilevel Modeling, and Latent Curve Analysis'. *Journal of Educational and Behavioral Statistics* 31 (4), 437–448.

Preacher, K., Rucker, D., and Hayes, A. (2007) 'Addressing Moderated Mediation Hypotheses: Theory, Methods, and Prescriptions'. *Multivariate Behavioural Research* 42 (1), 185–227.

Priem, R. L. and Butler, J. E. (2001) 'Is the resource-based 'view' a useful perspective for strategic management research? '. *Academy of Management Journal* 26 (1), 22–40.

Puranam, P., Singh, H., and Zollo, M. (2003) 'A bird in the hand or two in the bush? Integration trade-offs in technology grafting acquisitions'. *European Management Journal* 21 (2), 179–184.

Ramaswami, S. N., Srivastava, R. K., and Bhargava, M. (2009) 'Market-based capabilities and financial performance of firms: Insights into marketing's contribution to firm value'. *Journal of the Academy of Marketing Science* 37 (2), 97–11.

Reed, R. and DeFillippi, R. J. (1990) 'Causal Ambiguity, Barriers to Imitation, and Sustainable Competitive Advantage'. *Academy of Management Review* 15 (1), 88–102.

Reinecke, J. (1999) 'Interaktionseffekte in Strukturgleichungsmodellen mit der Theorie des geplanten Verhaltens: Multiple Gruppenvergleiche und Produktterme mit latenten Variablen'. *ZUMA-Nachrichten* 23 (1), 88–114.

Richardson, H., Simmering, M., and Sturman, M. (2009) 'A Tale of Three Perspectives: Examining Post Hoc Statistical Techniques for Detection and Correction of Common Method Variance'. *Organizational Research Methods* 12 (4), 762–800.

Rodan, S. (2002) 'Innovation and heterogeneous knowledge in managerial contact networks' *Journal of Knowledge Management* 6 (2), 152–163.

Rodan, S. and Galunic, C. (2004) 'More than Network Structure: How Knowledge Heterogeneity Influences Managerial Performance and Innovativeness'. *Strategic Management Journal* 25 (6), 541–562.

Rokkan, A., Heide, J., and Wathne, K. (2003) 'Specific Investments in Marketing Relationships'. *Journal of Marketing Research* 40 (2), 210–224.

Rosenberg, N. (1994) *Exploring the Black Box—Technology, Economics, and History*. New York: Cambridge University Press.

Rosenkopf, L. and Nerkar, A. (2001) 'Beyond local search: boundary-spanning, exploration, and impact in the optical disk industry'. *Strategic Management Journal* 22 (4), 287–306.

Rothaermel, F. T. (2001) 'Incumbent's advantage through exploiting complementary assets via inter firm cooperation'. *Strategic Management Journal* 22 (6–7), Summer Special Issue, 687–99.

Rothaermel, F. T. and Hess, A. M. (2007) 'Building Dynamic Capabilities: Innovation Driven by Individual-, Firm-, and Network-Level Effects'. *Organization Science* 18 (6), 898–921.

Rouse, M. J. and Daellenbach, U. S. (1999) 'Rethinking Research Methods for the Resource-Based Perspective: Isolating Sources of Sustainable Competitive Advantage'. *Strategic Management Journal* 20 (5), 487–494.

Rumelt, R. P. (1987) 'Theory, Strategy, and Entrepreneurship'. in *The Competitive Challenge: Strategies for Industrial Innovation and Renewal*. ed. by Teece, D. J. Cambridge, MA: Ballinger, 137–158.

Sanchez, R. (1995) 'Strategic flexibility in product competition'. *Strategic Management Journal* 16 (S1), 135–159.

Sanchez, R. (2004) 'Understanding competence-based management: identifying and managing five modes of competence'. *Journal of Business Research* 57 (5), 518–32.

Sanchez, R. and Heene, A. (1997) 'Reinventing strategic management: New theory and practice for competence-based competition'. *European Management Journal* 15 (3), 303–317.

Sanchez, R. and Mahoney, J. T. (1996) 'Modularity, Flexibility, and Knowledge Management in Product and Organization Design'. *Strategic Management Journal* 17 (Winter Special Issue), 63–76.

Sanchez, R., Heene, A., and Thomas, H. (1996) *Dynamics of Competence-Based Competition: Theory and Practices in the New Strategic Management*. Oxford: Elsevier.

Saunders, M., Lewis, P., and Thornhill, A. (2003) '*Research Methods for Business Students*', 3rd edn., Harlow: Pearson Education Limited.

Schreiber, J., Stage, F., King, J., Nora, A., and Barlow, E. (2006) 'Reporting Structural Equation Modeling and Confirmatory Factor Analysis Results: A Review'. *The Journal of Educational Research* 99 (6), 323–337.

Schreyögg, G. and Conrad, P. (2006) *Management von Kompetenz—Managementforschung*. 1st edn. Wiesbaden: Gabler.

Schreyögg, G. and Kliesch-Eberl, M. (2003) *Rahmenbedingungen für die Entwicklung Organisationaler Kompetenz*. Berlin: QUEM-Materialien.

Schreyögg, G. and Kliesch-Eberl, M. (2007) 'How Dynamic can Organizational Capabilities be? Towards a Dual-Process Model of Capability Dynamization'. *Strategic Management Journal* 28 (9), 913–933.

Schumpeter, J. A. (1934) *The Theory of Economic Development: An Inquiry into Profits, Capital, Credit, Interest, and the Business Cycle*. Cambridge, MA: Harvard University Press.

Sethi, R. (2000) 'New Product Quality and Product Development Teams'. *Journal of Marketing* 64 (2), 1–14.

Shane, S. and Venkataraman, S. (2000) 'The promise of entrepreneurship as a field of research'. *Academy of Management Review* 25 (1), 217–227.

Siggelkow, N. (2002) 'Evolution toward fit'. *Administrative Science Quarterly*, 47 (1), 125–159.

Singh, H. and Montgomery, C. A. (1987) 'Corporate acquisition strategies and economic performance'. *Strategic Management Journal* 8 (4), 377–386.

Sinkula, J. (1994) 'Market information processing and organizational learning'. *Journal of Marketing* 58 (1), 35–45.

Sirmon, D. G. and Hitt, M. A. (2003) 'Managing resources: Linking unique resources, management and wealth creation in family firms'. *Entrepreneurship Theory and Practice* 27 (4), 339–358.

Sirmon, D. G. and Hitt, M. A. (2009) 'Contingencies within Dynamic Managerial Capabilities: Interdependent Effects of Resource Investment and Deployment on Firm Performance'. *Strategic Management Journal* 30 (13), 1375–1394.

Sirmon, D. G., Gove, S., and Hitt, M. A. (2008). 'Resource management in dyadic competitive rivalry: The effects of resource bundling and deployment'. *Academy of Management Journal* 51 (5), 919–935.

Sirmon, D. G., Hitt, M. A., and Ireland, R. D. (2007) 'Managing Firm Resources in Dynamic Environments to Create Value: Looking Inside the Black Box'. *Academy of Management Review* 32 (1), 273–292.

Sirmon, D. G., Hitt, M. A., Arregle, J., and Campbell, J. T. (2010) 'The Dynamic Interplay of Capability Strengths and Weaknesses: Investigating the Bases of Temporary Competitive Advantage'. *Strategic Management Journal* 31 (13), 1386–1409.

Sirmon, D. G., Hitt, M. A., Ireland, R. D., and Gilbert, B. A. (2010) 'Resource Orchestration to Create Competitive Advantage: Breadth, Depth, and Life Cycle Effects'. *Journal of Management* 37 (5), 1390–1412.

Smith, K. G., Collins, C. J., and Clark, K. D. (2005) 'Existing knowledge, knowledge creation capability, and the rate of new product introduction in high-technology firms'. *Academy of Management Journal* 48 (2), 346–57.

Song, M., Droge, C., Hanvanich, S., and Calantone, R. (2005) 'Marketing and Technology Resource Complementarity: An Analysis of their Interaction Effect in Two Environmental Contexts'. *Strategic Management Journal* 26 (3), 259–276.

Song, X. M. and Parry, M. E. (1997) 'A Cross-National Comparative Study of New Product Development Processes: Japan and the United States'. *Journal of Marketing* 61 (2), 1–18.

Spector, P. (2006) 'Method Variance in Organizational Research: Truth Or Urban Legend?'. *Organizational Research Methods* 9 (2), 221–232.

Spender, J. C. (1996) 'Making knowledge the basis of a dynamic theory of the firm', *Strategic Management Journal* 17 (S2), 45–62.

Steenkamp, J. and Baumgartner, H. (2000) 'On the use of Structural Equation Models for Marketing Modeling'. *International Journal of Research in Marketing* 17 (2–3), 195–202.

Steenkamp, J. and van Trijp, H. (1991) 'The use of Lisrel in Validating Marketing Constructs'. *International Journal of Research in Marketing* 8 (4), 293–292.

Steinle, A., Mijnals, P., and Muckenschnabl, S. (2009) *Praxis-Guide Cross-Innovations: Wettbewerbsvorteile durch einen branchenübergreifenden Innovationsansatz.* 1st edn. Kelkheim: Zukunftsinstitut.

Stevenson, H. H. (1983) 'A Perspective on Entrepreneurship'. Harvard Business School Working Paper 9, 384–131.

Stopford, J. M. and Baden-Fuller, C. W. F. (1994) 'Creating Corporate Entrepreneurship'. *Strategic Management Journal* 15 (7), 521–536.

Straub, D., Rai, A., and Klein, R. (2004) 'Measuring Firm Performance at the Network Level: A Nomology of the Business Impact of Digital Supply Networks'. *Journal of Management Information Systems* 21 (1), 83–114.

Streiner, D. (2003) 'Being Inconsistent about Consistency: When Coefficient Alpha does and Doesn't Matter'. *Journal of Personality Assessment* 80 (3), 217–222.

Szulanski, G. (1996) 'Exploring Internal Stickiness: Impediments to the Transfer of Best Practice Within the Firm'. *Strategic Management Journal* 17 (Winter Special Issue), 27–43.

Teece, D. J. (1981) 'The Market for Know-how and the Efficient International Transfer of Technology'. *The Annals of the American Academy of Political and Social Science* 458 (1), 81–96.

Teece, D. J. (1982) 'Towards an economic theory of the multi-product firm'. *Journal of Economic Behavior and Organization* 3 (1), 39–63.

Teece, D. J. (2007) 'Explicating Dynamic Capabilities: The Nature and Microfoundations of (Sustainable) Enterprise Performance'. *Strategic Management Journal* 28 (13), 1319–1350.

Teece, D. J. (2012) 'Dynamic Capabilities: Routines versus Entrepreneurial Action'. *Journal of Management Studies* 49 (8), 1395–1401.

Teece, D. J., Pisano, G., and Shuen, A. (1997) 'Dynamic Capabilities and Strategic Management'. *Strategic Management Journal* 18 (7), 509–533.

Teece, D. J., Rumelt, R., Dosi, G., and Winter, S. (1994) 'Understanding corporate coherence: Theory and evidence'. *Journal of Economic Behavior and Organization* 23 (1), 1–30.

Ticehurst, G. W. and Veal, A. J. (1999) *Business Research Methods: A Managerial Approach.* 2nd edn. Frenchs Forest, N.S.W: Longman.

Turner, D. and Crawford, M. (1994) 'Managing Current and Future Competitive Performance: The Role of Competence'. In *Competence-Based Competition.* ed. by Hamel, G. and Heene, A. Chichester: John Wiley and Sons, 241–263.

Tushman, M. L. and Romanelli, E. (1996) 'Organizational evolution: a metamorphosis model of convergence and reorientation'. *Research in Organizational Behavior* 7 (1), 171–222.

Usher, A. P. (1954) *A History of Mechanical Inventions.* Cambridge, MA: Harvard University Press.

Uzzi, B. (1997) 'Social structure and competition in interfirm networks: The paradox of embeddedness'. *Administrative Science Quarterly* 42 (1), 35–67.

Van den Bosch, F., Volberda, H., and De Boer, M. (1999) 'Co-evolution of firm absorptive capacity and knowledge environment: Organizational firms and combinative capabilities'. *Organizational Science* 10 (4), 551–568.

Van den Putte, B., and Hoogstraten, J. (1997) 'Applying Structural Equation Modeling in the Context of the Theory of Reasoned Action'. Structural Equation Modeling 4 (4), 320–337.

Van Rijnbach, C. (2010) 'Innovation Commitment and Resource Allocation', [online] available from <http://www.business-strategy-innovation.com/wordpress/category/Cas par-van-Rijnbach/> [12/2010].

Van Wijk, R., Van den Bosch, F., and Volberda, H. (2001) 'The impact of knowledge depth and breadth on absorbed knowledge on levels of exploration and exploitation'. Paper presented at the annual meeting of the Academy of Management, Washington, DC.

Vandenberg, R. and Lance, C. E. (2000) 'A Review and Synthesis of the Measurement Invariance Literature: Suggestions, Practices, and Recommendations for Organizational Research'. *Organizational Research Methods* 3 (1), 4–70.

Veal, A. J. and Ticehurst, B. (2005) *Business Research Methods: A Managerial Approach.* Addison-Wesley Longman : Incorporated.

Velicer, W. and Jackson, D. (1990) 'Component Analysis Versus Common Factor Analysis: Some further Observations'. *Multivariate Behavioural Research* 25 (1), 97–114.

Venkataraman, S. (1997) 'The Distinctive Domain of Entrepreneurship Research: An Editor's Perspective'. in *Advances in Entrepreneurship, Firm Emergence and Growth.* ed. by Katz, J. A. and Brockhaus, R. H. Greenwich, CT: JAI Press, 119–138.

Verona, G. and Ravasi, D. (2003) 'Unbundling dynamic capabilities: An exploratory study of continuous product innovation'. *Industrial and Corporate Change* 12 (3), 577–606.

Wang, C. L. and Ahmed, P. K. (2007) 'Dynamic capabilities: A review and research agenda'. *International Journal of Management Reviews* 9 (1), 31–51.

Weick, K. E. and Roberts, K. H. (1993). 'Collective mind in organizations: Heedful interrelating on flight decks'. *Administrative Science Quarterly* 38 (3), 357–381.

Weis, C. and Steinmetz, P. (2002) *Marktforschung.* Ludwigshafen: Friedrich Kiehl Verlag.

Wernerfelt, B. (1984) 'A Recource-Based View of the Firm'. *Strategic Management Journal* 5 (2), 171–180.

Wiklund, J. (1999) 'The sustainability of the entrepreneurial orientation—performance relationship'. *Entrepreneurship Theory and Practice* 24 (1), 37–48.

Wiklund, J. and Shepherd, D. (2003) 'Knowledge-Based Resources, Entrepreneurial Orientation, and the Performance of Small and Medium-Sized Businesses'. *Strategic Management Journal* 24 (13), 1307–1314.

Wiklund, J. and Shepherd, D. A. (2009) 'The Effectiveness of Alliances and Acquisitions: The Role of Resource Combination Activities'. *Entrepreneurship: Theory & Practice* 33 (1), 193–212.

Wiklund, J., Eliasson, C., and Davidsson, P. (2002) 'Entrepreneurial Management and Schumpeterian Resource Recombination', Paper presented at the 21st Babson Entrepreneurship Research Conference, June 2002, Boulder.

Williams, L., Hartman, N., and Sturman, M. (2010) 'Method Variance and Marker Variables: A Review and Comprehensive CFA Marker Technique'. *Organizational Research Methods* 13 (3), 477–514.

Williamson, O. E. (1999) 'Strategy Research: Governance and Competence Perspectives'. *Strategic Management Journal* 20 (12), 1087–1108.

Winter, S. G. (2003) 'Understanding dynamic capabilities'. *Strategic Management Journal* 24, October Special Issue, 991–996.

Zahra, S. A. (1991) 'Predictors and Financial Outcomes of Corporate Entrepreneurship: An Exploratory Study'. *Journal of Business Venturing* 6 (4), 259–285.

Zahra, S. A. (1996) 'Technology Strategy and New Venture Performance: A Study of Corporate-Sponsored and Independent Biotechnology Ventures'. *Journal of Business Venturing* 11 (4), 289–321.

Zahra, S. A. and George, G. (2002) 'Absorptive Capacity: A Review, Reconceptualization, and Extension'. *Academy of Management Review* 27 (2), 185–203.

Zahra, S. A. and Wiklund, J. (2002) '*Top Management Team Characteristics and Entrepreneurial Resource Recombinations among New Ventures*'. Jönköping: Mimeo: Jönköping International Business School.

Zahra, S. A., Ireland, R. D., and Hitt, M. A. (2000) 'International Expansion by New Venture Firms: International Diversity, Mode of Market Entry, Technological Learning, and Performance'. *Academy of Management Journal* 43 (5), 925–50.

Zahra, S. A., Sapienza, H., and Davidsson, P. (2006) 'Entrepreneurship and dynamic capabilities: a review, model and research agenda'. *Journal of Management Studies* 43, 917–955.

Zander, U. and Kogut, B. (1995) 'Knowledge and the speed of transfer and imitation of organizational capabilities'. *Organizational Science* 6 (1), 76–92.

Zikmund, W. G. (2003) *Business Research Methods*. 7th edn. Mason Ohio: Thomson South-Western.

Zollo, M. and Winter, S. (2002) 'Deliberate learning and the evolution of dynamic capabilities'. *Organizational Science* 13 (2), 339–351.

Zott, C. (2003) 'Dynamic capabilities and the emergence of intraindustry differential firm performance: Insights from a simulation study'. *Strategic Management Journal* 24 (2), 97–125.

CPSIA information can be obtained
at www.ICGtesting.com
Printed in the USA
LVHW020445231121
704213LV00002B/96

9 783658 356651